THE NEW INTERNATIONAL
GREEK TESTAMENT COMMENTARY

Editors
I. Howard Marshall
and
W. Ward Gasque

THE PASTORAL EPISTLES

THE PASTORAL EPISTLES

A Commentary on the Greek Text

by

GEORGE W. KNIGHT III

WILLIAM B. EERDMANS PUBLISHING COMPANY
GRAND RAPIDS, MICHIGAN

THE PATERNOSTER PRESS
CARLISLE

First published 1992 jointly by Wm. B. Eerdmans Publishing Co. and
The Paternoster Press Ltd.,
P.O. Box 300, Carlisle, Cumbria CA3 0QS England

Printed in the United States of America

Reprinted 1996

Library of Congress Cataloging-in-Publication Data

Knight, George W. (George William), 1931-
The Pastoral Epistles: a commentary on the Greek text / by George W. Knight, III.
p. cm. — (The New international Greek Testament commentary)
Includes bibliographical references and indexes.
ISBN 0-8028-2395-5
1. Bible. N.T. Pastoral Epistles — Commentaries. I. Title. II. Series: New international Greek Testament commentary (Grand Rapids, Mich.)
BS2735.3.K55 1992
227′.8307—dc20 92-5467
CIP

Paternoster ISBN 0 85364 532 9

To all those who made this work possible
and especially
to my beloved wife, Virginia

CONTENTS

COMMENTARY ON TITUS

COMMENTARY ON 2 TIMOTHY

INDEXES

FOREWORD

While there have been many series of commentaries on the English text of the New Testament in recent years, it is a long time since any attempt has been made to cater particularly to the needs of students of the Greek text. It is true that at the present time there is something of a decline in the study of Greek in many traditional theological institutions, but there has been a welcome growth in the study of the New Testament in its original language in the new evangelical schools, especially in North America and the Third World. It is hoped that *The New International Greek Testament Commentary* will demonstrate the value of studying the Greek New Testament and help toward the revival of such study.

The purpose of the series is to cater to the needs of students who want something less technical than a full-scale critical commentary. At the same time, the commentaries are intended to interact with modern scholarship and to make their own scholarly contribution to the study of the New Testament. There has been a wealth of detailed study of the New Testament in articles and monographs in recent years, and the series is meant to harvest the results of this research in a more easily accessible form. The commentaries will thus include adequate, but not exhaustive, bibliographies. They will attempt to treat all important problems of history, exegesis, and interpretation that may arise.

One of the gains of recent scholarship has been the recognition of the primarily theological character of the books of the New Testament. This series will, therefore, attempt to provide a theological understanding of the text, based on historical-critical-linguistic exegesis. It will not, however, attempt to apply and expound the text for modern readers, although it is hoped that the exegesis will give some indication of the way in which the text should be expounded.

Within the limits set by the use of the English language, the series aims to be international in character; the contributors, however, have been chosen not primarily in order to achieve a spread between different countries but above all because of their specialized qualifications for their particular tasks. The supreme aim of this series is to serve those who are engaged in the ministry of the Word of God and thus to glorify his name. Our prayer is that it may be found helpful in this task.

I. Howard Marshall
W. Ward Gasque

PREFACE

I am thankful to the Editors for inviting me to contribute this volume to the series. Their patience over a number of years and their willingness to grant the time necessary is appreciated.

The format of the commentary series has been established by the preceding volumes, and I have sought to conform this volume to those already published. The text utilized as the basis for the commentary is that of the third edition (corrected) of *The Greek New Testament* published by the United Bible Societies (1983). I have followed the pattern of the commentary on Luke and given as full an account of the other occurrences of Greek words or phrases as would be helpful to the reader. On occasion I have listed all the occurrences in the NT, and this is indicated by a double asterisk ** after the word or phrase. At other times only the occurrences in the Pauline corpus or in the Pastoral Epistles are provided, and this is indicated by a single asterisk * after the abbreviation for Paul (Pl.) or for the Pastoral Epistles (PE). These listings will enable the reader to ascertain the usage of the word in the NT and to review the meaning and significance of the word in the NT. Since the building block of understanding is the word and its meaning, it is hoped that this will be an aid to the reader.

Like most exegetes, I am exceedingly indebted to those wordsmiths who have done a prodigious amount of work for the benefit of others. These have often been utilized but not specifically recognized because their contribution is so basic and well known. I have sought to rectify that injustice by constantly acknowledging my use of BAGD and other lexicons and theological dictionaries. If words are the building blocks, then the statement itself is the building that we are seeking to understand by entering into its meaning. For this aspect of the study the contributions of grammarians and other commentators are hereby gratefully acknowledged for the work that appears in the commentary proper. But since the task of the commentator is to comment on the text not on what others say about the text, I have not sought to constantly refer to those who hold differences of opinion but have sought rather to present arguments pro and con, and then to come to the most satisfactory conclusion as to the meaning of the text. However, at certain exegetical cruxes almost all the modern commentators are listed with an indication of the position taken. Similarly, not every known and available article on a subject or verse has been listed in the commentary (i.e., the bibliographical index card file has not been dumped into the book throughout), but rather a more selective (and, I hope, helpful) approach has been used. That is, the reader has been referred to those articles that contain a copious bibliography on the subject and to those articles that have provided the most help in understanding the matter under consideration. Between these two the reader will be adequately informed on the subject. In the Introduction, the interaction with the scholarly world has been more fully indicated and documented.

My debt to others is evident throughout the commentary, and I have sought to acknowledge that. Sometimes, of course, I have forgotten from whom I learned something or have come to the same conclusion through my own research. There have been so very many fine commentaries produced on the Pastorals that it would be odious to mention certain ones and thereby omit and neglect those not mentioned. But it would be derelict not to mention one person to whom I am most indebted in dealing with introductory questions regarding the Pastorals, particularly the question of authorship and especially those aspects relating to linguistics and pseudonymity. That person is Dr. Donald Guthrie. Even though his commentary in the Tyndale series (because of the nature of the series) is not technical, the Introduction and Appendix are gems of knowledge, as are his other works on the Pastorals and related subjects included in the bibliography. My indebtedness has been further increased by his gracious review of my Introduction and by the helpful comments and suggestions he has made. He must not, however, be held responsible for this writer's treatment of that subject, and particularly not for my treatment of Luke.

My indebtedness goes beyond individual scholars and their works. As indicated in the dedication, there are many who have helped make this volume a possibility. I take this opportunity to express my gratitude. I am very thankful to the board and to the administration of Covenant Theological Seminary for granting me two sabbaticals. The Libraries of Covenant Seminary and Concordia Seminary of St. Louis, and of Tyndale House and the University at Cambridge have been a rich source. I especially thank all the library staff at Covenant, particularly the former Librarian Dr. Joseph Hall (now my colleague at Knox), Mrs. Margaret Dye of Concordia, and Mr. David Deboys of Tyndale. To the Tyndale House I express my appreciation for a grant that made my stay in England possible, and for the use of an apartment and a study desk, which expedited my research and writing. A long overdue word of thanks goes to the Berean Class and to the Session of Central Presbyterian Church for their assistance during the first sabbatical. Friends whose private generosity should remain private as they wished it to be are nevertheless hereby thanked publicly for their kind support and encouragement. They know who they are, and I surely do. Former students, the Rev. Messrs. Lee Capper and Stephen Christian, Mrs. Gail MacNaughton, and Mr. Robert Wermuth, provided much valuable assistance in various ways, as did my daughter Jennie Rotherham in her work on the bibliography. My colleague, Dr. Robert Reymond, has graciously read certain portions of this work and his suggestions have been most helpful. The same goes for a previous NT colleague, Prof. Karl Cooper. Faculty secretaries Mrs. June Dare and Mrs. Eunice Lanz, the often unrecognized workers through whom a manuscript comes into its final form, have my deepest appreciation for their patient and skillful labors. I also want to express my great appreciation to Dr. John W. Simpson, Jr., of Eerdmans Publishing Co. for his gracious, skillful, and most helpful editing.

My family has been exceedingly supportive throughout the months of the sabbatical when my attention and activity have been single-mindedly directed toward the commentary. I thank my son-in-law and daughter, Simon and Jennie Rotherham, and my son, Hugh Knight, for the invaluable aid they provided in caring for my handicapped father so that I could have the time to do research and writing. But most of all I express thanks to my wife, Virginia. Words are inadequate to describe all her particular contributions to the completion of this task.

My thanks go above all to God the Father who not only saved me, but also, to paraphrase the words of Paul in the Pastorals, "put me into service." The privilege of working through material in which Paul is instructing Timothy (and Titus) has been an enormous spiritual benefit for me. It has reminded me again of the preciousness of the gospel and of the apostolic deposit, which must be correctly taught and faithfully passed on. It has given me new resolve to seek to serve the Lord Jesus Christ courageously and winsomely by means of the enabling grace of God and the powerful presence of his Spirit. It is my prayer that this commentary may faithfully communicate the apostolic message found in the Pastorals and that that message may have its intended beneficial effects on the readers of today as it did on those to whom it was originally sent.

Fort Lauderdale, Florida George W. Knight III
March, 1990

ABBREVIATIONS

A double asterisk (**) after a Greek word or phrase signifies that all occurrences of the word or phrase in the New Testament are listed or that it is identified as a New Testament hapax legomenon. A single asterisk (*) after Pl. (= Paul) or PE (= Pastoral Epistles) indicates that all occurrences of the word or phrase in Paul or in the Pastoral Epistles are cited. The frequency of a word or phrase in the New Testament, Paul, or the Pastorals is indicated by "x" preceded by a numeral (e.g., "Pl. 12x"). Works cited by author or author and short title are listed in the Bibliography. Abbreviations in text-critical discussions are from *UBSGNT*.

BOOKS OF THE BIBLE

OT — Old Testament

Gn., Ex., Lv., Nu., Dt., Jos., Jdg., Ru., 1, 2 Sa., 1, 2 Ki., 1, 2 Ch., Ezr., Ne., Est., Jb., Ps(s)., Pr., Ec., Ct., Is., Je., La., Ezk., Dn., Ho., Joel, Am., Ob., Jon., Mi., Na., Hab., Zp., Hg., Zc., Mal.

LXX — Septuagint

NT — New Testament

Mt., Mk., Lk., Jn., Acts, Rom., 1, 2 Cor., Gal., Eph., Phil., Col., 1, 2 Thes., 1, 2 Tim., Tit., Phm., Heb., Jas., 1, 2 Pet., 1, 2, 3 Jn., Jude, Rev.

par. — parallel Gospel passages

OTHER ANCIENT SOURCES

Adv. Marc. — *Adversus Marcionem* (Tertullian)
Adv. Val. — *Adversus Valentinianos* (Tertullian)
Ant. — *Antiquitates Judaicae* (Josephus)
Ap. — *Contra Apionem* (Josephus)

Apol.	*Apologia* (Tertullian)
B.J.	*De Bello Judaico* (Josephus)
De praesc.	*De praescriptione haereticorum* (Tertullian)
Dial.	*Dialogue with Trypho* (Justin)
Eph.	*Ephesians* (Ignatius)
HE	*Historia Ecclesiastica* (Eusebius)
Haer.	*Adversus Haereses* (Irenaeus)
In Ep. ad Rom.	*Commentaria in epistolam b. Pauli ad Romanos* (Origen)
Magn.	*Magnesians* (Ignatius)
Man.	*Mandates* (Hermas)
Paed.	*Paedagogus* (Clement of Alexandria)
Strom.	*Stromateis* (Clement of Alexandria)
Syr. Bar.	2 (Syriac) *Apocalypse of Baruch*

The standard abbreviations are used for the Qumran scrolls (see J. A. Fitzmyer, *The Dead Sea Scrolls: Major Publications and Tools for Study.* Missoula, MT, 1975, 1977).

REFERENCE WORKS, PERIODICALS, COLLECTIONS, AND SERIES

AnBib	Analecta Biblica
ASV	*American Standard Version*
BAGD	W. Bauer, *A Greek-English Lexicon of the New Testament and Other Early Christian Literature,* tr. W. F. Arndt and F. W. Gingrich. 2nd ed. rev. and augmented by F. W. Gingrich and F. W. Danker from Bauer's 5th ed. (1958), Chicago, 1979.
BC	F. J. Foakes-Jackson and K. Lake, eds., *The Beginnings of Christianity. Part I: The Acts of the Apostles* I-V. New York, 1920-33.
BDB	F. Brown, S. R. Driver, and C. A. Briggs, *A Hebrew and English Lexicon of the Old Testament.* Oxford, 1907.
BDF	F. Blass and A. Debrunner, *A Greek Grammar of the New Testament and Other Early Christian Literature,* tr. and rev. R. W. Funk from the 10th German ed. Chicago, 1961.
BET	Beiträge zur biblischen Exegese und Theologie
BGBE	Beiträge zur Geschichte der biblischen Exegese
BGU	*Aegyptische Urkunden aus den staatlichen Museen zu Berlin: Griechische Urkunden* I-VIII. 1895-1933.
Bib	*Biblica*

BJRL	*Bulletin of the John Rylands University Library of Manchester*
BSac	*Bibliotheca Sacra*
BSt	Biblische Studien (Freiburg, 1895-1930)
BST	The Bible Speaks Today
BT	*The Bible Translator*
BWANT	Beiträge zur Wissenschaft vom Alten und Neuen Testament
BZ	*Biblische Zeitschrift*
BZNW	Beihefte zur *ZNW*
CBQ	*Catholic Biblical Quarterly*
CC	Concordia Commentary
CGTC	Cambridge Greek Testament Commentary
CGTSC	Cambridge Greek Testament for Schools and Colleges
CNT	Commentaar op het Nieuwe Testament (continuing Kommentaar op het Nieuwe Testament)
ConNT	Coniectanea neotestamentica
CTJ	*Calvin Theological Journal*
DAC	J. Hastings, ed., *Dictionary of the Apostolic Church* I-II. Edinburgh, 1915, 1918.
DClA	O. Seyffert, H. Nettleship, and J. E. Sardys, *Dictionary of Classical Antiquities.* Revised ed., London, 1957.
DGRA	W. Smith, W. Wayte, and G. E. Marindin, *Dictionary of Greek and Roman Antiquities.* Vol. I, third ed., London, 1890.
EBC	F. E. Gaebelein, J. D. Douglas, et al., eds., *The Expositor's Bible Commentary* I-XII. Grand Rapids, 1978ff.
ÉBib	Études bibliques
EGT	W. R. Nicoll, *The Expositor's Greek Testament* I-V. Reprinted Grand Rapids.
Enc. Bib.	T. K. Cheyne and J. S. Black, eds., *Encyclopaedia Biblica* I-IV. London, 1899-1903.
Ev Q	*Evangelical Quarterly*
Expositor	*The Expositor*
Exp Tim	*Expository Times*
GNC	Good News Commentaries
HNT	Handbuch zum Neuen Testament
HNTC	Harper's (= Black's) New Testament Commentaries
IB	G. A. Buttrick, et al., eds., *Interpreter's Bible* I-XII. New York, 1951-57.
ICC	International Critical Commentary
ISBE	G. W. Bromiley, et al., ed., *International Standard Bible Encyclopedia* I-IV. Grand Rapids, 1979-88.

JAC	Jahrbuch für Antike und Christentum
JBL	*Journal of Biblical Literature*
JSNT	*Journal for the Study of the New Testament*
JTS	*Journal of Theological Studies*
Judaica	*Judaica: Beiträge zum Verständnis des jüdischen schicksals in Vergangenheit und Gegenwart*
KJV	*King James Version (Authorized Version)*
KNT	Kommentar zum Neuen Testament
LCL	Loeb Classical Library
LSJM	H. G. Liddell and R. Scott, *A Greek-English Lexicon,* rev. and augmented by H. S. Jones and R. McKenzie, with a *Supplement* by E. A. Barber. Oxford, 1968.
MeyerK	Kritisch-exegetischer Kommentar über das Neue Testament (initiated by H. A. W. Meyer)
MGM	W. F. Moulton and A. S. Geden, *A Concordance to the Greek Testament.* 5th ed. rev. H. K. Moulton, Edinburgh, 1978.
MHT	J. H. Moulton, W. F. Howard, and N. Turner, *A Grammar of New Testament Greek* I-IV. Edinburgh, 1908-76.
MM	J. H. Moulton and G. Milligan, *The Vocabulary of the Greek Testament.* London, 1930.
MNTC	Moffatt New Testament Commentary
NA^{25}	E. Nestle and K. Aland, eds., *Novum Testamentum Graece.* 25th ed., Stuttgart, 1963.
NA^{26}	K. Aland and B. Aland, eds., *Novum Testamentum Graece.* 26th ed., Stuttgart, 1979.
NASB	*New American Standard Bible*
NBD	J. D. Douglas, N. Hillyer, et al., eds., *New Bible Dictionary.* 2nd ed., Wheaton, IL, 1982.
NCBC	New Century Bible Commentary
NClarB	New Clarendon Bible
NEB	*New English Bible*
New Docs	*New Documents Illustrating Early Christianity*
NICNT	New International Commentary on the New Testament
NIDNTT	C. Brown, ed., *The New International Dictionary of New Testament Theology* I-III. Grand Rapids, 1975-78.
NIGTC	New International Greek Testament Commentary
NIV	*New International Version*
NovT	*Novum Testamentum*
NovTSup	*NovT* Supplements
NPNF	Nicene and Post-Nicene Fathers
NTAbh	Neutestamentliche Abhandlungen
NTC	New Testament Commentary

NTD	Das Neue Testament Deutsch
NTF	Neutestamentliche Forschungen
NTS	*New Testament Studies*
ÖBS	Österreichische Biblische Studien
P. Oxy.	*Oxyrhyncus Papyri*
PW	A. Pauly, G. Wissowa, and W. Kroll, eds., *Real-Encyclopädie der classischen Altertumswissenschaft.* 1893ff.
RB	*Revue Biblique*
RevExp	*Review and Expositor*
RNT	Regensburger Neues Testament
RSV	*Revised Standard Version*
RV	*Revised Version*
Sac Vb	J. Bauer, ed., *Sacramentum Verbi: An Encyclopedia of Biblical Theology.* New York, 1970.
SB	Sources bibliques
SB et T	*Studia Biblica et Theologica*
SBLDS	Society of Biblical Literature Dissertation Series
SBT	Studies in Biblical Theology
SNTSMS	Society for New Testament Studies Monograph Series
Str-B	H. Strack and P. Billerbeck, *Kommentar zum Neuen Testament aus Talmud und Midrasch* I-V. 3rd ed., München, 1956.
SNTU	*Studien zum Neuen Testament und seiner Umwelt*
TCGNT	B. M. Metzger, *A Textual Commentary on the Greek New Testament.* New York, 1971.
TDNT	G. Kittel and G. Friedrich, eds., *Theological Dictionary of the New Testament,* tr. G. W. Bromiley, I-X. Grand Rapids, 1964-76.
TDNT Abridged	G. W. Bromiley, *TDNT Abridged in One Volume.* Grand Rapids, 1985.
TDOT	G. J. Botterweck and H. Ringgren, eds., *Theological Dictionary of the Old Testament,* tr. J. T. Willis, G. W. Bromiley, and D. E. Green, I-. Grand Rapids, 1974-.
TEV	*Today's English Version (Good News Bible)*
THKNT	Theologischer Handkommentar zum Neuen Testament
TJ	*Trinity Journal*
TLZ	*Theologische Literaturzeitung*
TNTC	Tyndale New Testament Commentaries
TSK	*Theologische Studien und Kritiken*
TWNT	G. Kittel and G. Friedrich, eds., *Theologisches Wörterbuch zum Neuen Testament* I-X. Stuttgart, 1933-74.
TZ	*Theologische Zeitschrift*

UBSGNT	K. Aland, M. Black, C. M. Martini, B. M. Metzger, and A. Wikgren, *The Greek New Testament* (United Bible Societies). 3rd ed. corrected, Stuttgart, 1983.
VC	*Vigiliae Christianae*
VKGNT	K. Aland, ed., *Vollständige Konkordanz zum griechischen Neuen Testament.* Berlin, I/1, 2, 1983; II *(Spezialübersichten),* 1978.
WBC	Word Biblical Commentary
WUNT	Wissenschaftliche Untersuchungen zum Neuen Testament
ZNW	*Zeitschrift für die neutestamentliche Wissenschaft*
ZPEB	M. Tenney, et al., eds., *The Zondervan Pictorial Encyclopedia of the Bible* I-V. Grand Rapids, 1975-76.

BIBLIOGRAPHY

Works listed here are cited by author and short title except commentaries on one or more of the Pastoral Epistles, which are marked here with an asterisk (*) and are cited by author's name only.

Abbot, E., "On the Construction of Titus II.13," *idem, The Authorship of the Fourth Gospel and other Critical Essays.* Boston, 1888.

Abbott-Smith, G., *A Manual Greek Lexicon of the New Testament.* 3rd ed., Edinburgh, 1937.

Aland, K., "The Problem of Anonymity and Pseudonymity in Christian Literature of the First Two Centuries," *The Authorship and Integrity of the New Testament.* London, 1965, 1-13 (= *JTS* 12 [1961] 39ff.).

* Alford, H., *The Greek Testament* III. 5th ed., Cambridge, 1871.

Allan, J. A., "The 'In Christ' Formula in the Pastoral Epistles," *NTS* 10 (1963) 115-21.

Anton, P., *Exegetische Abhandlung der Pastoralbriefe S. Pauli.* Halle, 1753-55.

Balsdon, J. P. V. D., *Roman Women.* London, 1962.

* Barclay, W., *The Letters to Timothy, Titus, and Philemon.* Daily Study Bible; rev. ed., Philadelphia, 1975.

———, *More New Testament Words.* New York, 1958.

———, "Paul's Certainties VII. Our Security in God — 2 Timothy 1,12," *Exp Tim* 69 (1958) 324-27.

Barr, J., *Biblical Words for Time.* SBT 33; London, 1952; rev. ed., 1969.

———, *The Semantics of Biblical Language.* Oxford, 1961.

* Barrett, C. K., *The Pastoral Epistles.* NClarB; Oxford, 1963.

Bauckham, R. J., *Jude, 2 Peter.* WBC; Waco, 1983.

Baur, F. C., *Die sogennanten Pastoralbriefe.* Stuttgart, 1835.

* Bengel, J. A., *Gnomon of the New Testament,* tr. C. T. Lewis and M. R. Vincent, II. New York, 1864; reprinted Grand Rapids, 1971 as *New Testament Word Studies.*

Berdot, D. N., *Exercitatio theologica-exegetica in epistulam Pauli ad Titum.* 1703.

* Bernard, J. H., *The Pastoral Epistles.* CGTSC; Cambridge, 1899; reprinted Grand Rapids, 1980 (Thornapple Commentaries).

Bettenson, H., ed. and tr., *The Early Christian Fathers.* London, 1956.

Bjerkelund, C. J., *PARAKALÔ: Form, Funktion und Sinn der parakalô-Sätze in der paulinischen Briefen.* Oslo, 1967.

* Bouma, C., *De Brieven van den Apostel Paulus aan Timotheus en Titus.* Kommentaar op het Nieuwe Testament 11; Amsterdam, 1946.

Bratcher, R. G., *A Translator's Guide to Paul's Letters to Timothy and Titus.* Helps for Translators Series; London, New York, and Stuttgart, 1983.

Brooks, J. A., and Winbery, C. L., *Syntax of New Testament Greek.* Washington, 1979.

Brox, N., "Lukas als Verfasser der Pastoralbriefe?" JAC 13 (1970) 62-77.

* ———, *Die Pastoralbriefe.* RNT; 4th ed., Regensburg, 1969.

Bruce, F. F., *Commentary on the Book of the Acts.* NICNT; 2nd ed., Grand Rapids, 1988.

———, *The Epistle to the Galatians: A Commentary on the Greek Text.* NIGTC; Exeter and Grand Rapids, 1982.

———, *The Epistle to the Hebrews.* NICNT; 2nd ed., Grand Rapids, 1964.

———, *The Letters of Paul: An Expanded Paraphrase.* Exeter and Grand Rapids, 1965.

———, *New Testament History.* London and Garden City, NY, 1969.

———, *1 & 2 Thessalonians.* WBC; Waco, 1982.

Buck, C. D., *A Dictionary of Selected Synonyms in the Principal Indo-European Languages.* Chicago, 1949.

* Bürki, H., *Der erste Brief des Paulus an Timotheus.* Wuppertaler Studienbibel; Wuppertal, 1974.

* ———, *Der zweite Brief des Paulus an Timotheus, die Briefe an Titus und an Philemon.* Wuppertaler Studienbibel; 3rd ed., Wuppertal, 1979.

Burroughs, J., *The Rare Jewel of Christian Contentment.* 1648; reprinted London, 1964.

Burton, E. D., *The Epistle to the Galatians.* ICC; Edinburgh, 1921; reprinted 1952.

———, *Syntax of the Moods and Tenses in New Testament Greek.* 3rd ed., Chicago and Edinburgh, 1898; reprinted 1955.

Cadbury, H. J., "Erastus of Corinth," *JBL* 50 (1931) 42-58.

———, "Roman Law and the Trial of Paul," *BC* V, 297-338.

Calder, W. M., "A Fourth-Century Lycaonian Bishop," *Expositor* 7/6 (1908) 383-408.

* Calvin, J., *The Second Epistle of Paul to the Corinthians, and the Epistles to Timothy, Titus and Philemon,* tr. T. A. Smail. Calvin's New Testament Commentaries; Grand Rapids, 1964.

Chapman, J., "The Historical Setting of the Second and Third Epistles of St. John," *JTS* 5 (1904) 364ff. (357-68, 517-34).

* Chrysostom, J., *Homilies on the Epistles of St. Paul the Apostle to Timothy, Titus, and Philemon,* the Oxford translation ed. P. Schaff. NPNF first series XIII; reprinted Grand Rapids, 1956.

Clark, L. F., "An Investigation of Some Applications of Quantitative Methods to the Pauline Letters, with a View to the Question of Authorship." Unpublished University of Manchester M. A. Thesis, 1979.

Colson, F. H., "'Myths and Genealogies' — A Note on the Polemic of the Pastoral Epistles," *JTS* 19 (1917/18) 265-71.

Cook, D., "The Pastoral Fragments Reconsidered," *JTS* 35 (1984) 120-31.

Cranfield, C. E. B., *The Epistle to the Romans* I-II. ICC; Edinburgh, 1975-79.

Cremer, H., *Biblico-Theological Lexicon of New Testament Greek,* tr. W. Urwick. 4th English ed., Edinburgh, 1895; reprinted 1954.
Dana, H. E., and Mantey, J. R., *A Manual Grammar of the Greek New Testament.* New York, 1927.
Daube, D., *The New Testament and Rabbinic Judaism.* London, 1956.
———, "Evangelisten und Rabbinen," *ZNW* 48 (1957) 119-26.
De Boer, W. P., *The Imitation of Paul.* Kampen, 1962.
Deer, D. S., "Still More about the Imperatival *hina,*" *BT* 30 (1979) 148.
Deichgräber, R., *Gotteshymnus und Christushymnus in der frühen Christenheit.* Göttingen, 1967.
Deissmann, A., *Bible Studies,* tr. A. J. Grieve. Edinburgh, 1901.
———, *Light from the Ancient East: The New Testament Illustrated by Recently Discovered Texts of the Graeco-Roman World,* tr. L. R. M. Strachan. 2nd ed., London, 1927; reprinted Grand Rapids, 1978.
de Lestapis, S., *L'énigme des Pastorales de Saint Paul.* Paris, 1976.
Delling, G., "ΜΟΝΟΣ ΘΕΟΣ," *idem, Studien zum Neuen Testament und zum hellenistischen Judentum. Gesammelte Aufsätze 1950-1968.* Göttingen, 1970, 391-400 (= *TLZ* 77 [1952] 469-76).
de Vaux, R., *Ancient Israel.* London, 1961.
Dey, J., *ΠΑΛΙΓΓΕΝΕΣΙΑ. Ein Beitrag zur Klärung der religionsgeschichtlichen Bedeutung von Titus 3,5.* NTAbh 17/5; Münster, 1937.
Dibelius, M., "Ἐπίγνωσις ἀλήθειας," *idem, Botschaft und Geschichte. Gesammelte Aufsätze.* Tübingen, 1956, II, 1-13.
* Dibelius, M., and Conzelmann, H., *The Pastoral Epistles,* tr. P. Buttolph and A. Yarbro. Hermeneia; Philadelphia, 1972.
Dodd, C. H., *According to the Scriptures: The Sub-structure of New Testament Theology.* London, 1952.
———, *The Apostolic Preaching and Its Developments.* London, 1936.
———, "New Testament Translation Problems II," *BT* 28 (1977) 112-16.
* Dornier, P., *Les Épîtres Pastorales.* SB; Paris, 1969.
Doty, W. G., "The Classification of Epistolary Literature," *CBQ* 31 (1969) 183-99.
———, *Letters in Primitive Christianity.* Philadelphia, 1973.
Dubowy, E., *Klemens von Rom über die Reise Pauli nach Spanien.* BSt 19/3; Freiburg, 1914.
Duncan, J. G., "Πιστὸς ὁ λόγος," *Exp Tim* 35 (1923) 141.
du Plessis, P. J., *ΤΕΛΕΙΟΣ: The Idea of Perfection in the New Testament.* Kampen, 1959.
* Earle, R., "1 Timothy," *EBC* XI, 339-90.
* ———, "2 Timothy," *EBC* XI, 391-418.
* Easton, B. S., *The Pastoral Epistles.* New York and London, 1948.
Eichhorn, J. G., *Historisch-kritische Einleitung in das Neue Testament.* Leipzig, 1812.
* Ellicott, C. J., *The Pastoral Epistles of St. Paul.* 3rd ed., London, 1864.
Ellingworth, P., "The 'True Saying' in 1 Timothy 3.1," *BT* 31 (1980) 443-45.
Ellis, E. E., *Paul's Use of the Old Testament.* Edinburgh and London, 1957; reprinted Grand Rapids, 1981.

———, "The Problem of Authorship: First and Second Timothy," *RevExp* 56 (1959) 343-54.

Exler, F. X. J., *The Form of the Ancient Greek Letter of the Epistolary Papyri (3rd cen. BC–3rd cen. AD).* Chicago, 1923.

* Fairbairn, P., *The Pastoral Epistles.* Edinburgh, 1874.

* Falconer, R., *The Pastoral Epistles.* Oxford, 1937.

* Fausset, A. R., 1-2 Timothy, Titus in R. Jamieson, A. R. Fausset, and D. Brown, *A Commentary, Critical, Experimental, and Practical on the Old and New Testaments.* Grand Rapids, 1948, VI, 480-522.

* Fee, G. D., *1 and 2 Timothy, Titus.* GNC; San Francisco, 1984.

Field, F., *Notes on the Translation of the New Testament.* Cambridge, 1899.

———, *Origenis hexaplorum quae supersunt . . . fragmenta* I-II.Oxford, 1875.

Finegan, J., *Handbook of Biblical Chronology.* Princeton, 1964.

Foerster, W., "Εὐσέβεια in den Pastoralbriefen," *NTS* 5 (1958) 213-18.

* Freundorfer, J., *Die Pastoralbriefe.* RNT 7; Regensburg, 1965.

Friedrich, G., "Lohmeyers These über das paulinische Briefpräskript kritisch beleuchtet," *TLZ* 81 (1956) 343-46.

Funk, R. W., *Language, Hermeneutic and the Word of God.* New York, 1966.

Furfey, P. H., "ΠΛΟΥΣΙΟΣ and Cognates in the New Testament," *CBQ* 5 (1943) 241-63.

Gasque, W. W., *A History of the Criticism of the Acts of the Apostles.* BGBE 17; Tübingen and Grand Rapids, 1975.

* Gealy, F. D., "The First and Second Epistles to Timothy and the Epistle to Titus," *IB* XI, 341-551.

Godet, F., *Studies on the Epistles of St. Paul,* tr. A. H. Holmden. New York, 1889.

Grayston, K., and Herdan, G., "The Authorship of the Pastorals in the Light of Statistical Linguistics," *NTS* 6 (1960) 1-15.

Greeven, H., "Propheten, Lehrer, Vorsteher bei Paulus, zur Frage der 'Ämter' im Urchristentum," *ZNW* 44 (1952-53) 1-43.

* Gromacki, R. G., *Stand True to the Charge: An Exposition of I Timothy.* Grand Rapids, 1982.

Gundry, R. H., "The Form, Meaning and Background of the Hymn Quoted in 1 Timothy 3:16," *Apostolic History and the Gospel,* ed. W. W. Gasque and R. P. Martin. Grand Rapids, 1970, 203-22.

Guthrie, D., "The Development of the Idea of Canonical Pseudepigrapha in New Testament Criticism," *The Authorship and Integrity of the New Testament.* London, 1965, 14-39 (= *Vox Evangelica* [1962] 43-59).

* ———, *The Pastoral Epistles: An Introduction and Commentary.* TNTC; revised ed., Leicester and Grand Rapids, 1990.

———, *The Pastoral Epistles and the Mind of Paul.* London, 1956.

———, *New Testament Introduction.* 3rd ed., Downers Grove, IL, 1970.

———, "Timothy," *NBD* 1279f.

Haenchen, E., *The Acts of the Apostles,* tr. B. Noble, et al. Philadelphia and Oxford, 1971.

Hanna, R., *A Grammatical Aid to the Greek New Testament.* Grand Rapids, 1983.

* Hanson, A. T., *The Pastoral Epistles.* NCBC; London and Grand Rapids, 1982.

———, *Studies in the Pastoral Epistles.* London, 1968.
Harris, M. J., Appendix: Prepositions and Theology in the Greek New Testament," *NIDNTT* III, 1171-1215.
———, "Titus 2:13 and the Deity of Christ," *Pauline Studies: Essays Presented to Professor F. F. Bruce on His 70th Birthday,* ed. D. Hagner and M. J. Harris. Grand Rapids, 1980, 262-77.
Harrison, P. N., "Important Hypotheses Reconsidered: III. The Authorship of the Pastoral Epistles," *Exp Tim* 67 (1955-56) 77-81.
———, *Paulines and Pastorals.* London, 1964.
———, *The Problem of the Pastoral Epistles.* London, 1921.
* Hasler, V., *Die Briefe an Timotheus und Titus.* Zürcher Bibelkommentare; Zurich, 1978.
Hatch, E., and Redpath, H. A., *A Concordance to the Septuagint.* Oxford, 1897.
Haykin, M. A. G., "The Fading Vision? The Spirit and Freedom in the Pastoral Epistles," *Ev Q* 57 (1985) 291-305.
Hebert, G., " 'Faithfulness' and 'Faith,' " *Theology* 58 (1955) 373-79.
* Hendriksen, W., *Exposition of the Pastoral Epistles.* NTC; Grand Rapids, 1957.
* Hiebert, D. E., "Titus," *EBC* XI, 419-49.
Hillman, E., *Polygamy Reconsidered.* Maryknoll, 1975.
Hitchcock, F. R. M., "Latinity in the Pastorals," *Exp Tim* 39 (1927-28) 347-52.
———, "Philo and the Pastorals," *Hermathena* 56 (1940) 113-35.
———, "Tests for the Pastorals," *JTS* 30 (1928-29) 272-79.
* Holtz, G., *Die Pastoralbriefe.* THKNT 13; Berlin, 1965.
* Holtzmann, H. J., *Die Pastoralbriefe kritisch und exegetisch bearbeitet.* Leipzig, 1880.
Horsley, G. H. R., *New Documents Illustrating Early Christianity.* North Ryde, N. S. W., Australia, 1981ff.
Hort, F. J. A., *The Epistle of St. James.* London, 1909.
———, *Judaistic Christianity.* London, 1894; reprinted Grand Rapids, 1980.
* Houlden, J. L., *The Pastoral Epistles: I and II Timothy, Titus.* Pelican New Testament Commentaries; London, 1976.
House, H. W., "Biblical Inspiration in 2 Timothy 3:16," *BSac* 137 (1980) 54-63.
Hughes, P. E., *A Commentary on the Epistle to the Hebrews.* Grand Rapids, 1977.
———, *Paul's Second Epistle to the Corinthians.* NICNT; Grand Rapids, 1962.
Huizenga, H., "Women, Salvation and the Birth of Christ: A Reexamination of 1 Timothy 2:15," *SB et T* 12 (1982) 17-26.
Hull, W. E., "The Man — Timothy," *RevExp* 56 (1959) 355-66.
Hunt, A. S., and Edgar, C. C., eds. and trs., *Select Papyri* I. LCL; Cambridge, MA, and London, 1959.
Hunter, A. M., *Interpreting the New Testament: 1900-1950.* London, 1951.
———, *Paul and His Predecessors.* 2nd ed., London, 1961.
Hurley, J. B., *Man and Woman in Biblical Perspective.* Grand Rapids and Leicester, 1981.
* Huther, J. E., *Pastoral Epistles* (tr. of MeyerK 4th ed.). Edinburgh, 1893.
James, J. D., *The Genuineness and Authorship of the Pastoral Epistles.* London, 1909.

* Jeremias, J., *Die Briefe an Timotheus und Titus.* NTD IX; 8th ed., Göttingen, 1963.

———, "Das Lösegeld für viele," *Judaica* 3 (1948) 249-64.

———, "ΠΡΕΣΒΥΤΕΡΙΟΝ ausserchristlich bezeugt," *ZNW* 48 (1957) 127-32.

Johnson, L. T., "James 3:13–4:10 and the *Topos ΠΕΡΙ ΦΘΟΝΟΥ*," *NovT* 25 (1983) 327-47.

Johnson, P. F., "The Use of Statistics in the Analysis of the Characteristics of Pauline Writings," *NTS* 20 (1974) 92-100.

Jonker, G. J. A., "De paulinische formule 'door Christus,' " *TSK* 27 (1909) 173-208.

Karris, R. J., "The Background and Significance of the Polemic of the Pastoral Epistles," *JBL* 92 (1973) 549-64.

* ———, *The Pastoral Epistles.* New Testament Message 17; Wilmington and Dublin, 1979.

Käsemann, E., *Essays on New Testament Themes,* tr. W. J. Montague. London, 1964.

———, "Das Formular einer neutestamentlichen Ordinationspäranese," *Neutestamentliche Studien für Rudolf Bultmann,* ed. W. Eltester. BZNW 21; Berlin, 1957, 261-68.

Kee, H. C., "The Linguistic Background of 'Shame' in the New Testament," *On Language, Culture, and Religion: In Honor of Eugene A. Nida,* ed. M. Black and W. A. Smalley. The Hague, 1974, 133-74.

* Kelly, J. N. D., *A Commentary on the Pastoral Epistles.* HNTC; New York, 1963; reprinted Grand Rapids, 1981 (Thornapple Commentaries).

Kenny, A., *A Stylometric Study of the New Testament.* Oxford, 1986.

* Kent, H. A., *The Pastoral Epistles: Studies in I and II Timothy and Titus.* Chicago, 1958.

Kidd, R. M., *Wealth and Beneficence in the Pastoral Epistles.* SBLDS 122; Atlanta, 1990.

Kilpatrick, G. D., ed., *Η ΚΑΙΝΗ ΔΙΑΘΗΚΗ.* 2nd ed., London, 1958.

Kittel, G., "Die γενεαλογία der Pastoralbriefe," *ZNW* 20 (1921) 16-69.

Knight, G. W., III, "ΑΥΘΕΝΤΕΩ in Reference to Women in 1 Timothy 2.12," *NTS* 30 (1984) 143-57.

———, *The Faithful Sayings in the Pastoral Letters.* Kampen, 1968; reprinted Grand Rapids, 1979.

———, *The Role Relationship of Men and Women.* Revised ed., Phillipsburg, NJ, 1985.

Kümmel, W. G., *Introduction to the New Testament,* tr. H. C. Kee. 2nd ed., Nashville, 1975.

Lake, K., tr., *The Apostolic Fathers* I-II. LCL; London and Cambridge, MA, 1912-13.

———, tr., *Eusebius, The Ecclesiastical History* I (Books I-V). LCL; London and Cambridge, MA, 1926.

Lampe, G. W. H., *A Patristic Greek Lexicon.* Oxford, 1961.

Lane, W. L., "First Timothy IV.1-3: An Early Instance of Over-realized Eschatology?" *NTS* 11 (1965) 164-67.

Lategan, B. C., *Die Aardse Jesus in Die Prediking van Paulus volgens sy briewe.* Rotterdam, 1967.

* Leaney, A. R. C., *The Epistles to Timothy, Titus, and Philemon: Introduction and Commentary.* Torch Bible Commentaries; London, 1960.

Leivestad, R., "'The Meekness and Gentleness of Christ' II Cor. x.1," *NTS* 12 (1965-66) 156-64.

Lenski, R. C. H., *The Interpretation of St. Matthew's Gospel.* Columbus, OH, 1932.

* ———, *The Interpretation of St. Paul's Epistles to the Colossians, to the Thessalonians, to Timothy, to Titus and to Philemon.* Minneapolis, 1937.

* Liddon, H. P., *Explanatory Analysis of St. Paul's First Epistle to Timothy.* London, 1897.

Lightfoot, J. B., *The Apostolic Fathers,* part I, vols. I, II; part II, vols. I-III. London, 1869-90.

———, *Biblical Essays.* London, 1893.

———, *The Epistle of St. Paul to the Galatians.* London, 1884; reprinted Grand Rapids.

———, *Saint Paul's Epistle to the Philippians.* London, 1913; reprinted Grand Rapids, 1953.

* Lock, W., *A Critical and Exegetical Commentary on The Pastoral Epistles.* ICC; Edinburgh, 1924.

Lohmeyer, E., "Probleme paulinischer Theologie. I: Briefliche Grussüberschriften," *ZNW* 26 (1927) 158-73.

Lohse, E., *Die Ordination im Spätjudentum und im Neuen Testament.* Berlin, 1951.

Longenecker, R. N., "Acts," *EBC* IX. Grand Rapids, 1981.

Louw, J. P., and Nida, E. A., *Greek-English Lexicon of the New Testament Based on Semantic Domains.* 2 vols., New York, 1988.

Malherbe, A. J., "'In Season and Out of Season': 2 Timothy 4:2," *JBL* 103 (1984) 235-43.

Marshall, I. H., *The Acts of the Apostles: An Introduction and Commentary.* TNTC; Leicester and Grand Rapids, 1980.

———, *A Commentary on the Epistles to the Thessalonians.* NCBC; Grand Rapids and London, 1982.

———, "Faith and Works in the Pastoral Epistles," *SNTU* 9 (1984) 203-18.

———, *The Gospel of Luke: A Commentary on the Greek Text.* NIGTC; Exeter and Grand Rapids, 1978.

Mason, H. J., *Greek Terms for Roman Institutions: A Lexicon and Analysis.* Toronto, 1974.

Mayser, E., *Grammatik der griechischen Papyri aus der Ptolemäerzeit* I-II. Berlin and Leipzig, 1906-34.

McCasland, S. V., "Christ Jesus," *JBL* 65 (1946) 377-83.

McEleney, N. J., "The Vice Lists of the Pastoral Epistles," *CBQ* 36 (1974) 203-19.

McNamara, M., *The New Testament and the Palestinian Targum to the Pentateuch.* AnBib 27; Rome, 1966.

Meade, D. G., *Pseudonymity and Canon: An Investigation into the Relationship of Authorship and Authority in Jewish and Earliest Christian Tradition.* WUNT; Tübingen, 1986, Grand Rapids, 1987.

Meinertz, M., "Worauf bezieht sich die πρώτη ἀπολογία (2 Tim 4,16)?" *Bib* 4 (1923) 390-94.

Members of the Illinois Greek Club, *Aeneas, Tacticus, Asclepiodotus, Onasander.* LCL; London and Cambridge, MA, 1923.

Metzger, B. M., "A Reconsideration of Certain Arguments against the Pauline Authorship of the Pastoral Epistles," *Exp Tim* 70 (1958) 91-94.

———, *A Textual Commentary on the Greek New Testament.* London and New York, 1971.

Metzger, W., *Der Christushymnus 1 Timotheus 3,16.* Stuttgart, 1979.

———, *Die letzte Reise des Apostels Paulus: Beobachtungen und Erwägungen zu seinem Itinerar nach den Pastoralbriefen.* Stuttgart, 1976.

———, "Die *neôtérikai epithymíai* in 2. Tim. 2,22," *TZ* 33 (1977) 129-36.

Michaelis, W., *Pastoralbriefe und Gefangenschaftsbriefe: Zur Echtheitsfrage der Pastoralbriefe.* NTF 1/6; Gütersloh, 1930.

———, "Pastoralbriefe und Wortstatistik," *ZNW* 28 (1929) 69-76.

Michaelson, S., and Morton, A. Q., "Last Words: A Test of Authorship for Greek Writers," *NTS* 18 (1972) 192-208.

Michel, O., *Der Brief an die Römer.* MeyerK; 10th ed., Göttingen, 1955.

———, *Paulus und seine Bibel.* Gütersloh, 1929; reprinted Darmstadt, 1972.

Mickelsen, A., ed., *Women, Authority and the Bible.* Downers Grove, 1986.

Milligan, G., *St. Paul's Epistles to the Thessalonians.* Grand Rapids, 1959.

* Moellering, H. A., *1 Timothy, 2 Timothy, Titus.* CC; Saint Louis, 1970.

Moffatt, J., *Love in the New Testament.* London, 1929.

Moo, D. J., "1 Timothy 2:11-15: Meaning and Significance," *TJ* new series 1 (1980) 62-83.

———, "The Interpretation of 1 Timothy 2:11-15: A Rejoinder," *TJ* new series 2 (1981) 198-222.

Morgenthaler, R., *Statistik des Neutestamentlichen Wortschatzes.* Zürich, 1958, with *Beiheft zur 3. Auflage,* 1982.

Morris, L., *The Apostolic Preaching of the Cross.* 3rd ed., London, 1965.

———, *The First and Second Epistles to the Thessalonians.* NICNT; revised ed., Grand Rapids, 1991.

———, *New Testament Theology,* Grand Rapids, 1986.

Morton, A. Q., *Literary Detection: How to Prove Authorship and Fraud in Literary Documents.* New York and London, 1978.

Morton, A. Q., and McLeman, J. J., *Paul, the Man and the Myth.* London, 1966.

Moule, C. F. D., *The Epistles of Paul the Apostle to the Colossians and to Philemon.* CGTC; Cambridge, 1957.

———, *An Idiom-Book of New Testament Greek.* 2nd ed., Cambridge, 1959.

———, *The Meaning of Hope.* Philadelphia, 1963.

———, *The Origin of Christology.* Cambridge, 1977.

———, "The Problem of the Pastoral Epistles: A Reappraisal," *BJRL* 47 (1965) 430-52.

———, *Worship in the New Testament.* Ecumenical Studies in Worship 9; London and Richmond, 1961.

* Moule, H. C. G., *Studies in II Timothy.* London, 1905 (as *The Second Epistle to Timothy: Short Devotional Studies on the Dying Letter of St. Paul*); reprinted Grand Rapids, 1977.

Murray, J., *The Epistle to the Romans* I-II. NICNT; Grand Rapids, 1959, 1965.

Neumann, K. J., *The Authenticity of the Pauline Epistles in the Light of Stylostatistical Analysis.* SBLDS 120; Atlanta, 1990.

Norbie, D. L., "The Washing of Regeneration," *Ev Q* 34 (1962) 36-38.

O'Brien, P. T., *Introductory Thanksgivings in the Letters of Paul.* NovTSup 49; Leiden, 1977.

Oxford Society of Historical Theology, *The New Testament in the Apostolic Fathers.* Oxford, 1905.

Padgett, A., "The Pauline Rationale for Submission: Biblical Feminism and the *hina* Clauses of Titus 2:1-10," *Ev Q* 59 (1987) 39-52.

* Parry, R. S. J., *The Pastoral Epistles with Introduction, Text and Commentary.* Cambridge, 1920.

Pax, E., *ΕΠΙΦΑΝΕΙΑ, Ein religionsgeschichtlicher Beitrag zur biblischen Theologie.* München, 1955.

Pfitzner, V. C., *Paul and the Agon Motif: Traditional Athletic Imagery in the Pauline Literature.* NovTSup 16; Leiden, 1967.

Pherigo, L. P., "Paul's Life After the Close of Acts," *JBL* 70 (1951) 277-84.

Phillips, J. B., *The New Testament in Modern English.* London, 1959.

Pierce, C. A., *Conscience in the New Testament.* SBT 15; London, 1955.

Piper, J., and Grudem, W., eds., *Recovering Biblical Manhood and Womanhood.* Wheaton, IL, 1991.

* Plummer, A., *The Pastoral Epistles.* The Expositor's Bible; New York, 1888; reprinted Grand Rapids, 1943.

Prat, F., *The Theology of St. Paul,* tr. J. L. Stoddard, I-II. London, 1959.

Preisigke, F., *Wörterbuch der griechischen Papyruskunden* (completed by E. Kiessling) I-III. Berlin, 1925-31.

Prior, M. P., *Paul The Letter-Writer and The Second Letter to Timothy.* JSNT Supplement Series 23; Sheffield, 1988.

Quinn, J. D., "The Last Volume of Luke: The Relation of Luke-Acts to the Pastoral Epistles," *Perspectives on Luke-Acts,* ed. C. H. Talbert. Danville and Edinburgh, 1978, 62-75.

———, "𝔭46 — The Pauline Canon," *CBQ* 36 (1974) 379-85.

Radermacher, L., *Neutestamentliche Grammatik,* HNT 1/1. 2nd ed., Tübingen, 1925.

Ramsay, W. M., *The Church in the Roman Empire before* A.D. *170.* 5th ed., London, 1897.

———, *The Cities and Bishoprics of Phrygia,* I-II. Oxford, 1895-97.

* ———, "A Historical Commentary on the Epistles to Timothy," *Expositor* 7/7 (1909) 481-94; 7/8 (1909) 1-21, 167-85, 264-82, 339-57, 399-416, 557-668; 7/9 (1910) 172-87, 319-33, 433-40; 8/1 (1911) 262-73, 356-75.

Reicke, B., "Chronologie der Pastoralbriefe," *TLZ* 101 (1976) 81-94.

Reumann, J., "*OIKONOMIA*-Terms in Paul in Comparison with Lucan Heilsgeschichte," *NTS* 13 (1966-67), 147-67.

Ridderbos, H. N., "Kerkelijke orde en kerkelijk recht in de brieven van Paulus," *Ex auditu verbi (Feestbundel G. C. Berkouwer).* Kampen, 1965, 194-215.

* ———, *De Pastoral Brieven.* CNT; Kampen, 1967.

———, *Aan de Romeinen.* CNT; Kampen, 1959.

———, *Paul: An Outline of His Theology,* tr. J. R. De Witt. Grand Rapids, 1975.

Rienecker, F., *Sprachlicher Schlüssel zum Griechischen Neuen Testament.* 9th ed., Giessen and Basel, 1956.

Rienecker, F., and Rogers, C., *A Linguistic Key to the Greek New Testament.* Grand Rapids, 1980.

Riesenfeld, H., "The Meaning of the Verb ἀρνεῖσθαι," *In honorem Antonii Fridrichsen sexagenarii.* ConNT 11; Lund, 1947, 207-19.

Roberts, J. W., "The Bearing of The Use of Particles on the Authorship of The Pastoral Epistles," *Restoration Quarterly* 2 (1958) 132-37.

———, "Every Scripture Inspired of God," *Restoration Quarterly* 5 (1961) 33-37.

———, "Note on the Adjective after πᾶς in 2 Timothy 3[16]," *Exp Tim* 76 (1965) 359.

* Robertson, A. T., *The Epistles of Paul* (*Word Pictures in the New Testament,* IV). Nashville, 1931.

———, *A Grammar of the Greek New Testament in the Light of Historical Research.* 3rd ed., Nashville, 1919.

———, "The Greek Article and the Deity of Christ," *Expositor* 8/21 (1921) 182-88.

Robinson, H. W., "Hair," *DAC* I, 520.

Robinson, J. A. T., *Redating the New Testament.* London and Philadelphia, 1976.

Robinson, T. A., "Grayston and Herdan's 'C' Quantity Formula and the Authorship of the Pastoral Epistles," *NTS* 30 (1984) 282-88.

Roller, O., *Das Formular der paulinischen Briefe: Ein Beitrag zur Lehre vom antiken Briefe.* BWANT 4/6; Stuttgart, 1933.

Romaniuk, K., "L'origine des formules pauliniennes 'Le Christ s'est livré pour nous,' 'Le Christ nous a aimés et s'est livré pour nous,'" *NovT* 5 (1962) 55-76.

Sanders, J., "The Transition from Opening Epistolary Thanksgiving to Body in the Letters of the Pauline Corpus," *JBL* 81 (1962) 348-62.

Schlarb, E., "Miszelle zu 1 Tim 6 20," *ZNW* 77 (1986) 276-81.

* Schlatter, A., *Die Kirche der Griechen im Urteil des Paulus: Eine Auslegung seiner Briefe an Timotheus und Titus.* Stuttgart, 1936.

Schleiermacher, F. *Über den sogenannten Brief des Paulos an den Timotheos: Sendschreiben an J. C. Gass.* Berlin, 1807; reprinted in *Sämtliche Werke* I/1, 1836, 221ff.

Schott, H. A., *Isagoge Historico-critica in Libros Novi Foederis Sacros.* 1830.

Schwarz, R., *Bürgerliches Christentum im Neuen Testament? Ein Studie zu Ethik, Amt und Recht in den Pastoralbriefen.* ÖBS 4; Klosterneuburg, 1983.

Schweitzer, A., *Paul and His Interpreters,* tr. W. Montgomery. London, 1912.

Schweizer, E., *Church Order in the New Testament,* tr. F. Clarke. SBT 32; London, 1961.

———, *Lordship and Discipleship.* SBT 28, London, 1960.

* Scott, E. F., *The Pastoral Epistles.* MNTC; London, 1936.

Scott, W., ed. and tr., *Hermetica: The Ancient Greek and Latin Writings Which Contain Religious or Philosophic Teachings Ascribed to Hermes Trismegistus.* Vol. I, Oxford, 1924.

Sherwin-White, A. N., *Roman Society and Roman Law in the New Testament.* Oxford, 1963.

* Simpson, E. K., *The Pastoral Epistles: The Greek Text with Introduction and Commentary.* London, 1954.

Skeat, T. C., "'Especially the Parchments': A Note on 2 Timothy IV.13," *JTS* 30 (1979) 173-77.

* Smith, R. E., and Beekman, J., *A Literary-Semantic Analysis of Second Timothy,* ed. M. F. Kopesec. Dallas, 1981.

Smyth, H. W., *Greek Grammar,* rev. G. M. Messing. Cambridge, 1959.

Sohm, R., *Kirchenrecht* I. Leipzig, 1892.

———, *Wesen und Ursprung des Katholizismus.* 2nd ed., Leipzig, 1912; reprinted Stuttgart, 1967.

Sophocles, E. A., *A Greek Lexicon of the Roman and Byzantine Periods (from BC 146–AD 110)* I-II. New York, 1887.

Spence, R. M., "2 Timothy iii.15, 16," *Exp Tim* 8 (1896-97), 564f.

Spicq, C., "1 Timothée 5:23," *L'Évangile, hier et aujourd'hui. Mélanges offerts au Professeur Franz-J. Leenhardt.* Geneva, 1968, 143-50.

———, *Notes de lexicographie néo-testamentaire* I-II + Supplément. Orbis biblicus et orientalis 22/1-3; Fribourg, 1978, 1982.

———, "Saint Paul et la loi des dépôts," *RB* 40 (1931) 481-502.

* ———, *Saint Paul. Les Épîtres Pastorales* I-II. ÉBib; 4th ed., Paris, 1969.

———, "Le vocabulaire de l'esclavage dans le Noveau Testament," *RB* 85 (1978) 201-26.

Staab, K., *Pauluskommentare aus der griechischen Kirche.* Münster, 1933.

Stacey, W. D., *The Pauline View of Man.* London, 1956.

Stenger, W., *Der Christushymnus 1 Tim. 3,16. Eine structuranalytische Untersuchung.* Regensburger Studien zur Theologie 6; Frankfurt, 1977.

* Stott, J. R. W., *Guard the Gospel: The Message of 2 Timothy.* BST; Downers Grove and London, 1973.

Streeter, B. H., *The Primitive Church.* London, 1929.

Strobel, A., "Schreiben des Lukas? Zum sprachlichen Problem der Pastoralbriefe," *NTS* 15 (1969) 191-210.

Swete, H. B., "The Faithful Sayings," *JTS* 18 (1917) 1-7.

Tasker, R. V. G., ed., *The Greek New Testament;* being the text translated in The New English Bible. 1961. Oxford and Cambridge, 1964.

Taubenschlag, P., "The Legal Profession in Greco-Roman Egypt," *Festschrift Fritz Schulz,* ed. H. Böhlaus. Weimar, 1951, II, 189-91.

Thayer, J. H., *A Greek-English Lexicon of the New Testament.* 4th ed., Edinburgh, 1901.

* Theodore of Mopsuestia, *In Epistolas B. Pauli Commentarii: The Latin Version with the Greek Fragments, with an Introduction, Notes and Indices,* by H. B. Swete. Vol. II, Cambridge, 1882.

Theron, D. J., *Evidence of Tradition.* Grand Rapids, 1958.

Thrall, M. E., "The Pauline Use of Συνείδησις," *NTS* 14 (1967-68) 118-25.

Tischendorf, C., *Novum Testamentum Graece.* Leipzig, 1869. 8th ed. 1872.

Torrance, T. F., "One Aspect of the Biblical Conception of Faith," *Exp Tim* 68 (1957) 111-14.

Towner, P., "The Present Age in the Eschatology of the Pastoral Epistles," *NTS* 32 (1986) 427-48.

Trench, R. C., *Synonyms of the New Testament.* 9th ed., London, 1880; reprinted Grand Rapids, 1963.

Trummer, P., "Mantel und Schriften," *BZ* 18 (1974) 193-207.

———, *Die Paulustradition der Pastoralbriefe.* BET 8; Frankfurt, 1978.

Turner, N., *Grammatical Insights into the New Testament.* Edinburgh, 1965.

Usener, H., "Die Perle," *Das Neue Testament und die urchristliche Überlieferung, Theologische Abhandlungen C. von Weizsäcker gewidmet,* by A. Harnack, et al. Freiburg, 1892, 203-13.

van Bruggen, J., *Die geschichtliche Einordnung der Pastoralbriefe.* Wuppertal, 1981.

Van Elderen, B., "The Verb in the Epistolary Invocation," *CTJ* 2 (1967) 46-48.

* van Oosterzee, J. J., "The Pastoral Letters," *Commentary on the Holy Scriptures,* ed. J. P. Lange, translation ed. P. Schaff. Reprinted, Grand Rapids, 1960, vol. VIII.

van Unnik, W. C., "Dominus Vobiscum," *New Testament Essays: Studies in Memory of Thomas Walter Manson,* ed. A. J. B. Higgins. Manchester, 1959, 270-305.

Verner, D. C., *The Household of God: The Social World of the Pastoral Epistles.* SBLDS 71; Chico, CA, 1983.

* Vine, W. E., *The Epistles to Timothy and Titus.* London, 1965.

———, *An Expository Dictionary of New Testament Words.* Old Tappan, NJ, 1966.

Vogels, H. J., *Novum Testamentum Graece et Latine.* 4th ed., Freiburg, 1955.

Vögtle, A., *Die Tugend- und Lasterkataloge im NT.* NTAbh 16/4, 5; Münster, 1936.

von Campenhausen, H., *Ecclesiastical Authority and Spiritual Power in the Church of the First Three Centuries,* tr. J. A. Baker. Stanford, 1969.

* von Soden, H., *Die Briefe an die Kolosser, Epheser, Philemon; die Pastoralbriefe.* Hand-Commentar zum Neuen Testament 3/1; 2nd ed., Freiburg and Leipzig, 1893.

von Soden, H. F., *Die Schriften des Neuen Testaments in ihrer ältesten erreichbaren Textgestalt hergestellt auf Grund ihrer Textgeschichte,* I-IV. Berlin, 1902-13.

* Wallis, W. B., "The First Epistle to Timothy," "The Second Epistle to Timothy," "The Epistle to Titus," *The Wycliffe Bible Commentary,* ed. C. F. Pfeiffer and E. F. Harrison. Chicago, 1962, 1367-96.

* Ward, R. A., *Commentary on 1 & 2 Timothy & Titus.* Waco, 1974.

Warfield, B. B., *The Inspiration and Authority of the Bible.* Philadelphia, 1948 (virtually = *Revelation and Inspiration,* 1927).

———, *The Lord of Glory.* New York, 1907.

* Weiss, B., *Die Briefe Pauli an Timotheus und Titus.* MeyerK 11; 7th ed., Göttingen, 1902.

Wendland, P., *Die urchristlichen Literaturformen.* HNT 1/3 (bound with Wendland's *Hellenistisch-Römische Kultur in ihren Beziehungen zu Judentum und Christentum* [HNT 1/2]); Tübingen, 1912.

Westcott, B. F., and Hort, F. J. A., *The New Testament in the Original Greek.* Cambridge and London, 1881.

Wet[t]stein, J. J., *Novum Testamentum Graecum,* I-II. Amsterdam, 1751-52.

White, J. L., *The Body of the Greek Letter.* Missoula, 1972.

* White, N. J. D., "The Pastoral Epistles," *EGT* IV, 55-202.

Wilcox, M., *The Semiticism of Acts.* Oxford, 1965.

Wiles, G. R., *Paul's Intercessory Prayers.* SNTSMS 24; Cambridge, 1974.

Wilshire, L. E., "The TLG Computer and Further Reference to ΑΥΘΕΝΤΕΩ in 1 Timothy 2.12," *NTS* 34 (1988) 120-34.

* Wilson, G. B. *The Pastoral Epistles.* Edinburgh, 1982.

Wilson, R. M., *The Gnostic Problem.* London, 1958.

Wilson, S. G., *Luke and the Pastoral Epistles.* London, 1979.

Winer, G. B., *A Grammar of the Idiom of the New Testament, Prepared as a Solid Basis for the Interpretation of the New Testament,* tr. J. H. Thayer. Andover, 1872.

———, *A Treatise on the Grammar of New Testament Greek, Regarded as a Sure Basis for New Testament Exegesis,* tr. W. F. Moulton. 3rd ed., Edinburgh, 1882.

* Wohlenberg, G., *Die Pastoralbriefe.* KNT 13; 2nd ed., Leipzig, 1911.

Wright, D. F., "Homosexuals or Prostitutes? The Meaning of ΑΡΣΕΝΟΚΟΙΤΑΙ (1 Cor. 6:9; 1 Tim. 1:10)," *VC* 38 (1984) 125-53.

* Wuest, K. S., *The Pastoral Epistles in the Greek New Testament.* Grand Rapids, 1952.

Yamauchi, E., *Pre-Christian Gnosticism.* London, 1973.

Ysebaert, J., *Greek Baptismal Terminology: Its Origins and Early Development.* Graecitas Christianorum Primaeva 1; Nijmegen, 1962.

Yule, G. U., *The Statistical Study of Literary Vocabulary.* Cambridge, 1944.

Zahn, T., *Introduction to the New Testament,* tr. J. M. Trout, et al. Vol. II, reprinted Grand Rapids, 1953.

Zerwick, M., *Biblical Greek,* tr. J. Smith. Rome, 1963.

INTRODUCTION

THE NAME "PASTORAL EPISTLES"

The three letters 1 and 2 Timothy and Titus stand in very close relationship to one another. In contrast to the other Pauline letters,[1] which, except for Philemon, were written to churches, these three letters were written to fellow workers of the apostle Paul to give instruction concerning their pastoral duties. The similar content of the three letters also binds them together as a special group among the Pauline letters. Kümmel has put it tersely and well: "They presuppose the same false teachers, the same organization, and entirely similar conditions in the community. They move within the same relative theological concepts and have the same peculiarities of language and style."[2]

That they make up a special group and as such contain instructions for the conduct of the pastoral office has led to the collective designation of these three letters as "the Pastoral Epistles" (and thus the abbreviation PE used for them in this commentary), "Pastoral Letters," or simply "the Pastorals." As early as the Muratorian canon these Epistles were highly regarded for "the regulation of ecclesiastical discipline." But as far as we can ascertain, it was not until the eighteenth century that the designation "Pastoral Epistles" was applied to them. The earliest known use of the term was by Berdot, writing in 1703 and referring to Titus.[3] It was applied to all three letters in a work by Anton published posthumously in 1753-55.[4] The name has since then become a permanent fixture and serves today not only as an appropriate but also as a convenient way to refer to the three letters as a collective whole.

1. When referring to the other Pauline letters I shall be referring to the other letters of the known Pauline corpus, ten in number, found in the NT and bearing the name of Paul as their author. See n. 55 below.

2. Kümmel, *Introduction,* 367.

3. Berdot, *Exercitatio,* 3f.

4. Anton, *Abhandlung.*

SELF-TESTIMONY REGARDING AUTHORSHIP, RECIPIENTS, SETTING, AND PURPOSES

Since the three letters comprise a closely knit group, they may, in large part, be considered together with respect to questions regarding their authorship and related matters. Of course, the distinguishing qualities of each letter in regard to recipient and historical situation will have their own independent place in the composite picture. Before we turn to the modern critical evaluation of the question of authorship, it is only appropriate that a full account be taken of the self-testimony that the letters themselves afford.

AUTHORSHIP

The letters all claim to be by Paul the apostle of Christ Jesus (1 Tim. 1:1; Tit. 1:1; 2 Tim. 1:1), and this assertion is made in salutations similar to those in the other Pauline letters (see the commentary at 1 Tim. 1:1ff.). The description in 1 Tim. 1:12-14 of the author's former life as that of "a blasphemer and a persecutor and a violent aggressor" and of the change he experienced is in full accord with what we know of Paul from Acts and Paul's other letters (see the commentary at 1 Tim. 1:12-14 for comparison with the accounts in Acts of Paul's conversion). The recipients of the letters, Timothy and Titus, are addressed as spiritual sons and are instructed as those who work under the authority of the apostle; this description fits with what we know about them and their relationship to Paul from the other letters and from Acts (see the section below on **Recipients** and the commentary at 1 Tim. 1:2 and Tit. 1:4 for details and documentation). Paul's constantly recurring directions to Timothy and Titus are a pervasive note in these letters (cf. 1 Tim. 1:3, 18; 3:14; 4:6-16; 5:21-25; 6:11-14, 20; Tit. 1:5; 2:1, 6-8, 15; 3:12; 2 Tim. 1:3-8, 13-14; 2:1-3, 7, 14-16, 22-26; 3:1, 10-17; 4:1-5, 8, 11, 13, 15, 21-22).

The letters refer to specific events and places and are written in relation to these events. 1 Timothy says that Timothy was instructed to remain in

Ephesus to withstand false teaching and implies that it was written as a further reminder from Paul to carry out that instruction (1:3). Among the false teachers Hymenaeus and Alexander are singled out by name as specific examples (1:20). The letter is also written to give instructions in case Paul is delayed in his hoped-for visit (3:14, 15; cf. 4:13).

The letter to Titus relates that Titus was left on Crete to see that elders were chosen and installed in every city (1:5) and quotes the infamous statement about Cretans made by one whom they esteemed as a prophet (1:12). The letter asks Titus to join the author in Nicopolis when Titus has been replaced by either Artemas or Tychicus (3:12). It mentions two well-known fellow workers of Paul (Tychicus and Apollos) and with them two workers not mentioned elsewhere in the NT (Artemas and Zenas the lawyer, 3:12, 13).

There are references to the life and present situation of Paul and to Timothy's situation in almost every paragraph of 2 Timothy (see the extended list of verses above). Paul refers to himself as one who has suffered for the gospel and is now imprisoned for it (1:12) and as one through whom God has graciously communicated his gospel in the midst of all this difficulty (2:9). Paul appeals to his own example to show Timothy the necessity of suffering for the gospel and also to provide encouragement to Timothy: Just as God has enabled Paul so will he also enable Timothy (1:8, 12; 2:1, 3, 9). Paul recalls the faith of Timothy's mother and grandmother, both of whom he refers to by name (1:5), the training in the scriptures that Timothy has received (3:14, 15), and his awareness of the persecutions in Antioch, Iconium, and Lystra, out of which Paul had been delivered by the faithful and powerful Lord (3:11). As in the first letter, Paul mentions by name two false teachers (2:17) as well as two among all those from Asia who turned away from him (1:15). He praises at length the kindness of Onesiphorus toward him in Rome and Ephesus (1:16-18).

Paul spends nearly the whole last chapter of 2 Timothy speaking about his current condition and making various requests of Timothy, both general and specific, in view of this situation. Paul's vigorous charge to Timothy to fulfill his ministry (4:1-5) is made in the light of Paul's expected death (4:6-8). Twice he asks Timothy to come to him soon (vv. 9, 21), especially in view of the departure of all the other fellow workers except Luke (vv. 9-12, 20-21). He gives the names of the workers and the places to which they departed (vv. 10, 12, 20), mentioning that one had deserted him and one had been left sick at Miletus. He asks that Timothy bring along the cloak and books that he left in Troas (v. 13) and particularly that Timothy bring with him Mark, who "is useful to me for service" (v. 11). He thankfully reports the outcome of his first defense as the Lord stood by him (even though others did not) and strengthened and delivered him (v. 17) and then affirms that the Lord will bring him to his heavenly kingdom (v. 18, echoing the perspective of v. 8).

Paul concludes all three letters with a form of the "grace be with you" formula that marks all the Pauline letters, using the abbreviated form that made its first appearance in his letter to the Colossians.

These three letters certainly claim to be by Paul the former persecutor of Christians who was called to be Christ's apostle, who traveled far and wide in the Mediterranean world preaching the gospel and suffering for it, who continued to feel responsibility for the churches and for his apostolic delegates (cf. Phil. 2:18-23), and who continued to deal with actual situations and individuals in specific places. The self-testimony of the letters is most explicit in the identification of the author in the first verse of each letter, but it is also found in the repeated and pervasive personal references that the author makes about himself and about his relationships with the addressees and other individuals. On this background, it is not difficult to understand why the almost unanimous consensus of the church until the nineteenth century was that the letters were from Paul the apostle.

RECIPIENTS

The recipients of the letters are identified in the salutations as Timothy (1 Tim. 1:2; 2 Tim. 1:2) and Titus (Tit. 1:4). The personal references to these two men throughout the letters (note the second person singular imperatives and personal pronouns) are further corroboration that these individuals are the recipients. But alongside this, the church as a whole and specific groups of church members are instructed through Timothy and Titus, sometimes more directly (e.g., the church, 1 Tim. 2:1ff.; women, 2:9ff.; bishops and deacons, 3:1ff.; slaves, 6:1ff.), sometimes less directly (cf. the words in Tit. 2:6, which occur in the middle of Paul's instructions to men and women, "likewise urge the young men . . . ," and also those in 3:1, "remind them . . ."). By either method Paul is writing to the whole church as well as to his fellow workers Timothy and Titus — or through Timothy and Titus. This implicit fact surfaces in the plural "you" in the concluding benediction of each letter: "grace be with you" (1 Tim. 6:21; 2 Tim. 4:22), which in Titus is made even more explicit with the addition of "all" (Tit. 3:15). This broader address must be kept in mind even though it does not nullify the fact that the letters are written explicitly to Timothy and Titus.

Timothy

Timothy (Τιμόθεος**) is first mentioned in Acts 16:1, 2, where he is placed at Lystra during Paul's second missionary journey and is described as "the son of a Jewish woman who was a believer, but his father was a Greek" and as "well spoken of by the brothers in Lystra and Iconium." 2 Tim. 1:5 gives Timothy's mother's name as Eunice and his grandmother's as Lois, and indicates that both had a "sincere faith" (see the commentary). Acts 16:3 indicates that Paul "wanted this man to go with him," and, because of Jews who knew of his mixed family background, had him circumcised. From that point on he became Paul's assistant and continued as such to Paul's last imprisonment (2 Timothy).

Timothy and Silas (Silvanus) remained at Beroea (Acts 17:14) when Paul was sent away because of the agitation of the Thessalonian Jews, but then when Paul was in Athens he asked Timothy to come join him as soon as possible (v. 15). Paul moved on to Corinth, and there, according to Acts, Silas and Timothy were with him (18:5). There they also joined with him as proclaimers of Christ (2 Cor. 1:19). During this period Timothy and Silas, apparently as coworkers with Paul in establishing and building the Thessalonian church, are included with him as coauthors in both 1 and 2 Thessalonians (1 Thes. 1:1; 2 Thes. 1:1; note also the pervasive, but not exclusive, use of first person plural pronouns in these letters). In 1 Thessalonians we discover that Timothy had actually joined Paul already in Athens and was sent from there by Paul to strengthen and encourage the Thessalonians in their faith (1 Thes. 3:1-3) and then returned from there to Paul in Corinth bringing the good news of their faith and love (3:6-8).

Acts 19:22 indicates that Timothy was with Paul in Ephesus and Asia on the third missionary journey and that during Paul's stay in Ephesus he was again sent into Macedonia (cf. 18:5). 1 Corinthians, written while Paul was still in Ephesus, twice mentions Timothy being sent by Paul to Corinth (4:17; 16:10, 11). Later, Timothy was again with Paul and was included with Paul in the salutation of 2 Corinthians (1:1). When Paul reached Corinth and wrote to the Christians in Rome, he conveyed Timothy's greetings (16:21). Acts 20:4 includes Timothy among those who joined Paul at Troas at the end of the third missionary journey and who apparently accompanied him to Jerusalem. Timothy is again included in the salutations of the letters to the Philippians (1:1), Colossians (1:1), and Philemon (1:1), the so-called Prison Epistles, and from this we may deduce that he was with Paul in Rome (cf. also Phil. 2:19). In fact, Timothy is mentioned in all but three of the Pauline letters (Galatians, Ephesians, and Titus).

1 Tim. 1:2, 3 has Timothy remaining in Ephesus at the time of Paul's release from his first Roman imprisonment.[5] 2 Timothy finds him still at Ephesus (cf. 1:18; 4:9ff.), while Paul is in prison in Rome for the second and last time. Outside the Pauline letters and Acts we find a Timothy referred to in Heb. 13:23 as "our brother" and as being "released." It is thought, for good reasons, that this is the same Timothy (cf., e.g., Bruce, *Hebrews,* 390f. and the literature cited there).

5. Whether or not Paul was released from his Roman imprisonment will be considered below in the section on the Pastorals' **Relationship to Acts and the Other Epistles.**

Three things stand out about Timothy: (a) In regard to his background, Timothy had a strong religious heritage in his own family, biblical training from his youth, and a strong commendation already as a young man from the church, both his own congregation at Lystra and the neighboring congregation at Iconium (2 Tim. 1:5, 6; 3:14-17; Acts 16:1-3). (b) In regard to his service, Timothy was a faithful and consistent coworker with and assistant to Paul, who regarded Timothy as one of his most trustworthy and dedicated associates and one to whom he could assign difficult tasks (e.g., at Thessalonica, at Ephesus, and especially at Corinth; in addition to the passages cited above see especially Phil. 2:19-24, particularly 20-22; 1 Thes. 3:2, 6; 1 Tim. 1:18; 6:20; 2 Tim. 1:2 and all of 1 and 2 Timothy). (c) In regard to his personality and temperament, equally striking is Timothy's apparent timidity and need for encouragement[6] (cf. possibly 1 Cor. 16:10, 11; and the repeated notes in 1 and 2 Timothy, e.g., "God has not given us a spirit of timidity" [2 Tim. 1:7], "do not be ashamed" [1:8], "be strong" [2:1], "suffer hardship" [2:3], "let no one look down on your youthfulness" [1 Tim. 4:12], "do not neglect the spiritual gift" [4:14], "pay close attention to yourself and to your teaching" [4:16], "guard what has been entrusted to you" [6:20]). Timothy's timidity (and thus his need for encouragement) may have stemmed from a realistic appraisal of a difficult situation, from a natural propensity, or from both.

Paul addresses Timothy as his spiritual son (1 Tim. 1:2; 2 Tim. 1:2; cf. Tit. 1:4). That is, Paul writes to the younger man as his own spiritual convert, as one he has spiritually nurtured, and as one who serves under him as a son serves his father (see especially the commentary on the phrase Τιμοθέῳ γνησίῳ τέκνῳ ἐν πίστει in 1 Tim. 1:2).

Titus

Titus (Τίτος**) is the addressee of the letter bearing his name, as the salutation (1:4) indicates. He is referred to by name 12x in the NT (2 Cor. 2:13; 7:6, 13, 14; 8:6, 16, 23; 12:18; Gal. 2:1, 3; 2 Tim. 4:10; Tit. 1:4; Τίτ(ι)ος Ἰοῦστος [Acts 18:7] is someone else; see Bruce, *Acts*). He was a Greek who remained uncircumcised as a test case for the gospel with reference to the Gentiles (Gal. 2:3) and Paul's partner (κοινωνός) and fellow worker among the Corinthians (2 Cor. 8:23). He undertook several difficult assignments in Corinth as Paul's representative, including both the collection (8:6) and the responsibility of dealing with the tense situation that arose between Paul and the Corinthians (7:6, 7, 13-15; 12:18). From the letter to Titus it may be surmised that Titus accompanied Paul to Crete and was left there to strengthen and organize the work (Tit. 1:5ff.). Apparently Titus did rejoin Paul at Nicopolis as Paul requested (3:12), and we find him at the time Paul

6. For the development of this point see Hull, "Man."

wrote 2 Timothy north of Nicopolis in Dalmatia (2 Tim. 4:10). Eusebius reflects the tradition that Titus returned to Crete and served as a bishop there until his old age (*HE* 3.4.6).

Paul calls Titus his γνησίῳ τέκνῳ κατὰ κοινὴν πίστιν, "true child according to a common faith" (Tit. 1:4). This designation is almost identical to what Paul calls Timothy in 1 Tim. 1:2; the most noteworthy difference is the addition of "common" before "faith." The use here of κοινός (NT 14x), "common," for that which is communal or shared finds its closest counterpart in the NT in Jude 3, "common salvation." Paul may use it in reference to Titus, not to Timothy, because of a need to remind Titus, the churches on Crete, and the false teachers "of the circumcision" (1:10; cf. v. 14) that Titus the uncircumcised Greek and Paul the Hebrew of the Hebrews share the same faith (cf. Gal. 2:3, 4; 3:7-9, 14, 28-29). Titus, no less than circumcised Timothy, is Paul's spiritual son in this shared faith, and it is to him as such that Paul writes the letter.

SETTING AND CONCERNS

Historical Setting

From 1 Timothy and Titus one gathers that Paul is moving about freely and is not in prison, as he was when he wrote the "Prison Epistles" (Ephesians, Philippians, Colossians, and Philemon). 1 Timothy relates that he is on his way to Macedonia and implies some contact with Ephesus, where Timothy is, having been encouraged by Paul to remain there (1 Tim. 1:3), and that he hopes to come to Ephesus before long (3:14). The letter to Titus implies that Paul has been on Crete, where Titus is (Tit. 1:5), and says that he plans to winter in Nicopolis, some 200 miles northwest of Athens on the west coast of Greece, and have Titus come to him there. It also mentions that Paul will be sending Artemas or Tychicus, who are apparently with him at the time, to fill Titus's place when Titus leaves Crete (3:12). Zenas and Apollos, fellow evangelists, have probably been with Paul, since they are going through Crete, probably delivering Paul's letter, and he commends them to Titus (v. 13). There is no definite indication of where Paul is as he writes these two letters, and the evidence is not sufficiently interlocked that an itinerary emerges.[7] For the same reason the data at our disposal make it difficult to decide the order in which 1 Timothy and Titus were written. I have opted for the order 1 Timothy and then Titus, though others have chosen the opposite order.[8]

7. However, for a fascinating attempt to assemble such an itinerary see W. Metzger, *Die letzte Reise*.

8. Cf., e.g., Bruce, *Letters,* 289: "As between I Timothy and Titus, however, there are

It is clear, however, that 2 Timothy is the last written of the three letters, because of Paul's situation and expectation as he writes it: He is in prison in Rome (1:16, 17; 2:9; 4:16, 17) and has come successfully through his first defense, though no one supported him in it (4:16, 17). But he expects to die soon (vv. 6, 18), probably thinking that his second defense will lead to execution. As he writes, all his fellow workers have gone elsewhere (e.g., Titus to Dalmatia, v. 10) except Luke (v. 11). Before this imprisonment, Paul has apparently been to Troas, Corinth, and Miletus (vv. 13, 20). It appears from several references in the letter that Timothy is in Ephesus as Paul writes 2 Timothy, as he was when Paul wrote 1 Timothy (1 Tim. 1:3): In the context of his request that Timothy come to him (2 Tim. 4:9) Paul indicates that he has sent Tychicus to Ephesus (v. 12), presumably as Timothy's replacement. He also says that Timothy will know of the service Onesiphorus rendered at Ephesus (1:18), and he mentions Hymenaeus (2:17) and Alexander (4:14), who are elsewhere associated with Ephesus (cf. for both 1 Tim. 1:20 and possibly for the latter Acts 19:33, 34), and Prisca and Aquila (2 Tim. 4:19), who are in Ephesus in the last reference to them in Acts (Acts 18:18-19, 24-26). Paul asks Timothy to come to him soon (2 Tim. 4:9), before winter (v. 21), and to bring Mark (v. 11), his cloak, and some specific books (v. 13).

Purposes

Two broad concerns characterize all three letters: (1) Paul warns Timothy and Titus about a false teaching (see the separate section on **The False Teaching** below) and exhorts them to stand against it; (2) Paul gives instructions to the Christians of Ephesus and Crete, through Timothy and Titus, concerning their conduct and church life. In 1 Timothy and Titus the latter includes instructions concerning what sort of men are to be appointed to church leadership (1 Tim. 3:1-13; Tit. 1:5-9; cf. 2 Tim. 2:2). These concerns are not treated individually but are interwoven in the letters.

In 1 Timothy Paul especially seeks to encourage Timothy (in view of the latter's timidity, noted above) in regard to his responsibility over against the false teaching and his responsibility as the church's leader/teacher. Paul deals with the false teaching in 1:3-11, 18-20; 4:1-7; 6:3-10, 20-21, and gives specific instructions to the Christians about their conduct in 3:14, 15 and the bulk of the letter. He instructs and encourages Timothy as the leader/teacher in 1:3ff., 18, presents Timothy's responsibilities as leader/teacher in some detail in 4:6-16; 5:1-3, 17-25, interjects at key places in the text Timothy's responsibility to teach and apply the truths that Paul is communicating (5:7;

---

few criteria or none that could enable us to assign priority to the one or the other. Titus is placed first in the following pages simply so as not to separate I Timothy from II Timothy." For an argued statement of this same position see Doty, "Classification," 192-98.

6:2c), and concludes his instructions and admonitions to Timothy with a charge and a warning in 6:11-14, 20-21.

In the letter to Titus Paul warns Titus about the false teaching, exhorts him and the elders to refute it (1:9-16; 3:9-11), and communicates through the letter and through Titus himself instructions for the Christians on Crete. As with 1 Timothy, these concerns are intermingled, especially in the first chapter.

2 Timothy is especially marked by Paul's repeated urging of Timothy to suffer with him for the gospel in the strength of God (manifested in God's gift [1:6], his Spirit [1:7, 14], his power [1:8], and his grace [2:1]; see further 1:6-14; 2:1-13; 3:12; 4:5) and by his insistence that Timothy retain and guard the apostolic message (1:13, 14), that he pass it on to faithful men to teach others also (2:2), that he handle and teach it correctly (2:15), and that he be guided by it and by the OT in all his teaching and conduct (3:10-17). These two keynotes are intertwined and come together in a third, which is Paul's charge to Timothy to be the Lord's faithful servant who, relying on the Holy Spirit (1:14) and equipped with the God-breathed scripture, effectively and gently teaches the truth (2:24-26), who unceasingly preaches the word and applies its truths, and who does the work of an evangelist and fulfills his ministry (4:1-5).

Along with these instructions and exhortations the letters also give instructions regarding the comings and goings of Paul, Timothy, Titus, and their fellow workers (1 Tim. 1:3; 3:1; Tit. 3:12, 13; 2 Tim. 4:9, 11-13, 21). This aspect becomes particularly important in 2 Timothy, where it stands in the shadow of Paul's impending death (4:6).

The False Teaching

It appears that the false teachers and false teaching confronted in all three letters are of the same sort, since similar errors or tendencies are mentioned and similar terminology used, though not in every mention of them. As is often the case in Paul's letters (e.g., Colossians), one must put a number of pieces together in order to ascertain the nature of the false teaching. Paul is not interested in describing the teaching but in refuting it, so different aspects come up in different passages.

The false teachers are characterized by an interest in myths (1 Tim. 1:4; 4:7; Tit. 1:14; 2 Tim. 4:4) and genealogies (1 Tim. 1:4; Tit. 3:9), a concern with the law or a Jewish orientation (1 Tim. 1:7; Tit. 1:10, 14; 3:9), an interest in "antitheses" that they identify as "knowledge" (1 Tim. 6:20), a tendency toward controversy, argumentation, and speculation (1 Tim. 1:4, 6; 6:4, 20; Tit. 1:10; 3:9; 2 Tim. 2:14, 16, 23), deceptiveness (1 Tim. 4:1-3; Tit. 1:10-13; 2 Tim. 3:6ff., especially v. 13), immorality (1 Tim. 1:19, 20; Tit. 1:15, 16; 2 Tim. 2:16, 19; ch. 3), and a desire to get material gain by means of their teaching (1 Tim. 6:5; Tit. 1:11; 2 Tim. 3:2, 4). In addition to these aspects mentioned in all three PE (see also the list of parallels between 1 Timothy 1 and Titus 1 in the comments on Tit. 1:10-16), there is the harsh asceticism described in 1 Tim. 4:1-5, according to which some, in Ephesus at least, were apparently forbidding marriage and eating of meat, and a teaching that the resurrection had already taken place (2 Tim. 2:18; cf. 1 Tim. 1:19, 20). The false teachers were primarily but not exclusively Jewish (Tit. 1:10). Paul regarded their teaching as opposed to Christ's teaching and the apostolic teaching (1 Tim. 6:3; cf. 2 Tim. 4:15) and to the truth (2 Tim. 2:18).

Certain of these elements suggest that their teaching was along the line of, if not necessarily identical to, that of the false teachers opposed by Paul at Colossae (cf., e.g., philosophy and deception, Col. 2:8; Jewish regulations and the law, 2:16, 17; asceticism, 2:18-23). Paul sets the false teaching into the context of the difficulties of the last days (2 Tim. 3:1ff.) and is certain of its ultimate lack of success over against the church (2:19; 3:9). See the further discussion below of the PE's **Warnings against False Teaching**.

ATTESTATION IN THE EARLY CHURCH

The PE were known and regarded as Pauline in the early church.[9] There are a number of similarities between the PE and 1 Clement (ca. AD 96).[10] These similarities have been accounted for in different ways,[11] but Falconer is correct in saying that "the most probable explanation of the similarities, both in ideas and in language, between the Pastorals and I Clement is that the former, as they now are, were known to Clement."[12] Kelly notes that "several passages . . . in the Ignatian letters (*c.* 110) seem to echo passages in [the PE] so closely that only excessive caution refuses to admit direct dependence."[13] There are also indications that the Epistles were known and used by Polycarp (ca. AD 117), Justin Martyr (ca. AD 140), and others (see Bernard and White), and at about the same dates were included in Syriac and Latin versions.

The only exceptions to the early church's acceptance of all three of the PE as Pauline were the heretics Marcion, Basilides, and Tatian. Tertullian says of Marcion that "he rejected *[recusaverit]* the two Epistles to Timothy and the one to Titus."[14] But this in itself makes Marcion a witness to "the traditional place which the Epistles to Timothy and Titus occupied in orthodox circles at Rome about the year 140."[15] In his preface to Titus, Jerome

9. The documentation of this attestation has been set forth fully by Bernard (pp. xi-xxi) and N. J. D. White (pp. 75-81) with pages of quotations. For a full discussion of attestation in the early church cf. also James, *Genuineness,* 5-24.

10. See White, 76f.; Bernard, xix, the latter of whom presents the material from 1 Clement and the Pastorals in parallel columns.

11. A committee of the Oxford Society of Historical Theology (*NT in the Apostolic Fathers,* 37ff.) did not consider the similarities close enough to constitute proof of literary dependency. Streeter, however, who held that the PE were written later than 1 Clement, argued that they borrowed from Clement's letter (*Primitive Church,* 153).

12. Falconer, 5. Bernard (p. xix) came to the same conclusion: "Holtzmann explains these coincidences between Clement and the Pastorals to be due to 'the common Church atmosphere' in which they all originated; but it seems as if they were too close to admit of any other hypothesis save that Clement wrote with the language and thoughts of the Pastorals in his mind."

13. Kelly, 3.

14. *Adv. Marc.* 5.21. The sentence reads as follows: "I am surprised, however, that when he [Marcion] accepted this letter [Philemon], which was written but to one man, he rejected the two Epistles to Timothy and the one to Titus, which all treat of ecclesiastical discipline."

15. Bernard, xviii. Kümmel discounts this as evidence (*Introduction,* 370).

reports that Tatian (who died about 170) denied the authenticity of 1 Timothy because it conflicted with his asceticism, but recognized Titus, and that Basilides, like Marcion, rejected all three of the letters. Jerome implies in the same preface that "these adverse judgments were not critical in any true sense, but merely arbitrary."[16] Indeed, there are no traces in the writings of the time, or later in the early church, of discussion of the style of the PE or other such matters — though there are in the case of Hebrews. Clement of Alexandria states that some — apparently meaning those of a gnostic bent — rejected the PE because they did not like the expression ἡ ψευδώνυμος γνῶσις in 1 Tim. 6:20.[17] Thus it comes as no surprise that the *Gospel of Truth,* ascribed with some plausibility to Valentinus (ca. 150), does not quote the PE, even though it quotes all the other books of the NT.[18]

The Chester Beatty papyrus codex of the Pauline Epistles, 𝔭[46], which is generally dated about the middle of the third century,[19] presents a bit of a puzzle in that it does not contain the PE; but it is also not wholly preserved. As the document now stands there are seven leaves missing. Some doubt that space was available to include the PE in view of the number of words the scribe wrote on each page. Others suggest that the scribe was beginning to write smaller so as to fit more words on each page, as might be evidenced by a comparison of the earlier and later parts of the manuscript.[20] Others suggest that the scribe added pages to the codex that have since been lost, and still others that, since he also does not include Philemon, the scribe deliberately included only the letters to the churches.[21] In view of the several plausible explanations, it is probably best to leave this an unanswered puzzle. But it is hardly a testimony against the PE, since the papyrus documents that have been preserved and discovered are hardly the norm for what was canonical.[22]

By the time of Irenaeus (second century), when NT books are being quoted by the author's name, the PE are definitely regarded as Pauline.[23] Guthrie puts it well: "[their] attestation is as strong as most of the Pauline Epistles, with the exception of Romans and I Corinthians."[24]

16. N. J. D. White, 76.

17. *Strom.* 4.9.

18. Cf. Kelly, 4.

19. Second or third century according to *UBSGNT,* 913; ca. 200 according to *NA*^{26}, 686.

20. Jeremias, 4.

21. So, for example, Quinn, "𝔭[46]."

22. See the comments of Guthrie, *Introduction,* 587f.

23. Irenaeus, *Haer.* 1, preface 1; 1.16.3; 2.14.7; 3.3.3; 4.16.3. See also Clement of Alexandria (died 215), *Strom.* 1.350; Tertullian (died 220), *De praesc.* 6.25; *Adv. Marc.* 5.21. Cf. also the Muratorian canon. There seems to be a consensus on this point; cf., e.g., Kümmel, *Introduction,* 370, who says that "from the end of the second century on, however, the Pastorals are regarded without question to be letters of Paul."

24. Guthrie, 19f. Cf. also Falconer, 3.

RELATIONSHIP TO ACTS AND THE OTHER EPISTLES

INCONGRUENCIES

Most (but not all) of those who accept the self-testimony of the PE and the testimony of the early church to Pauline authorship acknowledge that the history and events of the PE do not seem to fit within the history of the life of Paul found in the book of Acts[25] and reconstructed from the other letters of Paul and that those events must, therefore, have taken place after the time period covered by Acts and the other letters. Of course, it cannot be absolutely proved that the PE cannot be fitted into the book of Acts, and several have sought to do so. The most recent attempts, which are very able indeed, are by de Lestapis,[26] Reicke,[27] and van Bruggen.[28] But as we examine the points at which Acts (with the other letters) and the PE might be referring to the same events, a number of incongruencies emerge:

1 and 2 Timothy place Timothy in Ephesus and 1 Timothy has Paul going to Macedonia (1:3). In Acts Paul does travel to Macedonia from Ephesus (Acts 20:1), but Timothy has not been left behind in Ephesus but sent ahead to Macedonia (19:22). Furthermore, Timothy accompanies Paul on his journey to Jerusalem (20:4). It is possible that Paul left Timothy with the Ephesian elders at Miletus, but when he would have done so the direction of Paul's journey was toward Jerusalem, not Macedonia (21:1-17). Paul came by Crete for a time during his journey to Rome (27:7-13), but we know

25. For discussion of the historicity of the events recorded in the book of Acts and an affirmation of such historicity see the introductions to Bruce, *Acts;* Marshall, *Acts;* and Longenecker, Acts; and Guthrie, *Introduction,* 354ff., and the literature referred to in these works. Cf. in particular Gasque, *History,* especially 251-309.

26. De Lestapis, *Énigme.*

27. Reicke, "Chronologie." For summaries of Reicke's and de Lestapis's arguments see Trummer, *Paulustradition,* 53-56. Cf. further the similar treatment of this question in J. A. T. Robinson, *Redating,* 67-85, which makes extensive use of Reicke's work. Cf. also Prior, *Paul the Letter-Writer,* which places 2 Timothy in the situation of Paul in Rome as reflected particularly in Acts and Philippians (p. 170).

28. Van Bruggen, *Die geschichtliche Einordung.*

nothing of the whereabouts of Titus at this time. It would be more than two years after that time (28:30) before Paul could have written to Titus that he planned to spend the winter in Nicopolis. This would seem to be an inordinate delay in writing a letter that has as one of its main purposes the reiteration to Titus of his responsibility to see to it that spiritual leaders are appointed for the churches (Tit. 1:5), unless of course Titus is meeting resistance and needs Paul's apostolic authority. 2 Timothy refers to Paul visiting Corinth, Troas, and Miletus (4:13, 20), and these events appear to be recorded to inform Timothy of them. In Acts, Paul visits the same places, but Timothy is with him (20:4) and does not need to be informed of these events (cf. 20:2f., 5ff., 15ff.). In Acts, Trophimus is not left sick at Miletus (2 Tim. 4:20) but continues with Paul to Jerusalem (Acts 21:29).

Similar incongruencies are seen if it is attempted to relate Paul's imprisonment in 2 Timothy to Acts and the Prison Epistles. In the Prison Epistles, which have historically been regarded as written from Rome during the imprisonment recorded at the end of Acts,[29] Timothy is included with Paul in the salutations (Phil. 1:1; Col. 1:1; Phm. 1). But in 2 Timothy, also written when Paul is in prison in Rome, Timothy is in Ephesus and is asked to come to Paul. Furthermore, while in 2 Timothy Paul's imprisonment is difficult (cf. 2 Tim. 1:16, 17), and he expects to die soon (4:6), in the Prison Epistles he expects to be released from prison and return to Philippi and Asia (Phil. 1:19, 25, 26; 2:24; Phm. 22). Acts itself does not mention the expectation found in the Prison Epistles, but it does present certain factors congruent with that expectation and with the realization of it: Even though he had kept Paul in prison for some time, the verdict of the Roman governor Porcius Festus was that Paul "had committed nothing worthy of death" (Acts 25:25). Festus asked Agrippa to hear Paul and to advise him what to write to Caesar, to whom Paul had appealed (v. 26). Agrippa's words to Festus after the hearing, "This man might have been set free had he not appealed to Caesar" (v. 32), are probably what Festus wrote to Caesar. If this is so, then the stage was set for the release expected in the Prison Epistles and, before that, for the two years of relatively loose house arrest described in Acts 28:16ff.

Therefore, when the same persons and places are mentioned in Acts (and the Prison Epistles) on the one hand and in the PE on the other hand, the same events are not being referred to, with the possible but doubtful exception of Crete. Of course, not every event in the period of Paul's life covered by Acts is, in fact, recorded in Acts (e.g., some of the events mentioned in 2 Cor. 11:24ff.), so we cannot absolutely rule out a solution that places the PE in that framework. But it is more likely that events as

29. For a defense of this position and a discussion of alternatives see Guthrie, *Introduction,* in his treatment of each of these letters and in his special section on "The Captivity Epistles." See also the literature cited by him.

significant as those standing behind the PE took place outside the Acts framework — after the Acts imprisonment and the expected release — than that they occurred during the period of time covered by Acts and merely escaped notice there.

THE RELEASE AND SECOND IMPRISONMENT

What, at any rate, might have happened at the end of the two-year period mentioned at the end of Acts? Parry suggests that the time reference and the use of aorist ἐνέμεινεν in Acts 28:30 "describes the period as past" and implies that "at the end of the two years he left Rome."[30] Paul's release might have come about in any of a number of ways: If the accusers did not appear the case would eventually lapse. It might also be that Paul was tried and acquitted or that the Roman government dropped the case against him.[31] The idea that Paul was released for one of these reasons and was later imprisoned in Rome again, this time with the expectation that he would be executed,[32] would be in accord with the expectations of the Prison Epistles, with the temper of Acts, particularly the statements of Festus and Agrippa recorded there (see above), and with the conditions reflected in the PE.

Also in support of this view is testimony from the early church that Paul was, indeed, released and then imprisoned again. The first possible witness is 1 Clement 5:6, 7 (ca. AD 96):

> Paul . . . preached in the East and the West, and won noble renown for his faith. He taught righteousness to the whole world and went to the western limit [ἐπὶ τὸ τέρμα τῆς δύσεως ἐλθών]. He bore witness before the rulers [καὶ μαρτυρήσας ἐπὶ τῶν ἡγουμένών], and then passed out of the world and went on to the holy place, having proved himself the greatest pattern of endurance.[33]

The question at issue here is the meaning of τὸ τέρμα τῆς δύσεως.[34] Those who argue that it refers to Rome say that Clement is writing from the

30. Parry, xv.

31. Marshall, *Acts,* 426, lists the possibilities named here, along with the suggestion that Paul was executed, which he finds unlikely. For an overview of the question with citations of the relevant discussions see Bruce, *History,* 361-64. For a more in-depth discussion with comments on the proposals of Lake and Ramsay and on the relation of the question to the practice of Roman law see Cadbury, "Roman Law." For a more recent treatment see Sherwin-White, *Roman Society and Roman Law,* 99-119.

32. Pherigo, "Paul's Life," argues that Paul was released from the imprisonment recorded in Acts and labored a few years longer. For a contrary view see Haenchen, *Acts,* 71.

33. The translation is that of Bettenson, *Early Christian Fathers,* 52. See also the translations in Lake, *Apostolic Fathers,* I, 17; Lightfoot, *Apostolic Fathers,* I/2, 274.

34. The various interpretations of the expression are dealt with by Dubowy, *Klemens,* 17-79.

standpoint of his eastern readers and that τέρμα refers to the conclusion of a course, which in the context and for Paul is Rome.[35] Those who regard the τέρμα as Spain argue that one writing from Rome would not regard Rome as the West and that furthermore "in the first century τὸ τέρμα τῆς δύσεως would be the Pillars of Hercules at the Straits of Gibraltar, that is, *Spain.*"[36] If Spain is meant, then a release from Paul's (first) Roman imprisonment is implied, after which he went to Spain and other places.

It has been said that this reference to τὸ τέρμα τῆς δύσεως only echoes Paul's hope and expectation expressed in Rom. 15:24, 28 and that it is not an independent testimony that Paul's plans were carried out. However, one writing from Rome not much more than thirty years after the purported event would certainly have independent evidence on the matter. Clement seems to have such evidence since he mentions in the same context something not found in the NT, namely, that Paul was in bonds "seven times" (v. 6). Some have responded that even if this were true, this passage in 1 Clement does not mention the journeys that the PE presuppose.[37] But 1 Clement speaks of Paul preaching "in the East and the West," which specifies neither the journeys of the PE nor any other, but which certainly does not rule them out and would in fact cover those journeys.

Therefore if 1 Clement 5:6, 7 is a testimony for Paul's release from his (first) Roman imprisonment, it provides testimony in accord with the PE. But if τὸ τέρμα τῆς δύσεως refers to Rome, then the passage is silent on whether Paul was released and traveled freely after his imprisonment (since on either view Paul dies in Rome), and no argument against the release and second imprisonment should be based on such silence.

The second main witness is that of the Muratorian canon (ca. AD 180):

> Luke described briefly "for" most excellent Theophilus particular [things], which happened in his presence, as he also evidently relates indirectly the death of Peter (?) and also Paul's departure from the city as he was proceeding to Spain.[38]

It is agreed that the Latin of the canon is not easy to understand, but it very clearly refers to a journey of Paul from Rome to Spain and gives the probable reason that this is omitted by Luke from Acts. The canon, unlike 1 Clement, speaks of "Paul's departure from the city [Rome] as he was proceeding to Spain," thus providing a witness to the release of Paul from his first Roman imprisonment. If the words about the journey to Spain are suspect, it does

35. E.g., J. Moffatt, *Enc. Bib.* IV, col. 5088; Harrison, *Problem,* 107.

36. James, *Genuineness,* 32. See also Lightfoot, *Apostolic Fathers,* ad loc.; *idem, Biblical Essays,* 423ff.; Zahn, *Introduction* II, 68ff. More recently this view has been held by Holtz (p. 18) and Brox (p. 30).

37. E.g., Kümmel, *Introduction,* 378.

38. As translated in Theron, *Evidence,* 109 (§96).

not necessarily follow that the reference to the release ("Paul's departure from the city") must also be suspect.

As with 1 Clement, it has been said of the Muratorian canon's reference to Paul's departure from Rome and journey to Spain that it is ultimately based just on the hope and expectation expressed in Rom. 15:24, 28.[39] Zahn's response to this view is still noteworthy:

> The groundlessness of the opinion that the tradition of the Spanish journey and of the second Roman imprisonment has arisen from Rom. xv.24, 28, can be seen from the fact that important defenders of the view that Paul was twice imprisoned in Rome do not mention Spain at all, but merely speak in general of a resumption of missionary preaching in the interval between the two imprisonments; so Eus. *H. E.* ii.22.2 . . . , the real Euthalius, *circa* 350 . . . , and Theodore. . . . Jerome also . . . only hints indefinitely at Spain in the words "in occidentis partibus. . . ."[40]

Eusebius, whom Zahn refers to, wrote in the early fourth century (*HE* 2.22.2, 7):

> Tradition has it [λόγος ἔχει] that after defending himself the Apostle was again sent on the ministry of preaching, and coming a second time to the same city suffered martyrdom under Nero. During this imprisonment he wrote the second Epistle to Timothy, indicating at the same time that his first defense had taken place and that his martyrdom was at hand. . . . We have said this to show that Paul's martyrdom was not accomplished during the sojourn in Rome that Luke describes.[41]

In 2.22.2, 3 Eusebius calls on what many regard as an erroneous interpretation of 2 Tim. 4:16 as confirmation of his report. "But the worthlessness of his own comment," Lightfoot observes, "does not affect the value of the tradition on which it is founded, and which must be held quite distinct."[42] Eusebius, as he himself says, is relating the common view held by those before him. After him a number of writers reflected this tradition (e.g., Athanasius, Epiphanius, Jerome, Theodore of Mopsuestia, Pelagius, and Theodoret).

There appears to be no testimony from the early church that contradicts this testimony to a release and an implied or explicitly mentioned second imprisonment and that insists, instead, that Paul died during the Roman imprisonment described in Acts. The first testimony is quite early (ca. AD 96) and is given by one living in and writing from Rome. Surely the Roman Christian community some thirty years after Paul's imprisonment was aware

39. E.g., Harrison, *Problem,* 108.
40. Zahn, *Introduction* II, 74.
41. As translated in Lake, *Eusebius,* 165, 167, 169.
42. Lightfoot, *Biblical Essays,* 425.

of what resulted from that imprisonment. The Muratorian canon is also associated with Rome, and Eusebius describes the release and second imprisonment as the accepted tradition and mentions no objections or alternative views.

This testimony to a release and second imprisonment is in accord with the self-testimony of the PE, with Paul's expectation in the Prison Epistles, with the description in Acts 28 of Paul's Roman imprisonment, and with what can be inferred from Acts concerning the manner in which his case went to Rome, so the various sources are mutually corroborative.[43] But even if one takes the view that what is said in 1 Clement has nothing to do with a release from imprisonment and that the Muratorian canon is based "on the legendary Gnostic Acts of Peter (A.D. *c.* 160-170)," as does Harrison,[44] the PE themselves still stand as valid testimony to the release and second imprisonment.

43. Lightfoot states the conclusion forcefully: "Indeed, so irresistible has this evidence appeared to impartial critics, that the release has been accepted as a fact by many writers who cannot be suspected of any bias towards this result — by Hug, for instance, who places the Pastoral Epistles earlier in St. Paul's life, and by Ewald, who denies their genuineness entirely" (*Biblical Essays,* 428).

44. Harrison, *Problem,* 107-8.

CRITICAL ARGUMENTS CONCERNING AUTHORSHIP

Questions and doubts about the Pauline authorship of the PE began to be raised in the nineteenth century and have continued until the present time. The first forceful challenge to Pauline authorship was made in 1807 by Schleiermacher, who disputed the Pauline authorship of 1 Timothy on the basis of its language and biographical statements.[45] Despite these bases to Schleiermacher's argument, Schweitzer astutely evaluated this challenge by saying that it was "not Schleiermacher the critic, but Schleiermacher the aesthete who had come to have doubts about 2 Timothy" and, on that basis, about 1 Timothy.[46]

Just a few years later, in 1812, Eichhorn extended Schleiermacher's judgment to all three PE on the basis of divergent religious language.[47] Baur (1835) and the "Tübingen school" extended this doubt about the Pauline corpus and came to the conclusion that there were only four authentic Epistles of Paul.[48] Holtzmann (1880) brought all the objections together and produced a most thoroughgoing criticism of the Pauline authorship of the PE.[49]

Since that time repudiation of the Pauline authorship of the PE has become a mark of critical orthodoxy. The position became widespread in the English-speaking world with the publication in 1921 of Harrison's well-known book, *The Problem of the Pastorals,*[50] which advanced its case on the basis of detailed linguistic and stylistic analyses. Because the self-testimony of the Epistles to Pauline authorship is so explicit and pervasive, those who object to Pauline authorship have either adopted the view that they are pseudonymous (so most of those who reject Pauline authorship, e.g., Dibelius-Conzelmann, Gealy, Barrett, Brox, and Hanson) or have concluded that they contain genuine Pauline fragments (so Harrison and, e.g., Falconer, Easton, and Scott).

45. Schleiermacher, *Über den sogenannten Brief.*
46. Schweitzer, *Paul,* 8.
47. Eichhorn, *Einleitung,* III/1, 137ff.
48. Baur, *Pastoralbriefe.*
49. Holtzmann, *Pastoralbriefe.*
50. Followed by the sequel, Harrison, *Paulines and Pastorals* (1964).

But while the Pauline authorship of the PE was being challenged and denied, there were able scholars who were affirming Pauline authorship and responding to the questions that were raised. In the nineteenth century this list of scholars included Alford, Ellicott, Huther, Plummer, Lightfoot,[51] Hort,[52] and Godet.[53] In the early and middle part of the twentieth century it included (among others) the commentators Bernard, Weiss, White, Parry, Wohlenberg, Lock, Robertson, and Schlatter, and Zahn in his *Introduction* and James in his monograph on the subject *(Genuineness).* From the middle of the twentieth century until the present date it has included the following commentators: Spicq, Jeremias, Simpson, Guthrie, Hendriksen, Kelly, Holtz, Ridderbos, Bürki, and Fee.

We have already mentioned the difficulty of coordinating the PE with Acts and the other letters of Paul, which for some (including Harrison) has figured in arguments against Pauline authorship of the PE (see above, **Relationship to Acts and the Other Epistles**). We concluded that there is strong evidence that Paul was released from the imprisonment described at the end of Acts and that the PE are from a later period of his life, after that release. In the sections below the other arguments against Pauline authorship of the PE will be laid out and an evaluation of each presented.

THE METHOD OF COMMUNICATION

Brox crystallizes and emphasizes an argument that has been brought against the Pauline authorship of the PE before, namely, that the method with which the writer of these letters communicates is quite different from that seen in the other letters of Paul.[54] In the other Pauline letters[55] Paul argues his case

51. Cf. Lightfoot's articles in *Biblical Essays:* "The Chronology of St. Paul's Life and Epistles" (213-33), "The Date of the Pastoral Epistles" (397-410), "Additional Note on the Heresy Combated in the Pastoral Epistles" (411-18), and "St. Paul's History After the Close of the Acts" (419-37).

52. Hort, *Judaistic Christianity,* 130.

53. Godet, *Studies,* 298-300.

54. Brox, 39-42.

55. We continue to use the designation "the other Pauline letters" to refer to those ten letters in the NT that bear the name of Paul as their author. This is not the time or place to marshall the arguments that have historically convinced the church that these letters are from Paul and that still convince a significant number of scholars. For the arguments for each letter see, for example, the relevant sections of Guthrie, *Introduction.* In any event, the fairest appraisal of whether or not the Pastorals are part of the Pauline corpus is to compare them with that corpus in its breadth not against a selected subgroup, such as the Tübingen School's four chief letters plus a couple of others. That kind of comparison can be a circular argument in its worse sense and a virtual self-fulfilling prophecy because the norm established in advance will automatically determine the result (cf. n. 155 below).

and interacts directly with those with whom he may differ or whom he seeks to correct. He sets forth his argument at some length and gives reasons for his position and answers objections that he presumes the readers would have. The author of the PE does not argue at any great length and appeals rather to compliance with the truth already known and given. In the PE the false teaching and teachers are warned against more than argued against. Except for Timothy and Titus, the members of the Christian community are dealt with indirectly through Timothy or Titus rather than directly.[56]

There is a large measure of truth in this analysis, even if the differences may be overdrawn. But the differences are what one would expect from an apostle dealing with and through his apostolic assistants. It would be strange indeed if he wrote to them in the way that he wrote to the members of a local church. Thus the differences in and of themselves are evidence not of non-Pauline authorship but of a more personal form of letters addressed to apostolic assistants. Paul's comments to the Ephesian elders at Miletus in Acts 20:17ff. can be taken as an example of the way in which Paul communicated with "leaders" of churches.[57] There also we see no development of teaching or of argumentation over against false teaching. Rather, Paul warns against false teachers that will arise and appeals to the leaders to be vigilant. He mentions what he has already taught, implying that his teaching has provided them that by which they can recognize and withstand the error that will arise, appeals to himself as an example for their own ministry, and commends them to God and his grace. The similarity between the method in this brief account in Acts and that in the PE, especially 2 Timothy, is quite remarkable and gives evidence that this method is as Pauline as that usually seen in the letters to the churches.

Furthermore, even in the other Pauline letters Paul sometimes does not develop his argument but simply appeals to the body of truth that has been given as the standard that his readers should uphold and act in accordance with (note the classic statement of Phil. 3:17, 18 and the discussion of it below under **Warnings against False Teaching**). Examples of this are Rom. 16:17 and 2 Thes. 3:6 (cf. 2:13; 3:14). One might even say that this is a pattern Paul follows where he is writing to the reader(s) concerning a third party. And in the PE it is often with third parties, especially false teachers, that Paul is dealing.

It would also be an overstatement to say that the PE only appeal to a known body of truth and do not develop from time to time the teaching presented. The rationale for prayer is a skillfully developed piece (see the commentary on 1 Tim. 2:1-7). The reason that women should not teach men and should learn in silence is more developed in 1 Tim. 2:11-15 than in

56. Cf. also Dibelius-Conzelmann, 2.

57. See n. 25 above for works affirming the historicity of this and other events in Acts.

1 Corinthians 14, though along the same lines. Why one should not follow the asceticism of the false teachers is answered by a theological gem of a statement (4:1-5). The arguments for slaves serving their masters (1 Tim. 6:1f.; Tit. 2:9, 10) is quite similar to those found in Ephesians and Colossians. These few but appropriate examples will suffice as illustrations of the point.

In summary, there are differences of method, but they are what one would expect in an apostle writing to his assistants and are, in fact, seen elsewhere in the NT where the apostle deals with church leaders. Furthermore, similarities to this method are also found in the earlier Pauline letters and in fact are more or less the norm there when Paul is dealing with a third party. Finally, one must recognize that the methods of the earlier letters are also utilized in the PE. Thus the method of writing fits the PE as letters of Paul to his assistants rather than being an incongruity that points away from Pauline authorship.

THE MANNER OF ADDRESSING AND INSTRUCTING TIMOTHY AND TITUS

It is further objected that the way in which the author addresses Timothy and Titus and deals with them is contrary to the historical situation that would have existed. Gealy, for example, points to the way in which they are addressed as Paul's children (1 Tim. 1:2; 2 Tim. 1:2; Tit. 1:4), are treated as still youthful (1 Tim. 4:12; 2 Tim. 2:22), and are instructed rather authoritatively. He insists that this is contrary to the fact that these men have been Paul's associates for a number of years and "occupy positions of responsibility and authority in the church next to 'Paul.' "[58] This objection to Pauline authorship, which seems on the surface quite valid, is probably a problem of perception and evaluation from the perspective of the nineteenth and twentieth centuries rather than one inherent to the situation.

We get a clearer perspective on this problem by observing that its various ingredients are all present in the earlier letters as well. Paul calls Timothy "my beloved and faithful child in the Lord" even when he writes to the Corinthians about Timothy's spiritual leadership in their midst (1 Cor. 4:17). He encourages them to listen to Timothy because he will remind them of Paul's "ways," which Paul "teaches." Furthermore, Paul summons and dispatches Timothy and Titus and other assistants at will, even sending a "command" (ἐντολήν) for them to come to him (Acts 17:15), and they come

58. Gealy, 344. Cf. also Hanson, who says (p. 4) of the instructions in the PE to Timothy and Titus that "this does not seem at all the sort of thing the real Paul would write to old and trusted colleagues."

and go as he calls or sends them (cf., e.g., Acts 19:22; 1 Cor. 4:17; and 2 Cor. 8:6; 12:18, where Paul twice "urges" Titus to do certain things). The need to alleviate Timothy's fears was apparently long-standing, since Paul asks the Corinthians to "see that he is with you without cause to be afraid" (1 Cor. 16:10) and says that no one is to "despise" Timothy (v. 11), just as later he was to write to Titus, "let no one disregard you" (Tit. 2:15).

The pattern found in the PE is, therefore, found in Paul's earlier dealings with these associates, though it may appear to be different because it is a more sustained presentation of what we see only glimpses of earlier. Furthermore, the references in the PE to the youthfulness of Timothy (1 Tim. 4:12; 2 Tim. 2:22) must be understood from the perspective of that day, when a man was considered youthful until he became old (see the commentary on these verses).

The nature of Paul's relationship to Timothy and Titus is a crucial element in understanding most of the differences between these letters written to his apostolic assistants and the earlier letters written to the churches. We have already noted some difference in Paul's method of communication. We will also note differences in content and subject matter, theological terminology, linguistic style, and vocabulary. We will often find that these are not disparate differences but aspects of one difference manifesting itself in interrelated ways. Thus, if in writing to an apostolic assistant rather than to a church the apostle uses at times a different method, his writing will most likely also show differences in content, both of which in turn will probably be expressed in part in different theological terminology, linguistic style, and vocabulary. Therefore, rather than having to explain the differences under the assumption that the PE are Pauline, one should *expect* that the letters to apostolic assistants will be noticeably different in comparison with those to churches. In fact one should think they were not genuine if they did not have these differences. This is especially the case when we have found that certain characteristics of these letters are also discovered in his dealings with these apostolic assistants and other spiritual leaders elsewhere in the NT. They may well be marks of authenticity rather than strange differences from the earlier Pauline letters.

WARNINGS AGAINST FALSE TEACHING

The Method of Addressing the Problem

A large part of the objection to the Pauline authorship arises from the way in which the false teaching and false teachers are handled in the PE. As was noted above, it is said that Paul uses a reasoned presentation concerning error in his other letters but that here that presentation is lacking and only warnings and appeals are given.[59] As was also indicated above, there is ultimately no difference of method, since both ways of addressing the problem of false teaching, are found in both the PE and the other letters, though differences of approach are seen, depending on who is addressed: When, as is usual, Paul is pleading with those who are in danger of being affected by false teaching, he does, indeed, seek to persuade them from that course. But where he has already made his case (in earlier teaching, for example) and wants to warn the Christians against the false teachers as a third party, his method of dealing with them in earlier Pauline letters is similar to that which we find in the PE.

Philippians 3 is a classic example. Early in the account he issues a strong warning against the false teachers, describing them in rather strong language (3:2). Near the end of the chapter, he returns to them, prefacing his remarks by an appeal to his own example as the standard to be observed and followed (v. 17). He then proceeds to say that the false teachers are "enemies of the cross" and that their god is their appetite (vv. 18, 19).[60]

What we find, for example, in Philippians cannot be called evidence of a non-Pauline approach when it appears in the PE. Moreover, that which Paul says he has done "often" (πολλάκις, Phil. 3:18), even if few or no other instances were to be found in the other Pauline letters, can hardly be called an adequate basis for declaring the PE non-Pauline. This is particularly true with regard to the PE in that they are addressed to Paul's apostolic assistants and Paul is dealing with the false teachers as third parties. His colleagues are not being allured by false teaching as so many Christians were who were the objects of his concern in his earlier letters. If lengthy arguments against following the false teaching appeared in the PE, as in the earlier letters, they would be an incongruity indeed[61] and a basis for considering the PE inauthentic.

The Nature of the Teaching

In addition to the arguments concerning the way in which the false teachers are handled in the PE, the argument is made that the false teaching itself does not fit into the time frame of the apostle Paul but into that of a later age. At this point our previous overview of the false teaching must be recalled (see above **Setting and Concerns: The False Teaching**). The teaching had

59. Cf. Hanson's summary statement of the evaluation of others with which he concurs: "Editors have also observed that the author of the Pastorals does not argue with his theological opponents as Paul does" (p. 4). Cf., e.g., Dibelius-Conzelmann, 2; Karris, "Background."

60. Cf. Gal. 6:12, 13 for a similar treatment of false teachers.

61. Cf. Lightfoot, *Biblical Essays,* who came to the same conclusion years ago: "St. Paul is writing to a friend, and instructing him to deal practically with the question. No lengthy exposition is necessary, nor would such be in place" (413).

certain Jewish aspects (e.g., its special handling of the law and its interest in specifically Jewish "myths"), it had certain esoteric aspects (myths and genealogies, controversial questions, and "antitheses" identified as knowledge [γνῶσις]), and in Ephesus at least it had strongly ascetic rules requiring abstention from marriage and certain foods — and two false teachers there maintained that the resurrection was already past.

Hanson has put the matter into perspective when he says that "the precise nature of the false teaching which [the author of the PE] opposes has given rise to much speculation." After commenting on the view of those who hold to Pauline authorship, Hanson goes on to say that "those who would put the Pastorals later suggest that the author was facing an early form of Gnosticism."[62] Several considerations are advanced to support this view. The first and most obvious is the use of γνῶσις in 1 Tim. 6:20 to describe the heresy.[63] Hanson himself asserts that "one feature of the heresy seems to fit Gnosticism better than anything else, and that is the references to genealogies in 1 Tim. 1:4 and Tit. 3:9." He makes this connection by observing that "the Gnostics did offer long accounts of the origin and hierarchy of aeons, which often included stories of how male and female aeons united to produce a litter of lesser aeons" and by concluding that this alternative makes sense of these terms and the significance of them as a heresy that was "offering a serious threat to the faith."[64]

But it is precarious to make too much of Paul's one use of γνῶσις in the PE since he has used it so widely and frequently before (some 22x) where Gnosticism is not in view and has also from time to time warned against a false view of the significance of "knowledge" in earlier contexts (cf., e.g., 1 Cor. 8:1, 2). Furthermore, the context of "myths and genealogies" in the PE suggests not gnostic aeons but matters relating to Jewish speculations and given an erroneous religious significance (see the commentary at 1 Tim. 1:4ff. and Tit. 3:9).

Brox connects the false teachers' doctrine that the resurrection had already taken place with a gnostic perspective.[65] Since errors had already arisen concerning the resurrection (1 Cor. 15) and the form of existence that Christians now have (1 Cor. 4:8) in the other Pauline letters, it is unnecessary to say that the error about the resurrection having taken place already is gnostic.

Our problem is compounded by the uncertainties that exist concerning

62. Hanson, 25.

63. Cf. Brox, 33f.

64. Hanson, 25.

65. Brox (36f.) makes this connection by saying that the rest spoken about as already come in logion 51 of the Gnostic *Gospel of Thomas* represents the same doctrine that one finds in Menander when he says (according to Irenaeus, *Haer.* 1.23.5) that by baptism one receives the resurrection and does not die.

the origins and development of Gnosticism[66] and concerning the relationship of the errors of the NT age to those of a later age. Dibelius-Conzelmann are probably on better ground in saying that the evidence that we have on "the opponents points not to the great Gnostic systems, but rather to a kind of Judaizing Gnosticism . . . as is found elsewhere."[67] They include Colossians here,[68] and this association with Colossians is probably the key to locating the false teachers of the PE temporally. The false teachers in Colossians have a Jewish orientation (Col. 2:16, 17), are interested in philosophy and human traditions (cf. v. 8), and are ascetic (vv. 18, 21-23). Although the terminology of the positions is not identical, the areas of interest and the concerns are so similar that the long-standing comparison between the two remains valid.[69]

Since the false teachers and false teaching can be so readily associated with similar patterns in the NT, i.e., in Colossians, it would seem more appropriate to look there than to insist that the error of the teachers is that of a later period. Kelly summarizes the question well when he says the following:

> It is in fact unrealistic to look to the well-known Gnostic, or near Gnostic, systems of the second century for light on the teaching that provoked the Pastorals. Everything suggests that it was something much more elementary; and it is significant that much of the writer's polemic is directed, not so much against any specific doctrine, as against the general contentiousness and loose living it encouraged. It is best defined as a Gnosticizing form of Jewish Christianity. . . . There is no need . . . to look outside the first century, or indeed the span of Paul's life, for such an amalgam of Jewish and Gnostic traits in the Levant.[70]

ECCLESIASTICAL ORGANIZATION

Some have argued that the ecclesiastical organization spoken of in the PE is so advanced that it does not fit with what existed in Paul's time.[71] It is

66. For a starting place on the discussion of Gnosticism see R. M. Wilson, *Gnostic Problem.* He classes the heresies of the NT as Gnosticism in embryonic form. Cf. also Yamauchi, *Pre-Christian Gnosticism.*

67. Dibelius-Conzelmann, 3. Ellis thinks that the condemned teaching reflects a gnosticizing Judaism characteristic of the apostolic age. His entire article is worth consulting ("Problem of Authorship").

68. Dibelius-Conzelmann, 3.

69. Cf. the still helpful and seminal works of Hort (*Judaistic Christianity,* 113ff.) and Lightfoot ("Additional Note on the Heresy Combated in the Pastoral Epistles," *Biblical Essays,* 411-18). Even though certain corrections may need to be made to their work in the light of further developments and research, they are still quite insightful.

70. Kelly, 12.

71. Hanson writes that, in contrast to the PE, "in Paul's day we do not find anything like a fixed institutional clergy" (p. 4).

stated that "Timothy" and "Titus" are monarchical bishops like those of a later age.[72] The concern for elders/bishops and deacons is either different from that of Paul or more advanced than Paul.[73] Finally, with regard to widows it is said that 1 Timothy already envisages an order of widows and thus goes far beyond anything known in the other Paulines.[74]

Church Leaders

Kelly, who was quite familiar with the age in which the monarchical bishop arose, indicated that Timothy and Titus are not presented as monarchical bishops and do not function as such. He wrote: "They are the Apostle's personal emissaries, with an *ad hoc,* temporary mandate." "Further," he added, "had the author intended to represent them as bishops, he would surely have avoided using the title in dealing with the other officials."[75] As Guthrie says, the functions that the addressees of the PE fulfill and that Easton cites as bases for identifying them as monarchical bishops "could just as well be executed by apostolic delegates, as Timothy is portrayed in Acts and both he and Titus in the other Pauline Epistles."[76]

The heart of the problem here is the widely accepted idea that Paul (and the NT as a whole) is unconcerned about recognized church leaders and that in the NT period spiritual gifts, not leadership, are the norm.[77] Various writers characterize the NT age in this way and also indicate that recognized leaders only came into existence later in the church when the vibrancy of the charismatic gifts were waning.[78] But Ridderbos has shown that "the contrast between

72. Easton, 177: "In 'Timothy' and 'Titus,' therefore, the Ignatian bishops are actually found in everything but the title." Cf. also Streeter, *Primitive Church,* 118f.; Gealy, 344f.

73. See von Campenhausen, *Ecclesiastical Authority,* 106-19.

74. Hanson writes that "another indication that the Pastorals are post-Pauline is the existence of an order of widows (1 Tim. 5:3-16), of which there is no sign in the other Paulines" (p. 4).

75. Kelly, 14. He goes on to make the following disjunction between the Pastorals and the hierarchy of the Ignatian letters: "What in any case the Ignatian letters reveal is a closely articulated hierarchy, with the functions of each order and their relation to each other clearly defined. Of this there is not a breath in the Pastorals, the whole atmosphere of which is much simpler and less sophisticated and indicative of a rather earlier stage in the growth of the ministry."

76. Quoting the first (1957) edition of Guthrie's commentary, 31; cf. also Lock, xix; E. F. Scott, xxix.

77. R. Sohm defended the thesis that every form of ecclesiastical polity is in flagrant conflict with the essence of the church (in his principal work, *Kirchenrecht,* I, later summarized in *Wesen und Ursprung des Katholizismus*).

78. Käsemann, for example, denies that the Pauline church at the time of the apostle could have known of a presbyterate and asserts that the development of it in the PE is an abandonment of the "Pauline conception of a church order based on charisma" (*Essays,* 88; cf. 83ff.). Schweizer regards any kind of act of appointment at the beginning of a specific ministry an impossibility with Paul (*Church Order,* p. 101).

the charismatic and institutional is at bottom just as false as that between charismatic and non-charismatic ministries in the church."[79]

Pastors and teachers, helps, and administrations (the *charisma* of governing) are in the first rank of the *charismata* that Christ gives to his church (Eph. 4:11; 1 Cor. 12:28). Thus Paul in one of his earliest Epistles can speak of a group of leaders who labor diligently among the Christians of Thessalonica and who "have charge over you in the Lord and give you instruction" (1 Thes. 5:12). He charges the Thessalonians to "esteem them very highly in love because of their work" (v. 13). Thus we see that from his earliest writings Paul is concerned about a simple but definite form of order and authority in the church and about those whom we may rightly designate spiritual leaders. Paul expressed a concern of this sort to nearly every church he wrote to (1 Thes. 5:12, 13; Gal. 6:6; Rom. 12:7, 8; 1 Cor. 12:28; 16:15, 16; Eph. 4:11, 12; Phil. 1:1; only the church at Colossae is not represented here). Other than when leadership is referred to in generic terms (i.e., Gal. 6:6; Rom. 12:7, 8), it is described in plural terms, indicating that local church leadership was done by groups (the remainder of the references just given above).

Such leaders are designated either in descriptive phrases as having charge over the Christians and giving instructions to them (1 Thes. 5:12, 13) and as those to whom Christians should be in subjection (1 Cor. 16:15, 16), or by such key terms as "teachers" (1 Cor. 12:28), "pastors and teachers" (Eph. 4:11), "bishops and deacons" (Phil. 1:1; the same two terms are in 1 Timothy 3 and the first in Titus 1). The descriptive phrases and the key terms "pastors, teachers, bishops" are virtually synonymous in meaning and significance. This pattern in the Pauline letters fits well with the activity of Paul described in Acts of returning to the cities he had gone to during his first missionary journey in order to appoint "elders in every church" (14:23; "elders" are also mentioned in 1 Tim. 5:17 and Tit. 1:5). If Paul regards the leaders in Thessalonica as responsible for caring for and teaching the people, it is understandable that he calls the Ephesian elders to him and discusses with them the same responsibilities (Acts 20:17ff.).

The PE are thus in accord with Paul's understanding of spiritual leadership in the local church. More, indeed, may be said in the PE about the leaders, including instructions regarding their qualifications, but the qualifications are an enlargement and specification of the general characteristics already required in the early days of the church (cf. Acts 6:3: "men of good reputation, full of the Spirit and of wisdom"). One may assume that these instructions were often given orally by Paul during the initial stages when a local church was being strengthened and established (cf. again Acts 14:23).

79. Ridderbos, *Paul,* 444. I am indebted to the entire section in this work, pp. 438-46 (§70), for the discussion above. See also Ridderbos's "Kerkelijke orde."

Paul now considered it important for Titus (and the local churches to whom he writes through Titus) to have the instructions in writing as elders were being appointed in every city. He apparently also thought that it would be good for Timothy (and the church at Ephesus) to have them in writing for the ongoing selection of elders in the church there, particularly since problems had arisen there with reference to elders (cf. 1 Tim. 5:19-25).

Paul may also speak for the first time in the PE of the laying of hands on those set apart to serve, but in doing so he reflects the practice of the early church whereby the Spirit's direction and enabling power was acknowledged (cf. Acts 13:2-4). Furthermore, the functions these elders/bishops in Ephesus are to perform are no different from those exercised by the leadership in Thessalonica (e.g., προΐστημι is used both in 1 Tim. 3:4, 5; 5:17 and in 1 Thes. 5:12; Rom. 12:8). From these considerations there seems to be no real substance to the charge that the officers in the PE are different from what one finds in the earlier letters (especially since the only other place in the NT in which ἐπίσκοποι and διάκονοι occur together is in Paul's letter to the Philippians [1:1][80]).

Provision for Care of Widows

Paul's treatment of widows (1 Tim. 5:3-16) is an advance on anything else written in the NT; the only other mention of the church's care of widows is the account of what the church at Jerusalem did in its very early days (Acts 6:1ff.). But even in that account we find some formal and recognized organization involved in their care. If the early church under the direct leadership of the apostles needed to make far-reaching adjustments to the ways in which the apostles initially cared for widows, then it is not surprising that Paul feels it necessary to give corrections and adjustments to the patterns that have developed in the church at Ephesus after so many years.

Essentially what Paul is doing is correcting the tendency toward institutionalization by restricting the care for widows to widows over sixty years of age who have no family members to care for them and who are spiritually qualified for any special service the church may ask of them. This approach, which emphasizes the family and curtails institutionalization while affirming the need for the family and the church to care for widows, is certainly moving in the opposite direction from that which developed later in the church.[81]

80. Ramsay (7/8, 17) takes the position that Phil. 1:1 testifies to the existence of the PE's type of church order in Paul's time.

81. Compare this treatment by Paul with that found in a church order book of the third century, the *Syrian Didascalia,* which among its elaborate rules permitted entry at the age of forty and prohibited remarriage altogether. It seems strange that Hanson, who refers to this work and its regulations (p. 98), which differ so much from the account in 1 Timothy 5, should also say that the latter's treatment of widows is post-Pauline (p. 4).

That it is only in the PE that Paul deals with widows does not mean that the PE cannot be from Paul. Arguments from silence are always dubious. One needs only to be reminded that the Lord's Supper is only dealt with once in the Pauline corpus (in 1 Corinthians) and that does not make that letter or that account suspect.

THEOLOGICAL DIFFERENCES

The perceived differences in theology between the PE and Paul's other letters are regarded by some as constituting one of the weightier arguments against authorship by Paul.[82] It is contended that the PE omit basic concepts that Paul uses, that they utilize the same words and terms but with different meanings, and, most significantly, that they utilize terms and concepts not used in Paul's other letters. We mention only in passing the charge that the PE teach only a "middle-class ethics," since this matter has been thoroughly investigated in the Schwarz's dissertation[83] and is dealt with in our comments on the relevant passages (e.g., 1 Tim. 2:2; Tit. 3:1ff.), both of which show that this charge is not only erroneous but also sets an inappropriate disjunction between the other Paulines and the PE.

Absence of Basic Pauline Concepts

It is rather more difficult to establish that the PE omit basic Pauline concepts than it might appear because, as a matter of fact, Paul does not always use in his letters those concepts that are most often associated with him. For example, the verb "to justify" (δικαιόω) is found in Romans, 1 Corinthians, Galatians, 1 Timothy, and Titus but not elsewhere. To make this point one must come up with a term or concept that Paul always uses and never omits. Easton charges that "the full Pauline use of 'faith' as the justifying principle is absent from the Pastorals,"[84] but then the same charge would have to be leveled against 1 Thessalonians and Philemon, to mention only two Pauline letters. As it is, the affirmation in 1 Tim. 1:16 about "those who would believe on him and receive eternal life," used in connection with the statement that "Christ Jesus came into the world to save sinners," refers to that kind of faith, as does the statement about "those who have trusted in God" (Tit. 3:8), which refers to those who have been "justified by his grace" (v. 7).

Hanson describes as "most startling" the absence in the PE of use of υἱός,

82. As recent examples see Hanson, 2f.; Brox, 51-55. For earlier examples cf. Gealy, 367; Easton, 11ff.

83. Schwarz, *Bürgerliches Christentum.*

84. Easton, 103.

"son," for Christ "and the total absence of any mention of the cross."[85] But υἱός is not used at all in Philippians or Philemon and is used of Christ only once each in 2 Corinthians, Ephesians, Colossians, and 1 and 2 Thessalonians. With regard to "cross" (σταυρός), it must be pointed out that it is also not found in Romans, 2 Corinthians, 1 and 2 Thessalonians, or Philemon.

Hanson concludes his list of key concepts in Pauline theology absent from the PE by citing Barrett's list of "words of great importance to Paul" absent from the PE: εὐανγελίζομαι, εὐχαριστέω, καυχάομαι, πνευματικός, σοφία, σῶμα, and ψυχή.[86] Barrett himself noted that "a list of this kind can prove little"[87]; each of these seven words is missing from at least one of the other Pauline letters, two are absent from five of the letters, two others from four of the letters, one from three of the letters, and one from two of the letters. Even those that are found in several letters are often found only once each in a few of them.[88] All this goes to demonstrate that not one of these terms is so Pauline that a letter of his could not be written without it. In fact, one is struck by the paucity of hard evidence in this area, by the fact that terms and concepts once proposed as so Pauline that their absence from a letter would demonstrate that it was not Pauline are not being repeated after being analyzed by others,[89] and by the fact that a new group of terms is being put forward that, like those listed above, represent at best matters of degree but not clear-cut matters of difference.

Terms Used in Non-Pauline Ways

We next turn to terms supposedly used in the PE in a "non-Pauline sense." Hanson cites as the first in a list of such examples ἀγάπη, "the key virtue in Paul," which is in the PE, Hanson says, "just one virtue among others."[90] ἀγάπη does occur in lists of other virtues in 1 Tim. 6:11; 2 Tim. 2:22, but then the same phenomenon occurs also in Gal. 5:22. Furthermore, ἀγάπη is hardly regarded as just one virtue among others in the key statement at the beginning of 1 Timothy: "the goal of our instruction is love (ἀγάπη)" (1:5).

85. Hanson, 3.

86. Hanson, 3, citing Barrett, 6.

87. Barrett, 6.

88. εὐαγγελίζομαι is not found in Phil., Col., 2 Thes., Phm., and appears once in 1 Thes.; εὐχαριστέω not in Gal., and once in 2 Cor., Phil., Phm.; καυχάομαι not in Col., 1 and 2 Thes., Phm., and once in Eph., Phil.; πνευματικός not in 2 Cor., Phil., 1 and 2 Thes., Phm., and once in Gal.; σοφία not in Gal., Phil., 1 and 2 Thes., Phm., and once in Rom., 1 and 2 Cor.; σῶμα not 2 Thes., Phm., and once in Gal., 1 Thes.; ψυχή not in Gal., 2 Thes., Phm., and once in 1 Cor., Eph., Col.

89. Cf. the items cited by earlier opponents of Pauline authorship that Guthrie, for example, patiently examines in *The Pastoral Epistles and the Mind of Paul,* 24ff.; in his commentary, 45ff.; and in his *Introduction,* 604f. Cf. also Kelly, 16-21.

90. Hanson, 3.

Similarly, Hanson says that πίστις is used differently in the PE and "tends to mean 'content of faith.' " He goes on to say that this is "a meaning not absent from Paul,"[91] which is, in fact, an adequate response, though it can be added that this meaning probably occurs less frequently in the PE than is generally thought (see the discussion of πίστις in the commentary below where it appears in the PE, especially under 1 Tim. 1:2).

Hanson repeats a concern that Easton raised earlier when he says that the author of the PE does not "seem to use the important phrase *en Christō,* ('in Christ') in the mystical way that Paul does."[92] Easton said that "Paul uses it to describe believers as so closely united with their Lord that the 'in' has an almost physical sense; in the Pastorals the phrase does not describe believers but gifts 'found in' Christ."[93] Allan also concludes that the formula is used in the PE in a way different from its usage in the Pauline letters.[94] Allan's article appears to be flawed, however, by his emphasis on the differences in usage and his discounting of similarities of usage — for example, those cases in which the formula is preceded by the definite article, a difference already found in the other Pauline letters.[95] As a response to Easton's comment above, though it is germane to Allan's article, Guthrie puts it well when he says that "it is difficult to see any difference of approach between 2 Timothy 1:13 'with faith and love in Christ Jesus,' and Colossians 1:4 'your faith in Christ Jesus.' " "Moreover," he continues, "if 'in Christ' is generally a synonym for 'Christian' in the Pastorals, it must also be considered in the same way in certain Pauline usages (*e.g.* the saints in Christ at Colossae, Col. 1:2)."[96]

Easton also maintains that the infrequent references to the Holy Spirit in the PE and the way in which it is referred to there shows that though the author of the PE accepted the doctrine it "meant little to him."[97] Infrequency can hardly be a safe and sure norm when in two of the other Pauline letters the Spirit is mentioned only once and in another it is not mentioned at all.[98] Haykin demonstrates that a vibrant pneumatology exists in the PE and that there is nothing concerning the Spirit in the PE that Paul could not have written.[99]

91. *Ibid.* Note how this usage of πίστις for "that which is believed" is found "as early as Paul" (not in the PE) by BAGD, 664.

92. Hanson, 3.

93. Easton, 12.

94. Allan, " 'In Christ' Formula."

95. Cf. Allan's treatment, p. 117.

96. Guthrie, 48. This and the preceding comment in the text are examples of the similarities to which Allan has given inadequate attention.

97. Easton, 22; so also Karris, xvi.

98. Once each in Col. (1:8) and 2 Thes. (2:13) and not at all in Phm.

99. Haykin, "Fading Vision."

The conclusion must be that the supposed differences are most often not differences at all, but are at best more fairly described as more intensive use of different nuances of terms already found in the other Pauline letters. And then differences in subject, recipients (the apostolic assistants), or other factors may explain these phenomena. Both in its own right and when considered in the light of other contributing factors, this objection is certainly an inadequate ground to deny Pauline authorship.

A Different Attitude toward Doctrine

It is also charged that the author of the PE cannot be Paul because of an entirely different attitude toward doctrine. Hanson sums up this criticism:

> The author of the Pastorals seems to have an attitude toward doctrine that is not Paul's. For him [the author of the PE] Christian doctrine is a *parathēkē,* "what has been entrusted to you" (1 Tim. 6:20). This deposit of faith has been delivered by Paul to Timothy and must be in turn handed on by Timothy to trustworthy successors (2 Tim. 1:13-14; 2:2; 3:14). . . . This is not the way the historical Paul handles Christian doctrine.[100]

But in fact Paul in his earlier Epistles does have this same attitude toward doctrine. Paul can speak of "the teaching that you have learned," which serves as the standard for identifying false teaching (Rom. 16:17). In 1 Cor. 15:1-3 the gospel itself is described as that which Paul himself has "received" (παρέλαβον), "made known," and "delivered" (παρέδωκα), which the readers "received" (παρελάβετε), in which they "stand," and which they must "hold fast" (κατέχετε). The verbs "receive" (παραλαμβάνω) and "deliver" (παραδίδωμι) are the language used of "handing on" a "tradition."[101] At an earlier point in 1 Corinthians Paul praises the readers because they "hold firmly (κατέχετε) to the traditions (τὰς παραδόσεις), just as I delivered (παρέδωκα) them to you" (11:2). He urges the Thessalonians to "hold to (κρατεῖτε) the traditions (τὰς παραδόσεις) that you were taught" (2 Thes. 2:15) and to take disciplinary actions "according to the tradition (τὴν παράδοσιν) that you received (παρελάβοσαν) from us (παρ' ἡμῶν)" (2 Thes. 3:6).

The only apparent difference is that in the earlier letters there is less explicit comment about passing the tradition on. Undoubtedly this is because the earlier letters were written to churches, not, like the PE, to fellow workers who were particularly responsible for the teaching ministry. Even in the PE this note is found only in the more personal last letter to Timothy, where

100. Hanson, 5-6.

101. See the articles on these words in BAGD and *TDNT* and the literature referred to in them.

this emphasis is appropriate. But even in the earlier letters this note is not completely absent. Timothy's task as Paul's ambassador to the Corinthians was to "remind you of my [Paul's] ways in Christ, just as I teach everywhere in every church" (1 Cor. 4:17). There we see the note of communicating a teaching.

The Use of Different Terms in the PE

But it seems that the articulation of this concern is done with different terms in the PE. Thus we have such expressions as "deposit" (παραθήκη), "sound doctrine" (ὑγιαίνουσα διδασκαλία), and "faithful is the saying" (πιστὸς ὁ λόγος), which are not found in the other letters. At this point our discussion begins to cross over to the discussion of differences in style and vocabulary, but this is inevitable since content on the one hand and style and vocabulary on the other are inextricably related in the PE (as all of those aspects are also related to who the recipients are). Even though these combinations of words are not used by Paul elsewhere, only παραθήκη and ὑγιαίνω themselves are absent from the other Pauline letters.

As significant as this may or may not be, a much more significant factor, which can be observed in the other letters, is Paul's use of a word or phrase in a couple of letters and not at all in the other letters. For example, he uses "tradition," παράδοσις, only five times in four letters and in a positive sense only in two letters — once in 1 Corinthians and twice in 2 Thessalonians. No one would say that the use of this word, which is unknown in nine of the Pauline letters and not used in a positive sense in eleven of the letters, could serve as an indicator that these two letters are not by the same Paul who wrote the others. The same norm should be applied to otherwise unused words and terms in the PE.

It might still be asked why Paul did not return to the use of παράδοσις in the PE rather than turning to the word παραθήκη. One cannot give dogmatic answers to such questions involving near synonyms. Perhaps the negative significance that παράδοσις could have for Paul (so Gal. 1:14; Col. 2:8) had finally had its effect and brought him to use a word that was not so encumbered. Perhaps Paul thought that παράδοσις was more appropriate for the congregation that primarily received the message and that παραθήκη was more appropriate for Timothy and other ministers whose responsibility was both to receive and to pass on faithfully that which they had received. Or perhaps the language of the context simply triggered the word παραθήκη (rather than παράδοσις) because the verb "guard" was used in all three contexts (1 Tim. 6:20; 2 Tim. 1:12, 14). Certainly in 2 Tim. 1:12 "deposit" is more appropriate than "tradition" for referring to Paul's own life (see the commentary), and then it was natural for Paul to use the same term when he turned to Timothy's responsibility. These very likely possibilities make it hazardous to put weight on the fact that a previously unused word occurs three times in the PE.

But what of the other words and phrases? Could not one say that the occurrences of several of these is more like a pattern than incidental occurrences? Again we need to ask if there is a plausible explanation that does not demand the denial of the claim of the letters to be Pauline. It is the first order of business to seek an explanation before one says that no explanation is possible and that the letters cannot therefore be by the same person. Might ὑγιαίνω with its medical associations have come into Paul's vocabulary through more prolonged contact with Luke the physician (except for one occurrence in 3 John, ὑγιαίνω occurs in the NT only in the PE and Luke)?[102] Or was ὑγιαίνουσα διδασκαλία something one was more likely to use speaking to colleagues than to a congregation?

Why are "faithful sayings" referred to in the PE and not in the other Paulines? Paul utilizes traditions in his other letters,[103] though he does not give them this designation. Perhaps more and more such sayings came into existence in the church before the time that the PE were written or were brought to his attention while he was in prison in Rome. Perhaps Luke, who was interested in what others said, collected these sayings and shared them with Paul so that Paul had more to draw upon than before.[104] Moreover, since in the PE Paul writes more briefly to colleagues than he did to churches, perhaps he found such sayings helpful in briefly summarizing what he wanted to say. Perhaps Paul had become more sensitive to and appreciative of the crystallizations of Christian teaching and wanted to share these with his colleagues.

Why also are the "faithful sayings" consistently designated as such in the PE? Perhaps this designation for such sayings had been recently developed and had come to be the convenient way of speaking of them. Or perhaps Paul himself devised this formula to call attention to the fact that they were sayings and to commend them. Unfortunately, we do not know which of these possibilities represents the actual state of affairs, though it is clear that there are a number of plausible explanations that do not demand the denial of the claim of the PE to be Pauline.

The Context of the Differences

We are left with the fact that the theological expressions in these letters of Paul to his colleagues are somewhat different from those in his letters to churches. They are not contradictory to the theology of the earlier letters nor

102. See **Was Luke Involved?** below.
103. Cf., e.g., Hunter, *Paul,* especially 14-40.
104. See **Was Luke Involved?** below.

do they introduce matters either of form or content that are unthinkable for Paul. Furthermore, these dissimilarities must be put in the larger context of the great similarities in theological viewpoint between the PE and the other Paulines. Kelly aptly sums up the echoes of what we know of Paul's teaching from his earlier letters that we find in the PE:

> This can surely be overheard in the author's heartfelt acknowledgement of the revelation of God's mercy in Jesus Christ and his own experience of it as a sinner and blasphemer (1 Tim. i.12-17; Tit. iii.3-7), in his clear affirmation that justification has nothing to do with man's deserts but depends wholly on God's grace (2 Tim. i.9; Tit. iii.5), and in his confession of Christ as the new man, the redeemer who gave himself a ransom for sinners (1 Tim. ii.5f.: cf. i.15). To these can be added his description of eternal life as both the goal to which Christians are called and as something they can enjoy here and now ([1 Tim.] vi.12: cf. 2 Tim. i.1; Tit. i.2; iii.7), and of faith in Christ as the means of attaining it (1 Tim. i.16). His conviction, too, that God called us by his grace before the world was made (2 Tim. i.9 f.; Tit. ii.11) is in line with Paul's teaching, and his attitude to such matters as . . . slaves (1 Tim. vi.1), and the state ([1 Tim.] ii.1 ff.; Tit. iii.1) is of a piece with the Apostle's.[105]

Scott, who does not advocate Pauline authorship, says of these teachings that "these are no mere perfunctory echoes of Pauline thought."[106] Without this pervasive similarity of basic truths and without the knowledge of Paul's own versatility and occasional use of terms and phrases that he did not use again, one might conceivably think that the differences were the crucial and deciding factor. But since both the similarities and the differences fit within the framework of Pauline practice, it does not point to a compelling argument against Pauline authorship.

VOCABULARY AND STYLE

We have already touched on vocabulary and style in discussing the use of different theological terms, since these matters, or at least those of vocabulary and theological terms, are inextricably interrelated. Harrison[107] and others have documented differences of greater or lesser magnitude for various aspects of style and for various ways of looking at vocabulary, mainly on the basis of numerical tabulations of word usage. These differences will be our concern here.

105. Kelly, 16f.
106. E. F. Scott, xxx.
107. Harrison, *Problem; idem, Paulines and Pastorals.*

Methodological Questions

Just as in most of the questions or objections examined above, here also one needs a norm or standard to determine what range of variation is beyond that of writers in general and of Paul in particular. Metzger raises this question most effectively, directing attention to the work of the statistician Yule.[108] Yule's volume deals with both the legitimacy and the limitations of using word counts to establish literary authorship and concludes that this approach is legitimate but needs certain controls. One control is that the treatise to be examined be about ten thousand words long.[109] Metzger observes that "since the sum total of the words in all three Pastoral Epistles is far less than this figure, the New Testament scholar who uses the statistical method on them must at the outset resign himself to accepting results that are less than generally trustworthy."[110]

Metzger also formulates the key methodological question that Yule's study addresses: "How *different* can the results of a particular analysis of the two texts be before they throw serious doubt upon the theory that they have a common author?"[111] He summarizes the transferable results of Yule's study as follows:

> The "allowed deviation" . . . must vary according to the text and subject matter, and may vary according to the change of a particular author's habits between the composing of two works. In this case we must take into account not only the amount of time that may have elapsed between the composition of two works, but also whether we are dealing with an author whose ways of writing fluctuate surprisingly. This latter question involves not only certain intangible considerations of the personality of the author, but even of the literary habits of the age in which he was living.[112]

In addition to calling attention to this most basic methodological point, Metzger also points out that others have raised questions about how the variables are calculated, again indicating a basic question of methodology.[113] "Hitchcock pointed out that when Harrison cites non-Biblical occurrences of words that appear in the Pastoral Epistles but not in the acknowledged Pauline Epistles, in many cases he does not cite the earliest appearance but the latest and thus creates the (erroneous) impression that these words occur only after the first century A.D."[114] Michaelis shows that Harrison would

108. B. M. Metzger, "Reconsideration," referring to Yule, *Statistical Study*.

109. Yule, *Statistical Study,* 281.

110. Metzger, "Reconsideration," 94.

111. *Ibid.,* 93.

112. *Ibid.,* 94.

113. Hitchcock, "Tests"; *idem,* "Philo"; Michaelis, "Pastoralbriefe."

114. Metzger's summary ("Reconsideration," 92) of the conclusion reached by Hitchcock, "Tests," 279.

have reached entirely different results if he had calculated the percentage of hapax legomena in relation to the total number of different Greek words per book rather than in relation to the number of pages of Greek text in a book. Using this other procedure Romans has nearly the same percentage of hapax legomena as 2 Timothy and Titus.[115]

Metzger concludes his article as a whole with a significant statement: "It seems, therefore, that a discreet reticence should replace the almost unbounded confidence with which many scholars have used this method in attempting to solve the problem of the authorship of the PE."[116]

The Arguments

The attempt to resolve the question of the authorship of Paul's letters has been taken up again by such scholars as Morton and McLeman,[117] and Grayston and Herdan (see below), and the methodology of the former two has been subjected to a great deal of criticism.[118] Two of the best critiques of the current use of statistical methodology in this area are those of Clark and Kenny.[119] Morton and McLeman have used sentence length among other criteria to determine whether a work should be considered non-Pauline. But their own study acknowledges that this criterion would rule out a section of Romans.[120] This test can hardly be adequate on that basis alone. But Kenny shows other serious flaws in their work and in the new work on the same subject by Morton.[121] Similar problems arise with the use of καί as a test.[122] Morton and Michaelson also proposed as another independent test the grammatical category of the last words of sentences.[123] The conclusions of their article were severely criticized in a later article in the same journal by P. F. Johnson.[124] Clark's conclusion after careful analysis of the work of Morton and McLeman probably can, unfortunately, be applied to Morton's later works (based on the impartial evaluation of others who have examined

115. Michaelis, "Pastoralbriefe," 73f.

116. Metzger, "Reconsideration," 94.

117. In a number of works, particularly *Paul, the Man and the Myth.*

118. See the list of articles in Guthrie, *Introduction,* 633.

119. Clark, "Investigation," to which I am particularly indebted in this section; Kenny, *Stylometric Study.*

120. As noted in Clark, "Investigation," 46.

121. Kenny, *Stylometric Study,* 101-11, taking into consideration the newer work by Morton, *Literary Detection.*

122. Clark, "Investigation," 179; Kenny, *Stylometric Study.*

123. Michaelson and Morton, "Last Words."

124. P. F. Johnson, "Use of Statistics," which in effect says that on the last words approach Paul could not have written sections of Romans. Kenny concluded his evaluation of this test by saying "that it was clear that to use the last-word test as a criterion of authorship would lead to absurd results" (*Stylometric Study,* 115).

those tests): "We have shown that none of [Morton and McLeman's] tests stand up completely to detailed study."[125]

Grayston and Herdan seek to state the linguistic argument of Harrison more precisely.[126] They replace the basic statistic used by Harrison, the number of words peculiar to an Epistle per page, with the ratio "C," which equals the words peculiar to a certain Epistle plus the words common to all Epistles divided by the vocabulary of the particular Epistle under consideration. Since this is a refinement of Harrison's tests, the "C" of the PE shows some divergence from the "C" of the other Paulines. But in the test run by Grayston and Herdan the PE are grouped together, whereas all the other Pauline letters (except the Thessalonian letters, which also showed as a group a divergence) were calculated separately. Grouping the PE together may anticipate the outcome by the way in which the calculation is framed. When Clark and Robinson ran the same test with the PE treated as separate letters, they both found that the PE fit well into the range set by the Pauline letters.[127] In fact, because of this outcome Robinson concluded that "until the time that a method is found that is much more discriminating than those before us, literary critics of the New Testament must recognize the possibility that there may exist no relationship between the percentage of hapax legomena in different works that could be used to detect a difference in authorship."[128]

The different variables that Harrison proposed and that Grayston and Herdan worked with must be considered in specific terms. Harrison's argument was based on four different groups of data: the hapaxes, other non-Pauline words found in the PE and shared with other NT writings, Pauline words or phrases absent from the PE, and grammatical and stylistic differences between the PE and the Paulines. Harrison concluded that the differences between the PE and the Paulines were such that they could not be by the same author. He then compared the linguistic evidence of the PE with second-century literature and concluded that the PE were written in that century. Harrison's arguments have been carefully summarized and meticulously examined in the appendix to Guthrie's commentary.[129]

125. Clark, "Investigation," 194. Kenny (*Stylometric Study,* preface, p. v) speaks for me when he says that although he has been critical of the methods and conclusions of Morton he "would like to pay tribute to the pioneering work he has done in stylometry, and the vigour with which, in his published writings, he has communicated the excitement of stylometric study."

126. Grayston and Herdan, "Authorship."

127. Clark, "Investigation," 138 (the statistics and the basis for the procedure are laid out on pp. 136-39); T. A. Robinson, "Grayston and Herdan's 'C.' "

128. Robinson, "Grayston and Herdan's 'C,' " 287.

129. "An Examination of the Linguistic Argument against the Authenticity of the Pastorals," Guthrie, 224-40. I am greatly indebted to this study as well as to Guthrie's earlier work, *The Pastoral Epistles and the Mind of Paul,* and to his *Introduction.*

Harrison demonstrated mathematically that the number of hapaxes in the other ten Paulines range between 3.3 and 6.2 per page and in the PE from 12.9 to 16.1, for a total of some 175 hapaxes in the PE. Harrison claims that the difference is inconceivable for one mind.[130] In addition, there are some 131 words that occur in the PE and in other NT books but not in the other Paulines. Therefore, there are some 306 words in the PE that are not found in the other Paulines. Harrison admits that Paul's working vocabulary consisted of more than the 2177 words of the other ten Paulines, but is sure that Paul would not have included all of these 306 words in that working vocabulary.

But are these words so unusual that Paul would not use them? If 131 are used by his Christian contemporaries, the other writers of the NT, all or nearly all with whom Paul had personal contact, is it not likely that Paul would have known these words too? Moreover, only 28 of the 306 words are unknown in other writings prior to AD 50.[131] Even Harrison admits that less than 20 were unknown before AD 90.[132] Finally, about 80 of the hapaxes are paralleled in the LXX.[133] These factors alone go a long way toward accounting for these words and the plausibility of their being known to Paul and serve as an adequate if not complete refutation of Harrison's contention that the vocabulary is that of the second century.[134]

To this must be added the fact that the great majority of the new words are found in sections dealing with new subject matter,[135] a phenomenon to be expected in letters to colleagues rather than to churches. The Latinity of some of the new words would suggest that Paul has been increasingly influenced by his environment.[136] Since several of the hapaxes are cognates of Pauline words and several are new compounds that have analogies in the other Pauline Epistles, the logical conclusion is that they point toward Paul as the author rather than away from him.[137] Paul often takes over the language of his opponents; perhaps this has also played a role in the PE. Finally, as shall see later, certain words are also shared with Luke his

130. Harrison, *Problem,* 23f.

131. So Hitchcock, "Tests," 278.

132. Harrison, "Important Hypotheses," 79.

133. For the list of words see Guthrie, *The Pastoral Epistles and the Mind of Paul,* 39f.

134. See Guthrie, *The Pastoral Epistles and the Mind of Paul,* 9-12, and his commentary, 226-28.

135. Observed already by Parry, cxi-cxxvi (1920), before Harrison's work was published.

136. Cf. Hitchcock, "Latinity"; Simpson, 20f., who gives a list of such words.

137. Guthrie, 229f. with n. 2 on 229, gives as a example of the former the Pauline ὠφελέω and ὠφέλεια and then the Pastorals' ὠφέλιμος, and of the latter the Pastorals' hapax κενοφωνία, which has only two analogous forms in the NT, both Pauline hapaxes, κενόδοξος and κενοδοξία. Other examples could be given, but are not necessary to make the point.

companion.[138] Our conclusion is that we expect Paul to use more new words when he writes to his colleagues (in contrast to his previous letters to churches) about new subjects and that the various factors listed above account adequately for a great number of the new words used.

Harrison cites a large number of words absent from the PE but present in anywhere from five to nine other Pauline letters,[139] and also whole groups of such words derived from a common root having approximately the same span of occurrence (with one group occurring in all of the other ten Epistles).[140] As impressive as it is to find four words that occur in nine of the other Pauline epistles and not in the PE, the fact that this happens for nine rather than ten speaks for itself. We cannot say that Paul must use any single word in any one of his letters. There is no word (leaving aside, as Harrison does, the article, conjunctions, etc., which are so common that they are not unique to a writer) that Paul always uses and must use in any letter that he writes. This should give us pause in evaluating the groups with a common root, for here there is one root that occurs in all ten of the other Paulines, the verb ἐνεργέω and its cognates. But since the most basic form of the root would be ἔργον rather than ἐνεργέω, it would not be right to say that the PE cannot be Pauline because they do not use some form of the root ἔργ- with ἐν-, even though they use ἔργον, ἐργάτης, εὐεργεσία, and other compound forms. It is, instead, more significant that the most basic form of the root of the one word grouping that is present in the ten other Paulines, namely the root form ἔργ-, is present also in the PE. As is often the case, the evidence against the Pauline authorship proves to be lacking in conclusiveness and points in the opposite direction.

Harrison also argued that a different style demonstrates the presence of a different author. His main argument in this area was that there are a great number of particles, prepositions, pronouns, etc., that appear in the other ten Paulines but not in the PE. This has become almost as significant to scholars as the differences in vocabulary, as with Hunter: "How are we to explain the fact that 'the connective tissue' (particles, etc. — a very subtle test of style) is clearly not Paul's?"[141]

Initially the argument seems quite impressive. Harrison lists 112 particles, prepositions, and pronouns, etc., that are in Paul's other ten letters but not in the PE.[142] But the impressiveness begins to wane when we realize that 58 of these occur in only one or two letters and three of the letters have less than 20 of them.[143] Furthermore, of the 112 words only 28 occur in at

138. See **Was Luke Involved?** below.
139. Harrison, *Problem,* 31f.
140. *Ibid.,* 33.
141. Hunter, *Interpreting,* 64.
142. Harrison, *Problem,* 36f.
143. Guthrie, *Introduction,* 610; cf. his commentary, 236.

least five Pauline Epistles.[144] Ephesians and Colossians, which are closely related, have in common only 6 particles.[145] Again, it needs to be noted that none of the particles appears in all ten of the other letters.[146] Thus there is no particle that Paul always uses and never omits.

The question of particles is put in a more complete perspective when it is recognized that there are 93 other particles, prepositional forms, etc., in the NT that are not included by Harrison (and are conveniently listed by Guthrie[147]). Of these 93, all but one (ἀνά) appear in the PE and all but 7 are also found in the other ten Paulines. A greater number of these 93 forms are found in five or more of the other Pauline Epistles than of Harrison's 112.[148] Of these 93 particles, 73 are in 1 Timothy, 61 in 2 Timothy, and 43 in Titus. In the other Paulines, aside from Philemon with 32, the numbers also range from the mid 40s to a high of 73.[149] Thus when we look at all the connective tissue we find that the PE and the other Paulines share a significant amount. But we always need to remember that neither list provides any word that is used by all of Paul's letters without exception.

The particles and other words that are part of the connective tissue are like all the other words at issue in that they are aspects of the content communicated and the method by which it is communicated.[150] We have already noted above that the style of the PE, just because they are written to colleagues, differs from that of the earlier letters (just as those letters also differ among themselves). White has pointed out that of some 24 characteristic Pauline particles more are found in the four great Epistles, which contain more rhetorical passages, and that less are found in the Prison Epistles, where rhetorical passages are less frequent.[151] We should expect this trend to continue in the even less rhetorical PE, and we should not be surprised that it does. To put the matter in its broadest perspective, we need to remind ourselves that there are 205 particles, pronouns, prepositional forms, etc., found in the NT, and 204 are found in one or more Pauline letters if we include the PE and 197 if we exclude the PE. It is true that a large number (112) do not appear in the PE. But that number is put into perspective

144. Roberts, "Bearing," 134. Roberts takes as an example of these 28 the particle ἄν, which occurs only twice in the ten Paulines outside Romans, 1 and 2 Corinthians, and Galatians, both times in constructions that were not needed in letters to colleagues. Roberts points out that thus one can understand why ἄν is not found in the Pastorals (134f.).

145. Guthrie, *The Pastoral Epistles and the Mind of Paul,* 14.

146. See the list in Harrison, *Problem,* 36f.

147. Appendix E of Guthrie's *The Pastoral Epistles and the Mind of Paul,* 41-44.

148. *Ibid.,* 13f.

149. For a complete list see *ibid.,* 13.

150. For example, although Luke uses τέ 159x in Acts he uses it only 8x in the Gospel. This was kindly brought to my attention by Colin Hemer (who was then intensely working on Acts) before his untimely death in 1987.

151. N. J. D. White, 71.

when one realizes that more than 112 particles, etc., do not appear in six of the ten other Paulines.[152] Thus the PE compare favorably with the other Paulines in the variety and number of particles, etc., or "connective tissue" (to use Hunter's phrase) that they use. Kenny's study of stylometrics (using a much wider base and including particles, etc.) came to the same conclusion regarding the PE regarded as a group.[153]

The PE do have certain differences in vocabulary and style from the other ten Paulines, but these differences are not out of the range of "a single, unusually versatile author," to use Kenny's designation of Paul.[154] They are differences in the midst of many similarities. When one takes into account the various factors that legitimately enter into these differences, they are adequately explained and in fact shown to be normal rather than abnormal. As we said earlier, the several differences between the PE and the Paulines are all interrelated and mutually explanatory parts of one overarching and comprehensive difference. These letters are written to different recipients about essentially different matters in a style and vocabulary consistent with these two factors and with any effect that the environment might have had on the author.[155]

152. Guthrie, *The Pastoral Epistles and the Mind of Paul,* 13.

153. Kenny, *Stylometric Study,* 100. "There is no support given by this table [displaying his test results] to the idea that a single group of Epistles (say the four major Tübingen Epistles) stand out as uniquely comfortable with one another; or that a single group (such as the Pastoral Epistles) stand out as uniquely diverse from the surrounding context" (98-100). Kenny uses 96 features as the test basis for comparing the Pauline Epistles (see pp. 123f.). Some may fault the fact that these are all weighted the same. On that basis, however, he sees "no reason to reject the hypothesis that twelve of the Pauline epistles are the work of a single, unusually versatile author." Only Titus remained for him under suspicion, but he graciously grants that "what is said of the authorship of the Epistles is in the end a matter for the Scripture scholar, not the stylometrist" (p. 100).

154. See the previous note.

155. Neumann's thorough review and critique of proposed stylostatistical procedures *(Authenticity)* was published too late to be considered in this section. The indices he uses classify the Pastorals as non-Pauline. But one may properly question the reliability of these indices, since they also place Revelation 2-3 with Paul (pp. 200, 213). Furthermore, 1 Timothy and 2 Timothy are grouped apart from one another under one of Neumann's sets of indices but together under the other set (pp. 200f.). Finally, one must note that the study uses as its norm of the Pauline style a restricted list of letters, but concludes that the disputed letters (other than the Pastorals) fall within the Pauline style as it is set by the restricted list (pp. 194-99). Even if these indices were adequate, on the basis of this outcome it would seem necessary to rerun the tests using the disputed letters now as part of the norm for the Pauline style, and also to rerun the tests without initially placing the Pastoral letters outside the Pauline corpus.

PSEUDONYMITY

The self-testimony to Pauline authorship in the PE and the specificity with which they refer to Paul and his circumstances, fellow workers, concerns, etc. (see above under **Self-Testimony regarding Authorship, Recipients, Setting, and Purposes**), pose a challenge to those who deny Pauline authorship. For this reason Harrison[156] and others regard some sections as genuine fragments written by Paul and incorporated into the letters by the pseudonymous writer. But this approach has had fewer defenders as time goes on. More often it is said that all the contents of the three letters were composed by a writer using the pseudonym of Paul.[157]

This more thorough pseudonymity view carries with it the problem of explaining why the author has included such details regarding Paul and other persons in his work. Some, Hanson for example, take the sections including these details as somehow preserving a genuine historical tradition.[158] Others take the material as "all fictional, invented by the author to give verisimilitude to his narrative."[159] Trummer, for instance, argues that the details that appear to be historical were invented to provide a model of how church leaders should live.[160] Meade continues further in the line of Trummer and others and argues that Paul has asked that he be imitated, with the implication that this warranted writing letters in Paul's name, since this was his way of communicating and passing on the tradition.[161] Hanson finds Trummer's argument unconvincing.[162] But to say, with Hanson, that these sections in the PE with apparent historical details represent genuine historical traditions, is still to say that they were included to "give verisimilitude" to the pseudonymous composition.

156. Harrison, *Problem,* 115-35, gives five fragments, which in *Paulines and Pastorals,* 106-28, he reduces to three, i.e., Tit. 3:12-15; 2 Tim. 4:9-15, 20, 21a, 22b; 2 Tim. 1:1-18; 3:10, 11; 4:12a, 5b-8, 16-19, 21b, 22a.

157. Cf. also Cook, "Pastoral Fragments." Cook concludes his study with these words: "The intermediate ground occupied by the defenders of the fragment hypothesis proves to be rather a no man's land not suited for habitation."

158. See, e.g., Hanson, 14ff., and those he cites.

159. The quotation is from Hanson, 14. Examples of those who take this view are Trummer and Hasler. Trummer gives his arguments regarding the reasons the author has done this in "Mantel und Schriften," and in *Paulustradition,* 81f.

160. See the previous note.

161. For a fuller statement of Meade's guiding principles and the arguments that he adduces with regard to the PE see *Pseudonymity,* 116-39, and especially the italicized statements on pp. 116, 127, and 139 as well as *passim.* One of the main weaknesses of his book is its initial assumption of pseudonymity in the NT, which it then proceeds to try to explain. As an example of this approach, Meade states that he will "assume," "with Ephesians and the Pastorals, that their pseudonymity is a foregone conclusion" (p. 118).

162. "We must conclude that Trummer's explanation of why these details are fictional is even more unconvincing than the attempts of some scholars to reconstruct an account of Paul's life that will harmonise all the details given in the Pastoral Epistles" (Hanson, 15).

This inevitably raises the ethical question of pseudonymous authorship. This is so even though those who take the pseudonymous position vigorously protest that questions of deception and untruthfulness are not germane to this practice, that it was accepted in that day and had no moral overtones, and therefore that to raise the question is to impose the standards of another day back on that day.[163] But is this really the case?

In 2 Thes. 3:17 Paul calls to the attention of his readers the "distinguishing mark," which is "the way he indicates that his letters are genuine,"[164] and indicates that the "mark" consists of the "greeting" that he writes "with his own hand." He further states that this distinguishing mark is "in every letter." He makes similar remarks about writing with his own hand in several of his other letters (1 Cor. 16:21; Gal. 6:11; Col. 4:18; Phm. 19), which he undoubtedly did, as in 2 Thessalonians, to authenticate his letters for their recipients. The reason for Paul's mentioning the "mark" most specifically in 2 Thessalonians may be gathered from his concern expressed in 2:2 that the readers not be shaken by "a letter as if from us" (2:2), that is, by a letter claiming falsely to be from Paul: The mark was intended to distinguish Paul's letter from any that were not his even if they claimed to be his.

Since Paul communicated to the church this concern that his letters be clearly authenticated and that other letters not from him not be mistakenly attributed to him, it would seem evident that he wanted the church members to have the same concern and to exercise appropriate safeguards against any pseudonymous letters. It is not too much to say that this perspective set the tone and the norm for the early church. Thus it is not accurate to characterize this perspective as foreign to the early church and imposed on it by those living in a later day. Rather, it is found in the apostle and communicated by him to the early church.

Therefore, the burden of proof is on those who advocate pseudonymity for letters that claim to be from the apostle Paul and that were accepted as canonical by the early church: It must be demonstrated not only that these letters are pseudonymous and not deceptive but also that the early church would accept letters known to be pseudonymous into the canon.

163. For comments like these see Gealy, 372; Harrison, *Problem,* 12; Easton, 19. The historical data relating to this question in the early church are too vast to be surveyed or adequately summarized here. The reader is therefore directed to the representative articles by Aland ("Problem"), who argues that pseudonymity was acceptable for a work that was to become canonical, and by Guthrie ("Development"), who argues that pseudonymity, particularly in letters, was not acceptable to the early church in works regarded as canonical. See also the primary and secondary sources referred to in these articles. See also Appendix C, "Epistolary Pseudepigraphy," in Guthrie's *Introduction,* 671-84, with the "Additional Note," 683f., which is a response to Aland's article.

164. Morris, *1-2 Thessalonians;* cf. also Bruce, *1 & 2 Thessalonians*.

WAS LUKE INVOLVED?

The Lucan Proposal

Another solution to the problem of the differences in vocabulary and style between the PE and the other Paulines is that a secretary or amanuensis wrote the letters under Paul's authority but did so in such a way as to have an impact upon the language and style of the letters.[165] A particular form of this solution proposed in recent years (albeit repeating an observation made long ago)[166] is that this secretary was Luke. This link with Luke has been suggested both by those who think that the PE are Pauline and by those who think that they are not, both agreeing that the PE and Luke have certain things in common.

C. F. D. Moule's stimulating lecture on "The Problem of the Pastoral Epistles: A Reappraisal" seems to have reestablished the Lucan proposal as a viable possibility. Strobel subsequently extended the argument with a detailed comparison of the language and style of Luke and Acts with that of the PE.[167] Brox criticized Strobel's presentation and argued that there is no evidence for Lucan authorship of, or even influence on, the PE.[168] Quinn suggested that the PE were originally short communications from Paul in which Luke collaborated and that they were subsequently edited and enlarged by Luke as a third volume to the Gospel and Acts.[169]

Wilson developed and modified the proposals of Moule and Strobel, taking into account Brox's criticisms, and argued that the PE were written by the author of Luke-Acts (who he claims is not the Luke of the NT, the companion of Paul) and that they are post-Pauline.[170] Wilson's book has received several thorough reviews, particularly noteworthy among them those of Quinn,[171] W. Larkin,[172] and I. H. Marshall.[173] Since Wilson's is the most thorough treatment to date of this hypothesis, we will analyze its argument, taking into account the criticisms, corrections, and suggestions found in the reviews.

Wilson's argument consists essentially of two parts. The first is based on

165. Cf., e.g., Jeremias, 7f.

166. In Schott, *Isagoge,* 35, quoted by Harrison, *Problem,* 52 n. 1, and cited by C. F. D. Moule, "Problem," 431.

167. Strobel, "Schreiben."

168. Brox, "Lukas."

169. Quinn, "Last Volume." Quinn indicates (p. 62) that this hypothesis is being used as he prepares his commentaries on 1 and 2 Timothy and Titus for the Anchor Bible.

170. S. G. Wilson, *Luke,* 3f.

171. *CBQ* 43 (1981), 488-90.

172. *TJ* 2 (1981), 91-94.

173. *JSNT* 10 (1981), 69-74.

similarities of language and vocabulary between Luke-Acts and the PE, the second on a common theological outlook, which Wilson develops under six topics. Since Dodd has already shown that the apostolic community had a common theological perspective[174] and this is seen to be even more widespread by the similarity of the "household tables" and other similar items in the Epistles, and even though this part of his argument seems as important for Wilson as the other, we will concentrate on the linguistic part of his argument as the most objective and arguably in the long run the most significant.

Wilson points out that Strobel listed 37 words common to Luke-Acts and the PE but absent elsewhere in the NT, admitting that some are used differently in the two bodies of literature. This is indeed remarkable considering the brevity of the PE and that only 62 words[175] are shared by Luke and Acts despite their common authorship. There are also 37 words common to the PE and Luke-Acts that are rare in the rest of the NT, Wilson again acknowledging that some are used differently.[176]

Wilson also lists stylistic traits that are found almost exclusively in Luke-Acts and the PE, of which some 4 are not found in the other ten Paulines.[177] He also mentions parallels in the use of verbs, of which 10 are not in the other ten Paulines.[178] Finally, he lists some random expressions and ideas shared by Luke-Acts and the PE, of which 10 are not found in the other ten Paulines.[179]

This commonality between the PE and Luke-Acts is impressive especially when it is compared with the other non-Pauline NT writings. Whereas the PE and Luke-Acts share 37 words exclusively, "the next most frequent are 10 shared with Hebrews and 7 with 2 Peter."[180]

The question is, however, how this compares with terms shared exclusively between the PE and the other ten Paulines? Marshall asks that crucial question and provides us with these figures: While Luke-Acts and the PE share *exclusively* 34 words out of the total of 554 common to both bodies of literature, the PE and the other ten Paulines share exclusively 55 words out of the total of 574 common to the two groups of Epistles.[181] These figures are all the more significant since Luke-Acts has a larger vocabulary than the Pauline corpus. On this basis the Pauline authorship of the PE is much more in line with the linguistic data than would be Lucan authorship.

174. Dodd, *Apostolic Preaching*.

175. This is Marshall's correction of Wilson's number of 42; cf. Marshall in *JSNT* 10 (1981), 71, and Wilson, *Luke,* 5.

176. Wilson, *Luke,* 6.

177. *Ibid.,* 7.

178. *Ibid.,* 8.

179. *Ibid.,* 9.

180. *Ibid.*

181. *JSNT* 10 (1981), 72.

The Relationship between Paul and Luke

Although this result is negative for Lucan authorship, there are two things to be gained from the comparative studies of Strobel, Wilson, and Marshall. The first is an increased awareness and appreciation for how similar the PE and the other Paulines really are. We have being dealing at length with differences between the PE and the other letters. This preoccupation with differences can put one's perspective out of kilter so that the differences loom larger than the similarities. But the differences are differences between groups that in large measure are quite similar, as the above statistics indicate. What we have then are letters that purport to be Pauline, that relate a great amount of personal information about Paul, and that share much of their vocabulary with the other Paulines, including a high number of exclusively shared words.

But the differences do remain and must be acknowledged as a difficulty. The comparisons with Luke-Acts may also point toward a solution to that problem. Although they failed to make the case for the Lucan authorship, they did establish that next to the Paulines the PE are much closer to Luke-Acts than to any other body of literature, in some ways significantly close. The very words, stylistic traits, and specific expressions in the PE that are not found in the Paulines (which are frequently regarded as inherently non-Pauline) are often those shared exclusively with Luke or shared with Luke and one or two other NT writers — some 68 such items by my count. Furthermore, my count of words occurring in the PE and in Luke-Acts but not in the other ten Paulines (based on Morgenthaler's *Statistik*) turned up 75 such words (including proper nouns but not some of the unique combinations of words that Wilson's list contains).[182]

If the PE share these characteristics with Luke-Acts, might it be a result of the shared lives of Luke and Paul? The "we" sections in Acts[183] imply that the author of Luke-Acts was personally present with Paul on a number of occasions and certainly during the two-year Roman imprisonment. Paul mentions Luke in two of his Prison Epistles (Col. 4:14; Phm. 24) and specifically says in 2 Tim. 4:11 that "only Luke is with me." The latter might indicate that Luke had become more and more a constant companion of Paul. It is clear, in any case, that he was a fairly constant companion of Paul, particularly during the first Roman imprisonment and afterward.

In their companionship Luke would have used his own vocabulary and style in conversation and would probably have shared with Paul any travel

182. E.g., in the εὐσεβ- word group, εὐσεβέω is found in the NT only in the PE and Acts and εὐσέβεια only in the PE, Acts, and 2 Peter. See the full discussion of εὐσέβεια in the commentary at 1 Tim. 2:2. Cf. also the comments made earlier about ὑγιαίνω and the "faithful sayings" in the section above on **Theological Differences.**

183. Acts 16:10-17; 20:5-15; 21:1-18; 27:1–28:16.

notes he might have made, which would come to be used in the composition of Acts, and any written material that would be used in his Gospel.[184] Even if there were no such sharing of written materials, it is to expected that some of Luke's vocabulary and style would have an effect on Paul and that as the companionship was extended and became more constant this would have been more and more a factor in Paul's linguistic reservoir.

The PE are what one would expect under these circumstances: They are primarily Pauline, but their second greatest element is what they share with Luke-Acts. This may have come about just through the linguistic impact that Luke had on Paul, but it might also be that Luke was the secretary whose language was sometimes utilized by Paul as he formulated the contents of the letters. In any case, the connections between Luke-Acts and the PE and between Luke and Paul are so striking and inherently interrelated that one must ask whether this may not be a significant factor in the solution to the linguistic phenomena of the PE.

CONCLUSION

The arguments against Pauline authorship of the PE, like the arguments for Lucan authorship, initially appear to be persuasive. But when examined more closely they fall far short of being convincing. Examination of both sets of arguments brings out relationships between the PE and the other Paulines that have been overlooked or not adequately appreciated. Thus the apparent problem areas have in the long run made their own contributions and have thus strengthened rather than weakened the pervasive self-testimony of the letters to their Pauline authorship. Differences remain between the PE and the other Paulines, but as suggested above, the differences are interrelated and mutually explanatory parts of one overarching and comprehensive difference: The PE were written to different recipients — colleagues not churches. When the apostle writes to his colleagues, much of what he writes about is different. Furthermore, his method of communication, style, and vocabulary are also different because of the difference in recipients and content. Thus the differences themselves are not unexplainable, but rather prove to be appropriate authenticating marks of letters by Paul to two of his colleagues.

But even though the different recipients and much new subject matter

184. Guthrie comments that "Luke had spent some time in Palestine while Paul was imprisoned at Caesarea. . . . It is a reasonable conjecture (although no more than a conjecture) that Luke collected up much of his own special material while at Caesarea, and it is an equally reasonable conjecture that he would have proceeded to write his Gospel soon after" (*Introduction,* 115).

go a long way in explaining the use of new vocabulary, the relationship between the vocabulary and style of Luke-Acts and that of the PE, along with the companionship of Luke with Paul, points to another factor in the different vocabulary. This helps to remove the question of possible influences on Paul's vocabulary from the realm of mere possibility to that of demonstrable possibility. Some form of the Lucan hypothesis short of exclusive Lucan authorship apart from Paul thus becomes a supporting element in the argument for Pauline authorship.

Our conclusion is that the PE were indeed written by the apostle Paul to his colleagues. This conclusion is based not only on the clear self-testimony of the letters to Paul as their author, their frequent personal references to Paul, their basic Pauline teaching, and their basic Pauline vocabulary and style, but also on the satisfactory resolution of the perceived or real differences, which in the end point toward rather than away from that authorship.

POSSIBLE DATES OF THE LETTERS

The chronology of Paul's life is constructed from various pieces of data found in the Acts and the Pauline letters, which are related to datable pieces of information, which serve as fixed reference points. It is our purpose here not to go over those data or to reconstruct that chronology[185] but to say what can be said regarding the relative and absolute dating of the three PE on the basis of the conclusions that have been made in this Introduction.

As argued above (see **Relationship to Acts and the Other Epistles**), the PE must be placed after the period in Paul's life covered by Acts and the other letters. A large consensus of those who still include the data from Acts in their calculations of Pauline chronology has narrowed the range for dating this later period of Paul's life to within a two- to three-year span. The dates suggested for Paul's two years of imprisonment in Rome (Acts 28:30) range from 59 (or 61) to 61 (or 63). The PE require that Paul was then released, involve certain journeys, and make reference to at least two winters (Tit. 3:12; 2 Tim. 4:21). 2 Timothy concludes with Paul back in prison in Rome before the second of those winters, expecting death.

That Rome was where Paul died is implied by 2 Timothy and supported by early church tradition. No other location for his death is suggested by the early church.[186] The remark in 1 Clement 5:7 that Paul "bore witness before rulers, and thus passed from the world" is the earliest allusion to Rome after 2 Timothy. Eusebius relates several accounts that point to Rome and to the time of Nero: Gaius, a Christian of Rome writing late in the second century, claims that he can point to the "trophies," the monuments marking the place where Paul and Peter died, and that Paul's is on the road from Rome to Ostia (*HE* 2.25.7). Gaius's contemporary Dionysius, bishop of Corinth, in a letter to the Roman church says that Peter and Paul taught in Rome and were martyred at the same time (2.25.8). Eusebius also writes that Origen stated in the third volume of his commentary on Genesis that Paul was martyred

185. Guthrie, *Introduction,* Appendix B: "The Chronology of the Life of Paul," 662-70, lays out the data, considers alternative views, and sets forth a possible chronology. For reconstructions of Pauline chronology see also, e.g., Kümmel, *Introduction,* 255; Finegan, *Handbook;* J. A. T. Robinson, *Redating.*

186. Cf. Bruce, *History,* 367.

in Rome (*HE* 3.1). He sums up the earlier writers and the consensus of tradition in these words: "It is related that in his [Nero's] time Paul was beheaded in Rome itself, and that Peter likewise was crucified, and the title of 'Peter and Paul,' which is still given to the cemeteries there, confirms the story" (2.25.5).

Assuming that this testimony about Paul's death under Nero is correct, the conclusion of Nero's reign in AD 68 makes that date or, more likely, the year before (AD 67) in order to accommodate the events referred to in 2 Timothy 4, the latest that 2 Timothy may be dated. Of course, Paul's death might have taken place earlier in Nero's reign and thus 2 Timothy could be dated a couple of years earlier, that is, as early as AD 64. In any event, 1 Timothy and Titus fall somewhere between Paul's release from his first imprisonment in Rome (as early as 61 or as late as 63) and the date of 2 Timothy (as early as 64 and as late as 67), i.e., from the latter part of the early 60s to the mid-60s.

COMMENTARY ON 1 TIMOTHY

SALUTATION: 1:1-2

The letter begins like other NT letters bearing Paul's name by indicating the author and the recipient and giving a greeting. This form, similar to Greek letters of the time, has been expanded in a noteworthy way by the apostle to express his Christian perspective, as is the case in all thirteen Pauline letters.

Except in 1 and 2 Thessalonians, Philippians, and Philemon, Paul refers to himself as an "ἀπόστολος of Jesus Christ," either in this brief form or in a more expanded form. In the PE the expanded form is used. In the letters to churches, except Galatians, the reference to the addressees refers to their relationship to Jesus Christ. The PE and Philemon, letters to "individuals," expand the reference to the addressees to indicate their relationship to Paul. In all thirteen Pauline letters, the greetings speak of "grace" (1 and 2 Timothy add "mercy") and "peace" "from God the Father and Christ Jesus our Lord" and are thus virtually identical.

This form of salutation reflects three factors: First, the teachings of the Christian faith have molded Paul's adaptation of the standard form. Second, there is a great uniformity in this molding, especially in the greeting section, which reflects a certain crystallization of his manner of expression of the essential Christian truths in these salutations. Third, there are certain variations that either reflect the recipients' situation and need or anticipate and emphasize that which will be presented in the letter proper.

On the salutations see Roller, *Formular,* 55ff., 147ff., 213ff., and the tables at the book's end comparing the PE and the other Paulines; Wendlund, *Die urchristlichen Literaturformen,* 342-58; Funk, *Language,* 250-74; Lohmeyer, "Probleme I"; Friedrich, "Lohmeyers These"; Cranfield, *Romans,* 45-48.

1:1 Paul begins with his name (Παῦλος; see the Introduction for responses to the challenges that have been made to Pauline authorship) and continues by indicating his office and authority (ἀπόστολος), the one whose apostle he is (Χριστοῦ Ἰησοῦ), and the basis of his apostleship (κατ' ἐπιταγὴν θεοῦ κτλ.). Παῦλος is the only name Paul uses to designate himself and is the only name used for Paul/Saul in other NT letters. In Acts Σαῦλος is used exclusively up to the statement in 13:9, Σαῦλος δέ, ὁ καὶ Παῦλος, after which the name Paul is used exclusively. On the relationship of these two names, what other names Paul might have had, and why only one name is used see Cranfield, *Romans,* 48-50 and the literature cited there.

Paul refers to himself as ἀπόστολος Χριστοῦ Ἰησοῦ in all his letters except 1 and 2 Thessalonians, Philippians, and Philemon. ἀπόστολος (NT 79x, Pl. 34x, PE 5x) designates one who is sent with the authority of and on behalf of the one sending (cf. Jn. 13:16; cf. further Hebrew *šālîaḥ* and and Aramaic *šᵉlîḥā',* which denote an authorized agent or representative). With only a few exceptions (e.g., 2 Cor. 8:23; Phil. 2:25, for messengers or delegates of the churches), the NT uses ἀπόστολος to refer to the inner circle of leaders appointed by Christ and usually referred to as "apostles of Jesus Christ" or known to be such, even without the addition of "of Jesus Christ." Paul uses the term in this sense, as is evidenced by his statement about his apostleship in Gal. 1:1 (cf. 1:11-17) and by the fact that in his use of ἀπόστολος in the salutations he always adds "of Jesus Christ."

For the discussion of ἀπόστολος see the articles in BAGD, *TDNT, NIDNTT,* and Cranfield, *Romans,* 51-52 and the literature mentioned there; for the basic discussion in regard to *šālîaḥ* and *šᵉlîḥā'* see Str-B III, 2-4.

For Paul that he was ἀπόστολος Χριστοῦ Ἰησοῦ meant that he was: (a) directly appointed by Jesus Christ and empowered and authorized by him (Gal. 1:1, 11-17; 2 Cor. 12:12; 1 Thes. 2:6), (b) an eyewitness of the resurrected Christ (1 Cor. 15:3-9; cf. Acts 1:22; 1 Cor. 9:1), (c) a foundation stone of the church along with the prophets as a bearer of the gospel and of God's revelation (Rom. 1:1; Eph. 2:20 and 3:4, 5; 1 Tim. 2:7; 2 Tim. 1:11), and thus (d) first in leadership and authority in the church along with the other apostles (1 Cor. 12:28; 2 Cor. 11:5; 12:11; Eph. 4:11; 1 Thes. 2:6; cf. Acts 15, especially vv. 23-29 and 16:4). Along with all this, in Paul's case an aspect of apostleship was to be especially responsible, under God, for the Gentiles (Rom. 1:5; 11:13; 1 Cor. 9:2; Gal. 2:7-9; 1 Tim. 2:7).

The addition of Χριστοῦ Ἰησοῦ is best explained in Paul's carefully chosen words in Gal. 1:1, where he makes it plain, on the background of his Damascus road experience (Acts 9:1-22; 22:3-21; 26:9-23), that both the origin (ἀπ') and mediation (δι') of his apostleship is solely διὰ Ἰησοῦ καὶ θεοῦ πατρός, and neither from nor through any human agency. The genitive here with no preposition has the same double sense of origin and mediation. It is with this awareness of authority as Christ Jesus' spokesman that Paul writes. Therefore he places this designation of himself at the beginning of the letter to express the authority by which he writes.

It has been objected that such an official title in a letter to a friend and colleague is surely out of place and is a sign of inauthenticity. But this is not just a friendly letter between colleagues, but a letter of instruction from an apostle to his assistant, even, perhaps, an official mandate (cf. 1:3, "I urged you . . . remain . . . in order that you may instruct"; 1:18, "this command I entrust to you"; 4:11-16, "prescribe and teach these things"; 6:13, "I charge you in the presence of God"; 6:20, "guard what has been entrusted to you"). This relationship is no different than that between the apostle and Timothy demonstrated elsewhere in the Pauline letters (cf., e.g., 1 Cor. 4:17; Phil. 2:19-23; and the remarks about Timothy here at v. 2).

Furthermore, this letter is also written so that Timothy can have apostolic authorization in the church and instruction for the church over against the false teachers. In effect the church is written to through Timothy. Thus the concluding benediction, "grace be with you" (6:21), is addressed to a plural "you," which fits with the fact that the church in its corporate capacity is instructed about prayer and worship (2:1-8), about the role of women (vv. 9-15), and about the qualifications for officers (3:1-13), and in general with the specific *raison d'être* of the letter (3:14, 15).

Therefore, Paul's use of his official title is no more strange here than in his other letters. The other letters were also written to friends and acquaintances but were also nonetheless written with apostolic authority.

The double designation, either Ἰησοῦ Χριστοῦ or Χριστοῦ Ἰησοῦ, is normal in Paul's writings (MGM, s.v.; for lists see Burton, *Galatians,* 393). The question arises as to the significance of such a double reference particularly on the background of the use of a single name for individuals in general in the NT and the fact that on some occasions Paul uses only one or the other by itself or with κύριος. The answer seems to be Paul's desire to identify Jesus as the Christ, i.e., as the Messiah promised in the OT, the anointed one of God. This identification is so important to him that the double designation predominates over all other designations except perhaps κύριος (which is, however, often used with the double designation).

That this identification of Jesus as the Messiah was significant for Paul is seen in his preaching in Acts. Luke indicates that Paul preached τὸν Ἰησοῦν ὅτι οὗτός ἐστιν ὁ υἱὸς τοῦ θεοῦ (9:20) and ὅτι οὗτός ἐστιν ὁ Χριστός (v. 22). Another summary giving the essence of Paul's preaching (17:2, 3) ends with the words ὅτι οὗτός ἐστιν ὁ Χριστός, [ὁ] Ἰησοῦς, ὃν ἐγὼ καταγγέλλω ὑμῖν (cf. 18:5).

Thus for Paul Ἰησοῦς (NT 905x; Pl. 203x) is the personal name and Χριστός is the title (NT 529x; Pl. 374x, just under 72% of the total NT occurrences, the next highest being Acts with only 25x; PE 32x; cf. Morris, *NT Theology,* 39). Hence the double designation Ἰησοῦ Χριστοῦ or Χριστοῦ Ἰησοῦ is to be understood as "Jesus the Christ" or "the Christ, Jesus."

All this assumes that Paul's use of Χριστός in Acts refers to the promised one of the OT, anointed by God (Hebrew *māšîaḥ,* transliterated as Μεσσίας** and translated as Χριστός). That this was the general understanding of the NT community is evidenced most directly by Jn. 1:41 and 4:25 and also in the Synoptics and in Acts where Paul is not in view (cf. Mt. 16:16 par. Mk. 8:29 par. Lk. 9:20; Acts 2:36; 3:18, 20; 18:28, etc.).

Within the Pauline corpus one finds a chronological transition from Ἰησοῦς Χριστός to Χριστὸς Ἰησοῦς, which is the rule in the PE and is, in fact, except in a few passages in Acts (3:20; 5:42; 24:24), found only in the Pauline corpus. Why did Paul reverse the order of the designation? Some, e.g., Hendriksen, have speculated that in a transition from a more Hebraic setting to a more Hellenic language setting Paul gradually changed from the translation form, "Jesus the Christ" (Ἰησοῦς Χριστός) to the form that better expressed the title and the name in Greek, "the Christ, Jesus" (Χριστὸς Ἰησοῦς). McCasland argues that this change would only come about if Χριστός remained an appellative or title (in his article "Christ Jesus").

I would suggest as another influence the significance and usage of the phrase ἐν Χριστῷ for Paul when used to express communion with Christ. Whenever this sense is found in Paul it is always with ἐν Χριστῷ or ἐν Χριστῷ Ἰησοῦ. It would appear that where communion or union is in view Χριστός is used, and where more than one name is used Χριστός occurs first. Is this so because Paul thinks of believers' union with their Lord more in terms of the representative work and status of Christ as the Messiah than in terms of identification of him as Jesus the man? If this is true, then this perspective would also have influenced Paul to write Χριστός before Ἰησοῦς more often because this union and communion became a more dominant thought for him.

Paul's growing preference for the order Χ. Ἰ. is already reflected in the salutations of his earlier letters, where this is almost the exclusive form. His prevailing practice would seem to indicate a preference for the order Χ. Ἰ. when referring to his own relationship to and servanthood of the Lord. The usage in the PE would seem to have brought to a culmination a usage that more and more appealed to Paul over the other order.

For the discussion and literature relating to the names Χριστός and Ἰησοῦς see the articles in BAGD, *TDNT,* and *NIDNTT* (K. H. Rengstorf, II, 330-48); McCasland, "Christ Jesus"; Burton, *Galatians,* 392-99; Knight, *Faithful Sayings,* 32-36; C. F. D. Moule, *Origin,* 1-10, 31-35, 54-69, 136.

κατ' ἐπιταγήν κτλ. indicates the ultimate basis of Paul's apostleship. As in Galatians, he is concerned not only to indicate that he is an apostle of Jesus Christ but that this apostleship has its origin in the will or command of both God the Father and Christ Jesus. The phrase contains four elements: (a) the idea of command or will; (b) the reference to God; (c) the joining of the name of Christ Jesus with that of God in a genitive construction linking them both to the one word ἐπιταγήν; and (d) a further qualification of both names, i.e., "our Savior" and "our hope."

Parts (a) and (b) of this pattern are similar to that found in the other Pauline salutations. In the other salutations, when Paul uses "apostle" he refers to God's decision, either with θέλημα (1 and 2 Corinthians, Colossians, Ephesians, and 2 Timothy) or ἐπιταγή (1 Timothy and also Titus in a much longer qualification), or to God's "will" without (Romans) or with (Titus again) a key term, or in Galatians no key word is used in the salutation but the idea is presented later in the letter in the defense of Paul's apostleship (cf. Gal. 1:15ff.; 2:7-9). The use in the PE of ἐπιταγή** (only in Paul, usually with κατά: Rom. 16:26; 1 Cor. 7:6; 2 Cor. 8:8; here; Tit. 1:3; twice without κατά: 1 Cor. 7:25; Tit. 2:15), which means "command," "order," or "injunction" (cf. MM and Spicq), rather than the more usual θέλημα, should probably be explained by Paul's desire to relate his being under orders to the need for Timothy and Titus to be under orders in carrying out the mandate from Christ's apostle. 2 Timothy, however, being a more personal letter, returns to θέλημα. Lock's summary is helpful: "Here it refers primarily to the choice of Paul as an Apostle (2^7, Acts 22^{14}). . . . It gives the commission in virtue of which he acts, and the rule and standard of his work."

Paul used θεός with astonishing frequency because God "was central in his thinking" (Pl. 548x, more than 40% of the NT's 1,314x, although Paul's writings make up only about a quarter of the NT; "far more often than does anyone else in the New Testament," Morris, *NT Theology,* 25; here the first of 21x in 1 Tim. and of 47x in the PE).

God the Father is referred to here as σωτήρ (NT 24x, Pl. 12x, PE 10x). For Paul the background is the OT concept of God as Savior, which he and other NT writers utilize in terms of God acting to save people through Jesus (cf. Thayer, *Lexicon,* s.v.). "Yahweh is presented as saviour in Deut. 32:15; 1 Chr. 16:35; Pss. 24(23):5; 25(24):5; 27(26):1, 9; 62(61):2, 6; 65(64):5; 79(78):9; 95(94):1; Prov. 29:25 *v.l.;* Mic. 7:7; Hab. 3:18; Is. 12:2; 17:10; 25:9; 62:11. Often the LXX speaks concretely of (e.g.) 'God my saviour [*ho theos ho soter mou*],' whereas the MT speaks of 'the God of my salvation'" (J. Schneider and C. Brown, *NIDNTT* III, 218; cf. G. Fohrer, *TDNT* VII, 1012f.; the plural "our" is used in 1 Ch. 16:35; Pss. 65[64]:5; 79[78]:9; 95[94]:1; and "your" in Is. 17:10; 62:11). The term was also applied to Hellenistic rulers and the Roman emperor and used by the mystery religions (cf. G. Fohrer and W. Foerster, *TDNT* VII, 1003-21). Although the OT background adequately explains Paul's usage (cf. *TDNT* VII, 1015), the term may also be used over against rival statements of the day, especially those with religious denotation.

God is referred to as "Savior" in the PE (6 of 10x) and Christ less frequently (the remaining 4). But in the other Paulines God is not referred to as Savior while Christ is. This has been highlighted as a noteworthy difference between the PE and the other Pauline letters. But the usage of the other Paulines amounts to only two instances (Eph. 5:23; Phil. 3:20), which is an inadequate basis for comparison. Furthermore, it should not be thought strange for Paul to refer to God in reference to salvation here, for, as Lock indicates, 1 Cor. 1:21 has already done so. Also, Paul is not the only one in the NT to refer to the Father as Savior; scant though the evidence may be, both Luke (1:47) and Jude (25) do as well. Finally, the PE do also, as we have seen, use the title for Christ (2 Tim. 1:10; Tit. 1:4; 2:13; 3:6), as do the earlier two Pauline occurrences.

The use of σωτήρ here with reference to God the Father reflects Paul's concern to communicate this reality of God as Savior as a corrective to the false teachers' perspective on God as less than the Savior of "all people." This emphasis on "all" will be highlighted in connection with prayers and evangelism (2:3ff., especially v. 4; cf. 4:10). This emphasis is present also in Titus, where God is again referred to as Savior (Tit. 1:3; and then especially 2:10, 11 and 3:1ff., especially vv. 2 and 4). Six of the eight NT references to God as Savior are in the PE, three each in 1 Timothy and Titus, one in each letter in the salutation. The remaining four in these two letters are in the bodies of the letters in contexts that emphasize the phrase "all people" (πάντες ἄνθρωποι); in three of these instances the connection with "God our Savior" is direct (1 Tim. 2:3, 4; 4:10; Tit. 2:10, 11) and in one it is less direct but still evident (Tit. 3:2, 4; see the commentary on this section; cf. W. Foerster, *TDNT* VII, 1016-18).

By means of the plural pronoun "our" (ἡμῶν), Paul joins his readers and himself in their union with each other as Christians, which is entailed in their mutual relationship to God as Savior and Father and Christ Jesus as Savior and Hope. In all the Pauline greetings this usage of ἡμῶν is present (with the likely exception of 1 Thessalonians).

The genitive construction θεοῦ σωτῆρος κτλ. joins the names of two persons to the noun ἐπιταγή so that the "command" is that of both God and Christ Jesus. Thus the apostleship of Paul is one that both God and Christ have conjointly commanded. Those that command as one, when one is said to be God, are considered on a par with one another (cf. v. 2) and have a certain unity in view of the fact that one command comes from both.

The special characteristic stated about Christ Jesus is that he is our "hope" (ἐλπίς). Paul's apostleship to "all people," Jew and Gentile, exists not only because God is Savior for "all people" but also because of the sure expectation Paul has for himself and for those who respond to the gospel embodied in Christ Jesus as our hope. In the NT, because ἐλπίς is based on the person and work of Christ Jesus, the word takes on a note of confident expectation, even if that expectation is not yet fully realized and is still in the future (cf. Rom. 5:2, 5; 8:24, 25; 15:4, 13; Tit. 1:2; 2:13; 3:7). Because the hope is that of the gospel (Col. 1:23) and is embodied in the one who brings the gospel, Christ Jesus (Col. 1:27, "Christ in you, the hope of glory"), Paul may speak of the bringer or basis of the hope of future salvation, which comes about at the return of Christ (Tit. 2:13), as the hope itself, as he does here (Χριστοῦ Ἰησοῦ τῆς ἐλπίδος ἡμῶν).

Although the noun "hope" does not occur again in 1 Timothy (1x in 1 Timothy; 3x in Titus: 1:2; 2:13; 3:7), the corresponding verb does, and thus it may be that the concept is chosen by Paul here at the beginning of the letter. When Paul focuses on the work of the ministry, a significant aspect of this letter, he says of both his and Timothy's ministries, "It is for this we labor and strive, because we have fixed our hope (ἠλπίκαμεν) on the living God, who is the Savior of all men [people] (σωτὴρ πάντων ἀνθρώπων), especially of believers" (4:10, *NASB*; cf. 6:13-19; especially v. 17). Thus Paul reflects on God as Savior of "all people" and on Christ Jesus as an unfailing object of hope not only because these truths are essential to his apostleship but also because they will be most helpful to Timothy in his ministry and the church in its situation.

On "hope" (ἐλπίς and related words) see the articles in BAGD, *TDNT,* and *NIDNTT* and C. F. D. Moule, *Meaning,* 58-71.

1:2 The name Τιμοθέῳ in the dative case designates the addressee (on the work and personality of Timothy see the Introduction under **Recipients**; see also D. Guthrie, "Timothy," *NBD,* 1201). As in all the Pauline letters (except Galatians), the addressee is further described in terms of his relationship to the Christian faith. In the letters to individuals (Philemon, 1 and 2 Timothy, Titus) this description also includes a reference to the close bond existing between the addressees and Paul. In the case of Timothy and Titus, Paul's younger assistants, the affectionate term τέκνον is used, preceded by a word that heightens or strengthens the kinship (γνήσιος here and in Titus, ἀγαπητός in 2 Timothy). In 1 Timothy and Titus τέκνον is followed by ἐν πίστει, indicating the realm in which the term τέκνον functions (in 2 Timothy this is not done but a stronger preceding word is used).

Paul thus gives appropriate encouragement and expresses the bond of spiritual kinship by describing Timothy as γνησίῳ τέκνῳ ἐν πίστει. The words are so interlocked that the meaning of each is determined by its setting among the others. The qualifications γνησίῳ and ἐν πίστει for τέκνον indicate that the relationship in view is in the spiritual realm. But is that spiritual relationship one of (a) spiritual paternity, i.e., Paul the evangelist and Timothy the convert; (b) spiritual adoption and training, i.e., Paul the nurturer and Timothy the son who grows under his adoptive father; or (c) simply of shared faith, with Paul being the older (the "father") in that faith and Timothy the younger?

At least two considerations may be advanced for the first of these options: (a) Timothy came from the very area Paul evangelized (Acts 16:1-3; cf. 14:6-23); (b) the likelihood that Timothy came to faith in Jesus under Paul's ministry is reinforced by the way, in 1 Cor. 4:15, that Paul uses and explains the language of paternity for those regenerated "in Christ Jesus through the gospel" as a result of his ministry and then (v. 17) calls Timothy "*my beloved and faithful child (τέκνον)* in the Lord." Paul uses τέκνον in the PE in reference to Timothy (1 Tim. 1:2, 18; 2 Tim. 1:2; 2:1), Titus (1:4), and the children of church officers (1 Tim. 3:4, 12; Tit. 1:6) and widows

(1 Tim. 5:4). Thus, if we understand the term to refer to spiritual paternity when it refers to Timothy and Titus, the usage would be uniform in both the spiritual and physical realms. But we may not say that the term is restricted to this aspect of sonship but may include (b) and possibly (c) as well.

Paul says not only that Timothy is a τέκνον but also that he is a true (γνήσιος) child. This note is found also when Paul refers to Timothy in 1 Cor. 4:17 ("faithful," πιστόν) and especially in Phil. 2:22, where of Timothy's worth and service it is said: ὡς πατρὶ τέκνον σὺν ἐμοὶ ἐδούλευσεν. This keynote of faithful service and proven worth is probably the significance of γνήσιος** here (2 Cor. 8:8; Phil. 4:3; 1 Tim. 1:2; Tit. 1:4), with its meaning of "genuine," although Schlatter has suggested that its other meaning, "legitimate" (cf. BAGD), is in view, and that it is an affirmation of Timothy's bona fide position, even if everyone knew that he had a Greek father and had not been circumcised until he joined Paul (especially in the setting of a church including some predisposed to genealogies). Schlatter further suggests that this is why the same term is used of Titus, who was a Greek and not circumcised at all (Gal. 2:3). The other two of the four NT occurrences would seem, however, to require the more general meaning "genuine" (2 Cor. 8:7, 8; Phil. 4:3; so also Louw and Nida, *Lexicon*, §73.1). MM indicate that the word has become "an epithet of affectionate regard" and say that it is doubtful that the note of legitimacy was still felt in normal usage since "most of the usages are wide of this" (128f., with a number of citations from the papyri).

ἐν πίστει demarcates the sonship as being in the realm of faith. Does Paul utilize πίστις here in the objective sense (for "the Christian faith") or in the subjective sense (for personal faith in Christ)? Tit. 1:4, which uses κατά in place of ἐν and adds κοινήν, might seem to tip the scales in terms of the objective understanding: "according to the common faith," namely, Christianity, which both Paul a Jew and Titus a Gentile share. But even this occurrence can be understood in the subjective sense. When one concentrates on πίστις in the PE (33x; 19x in 1 Timothy) a pattern does seem to emerge, and that is that πίστις without the article seems to be used in the subjective sense and πίστις with the article in the objective sense (just in 1 Timothy, without the article [those italicized with ἐν, as here]: 1:*2, 4, 5,* 14, 19a; 2:*7, 15;* 3:*13;* 4:*12;* 5:12 [?]; 6:11; and with the article: 1:19b; 3:9; 4:1, 6; 5:8; 6:10, 12, 21). Equally evident is the intertwining of these two forms so that the subjective and objective, or at least the usage with or without the article, are interrelated. It would thus appear that ἐν πίστει is used in 1:2 as elsewhere in 1 Timothy to designate the sphere of the trust relationship, which virtually amounts to the objective sense but still emphasizes the subjective, personal, and direct aspect of faith. So it is the response to and continuance in the gospel by faith that has brought Timothy to be considered a genuine son (cf. again 1 Cor. 4:15; Phil. 2:21, 22).

ἐν is not narrowly restricted to causal ("by," Jeremias and Schlatter) but is relational or local, designating the sphere (Ridderbos). The latter is certainly its significance in its next occurrence (1:4) and would appear to be most likely also in the other occurrences with πίστις (2:7, 15; 3:13; 4:12). Dibelius-Conzelmann assert that "the formulaic use of the expression 'in faith' (ἐν πίστει) is not found in the genuine Pauline epistles (1 Cor. 16:3; Gal. 2:20; 2 Thes. 2:13 are not analogous)." Contrary to this assertion, MGM (pp. 1067, 1083, 1086) designate 2 Cor. 13:5 (ἐν τῇ πίστει) as of the same category, relational, as 1 Tim. 1:2 and others in the PE, and τῇ πίστει in Col. 2:7 is also used in a similar way (although with textual variants).

Paul greets Timothy with "grace, mercy, and peace from God the Father and Christ Jesus our Lord." The greetings in all thirteen Pauline letters are nearly identical, with these minor differences: (a) 1 Thessalonians omits "from God our Father and the Lord Jesus Christ," which in that letter occurs immediately before the greeting; (b) Colossians omits (in the preferred reading) "and the Lord Jesus Christ" but has that phrase in the thanksgiving that immediately follows; (c) the PE omit "you" (ὑμῖν); (d) only 1 and 2 Timothy have the word "mercy" (ἔλεος); (e) Titus has "Savior" in place of "Lord"; and (f) in the PE "our" is shifted from Father to Lord (or Savior), probably because Lord (or Savior) is placed after "Christ Jesus" in the PE.

The overarching uniformity of this formula in the greetings indicates how significant these words are for Paul in communicating the essence of the Christian faith. The following analysis may help this become even more evident. To place this formula in the larger perspective of all the letters we will momentarily leave aside the term ἔλεος. Paul greets every church and individual in every letter with χάρις and εἰρήνη. The source of these both are always God and Christ Jesus, and the relationship that they have to the recipients of this grace and peace is that God is their Father and Jesus Christ is their Lord (or in Titus, Savior). The personal dimension of that relationship is indicated by the word "our," which signifies the recipients' relationship to God as Father and Jesus as Christ and Lord and also joins Paul and the readers in that common bond.

Use of the "grace and peace" motif is seen in most of the NT correspondence. Both Petrine letters (1 Pet. 1:2; 2 Pet. 1:2), 2 John (v. 3), and Revelation (1:4) also begin with "grace and peace," and Jude (v. 2) has "mercy and peace." All the Pauline letters include χάρις in their concluding remarks, as do the Petrine letters (1 Pet. 5:10, 12; 2 Pet. 3:18) and Revelation (22:21).

Trenkler has aptly caught both the focus and breadth of χάρις in his definition: ". . . grace is the soteriological activity of God, decreed from eternity, which is made manifest to man and effective in his salvation in Christ's act of redemption and which continues and perfects the work of redemption in us . . ." (*Sac Vb,* 344). Although χάρις is associated with the beginning of salvation in Paul (cf., e.g., Eph. 2:8), it would seem that the continuing and perfecting aspect is in view in his uniform greetings (and conclusions) to his letters, since those addressed are already recognized as saved. Thus the aspects of forgiving and enabling by instructing and giving life, strength, and ability (2 Cor. 1:12; 12:9; Eph. 2:7; 2 Tim. 2:1; Tit. 2:12) would seem to be the aspects in view in the greetings. Such well-known passages as Eph. 2:8ff. and Tit. 2:11ff., which begin with grace, uniformly conclude with emphasis on living a life of good works for which grace has saved and now enables us. Immediately after a greeting containing this term, Paul speaks of that grace enriching and equipping Christians with spiritual gifts and of God being faithful in this spiritual growth (1 Cor. 1:4ff.). In another context Paul says that "God is able to make all grace (πᾶσαν χάριν) abound to you, that always having all sufficiency in everything, you may have an abundance for every good deed" (2 Cor. 9:8). Grace is the work of God as the enabling Savior and Lord.

ἔλεος, "mercy," is not normally present in the Pauline greetings, although it is present in 2 Jn. 3 (between grace and peace as here) and in Jude 2 ("mercy and peace and love") and is found between grace and peace in both 1 and 2 Timothy. ἔλεος is not as frequent in the NT as χάρις (NT 27x, Pl. 10x,* PE 5x: Rom. 9:23; 11:31; 15:9; Gal. 6:16; Eph. 2:4; 1 Tim. 1:2; 2 Tim. 1:2, 16, 18; Tit. 3:5). It normally conveys the ideas of compassion and mercy to the unfortunate and needy (cf. Louw and Nida, *Lexicon,* §88.76). It should be noted that in Paul it is used in connection with salvation and in some of those contexts also in conjunction with χάρις, especially Eph. 2:4 and Tit. 3:5, in the context of which emphasis is given to the dire plight of sinners and hence their need for divine favor (cf. Tit. 3:3 and Eph. 2:1-3, which ends with the note of wrath; cf. Rom. 9:23, where vessels of mercy are contrasted with vessels of wrath, and 11:31, where mercy is related to disobedience). Paul's use of the verb ἐλεέω in the PE (1 Tim. 1:13, 16) also emphasizes the dire plight of sinners and their need for divine favor.

It would seem that a combination of factors has merged in Paul's use of "mercy" in the greetings of 1 and 2 Timothy. First, Timothy's Jewish background may well have played a role in Paul's utilizing this word with its OT background, since it translates *ḥesed̲* in the LXX. Secondly, and more importantly, it may well be that Paul sensed that Timothy needed this nuance of God's favor because he felt himself in special difficulty and needed not only a strength and enabling but also sympathy, tenderness, and comfort (see v. 1 and the Introduction regarding Timothy's timidity; cf. Phil. 2:27).

In distinguishing mercy and grace, the words of Lenski are helpful: ἔλεος ". . . always deals with what we see of pain, misery and distress, these results of sin; and *charis* (grace) always deals with the sin and guilt itself. The one extends relief, the other pardon; the one cures, heals, helps, the other cleanses and reinstates" (*Matthew,* 185; see also Trench, *Synonyms,* 156-61; R. Bultmann, *TDNT* II, 477-87; H.-H. Esser, *NIDNTT* II, 594-98).

"Peace" was the common greeting of the Semitic world (for OT usage cf., e.g., Gn. 43:23; Jdg. 19:20; 1 Sa. 25:6), and Jesus uses it to greet his disciples in his resurrection appearances (Jn. 20:19, 21, 26; cf. also Lk. 24:36). In the Semitic world it was used in epistolary salutations (examples in Str-B III, 25; and, e.g., Dan. 4:37c LXX; Dan. 6:26 Theodotion). As in Paul's usage, it is sometimes combined with another noun (cf. 2 Macc. 1:1; *Syr. Bar.* 78:2).

In the NT and Paul εἰρήνη denotes both tranquility and harmony (the Greek background and usage) and stability, welfare, and health (corresponding to the OT Hebrew *šālôm,* mediated to the NT community by the LXX). For Paul, as well as for the Gospels and Acts (e.g., Lk. 2:14; Acts 10:36), the primary emphasis is on human peace with God through Christ Jesus (Rom. 5:1). Peace with God brings with it an inner peace that enables the believer to relate to his problems with tranquility and stability (Phil. 4:6, 7; 2 Thes. 3:16; Rom. 8:6; 15:13; cf. Jn. 14:27; 16:33; 20:19, 21, 26). This Godward peace accomplished by Christ also enables the Christian church to live at peace and its members to continually pursue peace with one another (Eph. 2:14-18; Rom. 14:19; 2 Cor. 13:11; Gal. 5:22; Eph. 4:3; Col. 3:15; 2 Tim. 2:22). The Christian community in turn is to extend the peace of God to the hostile world, and Christians are to seek to live peacefully with individuals in the hostile world as much as the Christians themselves are able to do so (Rom. 12:18; cf. Mt. 10:13; Lk. 10:5, 6). A careful analysis of the passages listed here shows that there is an overlap between these categories in some contexts (cf., e.g., Eph. 2:14ff.).

This multiplicity of dimension and overlap is probably in view in Paul's use of this word in his greetings. It is doubtful that the Godward peace is still in view except insofar as it gives continual assurance and provides the basis for the other aspects. The inner peace and the interpersonal peace with fellow believers dominate Paul's usage in the body of his letters and overlap within them. Since Paul speaks of the peace of God or of Christ (cf., e.g., Phil. 4:7; Col. 3:15; and note this double connection in all the greetings) as well as the God of peace (Phil. 4:9; 1 Thes. 5:23; 2 Thes. 3:16; Rom. 15:33; 16:20; 2 Cor. 13:11), it is appropriate that we understand his usage here to be that of God's peace as mediated to Christians in all their needs and relationships.

With these three terms, then, Paul greets Timothy and the church: χάρις — God's ongoing forgiveness and enabling, ἔλεος — God's sympathy and concern, εἰρήνη — God's tranquility and stability within and among them as individuals and as a Christian community.

These three gifts are said to have one common source: God and Jesus; ἀπό occurs once and therefore includes both persons.

Paul uses θεός, as do all NT writers, as an all-encompassing term expressing monotheism (cf. for Paul especially Acts 17:22ff.; 1 Cor. 8:4-6) and including all the dimensions of Creator, Sustainer, Judge, etc. Although the term can embrace all three persons of the Godhead, especially the Father and Jesus Christ the Son (cf. again 1 Cor. 8:4-6 and, especially with reference to Christ, Rom. 9:5; Tit. 2:13), it is used primarily of the Father in distinction from Christ and the Holy Spirit (cf. once more 1 Cor. 8:4-6, where "Lord" is used for Jesus [v. 6] and θεός for the Father [v. 6], but both are included in the reference to God [θεός] as one [v. 4]). That this is the understanding in the Pauline greetings is evidenced by the fact that all but one of the greetings refer to God as "Father" (πατρός; 1 Thessalonians is the exception).

In what sense is God called "Father" (πατήρ) in reference to the recipients of the greeting? Paul and the other NT writers use "Father" to express the relationship of God with humans brought about by salvation through Jesus Christ. God is "Father" of those who are becoming new creatures in Christ and sons of God through the new birth and new beginning wrought by God. Paul speaks of Christians being adopted as sons and being given the ability by God's Spirit, which has come into them in connection with their sonship by faith in Christ, to say "Abba! Father!" (Rom. 8:14-17; Gal. 3:26–4:7). This specific sense of "Father" is also borne out by the use elsewhere of "our" with Father, which would be meaningless if it did not refer to a special relationship that Paul and his readers have with God.

Christ Jesus (see v. 1) is joined to God the Father as the source of the triple blessing by the use of καί and is called κύριος. This title is used in the NT with a broad range of meaning, from a polite or deferential "sir" to a virtual designation of deity. In the Pauline letters the latter usage carries with it a double aspect: It speaks both of Jesus' status in and of itself as deity and sovereign and of the relationship that Jesus has to human beings, which is acknowledged and recognized by those who confess him as Lord.

Although there are a number of passages in which the use of κύριος for Jesus "raises him above the human level" (BAGD s.v.; see the passages cited there), there are several that particularly stand out in doing so (e.g., 1 Cor. 8:4-6; 1 Tim. 6:14, 15; Rom. 10:12; 1 Cor. 2:8). In 1 Cor. 8:4ff. "Lord" is used under the rubric of one God (v. 4) and designates Jesus Christ as the one through whom all things originated (Creator) and through whom we now live (Sustainer, v. 6). 1 Tim. 6:14, 15 speaks of Christ's lordship as that of the Lord of lords and King of kings, the sole possessor of immortality, who dwells in unapproachable light. Rom. 10:12 speaks of Jesus as Lord of all; 1 Cor. 2:8 speaks of the crucified one as the Lord of glory. In the background of all this is the recognized usage of the LXX, in which κύριος is a title of God; use of "Lord" in the Orient as a title for God; and Jesus' crucial question of how the Messiah in Psalm 110 could both be David's son and be called "Lord" by David (Mt. 22:41-46 par. Mk. 12:35-37; Lk. 20:41-44). The title also carries with it a personal acknowledgment of that deity and sovereignty. Phil. 2:11 speaks of the day in which "every knee will bow and every tongue confess that Jesus Christ is Lord." Christians here and now willingly acknowledge that Jesus is Lord (Rom. 10:9-13; 1 Cor. 12:3). Furthermore, all activities of the Christian are done in the name of the Lord Jesus (Col. 3:17). The personal pronoun ἡμῶν in 1 Tim. 1:2 makes this personal recognition and connection explicit.

Is this greeting to be understood as a statement of fact, a blessing pronounced, or a prayer prayed? It is helpful to begin by noting the distribution of usages (see C. F. D. Moule, *Worship,* 79 n. 1). None of the opening Pauline greetings has a verb. Both of the Petrine greetings and Jude's opening greeting have optative πληθυνθείη ("be multiplied"). 2 Jn. 3 has future indicative ἔσται ("will be"). Paul's closing greetings are usually without a verb, although 1 Thes. 5:23 has optative ἁγιάσαι ("may sanctify") and τηρηθείη ("may be preserved") before the concluding blessing v. 28, which is without a verb; and 2 Thes. 3:16, just before the verbless v. 18, has optative δῴη ("may grant" or "give"). Although van Unnik argues against treating these forms as wishes rather than declarations (admitting the counterforce of 2 Thes. 3:16), and Moule (*Worship,* 78) says that the indicative is likely, and while Van Elderen may be right in his evaluation that it is "more than a wish . . . he expresses this with a strong confidence of fulfilment" ("Verb," 48), Wiles has probably analyzed the evidence best when he says that even though there is "no certainty" there is not enough evidence against "the usual assumption that the Pauline greetings should be understood in the optative or imperative" (*Paul's Intercessory Prayers,* 38; Wiles adds "or imperative" to acknowledge the force of the appraisals mentioned above and mentions the optative because of this unique situation; on 108 he argues that the understood verb in reference to the use of χάρις in Acts 14:26; 15:40; 20:32 is optative or imperative). Although there has been much study and interaction (cf., e.g., the writings listed below), most scholars have recognized that we can have no absolute certainty in answering this question.

For a fuller discussion of θεός and πατήρ and for the relevant literature see the respective articles in BAGD, *TDNT,* and *NIDNTT.* For a fuller discussion of κύριος and for the relevant literature see BAGD, *TDNT, NIDNTT,* C. F. D. Moule, *Origin,* 35-46, and especially the permanently significant Warfield, *Lord,* 202-39. On the verb understood in the greeting see van Unnik, "Dominus Vobiscum," 270-302; C. F. D. Moule, *Worship,* especially 78ff.; Van Elderen, "Verb," and Wiles, *Paul's Intercessory Prayers,* especially 38, 108-14.

PAUL'S COMMAND TO TIMOTHY TO WITHSTAND FALSE DOCTRINE AND TO FURTHER THE GOSPEL AND ITS GOAL, WHICH IS LOVE: 1:3-20

The remainder of this chapter is enveloped in Paul's command to Timothy to instruct "certain persons" not to teach strange doctrines (1:3; cf. 1:18ff.). Vv. 3-7 contain that command and a description of the false teachers. A reminder of the positive goal of the gospel, love, is set in the midst of this section. Paul then sets forth the lawful use of the law over against the false teachers' erroneous view and ends this section by correlating the law with the gospel (vv. 8-11). This reference to the gospel provides the transition to vv. 12-17, where Paul presents his own case as an example of God's saving mercy and thus as an encouragement over against the teaching of the false teachers. In vv. 18-20 Paul reiterates his general command to Timothy, this time reminding him of the need for personal struggle ("fight the good fight") and warning him by means of the bad example of Hymenaeus and Alexander of the danger of not holding faith and a good conscience.

In most of Paul's letters, in accordance with the style of his day, the body of the letter begins with a word of thanksgiving. But this is not the case here. Rather 1 Timothy and Titus (but not 2 Timothy) are more like mandates or official letters of his day (cf. Roller, *Formular,* 112ff.), as might be expected in letters written to Paul's associates and giving directions and instructions for them and the church.

For a discussion of the body of the Greek letter and its introductory sections and the corresponding phenomena in Paul's letters, see J. L. White, *Body* (especially 67ff. for an overview of previous studies); Funk, *Language,* ch. 10; Sanders, "Transition"; Roller, *Formular* (especially 112ff. on the similarity of Titus and 1 Timothy to the mandate [or official] letter form); Wendland, *Die urchristlichen Literaturformen,* 339-45; Deissmann, *Bible Studies,* 1-59, especially 55-59.

THE CHARGE, THE GOAL, AND A DESCRIPTION OF THE FALSE TEACHERS: 1:3-7

1:3 The letter proper begins with Paul's charge to Timothy to "instruct certain persons not to teach strange doctrines." Historical and geographical indicators are provided with the reference to Timothy remaining ἐν Ἐφέσῳ and with the reference to Paul having given this command πορευόμενος εἰς Μακεδονίαν. This raises the question of whether Paul was, when he urged Timothy to remain in Ephesus, himself in Ephesus but preparing to depart for Macedonia, or already on his way from Ephesus to Macedonia, or on his way to Macedonia without having been in Ephesus?

In favor of Paul being in Ephesus when he gives his charge to Timothy it is argued that "remain" implies that Timothy is to remain where he is when he first receives the charge and that the present participle πορευόμενος most likely refers to the same place and would therefore imply that Paul is going away from Ephesus and is giving the charge to Timothy while he is departing (possibly implied by the *NASB*). It has been argued on the other hand that all the text actually says about Paul's whereabouts is that he gave this charge (in writing? orally? by messenger?) while going to Macedonia. That Timothy was then in Ephesus and was urged to remain there is evident; where Paul was is not.

A related question is whether Paul returned to Ephesus after he was released from his first Roman imprisonment. If so, how does this relate to his statement to the Ephesian elders "that they should see his face no more" (Acts 20:38)? If he did not return to Ephesus, that would be prima facie evidence that the premonition proved to be correct. But if he did indeed go to Ephesus it may be that he was simply mistaken, or perhaps the particular elders to whom he spoke had died or moved elsewhere, or, more likely, perhaps he simply met Timothy alone in Ephesus or at Miletus for some compelling reason(s), just as previously there had been a compelling reason for him to meet with the Ephesian elders at Miletus (so Acts 20:16, 17). We leave the question there.

Another question is that of the sentence structure: Is the sentence incomplete, lacking a concluding element, which must be supplied, because Paul assumes that the very command to which he refers implies the operative verb? This practice is common with Paul (cf. Rom. 2:17ff.; 5:12ff.; 9:22ff.). BAGD indicate that with καθώς "the accompanying clause is somet[imes] to be supplied fr[om] the context" and cite this passage and compare Gal. 3:6. Thus that which he had previously urged, namely to instruct certain persons not to teach strange doctrines, is reiterated because that must still be done. On anacoluthon in Paul and the NT see Robertson, *Grammar,* 435-40.

The charge, "I urged you" (παρεκάλεσά σε), is both authoritative and personal. παρακαλέω in all its nuances (cf. PE* 1 Tim. 1:3; 2:1; 5:1; 6:2; Tit. 1:9; 2:6, 15; 2 Tim. 4:2) has the characteristic of personal concern, which is denoted in its basic idea of calling to one's side (cf. BAGD, *TDNT,* and Bjerkelund, *PARAKALÔ*). προσμένω means here "stay" or "remain." Ἔφεσος is where Timothy is located and the particular church to which this letter is sent. This letter (with 2 Timothy) thus provides a third perspective on the Christian community at Ephesus, along with Acts 19–20 and Ephesians (which, even if a circular letter, would indicate something of Ephesus).

The content of the charge is ἵνα παραγγείλῃς τισὶν μὴ ἑτεροδιδασκαλεῖν. The verb παραγγέλλω means "give orders, command, instruct, direct," and with an infinitive and μή comes to mean "forbid to (do something)." The indefinite plural pronoun τινές, "certain persons," indicates both that more than one is in view and that not all the teachers in Ephesus are meant. This use of the indefinite pronoun is normal in Paul (in PE cf. 1 Tim. 1:6, 19; 6:10, 21; 2 Tim. 2:18).

ἑτεροδιδασκαλεῖν** (only in 1 Tim. 1:3; 6:3 and not found in other literature of the day except in the later letter of Ignatius to Polycarp 3:1; cf. also 1QH 4:16) means literally "teach a different doctrine." This word was probably coined by Paul, given that he used ἕτερος already in Gal. 1:6 with reference to heretical teaching that differs from the gospel (cf. also the compound νομοδιδάσκαλος,** 1 Tim. 1:7; Acts 5:34; Lk. 5:17 as a similar pattern, so Spicq). Paul's comment in Gal. 1:6, 7 shows that he meant by ἕτερος that which was in contradiction to what he taught. Thus to teach ἑτερο- is to teach heterodoxy or, as translations put it, "false doctrine." In the only other occurrence of ἑτεροδιδασκαλεῖν (6:3) Paul virtually defines the term by the negation that follows it: "If any one advocates a different doctrine (ἑτεροδιδασκαλεῖ), *and does not agree with sound words, those of our Lord Jesus Christ, and with the doctrine conforming to godliness*" (*NASB,* italics added).

1:4 Although μηδέ is properly translated "nor," indicating a further aspect of the false teachers' activity, it also, in effect, begins a description of the content of their teaching, which in v. 3 is only described as "other" than true Christian teaching (cf. for μηδέ Rom. 6:13; 1 Cor. 5:8). However, "myths and endless genealogies" do not encompass all that was being taught, since vv. 6, 7 speak of the false teachers' desire to be "teachers of the law."

As is often the case with Paul's letters, one must put together the various comments he makes about the false teaching to ascertain its content, since he is not concerned to describe the teaching but to refute it. As seen in the Introduction above (see **The False Teaching**, under **Setting and Concerns**), certain elements of the false teaching opposed in all three PE suggest that it was similar to, if not necessarily identical with, the error opposed by Paul at Colossae.

προσέχω means "turn one's mind to": It is this paying attention to myths (μύθοι) that Paul opposes. μῦθος** is uniformly used in the NT to refer to a tale, legend, myth, or fable regarded as untrue. Here the myths (and genealogies) are said to give rise to mere speculation and to be contrary to the οἰκονομίαν θεοῦ; in 4:7 they are qualified by the designations "worldly" (βεβήλους) and "for old women" (γραώδεις); Tit. 1:14 designates them as "Jewish," 2 Tim. 4:4 as that which people turn to when they turn away from the truth (see also 2 Pet. 1:16). Hence "myth" for Paul (and Peter) is an unreal tale that only the gullible believe and follow, which produces nothing of value (see Spicq, 93-98).

γενεαλογία** (here, Tit. 3:9, and in LXX), "genealogy," has been understood in two different ways: As BAGD indicate, since Irenaeus (*Haer.* 1, preface 1) and Tertullian (*De praesc.* 7; 33; *Adv. Val.* 3) it has often been interpreted as referring to gnostic teachings, specifically to groups of Aeons (so also Alford and Bengel). The church fathers seem to be influenced in coming to this view by the fact that they regarded the PE passages using the word as virtual prophecies of the Gnosticism of their own time. Kelly shows the improbability of this gnostic view by a fourfold argument:

> *(a)* the Gnostic systems of aeons were never, so far as we know, called genealogies; *(b)* had he had them in mind, we should have expected the writer to go more fully into their content instead of being satisfied with a passing, imprecise allusion; *(c)* we should also have expected a much sharper, more far-reaching criticism than that they encouraged idle speculation and contentiousness; and *(d)* the fables are expressly labelled "Jewish" in Tit. i.14, while in [Tit.] iii.9, "genealogies" are lumped with "controversies about the law."

BAGD also indicate that the idea that "the errors in question have a Jewish background and involve rabbinical speculation" began in the commentaries of Ambrosiaster (cf. also on Tit. 1:14) and Chrysostom, and is "more or less favored" by Kittel, "γενεαλογία." This interpretation is also favored in the commentaries of Jeremias, Kelly, Lock, Schlatter, Simpson, Spicq (ad loc. and 99-104), Weiss, and Wohlenberg (30-44, arguing from *Jubilees*). Lock argues for the probability of Jewish reference from the teachers' claim to be νομοδιδάσκαλος, from the references in Titus to Ἰουδαΐκοῖς μύθοι (1:14) and γενεαλογίας καὶ ἔρεις καὶ μάχας νομικάς (3:9), and from Ignatius *Magn.* 8:1 (which may allude to 1 Tim. 1:4), where μυθεύμασιν παλαιοῖς πλανᾶσθαι is regarded as a sign of living κατὰ Ἰουδαϊσμόν.

Jeremias regards the "myths" as stories of creation and "genealogies" as the genealogies or generations of the patriarchs (so also Spicq) and appeals to Philo's designation of the history of the patriarchs as "genealogies." Lock understands μῦθοι as "defined by γενεαλογίαι, legendary stories about genealogies" (see also Hendriksen). Spicq points to "examples of this fantastic and unbridled hermeneutic" in rabbinic Haggadah, Philo's writings, the pseudo-

Philonic *Biblical Antiquities, Jubilees,* and in the Qumran writings (cf. 1QS 3:13-15). Dibelius-Conzelmann question the "alternative between Gnostic enumerations of aeons and Jewish, biblical speculations" and say that "we must think of early Jewish or Judaizing forms of Gnosticism" (so also Barrett and Ridderbos with reservations; one could appeal to 1 Tim. 4:1-4). With this comment Dibelius-Conzelmann appeal to the same phenomenon in Colossians. Appeals to Gnosticism must take into consideration that Gnosticism in any clearly recognized form is later than the NT, and only an incipient Gnosticism at best can be referred to in NT times (cf. Yamauchi, *Pre-Christian Gnosticism*). It seems rather certain, then, that the terms μῦθοι καὶ γενεαλογίαι are used in a Jewish setting, but it remains uncertain whether there is also some incipient Gnostic, or "pseudo-Hellenic," influence (cf. Colson, " 'Myths and Genealogies' "). Exactly what the terms refer to remains uncertain.

On γενεαλογία see Spicq; Kittel, "γενεαλογία"; F. Büchsel, *TDNT* I, 662-65. On μῦθος see G. Stählin, *TDNT* IV, 762-95.

ἀπέραντος** (NT hapax here but also found in LXX) means "endless" and is probably used not only "with a note of impatient scorn" (Lock), but also to highlight the uselessness of such genealogies, which because they have no end also have no result.

αἵτινες introduces a clause indicating the outcome and therefore the error of this occupation with "myths and genealogies," namely, speculation contrary to God's plan and intention for Christian maturity and growth. Paul opposes this teaching not only because it is "other" than the sound doctrine, but also because it has this contrary and disastrous result (cf. Calvin). παρέχω means "cause" or "give rise to." The fem. form of αἵτινες is probably in agreement with the nearest antecedent (γενεαλογίαις), but that is no reason to think that μύθοις is not also included, though genealogies may, in a relative sense, be more in view because myths, being false, would be more self-evidently harmful, but the same might not be seen with genealogies.

ἐκζήτησις** is a NT hapax here and appears only in Christian writings elsewhere, although ζήτησις is found elsewhere in NT and as a less strongly attested variant reading here. It has a pejorative meaning, "useless speculation" (BAGD). We are probably helped in our understanding of Paul's meaning here by the way in which he uses ζήτησις elsewhere in the PE (1 Tim. 6:4: ζητήσεις καὶ λογομαχίας; Tit. 3:9: μωρὰς ζητήσεις; 2 Tim. 2:23: μωρὰς καὶ ἀπαιδεύτους ζητήσεις) as always producing controversy or strife and as useless and by the two passages that indicate that these teachers and their efforts are devoid of truth (1 Tim. 6:4, 5; 2 Tim. 2:23-25). Paul is not saying that he is opposed to inquiry or controversy as such, but to speculation that is devoid of truth and has no good result. μᾶλλον ἤ "is here the equivalent of a negative in meaning (= comparative expressing exclusion . . .)" (BDF §185.2; cf. Robertson, *Grammar,* 666) and has the meaning "in contrast to" (BDF §245a; cf. also 2 Tim. 3:4).

οἰκονομίαν (ℵ A G and a few other Greek manuscripts, syr^{h}, TR) is to be preferred to the textual variant οἰκοδομήν (D* it vg syr$^{p, hmg}$ Irenaeus^{lat}; οἰκοδομίαν in D^{c}), "building" or "edification," not only as the more difficult reading but also as the best attested. The understanding of οἰκονομία** not only here but elsewhere (Lk. 16:2, 3, 4; 1 Cor. 9:17; Eph. 1:10; 3:2, 9; Col. 1:25) has presented a problem. Its literal, and original, meaning is the work performed by an οἰκονόμος, a "steward" or "manager." This idea of stewardship on God's behalf Paul applies to himself (1 Cor. 9:17; cf. also Tit. 1:7). The meaning "arrangement, order, plan" (BAGD), or more particularly, "God's plan of salvation," "his administration or order of salvation" (BAGD; O. Michel, *TDNT* V, 152) has also been proposed for the term; this view is influenced by the possible meaning of the word at some points in Ephesians (e.g., Eph. 1:10). A third meaning suggested for our passage (BAGD; Michel, 153), namely, "training or instruction," appeals to Clement of Alexandria, who uses the term in this way (*Paed.* 1, 8, 69; 70, 1). Perhaps a reexamination of the arguments in the light of the context can bring some resolution.

Alford argues that the predominant usage in the NT, and especially in Paul, as evidenced by Ephesians, is that of "plan" (so *TEV, NEB*). To the objection that the verb παρέχουσιν governs οἰκονομίαν and would seem to require not God's plan but its administration, it is answered that this is an example of zeugma (one verb having a different force with different subjects in a one context) and that the contrast here is more between God's plan and human folly than between human folly and a divinely given stewardship. Those favoring either "administration" or "training" argue that the verb is significant for determining the meaning. Those favoring "administration" or "stewardship" say that the divine outworking is what is primarily in mind in the use of the term in Ephesians and Colossians (cf., e.g., Col. 1:25: οἰκονομία has been given to Paul [τῆς δοθείσης μοι εἰς ὑμᾶς]) and is furthermore the meaning in the sole occurrence of the noun οἰκονόμος in the PE (Tit. 1:7).

Reumann, in a very helpful article ("*OIKONOMIA*-Terms") may, in his proposal for some of the usages in Colossians and Ephesians, have provided the clue for the meaning here. He proposes (as did C. F. D. Moule, *Colossians and Philemon*) that in Col. 1:25 οἰκονομία may refer to "God's administration, as well as the apostle's administrative activity" (p. 162). God's οἰκονομία is certainly in view in 1 Tim. 1:4, as the qualification θεοῦ makes plain (genitive of possession), but it is, at the same time, one that must be responded to and that is operative in the realm of faith (τὴν ἐν πίστει). Further, this οἰκονομία is in v. 5 called παραγγελία, i.e., "apostolic instructions with divine warrant." Since the concept seems to be set in such a context not only here but also in Ephesians, where it is spoken of as being brought to light or communicated (Eph. 3:9), it seems that neither of the two extremes is in view here, i.e., God's plan without reference to human stewardship, or

Paul's stewardship in the most specific sense. Rather, what is referred to is the outworking, administration, or stewardship of God's plan of salvation through the gospel and its communication (cf. 2 Tim. 1:9, 10: "God's purpose . . . revealed by . . . our Savior Christ Jesus . . . brought to light through the gospel," *NASB*).

The heterodoxy of the false teachers' speculation is, then, contrary to the furthering of God's administration, which is brought about not by speculation but ἐν πίστει (for πίστει with ἐν cf. 2 Thes. 2:13): With the definite article τήν Paul ties οἰκονομίαν with ἐν πίστει and indicates the realm in which the administration is accomplished. ἐν should not be taken as referring to initial saving faith only, but to the trust relationship that is the seedbed in which God works and produces growth. That this wider view of faith is in view is seen by the fact that it is returned to in v. 5 as one of the means that Christians must use to bring about the goal of the οἰκονομία and the attendant παραγγελία, namely, ἀγάπη.

1:5 Postpositive δέ, "but," contrasts the heterodox way (v. 4) and the apostolic way (v. 5). τέλος has here the meaning "goal" or "outcome toward which something is directed." The goal of Christian instruction is love manifested in the Christian's life through three channels, which are a pure heart, a good conscience, and a sincere faith.

Here love is the outcome of παραγγελία** (Acts 5:28; 16:24; 1 Thes. 4:2; 1 Tim. 1:5, 18). Some would relate παραγγελία to the specific charge of 1:3 (παρεκάλεσα . . . ἵνα παραγγείλῃς). This is correct, but is also a too restricted view (so likewise in 1:18). The other occurrence of the word in Paul, in 1 Thes. 4:2 (plural), speaks of commands handed on from Christ as requirements for the Christian's life. Since the context here speaks of Paul as an apostle according to commandment (1:1) and of Timothy being commanded by him in that capacity, παραγγελία is used here in the broader sense of *the* command of the Christian life seen in its entirety as God's charge to us (cf. Mt. 22:37-40; Mk. 12:31; 1 Jn. 4:21; 3:23). Not only does this understanding of the word fit with usage elsewhere in the NT, but more particularly it continues the emphasis on God's οἰκονομία (v. 4), which led to this statement in v. 5.

"Love" (ἀγάπη), says Paul, is the goal of the Christian teaching. This affirmation is in accord with Jesus' teaching (Mt. 22:37-40 par. Mk. 12:28-31; Lk. 10:27), which Paul seeks to communicate (cf. 1 Tim. 6:3), as do the other apostles and writers (cf., e.g., the Johannine passages listed above). "Love" is not defined in the NT but Paul does describe it in terms of Christ giving himself for the church (Eph. 5:25; cf. Rom. 5:8; cf. further Jn. 3:16; 14:23), in terms of the summary and fulfillment of the law (Rom. 13:8-10), and in the hymn of love in 1 Corinthians 13. In the first of these, Paul describes love in terms of Christ's self-giving to encourage husbands to love their wives by giving themselves for the good of their wives (cf. 1 Jn. 4:12, which also speaks of human love as the expression of God's love at work through us). When Paul speaks of love here, he probably has in mind love in this full-orbed sense (cf. further Gal. 5:6; Col. 3:14).

The love in view is said to come from (ἐκ) three sources, καρδίας, συνειδήσεως, and πίστεως, all three governed by one preposition and connected to each other by καί. With these three nouns and their adjectives Paul speaks of the inner being (καρδίας) and its continually cleansed status (καθαρᾶς), the life of obedience as an outcome of one's awareness of the responsibility to do what God asks believers to do (συνειδήσεως ἀγαθῆς), and sincere trust in God (πίστεως ἀνυποκρίτου), which enable a believer to love.

καρδία, "heart," is regularly used in the NT of the center of a person (cf. 1 Pet. 3:4), i.e., the person as he or she really is within himself or herself and before God. This usage reflects OT terminology (LXX ca. 650x, usually rendering *lēḇ*).

καθαρός (Pl.* 8x, all but one, Rom. 14:20, in the PE: 1 Tim. 1:5; 3:9; Tit. 1:15 [3x]; 2 Tim. 1:3; 2:22) means in a general sense "clean" or "pure." What is in view here is a condition in the personal realm analogous to what is spoken of in the Gospels with reference to cups and dishes (Mt. 23:25), i.e., having repeated defilement repeatedly cleansed away. Cf. also Jesus' spiritual application of washing the disciples' feet in relation to their essential and once-for-all cleansing (Jn. 13:5-11). The related verb (καθαρίζω) is used in 1 Jn. 1:7, 9 of God forgiving and cleansing from all sin and unrighteousness, through the blood of Christ, those who confess their sins (cf. Eph. 5:26). Thus the pure heart is the one cleansed by the forgiveness and cleansing that comes to those who continually confess their sins.

ἐκ καθαρᾶς καρδίας also appears in 2 Tim. 2:22: "Those who call on the Lord from a pure heart" are those with whom Timothy should pursue the virtues of godliness; καθαρᾶς refers to continued cleansing and inner transformation. Since both there and here in 1 Tim. 1:5 those who are already Christians are in view, that sense — continued cleansing and inner transformation — would be intended here too. Furthermore, Paul speaks elsewhere of putting off the old person and its deeds as a necessity for living the life of love (cf. Eph. 4:22ff. concluding with 5:1, 2; cf. Col. 3:3-14, especially v. 14).

συνείδησις** (NT 30x, Pl. 20x, PE 6x: Acts 23:1; 24:16; Rom. 2:15; 9:1; 13:5; 1 Cor. 8:7, 10, 12; 10:25, 27, 28, 29 [2x]; 2 Cor. 1:12; 4:2; 5:11; 1 Tim. 1:5, 19; 3:9; 4:2; Tit. 1:15; 2 Tim. 1:3; Heb. 9:9, 14; 10:2, 22; 13:18; 1 Pet. 2:19; 3:16, 21) means "consciousness," "moral consciousness," or "conscience," with the latter the predominant meaning in the NT. In the latter sense, the term indicates that one is self-conscious of the rightness or wrongness before God of one's actions and attitudes. Paul roots his view of conscience in the fact that mankind is made in God's image and that God is thereby inherently known and his standards thereby inherently present to the human conscience (cf. Rom. 1:18ff., especially v. 32, and then Rom. 2:15, where συνείδησις is correlated with "the work of the law written in their hearts"). Even when Paul recognizes that the conscience is not an altogether reliable instrument because of the effects of sin, speaking of it as "weak" (1 Cor. 8), "seared" (1 Tim. 4:2), or "defiled" (Tit. 1:15), he is at the same time affirming it as a moral self-evaluator.

For love to come to fruition Paul states that one's conscience must be "good" (ἀγαθῆς, PE 10x). Paul means by the "good conscience" an honest self-evaluation that one's conduct has been obedient rather than disobedient, as one evaluates the direction and perspective of one's life at the particular moment. Paul also speaks of serving God with a clear conscience (καθαρᾷ συνειδήσει, 2 Tim. 1:3), of deacons holding the faith with a clear conscience (καθαρᾷ συνειδήσει, 1 Tim. 3:9), and of false teachers rejecting a good conscience (ἀγαθὴν συνείδησιν, 1 Tim. 1:19) by their disobedient lives (ἀγαθή and καθαρά are virtual synonyms and the variation may be only stylistic). Paul's self-testimony in Acts is similar: "I have lived my life with a perfectly good conscience (πάσῃ συνειδήσει ἀγαθῇ) before God up to this day" (Acts 23:1; cf. 24:14-16), as also in 2 Cor. 1:12: "the testimony of our conscience, that in holiness and godly sincerity . . . we have conducted ourselves" (cf. 1 Tim. 4:2; cf. further Heb. 9:14; 13:18).

The third channel is a "sincere" or "unfeigned" faith (πίστεως ἀνυποκρίτου). πίστις here has the general NT and Pauline meaning of trust in God and reliance on him (cf. the two previous usages, 1:2 and especially 1:4). The last and ultimate requirement, then, is that one trust God to enable one to do such a sometimes difficult thing, i.e., love. The qualification "sincere" (ἀνυποκρίτος,** lit. "without hypocrisy") lays emphasis on the genuineness of that trust. Timothy's "sincere faith" (2 Tim. 1:5) gave reason (δι' ἣν αἰτίαν) for Paul to encourage him to "kindle afresh the charisma of God," "for God has not given us a spirit of timidity, but of power, love, and discipline" (vv. 6, 7); here again sincere love (cf. Rom. 12:9; 2 Cor. 6:6; 1 Pet. 1:22) requires genuine trust in God. Similarly James 1:5 makes undoubting faith a requisite for receiving wisdom.

See the articles relating to the key words in BAGD, *TDNT,* and *NIDNTT* and the literature referred to therein and in the supplementary volume of *TWNT* (X). On τέλος see especially du Plessis, *ΤΕΛΕΙΟΣ.* On συνείδησις see Pierce, *Conscience;* Thrall, "Συνείδησις." Pierce insists that conscience evaluates past actions and behavior (cf., e.g., p. 108) and thus ignores its function of evaluation and decision-making in the present and for the future (cf. in contrast Rom. 1:32; 13:5; 1 Corinthians 8 and 10; 1 Tim. 3:9; 1 Pet. 2:13, 19). Thrall provides a helpful balance by making the point this way: "Paul certainly begins with the secular meaning of the word but extends it further, so that conscience is thought of both as providing guidance for future moral action and also as being able to assess the actions of others" (p. 125; we dissent, however, from her view that conscience functions among the Gentiles as the law does among the Jews). Also against Pierce on this point are C. Maurer, *TDNT* VII, 898-919, especially 917; Stacey, *Pauline View of Man,* 206ff.

1:6 Paul returns to the specific problem at hand, namely, that some have strayed and turned aside from "these." ὧν, a plural relative pronoun, most likely refers to the three preceding concepts (cf. 1:19), though it may refer to the instruction and the piety that Paul has been speaking of. These people have not only substituted speculation for God's instruction, but have also wandered away from a concern for a pure heart, good conscience, and sincere faith. ἀστοχέω** means originally " 'miss the mark,' then 'miss, fail, deviate, depart' " (BAGD) with the genitive of that which is departed from, here ὧν. The verb is found in the NT only in the PE (1 Tim. 1:6; 6:21; 2 Tim. 2:18), referring to false teachers in every occurrence, but MM indicate that it is seen already in the third century BC. As a result of their departure (aorist participle, probably of antecedent action), "some persons" (τινες, cf. v. 3: probably the same people) "have turned themselves aside" (ἐκτρέπω,** 1 Tim. 1:6; 5:15; 6:20; 2 Tim. 4:4; Heb. 12:13, all passive with middle sense, with εἰς indicating that to which one turns [BAGD]) to ματαιολογία** (a NT hapax; cf. ματαιολόγος, Tit. 1:10), i.e., "empty, fruitless talk or discussion." For Paul's use of μάταιος elsewhere, see 1 Cor. 3:20; 15:17; and Tit. 3:9; cf. also Acts 14:15. The outcome is talk that is idle and useless.

1:7 The introductory participial phrase is related to the τινες of v. 6 and is a further description of these teachers. It indicates that they desire to be (θέλοντες followed by the infinitive εἶναι) "teachers of the law." The two other NT occurrences of νομοδιδάσκαλοι,** "teachers of the law" (Lk. 5:17; Acts 5:34), clearly refer to teachers of the Mosaic law, and there are contextual reasons to think that this is the meaning here: The "law" spoken of in vv. 8ff. would appear to be the Mosaic law because (a) Paul usually has the Mosaic law in mind when he speaks of "law"; (b) the law in view here has the same ethical concerns as those of the Mosaic law; (c) the pattern followed is very much like that of the Ten Commandments and like that of its application in Ex. 21:15ff. (see the comments below on 1:9ff.); (d) the correlation with the gospel in v. 11 would point in this direction; (e) Paul has already mentioned the false teachers' interest in (Jewish) myths and genealogies (v. 4; cf. Tit. 3:9). Furthermore, Paul's reference elsewhere to Jewish myths (Tit. 1:14) and circumcision (Tit. 1:10) when speaking of the false teaching would point to the same conclusion.

Along with this description Paul gives his evaluation of the false teachers. His verdict is that they do understand (νοέω) neither (1) "the things said" (ἅ, neuter plural relative pronoun, λέγουσιν) nor (2) their own confident doctrinal assertions about these things, i.e., about the laws. διαβεβαιόομαι** (middle deponent: "speak confidently, insist περί τινος . . . concerning or on something" [BAGD]) is used in the NT only in the PE (1 Tim. 1:7; Tit. 3:8). Paul is not criticizing confident speech as if such was inappropriate; in Tit. 3:8 he uses the same word to demand confidence of Titus in his teaching. He is, rather, criticizing the false teachers' failure to understand that about which they spoke so confidently. Thus incompetence and error are combined in them (for similar evaluations by Paul, cf., e.g., Col. 2:8, 18-23; Phil. 3:2, 18, 19).

LAWFUL USE OF THE LAW: 1:8-11

Reference to the false teachers' desire to be νομοδιδάσκαλοι and to their misunderstanding constrains Paul to set forth the proper use of the law. The key statement is the first, which begins with the affirmation "we know." That is to say, it is the common understanding of the Christian community that the law is "good," i.e., beneficial if used in the manner in which God intended. Paul goes on to apply this principle as a corrective to the misuse of the law by the false teachers.

The meaning of "law is not made for a righteous man" (v. 9, *NASB*) is crucial for understanding this passage. One view is that δίκαιος means "justified," i.e., the law does not apply to the Christian. This view acknowledges that the law functions to bring a person to Christ as a sinner, but then asserts that a saved person is not to be concerned with or directed by the law. It is my considered opinion that this view has misunderstood Paul here.

Although this is one of the most important questions connected with the passage, it is only one of several interrelated questions: (1) What law is in view, especially in v. 9? (2) What is the position that Paul is correcting? (3) What is the origin or source of the list in vv. 9, 10? (4) How is "according to the gospel" (v. 11) related to the preceding verses? Finally, (5) how are law and gospel related according to this passage? Each question will be handled as it comes up in the text.

1:8 Paul begins with a contrast (δέ, "but") and a claim, "we know" (οἴδαμεν), followed by a statement of what "we know" about the law, and concludes with the need for a right handling of the law, "if one uses it lawfully," all of which is set over against his evaluation of the would-be νομοδιδάσκαλοι (v. 7). Their mishandling of the law makes it necessary for him to set forth the proper use of the law. Their approach is wrong, *"but"* the law itself is good and can be used in a good way. οἴδαμεν is used by Paul to indicate that what he says is, in fact, the recognized Christian understanding of the subject, one that is commonly known, believed, and accepted (cf. for this use of οἴδαμεν, e.g., Rom. 2:2; 3:19; 8:22, 28; 1 Cor. 8:1, 4; 2 Cor. 5:1; 1 Jn. 3:2, 14; 5:18, 19, 20; cf. Michel, *An die Römer,* 86

n. 1, 174 n. 4; cf. further the only other first person plurals in the PE that include both Paul and other Christians: 1 Tim. 2:2; 6:7).

That which "we know" is "that the law is good" (ὅτι καλὸς ὁ νόμος; for the data on καλός see 2:3). The statement has striking similarities with several in Romans 7 (Rom. 7:14, 16; cf. v. 12, where the virtual synonyms ἅγιος and ἀγαθός are used). The point in 1 Tim. 1:8, as in Romans 7, is to affirm that the νόμος is intrinsically good because it is given by God (cf. Romans 2; 7:22; 8:4) and is not to be considered bad, though it can be mishandled, with bad results, as the νομοδιδάσκαλοι have done.

What νόμος is in view here? Although some say that in v. 9 νόμος as a general principle is in view, since the statement sounds like a general maxim (e.g., Bouma, Earle, Jeremias, Lock, Weiss, N. J. D. White, and Wohlenberg), most commentators recognize that νόμος in both v. 8 and v. 9 is the Mosaic law, particularly in its moral aspects (e.g., Bernard, Calvin, Ellicott, Fairbairn, Guthrie, Hendriksen, Kelly, Ridderbos, Schlatter, E. F. Scott, Simpson, and Spicq). Several considerations seem to establish this: (1) This section is a response to would-be νομοδιδάσκαλοι; this designation refers, as we have argued, to the Mosaic law, and the activity of these people had reference to the Mosaic law. (2) The ethical list in vv. 9-10 is similar to the Decalogue and the application of it in Exodus 21. (3) The reference to "gospel" in v. 11 points to the Mosaic law since that is the law in view elsewhere in the NT where law and gospel are discussed together, especially by Paul (cf. Romans 7–8; 3:19ff.; Galatians 3–4; Phil. 3:7ff.). (4) When Paul elsewhere speaks of "law" and gives ethical lists, it is the Mosaic moral law that is in view (cf., e.g., Rom. 13:9ff.). Furthermore, (5) it is usually the case that when Paul uses νόμος the Mosaic law is assumed (cf. W. Gutbrod, *TDNT* IV, 1069).

"If one uses it lawfully" indicates that for the law to have its proper effect it must be used in accord with its intent. This principle both exposes the error of the νομοδιδάσκαλοι and prepares the way for the following remarks.

Some have insisted that τις is a continued reference to the teachers (cf. the plural in vv. 3 and 6), but it is more likely used here as an indefinite reference to whoever uses the law. Indefinite τις is the subject in some forty ἐάν clauses in the NT. Furthermore, this understanding of τις is more likely in the present context. Paul is not saying how someone should teach the law, but how "anyone" should "use" it (χράομαι = "to make use of, employ," with dative, here αὐτῷ = τῷ νόμῳ [BAGD; cf. also Robertson, *Grammar,* 533]). The appearance of νομίμως here creates a play on words. Its nuance here is best explained by what follows (as εἰδὼς τοῦτο, v. 9, suggests). That is, why the law was given and for whom it was given indicate the law's "lawful" use. Thus "lawfully" means here in accordance with the intended use of the law.

1:9a εἰδὼς τοῦτο serves as a bridge from νομίμως χρῆται to the ὅτι clause that follows: τοῦτο represents the content of the ὅτι clause (cf. Robertson, *Grammar,* 699), and εἰδώς indicates that one must know that which follows in order to use the law lawfully (cf. H. von Soden). εἰδώς refers back to the singular τις and has "any" person in mind.

ὅτι δικαίῳ νόμος οὐ κεῖται, it has been argued, is a statement of principle about law in general (e.g., Bouma, Jeremias, Lock, Weiss, N. J. D. White, and Wohlenberg), because similar statements about law can be found elsewhere, and because νόμος is anarthrous and therefore, it is assumed, used in a general rather than a specific sense (see, e.g., Dibelius-Conzelmann ad loc. with notes). There are problems with this approach. νόμος is used by Paul of the Mosaic moral law without the article as well as with the article. The old attempt to make distinctions on the basis of the presence or absence of the article (beginning with Origen, *In ep. ad Rom.* on 3:7) has by examination of the evidence been shown incorrect (cf., e.g., Robertson, *Grammar,* 796: "In general, when νόμος is anarthrous in Paul, it refers to the Mosaic law, as in ἐπαναπαύῃ νόμῳ [Rom. 2:17]"; see the passages listed in MGM and cf., e.g., Rom. 2:25; 3:20; Gal. 2:19; 6:13; W. Gutbrod, *TDNT* IV, 1070; BAGD s.v., with the literature cited there). A further problem attends the understanding of νόμος as law in general and the clause here as a general principle, and that is the flow of the argument in vv. 9-11. The conjunction δέ relates this statement about "law" directly to a list of various sins that certainly seems to be based on the Mosaic law, all of them governed by the same verb (κεῖται) as that which governs the statement of principle (see below). The statement of principle and the list of sins are so tightly tied together that it is difficult not to think that they are both dealing with the Mosaic law.

κεῖμαι is used figuratively, as here, as a legal technical term meaning "be given, exist, be valid" with the dative for the person to whom a law is given (BAGD). Since there is no verb with the list of terms that follows, all of which are dative, it is evident that this verb governs them as well as δικαίῳ. Thus with this one verb Paul states both negatively and positively for whom the law is to function in this particular sense.

δίκαιος is understood by a number (Alford, BAGD, Freundorfer, Gealy, Guthrie, Jeremias, Kelly, Lock [?], Schlatter in particular, Spicq, and van Oosterzee) as referring to the justified Christian, so that the statement says that, contrary to the false teaching, the law has nothing to do with the Christian. It is argued that this is Paul's consistent use of δίκαιος and that elsewhere he indicates the freedom of the Christian from the law. Others (Barrett, Bernard, Calvin, Earle, Ellicott, Hendriksen, Ridderbos, Simpson, Weiss, N. J. D. White, and Wohlenberg) understand δίκαιος here in the ethical sense, the first sense given by BAGD: "upright, just, righteous, like *ṣaddîq* = conforming to human laws and the laws of God, and living in accordance with them."

The meaning of δίκαιος here would seem to be determined in large measure by its place preceding and contrasting with a list of terms concerned with moral behavior. Therefore, the point of this section is to emphasize, against the would-be νομοδιδάσκαλοι, that the law is given to deal with moral questions and not for speculation. The would-be νομοδιδάσκαλοι are not Judaizers like those of Galatians, since the PE give no evidence of that, but rather those who deal with God's law from the perspective of myths, genealogies, and disputes about it (v. 4; see Tit. 3:9). Thus Paul is saying that the law is not given to apply in some mystical way to people who are already "righteous," i.e., those already seeking to conform to the law. It is, rather, given to deal with people who are specifically violating its sanctions and to warn them against their specific sins (as the list in vv. 9b-10 goes on to do).

The "righteous" are, then, those living in conformity to the requirements of the law by the work of Christ wrought by the Spirit in them (cf. Rom. 8:4, "in order that the requirement of the law might be fulfilled in us [ἐν ἡμῖν], who . . . walk . . . according to the Spirit"). But Paul does not use "righteous" here in an absolutistic way such that he himself would have been inconsistent to refer to the law for the Christian (cf. Rom. 13:8-10), but in that less than absolute way which we see in Jesus — in a different situation and with a different nuance — but nonetheless in a nonabsolute way (Lk. 5:32: "I have come to call not the righteous but sinners to repentance").

The phrase δικαίῳ νόμος οὐ κεῖται turns out to be a foil to give emphasis to what follows, which is Paul's statement that the law's intention is to indicate to the lawless and rebellious that they should avoid sins. By thus identifying those for whom the law is given, Paul identifies the lawful use of the law (cf. v. 8). So concerned is Paul to make this ethical point that he does not even mention the law's soteriological use here.

1:9b, 10a The terms that follow in the list specify sins to be avoided and show that the law was given for a specific ethical use, not to be used in any other way with the righteous (v. 9a). The references to smiters of parents (with two words), murderers, sexual sinners (with two words), kidnappers (literally "stealers of people"), and liars and perjurers are a deliberate echo of the order of the second part of the Decalogue (Ex. 20:12-16). Furthermore, that some, indeed most, of the sins are stated in aggravated forms leads one to Ex. 21:15ff. (and elsewhere), where the commandments of Exodus 20 are specifically applied and worked out, where we have reference to striking of parents (v. 15), where there is a clear indication that "you shall not kill" is meant to prohibit murder (vv. 12-14), and where one of the forms of stealing is kidnapping (v. 16). By using these aggravated forms from Exodus 21, Paul may be showing the false teachers and the church that when the OT applied and worked out the principles of the law, it did so in this very specific way of dealing with people's sins. The list would therefore carry with it, then, a double-edged thrust: Its ethical application of the Decalogue echoes the OT itself and thus gives both an example of how the law is to function and a refutation of the would-be law-teachers.

Once it is recognized that from "strikers of father and mother" onward the order of the second part of the Decalogue is followed, then the question naturally arises whether the preceding part of the list in v. 9 corresponds to the earlier part of the Decalogue. An interesting correlation may well exist, especially if it is borne in mind that single words are used in the latter part of the list to refer to violators of a specific commandment, and therefore single words could also be used in the former part to characterize violators of the earlier commandments.

Let us test this possibility by beginning with the term immediately preceding the reference to fathers and mothers and working backward. Since the keynote of the sabbath command is to keep it holy (ἁγιάζειν, Ex. 20:8 LXX) and since Paul's list is in negative terms, the single term βέβηλος, "accessible to everyone, profane, unhallowed" (BAGD), might well characterize those who profane that day, putting the command negatively in terms of its violation (cf. Lv. 19:12 LXX, where the cognate verb for our term is used of profaning the Lord's name).

Likewise, those who take the Lord's name in vain (Ex. 20:7) might well be designated negatively by a single term as those who are "unholy" (ἀνόσιος [ἀν-οσιος]). This understanding is strengthened if the language associated with this command has been influenced by the petition of the Lord's Prayer that the Lord's name be hallowed or regarded as holy (Mt. 6:9; Lk. 11:2).

ἁμαρτωλός is often used in the NT with the broad meaning "sinner," as it is in 1 Tim. 1:15, the only other occurrence in the PE. At times, however, it is used in the NT more specifically of those who fail to keep the Mosaic law, particularly Gentiles, especially because of their idolatry (cf., e.g., BAGD: "irreligious, unobservant people, of those who did not observe the Law in detail Mt. 9:10f.; 11:19; Mk. 2:15f.; Lk. 5:30; 7:34; 15:1"). This usage is found also in Paul in Gal. 2:15 (cf. on idolatry Rom. 2:22). Thus one who violates the prohibition of making and worshipping idols (Ex. 20:4-6) might well be designated a "sinner" in the specific sense (so Ex. 20:5 LXX: ἁμαρτίας πατέρων).

ἀσεβής means "godless" or "impious." Since the first commandment of the Decalogue (Ex. 20:3) prohibits having other gods and abandoning God as the one and only true God, and since the NT uses σεβόμενοι (τὸν θεόν) of those who accepted the ethical monotheism of the OT (and of this commandment; cf. Acts 13:43, 50; 16:14; 17:4, 17; 18:7), then it is understandable how violators of this command could be designated by the ἀ-privative negative cognate of that concept, namely ἀσεβεῖς.

The order of the Decalogue seems, then, to give a satisfactory explanation of Paul's list from ἀσεβέσι onward. He may also have had an eye on the false teachers and their tendencies in his choice of various terms (cf. Vögtle, *Tugend- und Lasterkataloge,* 234f.), although this seems less likely.

This conclusion carries with it the recognition that the first two terms in the list, ἀνόμοις καὶ ἀνυποτάκτοις, are introductory. After the conjunction "but" (δέ) signals a contrast, these two general terms are used in contrast to δικαίῳ to summarily describe those for whom the law is given before the more specific list following the order of the Decalogue. ἄνομος is generally used in the NT of those who are without God's moral law or who do not act in accord with it, hence the wicked (cf. 1 Macc. 7:5). ἀνυποτάκτοις in its PE* usages (here and Tit. 1:6) designates those who are undisciplined, disobedient, or rebellious. These two terms bring into perspective those for whom the law is given, namely, those who need its discipline and restraint in their propensity for lawlessness and disobedience.

πατρολῴαις** and μητρολῴαις** are NT hapaxes here, neither of which appears in the Greek OT, though, as we have seen, their use here was influenced by Ex. 21:15. It is likely that they do not signify parricides but "smiters" (so Simpson and Ridderbos): The endings of the two terms are from the verb ἀλο[ι]άω, which has the ambiguous meaning "smite" (LSJM, 72; for variations in spelling of the two terms see LSJM, s.v.; Robertson, *Grammar,* 185). Since these terms seem to be influenced by Exodus 21, it is best to understand their meaning in accord with that chapter. Both the Hebrew text and the LXX speak of striking or smiting, not of slaying (hiphil of *nākâ,* according to BDB, 645, "smite (with a single, non-fatal, blow), strike"; LXX τύπτει, "beat, strike, smite" according to LSJM); in Exodus 21 a word referring to killing or dying is added where the striking is fatal, so that some blows are recognized not to be. This strong negative, expressed in just two words, rather than the positive phrase "honor your father and your mother," emphasizes the correcting and restraining character of the law and thereby brings out its serious ethical character.

ἀνδροφόνος** (a NT hapax, but cf. 2 Maccabees 9:28, the only LXX occurrence), "murderer," delineates the meaning of the sixth commandment of the Decalogue by its specificity, as does Ex. 21:12ff., which specifies that it refers to intentional manslaughter (cf. Lv. 24:17).

πόρνος is a general term in the NT for "sexual immorality." Here it reflects the seventh commandment of the Decalogue and its application later in the Mosaic law (e.g., Ex. 22:16, 17; Dt. 22:22-30; Lv. 20:10-21).

Paul's list also includes as representative of the seventh commandment ἀρσενόκοιτες** (also in 1 Cor. 6:9, cf. Rom. 1:27; for extrabiblical use see BAGD, MM, and LSJM; not in LXX and according to Morgenthaler not found in pre-Christian literature), "homosexuals," so that both heterosexual and homosexual aspects of immoral sexual activity are covered. The latter is in accord with Paul's approach elsewhere (Rom. 1:24, 26-28; 1 Cor. 6:9-11), where he writes about homosexuality as the perversion of the God-ordained orientation of sex and reflects the OT condemnation of homosexuality (cf. Lv. 18:22; 20:13; Dt. 23:18; and then also Gn. 18:20; 19:4-7; Ezk. 16:48-50, especially v. 50; Jdg. 19:22, 23).

The word Paul uses is composed of two components, ἀρσενο- and -κοιτης. The former is the specific word for male (ἄρσην) with "strong emphasis on sex" (BAGD). The latter means generally "bed" and is a euphemism for sexual intercourse (BAGD). The word does not refer, as some writers have alleged, only to sex with young boys or to male homosexual prostitutes, but simply to homosexuality itself (so Paul explicitly in Rom. 1:26, 27; cf. the article by Wright, "Homosexuals"). Paul writes elsewhere that the consequence for continued and unrepentant involvement in this, and other sins listed here, is exclusion from the kingdom of God and that deliverance from this, and the other sins, is an integral part of the gospel of Jesus Christ as Lord through the power of the Spirit of God (1 Cor. 6:9-11).

ἀνδραποδιστής** (a NT hapax; for its etymology and meaning see MM; not in LXX and not known in pre-Christian literature) means "slave dealer" or "kidnapper," though BAGD suggest that here perhaps it means "procurer" (for this term see also Spicq, "Vocabulaire de l'esclavage," especially 201-4). With this term the eighth commandment is represented, again in accord with the expansion and application of the law elsewhere in the OT, i.e., Ex. 21:16 (cf. Dt. 24:7). Paul hereby forbids, as does the OT, this particular act in regard to slavery but, like the OT elsewhere, also regulates the existing state of slaves and masters (cf. Eph. 6:5-9; Col. 3:22–4:1; 1 Tim. 6:1, 2; Tit. 2:9, 10). The apparent inconsistency may be explained by recognizing that in the latter case both the OT and Paul are only speaking of conduct appropriate within an existing social practice, without condoning that practice (cf. the analogy of divorce, Dt. 29:1ff.; Mt. 19:8).

ψεύστης (cf. Lv. 19:11 LXX: οὐ ψεύσεσθε) means "liar." ἐπίορκος** (a NT hapax that occurs once in the LXX, Zc. 5:3) means "perjurer," i.e., one who has sworn falsely (cf. LSJM). These two terms represent the ninth commandment's prohibition of bearing false witness against one's neighbor. With ἐπίορκος the specific focus of the ninth commandment is more directly in view, a focus taken up and developed in Ex. 23:1-3, 6-8 (cf. Zc. 5:3). The two concepts are combined in Lv. 19:11-16 (especially vv. 11, 12), which, with Zc. 5:3, may have influenced Paul's dual formulation here.

The tenth commandment, that against coveting, is not represented in Paul's list, which is concluded with the general clause, "and whatever else is contrary to sound teaching." Paul does include coveting in his only other list clearly reflecting the Decalogue, Rom. 13:9, which is, however, also incomplete, beginning with the commandment against adultery and omitting the commandment against bearing false witness. The only other clearly self-conscious list reflecting the Decalogue in the NT is that of Jesus in the

Synoptics (Mt. 19:18, 19 par. Mk. 10:19; Lk. 18:20), which is also incomplete and also omits the prohibition of coveting (cf. Marshall, *Luke,* ad loc.).

The omission of coveting from Paul's list may be explained by one or more of these possibilities: (1) Paul was influenced by Jesus' list, which does not include coveting; (2) the different NT lists mentioned above reflect a commonly utilized approach that did not quote the entire Decalogue, either (a) because it was understood that the hearers would complete the list, or (b) because enough of a sample was given for the lesson to be taught or the point to be made; (3) Paul has purposely omitted coveting here, which elsewhere he equates with idolatry (Eph. 5:5; Col. 3:5), either (a) because by this evaluation it is already included among the first three pairs, (b) because it is included in the general clause at the end of v. 10, (c) because, since it is inner and attitudinal, he omits it so that the list can highlight external sins, or (d) because he deals with it specifically later (6:9f. and context). (3c) is highly unlikely just because the same sort of sin is included in the first three pairs and in the concluding clause by its inclusiveness. (1) is probably ruled out by the fact that Rom. 13:9 does include coveting, even though Paul is influenced by the words of Jesus and his use of the Decalogue (cf. 1 Cor. 7:10). (2b) is probably inappropriate, since the list is so full and specific and especially because Paul goes to the trouble of adding the concluding clause. Either (2a), (3a), (3b), (3d), or some combination of these, seems to be the most likely reason that Paul omitted coveting from his list. But in light of the incomplete lists of Jesus and of Paul in Rom. 13:9, it cannot be assumed that this is a deliberate exclusion.

All the words in the list are masculine plural substantives: the list names not the sins forbidden by the law but the ones who do what is forbidden. But Paul preceded the list with singular δικαίῳ (v. 9a), probably as a generic term: When naming that for which the law is not given, the righteous, he speaks abstractly and comprehensively so that a generic singular is appropriate; when he names those for whom the law is given, he speaks concretely and particularly, so that the plurals are appropriate. However, in the summary concluding clause, he refers to any other sin (τι ἕτερον, neuter singular), a comprehensive generic. The list names not only specific sinners to whom and for whom the law was given, but also the principle, thus the indefinite generic singular, that the law was given to deal with sin — as is also the gospel (κατὰ τὸ εὐαγγέλιον, v. 11).

As we have seen, Paul's list follows the order of the Decalogue and utilizes the applications of those commandments found elsewhere in the OT. But the words themselves are rarely used in the LXX in connection with the Decalogue and its application (some, not all, are found elsewhere in the LXX). Two factors may account for this. The first is Paul's evident decision to express the commandments in single words, a phenomenon not present in the Hebrew OT and thus not in the LXX. The second may be his desire to express this list in the contemporary terms known to the hearers and the false teachers (cf., e.g., Colossians and the Corinthian letters), making use of terms found in lists of the day, which nonetheless express the truths of the biblical account, which he is so evidently following.

Other lists of sins (or vices) in Paul are Rom. 1:29-31; 13:13; 1 Cor. 5:10, 11; 6:9, 10; 2 Cor. 12:20, 21; Gal. 5:19-21; Eph. 4:31; 5:3-5; Col. 3:5, 8; 2 Tim. 3:2-5; Tit. 3:3. For a study that deals particularly with the vice lists of the PE see McEleney, "Vice Lists." McEleney concludes that the lists were written to address the real situations and are not formalized or stylized lists. He notes five influences operative in the formation of the lists, a chief one being the Decalogue, as we have demonstrated.

1:10b The concluding clause, καὶ εἴ τι ἕτερον κτλ., like καὶ εἴ τις ἑτέρα ἐντολή in Rom. 13:9, reminds the readers that the law's moral obligations are not circumscribed by this list that reflects OT application of the Decalogue (cf. other Pauline lists that include sins not mentioned in the Decalogue: Gal. 5:19-21; 1 Cor. 6:10; 2 Tim. 3:2-5; Tit. 3:3). Furthermore, the clause goes on to say that the "sound teaching" of the Christian faith has the same ethical perspective as the law, and that that teaching also points out sins that are contrary to it.

εἰ is not used to express doubt ("if"), but in connection with the indefinite pronoun τι and ἕτερον expresses a more general indefiniteness, as indicated by the translation "whatever else" (*NIV, NASB, RSV;* see for εἴτι BAGD s.v. εἰ VII [220]; Dana and Mantey, *Grammar,* 247; and the MGM listing and classifications). ἕτερον is used in this construction with its meaning "another" or "other," as is appropriate in a phrase that both extends and concludes a list (Robertson, *Grammar,* 749; BDF §306, which points to Mt. 15:30; Lk. 3:18; Rom. 8:39; 13:9 and, in Attic, Demosthenes 18.208, 219; 19.297). The implication is that the preceding sins are not the only ones, but that there are other sins ("whatever else") that are contrary to the sound teaching.

ἀντίκειμαι means "be opposed, in opposition to, or contrary to" and is possibly used here in wordplay with κεῖμαι (v. 9a). The law is made (κεῖμαι) for sinners, and for whatever else is contrary to (ἀντίκειμαι, cf. Gal. 5:17) "sound teaching," which by its very contrariety to sound teaching is marked as sinful. By this Paul indicates that law and "sound teaching" are together in opposing these sins and therefore have a common ethical perspective.

διδασκαλία** (Mt. 15:9; Mk. 7:7; Rom. 12:7; 15:4; Eph. 4:14; Col. 2:22; 1 Tim. 1:10; 4:1, 6, 13, 16; 5:17; 6:1, 3; Tit. 1:9; 2:1, 7, 10; 2 Tim. 3:10, 16; 4:3) is used here in its passive sense of "that which is taught." This concept is more widely utilized by Paul and the NT than the actual number of occurrences of this word would indicate, though an examination of the related words διδαχή, "teaching," and διδάσκω, "teach," do make this evident (cf. also παράδοσις, παραδίδωμι, and παραλαμβάνω, and other modes of expression that convey this concept but are not stereotyped, e.g., 2 Thes.

2:5ff.: "I was telling you these things"). Although Paul in earlier letters refers to the content of his teaching (cf. 2 Thes. 2:15; 3:6: the tradition received from him; Rom. 16:17: the teaching learned; Rom. 6:17: the form of teaching to which the readers were committed), it is not until the PE that the term διδασκαλία becomes generally used. Perhaps it was a replacement for the earlier and virtually synonymous διδαχή (Rom. 6:17; 16:17; 1 Cor. 14:6, 26; only 2x in PE: Tit. 1:4; 2 Tim. 4:2) that was able more definitely to speak of a teaching already given (which is more the case in the PE) rather than of that which was being given (as in the earlier letters).

Since διδασκαλία is neither intrinsically Christian teaching, nor, even when it claims a Christian framework, necessarily healthy (cf. 1 Tim. 1:3-7!), Paul adds the descriptive term ὑγιανούσῃ** (a participle from ὑγιαίνω used as an attributive adjective; cf. Robertson, *Grammar,* 1106). This is the first of several mentions of "sound teaching" (ὑγιαίνουσα διδασκαλία) in the PE (here and Tit. 1:9; 2:1; 2 Tim. 4:3). The phrase carries the figurative nuance of that which one knows to be healthy, i.e., "correct," although some have opted for the translation "health-giving" (e.g., Michaelis, *Pastoralbriefe und Gefangenschaftsbriefe,* 79f.; Bouma). But ὑγιαίνω means "be healthy or sound" (cognate to ὑγιής; cf. LSJM with examples), and not "make healthy" (= ὑγιάζω). Furthermore, the usage in Tit. 1:13; 2:2 of ὑγιαίνω (ἐν) τῇ πίστει would seem to point to the idea of "correct, sound, or true" in contrast with that which is incorrect or false.

In both of its occurrences in 1 Timothy ὑγιαίνω is used in a context that contrasts it with ἑτεροδιδασκέω (here and 6:3; cf. the similar contextual opposition to the false in Tit. 1:9, 13; 2 Tim. 4:3). Often ὑγιαίνω is used in relation to a norm or standard from which soundness is derived (cf., e.g., 1 Tim. 1:10, 11: sound teaching according to the gospel of God; 6:3: Christ's sound words; 2 Tim. 1:13: sound words heard from the apostle). This usage is in accord with the figurative nonphilosophical usage of the day. Thus the participle means "healthy" as opposed to false or sick (cf. U. Luck, *TDNT* VIII, 308-13, especially 312; and particularly D. Müller, *NIDNTT* II, 169-71, especially 169; and Ridderbos in an extended note, contra the one-sided excursus of Dibelius-Conzelmann, which appeals to philosophical usage in extrabiblical literature and says that the term should be understood in this philosophical sense as "rational"). This metaphorical use of a medical term may show the influence of the physician Luke.

1:11 With what is κατὰ τὸ εὐαγγέλιον connected? Bouma takes it with ἀντίκειται, Weiss with εἰδώς, and several commentators with οἴδαμεν and v. 8 or vv. 8-10 (e.g., Easton, Guthrie, Jeremias, Lenski, Lock, Simpson, Spicq, N. J. D. White, and Wohlenberg). Barrett takes it as "loosely attached to the paragraph as a whole" (from v. 5 on), so also Kelly, but in a way similar to the preceding group. Others take it with the "sound doctrine" of v. 10 (e.g., Bernard, Hendriksen, Ridderbos, *NEB, NIV*).

κατά means with the accusative, among other things, "according to, in accordance with, in conformity with, corresponding to," giving essentially the norm in view (BAGD s.v. II.5; see also M. J. Harris, *NIDNTT* III, 1200f.). κατὰ τὸ εὐαγγέλιον occurs 5x in the NT (Rom. 2:16; 11:28; 16:25; here; 2 Tim. 2:8). In the other passages the phrase indicates the norm for the main thought in closest proximity to it. Rom. 2:16 is especially instructive since it has to do with the law and is a longer passage, as here. κατὰ τὸ εὐαγγέλιον there does not refer back to the beginning of the statement nor does it serve as the norm for Paul's instruction about the law; it serves rather as the norm for the nearest main idea, i.e., that God will judge. Thus Paul's use of the phrase elsewhere would suggest that in 1 Tim. 1:11 also he refers to the main idea nearest at hand, i.e., the "sound teaching." Occurrences of κατά elsewhere in the PE also shed light: 1 Tim. 6:3 has κατ' εὐσέβειαν qualifying διδασκαλίᾳ by its very position; Tit. 1:9 shows a similar use of a κατά phrase.

Therefore, uses of κατά in the PE and the use of κατὰ τὸ εὐαγγέλιον by Paul both serve as indicators that the phrase here in 1:11 qualifies ὑγιαινούσῃ διδασκαλίᾳ. Furthermore, evidence is lacking for jumping over the nearer and more obvious correlation to somewhere else in the passage. That it is not through the gospel alone that mankind knows that the law is good or that it is made for sinners (cf. Rom. 1:32; 2:14, 15) makes the proposed more distant connection contrary to Paul's teaching elsewhere. Finally, contrary to Bouma, it is not the gospel itself that shows the opposition of these sins to sound teaching, but the sound teaching based on that gospel (cf. the dative form following the verb: "contrary to," indicating that to which it is contrary; Robertson).

κατὰ τὸ εὐαγγέλιον by its connection with ὑγιαινούσῃ διδασκαλίᾳ provides the norm for that teaching and for its soundness. The εὐαγγέλιον is the essence of the saving good news about the person and work of Jesus Christ, especially his death and resurrection, in relation to human sin (see 1 Cor. 15:1-4; 2 Tim. 1:8-11; Dodd, *Apostolic Preaching*).

Genitive τῆς δόξης may be understood either as an adjectival qualification, "the glorious gospel" *(KJV, RSV, NASB, NIV)* in Semitic style (cf. Eph. 1:17, ὁ πατὴρ τῆς δόξης), or as that which the gospel displays, "the gospel, which tells of the glory of God" *(NEB,* also *RV, TEV).* Although there is much to commend the first alternative in terms of Paul's usage of the descriptive genitive, it is more relevant to notice his correlation of εὐαγγέλιον and δόξα in the only other occurrence of the phrase, which, as here, is followed by a reference to a person of the Godhead (here τοῦ θεοῦ, there τοῦ Χριστοῦ): In 2 Cor. 4:4 the gospel tells or sets forth God's glory (cf. v. 6: "to give us the light of the knowledge of God's glory in Christ's face"); all the modern translations noted above that take the phrase as "glorious gospel" in 1 Tim. 1:11 render it "the gospel of the glory of Christ" here *(RSV, NASB, NIV,* as well as *RV, NEB, TEV;* cf. also Paul's comment in Acts 20:24: τὸ εὐαγγέλιον τῆς χάριτος τοῦ θεοῦ). Paul's previous usage would seem conclusive for the usage in 1 Tim 1:11. This is borne out by the usage of δόξα elsewhere in the PE* (1 Tim. 1:17; 3:16; Tit. 2:13; 2 Tim. 2:10; 4:18; cf. further the usage in the LXX; S. Aalen, *NIDNTT* II, 44-48, especially 44).

δόξα expresses here God's splendor and power (cf. G. Kittel, *TDNT* II, 247); the gospel causes us to see and know the divine splendor "in the face of Christ" (2 Cor. 4:6). We come to see and know that splendor in operation as a power that saves us (see the use of δόξα in reference to the new covenant, the gospel, in 2 Cor. 3:7-11; 4:4, 6) by God's grace (see Eph. 1:6: δόξης τῆς χάριτος αὐτοῦ; cf. Jn. 1:14). The result is that the gospel enables us to gain or share the glory of Jesus Christ in the future (cf. 2 Thes. 2:14; Tit. 2:13). Thus, as the *NEB* puts it, the gospel "tells the glory of God."

τοῦ μακαρίου θεοῦ is written with μακάριος between the article and the noun for emphasis (cf. Robertson, *Grammar,* 776). μακάριος (Pl. 7x: Rom. 4:7, 8; 14:22; 1 Cor. 7:40; 1 Tim. 1:11; 6:15; Tit. 2:13) is used only here and in 6:15, in both Testaments, as an attribute of God. With reference to God the concept is found among the Greeks and Greek-speaking Jews (for examples see BAGD; Wetstein, *NT Graecum;* Dibelius-Conzelmann; Spicq). The term itself means "blessed" or "happy" and therefore here designates "God as containing all happiness in Himself and bestowing it on men" (Lock; cf. *NEB:* "in his eternal felicity"). "Sound doctrine" is that which comes from and is in accord with the gospel that displays God's glory as the blessed one.

ὃ ἐπιστεύθην ἐγώ is Paul's typical and irresistible personal application of the previous statement (ἐγώ is emphatic; ὅ is accusative of the thing; its antecedent is τὸ εὐαγγέλιον; cf. Robertson, *Grammar,* 485). The gospel has been entrusted to Paul (cf. 1 Thes. 2:4; 1 Tim. 2:7; 2 Tim. 1:11; 2:9). ἐπιστεύθην is aorist passive of πιστεύω used in the sense of "entrust" (BAGD s.v. 3 [662]), as in Rom. 3:2 (with τὰ λόγια τοῦ θεοῦ); 1 Cor. 9:17 (with οἰκονομίαν, which has contextual reference to the εὐαγγέλιον, see v. 16); Gal. 2:7, 1 Thes. 2:4; (with τὸ εὐαγγέλιον, as here); and Tit. 1:3 (with κηρύγματι). In all of these occurrences it is God who entrusts and his message that is entrusted.

Paul has shown how the law may be used lawfully in accordance with its purpose as an ethical guide to warn against sin. He has demonstrated this by presenting a list that shows that the Decalogue is so understood in the OT. He has concluded by stating that this is also the ethical perspective of the truly healthy teaching based on the gospel, so that both it and a proper use of the law concur in terms of their concern for a righteous life and in their teaching against sin. Thus when the law is rightly applied as an ethical restraint against sin, it is in full accordance with the ethical norm given in the gospel as the standard for the redeemed life. A different use of the law, for example, in a mythological or genealogical application to the righteous, is thereby shown to be out of accord with the law's given purpose and the gospel and its teaching.

PAUL'S COMMISSION AND CONVERSION AS AN EXAMPLE OF THE TRUTH OF THE GOSPEL: 1:12-17

V. 11 with its assertion that the gospel was entrusted to Paul provides the setting for vv. 12-17. Paul demonstrates how this entrusting and his own reception of mercy and grace in Jesus Christ provides an illustration that the gospel is the power of God unto salvation for any sinner, because it has been that to him, a terrible sinner.

These verses spell out the central truths that Timothy and the church are to teach and hold on to over against the teaching of the false teachers (vv. 3-5) and at the same time serve as a bridge to vv. 18-20, where Paul returns to the charge laid on Timothy. Paul in turn entrusts the gospel and the teaching that flows from it to Timothy. Paul does so having known its power in his own life and also knowing that he is an example for other sinners who will be saved (v. 16). Aware of what the gospel can do for Paul, Timothy will be encouraged to stand for it, to hold on to it, and to engage in warfare against false teachers who would teach otherwise and who are thereby rejecting such a gospel (as their life indicates, vv. 18-20).

The form of this section is itself instructive in that the two subsections preceding the doxology in v. 17 (vv. 12-14, 15-16) give a twice repeated recounting of the gospel message and its application. In both subsections the account turns on the mercy shown to Paul and thus focuses on him as an example of God's mercy. In the first subsection v. 12 presents the work of Christ in Paul's life, v. 13a presents Paul's sin, and v. 13b the provision of mercy (ἠλεήθην), which culminates in "the faith and love that are in Christ Jesus" (v. 14). In the second subsection v. 15a presents the work of Christ in a faithful saying; this is followed by references to Paul's sin (v. 15b; cf. v. 13a) and the provision of mercy (v. 16a, ἠλεήθην, cf. v. 13b), which culminates with the reference to "Jesus Christ" and "those who would believe in him for eternal life" (v. 16b; cf. v. 14). Paul moves from the particular in the first subsection to the general in the second, from his own particular case (vv. 12-14, first person singular) to the general truth (v. 15: plural ἁμαρτωλούς; v. 16: plural τῶν μελλόντων πιστεύειν) and to himself as a prime example (v. 16a).

Vv. 12-14 begin their presentation of Paul's personal experiences with his statement of thankfulness for being strengthened and put into service by Christ (v. 12). They continue with his amazement that Christ would commission such a vicious sinner and personal opponent (v. 13) and conclude with Paul's forgiveness and reception into Christ and the sphere of faith and love in Christ (vv. 13b, 14). Having thus recounted his experience, Paul then cites the faithful saying that Christ came into the world for the very purpose of saving sinners (v. 15a) and moves to the general truth of which his own experience is an example: Since he as πρῶτος of sinners (v. 15b) has been shown mercy (v. 16a), his case serves as an example that Christ is so patient that he will receive sinners when they come to believe in him. Following this statement, Paul breaks into praise in v. 17.

1:12 The entrusting spoken of in v. 11 evokes the thankfulness of v. 12. χάριν ἔχω means "I thank" or "I am grateful to" (BAGD). It is usually followed, as here, by the one to whom one is grateful in the dative. The phrase is found 2x in the PE (here and 2 Tim. 1:3) and 2x with this meaning elsewhere in the NT (Lk. 17:9; Heb. 12:28). The phrase is not found elsewhere in Paul, but he does use χάρις with the meaning of thanks or gratitude (e.g., Rom. 7:25; 1 Cor. 10:30; 15:57; 2 Cor. 2:14; 8:16; 9:15). Since the phrase is used regularly in Greek, found frequently in the papyri, and could even reflect Latin *gratiam habere* as a result of Paul's recent and extended contact with Latin while in prison in Rome, it is probably used here as a virtual synonym for εὐχαριστέω, the form he uses more often.

The one to whom Paul is grateful is he who provided the basis for Paul's being entrusted with the gospel (v. 11), namely, he who "strengthened" Paul. Aorist ἐνδυναμώσαντί is the most strongly supported reading (*TCGNT* suggests that present ἐνδυναμοῦντι is influenced by recollection of Phil. 4:13, but copyists may have thought, apart from Phil. 4:13, that Paul should speak here of a continuous strengthening) and may have been utilized by Paul to express the activity of Christ prior to the entrusting to Paul and to all that follows in the ὅτι clause. ἐνδυναμόω is usually used of religious and moral strengthening, as in all the NT occurrences.

The one who strengthens Paul is Χριστῷ Ἰησοῦ τῷ κυρίῳ ἡμῶν. The fullness of the title may express Paul's continued reflection on his conversion and on the one who strengthened him (cf. the reflection in the accounts of his conversion in Acts 9:1-29; 22:3-16; 26:9-18 and in Gal. 1:11-17). Up to the time of his conversion Paul had denied that Jesus could be either the Christ or the Lord and had blasphemed against Jesus (v. 13; cf. Acts 9:5; 22:8; 26:15: "Who are you, Lord [κύριε]? . . . "I am Jesus, whom you are persecuting"); after his conversion, Paul proclaimed Jesus as Son of God and Christ (ὁ Χριστός, 9:20, 22; note the use of ἐνδυναμόω; cf. 26:23: "that the Christ was to suffer"). Paul identifies Christ who strengthens him as "*our* Lord" because he is aware that this lordship and strengthening is available for all who believe in Christ (cf. vv. 16, 18ff.; 2 Tim. 2:1; Eph. 6:10).

That for which Paul is thankful is stated in the ὅτι clause, which consists of two elements, namely, that Paul was considered faithful and put into Christ's service. The connection between the two seems to be that first Paul was considered faithful (the finite verb ἡγήσατο) and then (without a connecting καί) placed in Christ's service (a simple participle θέμενος following the verb and regarded by Robertson, *Grammar,* 1103, as "certainly circumstantial"). Hence the emphasis of his thankfulness is just as much on his being counted faithful as it is on being placed in service, but in essence is on both together as a whole.

πιστός could be taken as "believer" here, which it means elsewhere in Paul (2 Cor. 6:15; 1 Tim. 4:10; 5:16; 6:3a, b; Tit. 1:6). But that would make the reference to "faith" in v. 14 redundant. The preponderant meaning of πιστός in Paul's letters, including the PE, is "trustworthy" or "faithful," which fits this context. Furthermore, the use of πιστός in connection with the ministry in the sense of "trustworthy" or "reliable" is established in 1 Cor. 4:2; 7:25. According to BAGD, "When Paul explains in 1 Cor. 7:25 that the Lord graciously granted him the privilege of being πιστός, and uses this as the basis for his claim to be heard w[ith] respect, πιστός can hardly mean 'believing' . . . ; the apostle rather feels that in a special sense he has been called and commissioned because of the confidence God has in him (πιστός is almost like a title — 'trusted man, commissioner'; oft[en] in inscr[iptions] . . .)."

How can Paul have demonstrated his faithfulness, when this evaluation seems to have taken place at his conversion? The key would seem to lie in the earlier reference to strengthening; as 1 Cor. 7:25 puts it, Paul was "one who by the mercy of the Lord is trustworthy" (note the correlation of πιστός or διακονίας with ἔλεος in 1 Cor. 7:25; 2 Cor. 4:1; 1 Tim. 1:12, 13, 16). It is not that Paul at the time of his conversion had already proved his faithfulness, but that the Lord was willing to consider him then and there worthy of trust and therefore as one who would be faithful. Paul's gratitude is to the strengthening Christ who transformed him forthwith from the persecutor to the trustworthy servant. The aorist of ἡγέομαι ("think, consider, regard") refers back to the Lord's evaluation of Paul at his conversion before he was placed into that ministry (cf. Acts 9:15, 16; 22:19, 14, 15; 26:18-19).

That the Lord regarded him as faithful is evidenced in the Acts account by Paul's entering into the service in which the Lord placed him, and is expressed here by the words "putting me into service" (θέμενος εἰς διακονίαν). θέμενος (the aorist middle participle of τίθημι) expresses the past action of the Lord in "appointing" Paul, with εἰς διακονίαν indicating that into which or for which he was appointed. με, having already been used with ἡγήσατο, is understood and is not repeated. διακονία is a general word for "service," which Paul uses not only in its general sense but also to designate the ministry of a special office, as here (cf. 2 Tim. 4:5; Rom. 11:13; 1 Cor. 16:15; 2 Cor. 3:8, 9; 4:1; 5:18; 6:3; Col. 4:17; cf. Acts 1:17, 25; 6:4; 20:24; 21:19), as well as for the ministry of all the people of God (cf. Eph. 4:12; 1 Cor. 12:5). Paul may have chosen the general term here to emphasize the marvel that he had been placed in any service at all and so that he might be a more direct example for others (v. 16) and for Timothy (vv. 18-20).

1:13 Paul's gratitude to the Lord is that of one who was "formerly" (τὸ πρότερον, referring to his preconversion condition, as the following nouns make evident) the Lord's chief vicious adversary. τὸ πρότερον is used here as an adverb of time in the concessive sense, "even though" (so Robertson; with the neuter article [see BAGD], not the masculine [a poorly attested variant reading; see *NA*^{26}; see BDF §413.3 on the whole clause). The present participle ὄντα refers to antecedent, rather than simultaneous, time, since it is subservient to the preceding adverb of time (τὸ πρότερον), which refers to an antecedent time (see Robertson, *Grammar*, 1115).

Paul spells out the magnitude of his sin with three terms (βλάσφημον, διώκτην, ὑβριστήν), the appropriateness of which are evident in the Acts accounts of Paul's conversion. βλάσφημος designates "one who is slanderous or uses scurrilous words" (Acts 6:11), or "one who pronounces a defaming judgment" (2 Pet. 2:11). Here, and probably in 2 Tim. 3:2, it has more direct reference to God and the things of God (cf. Acts 6:11: Moses and God), as is usually the case in the LXX and with cognate words (cf. H. Währisch and C. Brown, *NIDNTT* III, 341-45; H. W. Beyer, *TDNT* I, 621-25). The most helpful passage for understanding the word as it is used here is Acts 26:9-11 ("I thought to myself that I had to do many things hostile to the name of Jesus of Nazareth. And this is just what I did . . . I tried to force them to blaspheme"; cf. also 22:19: "I used to imprison and beat those who believed in you").

διώκτης** means "persecutor" (a NT hapax; see in Paul elsewhere [and Acts] the usage of the related words διωγμός, 3x [2x], and διώκω, 18x [9x]). Persecution was the key issue in Jesus' confrontation with Paul, namely, that in Paul's activity against the people of Jesus Paul was, in fact, persecuting Jesus (Acts 9:4, 5; 22:7, 8; 26:14, 15). The cognate verb is the operative word with which Paul describes his activity in Acts: "I persecuted this way to the death, binding and putting both men and women into prison" (Acts 22:4; cf. 26:11). The last part of that description illustrates certain aspects of what Paul means here by ὑβριστής** (Rom. 1:30 and here; cf. ὑβρίζω and ὕβρις), "violent, insolent person" (BAGD, MM), which, Parry says, "emphasizes the element of outrageous disregard of other men's rights" (cf. again Acts 9:1, 2; 22:4, 5, 19, 20; 26:10, 11).

ἀλλὰ ἠλεήθην, "but I was shown mercy," i.e., but God took pity on me. The stark abbreviated simplicity of the statement makes it all the more forceful. ἀλλά indicates a contrast to what precedes and provides the appropriate abrupt turning point (as it often does in Paul and the NT in general). Passive ἠλεήθην (from ἐλεέω, which means essentially "be merciful, show mercy" to someone) means "be shown mercy." The passive voice assumes that the κύριος is the one who has shown mercy (cf. Jeremias). What it means concretely to be shown mercy is developed in all that follows: salvation from sin (v. 15; cf. Tit. 3:1-7, especially v. 5: κατὰ . . . ἔλεος ἔσωσεν ἡμᾶς), union with Christ in the sphere of faith and love (v. 14; cf. the connective δέ and the understood reference to the κύριος now made explicit), and eternal life through faith in him (v. 16), not to mention being counted trustworthy and being put in service (v. 12).

ὅτι ἀγνοῶν ἐποίησα ἐν ἀπιστίᾳ does not give the reason that Paul was shown mercy, as if his ignorance made him worthy and therefore elicited the mercy, nor is it written to indicate that what is described in v. 13a is not sin. This ὅτι clause explains, rather, why these sins were regarded neither as the defiant or high-handed sin mentioned in the OT (Nu. 15:30, 31, where interestingly enough such is described as "blaspheming the Lord," but is so described just because it is done defiantly) nor as the sin against the Holy Spirit described in the NT (Mt. 12:31, 32; Mk. 3:28-30; Lk. 12:10; cf. also Heb. 6:4-6; 10:26; 1 Jn. 5:16). Paul never wants to leave the impression that he is condoning sin, even when grace and mercy prevail (cf. Rom. 6:1ff.). That ignorance was the manner in which he did the things described (ἀγνοῶν being a circumstantial participle of manner: Robertson, *Grammar,* 1127; BDF §417; MHT III, 150) had a negative and a positive aspect. Negatively, Paul was truly ignorant of Jesus' true messianic status. Positively, he really thought he was serving God rightly by seeking to stamp out what he regarded as the false messianic sect of Christians, those of the Way (cf. the astonishment in "Who are you, Lord?" in Acts 9:5; 22:8; 26:15 and the sincerity reflected in each of the three Acts accounts, especially 22:3, 4: "being zealous for God . . . I persecuted this Way"; cf. also Rom. 10:1-3; Acts 13:27). ἐν ἀπιστίᾳ, "in unbelief," describes the condition in which Paul acted and provides the basis for the blindness of his ignorance (cf. 1 Cor. 2:8).

1:14 Postpositive δέ continues the line begun with ἠλεήθην and introduces a statement that speaks of the grace of the Lord in its superabundance, which brought Paul into a new status with Christ and out of the state of ignorance of and opposition to Christ. ὑπερεπλεόνασεν** is a NT hapax (see Morgenthaler, *Statistik,* 160, for Paul's preference for verbs prefixed with ὑπέρ, many of which are also hapaxes in the other Pauline letters [151]; note also that unprefixed πλεονάζω occurs only in Paul and once in 2 Peter) and means "be present in great abundance." In connection with a vessel it is rendered "to run over or overflow" (BAGD; cf. Hermas, *Man.* 5.2.5; MM). Paul is saying that when he was shown mercy, the grace of the Lord was poured out on him in abundance. This grace (χάρις, see 1:1) is from the Lord (τοῦ κυρίου ἡμῶν) and not only forgives and strengthens but brings one into a sphere described as "faith and love that are in Christ Jesus" and keeps one in that sphere.

With κύριος the implied person in view with the passive verb ἠλεήθην is now stated. κύριος is usually used by Paul as a title for Jesus and often to distinguish him from the Father, but also to acknowledge that he is on a par with the Father, to whom the title "God" is applied, so that "God" and "Lord" become their distinctive divine designations (cf., e.g., 1 Cor. 12:4-6: Spirit, Lord, God; 2 Cor. 13:14: Lord Jesus Christ, God, Holy Spirit). In 1 Timothy κύριος is usually in the same manner applied to Christ (1:2 [contrasted with Father], 12; 6:3, 14), but in 6:15 God the Father is most likely in view. In favor of it referring to Christ in 1:14 are the following considerations: (1) The verse beginning this section refers to Christ as "our Lord," and there is reason to think he is still in view, since he dominates the passage as the subject of the two immediately following verses. (2) This is the predominant usage in this letter (see above). (3) Elsewhere Paul refers to Christ as "Lord" in the phrase ἡ χάρις τοῦ κυρίου (ἡμῶν) (Rom. 16:20, 24; 1 Cor. 16:23; 2 Cor. 8:9; 13:13; Gal. 6:18; Phil. 4:23; 1 Thes. 5:28; 2 Thes. 1:12; 3:18; Phm. 25); in salutations that mention χάρις and where the Father is also in view, it is, again, Christ who is called κύριος.

In favor of κύριος referring to God the Father are the following considerations: (1) God the Father pervades the entire passage. The reference to "the gospel of God" and its being entrusted to Paul has sparked this section, and to "God" Paul returns in v. 17 with his doxology, so it would be appropriate to refer to the Father and his grace midway through. (2) God is spoken of in terms of lordship in the doxology in the phrase τῷ βασιλεῖ τῶν αἰώνων and perhaps in the reference to τιμὴ καὶ δόξα. (3) Twice in the PE (Tit. 2:11; 2 Tim. 1:9) χάρις is used of the grace of God the Father, although it must be admitted that once (2 Tim. 1:9) Paul goes on to speak of that grace revealed in Christ Jesus and that in 2 Tim. 2:1 he says of grace that it "is in Christ Jesus." (4) It would appear to be more natural to take κύριος as referring to God the Father here since "Christ Jesus" is mentioned by name later in the verse.

On balance the preference goes to understanding κύριος here as a reference to Christ. Arguments (1) and (2) for taking it as referring to the Father, though true, are not compelling and may be offset by the facts that the permanent work of Christ more fully pervades the passage and that Christ is the operative person in vv. 12, 15, and 16 (in showing patience), so that it may be assumed that he is in view in v. 14 as well. Argument (3) has within it its own weaknesses and shows that κύριος may equally well be associated with Christ. In response to argument (4) it is not inconceivable that Paul would refer to the grace of Jesus and then the faith and love of Jesus with different titles.

Furthermore, κύριος is the title that Acts has Paul using to address Christ during the Damascus road experience (9:5; 22:8; 26:15). Ananias also uses it of Jesus (9:17) when he brings the message of grace and says that Paul will be filled with the Holy Spirit — a concept similar to what the present verse speaks of. It would not be too much to say that Paul has the Damascus road experience in view as he writes.

That which is joined with (μετά) grace in its overflowing is πίστεως καὶ ἀγάπης. Paul is not only shown mercy, he is also by the Lord's grace brought to a new perspective of faith and a new attitude of love in a new relationship with Christ (*τῆς ἐν* Χριστῷ Ἰησοῦ).

Are the πίστεως and ἀγάπης shown by Jesus to Paul or by Paul to Jesus? Is the πίστεως "faith" or is it "faithfulness," and if the latter is it Jesus' or Paul's? πίστις is indeed used once by Paul for God's faithfulness (Rom. 3:3), but even though it has been argued that there are a number of other places in the NT where it refers to the faithfulness of God or Christ (Hebert, "'Faithfulness'"; Torrance, "One Aspect"), this has not been established and in fact has been refuted by a careful and detailed analysis (cf. Murray, *Romans,* I, 363-74).

Several factors point in the direction of πίστις being understood as "faith" and not "faithfulness," and of ἀγάπη being understood as the love that Paul shows because he is in Christ and not the love shown to him by Christ: (1) When πίστις and ἀγάπη are connected in Paul's letters, such as the thanksgiving sections, where Paul expresses thanks for what Christ has done, as here, it is the believer's faith and love in Christ that are in view (1 Cor. 13:13; Eph. 1:15; 1 Thes. 1:3; 3:6; 2 Thes. 1:3). (2) When in such passages and in similar circumstances ἐν appears with one or more of the titles or names of Jesus, the faith and love are those of the believer, which are rooted in Christ, not attributes that Christ himself exhibits to the believer (Eph. 1:5; Col. 1:4; 1 Tim. 3:13; 2 Tim. 3:15: πίστις ἐν; 2 Tim. 1:13: ἐν πίστει καὶ ἀγάπῃ τῇ ἐν Χριστῷ Ἰησοῦ; the one piece of contrary evidence is Rom. 8:28, where God's ἀγάπη is ἐν Χριστῷ Ἰησοῦ). (3) This understanding best fits the flow of the thought (cf. Calvin): Paul had earlier been in a state of unbelief (ἐν ἀπιστίᾳ) characterized by blasphemy, persecution, and insolence and violence (v. 13); God's mercy and grace moved him to the exact opposite, the state found only in Christ, that of faith and love, so that he serves as an example of those who will come to "believe in him" (v. 16). πίστις is placed between ἀπιστίᾳ and πιστεύειν ἐπ' αὐτῷ (v. 16) and therefore probably, like the other two terms, refers to the realm of faith and involves both the initial act (Paul a ὑποτύπωσιν, v. 16), and also the continuous sphere in which Paul now finds himself as a believer in Christ, no longer one ἐν ἀπιστίᾳ. (4) This section is also written as an encouragement for Timothy, concerning whom Paul speaks of "keeping faith" (v. 19), using πίστις with the meaning "faith, belief."

The object to which ἀγάπη (see also 1:5) is directed is not indicated. Since Paul's hatred had been directed against both Christians and the Lord, it may well be that both are in view by implied contrast. But in light of the evidence of Paul's usage elsewhere it probably has love for Christians in view as its primary, if not exclusive, focus. (In the πίστις καὶ ἀγάπη correlation elsewhere πίστις is directed to the Godhead and ἀγάπη to humans: e.g., Eph. 1:5; Col. 1:5; 2 Thes. 1:3; elsewhere in Paul ἀγάπη is directed toward mankind both explicitly, e.g., Rom. 13:8-10, and implicitly, 1 Cor. 13:4ff.; but there are places where the object is, as here, not specified: 1 Tim. 1:5; 2:15; 4:12; 6:11; Tit. 2:2; 2 Tim. 1:7, 13; 2:22; 3:10; 1 Thes. 3:6; 1 Cor. 8:1; Phil. 1:9; finally, ἀγαπάω is used by Paul of the believer's love for God or Christ: Rom. 8:28; 1 Cor. 2:9; 8:3; Eph. 6:29; cf. also 2 Tim. 4:8.)

Whether τῆς ἐν Χριστῷ Ἰησοῦ qualifies both πίστις and ἀγάπη or simply the latter is difficult to answer. That τῆς is singular presents no obstacle, since both items could be considered together as one (cf. 2 Tim. 1:13, where the repetition of the preposition makes it nearly certain that both are included). πίστις (τῆς) ἐν Χριστῷ Ἰησοῦ elsewhere in Paul (see the lists above) would favor the inclusion of πίστις. That the two nouns refer to similar categories and that both are governed by μετά and are joined together only with καί would also imply that that which identified the sphere of the second (ἀγάπη) also identified the sphere of the first (πίστις). Further, there is no reason for Paul to want to leave πίστις out of this construction.

By saying that ἀγάπη and πίστις are ἐν Χριστῷ Ἰησοῦ, Paul indicates that their sources are in Christ because of his being in Christ. Why Paul should say ἐν Χριστῷ Ἰησοῦ after referring to him as κύριος may be explained in terms of his conversion experience: It was when he acknowledged Jesus of Nazareth to be the Christ that he moved from unbelief to belief and from hatred to love.

Vv. 12-14 convey Paul's own experiences. But Paul's experience is not unique. V. 15 gives the general truth of which Paul's experience was a particular example.

1:15 The quotation-commendation formula πιστὸς ὁ λόγος occurs 5x in the PE (1 Tim. 1:15; 3:1; 4:9; Tit. 3:8; 2 Tim. 2:11) and nowhere else in the NT. In each occurrence the statement to which the formula refers has a "saying" quality. This, with the fact that λόγος can be used with reference to sayings (cf., e.g., BAGD, which cites extrabiblical literature and Jn. 4:37 as a NT example; cf. also G. Fries, et al., *NIDNTT* III, 1081-1123; A. Debrunner, et al., *TDNT* IV, 69-141; cf. Mt. 19:11; Rom. 13:9; 1 Cor. 15:54), leads one to regard the phrase as a quotation formula (for a fuller treatment of this formula and the sayings designated in the PE by it see Knight, *Faithful Sayings,* especially 4-22 for the formula). "Christ Jesus came into the world to save sinners" is, therefore, a quoted "saying."

πιστός (on the variant reading ἀνθρώπινος see *TCGNT;* Knight, *Faithful Sayings,* 31f.) serves as a commendation of the λόγος quoted. In Pauline usage πιστός is focused on correlation with God as the one who is faithful (2 Tim. 2:13; 1 Cor. 1:9; 10:13; 2 Cor. 1:18; 1 Thes. 5:24; 2 Thes. 3:3; cf. Heb. 10:23). Paul recognizes that God's faithfulness guarantees the faithfulness of God's message as it is given by God's messenger (see 2 Cor. 1:15-23). So when Paul states that the λόγος is πιστός, he is saying that it is a faithful presentation of God's message (cf. 2 Tim. 2:2).

Coupled with the quotation-commendation formula are the words καὶ πάσης ἀποδοχῆς ἄξιος, which also bear the characteristics of a formula. The likelihood that they constitute a formula is increased by their connnection to the previous formula and by the fact that they occur only here and in 4:9, both times with πιστὸς ὁ λόγος and sayings (cf. *Faithful Sayings,* 22-30). This additional formula expands on the πιστός evaluation by saying that the λόγος is "worthy" of a particular response, namely, "acceptance" (ἀποδοχή,** 1 Tim. 1:15; 4:9) or full personal appropriation and application to one's self. πᾶς states the degree of acceptance of which the saying is worthy, namely, the most complete and wholehearted acceptance (contra the understanding of πᾶς as indicating extent, i.e., "by all," for which cf. Spicq; cf. also *Faithful Sayings,* 25-29). So we may designate this a "personal appropriation formula."

This understanding of the phrase, with an appraisal of the differences between the "faithful sayings" where it is found (1 Tim. 1:15; 4:8) and those where it is not (Tit. 3:8; 2 Tim. 2:11), seems to provide the key to its presence or absence (leaving aside for the moment 1 Tim. 3:1). Where ἄξιος κτλ. is absent, the sayings are expressed in the first person, so that they include in themselves the aspect that this formula demands, namely, personal appropriation. The formula urging full acceptance is, however, present where the sayings are not expressed in the first person and so lack that note of appropriation (this would also be true if one took 1 Tim 4:10c rather than 4:8 as the saying in that context). 1 Tim. 3:1 with its third-person "anyone" (τις) also does not include the formula of personal appropriation. But this saying about the office of the bishop and desire for it cannot be personally appropriated by all, since not all are to seek the office and do not and should not expect to have the gift for it. We can conclude, therefore, that where the note of personal appropriation is not present in a "faithful saying" and would be appropriate, it is provided by the addition of the personal acceptance formula.

Since Paul wants to relate his own experience as a demonstration of the Christian truth, he quotes a saying that states what he had experienced as a general truth. The saying is introduced by ὅτι, used here, as it often is, to introduce direct discourse (ὅτι *recitativum,* virtually serving as our quotation marks; BDF §397.5; 470.1). The saying is Χριστὸς Ἰησοῦς ἦλθεν εἰς τὸν κόσμον ἁμαρτωλοὺς σῶσαι, to which Paul applies his own personal application in the words ὧν πρῶτός εἰμι ἐγώ (for a fuller analysis of the saying, substantiation of particular observations, and citation of linguistic parallels and alternative views see Knight, *Faithful Sayings,* 31-49).

Ἰησοῦς is the name given by God (Mt. 1:21 and Lk. 1:31; 2:21) indicating the bearer's calling. Χριστός indicates his role as the promised Christ (cf. the Father's testimony to his messianic role in the anointing by the Holy Spirit at Jesus' baptism: Mt. 3:16, 17; Mk. 1:10, 11; Lk. 3:21, 22; Jn. 1:25-34; cf. also the notes above on 1:1; Knight, *Faithful Sayings,* 32-36).

Although the concept ἦλθεν εἰς τὸν κόσμον is known by Paul (Rom. 5:12, with εἰσῆλθεν; the prepositional phrase without the verb in 1 Tim. 6:7; these are the only references in Paul), the expression (especially in application to Jesus) is not distinctly Pauline but is particularly Johannine (Jn. 1:9; 3:19; 11:27; 12:46; 16:28; 18:37; elsewhere not of Jesus: 6:14; elsewhere in the NT only Heb. 10:5; with a different form of the verb and a different nuance in 1 Jn. 4:1; 2 Jn. 7). Although it is true, as Dibelius-Conzelmann insist, that "coming into the world" need not demonstrate preexistence in and of itself (cf., e.g., Rom. 5:17; 1 Tim. 6:7; Jn. 6:14), it is equally true that when used of Jesus that is just what it does indicate, as the Johannine passages and their contexts specify, particularly with such clauses as "coming from the Father" and "going to the Father" (cf., e.g., Jn. 16:28; 1:9 in the context of 1:1, 14; 3:19 in the context of 3:16, 17; *Faithful Sayings,* 36-38). Thus when used with reference to Jesus here ἦλθεν εἰς τὸν κόσμον presumably carries the idea of coming from the Father into the world.

κόσμος, as used in the Johannine references to Jesus' coming into the "world," designates the sphere or habitation of humanity, i.e., the place where human beings live and sin and thus where a human needs to be met and humans redeemed (cf. especially Jn. 1:10; 3:17; 12:46, 47; 18:36, 37). Since our passage finds its parallel in those Johannine passages and their contexts (cf. again Jn. 1:9; 3:19; 11:27; 12:46; 16:28; 18:37; *Faithful Sayings,* 38-42), it is best to understand κόσμος here in the same sense. Aorist ἦλθεν specifies that the coming of Christ is that which has already taken place.

The purpose of his coming into the world is specified very simply in two words, ἁμαρτωλούς σῶσαι. ἁμαρτωλός (NT 47x; Mt. 5x; Mk. 6x; Lk. 18x; Jn. 4x; Pl. 8x; PE* here and 1:9 only), "sinner," designates human beings in their need and the state out of which they must be saved. Both Paul and the Synoptic Gospels (especially Luke) utilize the word to describe mankind as disobedient and unrighteous, as alienated from God and therefore lost. It is in this sense that Paul speaks of all having sinned (Rom. 5:19 and especially Romans 3, concluding with 3:23; 6:23; cf. Rengstorf, *TDNT* I, 328; Knight, *Faithful Sayings,* 42-45; cf. especially the usage in Lk. 15:7, 10; 18:13).

The keynote of the saying is the verb σῶσαι, which expresses the reason for Jesus' coming, namely, deliverance for sinners from their sin and from all its consequences. In its usage elsewhere it also denotes deliverance for a new and moral life here and now and for life eternal. Since Paul quotes this saying as a general statement of the gospel truth that he had experienced, it may be assumed that the salvation in view is the same as what he experienced, namely, deliverance from sin to faithfulness and service in the life of faith and love in Christ (vv. 12-14, 15c) and as what he would experience in the future (εἰς ζωὴν αἰώνιον, v. 16; see further *Faithful Sayings,* 45-47).

What is the origin of this saying? The most plausible suggestion is that it is an objectification and restatement of what Jesus said about himself, as it is recorded in the Gospels. The saying reflects phrases and concepts found both in the Synoptics (ἁμαρτωλοὺς σῶσαι, cf. above and note especially the self-testimonies of Jesus in Mt. 9:13; Mk. 2:17; Lk. 5:32; 19:10) and in John's Gospel (ἦλθεν εἰς τὸν κόσμον, see especially Jn. 12:46, 47; 16:28; 18:37 and note that this concept is almost exclusively Johannine). Paul quotes this brief objective statement based on Jesus' self-testimony to show that what he has experienced is what Jesus has come to do for all those who will respond in faith.

To make this correlation explicit, Paul adds the words ὧν πρῶτός εἰμι ἐγώ. Christ came to save sinners; therefore, in saving Paul a specific application took place and an example was provided. The example is even more significant because Paul is πρῶτος of sinners (for a list of possible meanings for this term and responses to each see Hendriksen). Paul does not mean the "first" in a sequence, since he was not the first one saved by Christ. He means, rather, that he (notice emphatic εἰμι ἐγώ) is first in the sense of "foremost" (see BAGD) in the category of sinners. This might seem like an exaggeration because of the apparently good moral life of Paul the Pharisee. This is not the perspective, however, from which Paul is judging his life and its sin, as v. 13 evidences (cf. Gal. 1:13), or the perspective of Christ as he spoke to Paul on the Damascus road of Paul persecuting Christ himself. Paul's use here of πρῶτος is focused on his having led the opposition to Christ and his people, his having sought to destroy God's plan. Paul regards this classification of himself as "foremost of sinners" as still valid (εἰμι, present tense); though he is fully forgiven, regarded as faithful, and put into service, he is still the notorious opponent who is so received. Elsewhere he writes (1 Cor. 15:9, 10): "I am [ἐγὼ . . . εἰμι] the least of the apostles, who am [εἰμί] not fit to be called an apostle, because I persecuted the church of God. But by God's grace I am what I am" (cf. Eph. 3:8).

1:16 Having highlighted his sinfulness, Paul again (see v. 13b) contrasts (ἀλλά) to it the mercy of Christ. διὰ τοῦτο, "for this reason," points forward to the ἵνα clause, which gives the specific purpose for which Christ showed mercy (on ἠλεήθην see v. 13) to Paul, thus showing the significance for others of Paul's salvation as πρῶτος of sinners. Christ's purpose was that Paul be an example of the application of Christ's redemption (for ἐν ἐμοί used here in the exemplary sense see H. C. G. Moule, 77). ἐνδείκνυμι here has its usual meaning of "show" or "demonstrate" (with God, or Christ [as here], the subject in Eph. 2:7; Rom. 9:17, 22).

Paul specifies that it is Christ who demonstrates his patience in being merciful to Paul. The designation Χριστὸς Ἰησοῦς continues the emphasis on "Christ Jesus" begun at v. 12, reflects the usage in the saying in v. 15, and also reflects Paul's conversion experience, where it is "Christ Jesus" who acts and speaks to Paul (cf. Acts 9:5, 6, 17; 22:8, 10; 26:15-18). It is difficult to make a decision between the readings Χριστὸς Ἰησοῦς and Ἰησοῦς Χριστός. If the latter is correct, and this is not certain, then the change may have been made by Paul, if not for stylistic reasons, then to emphasize that it was the man Ἰησοῦς, who is indeed the Christ, who met him on the Damascus road and demonstrated his patience in him. If this is the case, then the other sequence (which had been becoming customary for Paul) is momentarily reversed to emphasize this truth (cf. Lock).

τὴν ἅπασαν μακροθυμίαν is that which Jesus demonstrates in Paul. μακροθυμία has the meaning here of "forbearance" or "patience" toward others and is used of God (Rom. 2:4; 9:22; 1 Pet. 3:20; cf. for OT background Ex. 34:6; Nu. 14:18; Pss. 86:15; 103:8; Joel 2:13; Jon. 4:2) and of Christ (here and 2 Pet. 3:15). The patience of both God and Christ, in both Paul and Peter, has in view our sin and God's delay of judgment (cf. Rom. 9:22; 1 Pet. 3:20) and is used here of the occasion and opportunity for repentance and salvation (cf. Rom. 2:4: "kindness" leading to "repentance"; 2 Pet. 3:15: "salvation," cf. 3:9: "is patient [μακροθυμεῖ] toward you, not wishing for any to perish but for all to come to repentance"; Peter may have had 1 Tim. 1:16 in mind in 2 Pet. 3:15, where he refers to Paul writing of the Lord's patience toward them). So overwhelmed is Paul by the absoluteness of Christ's patience in the face of his sin that he adds ἅπας (used in place of πᾶς after consonants in Attic Greek and usually in the NT; cf. BAGD; BDF §275; and especially Robertson, *Grammar,* 771). BDF appropriately render the phrase, "The utmost . . . patience of which he is capable" (§275.7).

The ἵνα clause includes the prep. phrase πρὸς ὑποτύπωσιν as the culmination of its statement of God's purpose in showing such patience and, thereby, the significance of such a sinner being shown such patience. ὑποτύπωσις** (here and 2 Tim. 1:13 in the Greek Bible; cf. τύπος, particularly two passages where Paul is an "example": Phil. 3:17; 1 Thes. 1:7) means in this context "example": in Paul Christ has "sketched out" (this is the imagery of the term, though the phrase might possibly be translated "to give a word-picture"; cf. Simpson) what he will do for sinners who repent and believe.

τῶν μελλόντων is followed by a present infinitive as a periphrasis for the future tense. πιστεύειν means, as BAGD indicate fully (s.v. 2): "*believe (in), trust* of relig[ious] belief in a special sense, as faith in the Divinity that lays special emphasis on trust in his power and nearness to help, in addition to being convinced that he exists and that his revelations or disclosures are true." For Paul faith involves a recognition of the claims of Christ as to his person and work as well as a personal trust in him (cf. 3:16; 2 Tim. 1:12; Tit. 3:8; Rom. 1:16; 3:22, 4:11; 10:4, 9, 10, 11, 14; Gal. 2:16). Here αὐτῷ, which has Χριστὸς Ἰησοῦς as its antecedent, indicates that Christ is the object of faith.

πιστεύειν ἐπ' αὐτῷ is found in the NT elsewhere (aside from variant readings) only in Rom. 9:33; 10:11; 1 Pet. 2:6, which are quotations from Is. 28:16 LXX (ὁ πιστεύων ἐπ' αὐτῷ [in the LXX B omits ἐπ' αὐτῷ, but it is present in ℵ A Q]), which, J. Jeremias argues (*TDNT* IV, 272), has also influenced 1 Tim. 1:16. This is certainly possible because of the evident influence that Isa. 28:16 has had on Paul.

εἰς ζωὴν αἰώνιον indicates the final result of such faith in Christ (for εἰς used in this way see BAGD and cf. especially Rom. 10:10). αἰώνιος and ζωή are used together by Paul 9x or 10x (Rom. 2:7; 5:21; 6:22, 23; Gal. 6:8; 1 Tim. 1:16; 6:12, possibly v. 19; Tit. 1:2; 3:7). BAGD delineate one of the most significant aspects of the use of ζωή in the NT when they say that it is used "of the supernatural life belonging to God and Christ, which the believers will receive in the future, but which they also enjoy here and now" to which they later add as a more specific category "life in the blessed period of final consummation." This is its significance in Paul's usage (cf., e.g., 2 Tim. 1:9-10). αἰώνιον in this combination means "eternal" (BAGD) because it qualifies the life given by and lived with God; any other duration of time, although perhaps arguable elsewhere (cf. J. Guhrt, *NIDNTT* III, 827f.), is inappropriate here. In Paul, as in the NT as a whole (cf., e.g., Mt. 25:31-46), the focus of the concept αἰών/αἰώνιος is God himself (cf. 1 Tim. 1:17; Rom. 6:23; 16:26; 2 Tim. 1:8-10). For the literature on this subject see especially the bibliographies on the two words in BAGD, *NIDNTT,* and *TDNT.*

1:17 Paul ends on this note of having life eternal with God as a result of the work of Christ, whom God sent forth to bring this salvation (v. 15) to such undeserving sinners, then bursts into praise to God in a doxology (similarly, e.g., Rom. 1:25; 9:5; 11:36; Gal. 1:5; Eph. 3:21; Phil. 4:20; 1 Tim. 6:17). The doxologies in the NT usually consist, as does this one, of three or four component parts: the person designated and praised (usually in the dative), the statement of praise itself (usually with δόξα), a conclusion indicating the eternal duration of the praise (usually some variant of εἰς τοὺς αἰῶνας), and (in most cases) an ἀμήν (cf. Deichgräber, *Gotteshymnus,* 25).

δέ joins the doxology to what precedes and may be understood here as "now" (cf. BAGD; Dana-Mantey, *Grammar,* 244; *NASB; NIV*). The doxology designates God as king (βασιλεῖ τῶν αἰνώνων), continues with two attributes of his being (ἀφθάρτῳ, ἀοράτῳ) and with the statement that he is the μόνῳ θεῷ, and concludes with the honor and glory to be ascribed to him forever. Although the idea of kingship in reference to God finds its roots in the OT and pervades the NT, as evidenced by the phrase "kingdom of God," the word "king" (βασιλεύς) itself is not frequently used of God. Since βασιλεύς with αἰῶνος is found elsewhere in the Greek Bible only in Tobit 13:6, 10 and as a variant reading in Rev. 15:3 (see also Sirach 36:17) and since use of this concept is seen in Jewish writings (see Str-B III, 643; Dibelius-Conzelmann; Lock; Spicq [references to Josephus are in Dibelius-Conzelmann and Lock]), it is often proposed that the latter best explains its origins and inclusion here. As plausible as this is, it is equally plausible that Paul was directly influenced by the general teaching of the OT that God is king (cf., e.g., Is. 6:5; Je. 10:10: "everlasting king"; Pss. 10:16: "king forever and ever"; 74:12), or by the kingdom/king teaching of Jesus (cf., e.g., Mt. 5:35; 22:1-14).

ὁ βασιλεὺς τῶν αἰώνων can mean either "eternal king" or "king of the ages." Is the apostle saying, using a Hebraistic construction (a genitive modeled on a Hebrew construct state, *meleḵ ʿôlām;* cf. Str-B III, 320, 643; H. Sasse, *TDNT* I, 201), that God is an everlasting king *(NASB, NIV),* or is he saying that God is the King of all the ages of time *(RSV, NEB)?* If Paul is primarily influenced by current Jewish use of the terminology, which differs somewhat from the OT (cf. Sasse, *TDNT* I, 201, 204) and if he sees God as exercising his rule as king both now and into eternity, then "king of the ages" is his meaning. If he is primarily influenced by the OT use of the Hebrew construct state with the same use of a plural as here (cf. Je. 10:10), if a parallel doxology is of any significance (Rom. 16:26), and if the significance of the previous occurrence of αἰώνιον (v. 16) and the thrust of the conclusion of v. 17 itself (εἰς τοὺς αἰῶνας τῶν αἰώνων) are indicators of the meaning, then there seems to be a slight edge for the meaning "eternal king" (so Str-B and Sasse). In either case, the general meaning is that as king God rules in past, present, and future.

ἄφθαρτος describes God as one who is "not perishable," i.e., not subject to destruction, and therefore in the most absolute sense of the words "imperishable, incorruptible, and immortal" (cf. Rom. 1:23; cf. also 1 Tim. 6:16, which states that this characteristic is intrinsic to God). ἀόρατος expresses God's "unseenness" or, as the translations render it, that he is "invisible." The doxology in 1 Tim. 6:16 depicts this attribute in OT terms: "who . . . dwells in unapproachable light; whom no one has seen or can see" (ἰδεῖν). Since Paul knows and uses both of the previous concepts elsewhere and also expresses the latter in 6:16 in OT terms, we need not think that he has simply taken over concepts that are common in Greek philosophical descriptions of God.

The phrase μόνος θεός** is found in the NT without the article also in Jude 25 and with the article in Jn. 5:44 (also in Is. 37:20; Ps. 85[86]:10; 2 Ki.[4 Ki.] 19:15, 19; with ἀληθινός in Jn. 17:3; μόνος σοφὸς θεός in Rom. 16:27; ὁ μακάριος καὶ μόνος δυνάστης in 1 Tim. 6:15; ὁ μόνος ἔχων κτλ. in 6:16; cf. Rev. 15:4; BAGD). "The only God" reflects the monotheism of both Testaments (e.g., Dt. 6:4; Rom. 3:29; 1 Tim. 2:1-6; 1 Cor. 8:4, 5) and indicates to whom the doxology is offered (cf. Delling, "ΜΟΝΟΣ ΘΕΟΣ"). The addition of σοφός, which is not in the oldest manuscripts, in the Textus Receptus probably reflects the influence of Rom. 16:27 (see *TCGNT*).

τιμή (here and 1 Tim. 6:16 in Pauline doxologies) refers basically to the "honor" and "respect" that one is worth or has earned, which someone renders and thus the recipient enjoys and possesses. When used of God, as here, it designates that which rightly belongs to God, which those offering the doxology should recognize about him, so that they should seek to ascribe such honor to him (see J. Schneider, *TDNT* VIII, 169f., especially 177f.; cf. the use of the cognate verb τιμάω, especially in the commandment to "honor your parents," i.e., give them the respect due to them because of their parental status).

δόξα reflects the OT Hebrew *kāḇôḏ* (which it renders in the LXX), which indicates the luminous manifestation of God's person, his glorious revelation of himself (S. Aalen, *NIDNTT* II, 45). Used in a doxology it signifies desire either that God's radiance continue to be seen in its splendor and glory or that appropriate praise be given in response to it (see also BAGD; cf. use of the verb δοξάζω in this sense, e.g., Rom. 15:6, 9ff.; 2 Cor. 9:12-14); "The NT δόξαν διδόναι like the ancient phrase . . . , does not imply the adding of something not already present, it is rather predication in the sense of active acknowledgement (Ac[ts] 12:23; R[om]. 4:20; Rev. 16:9) or in doxologies as the extolling of what is (Lk. 2:14; 19:38; R[om]. 11:36; 16:27; Eph. 3:21; Phil. 4:20; 1 T[i]m. 1:17; Rev. 4:9; 7:12, etc.)" (G. Kittel, *TDNT* II, 248). Which verb form is to be understood, optative or imperative "be" (εἴη or ἔστω) or indicative "is" (ἐστιν)? The evidence of 1 Pet. 4:11 (ᾧ ἐστιν ἡ δόξα), which has ἐστιν between the dative and δόξα (the variant reading in A omits ἐστιν), points in the direction of ἐστιν (so BDF §128.5; G. Kittel, *TDNT* II, 248; cf. BAGD s.v. δόξα for further representatives of both views; for a full treatment of the question cf. Deichgräber, *Gotteshymnus,* 30-32).

εἰς τοὺς αἰῶνας τῶν αἰώνων** is used in the NT outside Revelation only in doxologies and frequently so in Revelation (Rom. 16:27 [variant reading]; Gal. 1:5; Phil. 4:20; 1 Tim. 1:17; 2 Tim. 4:18; Heb. 13:21; 1 Pet. 4:11; 5:11; Rev. 1:6 [variant reading], 18; 4:9, 10; 5:13; 7:12; 10:6; 11:15, 18; 14:11; 15:7; 19:3; 20:10; 22:5). That αἰών is plural and that it is repeated brings out more fully "the concept of eternity," i.e., the plural presupposes "a plurality of αἰῶνες . . . whose infinite series," here emphasized by the twofold use of the term, "constitutes eternity" (H. Sasse, *TDNT* I, 199).

ἀμήν concludes this doxology as it does most NT doxologies (cf. Rom. 1:25; 9:5; 11:36; 16:27; Gal. 1:5; Eph. 3:21; Phil. 4:20; 1 Tim. 1:17; 6:16; 2 Tim. 4:18; Heb. 13:21; 1 Pet. 4:11; 5:11; Jude 25). It expresses the writer's stated confirmation ("so let it be," "truly," or simply "amen"; cf. BAGD) of what he has expressed in the doxology (cf. Rev. 5:14), and most likely also seeks to invoke that response from the readers (cf. 1 Cor. 14:16; 2 Cor. 1:20; H. Schlier, *TDNT* I, 337; H. Bietenhard, *NIDNTT* I, 99).

The content of this doxology at first appears unusual in that, though it comes after a section in which stress has been laid on the mercy, grace, and patience shown in Christ Jesus, the doxology speaks of God in transcendent terms rather than in these same immanent terms. But perhaps the explanation is to be found in just that contrast. When Paul considers what the βασιλεὺς τῶν αἰώνων grants to the sinner, he thinks of how wonderful it is that the God who is transcendent (ἄφθαρτος, ἀόρατος), the only God (μόνος θεός), should come into the world to save sinners in Christ and in this marvelous act of condescension display his eternal glory (δόξα).

CHARGE TO TIMOTHY REITERATED WITH THE NEGATIVE EXAMPLE OF HYMENAEUS AND ALEXANDER: 1:18-20

Vv. 18-20 pick up the threads of this chapter and draw its main perspectives to a conclusion. Paul returns to the addressee of the letter (τέκνον Τιμόθεε, v. 18; cf. v. 2) and reiterates the task already referred to ("this charge," cf. vv. 3-7). He uses in v. 18 the concepts of Christ's entrusting and enabling, which he has just used with reference to himself (vv. 11, 12): "I entrust" (παρατίθεμαί σοι, v. 18) is to be understood in the light of Timothy's call and enabling (κατὰ τὰς προαγούσας ἐπὶ σὲ προφητείας). He appeals to Timothy to engage in a spiritual warfare (στρατεύῃ . . . τὴν καλὴν στρατείαν) adequately prepared for the task by faith and a good conscience (ἔχων πίστιν καὶ ἀγαθὴν συνείδησιν), which Paul has already shown is provided in Christ (v. 14). Knowing the gospel's power, which is the foundation for the charge (vv. 5, 18), and having been reminded of its reality in Paul's life as an example of its power for others (vv. 12-16), Timothy can be encouraged to wage such warfare (v. 18) even if there are opponents (vv. 19-20).

1:18 It is unlikely that "this charge" refers to the following ἵνα clause, "that you fight the good fight," since ἵνα indicates that the clause gives the result or purpose of the charge rather than its content. ταύτην refers, instead, to the charge given in vv. 3-5, though one may acknowledge that "fight the good fight" would be an apt summary of what is involved in carrying out such a charge, specifically that aspect of it which involves correction of false teachers and their false teaching. But the charge need not be restricted to correction, since in that earlier context Paul gave a wider and more positive perspective of the παραγγελία (v. 5), and also because now Paul appeals to "prophecies previously made concerning" Timothy, which more likely refer to Timothy's calling and ministry as a whole and not to this particular new development. Finally, there is the consideration that this charge to Timothy sets the stage for various appeals throughout the letter (e.g., 2:1), which would more readily follow from this statement if it were a general charge to Timothy.

παρατίθεμαι in this context has the meaning "entrust something to someone" (BAGD), which often has the double-sided nuance of both safekeeping and transmission to others (see 2 Tim. 2:2; cf. Lk. 12:48; 23:46). One may possibly say, therefore, that Paul is not only entrusting a παραγγελία to Timothy but also that he is entrusting to him the same παραγγελία that Paul himself has been entrusted with (cf. C. Maurer, *TDNT* VIII, 163). The designation τέκνον Τιμόθεε is one not simply of affection but rather one that a spiritual father uses with his spiritual son and disciple (cf. v. 2) and that conveys for Timothy his role and responsibility under Paul's apostolic authority.

Paul's charge to Timothy is κατὰ τὰς προαγούσας ἐπὶ σὲ προφητείας, i.e., "in accordance with" God's supernatural declaration communicated by the prophecies. προφητεία** (NT 19x: Mt. 13:14; Rom. 12:6; 1 Cor. 12:10; 13:2, 8; 14:6, 22; 1 Thes. 5:20; 1 Tim. 1:18; 4:14; 2 Pet. 1:20, 21; Rev. 1:3; 11:6; 19:10; 22:7, 10, 18, 19) is used uniformly in the NT of revelations (supernatural communications) from God (cf. also the occurrences of προφητεύω and προφήτης). The phenomenon is best explained by Acts 13:1-4, where we read that "the Holy Spirit said" that he was calling Barnabas and Saul for a work, and that in the context of reference to prophets. Plural προφητείας in 1 Tim. 1:18 seems to indicate that there was more than one prophecy. These "prophecies" are further described as προαγούσας ἐπὶ σέ. προάγω acquires its sense here from its use with ἐπὶ σέ: The prophecies "pointed forward" (so Ridderbos, contra BAGD; cf. also K. L. Schmidt, *TDNT* I, 130) to (ἐπί, BAGD) Timothy. As in Acts 13:2, a specific person is named in the prophecy. Paul's charge is in accordance with what prophecies have already said concerning Timothy.

What ministry did these prophecies indicate? The two most likely possibilities are a call to the ministry in general, or a call to a special service, e.g., to accompany Paul and to serve with him. Although either view is a possibility, in the light of other passages (particularly 1 Tim. 4:14; 2 Tim. 1:6) and of Timothy's situation, in which he is no longer with Paul and is removed from the specific place where the prophecies took place (cf. Acts 16:1-3), a general call to the ministry is probably in view here.

The ἵνα clause indicates what the charge entails. Military images are used elsewhere by Paul (cf., e.g., 1 Thes. 5:8; Eph. 6:11-18) and were widely known and used in the world of Paul's day (cf. Dibelius-Conzelmann, Lock). These factors make it virtually impossible to establish the specific origin of this statement (contra Dibelius-Conzelmann). In the NT military images are usually associated, as here, with service for Christ and the gospel (1 Tim. 6:12; 2 Tim. 2:3ff.; 4:7; 1 Cor. 9:7; 2 Cor. 10:3ff.; Phil. 2:25). By adding καλός to στρατεία (cf. 6:12, 13; 2 Tim. 1:14; 2:3; 4:7) Paul makes clear that the "fight" is a good and noble task and in accord with the gospel. The context depicts the fight in terms of a warfare against opponents such as Satan (v. 20) and, more concretely, those who abandon a good conscience and faith, who blaspheme (vv. 19 and 20), and who teach heterodoxy (vv.

4ff.). In his use of soldier imagery in 2 Tim. 2:3, 4 Paul elaborates, in effect, on what is involved in such a fight, namely, willingness to suffer hardship and to be completely faithful to one's commander. Paul again places a significant emphasis on these prophecies by inserting a reference to them in the midst of his words to Timothy, namely, "that by them (ἐν αὐταῖς) you may fight the good fight." Paul thus indicates that by remembering these prophecies Timothy will be aided in the fight (cf. 2 Tim. 1:6, 7).

1:19 To these objective and external calls from God and his apostle, Paul adds the personal activity of "holding" or "keeping" faith and a good conscience (ἔχων, a circumstantial participle indicating how the "fight" is to be carried out). Here it seems that faith as belief, the activity of trusting in God and his revelation, is in view, rather than as the faith, the body of truth, though elsewhere Paul relates these two aspects to one another: Faith is directed to a person of the Godhead on the basis of the teaching one has received about that person (cf. Rom. 10:14; 1 Cor. 15:1-4; 2 Tim. 2:18). Faith as believing has been the dominant theme of this chapter and is the setting for the appeal Paul now makes (see vv. 2, 4, 5, 14; cf. πιστεύειν in v. 16). Its correlation here with ἀγαθὴν συνείδησιν, one's self-conscious moral evaluation, would also seem to demand that πίστιν is also related to one's activity, i.e., faith. Furthermore, the phrase ἔχων πίστιν is used elsewhere with this meaning (Mt. 17:20; 21:21; Acts 14:9; Rom. 14:22; 1 Cor. 13:2; cf. 1 Tim. 3:9; cf. also 1 Cor. 15:2, where λόγῳ . . . κατέχετε is explained by and virtually equated with ἐπιστεύσατε).

To fight a good fight one must also have a "good conscience" (καὶ ἀγαθὴν συνείδησιν, see the notes at 1:5; cf. 3:9 for the correlation with πίστις; for the outworking of these two concepts and especially the latter see 4:6-16). A "good conscience" is a state in which one's moral self-evaluation accurately registers that one has been obedient to God.

The relative pronoun, ἥν, must have ἀγαθὴν συνείδησιν, and only it, as its antecedent: It is rejection of "good conscience," not rejection of faith, that causes shipwreck regarding faith. τινες is used here in the indefinite sense of "certain" or "some" to refer to those who are in the wrong (cf. vv. 3, 6). ἀπωθέω, which generally means "push aside," is used here figuratively in the sense of "reject" or "repudiate." To reject or repudiate a good conscience is to be willfully and self-consciously disobedient to God's requirements because a good conscience bespeaks a self-conscious obedience. The only concrete data we have about the actions involved are the reference to blasphemy in v. 20 and the description elsewhere of Hymenaeus as ungodly (2 Tim. 2:16) and as claiming that the resurrection has already occurred (v. 18), with possible oblique references to wickedness (v. 19), youthful lusts (v. 22), and a need for repentance (v. 25) on his part. Whatever disobedience is in view, Paul asserts that this activity led to and culminated in shipwreck in regard to (περί) τὴν πίστιν.

One could argue that the definite article (τήν) and the statement in 2 Timothy about Hymenaeus's straying from the truth, particularly with regard to the resurrection (2:17, 18), indicates that τὴν πίστιν is here that which is to be believed, not the belief. This is true enough (cf. Paul's evaluation of the false teachers as heterodox, 1:3). But it would still seem that here too Paul has the faith that believes in mind as he has all through this passage (vv. 2, 4, 5, 14, 19a). This would correlate with the personal and subjective element of rejecting a good conscience, as well as with the personal figure about the disaster of those who do so, namely, shipwreck "concerning [περί] faith" (not "shipwrecked the faith"). The definite article with πίστιν is most likely used here as the equivalent of a possessive pronoun ("their faith"). ναυαγέω, "to suffer shipwreck" (from ναῦς, ship, ἄγνυμι, to break: "to break a ship to pieces"; literal in 2 Cor. 11:25; figurative here), indicates in graphic terms the destruction wrought and provides a graphic negative lesson for Timothy and the listening church (cf. 6:20, 21; 2 Tim. 3:8).

1:20 Paul makes the lesson even more specific by naming Hymenaeus and Alexander as well-known examples. ὧν, "of whom," perhaps better, "among whom" (*NASV, RSV* [*NEB:* "among them"]), indicates that these individuals are some, but not all, of this category. The name Ὑμέναιος** appears in the NT only here and in 2 Tim. 2:17, and it is most likely that these two passages refer to the same individual. The latter passage indicates that Hymenaeus's error consisted particularly in "saying that the resurrection has already taken place." From 2 Tim. 2:18 (cf. 1 Tim. 1:3ff.) it would appear that not only Hymenaeus but also Alexander had been leaders in the Christian Church (cf. Gealy), but had come to be regarded by Paul as false teachers.

The name Ἀλέξανδρος occurs 5x in the NT: (1) Mk. 15:21, a son of Simon of Cyrene, who bore Christ's cross and whose sons are mentioned probably because they are known to the Christian community, perhaps as fellow Christians; (2) Acts 4:6, a Jew of the high-priestly family; (3) Acts 19:33, a would-be Jewish spokesman in Ephesus at the time of the riot; (4) here; and (5) 2 Tim. 4:14, 15, a coppersmith, presumably in Ephesus, who did Paul "much harm," and whom Timothy is warned to "be on guard against" because "he vigorously opposed our teaching." Alexander was a favorite name among Jews as well as Gentiles (BAGD). It is almost certain that (1) and (2) are not the same since a member of the high-priestly family would almost certainly not be forcefully drafted to carry a cross. It is unlikely but not impossible that (1) or (2) is the same as (3). (3), (4), and (5) are all associated with Ephesus. If (3) later claimed to have been converted to Christianity, he might be the same as (4). If he were a coppersmith, which might provide further reason that the Jews wanted him to speak and distinguish them from Paul and the Christians, he might be identified with (5). If both of these possibilities were true, then (3), (4), and (5) would be the same man. But we cannot be sure of this. The least that can be said is that it seems likely, because of the description of both (4) and (5) as opponents of Paul and his message and because of the extreme measures with which both cases are treated, that (4) and (5) are the same individual. If that be so, we have further insight into Alexander, namely, that "he *vigorously* opposed" (2 Tim. 4:15) Paul's teaching.

βλασφημεῖν is best rendered "to blaspheme." The dimensions of this word are seen in 6:1 where both God's name and Christian teaching are in view (cf. Tit. 2:5; Acts 13:8, 10), as well as 1:13, where Paul describes his own actions as being that of a "blasphemer." Hymenaeus and Alexander's rejection of a good conscience and their making shipwreck of their faith are why Paul speaks of them both as blaspheming. If we integrate with these actions the information that we are given about these men in 2 Timothy, namely, opposition to Paul's teaching (Alexander, 2 Tim. 4:15-16) and a seriously erroneous view of the resurrection (Hymenaeus, 2:17-18), we receive further confirmation for Paul's designating their views as blasphemy (cf., e.g., Gal. 1:6-12; Rom. 16:17-19; 2 Thes. 3:14; 1 Thes. 2:6, 13; 2 Tim. 2:24-26).

Paul has already "delivered over" (aorist παρέδωκα of παραδίδωμι) these two men (οὕς) to Satan "so that they might be taught not to blaspheme." παραδίδωμι is used by Paul in this sense especially when he speaks of God delivering people over to their sin (Rom. 1:24, 26, 28), i.e., of handing them over to that realm which they have already chosen (cf. Eph. 4:19: "have given themselves over to sensuality"). The closest parallel to the usage in 1 Tim. 1:20 is 1 Cor. 5:5: Delivering over to Satan is an act of discipline for unrepentant sin and involves putting the person out of the church, the fellowship of God's people, into the realm controlled by Satan (1 Cor. 5:2, 7, 11, 13). The apostolic determination to deliver such a person to Satan was accomplished by the church's act of discipline (cf. 1 Cor. 5:3-5), as was likely the case here also. Paul, like Jesus (e.g., Jn. 8:44) and the other NT writers, distinguishes "the domain of darkness" and "the kingdom of his [God's] beloved Son" (Col. 1:13; cf. 1 Jn. 5:19). Thus "delivering over to Satan" is inextricably involved in putting a person out of the church fellowship (cf. Mt. 18:17). Σατανᾶς (or indeclinable Σατάν), literally "the adversary" (Hebrew *śāṭān,* Aramaic *sāṭānā'*), is used in the NT specifically of "the enemy of God and of all those who belong to God" (BAGD; cf. H. Bietenhard, *NIDNTT* III, 468).

The ἵνα clause indicates the purpose in Hymenaeus and Alexander being delivered over to Satan, namely, that they might be taught not to blaspheme (cf. 1 Cor. 5:5). That God can use Satan and his works to his own end and for the good of his people is seen in Paul's description of his "thorn in the flesh," "a messenger of Satan to buffet me," which he acknowledges has an educative and positive value for him — "to keep me from exalting myself" (2 Cor. 12:7) and to enable him to appreciate the continuous need for and provision of God's grace (vv. 7-10). The whole concept of God using Satan's temptations for the good of his own begins in the NT with Jesus' temptation and continues with Paul (e.g., 1 Cor. 10:13), Peter (e.g., 1 Pet. 1:6, 7), and James (e.g., Jas. 1:12; for an OT example cf. Job 2:6).

How does Paul envision that a person is instructed (παιδευθῶσιν) "not to blaspheme" by being delivered over to Satan? Apparently this happens when the person realizes that such false belief and activity is so displeasing to God (cf. 1 Cor. 11:32) that it separates him from God, as is made evident by being separated from God's people and by being delivered unto Satan (cf. again 1 Corinthians 5). Elsewhere Paul says that breaking association with a person is done "so that he may be put to shame" (2 Thes. 3:14), i.e., that he may be ashamed of the evil he has done when he realizes that the people of God clearly see it as such (cf. v. 15: "admonish him"; see 2 Tim. 2:25; cf. 2 Cor. 2:1-11; 7:6-13 for the reconciliation and reception back into the Christian fellowship that Paul urges for one who has learned from his discipline and is repentant).

PRAYER FOR ALL; CONDUCT OF WOMEN: 2:1-15

Paul urges the church to pray for all people (2:1-8) and urges women to conduct themselves in accordance with their profession of godliness (vv. 9-15). His focus shifts from false teachers (which he returns to in 4:1-5; 6:3-5, 20, 21) to the church and its duties, "how one ought to conduct oneself in God's household" (3:15, where Paul has in mind at least chapters 2 and 3, and probably the rest of the book as well).

PRAYER FOR ALL URGED AND GROUNDED IN THE EXISTENCE OF ONE GOD AND ONE MEDIATOR: 2:1-8

The argument of this section is tightly knit and provides the basis for Paul's appeal. He urges prayers for all kinds of individuals (ὑπὲρ πάντων ἀνθρώπων, v. 1), specifically those in authority (v. 2a), with a view to civil peace (v. 2b), in which godly living may flourish (v. 2c). The grounds for such prayer is that it is good and acceptable to God (v. 3), and particularly so as we contemplate him as the Savior who desires all sorts of people to be saved (v. 4). That God would have all sorts of people be saved is a necessary corollary of the truth of monotheism and of the provision of only one mediator, the man Christ Jesus (v. 5), and of the extent of the provision of the mediator's ransom, which is for all sorts of people (v. 6). Paul's own career in proclaiming this gospel to Gentiles (not just to Jews) bears out that the "all" (πάντες, vv. 1, 4, 6) encompasses all sorts of people (v. 7). Since all these things are true, people in every place should pray with a godliness in accord with such a gospel (v. 8).

2:1 Paul begins with παρακαλέω (see 1:3) and uses it with the sensitivity of which he speaks in 5:1b. Using the word οὖν, "then," in the sense of "consequent command or exhortation" (MGM, 1104), he exhorts prayer (for a thoughtful treatment of οὖν, see, in addition to BAGD, Dana-Mantey, *Grammar,* 254-57).

"First of all" (πρῶτον) may mean either first in sequence or first in importance. The predominant usage of Paul elsewhere is that of sequence or time, although there are possible exceptions (e.g., Rom. 3:2; perhaps 1:8 [similar to our text]; according to BAGD also Rom. 1:16; 2:9f.; 2 Cor. 8:5, and our text). In the light of Paul's predominant usage, we should probably understand the word in a sequential sense here, but with the qualification that what is placed first in sequence may be so placed because it is also considered first in importance. This perspective is strengthened by the qualification of πρῶτον by the inclusive genitive plural παντῶν (the only occurrence of this combination in the NT and the LXX) so that what is "first" is "first of all" the matters about which he will exhort his readers in the body of the letter. In this particular situation and perhaps in any situation this is the first item of concern, though Paul's other letters do not begin their hortatory sections with exhortation to prayer. But Paul does offer prayer and thanksgiving as one of the first and most important items at the beginnings of his letters (see O'Brien, *Introductory Thanksgivings;* πρῶτον introduces thanksgiving in Rom. 1:8ff., but only there does it do so).

That which Paul urges is expressed by ποιεῖσθαι followed by four words for prayer in the accusative plural and then a prepositional phrase indicating on whose behalf prayers are to be made. The four words for prayer may be synonyms, repeated to give emphasis to the request, or, more likely, they may represent distinguishable nuances that Paul wanted to specify (the last term is certainly different from the others). All but one (ἐντεύξεις) occur elsewhere in Paul and the NT with some frequency and often in lists, as here (e.g., Phil. 4:6, where δέησις, προσευχή, and εὐχαριστία are also found; δέησις and προσευχή together in Eph. 6:18 and 1 Tim. 5:5 and in the LXX, e.g., Pss. 6:19; 17:1; 39:12; the classic treatment of these terms in relation to each other is Trench, *Synonyms* §li; for a more recent study with bibliography, see H. Schönweiss, C. Brown, and G. T. D. Angel, *NIDNTT* II, 855-85).

δέησις (in the NT only in reference to God) is the more specific word of the first two and indicates an "entreaty" (BAGD) for a particular benefit (Trench) or need (Ridderbos and Spicq, the latter with reference to the related verb δέομαι; cf. also H. Greeven, *TDNT* II, 40f.).

προσευχή is the more general word for prayer (cf. Greeven, *TDNT* II, 802: "with no narrower indication of its content"), although it can also be more focused when additional terms are added to it. It is most often found in contexts of petition, as here (cf. again O'Brien, *Introductory Thanksgivings,* 29f. n. 50), and may (cf. εὔχομαι, "I wish," "I pray") give emphasis to the desire to come to God, and in our context, to bring those for whom one is praying before God for his general blessing and care, whereas δεήσις would seem to focus on asking for some special need in that one's life.

ἔντευξις** (here and 4:5) means here "petition" or more appropriately "appeal" (BAGD; cf. ἐντυγχάνω in Paul, Rom. 8:27, 34; 11:2), with a note of both urgency and boldness of access (Trench). Prayers must manifest concern for others and perhaps particularly for their plight or difficulty. With ἔντευξις the image is that of one who comes to a king and appeals for the king's favorable response, here on behalf of "all" (for usage in the papyri see Spicq; BAGD; Deissmann, *Bible Studies,* 121, 146).

εὐχαριστία refers to "thanksgiving" or expressions of gratitude, here "thankfulness" or "gratitude" to God on behalf of all. The verb εὐχαριστέω is found in the introductory sections of all of Paul's letters except for Galatians and the PE (in 1 and 2 Timothy replaced by χάριν ἔχω). εὐχαριστία is included in his instructions about prayer in Phil. 4:6; Col. 4:2, as here (cf. also Eph. 5:20; Col. 3:15-17; 1 Thes. 5:18), to draw attention to the fact that requests are made always in the context of conscious expressions of thankfulness.

In summary, these four terms delineate aspects of what should mark prayers: δεήσεις, making requests for specific needs; προσευχάς, bringing those in view before God; ἐντεύξεις, appealing boldly on their behalf; and εὐχαριστίας, thankfulness for them. That the four words are plural points to more than one expression of prayer and suggests the involvement of a number of those in the congregation, as does plural τοὺς ἄνδρας in v. 8.

Paul desires that such prayers should be made "on behalf of all people" (ἄνθρωπος used here in the sense of human beings, not of males in contrast to females). ὑπέρ is often used in the sense of "for," "in behalf of," "for the sake of" (with the genitive, as here), especially after words for request or prayer (see BAGD s.v. ὑπέρ 1aα; s.v. δέησις; s.v. προσευχή).

What does "all people" (πάντες ἄνθρωποι, Acts 22:15; Rom. 5:12a, 18a, b; 12:17, 18; 1 Cor. 7:7; 15:19; 2 Cor. 3:2; Phil. 4:5; 1 Thes. 2:15; 1 Tim. 2:4; 4:10; Tit. 2:11; 3:2) mean? The repetition of ὑπέρ and further specification, as a subgroup, of civil rulers (v. 2) points in the direction of it meaning all *kinds* of people. This meaning would fit in the other occurrences of the phrase in 1 Timothy and Titus (especially Tit. 3:2) and would appear to be the understanding of the term when it was first presented to Paul as the perspective for his ministry (Acts 22:15). It is also the most natural understanding in a number of the Pauline passages where an absolute universalism is a virtual impossibility and a reference to all *kinds* of individuals is more likely (cf. Rom. 12:17, 18; 2 Cor. 3:2; Phil. 4:5; perhaps 1 Thes. 2:15; cf. also εἰς πάντας in Rom. 10:12; an absolute universalism for πάντες ἄνθρωποι is demanded only where the sin of "all people" is spoken of, Rom. 5:12a, 18a). That this is the significance of πάντες ἄνθρωποι here is also borne out by Paul's use of πάντες elsewhere to include different named categories of mankind (Gal. 3:28; Col. 3:11).

Does Paul request prayer for all kinds of people to counteract a narrowness on the part of the false teachers or because it is inherently part of the theology of one God and one mediator? Actually, this is not an either/or matter. In view of Paul's insistence on including "all" groups in the body of

Christ (Gal. 3:28; Col. 3:11), it would appear that the primary reason for this directive is theological and only secondarily the need to deal with trends in the opposite direction. But these trends may have been the occasion for the "all" being emphasized in this letter after references to the false teachers (here and vv. 4, 6 after chapter 1; 4:10 after 4:1-7). Paul's insistence that his message comes exclusively from God (Gal. 1:11, 12) would indicate that his teaching first unfolds truth and then corrects perceived error, rather than being simply a reaction to another view, even if that view may have served to call forth a clearer articulation of the truth.

2:2 The preposition ὑπέρ is repeated to specify one of the kinds of people, namely, civil authorities. They are singled out because of Paul's concern for God's ordained order in society (cf. Rom. 13:1-7) and more pragmatically in this text because (as the ἵνα clause indicates) the lives of all people, including Christians in their concern to proclaim the gospel and live a godly life, are affected by civil authorities. βασιλεύς is used in the NT generally in its strict sense of one who is a "king" or "monarch," but also sometimes in a figurative sense of the possessor of the highest power (see BAGD). Since the programmatic words of Acts 9:15 addressed to Paul ("to bear my name before the Gentiles and kings and the sons of Israel") are heard when Paul is before Agrippa (addressed as king) and finally before Caesar, the implication is that Paul understood Caesar and others, such as Agrippa, to be included in this term. Thus, with the anarthrous pl. βασιλεῖς Paul is referring to a category of supreme rulers.

He adds the inclusive statement, καὶ πάντων τῶν ἐν ὑπεροχῇ ὄντων, to make plain that his concern is for those in civil authority generally. πάντων is followed by the definite article τῶν, which indicates that a particular group is in view, which is then specified by ἐν ὑπεροχῇ ὄντων. ὑπεροχή** (here and 1 Cor. 2:1), literally "projection" or "prominence," is used in the NT only in figurative senses, here for a place of authority (cf. the use of ὑπερέχω in analogous contexts in Rom. 13:2; 1 Pet. 2:13).

Prayers for civil authorities have a very practical and significant purpose, which is indicated by the ἵνα clause. That purpose has to do with life itself (βίον διάγωμεν) in both proximate ("tranquil and quiet life") and ultimate ("in all godliness and dignity") goals. διάγω** (here and Tit. 3:3) is common in Greek and Jewish (e.g., 2 Maccabees 12:38; 3 Maccabees 4:8; Josephus, *Ap.* 2.229) writers both with and without βίον with the meaning "spend one's life, live" (BAGD). βίος (PE* 2x) refers here, as the correlation with διάγω also indicates, to earthly life in its various functions (BAGD; cf. 2 Tim. 2:4; Lk. 8:14). The first person plural verb διάγωμεν (others are in 1:8; 4:10; 6:8) probably has in view the entire Christian community, because of the reference to εὐσέβεια, a general term for Christian piety. The plural also probably reaches out to include all kinds of men and women, for whom the church is praying and for whom they desire, as does God (v. 4), salvation and godly living.

ἤρεμος** (hapax) means "quiet," "tranquil" (BAGD) in the sense of "untroubled from without" (Simpson and Ellicott). But as Buck observes (*Dictionary,* 840), even though a "state of rest" is the basic notion of this word, its "range" and "dominant application" differ. ἡσύχιος** (here and 1 Pet. 3:4) also means "quiet." An evaluation of Paul's own life leads one to realize that this "quiet" does not mean a sheltered life but rather freedom from the turmoil that threatened to thwart his ministry. A good example is the disquiet of the riot in the very city that he was writing to, Ephesus (Acts 19:23-41), which the rulers finally quieted. After this quiet came, Paul was able to gather and exhort the disciples (20:1; cf. also the case at Corinth, 18:12-18). But often the disquietude of riot and persecution would mean that Paul and his companions had to leave both church and city (Acts 13:50, 51; 14:5, 6, 19; 16:19-21, 39, 40; 17:8-10, 13, 14), and it was only the intervention of the Roman government that provided a measure of peace and tranquility for him to minister in Jerusalem and Rome (cf. 21:27-40 and the subsequent chapters, e.g., 28:16, 23ff., 30, 31, and the evidence of the Prison and Pastoral Epistles, e.g., Phil. 1:12, 13). Perhaps Paul has in mind the words of Je. 29:7 (LXX 36:7): "Seek the welfare of the city where I have sent you into exile, and pray to the Lord on its behalf; for in its welfare you will have welfare."

A tranquil life is to be prayed for as a setting in which the ultimate goal, πάσῃ εὐσέβεια καὶ σεμνότης, may be accomplished. εὐσέβεια** (Acts 3:12; 1 Tim. 2:2; 3:16; 4:7, 8; 6:3, 5, 6, 11; Tit. 1:1; 2 Tim. 3:5; 2 Pet. 1:3, 6, 7; 3:11) is aptly rendered by "religion," "piety," "godliness" (BAGD, cf. *NASB, RSV, NEB, TEV, NIV*) and has intrinsically the same range of meaning and application as do the English terms. The dynamic force and reality for a true εὐσέβεια is none other than Christ Jesus and his saving work in the hearts of believers (3:16; cf. 2 Pet. 1:3), without which any profession is merely a form lacking this power (2 Tim. 3:5; 1 Tim. 6:5). Just as earlier Paul spoke of one working out one's salvation with fear and trembling because God is at work within (Phil. 2:12, 13), so also εὐσέβεια is used to express the Christian's religion in action.

The word group that includes εὐσέβεια is well known in the LXX and in secular Greek (see BAGD and Spicq), and it is used by Luke as an appropriate term in reference to Peter and the Christians of Jerusalem (Acts 3:12) and Cornelius (10:2, 7). It is strange, therefore, that outside Acts it appears in the NT only in the PE and 2 Peter.

Fear of (or reverence toward) the Lord is a core concept of the OT (e.g., Ps. 103:17; in Pr. 1:7 the LXX uses εὐσέβεια) and appears, though infrequently, in Pauline theology (φοβέομαι and φόβος: Rom. 3:18; 2 Cor. 5:11; Eph. 5:21; Phil. 2:12; Col. 3:22; cf. also Acts 9:31). "God-fearers," i.e., "worshippers of God" (σεβόμενοι τὸν θεόν), was the common term for Gentiles who embraced the ethical monotheism of Judaism and is also used in Acts of those who became Christians (13:43; 16:14; 17:4, 17; 18:7). As more and more Christians came from a Gentile background and were therefore σεβόμενοι τὸν θεόν, Paul was increasingly involved in a culture where the related term εὐσέβεια was used more commonly. Finally, Luke may have influenced Paul in use of εὐσέβεια (Paul and Luke prefer εὐ-words more than other NT writers [Morgenthaler, *Statistik*, 162]). It is plausible to think that the PE reflects this combination of factors in its use of εὐσέβεια (and related words). Furthermore, if 2 Peter has been influenced by the PE, or at least by 1 Timothy (cf. especially 2 Pet. 3:15), then the use of εὐσέβεια in Acts (Luke), the PE, and 2 Peter finds a most satisfactory solution. (On εὐσέβεια see Knight, *Faithful Sayings*, 68-73; W. Foerster, *TDNT* VII, 175-85; *idem*, "Εὐσέβεια," and the literature cited in all three).

Paul emphasizes his concern for εὐσέβεια with the addition of πᾶς, which indicates that he wants godliness to come to full expression (a thought to which he returns in 4:7-10; cf. BAGD s.v. πᾶς 1aδ). πᾶς probably applies to σεμνότης as well.

σεμνότης** (1 Tim. 2:2; 3:4; Tit. 2:7; cf. σεμνός**: Phil. 4:8; 1 Tim. 3:8, 11; Tit. 2:2) means "dignity," "seriousness" and "connotes moral earnestness, affecting outward demeanour as well as interior intention" (Kelly). Lock puts it well by saying that ἐν εὐσεβείᾳ καὶ σεμνότητι is "an interesting Hellenic counterpart to the Hebraic ἐν ὁσιοτητι καὶ δικαιοσύνῃ" in Lk. 1:75. The two terms may well provide, as Bernard and Lock suggest, the more Godward and reverential perspective and the more manward and ethical perspective respectively.

Dibelius-Conzelmann assert that this "ideal of Christian citizenship . . . differs greatly from Paul's understanding of existence" in which he "lives in the tension between this world and God's world." They illustrate this difference by referring to Paul's statements concerning "his life's difficulties and dangers" in 2 Cor. 11:23-33. But Ridderbos points out that Rom. 13:1-7 (especially vv. 3 and 4) points to the same kind of "Christian citizenship" and is combined, in a way Dibelius-Conzelmann seem to think is impossible, with the awareness of "tension" expressed in 13:11-14. Furthermore, 2 Cor. 11:23-33 is also paralleled in the PE in 2 Tim. 4:6ff., 17ff.

2:3 Prayers are further encouraged by stating that they are pleasing to God, who is appealed to as "Savior" and particularly in terms of his desire that "all people be saved" (πάντας ἀνθρώπους θέλει σωθῆναι). "All people" echoes the designation of those for whom Christians are to pray (v. 1). The logic is that since God desires all to be saved, it must be good and acceptable to him that we pray for all, for we can surely use God as our model for concern in this area (cf. for the same argument Tit. 3:1-7). The logical connection is made explicit by γάρ after τοῦτο in most cursive manuscripts (though not in the oldest uncials), probably added to make explicit what is implicit, so that a scribe might do so almost automatically.

When Paul says "this is good," he probably means that it is so not only "before God," but also because of all that is involved in such prayer, such as concern for all people, and (as he implies in vv. 3ff.) for their salvation, as well as concern for civil government, tranquility, quiet, and a greater opportunity to live a life of Christian piety (cf. 2 Cor. 8:21). ἀπόδεκτος** (1 Tim. 2:3; 5:4, both with ἐνώπιον θεοῦ) means "acceptable" in the sense of pleasing (see BAGD). Spicq calls our attention to the formula "good and acceptable" before God in the LXX (Dt. 12:25, 28; 13:19; 21:9 — where, however, ἀρεστός is used rather than ἀπόδεκτος).

ἐνώπιον (neuter used as a preposition with the genitive; cf. MHT IV, 92) means simply "before." For our passage and for most of those in which θεός or κύριος are in view, BAGD indicates that the word has the nuance of "in the opinion or judgment of." That we pray for all people pleases God. As at the beginning of the letter, Paul is drawn to refer to God as σωτήρ (1:1, which see for notes on this word), since it is only when we remember that God is the Savior of all that we will be adequately urged to pray for all, sinners as they are. Paul adds ἡμῶν (as in nine of the ten occurrences of σωτήρ in the PE*: 1 Tim. 1:1; 2:3; Tit. 1:3, 4; 2:10, 13; 3:4, 6; 2 Tim. 1:10, but not in 1 Tim. 4:10) to remind those whom he urges to pray of their own salvation through God's mercy.

2:4 πάντες ἄνθρωποι is picked up from v. 1 to correlate God's attitude toward "all people" with the request that we pray for all. As in v. 1 Paul means by the phrase all *kinds* of people, all sorts of people, including civil authorities (cf. for a similar thought Tit. 3:1-7; note also Rom. 11:32, where the second "all" embraces Jew and Gentile, but not every person, cf. 9:6ff.; cf. again Gal. 3:28; Col. 3:11; 1 Cor. 12:12; Acts 22:15). "[God] wishes all people to be saved" expresses the truth for which Paul continually contended, especially against Jews and Judaizers, and that he and the other apostles were agreed on (see Galatians, especially chapter 2; Acts 10:34-36; 11:17, 18, where Peter expresses this same truth against the background of his vision of 10:9-23; 1 Tim. 2:7: "teacher of the Gentiles"; cf. for OT background Ezk. 18:23; 33:11; and especially the Abrahamic covenant, Gen. 12:3, reflected throughout Isaiah; G. Schrenk, *TDNT* III, 47f.).

σωθῆναι (see data at 1:15), as aorist passive, "to be saved," communicates, with the verb θέλει, that God wishes people to experience that which he would do for them, i.e., save them. The two focuses of this statement come to expression in two other uses of σῴζω in the PE: First, "And come to the knowledge of the truth" is reflected in 4:10, where from the human side those from "all kinds of people" who are saved are described simply as "believers" (cf. Romans 9–11; Gal. 3:28; Col. 2:11; 1 Cor. 12:13). Second, those who are saved are, from the Godward side, those "called" "according to [God's] purpose and grace, which was granted to us in Christ Jesus from all eternity" (2 Tim. 1:9; cf. Romans 9–11; Ephesians 1–2). These two focuses coalesce in the perspective of 2 Tim. 1:8-10, especially v. 10, where this eternal purpose is said to be brought about "through the gospel" (cf. Eph. 1:8-10).

καὶ εἰς ἐπίγνωσιν ἀληθείας ἐλθεῖν stresses the necessary noetic aspect of salvation, most simply put, knowledge of the person and work of Christ (cf. Rom. 10:12-14). Although ἐπίγνωσις ἀληθείας is found in Paul only in the PE (here, Tit. 1:1; 2 Tim. 2:25; 3:7 [all the occurrences of ἐπίγνωσις in the PE]; the phrase elsewhere in the NT only in Heb. 10:26), its component parts are found in Paul's earlier letters in the same sense. The phrase as used here indicates the process of coming to know and acknowledge the truth of the gospel (ἐπίγνωσις with genitive of the thing known). "'Recognition' (ἐπίγνωσις) designates not only rational comprehension but also acknowledgment, just as 'truth' (ἀλήθεια) is not merely a fact to be grasped theoretically, but also a state of affairs to be actualized. The phrase as a whole is a technical term for conversion" (Dibelius-Conzelmann; cf. Heb. 10:26; cf. further Dibelius, "'Ἐπίγνωσις ἀλήθειας").

This meaning for the phrase is borne out in the usage of the two words separately elsewhere in Paul. Bultmann asserts that "ἐπίγνωσις has become almost a technical term for the decisive knowledge of God which is implied in conversion to the Christian faith" (*TDNT* I, 707). Col. 2:2 (εἰς ἐπίγνωσιν τοῦ μυστηρίου τοῦ θεοῦ) is the most nearly parallel to our passage, although the experiential aspect is also evident in most of the other Pauline references, e.g., Eph. 1:17; 4:13; Phil. 1:9; Col. 1:9, 10; 3:10. ἀλήθεια means "true teaching or faith" and is used of the gospel in the earlier Pauline letters and probably here as well (cf. 2 Cor. 4:2; Gal. 5:7; 2 Cor. 6:7; Col. 1:5; Eph. 1:13; 2 Thes. 2:10-12; 2 Cor. 13:8; cf. 2 Jn. 1; 1 Pet. 1:22; Bultmann, *TDNT* I, 244; cf. also BAGD s.v. 2b, which gives the nuance here and elsewhere in the NT as "the content of Christianity as the absolute truth"). ἐλθεῖν, "to come," speaks of the personal and experiential response (see also 2 Tim. 3:7, the only other NT occurrence of εἰς ἐπίγνωσιν ἔρχεσθαι).

2:5 The basis for the preceding argument, as indicated here by γάρ and that which follows it, are the twin truths that there is one God (εἷς θεός) and one mediator (εἷς μεσίτης). Paul does not spell out why this provides a basis for his preceding argument, especially v. 4, but simply states it as being self-evidently the basis, which would be understood by Timothy and the church at Ephesus, probably because he has used it before (e.g., Rom. 3:30; 1 Cor. 8:4-6 [12:9, 13]; Gal. 3:20; Eph. 4:5, 6; cf. Jas. 2:19). That there is one God means that there are not other gods for non-Jews alongside the God of the Jews (cf. Acts 17:23-31; Rom. 3:30; 1 Cor. 8:6). God's concern for all was expressed in the Abrahamic covenant in the statement that "all the families of the earth shall be blessed" (Gen. 12:3). That covenantal promise has come to fruition in Christ (see Gal. 3:8-29, especially vv. 8, 14, 28). God's concern is further evidenced by his providing one mediator, with one sufficient ransom (1 Tim. 2:6), to be proclaimed to all people everywhere (cf. Paul's commission, v. 7; see also Gal. 2:7-9; Acts 9:15; 22:21; 26:16-18), through whom alone, by faith alone, people may be saved (1 Tim. 1:6; Rom. 3:21-30; Gal. 2:15, 16; 3:8, 14; cf. Acts 4:12; Jn. 14:6). So step-by-step from monotheism to the gospel itself Paul has argued that it is self-evident that God desires all people, Jew and Gentile, slave and free, ruled and ruler, etc., to be saved, and that such a perspective should elicit our prayers for all people.

Just as there is only one God, so there is only one mediator (μεσίτης; cf. εἷς with Christ: 1 Cor. 8:6; Eph. 4:5; most tellingly in Gal. 3:16, 28). μεσίτης is used here with the genitive of those between whom he mediates (for the nuances of the word see A. Oepke, *TDNT* IV, 598-624). The one God has provided one mediator between himself (θεοῦ) and humans (ἀνθρώπων, plural), who is himself human (ἄνθρωπος), namely, Christ Jesus (for Χριστὸς Ἰησοῦς see 1:1, 15). The humanity of the mediator is specified to emphasize his identity with those whom he represents as mediator (cf. "all people," πάντες ἄνθρωποι, vv. 1, 4; cf. also A. Oepke, *TDNT* IV, 619; for Paul's emphasis on the humanity of Christ see also 1 Cor. 15:21ff., 45-49; Rom. 5:15-21; Phil. 2:7, 8 — note that these passages speak of Christ's humanity in contexts where his deity is either implied, alluded to, or stated).

2:6 ὁ δοὺς ἑαυτὸν ἀντίλυτρον ὑπὲρ πάντων specifies the way in which Christ served as the mediator, namely, by giving up his life for all. The aorist substantival participle ὁ δούς (from δίδωμι) signifies a definite past action and may be rendered "the one who gave" or simply "who gave." It is related to the preceding nominative Χριστὸς Ἰησοῦς. The use of ἑαυτόν (in reference to Christ, as here, in Tit. 2:14a, which is almost identical, 14b; 2 Tim. 2:13), "himself," where τὴν ψυχὴν αὐτοῦ is found in Jesus' words (Mt. 20:28 par. Mk. 10:45, with δίδωμι) is what one would expect in a transposition of Jesus' statement about himself into a statement about Jesus (especially when the dynamics of the meaning of ψυχή in that setting are borne in mind; see BAGD s.v. ψυχή 1aβ; E. Schweizer, *TDNT* IX, 637f.; MHT I, 87, 105; see also Gal. 1:4 [ἑαυτόν with δίδωμι, as here]; 2:20; Eph. 5:2, 25 [παραδίδωμι with ἑαυτόν in all three]; Lk. 22:19).

ἀντίλυτρον** is a NT hapax found in pre-Christian literature (but see Field's note and conjecture on Ps. 48:9 in his edition of Origen's Hexapla, II, 170). It is a compound of ἀντί and λύτρον,** the latter of which appears 19x in the LXX and twice in the NT, both in the statement of Jesus noted in the previous paragraph (Mt. 20:28 par. Mk. 10:45: δοῦναι τὴν ψυχὴν αὐτοῦ λύτρον ἀντὶ πολλῶν). ἀντίλυτρον represents a price paid to free captives and thus means "ransom," or more appropriately, "substitute-ransom," as L. Morris renders it, noting the emphasis on the thought of substitution in the preposition (*Apostolic Preaching,* 51; cf. also F. Büchsel, *TDNT* IV, 349). "The addition of the prep[osition] *anti,* 'instead of,' is significant in view of the prep[osition] *huper,* 'in behalf of', used after it. Christ is conceived of as an 'exchange price' . . ." (Guthrie). On the prepositions see M. J. Harris, "Prepositions and Theology in the Greek New Testament," *NIDNTT* III, 1171-1215, for ἀντί, 1179f.

There are negative and positive aspects in NT contexts where λυτρ-words are used in connection with the death of Jesus and that which necessitated his death, i.e., human sins (e.g., Mt. 26:28; 1 Cor. 15:14). The concept is used negatively of redemption or ransom *from* sin (cf. Tit. 2:14), and this then brings into perspective the other aspects or consequences from which mankind in sin needs to be ransomed, namely death (both spiritual in the present, e.g., Rom. 6:1ff., and eternal, e.g., Rom. 6:23) and the wrath of God (e.g., Rom. 2:5; Col. 3:6; 1 Thes. 5:9; Gal. 3:10-14). The concept is used positively of ransom *to* God (e.g., Tit. 2:14; Eph. 1:14; 1 Cor. 6:20), and this brings into perspective that it is a ransom that results in life (e.g., Rom. 6:23), obedience (e.g., Romans 6 and 8, especially 8:2, 4), and sonship (e.g., Gal. 4:1-7, especially vv. 3 and 5). For the use of λυτρ- words outside the NT for manumission of slaves see BAGD; F. Büchsel, *TDNT* IV, 340ff.; Morris, *Apostolic Preaching,* 11-64.

ὑπέρ means, when expressing something that accrues to the person, as here, either "on behalf of" (representation) or "in the place of" (substitution). Since "on behalf of" or even the meaning "for the sake of" will fit in all three occurrences in close proximity (vv. 1, 2, 6), it is probably best to understand the preposition in that sense here. Thus we are to pray for all (ὑπὲρ πάντων) because this is in accord with the one mediator, himself a man, acting for the one God, who gave himself a ransom for all (ὑπὲρ πάντων). (On ὑπέρ see M. J. Harris, *NIDNTT* III, 1196f. and the literature referred to there; see also Robertson, *Grammar,* 630f.).

πάντων continues and concludes the emphasis of the passage on "all" kinds of people (cf. again Rom. 3:21-30, where ἀπολυτρώσεως τῆς ἐν Χριστῷ Ἰησοῦ, v. 24, is provided by the one God for both Jew and Gentile, vv. 29, 30). On the relationship of πάντων here to πολλῶν in Mt. 20:28 par. Mk. 10:45 see C. Brown, *NIDNTT* III, 197f. and the literature cited there; Jeremias, "Lösegeld," 260; *idem, TDNT* VI, 543f. If Jeremias is right in saying that πολλῶν reflects a Semitic background and means "all," this may help explain the consistent use of πάντων by Paul. It may also mean that the term on the lips of Jesus, as in Paul, points not to an absolute universalism (which Jeremias seems to think: *TDNT* VI, 543), but to a universalism including Gentile and Jew, etc., which would also seem to be the more natural understanding of the OT, Jesus, and Paul.

The question of πάντων and πολλῶν raises again the larger question of the relationship of the entire verse to the saying of Jesus in Mt. 20:28 par. Mk. 10:45. Paul knows of Jesus' life (e.g., Rom. 1:1-5; Philippians 2; 1 Tim. 6:13; 2 Tim. 2:8), quotes his sayings (e.g., 1 Cor. 7:10, 11), relates the specific words used in the institution of the Lord's Supper (1 Cor. 11:23ff.), and speaks elsewhere of Jesus' ministry and death in a manner like that of Jesus and the general apostolic kerygma (cf. Dodd, *According to the Scriptures; idem, Apostolic Preaching*), and his words here are as identical to the Gospel accounts as a restated objectification of a personal statement can be. These are compelling reasons to believe that this statement reflects that of Jesus. The answer to this question is beclouded, however, by the question whether vv. 5-6 are a "saying" in existence in the Christian community, which Paul here quotes, or words composed by Paul. Certainly the former is possible (cf. the faithful sayings, 1:15; 3:1; 4:9; Tit. 3:8; 2 Tim. 2:11; and also 1 Tim. 3:16) and, if so, would make the question of probability in regard to Paul's knowing Jesus' statement of almost no significance.

There is not a fully adequate basis to solve this last question, except to say that since each of the component parts of Paul's statement are an integral part of his argument, it is more likely that the parts, and the whole, were written by Paul. Furthermore, this kind of argument, or parts of it with the same or similar terms, is used elsewhere by Paul where a citation is less likely (cf. Rom. 3:21-30; Gal. 1:4; 2:20; Eph. 5:2, 25; Tit. 2:14a). That we do not know precisely how Paul knows the saying of Jesus that is behind our verse does not alter the fact that he does appear to know it and that he has manifested knowledge of other aspects of Jesus' person, work, and words.

On whether Paul's statement here implies that he believed that Jesus understood and spoke of his death in terms of the Suffering Servant of Is. 52:13–53:12 see the commentaries and other literature on Mt. 20:28 par. Mk. 10:45 and other passages (especially Lk. 24:25-27). If he did, it is possible that Paul's argument here receives further emphasis from his own commission and activity being based on the gospel of Jesus' death for all kinds of people interpreted according to Isaiah's — and Jesus' — perspective. This would be in accord with Paul's explicit use of Is. 52:13–53:12 elsewhere, always in the context of the free offer of the gospel to all people (for this connection, even if the specific words are missing, cf. Rom. 15:14-21, especially vv. 16, 20, 21, with Is. 52:13; Rom. 10:11-20, v. 11 with Is. 20:16, v. 15 with Is. 52:7, v. 16 with Is. 53:1, and note v. 12: "no distinction between Jew and Greek, for the same Lord is Lord of *all,* abounding in riches for *all* who call on him").

τὸ μαρτύριον is nominative or accusative absolute in apposition to the preceding clause (cf. τὸ ἀδύνατον in Rom. 8:3 and τὴν λατρείαν in 12:1; cf. Robertson). The question that arises is whether the giving of Christ himself is the testimony (so, e.g., Dibelius-Conzelmann, Jeremias, Ridderbos, Schlatter, Spicq), or whether the thought of a testimony being borne to that event is being introduced (so, e.g., Bouma, Wohlenberg, H. Strathmann, *TDNT* IV, 504). μαρτύριον is used by Paul in both senses.

καιρός means "time, i.e., point of time as well as period of time"

(BAGD; see Barr, *Biblical Words*). Is plural καιροῖς ἰδίοις "only an idiomatic usage, practically equivalent to the singular" (cf. Jer. 50[LXX 27]:26, 31; χρόνοι in Lk. 20:9; 23:8; γάμοι in Lk. 12:36), "*or* is the plural to be pressed?" (Lock on Tit. 1:3, who favors the latter view, though he provides evidence for the former). The usage of the plural phrase in 1 Tim. 6:15 and Tit. 1:3 (the only other occurrence of the two words together in the NT is singular in Gal. 6:9), both referring to the appearing of Jesus as a single event, would seem to warrant the understanding that it is "practically equivalent to the singular." A period of time, rather than a point of time, would seem to be in view when the reference is to Jesus' first coming, since Paul seems to regard the time from Christ's coming onward as part of the same time period (cf. the use of νῦν as the time indicator in 2 Tim. 1:10, where it encompasses both Christ's ministry on earth and the subsequent proclamation of that event). This comprehensive use of καιροῖς ἰδίοις best fits our text. ἴδιος has the general meaning of "one's own" and here is best rendered as "proper" ("the proper time," see BAGD, so *RSV, NASB, NIV,* cf. *NEB:* "the fitting time").

Who or what bears the testimony? (D* G and a few other manuscripts [see the *NA*[26] textual apparatus] remedied the obscurity by adding οὗ and ἐδόθη.) There are pointers to a possible, even if not certain, solution. First, the definite article with μαρτύριον would seem best understood as referring to Christ's giving of himself as "*the* testimony." Second, the idea of Christ's death as a demonstration of God's concern for humans is the argument of Rom. 3:21-30, which also uses the concept of one God for Jew and Gentile (= all people; cf. vv. 21, 25, 26). Third, though the two preceding considerations point to the self-giving of Christ as an act that itself bears testimony, the reference to Paul as having been appointed for this (εἰς ὅ ἐτέθην ἐγώ) would seem to understand the testimony as that borne by Paul (and others). The solution is probably to be found in a both-and rather than in an either-or understanding (in accord with the same correlation stated in Tit. 1:2, 3): The act of Jesus' self-giving for all bears witness to the desire of the one God that all be saved (cf. Jn. 3:16), and Paul was appointed to continue to bear testimony to this act (cf. 2 Tim. 1:9, 10, 11, the "purpose and grace" of God "now revealed by the appearing" of Jesus, who "brought life and immortality to light through the gospel, for which I was appointed . . ." [the basic structure and vocabulary of v. 11 is the same as our text]). On this understanding, the temporal dative καιροῖς ἰδίοις refers not only to the time of Christ's ministry but also to the time since, characterized as the era in which such a testimony can be borne (cf. the similar evaluation of οἰκονομία in 1:4).

2:7 As is Paul's practice elsewhere, having mentioned the person and work of Christ, he adds the fact that he was appointed to minister for Christ (twice already, 1 Tim. 1:11, 12; also 2 Cor. 5:18, 20; 6:1; Eph. 3:7, 8; Col. 1:25). Here the reference also carries with it the supportive evidence that his ministry brings to the argument. What he has just argued about "all people," he has proclaimed and taught as an apostle to the ἔθνη and as one appointed for that very task (Acts 9:15; 22:15 [cf. the very phrase πρὸς πάντας ἀνθρώπους], 21; 26:15-18 — all but 22:15 with the word ἔθνος; so also Gal. 1:15, 16; 2:7-9; Rom. 15:15ff.). And he has taught the Gentiles about (ἐν) the very things God has desired for all (v. 4), namely "faith and truth."

εἰς ὅ refers to that "for which" Paul was appointed (the only other Pauline occurrences of εἰς ὅ are in Phil. 3:16; Col. 1:29; 2 Thes. 1:11; 2:14; 2 Tim. 1:11, the last virtually identical to what follows here). Here, as in 2 Tim. 1:9, the word in question, here the "testimony," there the "gospel," is seen from two perspectives, namely, that which Christ did and that which Paul does. In 2 Tim. 1:9 Christ works through the gospel and Paul is appointed to it; here Christ bears the testimony, and it is for that task that Paul is appointed, i.e., to proclaim that same testimony (cf. 1 Tim. 3:16, where μυστήριον includes both Christ revealed and Christ proclaimed).

τίθημι (PE* 3x, here, 1:12; 2 Tim. 1:11; the passive has God or Christ in view, cf. 1:12) has the general meaning of "put" or "place" and is used here in the sense of "appoint," with the aorist tense indicating that the appointing was accomplished at a specific point in the past (cf. C. Maurer, *TDNT* VIII, 157; note that Paul applies Is. 49:6 to himself in Acts 13:46, 47). With the personal pronoun ἐγώ, "I," Paul makes the statement about his appointment quite emphatic (cf. the other PE occurrences: 1 Tim. 1:11, 15; 2:7; Tit. 1:3, 5; 2 Tim. 1:11; 4:6, all but the second and the last referring to Paul's appointment to ministry).

The three terms κῆρυξ, ἀπόστολος, and διδάσκαλος (all nominatives with the passive verb, "I was appointed") describe different, but not mutually exclusive or completely distinct, aspects of Paul's ministry. They do not represent different offices, since Paul elsewhere sees his office of apostle as encompassing the tasks of proclamation and teaching (only here and in 2 Tim. 1:11 does he refer to himself with all three terms together, though in the other letters he does use all three of himself).

κῆρυξ** (1 Tim. 2:7; 2 Tim. 1:11; 2 Pet. 2:5) signifies the "herald" or "proclaimer," and is known to Paul and his readers from the culture of the day in both secular and religious senses (see BAGD, MM). The word is known in the LXX (5x), and the proclaimer is an OT concept (e.g., Jon. 1:2; 3:2; Is. 40:1-6, though this word is not used in either passage; cf. also John the Baptist). Paul may use the word because of the interaction of these factors and as a consequence of his use (and that of the NT community) of the related words κήρυγμα and κηρύσσω. Perhaps the word occurs so infrequently because the NT so rarely speaks of the proclaimer and of the proclamation (κήρυγμα is also rare) but rather describes that which is proclaimed (thus the more frequent use of κηρύσσω). Only when Paul feels constrained to briefly crystallize his task with a noun, as here and in 2 Tim. 1:11, does he use κῆρυξ (much the same could be said of his use of κήρυγμα; cf. also G. Friedrich, *TDNT* III, 696; L. Coenen, *NIDNTT* III, 52).

Paul then calls himself an "apostle" (see 1:1 for the data and fuller discussion) in the special sense of one sent with the authority of Christ to be Christ's official spokesman (cf. Acts 11:14, 15; 26:16-18; 1 Cor. 15:8-10; Galatians 1). He immediately adds the note, ἀλήθειαν λέγω, οὐ ψεύδομαι (for speaking the truth in Paul cf. especially Rom. 9:1; Eph. 4:25; 2 Cor. 12:6, the first two in contrast with lying as here and Rom. 9:1 almost identical to our passage; ψεύδομαι, Pl.* 5x: Rom. 9:1; 2 Cor. 11:31; Gal. 1:20; Col. 3:9, and here; for textual variants see *UBSGNT; TCGNT*). Paul adds this comment over against those who might doubt or challenge his apostleship on the grounds that apostleship should be restricted to those who were apostles with Jesus during his early ministry or because they wanted to discredit Paul (cf. Galatians 1 and 2). Paul's apostleship was challenged in Galatia and continued to be challenged even where he had labored for some time, such as Corinth (cf. 1 Cor. 9:1, 2; 2 Cor. 11:5; 12:11, 12). Since he begins nearly every letter affirming his apostleship, we need not be surprised that he does so in 1 Timothy or that he insists on his truthfulness on the matter here, as in other letters (cf. Gal. 1:20; 2 Cor. 11:30). Spicq thinks Paul insists on his truthfulness in reference to his claim to be the "teacher of the Gentiles" and especially with reference to the word "Gentiles." Although this is a possibility and its plausibility is enhanced in this context by the word ἐθνῶν, on the whole this seems less likely in view of insistence on truthfulness elsewhere with reference to Paul's apostleship. The insistence on truthfulness places a break between ἀπόστολος and διδάσκαλος, which may explain why Paul writes διδάσκαλος without the intervening καί found between κῆρυξ and ἀπόστολος.

Paul applies διδάσκαλος to himself only here and in 2 Tim. 1:11. Elsewhere he either includes διδάσκαλοι in lists in such a way that they are distinguished from ἀπόστολοι (1 Cor. 12:28, 29; Eph. 4:11) or uses the word in a derogatory sense (Rom. 2:20; 2 Tim. 4:3). What has been observed above about κῆρυξ/κηρύσσω can also be applied to διδάσκαλος/διδάσκω, although to a considerably lesser degree. With the verb διδάσκω Paul says of himself "I teach everywhere in every church" (1 Cor. 4:17), which implies that he is a διδάσκαλος (but even this is a comparative statement, which in its fuller form emphasizes not so much Paul's identity as a teacher but the content of the teaching and the work of Timothy; cf., however, Col. 1:28; 2:7; Eph. 4:21; 2 Thes. 2:15; and διδαχή in Rom. 16:17). Perhaps Paul uses κῆρυξ and διδάσκαλος of himself in the two letters to Timothy because he wanted to refer to himself as a model with which Timothy could identify: Paul urges Timothy to "preach the word" (κηρύσσω, 2 Tim. 4:2), to "teach" (διδάσκω, 1 Tim. 4:11; 6:2), and to commit the teachings to "faithful men who will be able to teach others also" (διδάσκω, 2 Tim. 2:2). This explanation is strengthened by the fact that Paul has already expressly indicated that he is a model in 1:16, 18 and by the fact that this idea is present at the other occurrence of διδάσκαλος in the PE (2 Tim. 1:11; cf. 1:8, 13, 14; 2:1-3; 4:1-8).

The first and third of the three terms that Paul applies to himself (κῆρυξ and διδάσκαλος) seem to emphasize evangelism and exhortation on the one hand and instruction on the other, not only because these are the activities associated with these terms in the NT, but also because these activities are observable in connection with these terms in the PE (cf. the use of δίδασκε in 4:11; 6:2 and of κήρυξον in 2 Tim. 4:2). In addition to being evangelist and exhorter on the one hand and instructor on the other, Paul is Christ's authoritative eyewitness and spokesman (ἀπόστολος). Thus the three terms emphasize different aspects of Paul's ministry to "all people."

ἐθνῶν (without an article and thus probably qualitative; PE* 3[4]x: here; 3:16; 2 Tim. 1:11 [variant reading]; 4:17, all plural) is genitive to indicate to whom Paul's ministry is directed. Plural ἔθνη, which means "nation" in the singular, is not usually used by Paul to mean "nations" (although this nuance may possibly explain the occurrence in 3:16 and is in fact found in Rom. 15:11 and in Gal. 3:8, where πάντα is added), but rather, and especially when it is anarthrous as here, as the designation for non-Jews, the "Gentiles" (cf. K. L. Schmidt, *TDNT* II, 370: "some 100" passages in the NT; H. Bietenhard, *NIDNTT* II, 793-95; this understanding equates ἔθνη with Hebrew *gôyim,* as in the LXX; cf. Is. 49:6; Acts 13:46, 47, and the OT passages cited in Rom. 15:8-19; in addition to "Gentiles" BAGD suggest "pagans," "heathen," the latter of which Schmidt feels is possible [370 n. 19]). When Paul describes his ministry in relation to ἔθνη in earlier letters, it is to non-Jews in distinction from Jews (Rom. 11:13; 15:16; Gal. 2:7-9; Eph. 3:1, 7), so that this is probably the meaning here. Although ἐθνῶν most evidently goes with διδάσκαλος, the nearest word, it is likely that it qualifies the other two words, first, because Paul elsewhere sees his apostleship particularly in terms of the ἔθνη (Rom. 11:13; Gal. 2:7-9; cf. also Rom. 15:16; Eph. 3:1, 7), and second, because the particular point of referring to his ministry here is that the entire ministry, described by whatever terms, has been to ἔθνη, which here is virtually equivalent to πάντες (here the ambivalence of ἔθνη as "Gentiles/heathens" or as "nations" is significant because the term connotes on either view concern for "all people").

ἐν πίστει (see 1:2, 4, 5) καὶ ἀληθείᾳ (see v. 4) indicates that in which Paul instructs the ἔθνη; with the use of these two key words he says that his ministry seeks to accomplish what God desires for all people. πίστις corresponds to σωθῆναι (v. 4; cf. 1:14-16; Rom. 10:9ff.), and ἀλήθεια corresponds to ἐπίγνωσις ἀληθείας (v. 4; cf. Tit. 1:1; 2 Thes. 2:13).

2:8 Paul introduces his summary exhortation with "therefore" (οὖν), pointing back again to the preceding argument as the warrant for this charge.

The emphasis here is on prayer "in every place" (universality) and on practical holiness ("without wrath and dissension" — manifesting the proper attitude to others). βούλομαι (followed here and in 5:14; Tit. 3:8; Phil. 1:12; and Jude 5 by accusative plus infinitive) expresses an apostolic demand in the language of personal desire ("I want"; so *NASB* and *NIV; RSV* and *NEB* use equally strong "I desire"; note that the other Pauline uses of this verb denote the same strong sense: so BAGD; D. Müller, *NIDNTT* III, 1015-17; particularly G. Schrenk, *TDNT* I, 630-32, who relates the usage to Hellenistic Judaism, especially the LXX and Josephus, of the disposition of the royal will or of the lawgiver, and indicates that it refers here to "ordering by apostolic authority"). προσεύχεσχαι is used with the general meaning "to pray" and encapsulates the concern of v. 1.

τοὺς ἄνδρας (accusative plural as "subject" of the infinitive) means "men" here in distinction from women, as the use of γυναῖκας in the next verse implies. This distinction is borne out by the usage elsewhere in the PE* (1 Tim. 2:8, 12; 3:2, 12; 5:9; Tit. 1:6; 2:5). The plural (which seems to point beyond individual homes and families), coupled with the possible nuance of the following prepositional phrase and the wider context in vv. 1, 11, 12 (learning, teaching, exercising authority) and 3:14, 15 ("that you may know how one ought to conduct himself in the household of God"), all seem to point to public prayer by more than one individual in church gatherings. Men are specified here because it is their particular responsibility to lead the church and its worship service (cf. v. 12; 3:2, 5; 4:11-16; 5:17). Paul thus gives specific instructions to men here just as he will give specific instructions to women in the verses that follow (vv. 9ff.).

ἐν παντὶ τόπῳ, "in every place," may simply indicate that Paul wants prayer to be as universal as is its objects; but it is more likely that he is referring to the various meeting places of the church in, perhaps, house churches or other groups (cf. Rom. 16:3-5; 1 Cor. 16:19 [Ephesus]; Col. 4:15). The phrase has this significance in most of the other Pauline occurrences (cf. 1 Cor. 1:2; [2 Cor. 2:14]; 1 Thes. 1:8) and is perhaps also influenced by OT usage (e.g., Ex. 20:24; especially Mal. 1:11).

Paul is not only concerned that such prayer be offered in every place, but also about how it is offered, as is indicated by the participial clause of manner ἐπαίροντας . . . (Ellicott). ἐπαίρω means to lift up or hold up something, e.g., a staff, one's heel, one's voice, one's head, or, as here, hands in prayer (mentioned in the NT only here; cf. 2 Esdras 18[8]:6; Ps. 133[134]:2) or in blessing (Lk. 24:50; cf. Sirach 50:20).

χείρ is used with ἐπαίρω only here in the NT, even though it is also used with some thirteen other verbs in the NT and other early Christian literature (see BAGD s.v. 1 [880]). Raising of hands in prayer is known in the OT (Ex. 9:29; 17:11, 12; 1 Ki. 8:22, 54; Neh. 8:6; Pss. 28:2; 63:4; 141:2; 143:6; Is. 1:15; La. 2:19; 3:41; Hab. 3:10) and in Jewish (e.g., 2 Maccabees 3:20; 14:34; cf.

Spicq; Str-B II, 26) and Gentile literature (cf. Wetstein; Wohlenberg; Deissmann, *Light,* 414ff.; Spicq), as well as among Christians (in catacomb illustrations and in 1 Clement 29; Clement of Alexandria, *Strom.* 7.7; Tertullian, *Apol.* 30). Paul may want to emphasize here the posture or gesture as appropriate to the seriousness and urgency of prayer in general and prayer for all people and authorities in particular and as providing for a unity of body and mind in prayer (the body joining with the voice and heart in being lifted up to God). But this does not seem to be the focus of this passage (cf. the full list of various biblical prayer postures in Hendriksen). The reference to "hands" seems to be introduced to serve as a vehicle for conveying his concern for holiness (ὁσίους χεῖρας, as in many of the OT references), which is then further emphasized by the following phrase (χωρὶς κτλ.).

ὁσίους (the masculine ending with feminine χείρ as if it were an adjective of two endings) is used here in the religio-ethical sense of "holy" (BAGD), as evidenced by the following qualifying phrase (and as in the only other PE occurrence, Tit. 1:8; so also in the OT, which may have influenced Paul's usage here: cf. negatively Is. 1:15, 16; Job 16:17, positively Ps. 24:3, 4, 5; also note Jas. 4:8). ὅσιος is applied to the hands as the part of the body that both is associated with prayer and, more significantly, is the prime agent for human activities, that with which a person acts. Nevertheless the phrase as a whole is surely intended to stand for the entirety of human life, including particularly the central inner dimensions of heart and mind, as indicated by the following words (χωρὶς ὀργῆς καὶ διαλογισμοῦ; so also again the OT parallels and Jas. 4:8).

χωρίς is an adverb used in the NT most often as an improper preposition with the general meaning "without," as here, i.e., without expressing or practicing ὀργή or διαλογισμός. ὀργή (of the 36x in the NT only Eph. 4:31; Col. 3:8; Jas. 1:19, 20, and here does it refer to a human emotion, always with a pejorative denotation) designates "anger" or "wrath," in this context (as in Eph. 4:31; Col. 3:8) an attitude that should not be held toward one's fellow human beings and that, if it arises, should be first removed by forgiving that person for whatever has provoked the anger (so Col. 3:8, 13; Eph. 4:31, 32). Most likely the passage reflects the teaching of Jesus (cf. Mt. 5:22-24 [ὀργιζόμενος]; 6:14, 15; 18:21-35; Mk. 11:25).

διαλογισμός (some few and later texts [see *NA*²⁶ and Spicq] have plural διαλογισμῶν here, which Westcott-Hort slightly favored but which is best explained as a natural scribal "correction") means in general "thought," "opinion," or "reasoning" (BAGD) and then comes to mean more specifically either "doubt" or "dispute, argument" (cf. διαλογίζομαι, "consider and discuss," "argue"). A number of the Greek patristic exegetes, such as Theodore of Mopsuestia (and also moderns such as G. Schrenk, *TDNT* II, 98; Ellicott), interpreted the word as "doubt," with special reference to God (a meaning appropriate elsewhere in the NT and not inappropriate here); but since the context is concerned with one's attitude to other humans (cf. vv. 1-8: pray for all because God is concerned for all), since ὀργή is used here for anger toward people, and since the following strictures on women are concerned with their impact on others, it is likely, though not absolutely certain, that the word is to be understood here of "disputes" with others (so, e.g., Dibelius-Conzelmann, Lock, Weiss, *NASB, RSV, NEB, NIV;* cf. Phil. 2:14; Mk. 7:21; Mt. 15:19).

Avoidance of ὀργή and διαλογισμός is not intended to represent Paul's total understanding of the concept "holy" (other aspects are mentioned in the chapters that follow). Paul highlights rather (as did Jesus) the besetting sins of men that most affect their prayer for others by setting barriers between them and God (cf. 1 Pet. 3:7).

The question remains as to the relationship of this verse to the verses preceding and following (for the two main views and various decisions see the third edition of *UBSGNT* [1975; not the "corrected" third edition of 1983]). It may be argued that the reference to prayer in v. 8 beginning with οὖν picks up on and concludes the section in vv. 1-7 with a practical ethical perspective. On the other hand, vv. 9ff. have no main verb, and the verb βούλομαι (with or without προσεύχεσθαι) could well be understood as beginning this section. Since these are aspects that link this verse to both the preceding and the following, it is best to understand it as a transitional verse (*NA*[26] places breaks before and after the verse; Jeremias makes it a paragraph on its own). For the convenience of paragraph structure and analysis, we have placed it with vv. 1-7, as do some translations (cf. for a similar phenomenon Eph. 5:21).

INSTRUCTIONS FOR WOMEN: 2:9-15

Here Paul presents his instructions to women in parallel to his instructions to men in the preceding verse. A question that immediately arises is whether Paul is speaking to women in connection with the church gathered for prayer and instruction or in terms of the wider framework of the Christian community with the gathered church particularly, but not exclusively, in view. In favor of the former is that the church at prayer has just been mentioned (2:8) and that the one specific prohibition in this section envisages the community gathered for receiving (v. 11) and giving (v. 12) instruction. On the other hand, it is unlikely that the apostle is concerned for modesty and discretion in dress only in church worship services (cf. 1 Pet. 3:1-5) or that he limits "good works" (v. 10) to those that can be done only in the church service (cf. again 1 Pet. 3:1, 2, 4). The exercise of authority (v. 12), which may be related to the work of the bishops/presbyters (cf. 3:4, 5; 5:1, 2, 17; Tit. 1:9-13), extends beyond the worship service into family and individual relationships. Certainly the concluding reference to continuing "in faith and love and sanctity with self-restraint" (v. 15) has the Christian life in its widest sense in view.

That the context is the Christian community and not just the church service is also borne out by the self-conscious reflection in the key verse 3:15, where Paul says that he writes "so that you may know how one ought to conduct oneself in (ἐν) the household of God." Although it is possible that ἐν points to a gathering in which one is to behave in a certain mannner, it is more likely that it is the community ("household" more than "house") that is in view. Certainly this broader perspective is evident immediately preceding 3:15, where the qualifications and activities of church officers are spelled out in terms of the community (cf. especially 3:7) and not just in terms of the worship service. As the conduct and deportment of the officers relates to the community, so does the conduct and deportment of women.

Therefore, Paul's instructions to women, like the preceding instructions to men, are related to the context of the gathered Christian community but are not restricted to it. Men must always live holy lives that avoid wrath and dispute, particularly in connection with prayer for others; women are always to live in accord with their profession of godliness, dressing modestly and discreetly, and manifesting a proper relationship to men as regards the question of authority.

The argument is as follows: Paul enjoins modesty and discretion for women's apparel (v. 9a), indicates what should not characterize women's lives (v. 9b), and returns to the spiritual adornment, "good works," that befits their profession (v. 10). Next, he says that women are to learn, but, leading up to another prohibition, he emphasizes that their learning must be characterized by quietness and submission (v. 11). Specifically, he orders that women may not teach or exercise authority over men in the Christian community and its gatherings (v. 12). As grounds for this insistence, he appeals to the authority relationship established between man and woman in the representative man and woman, Adam and Eve, by means of the order of their creation (v. 13). This creation order is substantiated, or illustrated, by the great tragedy of the fall, when the leadership roles were reversed (v. 14). In conclusion Paul reminds women of God's great promise to the woman (Gn. 3:15) that she would be saved by means of her seed if she responds to that seed in faith, love, and sanctity, with submission to God's creation order, i.e., with self-restraint (v. 15).

Adornment and Good Works: 2:9-10

2:9a καί is found between ὡσαύτως and γυναῖκας in ℵ² D* F G K L, Origen, Chrysostom, Theodore of Mopsuestia, John of Damascus, and Ambrosiaster, and with τάς following in the Byzantine text tradition, and is absent in ℵ* A P 17 71, Clement, Origen. (It is bracketed in *UBSGNT,* indicating that the text is disputed; Tischendorf placed it in the eighth edition of his text, as did *KJV;* it is omitted by *NA*[25], Kilpatrick, Westcott-Hort, Tasker [the *NEB* text], *NASB, RSV,* and *NIV.*) The evidence is closely balanced, but since the two oldest manuscripts (with the majority of manuscripts and versions) omit it and addition can be explained more easily than omission, it can be concluded that the evidence favors omission.

ὡσαύτως (NT 17x; Pl. 8x) means "(in) the same (way), similarly," and most likely here, "likewise" (BAGD). Here, as elsewhere in the PE where it is used without a verb it assumes that the previous basic verb form is to be understood (the basic form of εἶναι understood in 3:8, 11 from 3:2; in 5:25 from 5:24; in Tit. 2:3 from 2:2). Here the understood verb is βούλομαι from v. 8. But is βούλομαι to be understood as followed (1) directly by the infinitive κοσμεῖν or (2) by the infinitive προσεύχεσθαι, also supplied from v. 8, which would in that case be itself followed by κοσμεῖν? In the first case the similarity indicated by ὡσαύτως would be that Paul has moral instructions for both men and women. But if βούλομαι προσεύχεσθαι is to be supplied, then the similarity is that both groups are to engage in the same activity, i.e., prayer.

In favor of the latter is that this gives unity to the passage. Men are to pray, mindful of their besetting sins, and women are to do likewise. It is sometimes argued that unless this approach is taken the passage must be read as if only men are to pray, which would be contrary to Paul's teaching elsewhere (1 Cor. 11:5ff.). The awkward construction that results from including προσεύχεσθαι with the understood verb is explained on the grounds that κοσμεῖν is added by asyndeton, that it has an explanatory or epexegetical force (e.g., Weiss), or that it is to be restricted to μετὰ αἰδοῦς καὶ σωφροσύνης, with ἐν καταστολῇ being governed by προσεύχεσθαι.

But it must be noted in this regard that the similarity that ὡσαύτως speaks of in the PE in relation to groups of people (here and 3:8, 11; Tit. 2:3, 6; cf. also Rom. 8:26 and its context) is that the groups in view are to be "like" those mentioned before in having certain qualifications, though not necessarily the same qualifications and activities. In each case the emphasis is on "similarity" rather than "sameness."

Furthermore, βούλομαι without προσεύχεσθαι fits vv. 9-10, is alone necessary, and seems intended. This natural understanding makes κοσμεῖν, then, the counterpart of προσεύχεσθαι in the preceding verse. Some suggest that Paul intended to parallel the previous ἐπαίροντας with the concept of κοσμε-, but this would necessitate κοσμε- being written as a participle. As an infinitive it is actually parallel to προσεύχεσθαι. Further, the unity of the passage is kept intact if προσεύχεσθαι is not understood along with βούλομαι: As elsewhere (5:1, 2; Tit. 2:1-6; Col. 3:18, 19; Eph. 5:21-33), Paul introduces the distinctions between men and women in their particular responsibilities in the midst of a discussion of the church as a worshipping community. Finally, just as the emphasis on women dressing modestly and discreetly does not mean that men are not to be concerned about this, so the emphasis on men, who have the responsibility for leading prayer in corporate worship, does not exclude women from praying as well (cf. again 1 Cor. 11:1ff.). But the concern for this question regarding women and men in regard to prayer must not dominate the discussion so that it obscures the construction of the passage and the emphasis Paul intends. On balance, the simpler solution, an understood repetition of βούλομαι, seems to be demanded both by ὡσαύτως and the lack of a finite verb before κοσμεῖν (so also *NASB, RSV, NEB, NIV*).

Although it may be conjectured why the reference to "men" has a definite article and that to "women" does not, no certain reason can be established. Just as ἀνήρ means "men" in distinction from women in v. 8 and does not have its more restricted and derived sense of "husbands," so here similarly γυναῖκας (accusative plural as "subject" of the infinitive κοσμεῖν) refers to women in distinction from men. Just as Paul was asking not only husbands but men in general to pray, so also he is enjoining women in general, not just wives, to dress modestly and discreetly, and to behave in accord with their womanliness in relation to men.

κοσμεῖν in the NT means (except in Mt. 25:7) "to adorn" and is related to "the basic sense of κόσμος, i.e., order or adornment" (H. Sasse, *TDNT* III, 867; cf. BAGD). ἑαυτάς refers back to γυναῖκας. Knowing that adornment and dress is an area with which women are often concerned and in which there are dangers of immodesty or indiscretion, Paul makes that the focal point of his warning and commands women "to adorn themselves" in keeping with their Christian profession and life.

ἐν is often used in the sense of "in" or "with" when used with reference to apparel as here (see BAGD s.v. 4b [p. 259] for a list of passages). καταστολή** (a NT hapax) is used of "deportment," both outward (expressed in clothing) and inward, and perhaps both together (BAGD s.v., with examples). The sentence as a whole is governed by the infinitive κοσμεῖν, which first governs ἐν καταστολῇ, then turns to a negation (μὴ ἐν, v. 9b), and ends with ἀλλὰ . . . δι' ἔργων ἀγαθῶν (v. 10). The emphasis first comes to expression in the adjective κόσμιος** (here and 1 Tim. 3:2; the adverb κοσμίως is found here in ℵ² D* F G H 17 33 1739 1881, etc.; κοσμίῳ is found in ℵ* A D Ψ it vg syr and Clement; in view of support by the earlier manuscripts and the fact that the adverb can be better explained as a correction from the adjective ["modestly" seeming to fit the statement better than "modest apparel," particularly if a scribe was also puzzled by the masculine ending with feminine καταστολή, not realizing that κόσμιος sometimes functions as a two-ending rather than a three-ending adjective] κοσμίῳ is to be preferred). κόσμιος has a general meaning of "respectable," "honorable," and when used in reference to women means elsewhere, as here, "modest" (BAGD cite

Epictetus, *Enchiridion* 40; Dio Chrysostom 5.14; one papyrus; cf. Dibelius-Conzelmann).

The prepositional phrase introduced by μετά denotes the state of mind or attitude necessary for one to be concerned about modesty and thus to dress modestly. αἰδώς** (a NT hapax [variant reading in Heb. 12:28] used with particular reference to women in extrabiblical literature in connection with the κοσμε-root but more particularly with σωφροσύνη; see BAGD s.v. σωφροσύνη; LSJM; MM; Spicq; and the monographs cited in BAGD s.v. αἰδώς; note especially the usage in Epictetus, e.g., 4.8; and also Josephus, *Ant.* 2.52; cf. αἰσχρός, which is synonymous with certain aspects of our word, especially 1 Cor. 11:6; 14:35) is used, according to LSJM, "as a moral feeling, *reverence, awe, respect* for the feeling or opinion of others or for one's own conscience, and so *shame, self-respect . . . sense of honour.*" Here it is that "which shrinks from overpassing the limits of womanly reserve and modesty, as well as from the dishonour which would justly attach thereto" (Trench, *Synonyms,* 71f.; cf. Ellicott and Bernard).

σωφροσύνη** (Acts 26:25; here; 2:15; common in extrabiblical Greek in reference to women and with αἰδώς, as here; see BAGD) has among its meanings the general one of "good judgment, moderation, self-control," which when seen as "a feminine virtue" is understood as *"decency, chastity"* (BAGD, 802). This word was used of one of the four cardinal virtues in Platonic philosophy (Plato, *Republic* 4.430e) and signified a command over bodily passions, a state of self-mastery in the area of the appetite. The basic meaning of the word has different nuances and connotations and represents "that habitual inner self-government, with its constant rein on all the passions and desires, which would hinder the temptation to [immodesty] from arising" (Trench, *Synonyms,* 72; cf. Spicq; Lock, 148; BAGD). In effect, Paul is saying that when such attitudes self-consciously control a woman's mind, the result is evident in her modest apparel.

2:9b Paul goes on to speak in negative terms, using μή, the usual negative particle after verbs of "will" (see Ellicott), κοσμεῖν and the reflexive pronoun ἑαυτάς being understood. He does so concretely, naming particular practices that violate the norm he just enunciated. The question arises of his intention with this specificity: Are the practices named intrinsically inappropriate to the lifestyle of a Christian woman? Is the negation hyperbolic, to be taken not absolutely but relatively, in connection with v. 10 (i.e., adorn your inner person not your outer; cf. 1 Pet. 3:3, 4 for a possible parallel)? Or is the apostle applying his general principle (v. 9a) to particular practices of the time that, because of the way they were used, were contrary to the Christian lifestyle? If so, should the same specific prohibitions be extended to other cultures, or might other practices fall more suitably into the same prohibited category in other cultures?

πλέγμα** (a NT hapax) is used of "anything," not just hair, "entwined, woven, braided" (BAGD s.v., with classical and Hellenistic references; cf. 1 Pet. 3:3 ἐμπλοκῆς τριχῶν; cf. T. K. Cheyne, *Enc. Bib.* II, 1941: "The Talmud . . . presents us with a word, for the woman's hairdresser [*m^e^gād^e^la'*] . . . and the verb from which it comes means 'to plait' "). χρυσίον (so A F G I P) like the variant reading χρυσῷ (א D K L Clement of Alexandria, Basil, Chrysostom, Theodore), over which it is to be preferred, means "gold" as a metal of great value. It is sometimes regarded (cf. Abbott-Smith, *Lexicon;* LSJM) as a diminutive of χρυσός and is understood as gold ornaments or jewelry here and in 1 Pet. 3:3; Rev. 17:4; 18:16 (see BAGD for Hellenistic references). μαργαρῖται, "pearls," were regarded as very precious (cf. Mt. 13:45, 46; Rev. 14:4; Usener, "Perle"; F. Hauck, *TDNT* IV, 472f.), in more demand even than gold (see BAGD for reference to Chares of Mitylene [fourth century BC]). ἱματισμός, "clothing" or "apparel," is qualified by πολυτελής** (cf. 1 Pet. 3:4), "very expensive" or "costly" (BAGD, cf. Mk. 14:3; used with reference to clothing in Xenophon, *Anabasis* 1.5.8; Philo, *De Sacrificiis* 21; Josephus, *B.J.* 1.605).

These items in this list are either plural (πλέγματα, perhaps because of the multiplicity of them in the extreme hair styles of the day, and μαργαρῖται) or generic singulars (χρυσίον is used in this way in many languages; ἱματισμός, perhaps emphasizing an outfit of clothing as a whole or thinking of each individual). More noteworthy are the connectives, καί between πλέγμασιν and χρυσίῳ (a variant is ἤ, but this is inadequately attested and can be explained as an attempt at uniformity) and then ἤ twice. καί may be used to connect braids with gold either because hair settings and jewelry are often taken together or because the gold in mind here is jewelry intertwined with the braid or a gold net over the hair. The first ἤ and the μαργαρῖται that follows either contrast with the hair and gold as a whole or with the gold as another form of ornate and sensuous ornamentation used in connection with the braiding of the hair. (1 Pet. 3:3, which is clearly parallel to 1 Tim. 2:9, omits pearls.) The second ἤ adds another ostentatious item, ἱματισμός πολυτελής.

The reason for Paul's prohibition of elaborate hair styles, ornate jewelry, and extremely expensive clothing becomes clear when one reads in the contemporary literature of the inordinate time, expense, and effort that elaborately braided hair and jewels demanded, not just as ostentatious display, but also as the mode of dress of courtesans and harlots (see Balsdon, *Roman Women,* 253-71; Str-B III, 427ff.; for braiding see especially *DAC* I, 520; for hair styles and jewelry see *DGRA* I, 496-502, especially 501; *DClA* 266-68; cf. also M. Stephan, "Haartracht," PW Supplement VI, 90-102; among ancient writers see, e.g., Pliny, *Natural History* 9.33.12; Juvenal, *Satires* 6.502-3; Ovid, *Ars Amatoria* 3.136ff.; Josephus, *Ant.* 8.185; Rev. 17:4; 18:12, 16). Philo (*De Sacrificiis* 21) speaks of "Pleasure" "languishing in the guise of a harlot or courtesan": "Her hair is dressed in curious and elaborate plaits," she wears "costly raiment," and "bracelets and necklaces and every other feminine ornament wrought of gold and jewels hang round her" (F. H. Colson and G. H. Whitaker's translation in LCL, II, 107, 109).

It is the excess and sensuality that the items connote that Paul forbids (cf. Jas. 5:1-6), not braids, gold, pearls, or even costly garments in and of themselves. This is borne out by the fact that the Christian community of the NT is quite willing to use these terms with positive connotations (gold: Mt. 2:11; 1 Cor. 3:12; Rev. 3:18; 21:18ff.; pearls: Mt. 7:6; 13:45, 46; Rev. 21:21; a bride adorned [κεκοσμημένην]: Rev. 21:2), as is the OT (e.g., the Song of Solomon).

Has Paul, however, merely taken up the criticism of women and their dress found in Greco-Roman and Jewish writers? That he might utilize their forms is not out of the question, since he believed that all people have a basic ethical understanding given them by God (Rom. 2:14, 15), sometimes even more admirable than what can be found among believers (1 Tim. 5:8; 1 Cor. 5:1); but his words are much more restrained than theirs (cf. especially Juvenal, *Satires* 6.502-3). It may be that Paul is applying to women Jesus' words in Mt. 5:28ff. and drawing on such OT passages as Is. 3:16ff. (cf. Judith 10:3ff., where the heroine sets out to seduce specifically by means of dress, hair, and jewelry). Whatever the origin of Paul's words, his concern is shared by the leaders of the Christian community (here and 1 Pet. 3:3). Just as Christian men needed to be warned that their interest in vigor and discussion should not produce strife and dissension (v. 8), so Christian women needed to be warned that their interest in beauty and adornment should not produce immodesty and indiscretion.

2:10 V. 10 carries this discussion to its conclusion. The ultimate adornment with which Christian women should be concerned is good works. ἀλλά contrasts good works with immodest attire. And since the preceding immodest practices are themselves already contrasted with modest apparel, we have a three-layered contrast (modest, immodest, good works). Therefore ἀλλά makes the ultimate emphasis fall on good works (cf. again 1 Pet. 3:1ff., especially v. 4). Paul is advocating not just modesty in dress, but also that more time and energy be spent on spiritual adornment.

To lead up to this final point he reminds the women of their own professed commitment. ὅ is the subject of the impersonal verb πρέπει, a collective used in anticipation of and in apposition to ἔργων ἀγαθῶν (cf. H. von Soden), which is kept to the last for emphasis. πρέπει means "be fitting, be seemly or suitable" (BAGD). The impersonal construction is followed by the dative of the persons (also Tit. 2:1; Eph. 5:3; cf. Xenophon, *Hellenica* 4.2.37), γυναιξίν, "for women. . . ."

Paul appeals to them as women ἐπαγγελλομένας θεοσέβειαν. ἐπαγγέλλομαι (only the middle occurs in NT) refers basically to the "announcement of a promise or offer" (the most frequent meaning) and the "announcement or proclamation about oneself or one's intention," meaning, therefore, "profess, lay claim to" (BAGD; J. Schniewind and G. Friedrich, *TDNT* II, 576ff.), with the latter in view here (and probably also in 6:21; for extra-biblical examples see BAGD and *TDNT*).

θεοσέβεια** (a NT hapax) means "reverence for God, piety, religion" (BAGD), and is used by both Greek and Jewish authors with a strong ethical note (cf. G. Bertram, *TDNT* III, 123ff.; Jn. 9:31: "if anyone is God-fearing, and does his will"). Paul uses the word perhaps to stress in particular the ethical here, since he uses εὐσέβεια elsewhere in the PE where that emphasis is not as strong. But perhaps he uses it also because the word's formation itself puts more direct emphasis on one's personal relation to God (θεός; cf. 1 Pet. 3:5). And perhaps Paul is utilizing a word already used by the false teachers who seek to influence the women (cf. 2 Tim. 3:6, 7; the word is used by Jewish writers [cf. G. Bertram, *TDNT* III, 124ff.], and the false teachers have a Jewish inclination; cf. again 1:3, 4, 7). The absence of the word from the NT otherwise may result from its use almost exclusively for the Jewish religion. Whatever the reason, it should not seem completely strange that one who has used words of the σεβ-stem, who utilizes compounds, and who has used θεοστυγής (hater of God, Rom. 1:30) should use this word here.

δι' ἔργων ἀγαθῶν, as the final phrase of this section, places the emphasis ultimately on "good works" in contrast to dress and adornment, now making specific what was in view in ὅ at the beginning of the verse. The verb construction to be understood is that which has governed v. 9 and which also carries over to v. 10, i.e., κοσμεῖν ἑαυτάς. These good works are not only the obedient deeds of wearing modest attire but also, as the plural implies, the wide spectrum of Christian obedience springing from faith in Christ Jesus (cf. in general Tit. 2:14 and in particular Eph. 2:10; 1 Tim. 5:10). διά here means "by means of." ἔργον, meaning generally "work," designates here in connection with ἀγαθόν the various deeds that flow from and give evidence of the power of Christ and the Spirit at work in one's life (again cf. Tit. 2:14; Eph. 2:10). ἀγαθόν describes the deeds as good in the moral sense (BAGD). That good deeds are an outcome and expression of salvation is as much a part of Paul's theology as is his repudiation of works as a basis for salvation.

The plural form of the phrase, ἔργα καλά/ἀγαθά, is found almost exclusively in the PE (Eph. 2:10; here; 1 Tim. 5:10, 25; 6:18; Tit. 2:7, 14; 3:8, 14), alongside a nearly equal number of instances of singular ἔργον καλόν/ἀγαθόν (Rom. 13:3; 2 Cor. 9:8; Phil. 1:6; Col. 1:10; 2 Thes. 2:17; 1 Tim. 3:1; 5:10; Tit. 1:16; 3:1; 2 Tim. 2:21; 3:17), though plural ἔργα is used elsewhere in Paul without καλά or ἀγαθά (e.g., Rom. 2:6, 7). Perhaps Paul's use of the singular in the earlier Epistles had already begun to give way to the plural by the addition of πᾶν to refer to good works in general (cf. 2 Cor. 9:8; Col. 1:10; 2 Thes. 2:17). Then in the PE the interchange between the singular and plural (cf. again Rom. 2:6, 7) came to its logical outworking in the plural phrase ἔργα καλά/ἀγαθά, without πᾶν (cf. plural τὰ καλά ἔργα in Mt. 5:16, the teaching of which may have been in Paul's mind). This interchange between the singular with πᾶν and the plural without πᾶν occurs within the PE (e.g., 1 Tim. 5:10: ἐν ἔργοις καλοῖς . . . εἰ παντὶ ἔργῳ ἀγαθῷ; Tit. 3:1, 8, 14: πᾶν ἔργον ἀγαθόν . . . καλῶν ἔργων).

We return to the broad questions posed at the beginning of v. 9: Is Paul dealing with a specific case, giving general remarks about these particular aspects of dress? Or is he making a hyperbolic statement for effect? The primary sources mentioned above allow us to see that Paul is forbidding a style of dress and hair that was known to his readers and that was particularly reprehensible because of both its immodesty and its cost in time, money, and effort. That his emphasis is on their effect and not on the items as such, is seen in the first part of v. 9, which sets out this concern as his guiding principle ("with proper clothing, modestly and discreetly"). It is with braided hair, gold, pearls, and very costly garments as violations of this principle, not with hair however arranged or gold, pearls, or garments in and of themselves that he is concerned. The possible exception to this evaluation would be the qualifying word, πολυτελεῖ, "very costly," which carries a note of opprobrium because of its inherent inappropriateness. Other than that, Paul's condemnation of particular practices and styles does have a hyperbolic cast to it. Paul knows the reader will understand that he does not mean hair styles, jewelry, and clothing as such but rather immodesty and indiscretion (cf. for a similar hyperbolic statement 1 Pet. 3:3: "Let not your adornment be external . . . putting on dresses").

Paul's argument as a whole is: "Let women dress modestly and discreetly, not with . . . , but by means of good works." What he wants to focus attention on is good deeds. Like an OT prophet who says "not sacrifice, but obedience," Paul prohibits specific practices because in their setting they are immodest and because he wants to motivate women to refocus their energy and attention (cf. again Mt. 5:16). What emerges is a statement of principle about women's dress (v. 9a), an application to the current situation in hyperbolic form (v. 9b), and a refocus of the argument to an ultimate and more important concern for good deeds (v. 10): principle, application, reorientation.

Prohibition of Teaching and Ruling Men Grounded in the Order of Creation: 2:11-15

Paul now turns to the learning/teaching/exercise of authority functions in reference to women and men in the church. He begins (v. 11) with an emphasis on silence (ἐν ἡσυχίᾳ) in women's learning as expressive of submission (ἐν πάσῃ ὑποταγῇ). Paul applies this concern to the functions of teaching and exercising authority by specifically not permitting women to do either in reference to men (διδάσκειν, αὐθεντεῖν, v. 12a). This prohibition is made even more clear by a return to the demand for silence (v. 12b). V. 13 indicates that the reason or basis for the prohibition is the creation order (γάρ), and v. 14 indicates how this is substantiated in the actions of the woman in the fall. As a concluding word (v. 15) Paul indicates that "salvation" (σωθήσεται) comes to women through that which is unique to them, διὰ τῆς τεκνογονίας, if they manifest an abiding trust evidenced in a life that does not overthrow God's order (μετὰ σωφροσύνης).

2:11 γυνή is used here, as it has been throughout the passage, to refer to women in general (see v. 9). Imperative μανθανέτω, "learn," is used here in the literal sense of learning through instruction (i.e., being present at and profiting from the edification of the service [1 Cor. 14:31], contra Babylonian Talmud *Ḥagiga* 3a: "The men came to learn, the women came to hear"). In anticipation of v. 12, the apostle insists that women's learning in public instruction is to be ἐν ἡσυχίᾳ** (Acts 22:2; 2 Thes. 3:12; 1 Tim. 2:11, 12), which means here "in silence" (as in Acts 22:2; cf. σιγάω, "be silent," in a parallel situation in 1 Cor. 14:34; see BAGD). This silence is a concrete expression of the principle of submission, which Paul articulates in the next prepositional phrase.

ὑποταγή** (2 Cor. 9:13; Gal. 2:5; 1 Tim. 2:11; 3:4) is used here in the passive sense of "subjection, subordination, or submission." With the related verb ὑποτάσσω (especially 1 Cor. 14:34; Eph. 5:21 [variant reading in v. 22], 24; Col. 3:18; 1 Pet. 3:1, 5) it is used in the NT of the submission of Christians to God the Father (Heb. 12:9; Jas. 4:7), of all things to Christ (present in Eph. 2:22; future in Phil. 3:21), of all Christians to one another in the fear of Christ (Eph. 5:21), and more particularly of the appropriate response of those under authority (1 Cor. 16:16; 1 Pet. 5:5; Rom. 13:1, 5; 1 Tim. 3:4; Tit. 2:9; 3:1; 1 Pet. 2:18), especially with regard to the relationship of wife to husband (Col. 3:18; Eph. 5:21-22; Tit. 2:5; 1 Pet. 3:1, 5; and thus ὑποτάσσω, ὑποταγή, and κεφαλή [cf. 1 Cor. 11:3, 4, 5, 7, 10; Eph. 5:23] are key words in this area of concern). In the relationship of husband and wife the concept of submission is used of a voluntary and willing compliance on the part of the wife, an equal, to one whom God has called to be the "head" in that relationship.

Here submission is, more broadly, the norm for the relationship of women to men in authority functions within the church. The addition of πάσῃ (ἐν πάσῃ ὑποταγῇ) to indicate "the highest degree" expresses in a heightened way the concern Paul has for this norm (for this sense of πάς see 4:9; 5:2; Tit. 2:15; BAGD s.v. laδ; the phrase is rendered "entire submissiveness" in *NASB;* "all submissiveness" in *RSV;* "full submission" in *NIV*). Paul is concerned that women's learning not become an occasion to overturn their role in relation to the authority role that men are to exercise in the church (as apparently in Corinth; cf. 1 Cor. 14:33ff., where Paul expresses the same concern). Therefore he has added the two qualifications, ἐν ἡσυχίᾳ and ἐν πάσῃ ὑποταγῇ.

2:12 Paul carries this injunction further by indicating that he does not permit women to teach and exercise authority over men. δέ is used here to indicate the contrast, "learn but not teach" (cf. 1 Cor. 14:34, where the desire to learn is not to be used to gain the privilege of speaking, and notice the close parallel of that passage, οὐ γάρ ἐπιτρέπεται αὐταῖς λαλεῖν, to our passage). ἐπιτρέπω (NT 17x) means "allow, permit" someone (dative) to do something (infinitive; BAGD).

Some have suggested that Paul conveys here only a note of personal disinclination (cf. Phillips's translation: "Personally, I don't allow"). But such a suggestion misunderstands the authoritativeness of ἐπιτρέπω when used by Paul (cf. Robertson: "Paul speaks authoritatively"), which is demonstrated by a close analysis of the three occurrences in Paul (1 Cor. 14:34, a parallel; 16:7, an action of the Lord; here). The strength of the prohibition here is underlined by Paul's appeal to the creation order (v. 13, γάρ); in 1 Cor. 14:34 the prohibition is correlated to "the law" (undoubtedly the same OT teaching as here in v. 13) and is further delineated by his covering statement in v. 37, "the things that I write to you are the Lord's commandment."

It has also been suggested that the present indicative form of ἐπιτρέπω indicates a temporal limitation and thus limits Paul's statement to the then and there of Ephesus. An examination of other occurrences of Paul's use of first person singular present indicative (Rom. 12:1, 3; 1 Cor. 4:16; 2 Cor. 5:20; Gal. 5:2, 3, Eph. 4:1; 1 Thes. 4:1; 5:14; 2 Thes. 3:6; 1 Tim. 2:1, 8) demonstrates that he uses it to give universal and authoritative instruction or exhortation (cf. especially Rom. 12:1; 1 Tim. 2:8).

As in vv. 9 and 11, so also here γυνή refers generally to any "woman," and this is probably highlighted by the use of anarthrous forms for both γυνή and ἀνήρ. Just as it was womanhood that required silence and submission in v. 11, so here also it is womanhood (vis-à-vis men) that is in view in the prohibition.

That which is not permitted is first of all διδάσκειν, "to teach," but not as an unqualified prohibition since the object "man" indicates a limitation, as does the immediate context, which has been dealing with religious instruction in the life of the church. To this can be compared Paul's commendation of women teaching other women (Tit. 2:3-5) and teaching their children and sons (2 Tim. 1:5; 3:14, 15; cf. Acts 16:1); he apparently also approved of the team effort of Priscilla and Aquila in explaining in private conversation ("they took him aside") to Apollos "the way of God more accurately" (Acts 18:25, 26). Just as v. 11 was not a demand for all learning to be done in silence, as an unqualified absolute, but was concerned with women's learning in the midst of the assembled people of God, so also the prohibition of teaching here has the same setting and perspective in view.

διδάσκειν (Pl.* 15x) means generally "to teach or instruct." Here the religious subject matter is assumed, and the persons (not) to be taught are "men," the implication being that women may not teach or exercise authority in or over the church (of which men are a part; cf. 1 Cor. 14:34, 35: "in the churches," "in church"). Other uses of the verb in 1 Timothy are in settings where Timothy is urged to teach as part of his ministry (4:11; 6:2), and others are also so urged in 2 Timothy (2:2), though in Titus (1:11) the activity may be somewhat more general. A similar authoritative note is found in Rom. 12:7; 1 Cor. 4:17; Gal. 1:12; [Eph. 4:21?]; Col. 1:28; 2:7; 2 Thes. 2:15. In Col. 3:16 Paul does not restrict teaching to ministers in distinction from other Christians, and in other places he uses the verb in the most general sense (but still with a certain note or overtone of authority indicated [1 Cor. 11:14] or implied [Rom. 2:21]). In 1 Cor. 14:34, 35, the instruction that women "keep silence" is given in the context of various Christians getting up and speaking. Both there and here Paul's prohibition of women teaching would prevent them from serving as elders or ministers, but it is unwarranted to limit it to such a restriction from office-bearing. Paul uses functional language ("to teach") rather than office language ("a bishop") to express the prohibition. Here he prohibits women from publicly teaching men, and thus teaching the church.

οὐδέ joins the second infinitive to the first under οὐκ ἐπιτρέπω, whose negative is now conveyed in οὐδέ itself. Robertson (*Grammar,* 1185) indicates that "in accord with the copulative use of δέ we frequently have οὐδέ and μηδέ in the continuative sense, carrying on the negative with no idea of contrast" (cf., e.g., Mt. 6:26). Therefore, οὐδέ here may be rendered "nor" *(KJV, NEB)* or for English stylistic reasons "or" *(NASB, RSV, TEV, NIV).*

αὐθεντεῖν** (a biblical hapax; see Knight, "ΑΥΘΕΝΤΕΩ" and the response by Wilshire, "TLG Computer"), once thought to be unique to Christian literature (e.g., Thayer, *Lexicon*), occurs in the papyrus *BGU* 1208:38 (27 BC) and in Philodemus, *Rhetoric* 2 (first century BC; see BAGD for further documentation and later occurrences) and is referred to as Hellenistic (Ἑλληνικῶς) over against Attic αὐτοδικεῖν by the second-century AD Attic lexicographer Moeris (ed. J. Pierson [1759], 58; [43 in 1831 edition]; cf. also the account of the word and its meaning and that of related words, especially αὐθέντης, in MM; Deissmann, *Light,* 88f.; Robertson, IV, 570; MHT II, 278). Contrary to the suggestion of *KJV*'s "to usurp authority" and BAGD's alternative, "domineer" (so also *NEB*), the use of the word shows no inherent negative sense of grasping or usurping authority or of exercising it in a harsh or authoritative way, but simply means "to have or exercise authority" (BAGD; LSJM: "to have full power or authority over"; cf. Preisigke, *Wörterbuch* I, 235f., giving three nuances for four different papyri, all in the sphere of the above definition; cf. finally Lampe, *Lexicon,* whose four main meanings are in the same orbit; so *NASB, RSV, TEV, NIV:* "to have authority").

Paul refers, then, with αὐθεντεῖν to exercise of a leadership role or function in the church (the contextual setting), and thus by specific application the office of ἐπίσκοπος/πρεσβύτερος, since the names of these offices (especially ἐπίσκοπος) and the activities associated with them (cf., e.g., 3:4, 5; 5:17; Tit. 1:9ff.; Acts 20:17, 28ff.) indicate the exercise of authority. It is noteworthy, however, that Paul does not use "office" terminology here (bishop/presbyter) but functional terminology (teach/exercise authority). It is thus the activity that he prohibits, not just the office (cf. again 1 Cor. 14:34, 35).

ἀνήρ is used here, as in v. 8, to refer to "man" in distinction from woman, not in its more restricted sense of "husband." The singular refers to men in general, just as γυνή refers here and in v. 11 to women in general. The genitive case of ἀνδρός agrees with the nearer infinitive, which like other verbs of ruling and governing takes the genitive (BDF §177; Robertson, *Grammar,* 510), though the noun qualifies not only the second infinitive, αὐθεντεῖν, but also the first, διδάσκειν, in accordance with normal Greek usage (cf. Acts 8:21, where as here οὐδέ is used; see also Smyth, *Grammar* §1634, which gives an example of two infinitives joined by οὐδέ with a common object written only once).

That a woman may not teach in the church, or teach a man, is underlined by the addition of ἀλλ' εἶναι ἐν ἡσυχίᾳ. The adversative particle ἀλλά indicates that this clause is contrasted with what precedes (not to teach or exercise authority *but* to be in silence). Some have suggested that Paul is only ruling out teaching or exercise of authority apart from a man's oversight, or just a certain type of authoritative teaching. The insistence here on silence seems to rule out all these solutions. The clause as a whole describes the status of a woman not in relation to every aspect of the gathered assembly (i.e., praying, prophesying, singing, etc.; cf. again 1 Cor. 11:5) but specifically in respect to that with which it is contrasted, i.e., teaching (and the exercise of authority), just as the first occurrence of ἐν ἡσυχίᾳ applied to the learning/teaching situation (v. 11).

2:13 The ground for the prohibition is now given: It is the order of the creation of Adam and Eve as the archetypes of man and woman and the implication of this order for headship and submission in such relationships. (The conjunction γάρ signifies that the statement that follows provides the reason for the previous command; cf. BAGD s.v. 1.) The verse is a terse statement of an argument that Paul has used before in connection with the headship of man to woman in 1 Cor. 11:3ff.

'Αδάμ is the transliteration of the Hebrew word used in Genesis as the name of the first man created by God (first in the Hebrew text at Gn. 1:26; first in the LXX at Gn. 2:16; cf. 1 Cor. 15:45: "the first man, Adam"). It is used in our passage not of generic "mankind," as in Gn. 1:26, 27, but of man = male, as distinct from Eve (cf. especially Gn. 2:20ff.). πρῶτος, used here as a predicate adjective (cf. BAGD s.v. 1a; Robertson, *Grammar,* 657; BDF §243), indicates both the absolute priority of Adam in God's creation and, most of all, in the contrast here of Adam to Eve (εἶτα Εὕα), his priority to her. πλάσσω** (Rom. 9:20; 1 Tim. 2:13; both seem to reflect the OT usage) means "form" or "mold" and is the verb used by the LXX in Gn. 2:7, 8, 15 (v. 15 without a Hebrew equivalent) of the creation of Adam. εἶτα (NT 13x) is used here, as is predominantly the case in the NT, as a temporal adverb meaning "then." It is found in the "first . . . then . . ." construction here and in 3:10 (BAGD s.v. 1). Εὕα** (2 Cor. 11:3; 1 Tim. 2:13) is the Greek transliteration (sometimes Εὕα) of Hebrew *ḥawwâh,* the name of the woman formed from Adam (first so named in Gn. 3:20, where the LXX renders it Ζωή: the first use of Εὕα in the LXX is in 4:1).

It is evident, then, that Paul has Genesis 2 in mind here, just as he has Genesis 3 in mind in the next verse, as is evidenced by his use of LXX terms (especially πλάσσω). The appeal to what God does (or says) with Adam and Eve in the creation account as an indication of God's will with reference to men and women in general is similar to the argument Jesus uses in demonstrating that God intends permanence for marriage between men and women (Mt. 19:4-6).

With this brief statement on the order of creation Paul appeals to the whole of the creation narrative, as is indicated by his fuller treatment in 1 Cor. 11:8-9 (cf. Dodd, *According to the Scriptures*). This whole account would include "a helper suitable for him [i.e., for man, Adam]"; (Gn. 2:18) and the significance of the naming of the woman: "She shall be called Woman, because she was taken out of Man" (2:23). Paul explicitly specifies that the woman was "taken out of" (ἐκ) the man and created to help, or to be "for" (διά), the man in his fuller statement in 1 Corinthians. So it is not mere chronology ("first . . . then . . .") that Paul appeals to here but what is entailed in this chronology. (That drawing such implications from chronological priority is not foreign to the OT is seen from the similar, but different, appeals to the rights of primogeniture [see I. H. Marshall, *NBD* 377f.; J. E. Rosscup, *ZPEB* II, 540f.; R. de Vaux, *Ancient Israel,* 41f.].)

2:14 καί joins this verse to the preceding. Paul now appeals to the fall as an event that demonstrates in the most absolute way the dire consequences of a reversal of leadership roles. Just as v. 13 reflects the events and terminology of Genesis 2, so v. 14 reflects Genesis 3 and the terms used there (especially ἀπατάω).

ἀπατάω** (Eph. 5:6; here; Jas. 1:26) means "deceive" or "mislead" and occurs in the LXX of Genesis only at 3:13 in the woman's statement: "The serpent deceived me." καὶ 'Αδὰμ οὐκ ἠπατήθη is not meant to deny Adam's sin or participation in the fall (cf. Rom. 5:12ff.; 1 Cor. 15:21, 22) but to indicate, as the Genesis narrative does, that he sinned willfully, not as a result of deception (Gn. 3:6, 12). To this Paul contrasts (δέ = "but") the woman's deception. ἡ γυνή is probably used instead of "Eve" because it is used in the LXX of the Genesis 3 account (vv. 1, 2, 4, 6, 12, 13, 15, 16, 17; "Eve" appears in v. 20, only after the temptation/fall/judgment account) and also perhaps to begin to make the transition from Eve as a type to women in general (to whom this section is addressed). (γυνή is used in the statement about the seed of the woman in Gn. 3:15 [cf. both Hebrew and LXX].) The argument would then proceed in three steps: from "Eve" to "the woman" (singular as a transition from "Eve" to "women") to plural "women" in v. 15 (cf. Ridderbos). The compound form ἐξαπατάω, which similarly means "deceive" or "lead astray," may be used with regard to "the woman" in contrast with the preceding uncompounded form (with "Adam") for emphasis; but it also may simply be a stylistic change reflecting Paul's preference, since he uses the same compound verb in reference to Eve in 2 Cor. 11:3 as well. The basis for Paul's affirmation is the woman's statement in Gn. 3:13: "The serpent deceived me, and I ate."

The last part of the verse indicates the state of affairs resulting from the deception: the woman "fell into transgression" (*NASB*; cf. BAGD s.v. ἐν 14d) or "became a transgressor" (*RSV;* BAGD s.v. παράβασις [612]). παράβασις is used of the overstepping of set limits and therefore more tersely "transgression," in the NT always transgression against God's law or standard. Eve, by being deceived, took and ate the prohibited fruit and thus came into transgression. γέγονεν (perfect tense) indicates, with the prepositional phrase, the new condition into which she entered.

V. 14 thus shows by a negative example the importance of heeding the respective roles established by God in the creation of Eve from Adam. This adds to v. 13 (with καί) an example rather than a separate basis for Paul's argument. Thus Paul argues not from creation and fall but from creation, and then illustrates this argument, albeit negatively, from the fall (cf. God's judgment on Adam: "Because you have listened to the voice of your wife," Gn. 3:17).

2:15 Paul brings the section addressed to women to a conclusion with a note of encouragement (the main verb is σῴζω, "save") and an emphasis on continued Christian faith and godliness (repeating σωφροσύνης from v. 9, so that the section begins and ends with this motif).

The exegetical cruxes in this verse are the meanings of σωθήσεται and διὰ τῆς τεκνογονίας in connection with the following ἐάν clause. These questions are further encumbered by the shift from singular (σωθήσεται) to plural (μείνωσιν) and the attendant problem of identifying the subjects of these verbs.

Essentially two views have been followed on the use here of σωθήσεται: The reference is to either (1) salvation in the spiritual sense or (2) salvation in the physical sense of preservation. Similarly, essentially two views have been taken with regard to διὰ τῆς τεκνογονίας: It is a reference to either (1) the birth of Messiah or (2) childbearing in general. Various combinations of these solutions have been suggested.

It would be contrary to Paul's teaching elsewhere and to the emphasis of this letter (cf. 1 Tim. 1:15, 16; 2:3-6) and the other PE (cf. especially Tit. 3:3-7; 2 Tim. 1:8-10) to understand σωθήσεται as referring to spiritual salvation if διὰ τῆς τεκνογονίας is taken as referring to childbearing in general. This would make salvation for women conditional on a work, and specifically a work not all are able to perform.

Some suggest that we take σωθήσεται to mean "preserve" in the physical sense and διὰ τῆς τεκνογονίας to refer to childbirth (Barrett, Dibelius-Conzelmann [?], Guthrie, Simpson), on the grounds that this passage then would relate to the same problem as Gn. 3:16. But this suggestion also raises the question of how the ἐάν clause then functions. Is the clause saying that all who come through childbirth do so because they believe, implying that all who die in childbirth do not believe? This seems extremely unlikely. Furthermore, the problem of being preserved through childbirth is not part of the context in 1 Timothy, and it is doubtful whether σῴζω was ever used by Paul in this sense.

Another view (with some variations, Alford, Bernard, Calvin, Falconer, Scott, and White) understands σωθήσεται in the spiritual sense and τεκνογονία in the physical, but understands the connection of the former with the latter (διά) in terms of deliverance from (cf. 1 Cor. 3:15, "through fire") the pain of childbirth, which is understood as the sign of woman being in transgression (cf. Gn. 3:16). Women then are being encouraged to fulfill the role of motherhood, even though that very role reminds them of the fall and its consequence for them, because God will save them out of all such one day, if they continue, etc. But this understanding of διά is strained in this context, and the understanding of τεκνογονία taken in this view is far more negative than is appropriate to the context in both 1 Timothy and Genesis 3, almost as if childbearing were a hindrance to salvation (cf. the positive use of τεκνογονέω in 5:14; cf. also Gn. 4:1). Furthermore, it is doubtful whether Christian women ever faced the dilemma assumed by this position.

Another view (cf. with variations Chrysostom, Gealy, Hendriksen, Huther, Jeremias, Kelly, Parry, Ridderbos, Robertson, Ward, Weiss, and Vine) understands the salvation referred to predominantly in the spiritual sense and the reference to childbearing as typical of the feminine role. Thus, the way to salvation is not found by seeking a masculine role or by repudiating a feminine role but simply in being a woman (typified by childbearing) and responding to God in faith. The particular difficulty with this is the ambiguity in the understanding of σῴζω, especially in its relationship to childbearing and the feminine role, so that the significance of the latter, and especially the διά phrase, for σῴζω is quite unclear.

Yet another view falls somewhat in between in its understanding of the terms: The woman shall be saved or preserved from the error of becoming the dominant religious figure (v. 12) by assuming the feminine role, here typified symbolically (but not literally) by the expression διὰ τῆς τεκνογονίας, but only when assuming this role is coupled with faith and godliness (see Hurley, *Man and Woman*). Attractive as this position is in tying the conclusion to the argument, it still has difficulties in adequately explaining the fact that σωθήσεται (singular) appears to have ἡ γυνή as its subject, the meaning of σωθήσεται, and the use of a prepositional phrase in this uniquely typical and symbolic way.

The most likely understanding of this verse is that it refers to spiritual salvation through the birth of the Messiah. Some commentators (Alford, Bernard, Guthrie, Ward) have rejected this view without giving adequate reasons. But good reasons exist for adopting it (so Ellicott; Lock; H. von Soden; Wohlenberg; Huizenga, "Women"; cf. *RV, RSV* margin, *NEB* margin; with undue emphasis on Mary, Ignatius, *Eph.* 19; Irenaeus, *Haer.* 5.19; Justin, *Dial.* 100).

First, the context: V. 14 summarizes the woman's fall into sin (ἐν παραβάσει γέγονεν) described in Genesis 3. The one about whom it speaks is "the woman" (ἡ γυνή), Eve, and this one is the natural subject to be understood in v. 15, "she will be saved" = the woman, Eve, will be saved. From what does Eve need to be saved (in both 1 Timothy 2 and Genesis 3)? From ἐν παραβάσει γέγονεν, the last words preceding this verse. In the protevangelium of Gn. 3:15, which speaks of "her seed" and says "He [the seed] shall bruise you [the serpent = Satan] on the head," salvation is announced in terms of a child to be borne by the woman.

Furthermore, this understanding fits the flow of Paul's argument. He points out that Eve (ἡ γυνή) brought herself into transgression by abandoning her role and taking on that of the man. But by fulfilling her role, difficult as it may be as a result of sin (Gn. 3:16), she gives birth to the Messiah, and thereby "she" (ἡ γυνή, fulfilled, of course, in Mary; cf. Gal. 4:4) brings salvation into the world. The conditional clause (ἐὰν μείνωσιν κτλ.) signifies that the previous statement is true only when conditions are met, and σωθήσεται, understood as referring to spiritual salvation, would seem to be the only understanding that fulfills that requirement. Thus deliverance from transgression comes to those who have a true and sincere faith, which points to the usual correlation between salvation and faith in Paul and the attendant and abiding manifestation of faith in a godly life (cf. Romans 6 and 8). There is thus a transition from Eve (ἡ γυνή, singular σωθήσεται) back to women in general (μείνωσιν, plural); in this way the passage serves to show women the importance of their role and of carrying it out in an obedient way, the note on which the passage ends (ἁγιασμῷ μετὰ σωφροσύνης; cf. Mary's words in Lk. 1:38).

Second, the vocabulary, consideration of which brings us to the detailed examination of the text on the basis of which the view presented above can be tested. δέ here suggests the contrast between vv. 14 and 15. The subject of σωθήσεται is "the woman" (Eve, but also as typical woman) "in transgression."

That σωθήσεται is passive indicates that the deliverance is wrought for her by another. That its tense is future points forward from Eve to the promised future deliverance by means of the seed of the woman, which is Christ (Gn. 3:15). σῴζω (NT 106x; Pl. 29x) is used by Paul in the sense of "*save* or *preserve from eternal death,* from judgment, and from all that might lead to such death, e.g., sin, also in a positive sense, *bring* Messianic *salvation, bring to salvation*" (BAGD s.v. 2 [798], which places all Pauline occurrences in this category [Rom. 9:27 and 1 Cor. 3:15 being placed both in this category and in another]; cf. also J. Schneider, *NIDNTT* III, 214f.; W. Foerster, *TDNT* VII, 992-95). In line with this comprehensive evaluation is the usage of σῴζω (1:15; 2:4) and πίστις (1:2, 4, 5, 14, 19[2x]; 2:7) in 1 Timothy up to this point in the flow of the argument.

διά with the genitive is used here to express means, instrument, or agency (cf. BAGD s.v. A.III.1d [180]). There are seven occurrences in the NT of the verb σῴζω with διά (Acts 15:11; Rom. 5:9; 1 Cor. 1:21; 3:15; 15:2; here; 1 Pet. 3:20), all except 1 Cor. 1:21 passive and all except 1 Cor. 3:15 (which has δὲ ὡς and thus has a different relationship) and 1 Pet. 3:20 (leaving 1 Tim. 2:15 aside for the moment) indicating with διά the means through which salvation is brought, accomplished, or appropriated (where an element is mentioned, i.e., fire or water [1 Cor. 3:15; 1 Pet. 3:20], salvation is brought through these elements, not by them). Since τεκνογονία may well indicate the seed of the woman, Jesus (cf. especially Rom. 5:9), it would be in accord with Paul's usage to understand διά with the passive form of σῴζω in this same manner, which is a normal understanding of διά and fits best with the interpretation being proposed.

That through which, or by means of which, the woman will be saved is τεκνογονία** (a biblical hapax), "bearing a child." Although it is not certain that the definite article is to be stressed (the article is absent in *Stoicorum Veterum Fragmenta* [ed. J. von Arnim] III, 158, 5; in Galen, *Corpus Medicorum Graecorum* V/9/1, 27, 12; and in a textual variant here), if it is, then the noun plus article would refer to "*the* bearing of a child"; but even without such a stress the reference to "bearing a child" could well stand for the birth of the promised seed of the woman (cf., e.g., Ellicott).

Although the salvation is objectively accomplished and provided, it is not thereby automatically experienced. To experience it requires a living and abiding faith (ἐὰν μείνωσιν ἐν πίστει) manifested and expressed in holiness of life appropriate to women (καὶ ἀγάπῃ . . . μετὰ σωφροσύνης). With a shift to the plural (μείνωσιν) and a conclusion utilizing one of the key opening terms (σωφροσύνη, vv. 9, 15), Paul returns to women in general. Although it could be argued that this clause could apply to men and children as well, here it is applied specifically to women.

The ἐάν clause indicates the condition necessary to receive the salvation and remain in it and states it as a fact assumed to be true (cf. BAGD s.v. 1 [211]; BDF §371.4; 373). μένω is used figuratively here of abiding in a realm or sphere (BAGD s.v. 1a, b [503f.]; cf. 2 Tim. 3:14; 1 Cor. 7:8, 11, 20, 24, 40). The concept of "remaining" or "continuing" would also seem to tie the subject of this verb to the subject of the previous clause (γυνή); one does not talk about "continuing" with a new subject but with a continuation of the previous subject. The same emphasis on the need for permanence and perseverance is sounded in 1 Cor. 15:2, which speaks of salvation (σῴζω) through (διά) Christ's work, if (εἰ) "you hold fast" (κατέχετε; cf. also μένω in Jn. 15:4-10).

πίστις (cf. 1:2) in the flow of the letter and in connection with σῴζω undoubtedly means "*trust, confidence, faith* in the active sense = 'believing' " (BAGD s.v. 2 [662]), with ἐν indicating the sphere or realm in which women are to continue. Joined to πίστις are ἀγάπη and ἁγιασμός, the first of which is joined to πίστις in 2:14 (cf. 1:5) and in Gal. 5:6 to express the essence of the response called for by the gospel of grace, in contrast to a salvation that relies on works. The addition of ἁγιασμός is in accord with Paul's practice of correlating two, three, or more items in which faith and love are usually the constants (1 Cor. 13:13; Gal. 5:22, 23; Eph. 6:23; 1 Thes. 1:3; 3:6; 5:8; 2 Thes. 1:3, 4; 1 Tim. 1:5, 14, 19; 4:12; 6:11; 2 Tim. 1:13; 2:22; 3:10; Phm. 5). The note of ethical concern, as here, is usually found either in the list or its context (cf. especially 1 Tim. 4:12: ἐν λόγῳ, ἐν ἀναστροφῃ, ἐν ἀγάπῃ, ἐν πίστει, ἐν ἁγνείᾳ).

ἁγιασμός (NT 10x) means in the NT "*holiness, consecration, sanctification;* the use in a moral sense for a process or, more often, its result (the state of being made holy)" (BAGD s.v. [220]). Its use here to denote a state or process in which women must continue as a condition for salvation is in accord with 2 Thes. 2:13, where the brethren are chosen by God "for salvation through sanctification by the Spirit," and especially Rom. 6:19, 22: In Romans 6 Paul responds to the question whether one may continue in sin with the answer summed up in vv. 22, 23. Just as he says there that salvation in Christ must be demonstrated in a living faith through ἁγιασμός, so also he says the same to women in 1 Tim. 2:15 (cf. Heb. 12:14). It may be that ἁγιασμός in 1 Tim. 2:15 has particular reference to both v. 9, with its emphasis on modesty, and the "good works" mentioned in v. 10.

μετὰ σωφροσύνης, "with self-restraint" (see v. 9), brings into perspective the need for this virtue in addition to the general call for ἁγιασμός. It probably refers not only to restraint and discretion in regard to clothing and adornment, but also, in connection with vv. 11-14, a woman's role vis-à-vis men and the church. It is thus a reminder that not only sin (vv. 9, 10) but also the creation order necessitates self-restraint and that true faith, love, and sanctity will manifest itself in a lifestyle and attitude that restrains itself from immodesty or ostentatiousness and from violating the order of the Creator-Savior.

The understanding and application of vv. 12-15 are much in discussion, and the literature must be consulted as it appears. For a discussion of the question as a whole with references to the main body of literature up to that time see Knight, *Role Relationship;* see especially also Moo's thorough exegetical study, "1 Timothy 2:11-15," and, responding to P. Payne's response, Moo's "Interpretation of 1 Timothy 2:11-15." Since the literature on the subject as a whole is voluminous and grows constantly, rather than giving a bibliographical note here I would refer the reader to two representative collections of essays that carefully present the arguments on both sides, interact with one another, and refer to much of the current literature: Mickelsen, ed., *Women;* Piper and Grudem, eds., *Recovering.*

QUALIFICATIONS FOR BISHOPS AND DEACONS: 3:1-16

This chapter gives the qualifications for two groups of officers, bishops and deacons, and then gives the pastoral reason for the instructions of this letter (Paul's delay and the need for such instruction now, vv. 14, 15) and the theological perspective that necessitates such instructions and permeates them (the church is the household and dwelling place of the living God, committed to uphold and practice God's truth, vv. 15, 16).

A number of questions arise concerning the identity of these two groups of officers: Who held these offices? What were their functions? How were the two offices related to each other? Are they mentioned elsewhere in the NT, and, if so, how are the various references to them related and what picture of the NT situation do they give? Although these questions must be addressed further in the detailed examination below of this section of the letter, it will be helpful to have a general perspective on these two offices as a working hypothesis. Three factors present some means of identification and differentiation: (1) the names, (2) the further delineation of the bishop's task in Titus 1, and (3) the differences in the qualifications between the ἐπίσκοπος and διάκονοι.

The name of the office of ἐπίσκοπος, "bishop," "overseer," indicates that oversight is a major aspect of the position. This is further delineated in the parallel passage, Tit. 1:5ff. Therefore, the πρεσβύτεροι spoken of in 1 Tim. 5:17 as ruling (προεστῶτες) and teaching are ἐπίσκοποι. These same two functions of ruling and teaching distinguish the ἐπίσκοπος and the διάκονοι (plural in 1 Tim. 3:8 in contrast to singular ἐπίσκοπος in v. 2) in the descriptions of the functions of the two offices here in 1 Timothy 3. It is said of the ἐπίσκοπος, but not of the διάκονοι, that he must be "able to teach" (διδακτικόν, v. 2), and it is specified (in a rhetorical question) that the ἐπίσκοπος will "take care of the church of God" (v. 5). In Titus 1 also it is said that the ἐπίσκοπος/πρεσβύτερος must "be able to exhort in sound doctrine and to refute those who contradict" (v. 9), i.e., give spiritual instruction and exercise spiritual authority or oversight. It is also said that the ἐπίσκοπος as well as Titus must silence false teachers who are "upsetting whole families" (v. 11) and "reprove them severely that they may be sound in the faith"

(v. 13). This picture of the ἐπίσκοπος as one who exercises oversight in the church particularly in ruling and teaching is reflected in Acts 20:28 ("to shepherd the church of God"; cf. also the mention of ἐπίσκοποι in Phil. 1:1 and the description of Christ as ἐπίσκοπος in 1 Pet. 2:25).

διάκονοι seems to be used here in a more technical sense than elsewhere, since it goes beyond the more general sense of one who serves the church as a minister. That latter role is expressed here by ἐπίσκοπος, and here the διάκονοι are distinguished from the ἐπίσκοπος. The position of the διάκονοι is so characterized by service, as its main function, that the word has become a technical term for those carrying out such service (cf. H. W. Beyer, *TDNT* I, 88-93; see Acts 6:1-7).

So the working hypothesis, provided primarily by the self-defining terms, is that the ἐπίσκοπος is an "overseer," one carrying out a ministry of oversight, while διάκονοι are "servants," those carrying out a ministry of service (cf. also the mutually exclusive description in Acts 6:2-4). See the **Excursus: Bishops/Presbyters and Deacons** below for an analysis of the NT as a whole on this subject.

Dibelius-Conzelmann and others, particularly those of the history of religions school, have asked whether the lists of qualifications of bishops and deacons in this chapter might represent a common stylized list that was used in the non-Christian world to describe all sorts of leaders and that was not drafted by Paul with the particular offices in mind. Dibelius-Conzelmann give examples of such lists of qualifications, especially the description of the military general in Onasander (= Onosander), *De Imperatoris Officio* (pp. 374ff. in the LCL edition translated by Members of the Illinois Greek Club), quoted at length by Dibelius-Conzelmann, 158-60. Of the eleven qualifications in Onasander's list, two words are also found in 1 Timothy 3 (σώφρων in v. 2, ἀφιλάργυρος in v. 3, both of the bishop) and three are similar to terms used in 1 Timothy 3 (self-restrained [ἐγκρατῆ], being a father [though entirely different considerations are adduced], and "a man of good reputation").

On the other hand, several items in Paul's list of qualifications for the bishop are directly related to that ministry ("able to teach," v. 3; ability to govern the church proven by governing of one's family, vv. 4, 5; and "not a new convert," v. 6) and other elements that are distinctly Christian (references to the διάβολος, vv. 6, 7; the distinctly Christian element of gentleness expressed by a cluster of terms, three negative and one positive, v. 3; in the list for deacons, faith and conscience, v. 9, standing and confidence in the faith that is in Christ Jesus, v. 13). Furthermore, the lists for the bishop and the deacons share certain distinctive concepts that are appropriate for the particular ministry of that group and do not appear to be a mere echoing of some existing list.

As one analyzes these lists, one gains the distinct impression that they are not stylized but that the aspects are appropriate to leadership in the church in general and to the specific office in particular. Those aspects of similarity with lists in the non-Christian world may be explained by the fact that leadership, whether in different religions or in the military or in the church, must have certain common characteristics, as is evident in part from the similar items in the list for the bishop and the deacons. Paul self-consciously incorporates an awareness and appreciation of that fact when he says of the bishop that "he must have a good reputation with those outside" the church (cf. his earlier recognition of the non-Christian's awareness of certain things that are right, Rom. 2:14, 15). It would have been strange for one who earlier appealed to the instruction that the natural order provided (1 Cor. 11:14) not to have had some overlap in his list with those drawn up outside the church. What is most noteworthy, however, is the distinctiveness of his lists in spite of this fact and their distinctly Christian character (see above) and appropriateness to the officers of the church.

Also against considering these lists as merely borrowed from the secular milieu is their basic similarity in essence with the primitive list in Acts 6:3, which in effect is explicated in 1 Timothy 3 and Titus 1. Furthermore, there are differences among the similarities among the four lists in the PE, three in 1 Timothy 3 (for the bishop, for deacons, and for "women") and one in Titus 1. A mere borrowing cannot explain the uniqueness and particular appropriateness of the lists respectively for the bishop and for the deacons. The lists seem to be constructed from a distinctly Christian and ecclesiastical perspective (for this same evaluation see also Ridderbos and Spicq, contra Brox).

BISHOPS: 3:1-7

3:1 Does πιστὸς ὁ λόγος, "the saying is faithful" (on the formula's meaning see 1:15), refer to what precedes or to what follows (for a fuller treatment of this question see Knight, *Faithful Sayings,* 50-54; see also Spicq; the punctuation apparatus of *UBSGNT*). The argument most often presented for referring the formula to what precedes in 2:15 is the claim that sayings attached to the formula elsewhere are always concerned with salvation (note σωθήσεται in v. 15). This argument is sometimes coupled with or replaced by a view that 3:1 cannot be, or is not worthy of being, designated by the formula (though Scott argues similarly against 2:15). The criterion of soteriology would be decisive were it certain, but here the very question whether it constitutes such a criterion is under discussion, even if it is true that most or all of the other texts are soteriological (cf. the contexts of 1:15; 4:9 [preceding or following?]; Tit. 3:8; 2 Tim. 2:11).

What is clear is that 3:1b is recognized as a "saying" by most, even by those who take πιστὸς ὁ λόγος as referring to what precedes. That it is a "saying," perhaps coupled with prejudice against the significance of the saying, most likely explains the weakly attested textual variant ἀνθρώπινος/*humanus,* "human," "common," "popular," for πιστός (ἀνθρώπινος in D*; *humanus* in it[d, m, mon g], Ambrosiaster [manuscripts according to Jerome], Augustine, Sedulius Scotus), which thus provides some early testimony that 3:1b was considered to be the saying connected with the formula in 3:1a (Westcott-Hort, in their "Notes on Select Readings"). (It is sometimes argued [e.g., Wohlenberg, Easton, and Lock with hesitation; cf. *NEB*] that ἀνθρώπινος is the original reading, that it can explain πιστός but not vice versa, and further that what follows is manifestly a "common" proverb. But this is complicated by the fact that the saying's key term ἐπισκοπή is found only rarely in secular sources and then not in the sense of "office" [as pointed out by Weiss; Zahn, *Introduction,* §37, n. 6; see Knight, *Faithful Sayings,* 56, 58ff.]. Both manuscript evidence and internal considerations show πιστός to be the correct reading.)

To say that the saying in 3:1b could not have arisen in the early church or that Paul would not use this formula to refer to it is to misunderstand both. That there was a lively and deep interest in church order is evidenced not only by 1 Timothy 3 itself (vv. 14, 15), along with 5:17ff. and Tit. 1:5ff., but also by many passages throughout Acts, Paul's letters, and other NT letters (cf. Acts 6:1ff.; 14:21ff.; 20:17ff.; Rom. 12:6ff.; 1 Cor. 12:28; Phil. 1:1; 1 Thes. 5:12ff.; Heb. 12:7; 1 Pet. 5:1ff., etc.). Furthermore, the "saying" in 3:1b seems much too abrupt an introduction to the verses that follow without the formula, but seems in place with the formula. Therefore the verdict must be entered with most Greek NT editors (except Westcott-Hort, the "corrected" edition of *UBSGNT,* and *NA*[26]), the text of most modern English translations, and most commentators that πιστὸς ὁ λόγος refers to 3:1b (so also Ellingworth, "'True Saying'").

The formula is used here, then, both to cite a "saying" concerning the office of bishop and to commend the saying's evaluation of this office and thus to introduce Paul's presentation of the qualifications for the office. The saying itself, in the form of the conditional sentence, commends the office as a good work and therefore seeks to encourage men to seek the office (for a fuller discussion of the saying see Knight, *Faithful Sayings,* 55-61). The terms of the first clause are quite general (εἴ τις, "if any man"). The effect is to recommend that "anyone" meeting the qualifications listed afterward aspire to the office, with the understanding given in the second clause that such an aspiration is desire for a "good" task or assignment.

That the verb ὀρέγεται in the first clause is indicative signifies that the condition is assumed to be true (BAGD; Robertson; Burton, *Syntax,* 100ff.). ἐπισκοπῆς** (Lk. 19:44; Acts 1:20; 1 Tim. 3:1; 1 Pet 2:12; genitive with ὀρέγεται, Robertson, *Grammar,* 508; BDF §171.1), the key word in the saying, occurs rarely in secular Greek and is used there in the sense of "visit" (as in Luke and 1 Peter), "care," "charge," or "foresight" (see BAGD; H. W. Beyer, *TDNT* II, 606-8). The meaning "office" is in view in two passages in the LXX, Nu. 4:16 and Ps. 108[109]:8, the latter of which is utilized in Acts 1:20, the only place in the NT where the word has the general sense of "office." Since the term is not known in secular Greek in this sense and since in Acts 1:20 it is used in a more general sense while here it is used in a very specific sense, Beyer has evaluated the situation appropriately when he says: "The term ἐπισκοπή in 1 Tim. 3:1 does not derive from Acts 1:20 or its OT original. It is newly coined on the basis of the title ἐπίσκοπος, which had meantime established itself in the early church. This is the more easily possible, of course, because ἐπισκοπή is clearly used for 'office' in the language of the LXX" (*TDNT* II, 608). This relationship between ἐπισκοπή and ἐπίσκοπος is most evident in vv. 1-2 (note οὖν).

ἐπισκοπή is thus used here with the meaning "position (or office) of an ἐπίσκοπος," i.e., the position of an overseer or bishop in the church (see again BAGD and Beyer). (The word is also found in a fourth-century Christian inscription from Lycaonia that describes a bishop: See MM; Ramsay, *Phrygia* II, 543; and especially Calder, "Fourth-Century Lycaonian Bishop" [text and translation]. 1 Clement 44:1, 4 and context relates the word to οἱ πρεσβύτεροι.)

The attitude commended toward the office of the ἐπίσκοπος is expressed in the verb ὀρέγομαι** (here; 6:10; Heb. 11:16, all three middle and figurative), literally "stretch oneself, reach out one's hand," figuratively "aspire to, strive for, desire" with genitive of the thing desired (BAGD; see also Thayer, *Lexicon*). Field elicits several examples from Greek writers to show that the word "has a special application to such objects as a man is commonly said to *aspire to*" and therefore repudiates "the idea of an *ambitious seeking* which does not belong either to the word itself or to its connexion" (*Notes,* 204; in 1 Tim. 6:10 it is the context, not the word, that indicates otherwise). Here καλοῦ ἔργου ἐπιθυμεῖ shows that the aspiration is being commended.

ἐπιθυμέω means "desire" or "long for," with genitive of the thing desired (BAGD; Robertson, *Grammar,* 508; BDF §171.1) and is comparable to the expression "set one's heart on" (see LSJM and Thayer). Used here with καλοῦ ἔργου and commended by the formula, it is evidently intended in a good sense (as in, e.g., Heb. 6:11). It may provide a stylistic change from the nearly synonymous ὀρέγεμαι, or it may be used to emphasize the inner desire for the good work.

That which one desires when one aspires to the office of bishop is a καλὸν ἔργον, a "good work, task, or activity." ἔργον is not being used in its more general sense of work as deed or action, but either in the sense of work as "occupation" or "task," perhaps even "office" (BAGD s.v. 2), or in the most weakened sense of "thing or matter" (BAGD s.v. 4), the former being more likely (cf. Acts 13:2: "for the work to which I called them"; 14:26; 15:38; 1 Thes. 5:12, 13; 2 Tim. 4:5: "the work of an evangelist"; also Eph. 4:12). The word "task" gives the best nuance, though "work" appropriately renders the Greek.

The task is commended as καλός. Even though use of καλός with ἔργον in the plural is attested in the PE, as is the synonym ἔργον ἀγαθόν in the singular, καλός with ἔργον in the singular exists in only three other places in the NT. This highlights both the saying quality and also the significance of the phrase as one that refers not to one of many good deeds but to a task that is good, i.e., excellent (BAGD s.v. 2cβ). The second clause of the saying thus emphasizes desiring this good task (cf. Tit. 1:7: "God's steward"). (A number of the early church fathers stress that it is a work and not a dignity or an exalted position: See the commentary of Theodore of Mopsuestia, ad loc., and the editor's summary of the views of others in note 16 of the same work.)

3:2 Because of the nature of the task, there is "therefore" the consequent necessity that such an overseer be above reproach. οὖν indicates that an inference is to be drawn. δεῖ, which denotes compulsion in the sense of what is necessary or one must do, states the inference to be drawn by means of the accusative and infinitive that follow.

The one who enters into the ἐπισκοπή is now designated the ἐπίσκοπος** (Acts 20:28; Phil. 1:1; 1 Tim. 3:2; Tit. 1:7; 1 Pet. 2:25), "overseer." Both terms imply a fixed office with a definite function (see BAGD). ἐπίσκοπος is used in secular Greek in a general sense of civil functions (LSJM) and in a religious sense (see Deissmann, *Bible Studies,* 230f.). In the LXX it occurs 14x, most often representing the root *pqd* but also two others (see Abbott-Smith, *Lexicon* s.v.). Aside from its reference to Jesus in 1 Pet. 2:15, the word is used in the NT in a Pauline and Gentile church setting as a designation for a church officer who is one of a group (ἐπίσκοποι: Acts 20:28, cf. 17 [πρεσβύτεροι]; Phil. 1:1; following πρεσβύτεροι in Tit. 1:5, 7; see the excursus in Lightfoot, *Philippians;* a textual variant at 1 Pet. 5:2 uses the participle ἐπισκοποῦντες of the work of the πρεσβύτεροι; for other bibliography see BAGD; H. W. Beyer, *TDNT* II, 599ff.; *TWNT* X s.v.). The parallel passage Tit. 1:5-7 has the only other NT occurrence of the word in the singular; there the singular is generic, as is evidenced by its correlation with the plural πρεσβύτεροι, in accord with the use of the plural elsewhere. Thus the word in the singular refers to the category of those who give oversight to and teach the church. Kelly suggests that here "the singular may have been prompted by the singular . . . [τις] . . . in [v.] 1."

The general characteristic of the bishop is that he must be ἀνεπίλημπτος** (1 Tim. 3:2; 5:17; 6:14; in 3:10 and Tit. 1:6 the synonym ἀνέγκλητος is used), "irreproachable," in the sense of not open to attack or criticism (see

LSJM) in terms of his Christian life in general and in terms of the characteristics that follow in particular. By God's grace the pattern of the bishop's life conforms to both the general and specific characteristics and he is not objectively chargeable.

Following this overarching characteristic, the specifics for a bishop are now delineated. The items focus on two areas: (1) personal self-discipline and maturity, and (2) ability to relate well to others and to teach and care for them. These two are intertwined, although there seems to be a tendency to move from the personal to the interpersonal. V. 2 begins with items of self-discipline and maturity such as "husband of one wife, temperate" and ends with "hospitable, able to teach." V. 3 begins with "not addicted to wine" and ends with "not a lover of money," while the center section speaks of gentleness in relating to others. V. 4 makes the managing of one's household and children with dignity a requisite since this will indicate (v. 5) how a man can take care of the church. V. 6 returns to the question of personal maturity and mandates that a bishop not be a new convert, lest he become conceited. V. 7 ends with the emphasis on how a man relates to and is regarded by those outside the church. In the last two, the danger of the devil using either as an occasion for sin is emphasized. In effect the list spells out the brief and essentially twofold requirement laid down in Acts 6:3: "full of the Spirit and of wisdom," the personal, and "of good reputation," the interpersonal.

The list in Tit. 1:6-9 has essentially the same pattern but is arranged somewhat differently. It begins by joining marriage and the family together (v. 6), then states what a bishop should not be (v. 7), affirms with a positive list what he should be (v. 8), i.e., "just and devout," and ends by enlarging on the concepts of teaching and caring for the church (1:9). Not in the list in Titus are the requirements that a bishop not be a new convert and that he have a good report from those outside the church. The following list correlates the words and phrases of 1 Tim. 3:2-7 and Tit. 1:5-9 in the order of 1 Timothy.

1 Timothy	**Titus**
ἀνεπίλημπτος	ἀνέγκλητος / ὡς θεοῦ οἰκονόμου
μιᾶς γυναικὸς ἀνήρ	μιᾶς γυναικὸς ἀνήρ
νηφάλιον	? ἐγκρατής
σώφρων	σώφρων
κόσμιος	? φιλάγαθος
φιλόξενος	φιλόξενος
διδακτικός	ἀντεχόμενος τοῦ κατὰ τὴν διδαχὴν πιστοῦ λόγου, ἵνα δυνατὸς ᾖ καὶ παρακαλεῖν ἐν τῇ διδασκαλίᾳ τῇ

	ὑγιαινούσῃ καὶ τοὺς ἀντιλέγοντας ἐλέγχειν
μὴ πάροινος	μὴ πάροινος
μὴ πλήκτης	μὴ πλήκτης
ἐπιεικής	μὴ αὐθάδης
ἄμαχος	μὴ ὀργίλος
ἀφιλάργυρος	μὴ αἰσχροκερδής
τοῦ ἰδίου οἴκου καλῶς προϊστάμενος, τέκνα ἔχοντα ἐν ὑποταγῇ	τέκνα ἔχων πιστά
μετὰ πάσης σεμνότητος	μὴ ἐν κατηγορίᾳ ἀσωτίας ἢ ἀνυπότακτα
μὴ νεόφυτος	
μαρτυρίαν καλὴν ἔχειν ἀπὸ τῶν ἔξωθεν	
	δίκαιος
	ὅσιος

The first specific characteristic in the 1 Timothy list is μιᾶς γυναικὸς ἄνδρα, literally "a man of one woman," or "a husband of one wife." ἀνήρ and γυνή, the common NT words for "man" and "woman," take on the meanings "husband" and "wife" in contexts such as here. Various interpretations have been proposed for this phrase from the patristic period until today (for a summary of the patristic discussion including a synopsis of the elaborate discussion by Theodore of Mopsuestia see Dodd, "NT Translation Problems II"): It has been suggested that it requires that a bishop (1) be married, (2) have only one wife his entire life, (3) be monogamous, or (4) be faithful in the marital and sexual realm.

With regard to (1), it is exceedingly doubtful that Paul intended that these words and the words about "children" (plural, vv. 4, 12) be understood as mandating that only a married man with at least two children could be an officer in the church. Probably he wrote in terms of the common situation, i.e., of being married and having children, and then spoke of what should be the case when this most common situation exists in an officer's life. Paul, like Peter (cf. 1 Pet. 5:1), regarded himself as a fellow elder or bishop and wrote of his singleness and his apostolic ministry without regarding them as mutually exclusive (cf. 1 Cor. 9:1ff., especially v. 5; see also 7:7, 8). In fact, he commended singleness, using himself as an example, as a state where one would have more freedom to serve the Lord (1 Cor. 7:32ff.).

With regard to (2), it would be strange for the apostle of liberty, who considered widows and widowers "free to be married . . . , only in the Lord" (1 Cor. 7:39) and who used this principle of freedom to illustrate his teaching on the law (Rom. 7:1-3), to deny this freedom to a potential church officer whose spouse has died. Likewise, the freedom to remarry granted to the "innocent" party when a marriage has been terminated as a result of sexual unfaithfulness (as I believe Mt. 19:9 should be understood) or when an unbelieving spouse has abandoned a believing spouse (1 Cor. 7:15) does not seem to be restricted so that they could not apply to a potential officer. Only if the phrase under consideration could *only* be understood in the sense of (2) above would this evidence be excluded. An interpretation, however, that included those other considerations would do more justice to the totality of the evidence.

With regard to (3), polygamy, which existed among Jews of the NT age (see Str-B ad loc. for documentation; they cite, among many others, Josephus, *Ant.* 17.14; *B.J.* 1.477), is certainly ruled out by the sense of the phrase. In AD 212 the *lex Antoniana de civitate* made monogamy the law for Romans but Jews were excepted. In AD 393 Theodosius enacted a special law against polygamy among Jews, since they persisted in the practice (Hillman, *Polygamy,* 20f.). Two Greek marriage contracts have been found that seem to be concerned to prohibit polygamy: "It shall not be lawful for Philiscus to bring in another wife besides Appolania" (92 BC); "Ptolemaeus . . . shall not . . . insult her nor bring in another wife" (13 BC, both in Hunt-Edgar, *Select Papyri* I, 7, 11).

The question remains, however, whether the phrase is intended to exclude only polygamy or all violations of marital and sexual fidelity (4). Two considerations make it doubtful that polygamy is exclusively in view: The first is the insight obtained (*pace* Str-B) from the occurrence of the counterpart phrase ἑνὸς ἀνδρὸς γυνή in a similar context, 1 Tim. 5:9 (the only other NT occurrences of this kind of phrase are μιᾶς γυναικὸς ἄνδρα here, in 3:12 [ἄνδρες in v. 12], and in Tit. 1:6 [ἀνήρ]). The phrase in 5:9 affirms marital and sexual fidelity in monogamous terms, but does not imply polyandry as the intended contrast, since polyandry was not practiced in the first-century Greco-Roman world. Doubtless the phrase in 5:9, following after 3:2, 12 and in a similar list of qualifications, is used in a similar way as its counterpart in 3:2, 12. The implication is that the phrase in 3:2, 12 is therefore not intended to exclude only polygamy. Furthermore, that men could have sexual relations with women other than their wives seems to have been accepted among Greeks and Romans, so that this would be an issue important to address.

The second consideration in favor of (4) is that this statement (3:2) positively affirms sexual fidelity couched in monogamous marital terminology ("husband of one wife"). It is analogous, therefore, to the command "You shall not commit adultery," which is also couched in marital language but which encompasses other sexual sins, as the outworkings of that command in the chapters following Exodus 20 evince. "The natural meaning of μιᾶς γυναικὸς ἀνήρ is surely, as Theodore [of Mopsuestia] says, 'a man who having contracted a monogamous marriage is faithful to his marriage vows,' excluding alike polygamy, concubinage and promiscuous indulgence" (Dodd, "NT Translation Problems II," 115). "Promiscuous indulgence" would encompass Jesus' words on wrongful divorce and remarriage in Mt. 5:32; 19:9.

This characteristic, like the others, is the result of God's grace in Christ (cf. especially 3:6, 9) and thus has reference to a man's status and conduct from the time of his conversion. So just as one is called on to look back on a widow's earlier life (when she was living with her husband) to ascertain her marital and sexual fidelity in having been "the wife of one husband" (5:9), so also (cf. 5:22, 24, 25) for the bishop (3:2) and deacon (3:12): One must look back over his life from the time of his conversion to ascertain his marital and sexual fidelity in having been "the husband of one wife."

Since two words in this list could refer to use of alcohol, i.e., νηφάλιον (here) and πάροινον (v. 8), it is unlikely that both are meant literally. So even though νηφάλιος** (also in 3:11; Tit. 2:2) does mean "temperate in the use of alcoholic beverages," it probably means here, as is also the case with "sober" in English, "sober in the sense of clear-headed, self-controlled" (BAGD). Since both this word and σώφρων have the nuance of "self-controlled" (cf. also ἐγκρατής in Tit. 1:8, which is coupled with σώφρων), different aspects of self-control are probably emphasized in each. For νηφάλιος it is the sober, clear-headed aspect.

σώφρων** (also in Tit. 1:8; 2:2, 5) represents a word group that is not frequently used in the NT (σωφρονέω** in Mk. 5:15; Lk. 8:35; Rom. 12:3; 2 Cor. 5:13; Tit. 2:6; 1 Pet. 4:7; σωφρονίζω** in Tit. 2:4; σωφρονισμός** in 2 Tim. 1:7; σωφρόνως** in Tit. 2:12; σωφροσύνη** in Acts 26:25; 1 Tim. 2:9, 15; see U. Luck, *TDNT* VII, 1097-1104). This particular term denotes "the prudent, thoughtful" aspect of self-control (BAGD).

κόσμιος** (also in 2:9) is used in classical Greek (LSJM) and in the inscriptions (MM) to describe a person as "orderly" (cf. κοσμέω, κόσμος), "well-behaved," or "virtuous," which is the sense that it bears here: that which causes a person to be regarded as "respectable" by others (see Trench, *Synonyms,* 344-46). To be "hospitable" (φιλόξενος,** Tit. 1:8 of the bishop; 1 Pet. 4:9 of Christians in general) is the duty of all Christians (see also φιλοξενία, Rom. 12:13; Heb. 13:2; cf. 3 Jn. 5ff.) and must be evident, as is true of the other characteristics, in a heightened way in the bishop. He who must teach others and take care of and exercise oversight over them must be open and loving to them.

The key to διδακτικός** (2 Tim. 2:24), "skillful in teaching" (BAGD), is found in the parallel Tit. 1:9, where that responsibility is spelled out: "that he may be able both to exhort in sound doctrine and to refute those who contradict." The other NT occurrence of this word (2 Tim. 2:24) is also explicated by the statement following it, "with gentleness correcting those who are in opposition" (2 Tim. 2:25). The usage in the PE is more significant than the usage in Philo ("consisting or expressing itself in learning" according to K. H. Rengstorf, *TDNT* II, 165, who gives "able to learn" as the meaning in 1 Tim. 3:2; 2 Tim. 2:24; Dibelius-Conzelmann, however, take διδακτικὴ ἀρετή in Philo as "virtue attained by means of teaching"). The meaning "skillful in teaching" is also reflected in most modern English translations *(RSV, TEV, NASB, NEB, NIV)*.

3:3 The δεῖ εἶναι construction continues and is carried on through v. 6 (Robertson, *Grammar,* 1172). V. 3 is dominated by negations, which state what the bishop must not be: The first two words are negated by μή, and the last two words are negative in form, with ἀ-privative. The total impact, however, is positive, as seen in the contrast of the positive ἐπιεικῆ with the preceding μὴ πλήκτην and the inherently positive meaning of the following ἄμαχον. In short, the bishop's life is not to be dominated or controlled by wine or money, nor may it be one of strife, but rather it must be one of peace and gentleness.

μὴ πάροινον** (Tit. 1:7), "not addicted to wine" (BAGD, *NASB*), "not given to much wine" *(NIV)*, is best explained by the synonymous and more explicit expression in v. 8. The parallel tips the scales in favor of this literal meaning over a figurative interpretation (e.g., "drunken violence," which MM recognize among the verbal usages; Lock suggests "blustering," "abrasive" with documentation). μὴ πλήκτην** (Tit. 1:7) indicates that the bishop must not be a pugnacious man. ἀλλά ("but") after the negative indicates the positive contrast afforded by ἐπιεικῆ. ἐπιεικής** (Phil. 4:5; Tit. 3:2; Jas. 3:17; 1 Pet. 2:18) means "gentle, kind," with a concomitant note of graciousness (see ἐπιείκεια,** Acts 24:4; especially 2 Cor. 10:1 in which the quality is ascribed to Christ). Spicq proposes "un sympathique équilibre" in his commentary (see his study of both words in *Notes* I, 263-67; also H. Preisker, *TDNT* II, 588-90). ἄμαχος** (here and Tit. 3:2 paired with ἐπιεικής) means "peaceable" in the sense of "uncontentious" (cf. 2 Tim. 2:23, 24: δοῦλον δὲ κυρίου οὐ δεῖ μάχεσθαι).

The implication of ἀφιλάργυρος,** "not loving money," "not greedy," is best ascertained in the contrasting words in Heb. 13:5 (the only other NT occurrence), "being content with what you have." As in Heb. 13:5 so in 1 Tim. 6:6-10 (ἡ φιλαργυρία,** v. 10) contentment with God and his provision is commended as the antidote to love of money and the insatiable desire to get rich. Although this quality appears without exception as a requirement for both bishops and deacons in the PE (in 3:8 and Tit. 1:7 as μὴ αἰσχροκερδής**) and in 1 Pet. 5:2 (μηδὲ αἰσχροκερδῶς**), and although there are peculiar temptations for these officers (see 3:8; Tit. 1:7) of such force that they characterize false teachers (Tit. 1:11: αἰσχροῦ κέρδους χάριν), this temptation is common to mankind (6:6-10; 2 Tim. 3:2: φιλάργυρος,** see also Lk. 16:14), and is addressed by Jesus in Lk. 16:13 and more fully in Mt.

6:24ff. as a choice of which master one will serve, God or money. For the church's overseer this answer must not be in doubt. (For a thorough consideration of both αἰσχροκερδής and ἀφιλάργυρος together see Spicq, *Notes,* I, 53-56.)

3:4 The leadership and caring abilities of the ἐπίσκοπος are evaluated on the basis of his management of his household (τοῦ ἰδίου οἴκου). V. 4a states that this management must be done "well" (καλῶς). V. 4b indicates what that means by speaking of a man's having his children ἐν ὑποταγῇ. V. 4c indicates how that is accomplished: μετὰ πάσης σεμνότητος.

οἴκου (genitive with προΐστημι) is used here in the sense of "household" or "family" (BAGD s.v. 2) as it is throughout the PE* (3:4, 5, 12, 15[?]; 5:4; Tit. 1:11; 2 Tim. 1:16; 4:19) and elsewhere in Paul (1 Cor. 1:16). προΐστημι** in the NT (only in Paul) emphasizes the leadership role of one who has been placed at the head of the family or church and who is therefore responsible to "rule, direct and lead" (cf. 3:4, 5, 12; 5:17; Rom. 12:8; 1 Thes. 5:12). The explication given by the key phrase ἐν ὑποταγῇ also points in this direction. The correlation of προΐστημι and ἐπιμελέομαι (care for, take care of) in 3:5, however, reminds us to include the secondary sense of προΐστημι as well, i.e., "be concerned about" or "care for" (as in Tit. 3:8, 14). BAGD present the two meanings as mutually exclusive alternatives for 1 Thes. 5:12 and Rom. 12:8; when, however, they may both be present (so B. Reicke, *TDNT* VI, 701f.). This the bishop must do "well" (καλῶς, in the PE* exclusively as the measure of one's ministry in the family [3:4, 12] and in the church [3:13; 5:17]).

The determination of this ability "to rule" is seen (1) in the submission of a man's children (v. 4b) and (2) in the way in which this submission is manifested (v. 4c). To the question whether this statement requires one to have children to be an ἐπίσκοπος (or a διάκονος), or is rather stating what must be true in the usual situation, the reader is referred to the related question in regard to a wife and the negative answer given above at 3:2.

Although τέκνον can be used of an adult (e.g., 1:2, 18; 5:4), the qualification ἐν ὑποταγῇ indicates that the "children" in view are those under authority and therefore those not yet of age (cf. the ὑπο- concept in Gal. 4:2ff.: ἄχρι τῆς προθεσμίας τοῦ πατρός). ὑποταγή** (2 Cor. 9:13; Gal. 2:5; 1 Tim. 2:11; 3:4) is used in the NT only in the passive sense of "subjection, subordination, or obedience." Since the word is used in its four NT occurrences of different situations, the nuance of meaning for ὑποταγή in each situation differs accordingly. For the phrase τέκνα ἐν ὑποταγῇ the note of obedience may be presumed in the light of Eph. 6:1ff. and Col. 3:20 (τὰ τέκνα ὑπακούετε).

The subjection shown by the children must reflect the character of their father's leadership: It must be μετὰ πάσης σεμνότητος. σεμνότης** (here; 2:2; Tit. 2:7) when used in reference to males has as its range of meanings "reverence, dignity, seriousness, respectfulness, holiness, probity" (BAGD s.v. 1). The particular aspects of this range that are in view depend in part on how the prepositional phrase is construed here. Does it focus on the father and indicate how he has his children in submission (so, e.g., Bouma)? Does it focus on the children and indicate their attitude in submission (so, e.g., Ridderbos)? Or does it serve as an evaluation of the relationship as a whole? In saying that it refers to the children, appeal may be made to the additional words in the otherwise parallel phrase in Tit. 1:6. There the focus is on the children's conduct. In saying that it refers to the father, appeal may be made to the use of the concept expressed by the related word σεμνός from this point on in the PE* (3:8, 11; Tit. 2:2). In these passages the concept is characterizing respectively deacons, women, and older men. Furthermore, σεμνός is the first requirement listed for deacons, and it follows the designation "likewise" (ὡσαύτως), presumably meaning that deacons must be σεμνός just as bishops must be. Since 3:4 is the only use of the related word in the statement about bishops, this ὡσαύτως might seem to clinch the reference of σεμνότης to fathers here. However, σεμνός and ὡσαύτως used with reference to the deacons may also refer to other items in the list for bishops for which σεμνός is a synonym.

It is difficult, therefore, to be sure of the reference of μετὰ πάσης σεμνότητος. Perhaps Paul sought to describe that which characterized the relationship from both sides. Submission on the part of the children marked by a relationship of dignity and seriousness is that which reflects on the ability of a man to be a bishop. And this needs to be not just an appearance of σεμνότητος, but πάσης σεμνότητος, a full demonstration of it (for πᾶς in this kind of combination in the PE see 2:2b, 11; 4:9; 5:2; Tit. 2:15; for further references in Paul and the NT see BAGD s.v. laδ).

3:5 Here Paul tells why such a caring leadership is essential. If this ability is lacking, "how will he take care of the church of God?" The argument moves from the "lesser" to the "greater," in analogous realms, i.e., from the family to the family of God, and states that inability in the former makes ability extremely doubtful in the latter. V. 5 is parenthetical since it does not depend on the δεῖ εἶναι of v. 2, as the preceding verses do and as the following μὴ νεόφυτον of v. 6 does. But its intrinsic significance is not parenthetical. For the various ways of indicating this see the punctuation apparatus in *UBSGNT*.

δέ introduces a contrast to the requirement just given by means of a conditional statement, of which the "if" clause is assumed to be true, and the conclusion is in the form of a rhetorical question expecting a negative answer (Robertson; on εἰ . . . τις see v. 1). The first clause repeats v. 4 (with slight variations) and thus provides the basis for the rhetorical question.

οἶδα followed by the infinitive means "know or understand how" (for NT and extrabiblical examples see BAGD s.v. 3). This construction is then picked up by the introductory "how" (πῶς) of the rhetorical question. If a man does not "know how" to rule his own house, "how" can he take care of the church of God? The οὐκ of the conditional clause implies a negative answer for the question.

πῶς (in the PE* here and 3:15) introduces the rhetorical question that elicits a negative to its own statement (BAGD s.v. 1d; cf. 1 Cor. 14:7, 9, 16). The question speaks of the very task that the bishop is called to do, namely, ἐκκλησίας θεοῦ ἐπιμελήσεται. ἐπιμελέομαι** (Lk. 10:34f.) means "care for" or "take care of" (with the genitive). The personal and thorough care given by the Good Samaritan, the only other NT occurrence of the verb, cannot help but serve as a pattern, even though the contexts differ. ἐκκλησία in the PE* (here; 3:15; 5:16) consistently refers to the Christian church (for bibliography see BAGD; K. L. Schmidt, *TDNT* III, 501-36; *TWNT* X s.v.). The anarthrous form of ἐκκλησίας here emphasizes that this is a general principle about an "overseer's" relationship to any church. Genitive θεοῦ with ἐκκλησία, an essentially Pauline usage (1 Cor. 1:2; 10:32; 11:16, 22; 15:9; 2 Cor. 1:1; Gal. 1:13; 1 Thes. 2:14; 2 Thes. 1:4; 1 Tim. 3:5, 15; Acts 20:28), gives ἐκκλησία its Christian orientation and provides for its special meaning. The ἐκκλησία belongs to God, and only those evidently equipped and qualified are to be entrusted with its care. The rhetorical question indicates that anything else is unthinkable and is to be denied.

3:6 The requirement of maturity is now introduced with the insistence that the bishop not be a new convert, followed by the reason for this. νεόφυτος** meant literally "newly planted" but is used figuratively, only in Christian literature, of one "newly planted" in the Christian church, or "newly converted" (BAGD; cf. our word "neophyte").

The reason that a νεόφυτος is not to be a bishop is given in a clause introduced by ἵνα μή, a combination used to designate a purpose clause with a negative intent and rendered "in order that not" (BAGD s.v. μή 2) or sometimes "lest" *(NASB)*. The clause indicates what one seeks to prevent and what would likely happen if a neophyte were made a bishop, i.e., "in order that he may not become conceited and fall into the condemnation incurred by the devil." τυφόω** (here; 6:4; 2 Tim. 3:4) is used only in the passive and in a figurative sense in the NT and early Christian literature and has the meaning here of "be puffed up or conceited." ἐμπίπτω, "fall in or into," used literally in the Gospels (Mt. 12:11; Lk. 6:39; 10:36), is used with reference to sin and its consequences in the PE (here; v. 7; 6:9).

The understanding of the remainder of the verse depends in part on the meaning of τοῦ διαβόλου and the significance of the genitive construction. Although διάβολος in its adjectival plural form is used of human beings (3:11; Tit. 2:3; 2 Tim. 3:3), in the NT the articular substantival form refers specifically, as here (contra Weiss), to the "devil" (a usage already current in the LXX translation of *haśśāṭān*, e.g., Jb. 2:1; Zc. 3:1f.; 1 Ch. 21:1; cf.

BAGD s.v. 2). Of the thirty-seven occurrences of διάβολος in the NT the thirty singular articular forms (like two others that are not articular: Rev. 12:9; 20:2) refer to the evil one, the devil, as here and 2 Tim. 2:26.

Is the κρίμα that which the devil has received (so that οὗ διαβόλου is objective genitive; so Calvin, Bengel, Robertson, Lenski, and Hendriksen) or is it that which he gives (subjective genitive; so Wohlenberg, von Soden, Gealy, Kelly, Lock, Spicq, and Ridderbos)? The argument for the latter appeals to the subjective genitive in v. 7, the absence of an article before κρίμα, the appropriateness of κρίμα being the onslaught of one who is a slanderer (διάβολος), and the parallel to 1 Tim. 1:20; Job 1 and 2; Rev. 12:10, etc. The argument for objective genitive responds that the usage of v. 7 with a different kind of word is not decisive, even though the verb is the same, that the article is not present because the judgment that falls on humans is not the same as that which falls on the devil but only similar, and with Calvin notes that κρίμα rarely means "slander" but rather a "judicial verdict" and here "condemnation" (BAGD s.v. 4b; see especially Rom. 3:8; PE* 2x, here and 5:12). Furthermore, the reference to 1:20 seems inappropriate, because it speaks of the result of church discipline — of that which is regarded as salutary, whereas in 3:7 judgment is not such a result and is something to be avoided. When one correlates "conceit" or "pride" (τυφωθείς) with falling into κρίμα, the OT passage that has just been in Paul's mind in 2:13-14, namely Genesis 2 and 3, particularly Gn. 3:14, 15, would seem to provide the background for our text. In Genesis the serpent receives condemnation because he tempted Eve to be like God (Gn. 3:5). That act reflected his own previous pride, arrogance, and enmity against God. In the light of all these considerations, τοῦ διαβόλου is more likely to be objective genitive.

3:7 The final requirement of the bishop is "a good reputation with those outside." The reason for this requirement is given in a grammatical form similar to that of v. 6 (ἵνα μή): "so that he may not fall into reproach and the snare of the devil." The list ends with the note of necessity (δεῖ, see v. 2) with which it began and which set the tone for the intervening qualifications. This final requirement is joined to those that precede it by the particle δέ (aside from the parenthetical v. 5 the only occurrence of δέ in this list) and the emphatic καί ("also" in *NIV;* "moreover" in *RSV, NEB*), which together indicate that this characteristic is equally important.

ἔξωθεν is an adverb of place used 13x in the NT, as a substantive twice with a neuter singular article (Mt. 23:25; Lk. 11:39f.) and here with a masculine plural article (as in the variant reading of Mk. 4:11). A literal rendering is simply "outsiders" *(RSV, NIV).* Since the discourse in this passage is speaking of the church (vv. 5, 15), those who are outside are "those outside *the church*" *(NASB),* or non-Christians (BAGD; *NEB:* "the non-Christian public"). Paul* has used the synonymous οἱ ἔξω (1 Cor. 5:12,

13; Col. 4:5; 1 Thes. 4:12; cf. Mk. 4:11), and the variant ἔξωθεν may be used here because of the preposition ἀπό (so Simpson).

The μαρτυρίαν καλήν is said to be ἀπὸ τῶν ἔξωθεν with ἀπό indicating "the originator of the action denoted by the verb" so that ἔχειν τι ἀπό τινος means "to have (received) something from someone" (BAGD s.v. ἀπό 4; cf. 1 Cor. 6:19; 1 Jn. 2:20; 4:21). "ἀπό is equivalent not to 'among,' but to *'from'*; the testimony comes from those who are not Christians" (Huther). μαρτυρία (Pl.* 2x: here and Tit. 1:13) is used here with the meaning "testimony" in the sense of "a judgment on relig[ious] or moral matters, passed by one person upon another" (BAGD s.v. 2c). An English idiom for "testimony from" is "reputation with" *(NASB, NEB, NIV)*. Paul is concerned that those who may judge less sympathetically but perhaps also more realistically and knowledgeably will render a "good" (καλήν, see 1:8) verdict both from the perspective of their own consciences (cf. Rom. 1:18ff., 32; 2:14f.) and also from their awareness of the particular man's commitment and consistency in terms of his Christian faith. Is he in their eyes ἀνεπίλημπτον (3:2) from these perspectives, and do they, albeit grudgingly or in opposition, render that testimony? Thus the "good" (καλήν) that marks their testimony concerning him is that which the church, and Paul, will also regard as καλήν.

The reason for this requirement, stated in a ἵνα clause, is concern for what will happen to a leader who is not so regarded by those outside the church. The first aspect of this concern is that he will fall into "reproach" (ὀνειδισμός). From whom will the reproach come? That is to say, is ὀνειδισμός qualified by the genitive τοῦ διαβόλου or is it used absolutely? For the former, it is argued that the preposition εἰς is not repeated before παγίδα. For the latter, it is argued that the reproach follows from the potential bishop not having a good testimony from those outside and so is not restricted exclusively to the διάβολος. That consideration is more in line with the context.

ὀνειδισμός** is a reproach or reviling that is a disgrace or insult (BAGD). The other NT occurrences use ὀνειδισμός to relate what Christ (Rom. 15:3) and his people have borne (Heb. 10:33; 11:26) and must bear (Heb. 13:12). Here, however, the issue is not bearing up under reproach but falling into it, in the sense of being tempted to sin and adversely affected by it. ἐμπίπτω in all its figurative occurrences in the NT has a negative meaning (cf. Lk. 10:36; Heb. 10:31; and especially 1 Tim. 6:9: "fall into temptation," a most apt parallel also followed by παγίδα). Kelly indicates in part what is involved in ὀνειδισμός when he says that "unsympathetic outsiders will put the most unfavourable interpretation on [the man's] slightest word or deed." Either their making such an evaluation justly or his inappropriate reaction to an unjust evaluation will lead him to fall and to be caught in the snare of the devil.

The "snare" (παγίς**) is literally a trap, often one used to catch birds.

As elsewhere (Rom. 11:9; 1 Tim. 6:9; 2 Tim. 2:26; cf. Lk. 21:35 [34 in English versions], where the literal sense is used comparatively), the word is used figuratively "of things that bring danger or death, suddenly and unexpectedly" (BAGD). Here and in 2 Tim. 2:26 it is used with the qualification τοῦ διαβόλου. Although a διάβολος could be a human slanderer, the indication of 2 Tim. 2:26 that the snare of the διάβολος has reference to the evil one and the rather uniform usage of διάβολος with that meaning elsewhere in the NT and Paul (see above on v. 6) suggest that the evil one is meant here also. The παγίς τοῦ διαβόλου is that which he sets for others, not that which is set for him, as 2 Tim. 2:26 makes clear with the words "having been held captive by him to do his will" and by speaking of those who escape the snare by coming "to their senses." A man without a good testimony from outsiders could "lose his head" or "senses" when he fell into reproach and thereby be ensnared to obey the evil one and disobey God.

Vv. 6 and 7 seek to protect both the man and the church's leadership from self-righteous pride and cowardly disobedience. To avoid both demands a mature believer with an established reputation.

The qualifications given in this list are all either self-explanatory or explained by Paul. They call on the church to evaluate a potential bishop by means of characteristics that the members are aware of. They speak of time for a potential bishop to grow so that he can see himself and the office without pride (v. 6), of a man's control of besetting sins that compete against the lordship of Christ, of his ability to share himself and the teaching of the Word with others (v. 2), of his ability to live peaceably with people and not materialistically or contentiously (v. 3), of his family life as an indicator of his leadership ability (vv. 4, 5), and of testimony by outsiders regarding him that can indicate the genuineness, reality, and stability of his new life in Christ (v. 7). These touchstones coupled with those marks that should characterize all Christians are those things concerning which he should be "above reproach." It would appear that this list is given for the same purpose as the brief list of Acts 6:3, namely, to provide a basis for the people of the church to select the one God would have lead them, since such qualifications are the outworking of God's grace.

DEACONS: 3:8-13

With v. 8 the apostle introduces another office and its qualifications, that of the διάκονοι (Phil. 1:1 also mentions both bishops and deacons; cf. also the similar twofold structure [the apostles and their ministry and the Seven and theirs] in Acts 6). The new section is signaled by the appearance of three elements: (1) first and foremost the term διάκονος itself, (2) the adverb ὡσαύτως, and (3) the similar but, in certain ways, different list of qualifications. These together indicate that a different office is being presented.

The list of qualifications is analogous to that for the bishop but also uniquely fitting for the particular service of the διάκονοι. Like the bishop a deacon must be "beyond reproach" (ἀνέγκλητος, v. 10, a synonym of ἀνεπιλήμπτος in v. 2). The qualifications are expressed both positively and negatively (vv. 8 and 9). Negatively, a deacon must evidence a control of besetting sins, which include, as with the bishop, problems related to drink, money, and personal speech (v. 8). The brevity of this list may compress in the one word σεμνούς several of the positive items specified for the bishop and may also allude to such items by speaking of the deacon "holding to the mystery of the faith" "with a clear conscience" (v. 9). As for the bishop, so also for the deacon the family serves as a crucial test of his qualifications, both in regard to marital fidelity and to his managing his children (v. 12). The statement "husbands of one wife" is preceded by a verse (introduced by ὡσαύτως) setting forth the qualifications of γυναῖκες, "women."

There are items in the list for the bishop that are not present in this list for deacons, most noteworthy being the requirements that the bishop be "able to teach" (v. 2) and "take care of the church of God" (v. 5). It would seem that these two are omitted because they are not part of the role of the deacons. Similarly not mentioned is the need to be gentle and not contentious in interpersonal relationships (v. 3). Again, this may reflect the fact that the deacon is not in the role of one who must give oversight and direction, as well as discipline, in sometimes difficult situations that make such qualifications imperative. A concern for the new convert's potential conceit is also not mentioned, nor is concern for the testimony from outsiders or the danger of falling into reproach. Although the reference to testing (v. 10) may in itself indicate that a deacon is not to be a new convert, it may be that a ministry of service rather than oversight is less liable to those temptations and assaults. At any rate the note of caution is sounded in different ways for the two offices. The whole passage on bishops and deacons begins and ends with commendation of and appreciation for men who serve faithfully in these two offices, though the note of encouragement for deacons who serve well (v. 13) is more explicit in its praise than that which is addressed to the bishop (v. 1).

3:8 διάκονοι (PE* 3x: here; 3:12; 4:6), as it is used here in distinction from ἐπίσκοπος (so also in Phil. 1:1), is the technical designation of those who have the serving office in the church and is commonly translated as "deacons" (see BAGD s.v. lc). This is the most specialized usage of the term, which in general usage simply means "servant." διάκονος is used of the apostles and those like them (Mt. 20:26; Mk. 10:43; cf. Mt. 23:11; Mk. 9:35) and generally of officers in the church, such as Timothy (1 Tim. 4:6), probably because of Jesus' identification of his own work as that of one who serves (διακονῆσαι, Mt. 20:28; Mk. 10:45). Thus the common NT designation of a Christian leader (and of Paul himself) is διάκονος (e.g., 1 Cor. 3:5; 2 Cor. 3:6; Eph. 3:7; 6:21; Col. 1:23, 25; 4:7), sometimes with the qualification θεοῦ or Χριστοῦ (4:6; 2 Cor. 6:4; Col. 1:7; 1 Thes. 3:2), and when used in this way the designation is commonly rendered "minister." Within the category of "ministers" (διάκονοι) some are distinguished from other fellow ministers as ἐπίσκοποι, and the others are designated διάκονοι (as here and in Phil. 1:1). Apparently the ministry of the latter is so specifically and exclusively that of service that the name designating their function becomes uniquely theirs, even though later in this same Epistle (as elsewhere in Paul's letters) the broader usage for others in "ministry" still occurs (4:6).

As in the case of the ἐπίσκοπος, the noun διάκονος is both the designation of an office and a descriptive indication of what one who holds the office does. The plural here (and in Phil. 1:1) indicates that several men are to undertake this office and its work in the congregation (cf. the Seven in Acts 6:1ff.).

The adverb ὡσαύτως (see 2:9) with its meaning of "likewise" both distinguishes the διάκονοι from the ἐπίσκοπος and compares the two. The διάκονοι, like the ἐπίσκοπος, must "likewise" have qualifications, namely those that follow. ὡσαύτως in vv. 8 and 9, as elsewhere, requires that a verb be understood or supplied (see 2:9). Both here and in v. 11 the verb is that found at the beginning of, and presumed throughout, the list of qualifications for the bishop, i.e., δεῖ εἶναι (v. 2). The accusative form of διακόνους and of the following qualifications is required by their relationship to the understood infinitive εἶναι.

σεμνός** (here; v. 11; Tit. 2:2; Phil. 4:8; see W. Foerster, *TDNT* VII, 191-96) means, when used of a person (as in the PE), that the person is "worthy of respect," or as Foerster (p. 195) puts it, "serious and worthy." "σεμνός in 1 Tim. 3:8 embraces what is put separately in the portrait of the bishop" (Foerster, 195), i.e., the positive traits of the bishop's list in 3:2-3.

To this positive trait are added three negative traits to be avoided. In all three the quality of self-control is spelled out — with reference to speech, appetite for drink, and perspective on money, all of which the deacon must have under control rather than being controlled or betrayed by them. μὴ διλόγους** (a biblical hapax not found with the Pauline sense in Greek writers before the Christian era; see BAGD and MM) must mean here "double-tongued" in the sense of "insincere" (BAGD); *NEB* aptly renders it "indulging in double talk" (cf. 2 Cor. 1:17, 18). μὴ οἴνῳ πολλῷ προσέχοντας says for the deacons what μὴ πάροινον (v. 3) said for the bishop. The emphasis on not being controlled by wine (οἶνος, 1 Tim. 5:23; Tit. 2:3) is heightened by the addition here of the adjective πολλῷ and by the sense of the verb; προσέχω has the general meaning in the active voice of "turn one's mind to" and here of "occupy oneself with" or "devote oneself to" (BAGD). Tit. 2:3 expresses the idea well with "not enslaved to much wine."

μὴ αἰσχροκερδεῖς** (also in Tit. 1:7) represents a concern that is always present in the lists of requirements for officers in the PE (see the synonymous ἀφιλάργυρον in 3:3 and the notes there) and in 1 Pet. 5:2 (αἰσχροκερδῶς**). This being "greedy for money" (BAGD) is illustrated in Lysias (12.19) by those who took from others even though they already had an abundance of what they took. When this concern is addressed again in 1 Tim. 6:5-10, the antidote is said to be "contentment" with the food and covering one has. The attitudinal character of this problem is illustrated by the contrasting term in 1 Pet. 5:2, προθύμως, "willingly and eagerly." What is spoken of, therefore, is ministry not motivated by financial gain but by desire to serve God and his people.

3:9 This verse concludes the initial statement about the διάκονοι by adding the important item relating the deacon's faith to his life. ἔχοντας τὸ μυστήριον τῆς πίστεως indicates both that deacons have embraced the faith (ἔχοντας) and what it is that they embrace (τὸ μυστήριον τῆς πίστεως). The concluding words, ἐν καθαρᾷ συνειδήσει, signify that the genuineness of their faith is evident in their godly life.

ἔχω here means "keep" or "preserve" (BAGD s.v. I.1cβ). The ongoing governing force of δεῖ (v. 2) brings the note of necessity to this statement (cf. *NIV:* "they must keep hold of the faith"). μυστήριον (PE* 2x: here and 3:16) in the NT is used of "the secret thoughts, plans, and dispensations of God that are hidden from the human reason, as well as from all other comprehension below the divine level, and hence must be revealed" (BAGD). The phrase (τὸ μυστήριον τῆς πίστεως) may thus be paraphrased as "the revealed truth of the Christian faith" with πίστις referring here to that which is believed (cf. BAGD s.v. 3). Since ἔχοντας has already expressed the subjective side of faith, and the phrase is not redundant, the objectivizing of the concept of "faith" must be in view here (cf., e.g., Gal. 1:23; 1 Tim. 4:1, 6; 6:10, 21; 2 Tim. 3:8; 4:7).

The emphasis is on the concluding words, ἐν καθαρᾷ συνειδήσει, for without the life the profession is empty. συνείδησις (see 1 Tim. 1:5) in the NT indicates the moral self-consciousness that a person has as one made in God's image (cf. Rom. 2:15). This moral self-consciousness is strengthened and instructed by the redeeming work of Christ and the illuminating work of the Spirit. The previous two occurrences of συνείδησις in 1 Timothy are qualified by ἀγαθή. Here the qualifier is καθαρά in the sense of "clean" or "clear" (as in 2 Tim. 1:3, the only other NT occurrence of καθαρά with συνείδησις, but cf. καθαρίζω with συνείδησις in Heb. 9:14). That the deacon's moral self-consciousness is καθαρά means that he seeks to live according to the ethical demands of the revealed faith that he holds fast (cf. in contrast 1:19).

3:10 With καί ("also") before οὗτοι "these" (the deacons) are compared with the bishop. With the verb δοκιμαζέσθωσαν we are reminded of the tests implied in vv. 4-7. For the bishops/presbyters Paul will return to the note of testing and caution in 5:22, 24, 25 and warn against a hasty laying on of hands that does not allow time to consider the positive and negative evidence that a man's life affords. Both here and there Paul insists on an orderly and careful evaluation. That this evaluation take place first is signified by the temporal πρῶτον — εἶτα construction with the second clause qualified by ἀνέγκλητοι ὄντες.

The passive imperative form of δοκιμάζω means here that the deacons are to be "put to the test" or "examined" with reference to the items mentioned. How this is to be done is not specified. The letter itself makes the requirements public, and 5:22ff. indicates that time must be given to appraise a man's life. From this we can conclude that the testing is to be a thoughtful and careful evaluation of a man's life by a congregation aware of these needed qualifications. The hoped-for positive outcome of the testing is expressed in the present active imperative of διακονέω (PE*: here; v. 13; 2 Tim. 1:18), which means generally "serve" but in this context most likely means "serve as a διάκονος," i.e., enter into the church office for which they have been tested (so also BAGD s.v. 5). This use of the verb helps us to understand how a group of church officers received as their title the noun διάκονος, which states in a substantive the task that the verb διακονεῖν says they are engaged in. The relationship of noun and verb may well indicate a semantic link with the Seven of Acts 6, whose official task for the church was designated with the verbal phrase διακονεῖν τραπέζαις (Acts 6:2).

ἀνέγκλητοι ὄντες specifies what the outcome of the testing must be before the potential candidates may enter into service as deacons. Prospective deacons will be ἀνέγκλητος** (1 Cor. 1:8; Col. 1:22; Tit. 1:6, 7; the synonym of ἀνεπίλημπτος in 3:2), "beyond reproach" or "blameless" in the moral realm if a fair appraisal judges that they have each of the listed positive qualifications and none of the listed negative traits as characteristics of their life.

3:11 With this verse γυναῖκες ("women" or "wives") are introduced into the pericope. They are distinguished from and compared with the preceding category of διάκονοι by the adverb ὡσαύτως with its comparative sense of "likewise," just as the διάκονοι have been previously distinguished from and compared with the ἐπίσκοπος by the same word (v. 8; see the discussion of this word above in 2:9). Those with whom the γυναῖκες are compared and from whom they are distinguished are designated διάκονοι in v. 8 and again in v. 12 and are assumed to be men (μιᾶς γυναικὸς ἄνδρες). The "women" are, therefore, distinguished from the deacons.

The question still remains (and has become even more significant): Why are γυναῖκας introduced in the midst of this pericope on διάκονοι and introduced in a parallel way (ὡσαύτως) to the διάκονοι and with a comparable list of qualifications (cf. v. 11 with vv. 8, 9)? In general terms, the answer would appear to be that they are in some way involved in the diaconal service that the διάκονοι are called to perform. But what is the nature of their involvement? Essentially four positions have been taken: (1) The women are inherently part of the διάκονοι, (2) they are "deaconesses" distinguished from but comparable with the διάκονοι, (3) they are female assistants to the διάκονοι, or (4) they are the wives of the διάκονοι.

Those in v. 11 are too clearly and definitely distinguished from the διάκονοι (again by ὡσαύτως, the title διάκονοι, and the qualification μιᾶς γυναικὸς ἄνδρες for the διάκονοι) for (1) to be the meaning intended by Paul. (3) is preferable to (2) because the title διάκονοι is not used in v. 11 and seems to be used so self-consciously before and after v. 11 and in unmistakable male categories (μιᾶς γυναικὸς ἄνδρες). The solution would seem to narrow down to either (3) or (4), either of which would presume the same activity of diaconal service but would understand a more general or more specific reference for γυναῖκες, i.e., either "women" assistants, or "wives" of the διάκονοι.

γυνή, both singular and plural, has the general meaning "woman/women," but is also often used to mean "wife/wives" (see BAGD). Both usages occur in the PE and especially in 1 Timothy ("woman" in 2:9, 10, 11, 12, 14; "wife" in 3:2, 12; 5:9; cf. Tit. 1:6). Here it seems likely that the term is used in v. 11 in the same way that it is used in the immediately following verse, and as it was used in the preceding occurrence in v. 2, i.e., as "wife."

γυναῖκας is accusative because it, like διακόνους in v. 8, is governed by the understood δεῖ. With the bishop and the deacons it is the role that gives warrant for the δεῖ εἶναι. Therefore, the γυναῖκας in v. 11 are urged to manifest the four characteristics listed there, not because all women in the church must manifest these characteristics, but because of a special role that these "women" in particular have that demands these characteristics. As spouses of the deacons they are to be involved with their husbands as their husbands seek to fulfill their diaconal service. The translation "wives" expresses this unique relationship and responsibility. Further, it is also more likely that Paul, who was wise concerning sexuality (cf., e.g., 2:9; 5:11, 15; and perhaps 5:6), would propose the deacons' wives as their assistants rather than women in general.

Another consideration that favors the understanding "wives" in v. 11 is the omission of any reference to their marital status and fidelity (i.e., "the wife of one husband"), as is found with reference to the bishops and deacons (vv. 2, 12) and in the qualifications for enrollment for older widows (5:9). This omission is significant because this qualification is always mentioned in the PE where positions of ministry or service are in view and because it stands out as such a striking difference between the otherwise nearly parallel qualifications of the διάκονοι and the γυναῖκες. The omission can, however, be explained if the requirement is inherent in their position as wives of the διάκονοι.

Furthermore, this understanding of γυναῖκες as "wives" also provides the solution for the reference to γυναῖκες at this place in the pericope. If it is wives that are in view, then the verse fits here as another qualification necessary for one who would be a deacon and who would conduct his ministry with his wife's assistance. Thus the wife's qualifications are part and parcel of his qualifications for the office of διάκονος. And after giving the qualifications for the deacon's wife, Paul then goes on to the deacon's fidelity to his wife and his children and thereby completes the picture of his family life (v. 12).

It has been objected to this understanding of γυναῖκες that no indication of relationship is found in the text, not even a definite article before γυναῖκας. It may be responded that in the whole pericope Paul refers to people anarthrously (διακόνους, v. 8; διάκονοι, v. 12; τέκνων, v. 12; τέκνα, v. 3; γυναικός as "wife," v. 12 as in v. 2, in both cases preceding anarthrous words, ἄνδρες in v. 12, ἄνδρα in v. 2; τὸν ἐπίσκοπον, v. 2, is the sole exception, probably because of its generic usage). If v. 11 had been written after v. 12, the understanding of γυναῖκες as wives, even without any qualification, would likely be more apparent just because of the order and the usage of the anarthrous γυναικός, which would have been immediately preceding. However, the effect of v. 12 on our understanding of v. 11 still remains, even with the order of the verses as we have them.

The qualifications for the deacons' wives, who are engaged with the deacons in diaconal service, are virtually synonymous with the qualifications of the διάκονοι (vv. 8, 9): σεμνάς corresponds to σεμνούς, μὴ διαβόλους to μὴ διλόγους, νηφαλίους to μὴ οἴνῳ πολλῷ προσέχοντας and perhaps also μὴ αἰσχροκερδεῖς, and finally πιστὰς ἐν πᾶσιν to the entirety of v. 9. On σεμνάς see v. 8 (σεμνούς)

διάβολος (see v. 6) is usually used in the NT in the singular as a substantive indicating the slanderer, the devil. Here, as in two other places in the PE (Tit. 2:3; 2 Tim. 3:3), it is used in the plural as an adjective. The idea of "slanderer" *(RSV;* cf. *NEB)* remains, although probably what is in mind is the activity of "malicious gossips" *(NASB)* or "malicious talkers" *(NIV).* Here and in Tit. 2:3 (with the identical construction) this concern is related specifically to women, but 2 Tim. 3:3 regards it as a problem of the day without regard to sexual identification. Its usage here rather than the parallel διλόγους of v. 8 may be an indication of emphasis in terms of the besetting sins of the tongue that were regarded as characterizing each sex.

νηφαλίους** (also in 3:2 [which see]; Tit. 2:2), since the list is so brief and compressed, probably encompasses here its various meanings and nuances, i.e., "temperate in the use of alcoholic beverages, sober, clear-headed, self-controlled," with emphasis on the latter as including the former.

The list of qualifications concludes with πιστὰς ἐν πᾶσιν. πιστός (see

1:12) is used here in its passive sense of "trustworthy, faithful, or dependable" (see BAGD s.v. 1a). ἐν πᾶσιν indicates the extent of that fidelity, as does the phrase παντὶ ἔργῳ ἀγαθῷ in relationship to the enrolled widow in 5:9.

The similarities and differences between the γυναῖκες and διάκονοι must be noted and evaluated. The wives of deacons must be as committed and serious as their husbands, as in control of tongues and attitudes, as self-controlled and as faithful, for them to be responsible laborers with their husbands. Although this is all true, it is not said of the γυναῖκες that they must be first tested and be beyond reproach, because it is not they, but their husbands, who are being elected to and put into office. Thus certain qualifications are left out of consideration, which thus in itself gives further corroboration to the conclusion that those in view in v. 11 are "wives" who assist the διάκονοι, their husbands.

3:12 Paul returns to the διάκονοι themselves, as is indicated by his repetition of their title and by the first requirement named in this verse, which involves the διάκονοι being men. The imperative ἔστωσαν substitutes for δεῖ εἶναι, which has been understood since its appearance in v. 2. Sexual and marital fidelity and good management of his children and household are demanded of the deacon. In vv. 2 and 4 (see above on those verses for the meanings of the terms) identical terms are used in regard to the ἐπίσκοπος. The one noteworthy difference is the absence of the concluding phrase of v. 4 and of the corresponding deduction in v. 5. Both the similarity and the difference are significant: The similarity indicates that the home is the proving ground of fidelity for all officers. The difference indicates that the implication spelled out in v. 5 is not drawn for the διάκονοι because they are not ἐπίσκοποι, overseers of the church.

3:13 The third chapter began with a word of encouragement for anyone aspiring to the office of bishop. The section for the deacons ends with such a word of encouragement. γάρ points forward to the second half of the verse, which gives the reason for the good service described in the first half.

Although it is possible to take διακονήσαντες in the general sense of serving and thus include the ἐπίσκοποι of vv. 1-8 under this term, it is more likely that following the use of διάκονοι in the technical sense in vv. 8 and 12 and the use of the verb in that technical sense in v. 10 the verb would be used here in that same sense to refer to the deacons. Those who gain the standing and confidence of which the latter part of the verse speaks are indicated by the articular aorist participle οἱ διακονήσαντες, "those who have served." But it is not perfunctory office bearing but rather serving "well" (καλῶς) as a deacon that results in that good outcome. καλῶς in the sense of "in the right way" and thus "commendably" permeates Paul's treatment of church officers (cf. vv. 4, 12 and especially 5:17). Those who serve well gain (περιποιέω, with the reflexive pronoun ἑαυτοῖς and in similar senses here and Acts 20:28) for themselves a standing (βαθμός) characterized as good (καλόν) and confidence (παρρησία) that is great (πολύς).

Are the "standing" and "confidence" what a deacon can have before God or before humans? Do they refer to spiritual standing or church position? Might it even be that one refers to the former and the other to the latter? How does ἐν πίστει κτλ. qualify what precedes?

βαθμός** (a NT hapax) means "step" or "threshold" and is used figuratively to mean "step" or "standing" (see LSJM). It can also be used to refer to a "grade" or "rank" (see BAGD for all these nuances). It is doubtful that the latter sense is meant, as if good service as a deacon would acquire for the deacon the rank of an ἐπίσκοπος. The qualifier καλός is probably against that understanding since it would then imply that the position of διάκονος was not καλός, so that this would hardly be a word of encouragement for faithful service as a διάκονος. The literal meaning "step" is also self-evidently excluded, and thus one is left with the understanding that good service as a deacon gains a "good standing." If we may anticipate our later discussion and say that ἐν πίστει κτλ. qualifies this concept as well as παρρησία, then what is spoken of here is standing in the Christian faith.

παρρησία (Pl.* 8x, qualified by πολλή here and in 2 Cor. 3:12; 7:4; Phm. 8 and by πᾶσα in Phil. 1:20) indicates a freedom to speak that carries with it the nuances of confidence and boldness (see BAGD; H. Schlier, *TDNT* V, 871ff.; H.-C. Hahn, *NIDNTT* II, 734ff.). The παρρησία that comes to the Christian "in Christ Jesus" "through faith in him" (Eph. 3:11, 12) is, therefore, increased and enlarged (πολλὴν παρρησίαν) by the Christian's faithful service for Christ (cf. Phil. 1:12, 13).

The realm or sphere in which the πολλὴν παρρησίαν is expressed and is active is indicated by the first ἐν of the following prepositional phrase: It is the sphere of πίστις, here used in the sense of "faith" as trust in Christ, as the emphatic τῇ makes clear. On Χριστῷ Ἰησοῦ see 1:1.

Since πολλὴν παρρησίαν is qualified by ἐν πίστει and gets its frame of reference from that phrase, we may ask whether βαθμὸν καλόν, which is joined to πολλὴν παρρησίαν by καί, and having no other expressed frame of reference, is not also qualified by ἐν πίστει. Since this kind of construction with a prepositional phrase is quite normal, we may construe this as the intention of Paul.

Thus the encouragement given to deacons who serve faithfully is progress (βαθμὸν καλόν) and confidence or boldness (πολλὴν παρρησίαν) in the sphere of faith in Christ, in which they already stand (cf. Rom. 5:1). The encouragement is spiritually delineated and is not limited in any other way. As to whether this is experienced in relation to people or God, it may only be answered that neither is indicated. Furthermore, examination of the other NT occurrences of παρρησία shows that it has significance in both directions, both human and divine, within the framework of πίστις ἐν Χριστῷ Ἰησοῦ.

EXCURSUS: BISHOPS/PRESBYTERS AND DEACONS: 3:1-13

1 Tim. 3:1-13 thus presents a twofold pattern for the official ministry of the church, that of oversight (ἐπίσκοπος) and that of service (διάκονος). This same twofold pattern is also seen in Phil. 1:1 and seems to be reflected in the early division of labor at Jerusalem between the oversight ministry of the apostles (of prayer and of the ministry of the Word, Acts 6:1, 4) and the aid to widows on the part of the Seven (vv. 1-3). The early Jerusalem community presents not only a conceptual parallel but also linguistic parallels: (1) Peter, one of those apostles, can refer to himself as a "fellow elder" (συμπρεσβύτερος, 1 Pet. 5:1). That "elder" (πρεσβύτερος) was a synonym for ἐπίσκοπος is clear from Tit. 1:5, 7 and Acts 20:17, 28 (cf. 1 Pet. 5:2; 1 Tim. 5:17; see the still valid study of Lightfoot, "The Synonyms 'Bishop' and 'Presbyter,'" *Philippians,* 95-99). (2) The responsibility for which the Seven were elected is referred to as the daily διακονία without further qualification, and their activity is described as διακονεῖν τραπέζαις (Acts 6:12). The linguistic connections with those who are in 1 Tim. 3:8-13 described with the noun διάκονοι and the verb διακονεῖν (used in a technical sense) is striking and is in accord with the division of labor in conceptual terms in Acts 6. These three passages show, then, a twofold division of labor in early, middle, and later time periods in the NT church, in key cities in three various geographical areas (Palestine, Greece, and Asia Minor), and in both Jewish and Greco-Roman settings.

But it is puzzling that such an early and widespread phenomenon is otherwise virtually absent from the rest of the NT, at least in terms of the διάκονοι, although not entirely so in terms of the ἐπίσκοποι/πρεσβύτεροι. The fundamental difference between the parallel instructions of Titus 1 and 1 Timothy 3 provides one clue regarding this difficulty. Tit. 1:5 suggests that the church in Crete had been established only a short time and was still virtually unorganized. In such a situation, only the initial rank of officers is prescribed, i.e., the bishops/presbyters, while 1 Timothy 3 refers to both bishops and deacons. Apparently, as in Jerusalem with the apostles, it was assumed that in Crete the bishops/presbyters would also care for the needy until such time as the work became too great and men qualified to serve as διάκονοι were available. The same approach was followed in Paul's first missionary journey (Acts 14:23), and concern for "the weak" was still perceived as the responsibility of the bishops/elders in Miletus (Acts 20:35), whether these men administered such aid or not.

The NT letters do not often refer to officers at all (Phil. 1:1 being the notable exception), because the letters are ministering directly to the entire congregation through instruction and persuasion, and thus have very little reason to refer to officers. When officers are referred to, it is usually in terms of their leadership responsibilities and the significance of that in terms of the congregation's response, rather than in terms of diaconal duties (cf. 1 Thes. 5:12, 13; Heb. 13:17; 1 Pet. 5:1-4). Therefore, those to whom the congregation is to respond are referred to, i.e., leadership officers, and there is no reason to refer to service officers.

Finally, there may be at least one reference to the diaconal office that is overlooked because a different designation is utilized, just as there are a number of other references in the NT to the leadership offices using other designations than ἐπίσκοποι. 1 Cor. 12:28 is the most noteworthy example. In this list are both those who have some sort of office, i.e., apostles, prophets, teachers, helps, and administrators, and those whose gifts are not what would be associated with an office, i.e., miracles, gifts of healings, and tongues. Leaving aside the foundational gifts of apostles and prophets (Eph. 2:20) and the nonoffice gifts, we arrive at a threefold designation: teachers (διδάσκαλοι), helps (ἀντιλήμψεις), and administrators (κυβερνήσεις). We have seen from 1 Timothy 3 that the office of ἐπίσκοπος involves two duties: teaching (v. 2) and caring/ruling (vv. 4, 5), which are paralleled in the teachers and administrators of 1 Cor. 12:28, leaving "helps," which would be a designation for deacons. It is likely, therefore, that the Corinthian church had διάκονοι who were referred to as ἀντιλήμψεις and ἐπίσκοποι/πρεσβύτεροι referred to as διδάσκαλοι and κυβερνήσεις (see BAGD; H. W. Beyer, *TDNT* III, 1036).

ἐπίσκοποι/πρεσβύτεροι are mentioned in the plural in regard to Ephesus (Acts 20:17, 28), Philippi (Phil. 1:1), and each city church on Crete (Tit. 1:5). Furthermore, Paul moves from plural πρεσβύτεροι in Tit. 1:5 to generic singular ἐπίσκοπος in Tit. 1:7 and from generic singular ἐπίσκοπος in 1 Tim. 3:2 to plural πρεσβύτεροι in 1 Tim. 5:17. This plurality of ruling officers is also seen in the references to πρεσβύτεροι in Acts 11:30; 14:23; 15:2, 4, 5, 22, 23; 16:4; 20:17; 21:18; 1 Tim. 5:17, 19 (in correlation with v. 17); Tit. 1:5; Jas. 5:14; 1 Pet. 5:1, 5 (excluding 2 Jn. 1 and 3 Jn. 1, because they refer to individuals and not to a situation of church government, and the references in Revelation, because of their symbolic and heavenly orientation; cf. also the collective term πρεσβυτέριον in 1 Tim. 4:14).

When attention is paid to this concept of oversight by a plurality of leaders involving instruction and care, we ascertain that other passages refer to such a group using other terms that are synonymous to the slightly more frequent terms ἐπίσκοποι and πρεσβύτεροι, i.e., 1 Thes. 5:12, 13 (προϊστάμενοι; see for this term 1 Tim. 3:4, 5; 5:17); Heb. 13:7, 17 (ἡγούμενοι; cf. the description of their duties); 1 Cor 12:28 (διδάσκαλοι and κυβερνήσεις, mentioned above); Eph. 4:11 (ποιμένες καὶ διδάσκαλοι, representing the twofold duties of the elders; so Lightfoot, *Philippians,* 194).

An analysis of the data seems, therefore, to indicate the existence of oversight by a plurality of church leaders throughout the NT church in virtually every known area and acknowledged or commended by virtually every NT writer who writes about church leadership. In the Apostolic Council the apostles acknowledge and submit to the government of elders, as do the Jerusalem church, the Christians in Antioch, which was center for the Gentile mission, and the churches established on the Gentile mission (Acts 15, especially vv. 2, 4, 6, 22, 23; 16:4; cf. 21:25). Every church in which leadership is referred to in Asia Minor either under Paul and his associates or under Peter's ministry has a plurality of leadership (Acts 14:23; 20:17, 28; 1 Tim. 3:1ff.; 5:17; Eph. 4:11; 1 Pet. 5:1-4, note 1:1 for the provinces of Asia Minor where the addressees lived). Key churches of Achaia and Macedonia have such a leadership, i.e., Philippi (Phil. 1:1), Thessalonica (1 Thes. 5:12, 13), and Corinth (1 Cor. 12:28). The island of Crete is urged to establish such a pattern (Tit. 1:5ff.), and the communities written to by James (5:14) and the writer of Hebrews (13:7, 17) know the same pattern. We may assume that Barnabas continued the same pattern that he and Paul had established at Lystra, Iconium, and Antioch (Acts 14:23) when he returned to Cyprus (Acts 15:39). Only Rome and its geographical area provide us with no explicit information because Paul's letter does not deal explicitly with the subject. But it may well be that Paul's very general list of personal gifts in Rom. 12:6-8 implies a similar approach to that of 1 Cor. 12:28 with the terms ὁ διδάσκων, ὁ προϊστάμενος, and διακονίαν.

Since the pattern of twofold ministry and plurality of bishops/elders is found in the PE, as in the rest of the NT, including Paul in his other letters and in Acts, why was it necessary for him to speak of these ministries to trusted colleagues, especially to Timothy in the settled situation in Ephesus? Tit. 1:5, in its reference to the fact that Paul has already directed Titus to do these things (ταῦτα), points the way to the answer. It seems to be Paul's long-standing practice to reiterate or call to remembrance things he has taught and wants to have practiced. In this respect 1 Tim. 3:1ff. is similar to Tit. 1:5ff., and this pattern of recalling earlier teaching is seen throughout his writings from the very earliest (cf., e.g., 1 Thes. 4:1, 2, 10; 2 Thes. 2:5; 3:10; Gal. 3:21; especially Phil. 3:1). That he thus recall earlier teaching was especially appropriate in the unorganized situation on the island of Crete, so that Titus and the churches might have the qualifications for officers in writing. Though Ephesus had had a Christian church for some time, it seems that problems had arisen there with reference to the elders (cf. 1 Tim. 5:19-25), which may have been the catalyst for Paul putting the qualifications for officers in writing to Timothy. It is also possible that since Paul was writing in general about the way in which the church was to order and conduct itself (cf. 1 Tim. 3:14, 15), he may have felt that it was appropriate to put into writing for his young associate and for the church the qualifications for officers.

THE BASIS FOR THESE INSTRUCTIONS: 3:14-16

Paul has written "these things" (v. 14), i.e., the instructions regarding church offices, because he anticipates a possible delay in his arrival (ἐὰν δὲ βραδύνω, v. 15a), and because he wants conduct appropriate to God's house to be known now (v. 15b). The seriousness concerning the conduct is determined by the fact that the place of such conduct is the church, which is the possession and dwelling place of the living God (v. 15c). The living God has established his church to display the embodiment of his truth (v. 15d). The truth that the church publicly acknowledges and from which its godliness derives is manifested in the revelation of Christ Jesus (v. 16).

In this section alone in 1 Timothy does Paul refer directly to himself writing (γράφω, v. 14), even though he has earlier (1:3ff., 18) referred to concerns he has in writing. His use of γράφω here makes this statement a more self-conscious specification of his reason for writing. Such a deliberate statement also emphasizes the attendant theological description of the church (v. 15) and of the truth or mystery of godliness that the church confesses (v. 16).

3:14 The setting for writing is delineated in this verse and the following. Although Paul anticipates being with Timothy and the church shortly, he does not want to delay the instruction necessary for conduct in God's house. So he writes "these things" now. ταῦτα is a plural demonstrative pronoun referring to something comparatively near at hand. From the other occurrences of ταῦτα in 1 Timothy, it would appear that the reference is to that which precedes (PE* 13x: 1 Tim. 3:14; 4:6, 11, 15; 5:7, 21; 6:2, 11; Tit. 2:15; 3:8; 2 Tim. 1:12; 2:2, 14). Since chapters 2 and 3 both relate to conduct in God's house, the reference probably includes chapter 2 as well as chapter 3. For a fuller treatment of the question of what ταῦτα refers to, considering the pattern in the PE, see the notes on 4:11 and 6:2.

σοι indicates that Timothy is the one addressed. The singular is continued in v. 15 (εἰδῇς). Since, however, Timothy is to be a model for believers (4:12, 15), and is also to relay to the church that which Paul addresses to him (cf. 4:11; 6:2), "these things" are instructions communicated to Timothy for each individual member of the church. The nature of the instructions in chapters 2 and 3 evidences that they are not meant for Timothy alone but for Timothy as Paul's representative in the leadership of the church. This combination of direct address to Timothy coupled with communication to the church ministered through him is seen in the concluding words of the book: "O Timothy" (6:20) followed by "Grace be with you [plural]" (6:21).

Although this verse contains the only occurrence of γράφω in the PE, the verb is common in most of Paul's letters (Pl. 63x). He uses it elsewhere in the same sense of communicating his instructions as an apostle by means of the letter he is writing (cf. Rom. 15:15; 1 Cor. 4:14; 5:9; 14:37; 2 Cor. 2:9; 7:12; Phil. 3:1).

The remainder of the verse consists of a participial clause that functions concessively (Dana-Mantey, *Grammar,* 193, contra Lock), which for clarification could be paraphrased as "even though I hope to come to you before long" (*NIV:* "although"). The participle ἐλπίζων with the aorist infinitive ἐλθεῖν indicates what Paul hopes for, i.e., that he might come and be with Timothy (cf. similarly Rom. 15:24; 1 Cor. 16:2; Phil. 2:19, 23). *NA*[25] has τάχιον (in accord with ℵ D[2] F G and the "Koine" recension), which is replaced by ἐν τάχει (A C D* P Ψ 33 81, etc.) in *UBSGNT* and *NA*[26]. Both τάχιον, the comparative form of the adverb ταχέως, and the noun τάχος in an adverbial phrase with the preposition ἐν mean "soon."

3:15 This verse concludes the point begun in v. 14. The main thrust of the sentence is expressed in the beginning of v. 14 and the ἵνα clause of v. 15: Paul writes so that Timothy may know how one ought to live within and as a member of God's house.

The conditional (ἐάν) clause, "if I am delayed," assumes that Paul probably will in fact be delayed and thus restates more negatively what the concessive clause at the end of v. 14 conveyed more positively (I hope to come). δέ sets up a contrast between the two clauses and is best rendered here as "but," indicating that the conditional of v. 15 is more likely than the concessive of v. 14. ἐάν with the subjunctive expresses that note of probability, indeed of likelihood (but not quite certainty), with reference to the delay. βραδύνω is best rendered "I am delayed" *(RSV, NEB, NIV).*

The ἵνα clause then introduces the reason for Paul's writing: so that Timothy and the church may know what is proper conduct for God's household — with the implicit understanding that such knowledge will result in that kind of conduct.

Paul writes to communicate not theoretical knowledge but "how to" knowledge (he uses πῶς with οἶδα also in Col. 4:6; 2 Thes. 3:7). The conduct the apostle demands is that which one "ought" (δεῖ; see BAGD) to do. The passive form of ἀναστρέφω is used in its reflexive and figurative sense in reference to human conduct, "in the sense of the practice of certain principles" (BAGD s.v. 2b). The verb is "a comprehensive one and aptly covers the conduct expected from, and the mutual relations of, all the groups discussed. To understand it as applying to the Ephesian church generally also consorts better both with the semi-public character of the letter and also with the idea of the congregation as God's family" (Kelly; cf. also Ridderbos).

ἐν οἴκῳ θεοῦ describes the church under the familiar "house" image (οἶκος, PE 8x; cf. οἰκία, PE 2x), which is seen in other NT writers (Heb. 3:6; 10:21; 1 Pet. 2:5ff.; 4:17) and elsewhere in Paul with related terms such as οἰκείος and οἰκοδομή (cf., e.g., Gal. 6:10; Eph. 2:19-21). Paul also speaks of the minister as an οἰκονόμος of God (Tit. 1:7; 1 Cor. 4:1, 2) and of God's plan of salvation as an οἰκονομία (Eph. 1:10; 3:29; Col. 1:25; 1 Tim. 1:4).

The translation "house" for οἶκος might seem preferable to "household" here since building terms, στῦλος and ἑδραίωμα, are used, so that the church is depicted as the place where the living God dwells with his people (cf. also οἰκέω, used in 1 Cor. 3:16 of God's Spirit dwelling in his people, who are his temple; cf. further Eph. 2:21, 22). But an absolute distinction between "house" and "household" cannot be made for the word and the concept it represents as it is employed both here and elsewhere in the NT. In Eph. 2:19ff., for example, the concept embraces both the building (vv. 20, 21, 22) and the human "household," the "fellow citizens" (v. 19, similarly 1 Pet. 2:4ff.). So even though building terminology is utilized, since the conduct in view relates to the interaction of the members of God's family, modern translations have opted for "household" *(RSV, NASB, NEB, NIV)*.

Whichever English term is chosen, the breadth of the concept as used in the NT must be preserved. The standards of conduct prescribed are no mere rules of etiquette, they are standards for the house/household that is none other than God's (ἐν οἴκῳ θεοῦ). They provide directions for conduct in his temple, where he dwells by his Spirit, and they provide directions for relationships among his people. (See the helpful analysis and critique of Verner, *Household,* by Kidd in *Wealth and Beneficence,* 78-87, especially 80, 102, 104. According to Verner's reconstruction, the Pastorals argue that the church should be patterned after the household so that the governing principles of domestic life are transferred directly to ecclesiastical life. Kidd [104], in one of his telling criticisms, notes, however, the careful distinction that Paul makes between the family caring for its widow rather than the church.)

The awesomeness and responsibility of this conduct are underscored by the relative clause introduced by ἥτις (the antecedent of which is masculine οἶκος, the feminine gender coming by attraction from ἐκκλησία). The awesomeness is highlighted by restating what the house/household is (ἐκκλησία θεοῦ ζῶντος) and especially by emphasizing that God is the "living God." The responsibility is highlighted by referring again to the architectural metaphor in terms of the components of the "house" that undergird and uphold "the truth" (τῆς ἀληθείας).

An analogy had already been drawn between οἶκος and ἐκκλησία at the first occurrence of both in 1 Timothy (3:4, 5). Now what was implicit is made explicit: God's οἶκος is his ἐκκλησία. The three occurrences of ἐκκλησία in the PE* (all in 1 Timothy: 3:5, 15; 5:16) provide a description of the church similar to what we see elsewhere in Paul and the NT. 3:5 depicts the church as a family under the oversight of the ἐπίσκοποι, 3:15 depicts it as the house/household of God and on that basis calls for godly conduct on the part of those who are the possession and locale of the living God and the structure undergirding God's truth, and 5:16 depicts the church as the caring community (next to the actual family itself). Since the whole letter is about the church, it would be inappropriate to restrict the description of the church in it to the three occurrences of ἐκκλησία, but the emphasis on order and oversight, on godly conduct and on God's people upholding his truth, and on caring for those in need is striking and noteworthy.

With θεοῦ ζῶντος, a form of the phrase (ὁ) θεὸς (ὁ) ζῶν** (see BAGD s.v. ζάω 1aε; R. Bultmann, *TDNT* II, 862), Paul utilizes a concept found in the OT (e.g., Jos. 3:10; 2 Ki. 19:4, 16; Ps. 42[LXX 41]:2[3 in Hebrew]; Is. 37:4, 17; Ho. 1:10[2:1 in Hebrew]; Dn. 6:20[21 in Hebrew]; with Hebrew *ḥay* standing behind Greek ζῶν) and used 14x elsewhere in the NT. ζῶν emphasizes that God is the only God and is himself the source of life. In this Epistle the emphasis on God's "immortality" in 1:17 and 6:16, coupled in both instances with the concept "one," affirms this truth in other words (cf. Jn. 5:26). That God is living (and true) contrasts with the deadness (and falseness) of idols (cf. 1 Thes. 1:9 and Paul at Lystra, Acts 14:15). The living God communicates life and salvation to believers in Christ (1 Tim. 1:16; 4:8-10) and gives them the vitality of life for service and obedience (1 Thes. 1:9; cf. Heb. 9:14). The correlation suggested by the phrase "living God" between who God is and the significance of that fact for believers in terms of their conduct was articulated earlier by Paul in 2 Cor. 6:16 and its context.

The house/church of God is further described with the structural terms στῦλος καὶ ἑδραίωμα. στῦλος** (also in Gal. 2:9; Rev. 3:12; 10:1) means "pillar" or "column" and is used in the LXX of an important part of Solomon's temple (see 1 Ki. 7:15ff., where two pillars are named Jachin and Boaz, i.e., "he shall establish" and "in it is strength"; see also 2 Ki. 25:13ff.; 2 Ch. 3:15ff.; 4:12ff.). Here Paul describes the church as the pillar or column τῆς ἀληθείας. ἑδραίωμα** (a NT hapax found only in Christian writings and occurring here first), used with στῦλος, must be some component of a building, but its exact meaning is less clear. Translations have included "foundation" (BAGD, Phillips, *NIV*) or "ground" *(KJV, RV),* or, taking it differently, "mainstay" (BAGD) or "support" *(NASB),* or, differently again, "bulwark" *(RSV, NEB).* Hanson (*Studies,* 5ff.), following a clue provided by Spicq, thinks that OT (and NT) parallels point in the direction of "foundation" rather than "prop" or "stay."

ἀληθεία (PE* 14x: 1 Tim. 2:4, 7 [2x]; 3:15; 4:3; 6:5; Tit. 1:1, 14; 2 Tim. 2:15, 18, 25; 3:7, 8; 4:4) is used here of "the content of Christianity as the absolute truth" (BAGD), as in the other PE occurrences (except 1 Tim. 2:7a) and often in Paul (cf. Gal. 2:5, 14; 5:7; Eph. 4:21; Col. 1:5; 2 Thes. 2:12, 13). To remind the church that it is a structure called to uphold the truth of Christianity is also to remind it that it is a household called to manifest that truth in its conduct and to conform to it (cf. 4:1-5, where godly conduct is shaped by belief and knowledge of the truth [v. 3]; cf. also Tit. 1:1: "the knowledge of the truth that is according to godliness").

In summary, Timothy and the church will conduct their lives appropriately if they remember that they are the home built and owned by God and indwelt by him as the living one, and also remember that they are called on to undergird and hold aloft God's truth in word and deed.

3:16 Having ended the last verse with emphasis on the truth of the gospel, Paul now writes of the confessed grandeur of the gospel in terms of him who is its reality. It is the revelation (μυστήριον) of true godliness (εὐσεβείας), a godliness seen and known in Jesus Christ. In six balanced lines he delineates τὸ τῆς εὐσεβείας μυστήριον. Spicq suggests that the καί at the beginning of v. 16 is emphatic ("indeed," *RSV*), as καί is frequently in the papyri (cf. Mayser, *Grammatik,* II/3, 141, 144). On this understanding, v. 16 brings vv. 14-16 to an end with an emphatic affirmation.

ὁμολογουμένως** (a NT hapax but a common Hellenistic term; see BAGD; MM; O. Michel, *TDNT* V, 213; and especially *Epistle to Diognetus* 5:4) contains both the positive aspect of agreement by all ("confessedly, most certainly," BAGD) and the negative aspect of that which is beyond question or denial ("undeniably," BAGD), both of which amount to the same thing. Because this can be stated idiomatically in various ways and with a more positive or more negative cast, various English translations seem on the surface to be opting for different meanings or nuances when in fact they are all saying essentially the same thing. That which is "beyond all question" is that "the mystery of godliness" is μέγα, "great" in the sense of sublime or important (see BAGD s.v. 2bβ; cf. Eph. 5:32, where Paul gives the designation "great" to the μυστήριον). It is possible that the pagan confession "Great is Artemis of the Ephesians" (Acts 19:28) helped evoke a self-conscious awareness that the Christian confession concerning "our great God and Savior, Christ Jesus" (cf. Tit. 2:13) is itself, without doubt, great.

The "great" μυστήριον is qualified by the genitive τῆς εὐσεβείας (see 1 Tim. 2:2). The *RSV* and *NEB* have captured the sense well in their rendering "the mystery of our religion" (cf. BAGD: "the duty that man owes to God, *piety, godliness, religion*"). Thus the concern of v. 15 for both "truth" and "conduct" is restated in this phrase.

The content of the μυστήριον is set forth in a sixfold statement that describes the pivotal points of Christ's earthly ministry and the continuing results of that ministry (cf. Rom. 16:25). This statement is introduced by either ὅς (a relative pronoun referring to Christ), ὅ (a relative pronoun referring to μυστήριον), or θεός ("God"). Metzger's arguments and thus his conclusion *(TCGNT)* seem to be correct: "The reading which, on the basis of external evidence and transcriptional probability, best explains the rise of the others is ὅς."

This sixfold statement appears to be a citation of a statement of the apostolic church. The evidence for this evaluation is that (1) the introductory word ὅς does not seem to be connected to what precedes, i.e., it has no apparent antecedent; (2) the six lines are almost identical in form (aorist passive third person singular verb, ἐν [except once], and dative noun); (3) this section is distinctly different from what precedes and what follows; and (4) because of its content, the statement appears to be liturgical. One may debate whether the statement is more like a creed or more like a hymn, but absolute certainty seems elusive. ὅς seems to refer to an antecedent that has not been included in what is cited from a larger context.

How are these six lines related to one another? (For the following overview I am indebted to Gundry, "Form," 210-22.) Alford and Barrett treat them as somewhat separate items but in chronological progression. For Alford all six lines refer to Jesus' earthly ministry with the sixth referring to the ascension. For Barrett the lines include postresurrection activity and the sixth refers to the parousia. Barrett recognizes the problems of Alford's restriction to Jesus' earthly ministry and gives an adequate refutation of that view. However, the noun and verb concept in item 6 are more naturally taken to refer to the ascension rather than the parousia (see also Wallis).

Lock, von Soden, Scott, and Falconer are examples of those who see the quotation as two strophes of three lines each and also take them to be chronologically arranged. The format suggested is either that of strophes of three lines each or of two lines with the third line as a refrain in each case. All but Falconer relate the first strophe to Christ's life on earth and the second to his life on earth through the church and its proclamation. In response to this view it must be noted that the often-noted antitheses between adjacent lines (1-2, 3-4, 5-6) is ignored, with one pair (3-4) separated, and that line 6 again makes even this chronology out of place. On this view, it may be said, line 6 should be placed before line 4.

Falconer's unique expression of this view draws parallels between the respective lines of each strophe, i.e., 1 and 4, 2 and 5, 3 and 6. But should more remote, and sometimes less obvious, contrasts be taken as significant rather than the contrasts between adjacent lines?

These contrasts between adjacent lines have brought the majority of current commentators to favor division of the quoted statement into three couplets (e.g., Dibelius-Conzelmann, Jeremias, Kelly, Ridderbos, and Spicq; also *NA*[26] in apparent contrast to *UBSGNT*). The contrasts are between flesh and Spirit, angels and nations, and world and glory and may be summarized as repetitions of the one antithesis of earthly and heavenly. Furthermore, if this analysis is correct, the six lines present also a chiastic pattern of a-b, b-a, a-b. The first of the three couplets presents Christ's work accomplished, the second his work made known, and the third his work acknowledged.

Gundry suggests, on the other hand, that the hymn is framed by lines 1 and 6 and filled out by synthetically parallel lines 2-3 and 4-5. For all the insightfulness and plausibility of this view, it does not seem more plausible than the analysis of the statement into three pairs of contrasting couplets.

The linkage of lines 1 and 6 is not readily evident over that between 1 and 2 and between 5 and 6.

Finally, attention must be drawn in this brief summary to the fullest modern discussion of this verse, by W. Metzger *(Christushymnus)*. Especially noteworthy is his plausible reconstruction (see pp. 141f.) of the enlarged hymn from this verse and fragments cited elsewhere in 1 Timothy (2:2-6; 1:15; 3:16; 6:14b-16).

Jeremias has suggested that this hymnic quotation is patterned after the enthronement ceremony for the king in ancient Egypt: (1) reception of divine attributes, (2) presentation, and (3) enthronement. Kelly believes that the resemblance is superficial and coincidental, Gundry points out (p. 207) that the parallels do not really tally, and E. Schweizer (*Lordship,* 65f.) points out that in the Egyptian ceremony the order and content were somewhat different from Jeremias's reconstruction. Certainly the ideas in the three couplets — revelation of Christ, proclamation of Christ, and reception of Christ — are so inherent in the Christian mystery that they would have had their own formative force, which provides a much better hypothesis than that of borrowing from a cultic event quite distantly related, both geographically and religiously.

(Line 1) ὅς, as indicated above, probably has its antecedent in a section of the cited liturgical document that is not included here, not in the previous section of 1 Timothy, which presents nothing appropriate. That antecedent would seem to have been the name of or a reference to Christ, as the descriptions in the six lines indicate.

ἐφανερώθη depicts Christ as one who is "made known" by another, i.e., God the Father. The emphasis is thus on revelation and the implication is that he who is revealed previously existed but was unknown (cf. the other PE* occurrences of the verb, 2 Tim. 1:10; Tit. 1:3; see also this same verb form used of Jesus' incarnation in 1 Pet. 1:20; Heb. 9:26; 1 Jn. 1:2; 3:5, 8). ἐν σαρκί designates his becoming human; σάρξ thus has here the same significance as in Jn. 1:14 (cf. Phil. 2:7, 8; Christ as the second Adam in Rom. 5:12ff.; 1 Cor. 15:20ff., 45ff.). The manifestation of Christ takes place, therefore, by means of the incarnation (cf. especially Heb. 2:14, 15, 17).

(Line 2) ἐδικαιώθη is used here to mean "vindicated" (so *RSV, NASB, NEB, NIV*), in the general sense of the word found also in Mt. 11:19; Lk. 7:29; Rom. 3:4. This vindication is related to Christ's claim to be the promised Messiah and Son of God (see the Son of Man passages in the Gospels, the confession of Peter, and Jesus' assent at his trial to the charge that he made such claims; cf. G. Schrenk, *TDNT* II, 215).

The vindication takes place ἐν πνεύματι. Rom. 1:4 serves as the best commentary on this compact statement (see the commentaries on Romans by Cranfield, Murray, and Ridderbos, ad loc.). In Rom. 1:4 the πνεῦμα would appear to be the Holy Spirit. There, too, a vindication or demonstration is in view ("declared to be the Son of God with power") and the means of the declaration is "by resurrection from the dead." Likewise Rom. 8:11 speaks of "the Spirit of Him who raised Jesus from the dead." If these are true parallels, then here Paul is speaking of the vindication of Jesus by the Holy Spirit through his resurrection. The next use of πνεῦμα in the PE (4:1, without qualification, as here) refers to the Holy Spirit (see also Tit. 3:5; 2 Tim. 1:14; probably 1:7) and not the human spirit (as indicated by ὑμῶν in 2 Tim. 4:22), and there is no indication of shift in meaning, which favors that same identification here. If this understanding is correct, then ἐν is used with the meaning "by," indicating means, in contrast to the preceding line where it is used with the meaning "in," indicating place. The nearly identical format of each line should not be construed as requiring the same meaning for each instance of ἐν and for each dative. The form is a vehicle for the sense, and when the form will not convey the sense, i.e., in line 3, ἐν does not appear.

(Line 3) ὤφθη is used here in the sense of "(was) seen" *(RSV, NEB, NIV)*. All other NT occurrences of ὤφθη used with reference to Jesus refer to his resurrection appearances (Lk. 24:31; Acts 13:31; 1 Cor. 15:5, 6, 7, 8; cf. ὤφθην in Acts 26:16). Probably, therefore, the word refers here to the resurrection appearances rather than to the ascension only, although the ascension need not be ruled out. The NT nearly always uses ἄγγελοι of supernatural powers (angels) rather than humans, specifically good rather than evil powers (see BAGD). That angels are intended here as well is suggested strongly by the contrast in lines 3 and 4 between ἀγγέλοις and ἔθνεσιν, the one heavenly, supernatural, and angelic, the other earthly, natural, and human. Angels are referred to here apparently to emphasize the cosmic nature of Christ's work and its significance. Here the aspect of Christ's victory being known from the time of the resurrection on is affirmed (cf., e.g., 1 Pet. 1:12; see also Eph. 3:9-11; then further Phil. 2:10, 11; Eph. 1:21; Col. 2:10, 15; 1 Pet. 3:18, 19; Rev. 5:11, 12). The angels, as those who saw it, became messengers of Jesus' resurrection (Mt. 28:5-7; Mk. 16:5-7; Lk. 24:4-7; cf. Jn. 20:11-13), as they became of his ascension (Acts 1:9-11). The brief statement does not indicate the conditions under which Christ was "seen by angels." ἐν is not used here apparently because it does not quite give the right sense, and the dative by itself can express the idea more clearly.

(Line 4) Whereas for the ἄγγελοι the means of communication is that of sight (ὤφθη), i.e., as supernatural beings they beheld Jesus and his victory, for ἔθνη it is that of proclamation and announcement (ἐκηρύχθη). κηρύσσω with Christ as the subject matter is frequent in the NT (Acts 8:5; 9:20; 19:13; 1 Cor. 1:23; 15:12; 2 Cor. 1:19; 4:5; 11:4; Phil. 1:15; 1 Tim. 3:16). Lk. 24:47 adds εἰς πάντα τὰ ἔθνη. Those "among" (ἐν) whom Christ is announced are the ἔθνη (see comment on 2:7 above), which refers to "all peoples, as is often made clear by the epithet *panta,* all (cf. Matt. 24:9; 28:19; Mk. 11:17; Lk. 21:24; Rom. 15:11)" (H. Bietenhard, *NIDNTT* II, 793). Thus the common

English translation "nations" *(RSV, NASB, NEB, NIV)* is appropriate, as would be "peoples," rather than "Gentiles" (cf. K. L. Schmidt, *TDNT* II, 364-72, who seems to absolutize the case in this direction; cf. 2:7 above for further discussion of the word). It is the universalism demanded and promised by Jesus that is confessed here.

(Line 5) Lines 5 and 6 present the response in the world and in the heavenly realm of glory. Passive ἐπιστεύθη is used only here and in 2 Thes. 1:10 in the sense of "be believed" (see above at 1:16 on πιστεύειν = "believe"). ἐν κόσμῳ is used here apparently of the response to Christ's being "proclaimed among the nations" (line 4; cf. Col. 1:6, 23) and as a contrast with ἐν δόξῃ. Thus κόσμος here represents the world of humans in contrast to heaven (cf. BAGD s.v. 4c).

(Line 6) ἀναλαμβάνω has the general meaning "take up" and is used elsewhere of Christ's ascension and exaltation (cf. Acts 1:2, 11, 22; Lk. 9:51), as here. δόξα indicates brightness, splendor, or radiance and denotes in particular the glory, majesty, and sublimity of God (BAGD s.v. 1a). To enter into God's presence is thus to enter into glory, and so the NT speaks of entrance into the next life as entrance into glory (with reference to Christ: Lk. 24:26; cf. 1 Pet. 1:11; see further Jn. 17:5; BAGD s.v. 1b). This line speaks of Christ's ascension as an entrance into the exalted realm of δόξα. It says compactly what the NT says elsewhere more fully, i.e., that Christ is exalted and given power and authority (cf., e.g., Phil. 2:9-11; Eph. 1:20-23).

Even though there is not a strict chronology in the liturgical statement of v. 16, we may speak of a sense of theological direction. The first couplet speaks of the accomplishment of Christ's work, the second of the accomplishment made known, and the third of the response to the accomplishment made known. It is this great mystery of godliness that the church confesses, that the church, as the pillar and support of the truth, holds aloft, and that shapes the church's conduct before the living God. The preceding (and following) instructions have as their theological basis this great truth concerning the cosmic Christ who is the Lord and Savior of his church.

APOSTASY; A GOOD MINISTER'S DISCIPLINE: 4:1-16

Paul turns from instructions for Timothy and the congregation to warning against an apostasy that involves false asceticism, mentioned for the first time here. The ultimate source of this apostasy is "deceitful spirits and doctrines of demons" (4:1), working "by means of the hypocrisy of liars" (v. 2). By prohibiting marriage and certain kinds of food, it forbids what God created to be received and shared in (vv. 3, 4). The church, however, is not caught unawares by this phenomenon because the Spirit has previously spoken about the apostasy (v. 1). The remedy for this error is recollection that "everything created by God is good," which will keep one from rejecting God's good creation and cause one to receive it with prayer and thanksgiving (vv. 4, 5).

Vv. 6-16 urge Timothy to point out these truths to his fellow Christians, to avoid such errors himself, and to engage in godly self-discipline (vv. 6-10). In his ministerial life he is to take heed to two things, his public duties and his personal piety. He is to give attention to "reading, exhortation, and teaching" (vv. 13, 16), be an example to believers (v. 12), and not neglect the spiritual gift within him (v. 14). He is to progress in both public duties and personal piety, and persevere for his own good and that of those who hear him (vv. 15, 16), all the while prescribing and teaching "these things" (v. 11), in particular the hope that can be placed in the living God as Savior of all believers (4:10).

APOSTASY AND ITS FALSE ASCETICISM: 4:1-5

4:1 "But" — and here the δέ serves most pointedly — the apostasy that Paul now warns of and its source were spoken of beforehand by the Spirit. τὸ πνεῦμα here refers to the Spirit of God as it does in 4 or 5 of the 7 PE occurrences (1 Tim. 3:16; 4:1 [1x]; Tit. 3:5; 2 Tim. 1:7 [?], 14). The definite article with πνεῦμα (see the list in BAGD s.v. 5d) and the following λέγει are further indicators of that fact: *The* Spirit that *speaks* is in the NT the Spirit of God (see, e.g., the repeated τὸ πνεῦμα in Rev. 2:7, 11, 17, 29; 3:6, 13, 22). Paul expresses the present reality of the Spirit's communication by using present tense λέγει. This use of the present tense when referring to the communication of God, even when the communication was given in the past, is seen elsewhere in this letter in "the Scripture says" (1 Tim. 5:18) and conveys a constantly present authority. ῥητῶς** (a NT hapax), "expressly, explicitly," emphasizes that the Spirit has communicated in no uncertain terms. The ὅτι clause contains the Spirit's message, i.e., that there will be a falling away from the faith. Paul explicates the ultimate origin of that apostasy in the remainder of v. 1 and describes how it is taking place specifically at Ephesus in vv. 2 and 3.

How, when, and where did the Spirit give this message? The numerous occurrences of τὸ πνεῦμα λέγει in Revelation (2:7, 11, 17, 25; 3:6, 13, 22) demonstrate that this phrase can be used to refer to the revelation given by Jesus Christ (cf. Rev. 1:1-3, 9-20, especially vv. 1, 19, 20). Such usage brings to mind the warning of Jesus concerning apostasy in Mt. 24:10, 11 and Mk. 13:22. The warning of Jesus is conceptually the closest to this clause in that both speak of "falling away" (1 Tim. 4:1 with ἀφίστημι, Mt. 24:10 with σκανδαλίζω; these words can be used interchangeably as in Lk. 8:13 [ἀφίστημι] par. Mt. 13:21; Mk. 4:17 [σκανδαλίζω]). It is therefore most likely that Paul has this source in view. That he writes τὸ πνεῦμα λέγει emphasizes the ongoing and present significance of this warning, which has been reiterated by the Spirit through him and others (cf., e.g., Acts 20:28-31; 2 Tim. 3:1ff.; 4:3, 4).

The ὅτι clause communicates what will happen and when it will happen. The what is that "some will fall away from the faith." The when is "in later times." ἀφίστημι means here, as often in the LXX (see BAGD s.v. 2a), "fall away" from God, and here from whom or what one falls away is expressed by genitive τῆς πίστεως. "*aphistēmi* thus connotes the serious situation of becoming separated from the living God after a previous turning towards him, by falling away from the faith" (W. Bauder, *NIDNTT* I, 608). Jesus describes those who fall away as those who "have no root" (Lk. 8:13; cf. also Heb. 3:12ff.; 6:4ff.; 10:26ff.; 12:25ff.; Hughes, *Hebrews,* ad loc.). Articular πίστις is used here with the same nuance as in 1:18-20, i.e., primarily subjective but with an objective overtone. The one falling away falls away from faith, a subjective relationship, but at the same time from that which may be objectively referred to as ἡ πίστις.

This will take place "in later times," ἐν ὑστέρους καιροῖς (the phrase is a NT hapax). The virtually synonymous phrase ἐν ἐσχάταις ἡμέραις is used in 2 Tim. 3:1. The NT community is conscious of being "in the last days" (Acts 2:16, 17), i.e., the days inaugurated by the Messiah and characterized by the Spirit's presence in power, the days to be consummated by the return of Christ (see Ridderbos, *Paul,* 44-49). The phrase with the verb in the future tense (ἀποστήσονται) might at first incline one to think that Paul is warning about something *yet* to come. But the NT community used futuristic sounding language to describe the present age. Furthermore, when this word was originally said the phenomenon was in a relative sense future, and thus "later." Therefore, Paul is speaking about a present phenomenon using emphatic future language characteristic of prophecy. That he goes on to an argument addressed to a present situation (vv. 3-5) and that he urges Timothy to instruct the church members in this regard here and now (v. 6) substantiate this understanding.

The ultimate cause of such falling away is that people "pay attention to deceitful spirits and doctrines of demons." "Paying attention" means giving heed to and following (προσέχοντες with dative). πνεύμασιν πλάνοις** (the phrase here only in the NT) are spirit beings whose wickedness is characterized as "deceitful" and thus as "leading astray" (BAGD s.v. πλάνος; cf. 2 Cor. 11:13-15). The teachings are those of "demons" (δαιμονίων, Pl.* 5x: 1 Cor. 10:20 [2x], 21 [2x]; 53x in the Gospels, usually in the words of Jesus).

4:2 These "teachings" are mediated (ἐν) "by means of" *(NASB;* "through" in *RSV, NEB, NIV)* human beings as the proximate source. These teachers are said to be ψευδολόγοι** (a biblical hapax), i.e., those who speak falsely or lie. This substantival adjective is appropriately rendered by the noun "liars." Their teaching is said to be ἐν ὑποκρίσει because "they contradict the words of the truth of God (cf. 4:3; 6:5; 2 Tim. 3:8; 4:4; Tit. 1:14) and this is ὑπόκρισις" (U. Wilckens, *TDNT* VIII, 569; see especially Gal. 2:13). But further, "Paul is insinuating that their air of devotion and ethical rigour is only a specious mask" (Kelly).

κεκαυστηριασμένων** (perfect passive participle of καυστηριάζω, a NT hapax [following the *UBSGNT* reading rather than καυτηριάζω]) has been explained as "branded" as slaves were, with the mark of Satan to indicate ownership (Robertson, Lock, Kelly), as "branded" with a penal brand as transgressors (Liddon, Bernard), or as "cauterized," i.e., made insensible to the distinction between right and wrong (Spicq; see Eph. 4:19). The last of these seems more in accord with Paul's evaluation in Rom. 1:18, 28-32, of conduct contrary to God's moral standards, where a sense of self-consciousness is also present, as here, i.e., τὴν ἰδίαν συνείδησιν. ἰδίαν means "their own" and emphasizes the self-deception of sin within their own moral evaluator, ἡ συνείδησις (see 1:5), "the conscience." This concluding participial phrase gives the inner basis for the conduct just described as ἐν ὑποκρίσει ψευδολόγων.

4:3 This verse states that the two actions mandated by the false teachers are abstention from marriage and from certain foods, and then indicates why this mandate is so wrong, i.e., because God has created these things to be received with thanksgiving.

κωλυόντων (genitive to agree with ψευδολόγων) is from κωλύω, which means generally "hinder, prevent, forbid" (BAGD), here "forbid." The false teachers are forbidding marriage (γαμεῖν, Pl.* 12x: 1 Cor. 7:9, 10, 28, 33, 34, 36, 39; 1 Tim. 4:3; 5:11, 14). Although Paul commended singleness as an estate in which one could give more time and energy directly to serving the Lord (1 Cor. 7:32, 35), he always insisted that marriage was not wrong (1 Cor. 7:28) and that God had indeed gifted many to marry (1 Cor. 7:7; contra Dibelius-Conzelmann). These errorists forbid marriage as inherently wrong.

The construction ἀπέχεσθαι βρωμάτων following κωλυόντων is a zeugma, "a special type of ellipsis requiring a different verb to be supplied . . . , i.e., *one* verb is used with two objects (subjects) but suits only one . . ." (BDF §479.2). ἀπέχω means in the middle "hold oneself away from" (Robertson), with the genitive of what one holds away from (BAGD), here βρῶμα, which has the general meaning of "food." The word is used in a specialized sense in Romans 14 and 1 Corinthians 8, as indicated by its replacement with κρέα, i.e., "meat," in Rom. 14:21 (cf. also v. 2: "eats vegetables") and 1 Cor. 8:13 (where the interchange of terms is made in a single verse). It is likely that βρῶμα is used in that specialized sense here. If so, the false teachers are urging abstention from meat as something intrinsically wrong. It is this evaluation of meat as intrinsically evil that distinguishes the false teachers from the "weak" in Romans 14 and 1 Corinthians 8 and that elicits condemnation and refutation (cf. Col. 2:16ff., 21ff.).

With ἃ ὁ θεὸς ἔκτισεν . . . Paul indicates the error of this prohibition: It is directly contrary to God's purposeful action (cf. Lane, "First Timothy IV.1-3"). ἅ agrees with the nearest possible antecedent, βρωμάτων, but it may also include γαμεῖν indirectly if not directly. What Paul argues here and in vv. 4 and 5 applies also to marriage, even though his emphasis may be on the nearer antecedent. If his focus is more on the question of food, this may be because marriage is so clearly upheld and affirmed elsewhere in the letter (see 1 Tim. 3:2, 12; 5:9, 14; cf. the remarks in a letter known to this congregation, Eph. 5:22-33) and because the false teachers' view of marriage is so self-evidently wrong.

The keynote of Paul's refutation is that these things are what "God created to be gratefully shared in," i.e., that the personal response appropriate to God's creation of them is reception with thanksgiving. The implication to be drawn from the fact that God created these things is stated in v. 4a, ὅτι πᾶν κτίσμα θεοῦ καλόν. The action proposed by the false teachers is therefore repudiated, καὶ οὐδὲν ἀπόβλητον, v. 4b.

The use of ὁ θεός (see 1:1, 2) in this sentence states specifically that it is God who has created these things. κτίζω (see especially Eph. 3:9; Rev. 4:11) is used in early Christian literature "of God's creative activity" (BAGD). The purpose for which God created these things is stated in the prepositional phrase εἰς μετάλημψιν** (a NT hapax), "to be received" *(RSV, NIV)*. The attitude of the recipients is to be μετὰ εὐχαριστίας, "with thanksgiving" *(NIV)*, an attitude so important that it is repeated in v. 4, perhaps even a third time in v. 5 in the reference to prayer. εὐχαριστία (the prepositional phrase μετὰ εὐχαριστίας is found in Acts 24:3; Phil. 4:6; 1 Tim. 4:3, 4) is a term repeatedly used by Paul of the gratitude humans should have toward God for his good gifts to them (see also 2 Cor. 9:11, 12).

The concluding words of v. 3, τοῖς πιστοῖς καὶ ἐπεγνωκόσι τὴν ἀλήθειαν, demonstrate "that what was created for all men must therefore be legitimate for Christians" (Guthrie). The one article τοῖς indicates that the two designations, πιστοῖς καὶ ἐπεγνωκόσι, have a certain unity, i.e., they are two ways of referring to one group, namely, Christians (Zerwick, *Biblical Greek* §184). πιστοῖς is used here in the active sense of "those who believe" (BAGD s.v. 2). To this affirmation of their trust in God and Christ is joined the affirmation that they "know the truth" (ἐπεγνωκόσι τὴν ἀλήθειαν; see 2:4 for the similar phrase ἐπίγνωσιν ἀληθείας; the only other occurrence of the phrase found here is in 2 Jn. 1). The perfect active participle is probably used to emphasize the abiding awareness believers have of the truth that Paul is emphasizing, i.e., that God has created these things, that they are good, and therefore that they should be gratefully received (cf., e.g., Acts 14:15-17; 17:24, 25; also Jas. 1:17, 18).

4:4 With πᾶν κτίσμα θεοῦ καλόν Paul states the intrinsically good quality of everything created by God (cf. Gn. 1:31; Rom. 14:14, 20; Mk. 7:18, 19). In these words Paul both draws the conclusion implied in the statement of v. 3, "which God has created," and also states, with this ὅτι clause, the ground for the further statement of v. 3 that these things are "to be gratefully shared in."

πᾶν with a singular anarthrous noun, as here, emphasizes the individual members of the class denoted by the noun, i.e., "every" (cf. BAGD s.v. 1aα, β). Since the class denoted by κτίσμα is that which is created, the combination πᾶν κτίσμα designates everything existing. The explicit θεοῦ (see 1:1, 2) reiterates the truth of v. 3 that the created things come from none other than God. Paul asserts of these created things the verdict given by God himself in Gn. 1:31, i.e., that every one of them is "good" (καλόν; note the LXX of Gn. 1:31: καὶ εἶδεν ὁ θεὸς τὰ πάντα, ὅσα ἐποίησα, καὶ ἰδοὺ καλὰ λίαν).

καὶ οὐδὲν ἀπόβλητον expresses Paul's repudiation of the actions taught by the false teachers (κωλυόντων γαμεῖν, ἀπέχεσθαι βρωμάτων). καί links this phrase to the preceding, and the absolute negative "nothing," οὐδέν, picks up the previous πᾶν κτίσμα. ἀπόβλητον (a NT hapax) is a verbal adjective related to ἀποβάλλω and means "rejected" (BAGD).

The adverbial participle of condition (λαμβανόμενον) and its prepositional phrase (μετὰ εὐχαριστίας, see v. 3) are together equivalent to a conditional clause ("*if* it is received with thanksgiving," Burton, *Syntax* §436).

This repeated emphasis (vv. 3, 4, and 5) reminds the readers that it is thankful acceptance of God's good gifts that is being defended (cf. 6:6-10), not an autonomous materialism or hedonism (cf. also Col. 3:17; Eph. 5:20). The antidote to rejection is not mere reception but rather reception with thankfulness to God as the acknowledged giver of these good gifts. It is God's goodness more than human freedom that Paul defends here, even though the conduct he defends is human, i.e., marriage and eating of certain foods.

4:5 ἁγιάζεται γὰρ διὰ λόγου θεοῦ καὶ ἐντεύξεως, rather than adding a new thought, summarizes and reiterates the argument of vv. 3 and 4 and thereby repeats the reason (γάρ) for receiving God's good gifts of creation with thankfulness (v. 4). ἁγιάζεται is used here in the general sense of being declared fit, acceptable, or good for use or consumption, with the third person singular referring back to πᾶν κτίσμα. Thus ἁγιάζεται is restating the divine declaration of καλόν and the human response expected in εἰς μετάλημψιν and λαμβανόμενον and probably even includes the expressed overtones of thankfulness.

The means by which (διά, C. F. D. Moule, *Idiom Book*, 57) this declaring fit happens is stated in the prepositional phrase διὰ λόγου θεοῦ καὶ ἐντεύξεως, with λόγου θεοῦ being the objective means and ἐντεύξεως the subjective. λόγος θεοῦ (the phrase occurs in the NT 45x, in Pl.* 11x, in the PE 3x: Rom. 9:6; 1 Cor. 14:36; 2 Cor. 2:17; 4:2; Phil. 1:14; Col. 1:25; 1 Thes. 2:13 [2x]; here; Tit. 2:5; 2 Tim. 2:9) would seem to be used here, as elsewhere in Paul, with reference to a statement or message from God (G. Kittel, *TDNT* IV, 114-16). This phrase would thus appear to be an abbreviated way of recalling those truths that God has communicated, namely, that every created thing was made by him and is therefore good (vv. 3 and 4; cf. again Gn. 1:31). ἔντευξις** (see 2:1) is a general word for prayer but approaches the meaning "prayer of thanksgiving" (= εὐχαριστία in vv. 3, 4, as suggested in BAGD s.v. 2c). Just as the phrase λόγος θεοῦ succinctly reminds the reader of the objective truths from God communicated in vv. 3 and 4, so ἔντευξις reiterates succinctly the repeated emphasis on the attitude necessary, i.e., receiving these gifts μετὰ εὐχαριστίας (vv. 3 and 4; cf. Mk. 8:6, 7, where Jesus gives thanks, εὐχαριστήσας).

Vv. 1-5 are a compact unit. V. 1 indicates that apostasy has been spoken about by the Spirit and that the ultimate source of such teaching is evil spirits (demons). V. 2 indicates that the teaching is mediated by hypocritical liars whose consciences have been seared. V. 3a indicates that the false teaching consists of the requirement of abstention from marriage and certain foods. The latter part of v. 3 shows how inappropriate this teaching is on the grounds that God created everything to be received with thanksgiving. V. 4 indicates the implied middle link, i.e., everything God created is good and therefore nothing may be rejected but rather received with thanksgiving. V. 5 reiterates and summarizes the aforementioned teaching of God, and the prayerful and thankful acceptance make each created thing truly consecrated for human use. In short, the truth of the good creation of God, whose purpose is to provide for people's needs, coupled with an appropriate response and acceptance is the correct teaching and the antidote to the false teaching.

A GOOD MINISTER'S DISCIPLINE: 4:6-16

The remainder of the chapter takes its point of departure from the false teaching just mentioned and from Timothy's responsibility to instruct the church members about the truths just set forth (v. 6). In doing so Timothy himself must be nourished on the truths that he teaches (v. 6), must himself turn away from untruthful fables (v. 7a), and must train himself in godliness (vv. 7b-9), having his hope set on God, the Savior of all who believe in him (v. 10). Vv. 6-10 thus urge Timothy the minister to teach the good doctrine and train himself to live in a more godly manner.

Vv. 11-16 continue in the same vein but with variations. V. 11 commands as a general principle what Timothy was asked to do more specifically in v. 8, i.e., it charges him to prescribe and teach these things. In the accomplishment of this task he is urged to be an example (v. 12), to pay special attention to his responsibilities in his public ministry of scripture reading, edification, and exhortation (v. 13), not to neglect his spiritual gift (v. 14), and finally to give close attention himself to what he teaches, by persevering in the teachings and by progressing in holiness (vv. 15, 16). Vv. 11-16 thus emphasize the minister's example, public ministry, and personal growth.

Teach These Things and Undergo Training to Become More Godly: 4:6-10

4:6 This section, oriented to the previous section(s) by ταῦτα, is directed to Timothy (ἔσῃ) but is concerned ultimately for the entire church (τοῖς ἀδελφοῖς). We see again what is true of the whole Epistle, namely, that it is written to Timothy but with the intention that its contents be taught to and heard by the church.

ταῦτα, "these things," refers primarily, but perhaps not exclusively, to the immediately preceding verses (see also v. 11). ὑποτίθημι** (Rom. 16:4) has in the middle voice the general, but significant, meaning of "point out" something to someone; here, as BAGD indicate, it has the more definite meaning "teach." The forcefulness of the word can be gathered from the meaning of the active form ("risked their own necks," Rom. 16:4) and from the importance of the teachings in vv. 1-5, which Timothy is to "point out." The participial form may imply a conditional significance ("if," so *RSV, NIV*), or, more likely, a modal significance ("in," *NASB;* "by," *NEB*).

Those to be taught are called ἀδελφοί, "brothers," as fellow members of the family of God (1 Tim. 3:15). Jesus used this term for everyone who was devoted to him (cf. Mt. 12:50; Mk. 3:35; also Mt. 28:10; Jn. 20:17), and it became a term used by Christians in their relations with each other (cf. Rom. 8:29; 1 Cor. 5:11; Eph. 6:23; 1 Tim. 6:2; Acts 6:3; 9:30; 10:23; Rev. 1:9; 12:10). This is the meaning found in three of the four PE occurrences (here; 6:2; 2 Tim. 4:21).

If Timothy carries out the task of instruction prescribed in v. 6a, he deserves the evaluation spelled out in v. 6b: καλὸς ἔσῃ διάκονος Χριστοῦ Ἰησοῦ. διάκονος ("servant," *NASB, NEB,* or "minister," *RSV, NIV*) is used here of Timothy's role as the leader who leads by serving and teaching (cf. 4:14; Mt. 20:26; 23:11; Mk. 10:45; 1 Cor. 3:5; 2 Cor. 3:6; 6:4; Eph. 3:7; 6:21; Col. 1:7, 23, 25; 4:7; 1 Thes. 3:2). Just as Paul regards himself as the apostle "of Christ Jesus" (1:1) so Timothy is designated the "minister of Christ Jesus."

The participial phrase ἐντρεφόμενος . . . in v. 6c delineates the nourishment necessary for a good minister if he is to instruct others. ἐντρέφω** (a NT hapax) was used by Plato (*Leges* 7.798a) of those who are "nourished in the laws" (Robertson). The present participle indicates continual nourishment (Lock, Guthrie). That in which (dative, see Epictetus 4.4.48; Dibelius-Conzelmann) the minister is being nourished is τοῖς λόγοις. Plural λόγοι occurs in the PE only here and in 6:3; 2 Tim. 1:13; 4:15. In 6:3 the "sound words" are "those of our Lord Jesus Christ" (τοῖς τοῦ κυρίου ἡμῶν Ἰησοῦ Χριστοῦ). The 2 Timothy passages describe the "words" as those of the apostle Paul ("which you have heard from me," 2 Tim. 1:13; "opposed our teaching," 4:15). The evidence thus indicates that Paul is referring to the teaching of Jesus and the apostles when he uses plural λόγοι.

τοῖς λόγοις is qualified by two genitives, τῆς πίστεως καὶ καλῆς διδασκαλίας. πίστις is used here with the same objective sense it has elsewhere in Paul (cf., e.g., Gal. 1:23, "preaching the faith"). Since the essential response demanded by Christianity is πίστις, Christianity itself and the sum of its message are appropriately called πίστις (cf. substantive use of the participle of the cognate verb πιστεύω of Christians, i.e., "believers," Acts 2:44; 4:32; 19:18; 21:20; Rom. 3:22; 1 Cor. 14:22, 1 Thes. 1:7; 2 Thes. 1:10). The movement from the more subjective use of the word ("faith") to the more objective ("the faith") is evident in the PE as elsewhere in Paul (cf. 1 Tim. 1:2; 3:9; 4:1). The movement is not in one direction, for the usage goes back and forth (cf. the immediately following subjective usage in 4:12), but the more objective use will occur a few more times in 1 Timothy (5:8 [?]; 6:10, 12 [?], 21) and the other PE (Tit. 1:4 [?]; 1:13 [?]; 2 Tim. 2:18 [?]; 3:8; 4:7).

The "words" are also described in terms of their purpose (τῆς καλῆς διδασκαλίας). διδασκαλία is used here in the passive sense of "that which is taught," or "teaching," and is qualified by the adjective καλή, "good," to distinguish it from the erroneous teaching just described (v. 1). This "good teaching" is that which (ᾗ) Timothy has followed and continues to follow (the perfect tense of παρακολουθέω**), in the sense of "follow with the mind, understand, make one's own" (BAGD; with dative of that which is followed; see the other occurrences in 2 Tim. 3:10; Lk. 1:3).

4:7a The good minister must also refuse the untruthful. This is now asserted with δέ, "but." The imperative form παραιτοῦ is used in the NT only in the PE (here and 2 Tim. 2:23 of things; 1 Tim. 5:11; Tit. 3:10 of persons) and means generally in its negative sense "decline," and with reference to things, "reject," "avoid" (BAGD s.v. 2b; see also LSJM s.v. II.2). Timothy is to reject μύθοι (see 1:4), which are fables that are both unhistorical and untruthful. They are here further characterized as both βέβηλος and γραώδης. βέβηλος meaning "profane" or "godless," the latter communicating best the ethical and religious significance of the term in the NT (cf. BAGD). γραώδης (a NT hapax), "characteristic of old women," is "a sarcastic epithet which was frequent in philosophical polemic and conveys the idea of limitless credulity" (Kelly), not carrying any negative overtones about either age or sex (cf., e.g., 5:1 for Paul's own insistence that there be no negative attitudes relating to these matters).

Athletic imagery in 4:7b, 8a. γυμνάζω and related words refer literally to the physical training of athletes (see BAGD and MM). But to what do γύμναζε (v. 7b) and σωματικὴ γυμνασία (v. 8a), the "bodily exercise" said to be "of little profit," refer (for discussion and bibliography see Knight, *Faithful Sayings,* 65-68)?

Some argue that by "bodily exercise" Paul refers to the asceticism repudiated in vv. 1-5, contending that the aim of those verses is continued here (A. Oepke, *TDNT* I [s.v. γυμνασία], 775f.; Pfitzner, *Agon Motif,* 172f.; Towner, "Present Age," 433; commentaries by Bernard, Brox, Calvin, Dibelius-Conzelmann, Easton, Ellicott, Fausset, Hiebert, Houlden, Jeremias, Lenski, Ridderbos [?], Schlatter, H. von Soden, Weiss, White). Though some say that athletic exercise "is foreign to the context" (e.g., Bernard), more often the athletic imagery is acknowledged by those who connect it with the asceticism described in the earlier verses (Dibelius-Conzelmann: "It [the saying] was doubtless originally directed against the physical training [ἄσκησις] of athletes"; Pfitzner, *Agon Motif,* 172, agreeing with this observation; White, acknowledging the aptness of Lightfoot's appeal to Seneca, *Epistulae Morales* 5.2.5). It is argued under this view that the reference to μύθοι in v. 7a also has in view the teachings repudiated in vv. 1-5 (e.g., Towner, "Present Age," 433, with a reference to Tit. 1:14) and, therefore, that vv. 6ff. are still dealing with the subject matter of vv. 1-5.

Use of athletic imagery to encourage a proper ἀγών in one's Christian life is typical of Paul (cf. especially 1 Cor. 9:25; in the PE, leaving aside the present text for the moment: 2 Tim. 2:5; 4:7; see Pfitzner, *Agon Motif,* and works referred to there). This points to a broader view of 1 Tim. 4:6ff. The connection with vv. 1-5 is not a continuation of the specific point made there but a broadening of the perspective in terms of the Christian minister's life and work. Not only should the minister and his people repudiate the error of the asceticism described in vv. 1-5, he should reject all erroneous teaching (μύθοι, a reference back to 1:4 and the false teaching in general rather than just to vv. 1-5) and should be nourished by all the words of the faith and of the good teaching (v. 6), not just the words and teaching of vv. 4 and 5. Furthermore, even though the asceticism described in vv. 1-5 is radically and absolutely repudiated, there is still, in v. 7b, a demand for γυμνασία in the Christian minister's life — not a γυμνασία of the athlete but of and toward godliness. The connection with vv. 1-5 is therefore once removed.

In this view the "exercise" said to be "of little profit" (v. 8a) is literal athletic training (so Alford, Bengel, Bouma, Chrysostom, Fairbairn, Falconer, Gealy, Guthrie, Hendriksen, Huther, Kelly, Kent, Liddon, Lock, Parry, Spicq, MM s.v. γυμνασία). It is unlikely that asceticism like that spoken of in v. 3 should now be regarded as profitable, even "of little profit," after the absolute rejection of it in vv. 1-5. Also, if v. 8a is part of a "faithful saying" (see v. 9), it is much more likely that it refers literally to athletics than figuratively to asceticism: It is unlikely that a saying would arise contrasting asceticism, especially under this phrase, with εὐσέβεια (cf. Gealy), and 1 Timothy itself, especially 4:1-5, shows that the church was not sufficiently conscious of the need to eschew such asceticism to have developed a saying against asceticism. Finally, note must be taken of the progress of the passage from v. 7b to v. 10 and how σωματικὴ γυμνασία fits in that context. The literal understanding of σωματικὴ γυμνασία fits with the use of the related verb in v. 7b and the continuation of the imagery of vigorous bodily exertion in v. 10 with the verbs "labor" (κοπιῶμεν) and "strive" (ἀγωνιζόμεθα).

Some who propose that Paul has asceticism in mind with σωματικὴ γυμνασία mean by asceticism not what has been repudiated in vv. 1-5, but rather the commendable self-restraint of bodily appetites seen in passages such as Rom. 13:14; 1 Cor. 8:13; and especially 1 Cor. 9:27 (cf., e.g., Ridderbos). But this sort of self-restraint should not be called asceticism. The "profit" of the "bodily exercise" mentioned in 1 Tim. 4:8 is "little," and the "exercise" is itself contrasted with εὐσέβεια, of which self-restraint would seem to be an expression. Self-restraint is described in 1 Cor. 9:24-27 according to athletic imagery, but is not regarded as a form of asceticism. There the concern is the same as that of the exercise unto εὐσέβειαν in 1 Tim. 4:7b, not that of the "bodily exercise" πρὸς ὀλίγον. The self-restraint spoken of in 1 Cor. 8:13 does not have ascetic purposes but is pursued out of concern for fellow Christians, as an act of godliness. And the restraint spoken of in Rom. 13:14 is a result of "putting on" Jesus and consists of restraining oneself from evil desires. Thus these passages speak not of what is called "bodily exercise" in 1 Tim. 4:8a, but of aspects of the "exercise unto εὐσέβεια" spoken of in 1 Tim. 4:7b.

4:7b With this part of the verse a new section begins that runs through v. 8 (cf. the punctuation in *UBSGNT* and the break in *NA*[26]). δέ is a simple connective that need not be translated (so BAGD, *RSV, NEB, NIV*). γυμνάζω means literally "exercise naked, train" and is also used figuratively "of mental and spiritual powers" in extrabiblical literature, as here and consistently in the NT (BAGD; cf. for the same concern, although without this word, 1 Cor. 9:24-27; Phil. 2:12; 3:12ff., according to A. Oepke, *TDNT* I, 775). Although a false asceticism is repudiated (vv. 1-5), γυμνάζειν is required of the minister. σεαυτόν, "yourself," brings the imperative forcefully to bear on Timothy (cf. the twofold σεαυτόν in v. 16). Vv. 6-8 thus establish a pattern for this section. V. 6a demanded that the minister communicate the truth to others. V. 6b demanded that he himself appropriate revealed truth in order to be equipped to minister. V. 7b demands the vigorous outworking of that truth (cf. v. 16), with the implication that other Christians should do the same.

εὐσέβεια (see 2:2; 3:16; Knight, *Faithful Sayings,* 68-73) is best rendered as "godliness" here. It is a Greek term for religion used in the LXX and then in Acts, the PE, and 2 Peter of the Christian faith. As Barclay puts it, this word and others from the same root refer to awe and reverence, which imply a worship that befits that awe and a life of active obedience that befits that reverence (*More NT Words,* 67). "But the εὐσέβεια is no longer, as in Greek thought, a general religious piety. It is now a εὐσέβεια rooted in the mystery of εὐσέβεια, Jesus Christ. It is now a distinctly Christian εὐσέβεια, which is not just an external form, but which has an inner power (2 Tim. 3:5). That inner power is appropriated in Christ (*cf.* 2 Pet. 1:3)" (Knight, *Faithful Sayings,* 70).

Ridderbos's suggestion that πρός should be understood to indicate that εὐσέβειαν is that *in* which one exercises, and not just that toward which one exercises, seems to be correct, as is evidenced by v. 8, where εὐσέβεια is placed in parallel with σωματικὴ γυμνασία itself. One may speak paraphrastically of exercising one's godliness with the purpose of being more godly. Therefore, the εὐσέβεια that one has in Christ is to be developed by γυμνάζειν in εὐσέβεια (cf. Phil. 2:12, 13: "work out your salvation with fear and trembling; for it is God who is at work in you, both to will and to work for his good pleasure").

4:8 γάρ joins this verse to v. 7b and provides the grounds for the exhortation of v. 7b. It is surprising that v. 8a refers to σωματικὴ γυμνασία since the words of v. 8b concerning the profitability of εὐσέβεια would have provided an adequate reason in itself for the exhortation. This coupled with the words of v. 9, πιστὸς ὁ λόγος, raises the question of whether part or all of v. 8 or part or all of v. 10 is the "faithful saying" (see Knight, *Faithful Sayings,* 9, n. 1, 62-65).

The following considerations have convinced me that v. 8 is the saying: V. 8 looks like a proverbial saying, a point acknowledged by those who opt for v. 10. It contains two unique words, γυμνασία (a NT hapax) and σωματικός (only here and Lk. 3:22 in the NT), whereas v. 10 contains none, and it is more stereotyped in form than v. 10. V. 9 urges a personal response to the saying with the words "worthy of full acceptance," words that are only added to the citation-commendation formula when the note of personal response is not contained in the saying itself (see the comments on 1:15; *Faithful Sayings,* 30, 143f.), which is the case with v. 8, but not with v. 10, with its first person plural ("we") verbs. Some have suggested that the saying is only the latter part of v. 10, beginning with ὅτι ἠλπίκαμεν. But this would remove the saying from the formula πιστὸς ὁ λόγος by intervening words, unlike no other instance of a "faithful saying" in the PE. V. 10 does seem to be a more lofty theological statement than v. 8 and does include the note of salvation found in other "faithful sayings" (e.g., 1 Tim. 1:15), but certainly v. 8 is equally significant as a theological statement, and the concept of salvation is not present in all the "faithful sayings" (e.g., 1 Tim. 3:1; cf. also 2 Tim. 2:11-13). And form is a surer guide than content. Finally, the foil statement in v. 8a, ἡ γὰρ σωματικὴ γυμνασία πρὸς ὀλίγον ἐστὶν ὠφέλιμος can be better explained as part of a "saying." Although the vast majority of commentators (see *Faithful Sayings,* 62, n. 1) agree that part or all of v. 8 is the saying, some modern English translations surprisingly identify v. 10 as the saying (*NIV* most decisively, *NEB* in the text with v. 8 as a marginal alternative; the punctuation apparatus of *UBSGNT* seems on the surface to represent the two alternatives, but closer analysis will indicate that this is not the case).

The saying in v. 8 begins with a nearly perfect internal parallelism to which is then added the content of the πρὸς πάντα of the εὐσέβεια in terms of the promise concerning the ζωή now and in eternity. That parallelism is of such a nature that the words are in relationship to one another in almost the same order throughout both halves of the statement:

ἡ γὰρ	σωματικὴ	γυμνασία	πρὸς ὀλίγον	ἐστὶν ὠφέλιμος
ἡ δὲ		εὐσέβεια	πρὸς πάντα	ὠφέλιμός ἐστιν

γάρ introduces the whole saying and, as Ellicott says, "confirms the preceding clause by putting σωματικὴ γυμνασία, the outward and visible, in contrast with γυμνασία πρὸς εὐσέβ., the internal and unseen." It was not, however, originally part of the saying but was added by Paul to connect the saying with his own previous words γυμνασία κτλ. (as pointed out by Swete, "Faithful Sayings," 4).

On the meaning of the phrase σωματική** (Lk. 3:22; 1 Tim. 4:8) γυμνασία** (1 Tim. 4:8) see the discussion above of **Athletic imagery in 4:7b, 8a,** where the literal meaning "bodily training," i.e., athletics, is acknowledged to be present here. Of this σωματικὴ γυμνασία the saying affirms that it is ὠφέλιμος** (twice in this verse; Tit. 3:8; 2 Tim. 3:16), "useful" in the sense of "beneficial, advantageous τινί for someone or for someth[ing]" (BAGD; cf. *RSV, NIV:* "of . . . value"; *NASB:* "profitable"; *NEB:* "does bring . . . benefit").

The usefulness of σωματικὴ γυμνασία is πρὸς ὀλίγον. πρός indicates the goal or purpose aimed at or striven toward (BAGD s.v. III.3c). Here πρὸς ὀλίγον might mean "for a little," i.e., that "bodily exercise is of some value," or "for little," i.e., that it is of no value at all. The consensus (e.g., MM, BAGD, *RSV, NEB, NIV,* most commentators) is that Paul is comparing the limited benefit of σωματικὴ γυμνασία (πρὸς ὀλίγον) and the limitless benefit of εὐσέβεια (πρὸς πάντα): The smallness of the former as a foil for the latter (cf. similarly 1 Cor. 9:25). The saying does not elaborate on the ὀλίγον and thus is not concerned with identifying the "little" but with the πάντα and ζωή of the εὐσέβεια.

In contrast (δέ) with the little value of σωματικὴ γυμνασία is exercise in εὐσέβεια. Actually we have a brachylogy (BDF §483) in that εὐσέβεια itself is contrasted with σωματικὴ γυμνασία. Exercise in εὐσέβεια, or εὐσέβεια itself, is commended in that it is profitable πρὸς πάντα and in that this πάντα involves a promise that encompasses life now and in the future. πάντα means here "all things," "everything" in an absolute sense (BAGD s.v. 2aδ; cf. use of πάντα in 1 Cor. 3:21-23; Rom. 8:28, 32) and is used to indicate the absolute value of εὐσέβεια over against the relative value of σωματικὴ γυμνασία. Thus any attempt to limit the πάντα would be a misunderstanding and a partial negation of its scope.

ἐπαγγελίαν ἔχουσα κτλ. is equivalent to a causal clause, "because it has promise" (cf. Burton, *Syntax,* §439; Robertson, *Grammar,* 1128; see also Col. 1:3, 4; Mt. 2:3, 10; Acts 9:26), and is therefore a further affirmation of the significance of εὐσέβεια. That the εὐσέβεια "has" (ἔχουσα) the "promise" (ἐπαγγελίαν) means that this promise is inherent to the nature of εὐσέβεια. The one who promises is understood to be God (BAGD s.v. 2a; cf. Heb. 9:15), which is explicated in v. 10: One labors and strives, i.e., exercises in εὐσέβεια, because one has put one's hope in the living God who has promised life and who gives it in the Savior, Jesus Christ.

The words τῆς νῦν καὶ τῆς μελλούσης and the preceding ἐπαγγελίαν indicate the nature of the "life" in view. The temporal terms indicate that the ζωή is that which is both now and in the future. But mere existence is not the point here (see Knight, *Faithful Sayings,* 75f.). It is true that Eph. 6:1-3 does correlate longevity with that godliness which honors parents, but even there it is associated with the significant promise "that it may be well with you." Thus although the NT is thankful to God for life as existence and for longevity, it does not regard biological existence as the ἐπαγγελία of God, since all people exist now without any reference to εὐσέβεια.

A decisive factor in determining the significance of ζωή is the key word ἐπαγγελία. The only other place in the NT where the phrase ἐπαγγελίαν ζωῆς is found is 2 Tim. 1:1. There it is stated that the life is ἐν Χριστῷ Ἰησοῦ. That is to say, the promise of life now and in the future is that of the life that one has in union with Christ. That same chapter also indicates how that ζωή is brought to mankind: It is "our Savior, Christ Jesus, who abolished death and brought life (ζωή) and immortality to light through the gospel" (2 Tim. 1:10). Thus the ζωή that is the promised possession of the believer is the opposite of the death in which he or she has lived, "a perfect and abiding antithesis to death" (Cremer, *Lexicon,* s.v. ζωή). Therefore, the one word ζωή may be used to refer to the "life" that the believer has now and hereafter because "the distinction is not between two kinds of life, but the two conditions under which the one life is lived" (Parry). Paul and the Christian community here, and elsewhere, have stated in other words what Jesus indicated he came to accomplish when he said that he came "that they may have life" (ζωή) and "may have it abundantly" (περισσόν). So in 4:8, as in 6:19, that same ζωή is in view. Since the εὐσέβεια in which one exercises is the εὐσέβεια of which Christ is the revealed truth and power (see 1 Tim. 3:16), to exercise in εὐσέβεια is to work out one's salvation according to the power of Christ who works within.

We have already touched on another closely related question, that of the relationship between ἐπαγγελία and the word that follows it in the genitive case, ζωῆς (see Knight, *Faithful Sayings,* 74f.). Is life itself that which is promised or is the content of the promise that which one may receive within this life and the next? The usage elsewhere of ἐπαγγελία in the singular followed by a genitive (2 Tim. 1:1; 2 Pet. 3:4; Heb. 9:15) indicates that the genitive signifies the thing promised (BAGD s.v. ἐπαγγελία 2a), as does the usage of ἐπαγγελία elsewhere with other constructions (Heb. 4:1; 1 Jn. 2:25; Rom. 4:13). Furthermore, the only other occurrence of ἐπαγγελία in the PE (2 Tim. 1:1: ἐπαγγελίαν ζωῆς τῆς ἐν Χριστῷ Ἰησοῦ), with its specifying article, and the only occurrence of the verb ἐπαγγέλλομαι with ζωή in the PE (Tit. 1:7, ἐπ' ἐλπίδι ζωῆς αἰωνίου, ἣν ἐπηγγείλατο ὁ ἀψευδὴς θεός) both point to an understanding of ζωή as the content of the promise.

The life that now is, ζωῆς τῆς νῦν, is "life" in this present earthly realm (see 2 Tim. 1:10). This "life," which is here and now already entered into, is also the "life" that will be fully realized and enjoyed in the age to come; the ζωή that is νῦν is also καὶ τῆς μελλούσης. The participial form μελλούσης, used absolutely, means "future, to come" (BAGD s.v. μέλλω 2). G. Stählin aptly says that it is "(divine) life in which we already participate in the period of Christ, and to which we look forward in fulness then. This thought of twofold fulfillment runs through the whole of the NT (cf., e.g., Eph. 1:13f.)" (*TDNT* IV, 1120).

The closest conceptual NT parallel are the words of Jesus in Lk. 18:29, 30 (par. Mk. 10:29, 30; Mt. 19:29), where the similarity to the double reference of ζωῆς in 1 Tim. 4:8 is the idea of a double blessing, "at this time" and "in the age to come eternal life." The note of promise is evident in the dominical phrase, "Truly I say to you," and in the assurance that "there is no one . . . who shall not receive." The reference to "promise" (ἐπαγγελίαν) in 1 Tim. 4:8 causes Parry to state that there is a reference to Jesus' utterance. It is thus possible that the Christian community reflected on Jesus' words in Lk. 18:29, 30, generalized them, and produced the saying about εὐσέβεια in 1 Tim. 4:8. Kelly summarizes the matter well: 1 Tim. 4:8b "seem[s] to echo words of our Lord recorded in the gospel tradition which offer precisely this reward to those who renounce all for his sake. . . ."

One may also postulate the influence of the gymnastics of the day and of the Ephesian situation. Swete ("Faithful Sayings," 3), Spicq (Excursus vii), and others bring out the special importance that γυμνασία had in the training of the youth of Ephesus, such that it was entrusted to an officer of high rank and was central in the agonistic festivals that abounded in the Ephesian calendar. Swete (loc. cit.) also points out that the εὐσέβεια family of words bears an almost technical sense in Ephesian inscriptions.

Swete (op. cit., 4) has put most of these elements together, unfortunately omitting, however, the impact of the words of Jesus, in the following hypothesis: "In the Christian at Ephesus, Christ has taken the place of Artemis and the Church that of the Artemisian, and the self-control and self-sacrifice of the new life in Christ, which were good for both worlds, were the Christian substitute for the drill of the gymnasium, which was serviceable only for the life that now is" (see also Knight, *Faithful Sayings,* 76-79). Whatever the origins of the saying, it commends εὐσέβεια in terms of its intrinsic absolute value and also of its absoluteness in comparison with σωματικὴ γυμνασία.

4:9 With the citation-commendation formula πιστὸς ὁ λόγος Paul designates what precedes as a saying (λόγος) and commends it as trustworthy (πιστός). With καὶ πάσης ἀποδοχῆς ἄξιος he also urges a full personal appropriation of the saying (see comments above on 1:15).

A question that remains is the punctuation at the end of this verse (see the *UBSGNT* apparatus). This question is related to the identity of the saying and is inevitably intertwined with it (see the solution given in the discussion of v. 8 above). A period before and at the end of the verse (*RSV, NASB, NEB* margin) distinguishes it and its formula from both v. 8 and v. 10 and does not commit the translation either way with regard to the identification of the "saying." But a colon at the end of the verse (*NEB* text) virtually identifies v. 10 as the "saying" (*NIV* parenthesizes the first clause of v. 10 and places a paragraph break between vv. 8 and 9, thereby identifying the rest of v. 10

as the "saying"). For reasons given above, the "saying" should, however, be identified as v. 8. A comma at the end of v. 9 would present v. 10 as a more personal (note first person plural "we") and theological concurrence with the formula of v. 9.

4:10 This is Paul's personal theological affirmation of the truth of the saying in v. 8. Because godliness has the promise of life, "we" "labor and struggle" (v. 10a). Such effort is undertaken ultimately because our hope is fixed on θεῷ ζῶντι, who can give such ζωή (v. 10b) as the Savior of all who believe on him (v. 10c).

V. 10 begins with two transition terms, εἰς τοῦτο and γάρ. εἰς τοῦτο (this combination 4x in Pl.*: Rom. 14:9; 2 Cor. 2:9; 1 Thes. 3:3; 1 Tim. 4:10) has reference to the promise and its content. γάρ "shows that this verse is to serve as a reason or confirmation of the preceding thought that godliness is profitable for all things . . ." (Huther). Both terms bridge over v. 9 to v. 8 and tie v. 10 very closely with v. 8.

The words that follow, κοπιῶμεν καὶ ἀγωνιζόμεθα, are reminiscent of Col. 1:29 (cf. also Col. 2:1). Paul now speaks of his own and his colleagues' spiritual struggle and exercise, not only in terms that apply to every Christian believer, but in terms that he also applies to the activities of the ministers (διάκονοι) who are the leaders within the congregation. κοπιάω (PE* 3x) means "work hard, toil, labor" and may indicate mental and spiritual as well as physical exertion. It is used here of the spiritual exertion of Paul and other leaders, as it is elsewhere (cf., e.g., 1 Cor. 15:10; 16:16; Gal. 4:11; Col. 1:29; 1 Thes. 5:12; both occurrences in 1 Timothy, 4:10 and 5:17; and by analogy 2 Tim. 2:6; on the significance of κοπιάω see also Pfitzner, *Agon Motif,* 102f., interacting with the earlier studies of Deissmann, Harnack, and Lightfoot; see also F. Hauck, *TDNT* III, 829).

ἀγωνιζόμεθα is to be preferred over the textual variant ὀνειδιζόμεθα ("suffer reproach"), "partly because it has slightly better attestation and partly because it seems better suited to the context" (*TCGNT;* for textual evidence see *NA*[26]). ἀγωνίζομαι means generally "struggle or strive" and may be used more specifically of an athletic contest or of fighting with weapons. Here the emphasis falls on striving after a goal (εἰς τοῦτο; see E. Stauffer, *TDNT* I, 136-39; Pfitzner, *Agon Motif,* 109f.). The two present tense verbs taken together speak of the continual "tremendous efforts and exertions in the proclamation of the gospel" (Rienecker-Rogers, *Linguistic Key,* ad loc.) on the part of Paul and his associates (note the first person plural).

ὅτι introduces the ultimate ground for this labor and striving, i.e., hope in the living God. This hope placed in God is a hope aware of the fact that he is the "Savior of all." The perspective of the verb ἐλπίζω "embraces at once the three elements of expectation of the future, trust, and the patience of waiting" (R. Bultmann, *TDNT* II, 531). The perfect tense here describes a past action with a continuing significance: Such expectant trust has given

Paul and his associates confidence to continue laboring and striving. ἐπί indicates specifically that their hope is placed "on" God. Paul refers to God as "living" (ζῶντι; see 3:15). They may place their hope on "the living God" because as such he is the source and giver of life and is able to fulfill the promise of ζωή (cf. especially 1:16, 17).

The assumption of the previous clause is now made explicit: we hope in the living God as the one ὅς ἐστιν σωτὴρ πάντων ἀνθρώπων. Although the phrase σωτὴρ πάντων ἀνθρώπων occurs only here in the NT, the concept has been set forth earlier in 1 Timothy in nearly identical words (2:3, 4; see the notes there, especially on πάντες ἄνθρωποι). Here, as in 2:1-7, the phrase πάντες ἄνθρωποι designates "all sorts of people." σωτήρ means "Savior" in the soteriological sense that it has elsewhere in 1 Timothy and the PE (PE* 10x: 1 Tim. 1:1; 2:3; 4:10; Tit. 1:3, 4; 2:10, 13; 3:4, 6; 2 Tim. 1:10). The focus on the promise of ζωῆς, τῆς νῦν καὶ τῆς μελλούσης, and on a hope set upon θεῷ ζῶντι, demands that understanding of σωτήρ here. But to understand σωτὴρ πάντων ἀνθρώπων in the sense that all people are actually and surely saved would be contrary to Paul's teaching elsewhere since Paul clearly regards some people as bearing God's retribution and punishment in the penalty of eternal destruction (cf., e.g., 2 Thes. 1:7-10; 1 Thes. 1:10). Thus another understanding has been suggested in connection with πάντων and that is that σωτήρ is used in the broadest sense as Preserver and Giver of life for all people and then, in addition to that, as Savior in the spiritual sense for believers. This is certainly possible, and appeal could be made to 6:13 (cf. Acts 14:15-17; 17:24-28). But a better solution may be had by an alternate understanding of μάλιστα.

The phrase μάλιστα πιστῶν contains the one qualification that Paul and the NT always posit for receiving God's salvation, i.e., "trust" in God as the only Savior. Absolute πιστῶν, as used here and elsewhere in the NT, refers to those who believe in Christ, i.e., Christian believers (BAGD s.v. 2; e.g., Acts 16:1; 2 Cor. 6:15; 1 Tim. 5:16; 6:2a, b; cf. τῶν πιστῶν in 1 Tim. 4:12; thus five of the seven plural occurrences of πιστός in the PE have the meaning "believers," i.e., 1 Tim. 4:3, 10, 12; 6:2 [2x]). μάλιστα** (NT 12x, Pl. 8x, PE 5x: Acts 20:38; 25:26; 26:3; Gal. 6:10; Phil. 4:22; 1 Tim. 4:10; 5:8, 17; Tit. 1:10; 2 Tim. 4:13; Phm. 16; 2 Pet. 2:10) has usually been rendered "especially" and regarded as in some way distinguishing that which follows it from that which goes before it. Skeat ("Especially the Parchments") argues persuasively that μάλιστα in some cases (2 Tim. 4:13; Tit. 1:10, 11; and here) should be understood as providing a further definition or identification of that which precedes it and thus renders it by such words as "that is." He cites several examples from papyrus letters that would seem to require this sense and that would in their particular cases rule out the otherwise legitimate alternate sense. If his proposal is correct here, which seems most likely, then the phrase μάλιστα πιστῶν should be rendered "that is, believers." This understanding is also in line with Paul's assertion that all sorts and conditions of people are in Christ (even at times using πάντες) and with his insistence in those contexts that all such are in Christ and have salvation by faith (cf., e.g., Gal. 3:26-28).

Show the Believers by Example How They Should Conduct Themselves as You Continue to Conduct Yourself Well and Teach Good Doctrine: 4:11-16

This is a subsection of vv. 6-16. V. 11 is a transition verse and could be taken as the conclusion of what precedes or as the beginning of this section. Since v. 6 makes a similar request, it is best to see v. 11 repeating that note as the beginning of this subsection. Timothy must exemplify what he teaches and thus remove any barrier his youth may cause (v. 12), and he must concentrate on and carry out effectively his public ministry responsibilities (v. 13). He must not neglect God's spiritual gift within him (v. 14) and must be diligent in these things so that his progress may be evident to all around him (v. 15). In a concluding admonition, Timothy is again urged to attend to his own life and to his teaching, and to persevere in them, being mindful of the fact that by this means his hearers and he himself will be saved (v. 16).

This subsection intertwines the necessity for faithfulness in Timothy's public ministry with faithfulness in his personal life. In distinction from the previous section, it is more of a personal directive to Timothy, whereas the previous section had the more generalized "saying" (vv. 7b, 8) and "we" statement (v. 10). At the same time this section continues the trend set in the previous section to speak in terms of principle.

4:11 With παράγγελλε ταῦτα καὶ δίδασκε Paul urges Timothy to communicate that which he has written (cf. 6:2). These words pick up a phenomenon begun in v. 6 and repeated in the same, or similar, terms several times in the letter (ταῦτα παράγγελλε, 5:7; ταῦτα δίδασκε καὶ παρακάλει, 6:2; παράγγελλε, 6:17; similarly in Titus: σὺ δὲ λάλει ἃ πρέπει τῇ ὑγιαινούσῃ διδασκαλίᾳ, 2:1; παρακάλει, 2:6; ταῦτα λάλει καὶ παρακάλει καὶ ἔλεγχε, 2:15; καὶ περὶ τούτων βούλομαί σε διαβεβαιοῦσθαι, 3:8). The fact that the exhortation recurs and that it often has a ταῦτα (4:6, 11; 5:7; 6:2; see v. 6) makes it likely that the ταῦτα to be taught and prescribed is the section closest at hand. Here the preceding section seems most appropriate, since it consists of general truths for believers, whereas the section following is directed almost exclusively to Timothy. παραγγέλλω means generally "give orders, command, instruct, direct" and is used "of all kinds of persons in authority" (BAGD). The apostle of Christ (1:1) commands the servant of Christ (4:6) to continually command (παράγγελλε, present imperative) that which the apostle has communicated (cf. 4:6). δίδασκε refers to the communication of the truth to which παράγγελλε seeks obedience. ταῦτα indicates the content to be taught, and "the brothers" (understood, see 4:6) are those to be taught. These two imperative verbs require continual engagement in commanding and teaching the apostolic instructions.

4:12 V. 11 sets the stage for v. 12 and explains why v. 12 is necessary (and thus indicates a closer relationship to v. 12 than to the preceding verses). The admonition and instruction demanded by v. 11 may evoke resistance and may raise questions and doubts, especially when the one commanding and teaching is νεότης. This youthfulness may provide an excuse for some to look down on Timothy and on his instruction (cf. Tit. 2:15). Paul urges Timothy not to let that happen and says he may overcome such by being a good example.

μηδείς is used here as a substantive with the meaning "no one." νεότης** (Mk. 10:20; Lk. 18:21; Acts 26:4) and the related adjective νέος are used of "children, youths, and of men at least as old as 30" (LSJM s.v. νέος). The phrase "wife of your youth" (ἐκ νεότητός σου) is used in the LXX (Pr. 5:18; Mal. 2:14) and shows the second category of usage. The third category extends into and somewhat beyond the age of thirty and is evidenced by the following: Polybius (18.12.5) speaks of Flaminius as "young" because he is only thirty, and Irenaeus (*Haer.* 2.22.5) explicitly says that one could be called "young" up to forty (cf. Bernard, Simpson, Kelly). Simpson points out that in Aulus Gellius (10.28) soldiers "are reckoned *iuniores* up to forty-six." Luke called Paul a "young man" (Acts 7:58) when he was of the same age range as Timothy is now. Timothy's age, in his thirties (the estimate most would agree on), might seem to be a handicap in the Ephesian community, where some of the other believers and other elders are older. The tendency is for νεότης "to be looked down on" (cf. BAGD s.v. καταφρονέω 1). The admonition of the apostle is that Timothy not let this become a factor, since the apostolic instruction and admonition are at stake.

The antidote given is to overcome the tendency of others to look down on youth by demonstrating a maturity in life and conduct. Thus Timothy is urged to be an "example" or "pattern" (τύπος, Pl.* 8x: Rom. 5:14; 8:17; 1 Cor. 10:6; Phil. 3:17; 1 Thes. 1:7; 2 Thes. 3:9; Tit. 2:7; in all the Pauline passages except the first two, the idea of a model or example for others is evident; see L. Goppelt, *TDNT* VIII, 248-50; De Boer, *Imitation,* 21-23, 86-89). Some think that the genitive construction τῶν πιστῶν following τύπος means that Timothy must be an example *of* believers (*NASB:* "an example *of* those who believe"). However, the parallel usage in 1 Pet. 5:3 (τύποι γινόμενοι τοῦ ποιμνίου), which requires the understanding "be examples *to* the flock" (so *NASB*), demonstrates that *to* or *for* is appropriate here (so *NEB, NIV*). The adjective πιστῶν is used in an active sense here (as in v. 10) as a substantive designating "those who believe" in Christ, i.e., "believers" (see vv. 3, 10). With the definite article (τῶν) it designates the specific believers among whom Timothy lives.

In five prepositional phrases with ἐν the apostle indicates the qualities in which Timothy is to be a τύπος. ἐν πνεύματι (which would be a sixth such phrase) is not found in the best representatives of both the "Alexandrian" and "Western" text-types (see *NA*[26]; *TCGNT*). The five phrases appear in a certain order: First are the two basic realms of word and deed (ἐν λόγῳ, ἐν ἀναστροφῇ). Then appear the necessary basic qualities (ἐν ἀγάπῃ, ἐν πίστει, ἐν ἁγνείᾳ). λόγος is used here without the article in the sense of "speech," as in Colossians and Ephesians, where Paul indicates both negatively (Eph. 4:25, 26, 29, 31; 5:4; Col. 3:8, 9) and positively (Eph. 4:25, 29, 32; 5:4, 19, 20; Col. 3:12, 13, 16, 17) ways of speaking to be avoided (falsehood, anger, bitterness, slander, malice, abusive speech, filthy talk) and to be sought (truth, edification, admonition, tenderness, forgiveness, and thanks, especially to God in Jesus Christ). Similarly the ἀναστροφή, i.e., "way of life," "conduct," or "behavior," appropriate for the Christian is indicated in those same letters. For in them also, as elsewhere in Paul, he is concerned for "word or deed" (Col. 3:17). The radical change expected of the Christian is that "in reference to your former manner of life (ἀναστροφήν), you lay aside the old self . . . and that you be renewed in the spirit of your mind, and put on the new self, which in the likeness of God has been created in righteousness and holiness of the truth" (Eph. 4:22-24).

One is not surprised to find ἀγάπη (see 1:5, 14; 2:15) as the first of the qualities mentioned. It is the centerpiece of the Colossian and Ephesian passages cited above (Eph. 4:2, 15, 16; 5:2; Col. 3:14), with the admonitions "beyond all these things put on love" (Col. 3:14) and "walk in love, just as Christ also loved you" (Eph. 5:2) expressing that central concern. In virtually all of Paul's letters, love is said to be a decisive quality for a Christian's life (cf., e.g., Rom. 12:9; 13:9, 10; 14:15; 1 Cor. 8:1; 13; 16:14; Gal. 5:6, 13; Phil. 1:9; 2:1, 2; 1 Thes. 3:12; 2 Thes. 1:3). 1 Cor. 16:14 captures this concern when it says, "Let all that you do be done in love."

πίστις signifies here a Christian virtue, just as it does elsewhere in Paul coupled with ἀγάπη (1 Thes. 3:6; 5:8; 1 Tim. 1:14; 2 Tim. 1:13; Phm. 5) and with other concepts such as ἁγνεία (2 Cor. 8:7; Gal. 5:22; Eph. 6:23; 1 Tim. 2:15; 6:11; Tit. 2:2; 2 Tim. 2:22; 3:10). The meaning of πίστις in these cases is always difficult to ascertain with certainty (e.g., *NEB:* "fidelity"; *RSV, NASB, NIV:* "faith"). The previous and following usages of πίστις as a Christian virtue coupled with ἀγάπη and other virtues in the PE (see above) incline one to understand πίστις here as "faith," i.e., "trust," as do the preponderance of cases elsewhere in Paul (e.g., 1 Tim. 2:15; 6:11; 2 Tim. 2:22; 3:10; Gal. 5:6, 22, but for a contrary view on Gal. 5:22 cf. the commentaries of Burton and Bruce).

The third quality is ἁγνεία** (also in 5:2), which means generally "purity" and more specifically "chastity." Here the general meaning, which would include the specific, is probably intended. This word seems to be used here in the place of other terms that are used in combination with ἀγάπη and πίστις elsewhere in Paul and in the PE (for the PE note ἁγιασμῷ μετὰ σωφροσύνης, 2:15; δικαιοσύνην, εὐσέβειαν, 6:11; δικαιοσύνη, 2 Tim. 2:22). By having these qualities, Timothy will be an example for believers and will demonstrate thereby that he is spiritually mature and warranted to lead and to "command and teach these things."

4:13 Paul specifies the tasks to which he commands Timothy to devote himself in his public ministry. ἕως ἔρχομαι, "until I come," indicates a time frame and implies that Timothy may be assigned other tasks when Paul arrives and perhaps that Paul himself will take over (some of) these responsibilities. Turner asserts that "ἕως clauses are invariably post-positive" and thus we must take the clause "with what precedes" (MHT III, 344, rendering our passage with "Make yourself an example until I come" [n. 1]). But Hanna *(Grammatical Aid)* indicates that Mt. 5:18 and 2 Cor. 3:15 are exceptions to this rule and that our passage can be also (cf. the consistent punctuation of *UBSGNT, NA*^{26}, *RSV, NEB, NASB, NIV*). Robertson (*Grammar,* 976) suggests that ἕως with the indicative here means "while," rather than "until," but even if this doubtful view were correct the meaning would remain virtually the same (for "until" see BAGD and cf. the only other occurrence of the phrase ἕως ἔρχομαι, Jn. 21:22, 23, which virtually demands "until"). προσέχω (see 1:4) means generally "turn one's mind to" and is used here for the first and only time in the PE in a positive sense with the special nuance (appropriate to the imperative) of "occupy oneself with, devote or apply oneself to" (BAGD s.v. 1c).

The first of the three activities to which Timothy is to devote himself is ἀνάγνωσις (cf. ἀναγινώσκω), "reading," "public reading," used here and in its other two NT occurrences of public reading in a religious gathering (Acts 13:15; 2 Cor. 3:14 refer to reading of the OT in the synagogue; cf. the synagogue inscription in Jerusalem, *Supplementum Epigraphicum Graecum,* ed. J. J. E. Hondius, VIII, 170, l. 4: συναγωγὴν εἰς ἀνάγνωσιν νόμου). The following word, παράκλησις, by analogy with Acts 13:15, where the reading aloud of the OT is followed by a "word of exhortation" (λόγος παρακλήσεως), signifies that the reading here is a public reading. The "reading," like that of the other two NT occurrences, would be of those writings that were regarded as authoritative, and, in addition to the OT, would include extant NT writings (cf. the admonitions of Paul to the congregation to read the letters he wrote to them and to others with the related verb ἀναγινώσκω: 1 Thes. 5:27; Col. 4:16; cf. also Acts 15:31; Rev. 1:3; cf. further 1 Tim. 5:18, where a statement of Jesus found in Mt. 10:10 and Lk. 10:7 may be quoted under the rubric of "scripture says," λέγει γὰρ γραφή).

παράκλησις is used in correlation with ἀνάγνωσις here as in Acts 13:15. There the content of the παράκλησις is that Jesus is the promised Messiah of the OT and that those who believe in him receive forgiveness of sins.

παράκλησις is associated with the OT in Rom. 15:4 and Heb. 12:5 and with the letter of the Apostolic Council in Acts 15:31, and is used by the author of Hebrews to describe his letter (13:22). These uses manifest the three senses recognized as inherent in the word's meaning, i.e., "to summon or ask, to exhort, and to comfort" (see O. Schmitz and G. Stählin, *TDNT* V, 773-99; G. Braumann, *NIDNTT* I, 569-71). Here Timothy is to summon his hearers to respond to the scripture that has been read. Whether he does so in exhortation or in comfort will depend on the message of the passage, but common to these two senses is the note of encouragement inherent in this term (cf. Rom. 15:4).

διδασκαλία (see 1:10 and 4:6) "bears an unmistakable intellectual character" (K. H. Rengstorf, *TDNT* II, 160). It is the teaching of the scripture read, analogous to the use of παράκλησις (cf. 2 Tim. 3:16: πᾶσα γραφή . . . ὠφέλιμος πρὸς διδασκαλίαν; Rom. 15:4). Thus Paul urges a public ministry that reads the scriptures to the gathered Christians, exhorts them to respond appropriately, and teaches them its principles.

4:14 Paul also urges Timothy not to neglect the spiritual gift within him (τοῦ ἐν σοὶ χαρίσματος), i.e., the gift from God (cf. 2 Tim. 1:6: τὸ χάρισμα τοῦ θεοῦ). With this we come to the source of power for the conduct (v. 12) and ministry (v. 13) urged on Timothy (cf. Phil. 2:12, 13; 1 Cor. 15:10; 2 Tim. 1:14; 2:1). Paul points to those public episodes that were associated with the recognition of Timothy and with his having received this gift from God, i.e., the prophetic utterances and the laying on of hands, and he does so as an encouragement for Timothy.

ἀμέλω means here "neglect." τὸ χάρισμα is generally a gift freely and graciously given (BAGD), and usually in Paul a special nonmaterial gift bestowed by God's grace and Spirit on individual Christians. ὃ ἐδόθη σοι specifies that the χάρισμα is that given with Timothy's calling and appointment to his special ministry, i.e., a gift equipping him for that ministry (cf. Rom. 12:6; especially 1 Cor. 12:4ff.: "varieties of gifts . . . varieties of ministries"; 2 Tim. 1:6; 1 Pet. 4:10). The gift is now resident in Timothy (τοῦ ἐν σοὶ χαρίσματος). Aorist passive ἐδόθη indicates that the gift "was given" by God (cf. 2 Tim. 1:6).

διὰ προφητείας μετὰ ἐπιθέσεως τῶν χειρῶν τοῦ πρεσβυτερίου indicate the public testimonies to that internal work of God. προφητεία (Pl.* 9x: Rom. 12:6; 1 Cor. 12:10; 13:2, 8; 14:6, 22; 1 Thes. 5:20; 1 Tim. 1:18, which see; 4:14) means "prophecy" and is used consistently by Paul and the NT of a revelation given by God. διὰ προφητείας (probably accusative plural, as in 1:18, rather than genitive singular) expresses the truth already articulated in 1:18, namely, that "the prophetic utterances . . . pointed to you" *(RSV),* i.e., they showed Timothy to be gifted by God for the task and thus called by the Holy Spirit (cf. Acts 13:1, 2). The testimony of the prophecy points to that inner reality.

The prophecy was obediently accompanied by laying on of hands (cf. BAGD s.v. μετά III.2). Similarly Acts 13:2, 3 indicates that "the Holy Spirit said, Set apart for me Barnabas and Saul for the work" and records "then, when they . . . laid their hands on them, they sent them away." The phrase ἐπίθεσις τῶν χειρῶν** is found 4x in the NT (Acts 8:18; here; 2 Tim. 1:6; Heb. 6:2), and the same action is expressed with the clause ἐπιτίθημι χεῖρά (or χεῖρας) τινι (or ἐπί τινα, ἐπί τι) some 20x, although only 3x does the expression parallel the activity here (Acts 6:6; 13:3; 1 Tim. 5:22; see C. Maurer, *TDNT* VIII, 160; E. Lohse, *TDNT* IX, 431ff., and the literature cited in these articles and in BAGD). Both the phrase and the clause refer to "laying on of hands," which refers here to what we call an act of ordination, as in 2 Tim. 1:6; Acts 6:6; and most likely 1 Tim. 5:22 (Acts 13:3 would be a commissioning of those already "ordained"; Heb. 6:2 may well fit into this category; cf. Nu. 27:18-23, where Moses lays hands on Joshua to commission him; see Lohse, *TDNT* IX, 429, for the impact of that act on the practice within Judaism).

The phrase is qualified by genitive τοῦ πρεσβυτερίου** (Lk. 22:66; Acts 22:5; here; Theodotion's text of Susanna 50; not found in pre-Christian literature). In its NT usage this word refers generally to a council or college of elders (BAGD; LSJM; G. Bornkamm, *TDNT* VI, 654) with the Lukan passages referring to the Jewish court in Jerusalem, and our passage referring to Christian πρεσβύτεροι (as 13x in Ignatius, see BAGD). Daube (*NT and Rabbinic Judaism,* 224-46, especially 244f.; "Evangelisten," especially 125) and Jeremias ("ΠΡΕΣΒΥΤΕΡΙΟΝ") propose that the term be understood, with the preceding words, as ordination "to the presbyterate," i.e., as a genitive of purpose. They argue that Susanna 50 (Theodotion) has this sense and also that such an understanding eliminates a conflict between the present passage and 2 Tim. 1:6.

G. Bornkamm (*TDNT* VI, 666, especially n. 92) and Hanson (94) set forth a number of arguments against Daube's and Jeremias's suggestion that appear cogent and compelling: πρεσβυτέριον is used elsewhere in the NT of a body of elders (since Luke is Paul's close associate this is even more significant), and this usage with reference to a body of Christian elders appears not many years later in Ignatius. Susanna 50 (Theodotion) is the only known use of the word for an abstract office, and it "implies membership of a specific corporation and is thus unable to sustain the hypothesis" (Bornkamm, 666, n. 92). Elsewhere the genitive after the phrase ἐπίθεσις τῶν χειρῶν is subjective, indicating those that lay on hands (cf. 2 Tim. 1:6; Acts 8:18). "The difference between 1 Tim. 4:14 and 2 Tim. 1:6 is adequately explained by the difference in character between the two letters (congregational rule/apostolic testament)" (Bornkamm, 666, n. 92). Hence we may say that this passage does refer, as Hanson indicates, to ordination by the group of presbyters (cf. Acts 6:6; 13:3; cf. also Lohse, *Ordination,* especially 64-66, 89-101).

4:15 Vv. 15 and 16 bring these admonitions to a close. Paul reiterates in v. 15 that Timothy must do these things, and indicates in v. 16 why such perseverance is important, namely, because it has as its outcome salvation for Timothy and his hearers.

ταῦτα, as in vv. 6 and 11 (which see), refers to the preceding items. μελετάω** (also in Acts 4:25) "can signify either *to study* or *practice,* and which to choose in this context is a puzzle" (Simpson; see also MM). If the word means "practice," then the previous reference to exercise is reiterated. But perhaps a more basic and comprehensive meaning may be intended here: cf. *NEB:* "make these matters your business," *NASB:* "take pains with these things," and *NIV:* "be diligent in these things" (cf. also μὴ ἀμέλει, v. 14). ἐν τούτοις picks up the preceding ταῦτα. The exhortation continues with ἴσθι (present imperative of εἰμί). ἐν τούτοις ἴσθι has been variously expressed: "be wrapped up in these things" (MHT I, 184), be "occupied in (ἐν) these things" (MHT III, 265), "be absorbed in them" *(NASB,* cf. *NEB),* "devote yourself to them" *(RSV),* "give yourself wholly to them" *(NIV).* Each attempt seeks to capture in English idiom the total involvement and intensity of the exhortation.

The ἵνα clause states the purpose ("so that") of the imperatives. What is important is ἡ προκοπή** (also in Phil. 1:12, 25), "progress or advancement," with "in the faith" understood (as Phil. 1:25 demonstrates; προκοπὴν καὶ χαρὰν τῆς πίστεως; cf. 1 Tim. 4:12; Tit. 2:7). Timothy's progress (σου) is to be φανερὰ πᾶσιν. This echoes the note in 4:12 (τύπος γίνου τῶν πιστῶν), but πᾶσιν here encompasses a wider audience (cf. v. 16: τοὺς ἀκούοντας σου). φανερά means here "visible, clear, evident, plainly to be seen." πᾶσιν (see 2:1, 2, 4, 6) indicates all those before whom Timothy lives.

4:16 This verse presents the final exhortation of the section: ἔπεχε σεαυτῷ καὶ τῇ διδασκαλίᾳ, ἐπίμενε αὐτοῖς. With this exhortation comes the reason why Paul is so persistent and so concerned, because what is at stake is salvation for Timothy and his hearers.

ἔπεχω in its intransitive form takes the dative of the "thing" and means here "give attention to." There are two things to which Timothy is to give attention (cf. Acts 20:28). The first is himself (σεαυτῷ), reflecting what Paul expressed in v. 7 (γύμναζε δὲ σεαυτὸν πρὸς εὐσέβειαν), and the second is διδασκαλίᾳ, the "teaching" that Timothy has received and followed (see v. 6), that he is to communicate from the scriptures (v. 13), and that ultimately is from Christ (6:3).

ἐπιμένω used figuratively, as here (ἐπίμενε αὐτοῖς), means to "continue, persist (in), persevere" (with dative, BAGD). Plural αὐτοῖς probably refers to the nearest possible antecedents, σεαυτῷ καὶ τῇ διδασκαλίᾳ, although it may refer to the several items in vv. 6-15. But even these items may be summarily referred to as personal piety (vv. 7ff., 12) and public ministry (vv. 6, 11, 13), which could be succinctly stated as σεαυτῷ καὶ τῇ διδασκαλίᾳ, so that either understanding amounts to the same thing. ἐπιμένω with reference to διδασκαλίᾳ refers to persistent fidelity to the teaching and a constant urging of it upon his hearers, as Luke records Paul and Barnabas doing: "Speaking to them, were urging them to continue in the grace of God" (Acts 13:43; cf. Rom. 11:22). Paul is reminding Timothy that he must embrace and personally persevere in that which he teaches (cf. 1 Cor. 9:24-27).

The concept of perseverance as essential to salvation, which Paul presents in the concluding words of this verse, has been stated by Paul with this same verb ἐπιμένω in both Rom. 11:22 ("if you continue in his kindness; otherwise you also will be cut off") and Col. 1:22, 23 ("to present you before him holy and blameless and beyond reproach — if indeed you continue in the faith firmly established and steadfast, and not moved away from the hope of the gospel that you have heard") and with a different verb in 1 Cor. 15:1, 2 (but with σῴζω as here; cf. in Heb. 3:6, 14). Paul's insistence on holding fast the "word" in 1 Cor. 15:2 and on perseverance in the "teaching" (διδασκαλίᾳ) are synonymous concepts.

That which Paul has so forcefully exhorted Timothy to do (τοῦτο γὰρ ποιῶν) will bring about the much to be hoped for outcome: καὶ σεαυτὸν σώσεις καὶ τοὺς ἀκούοντάς σου. γάρ governs the main clause with its key verb σώσεις, and not the participial phrase, τοῦτο ποιῶν, which serves as an introductory recapitulation of the preceding words. Thus γάρ, "for," introduces the ultimate conclusion of the section and affords the reason for such exhortation. τοῦτο, which usually refers to something comparatively near at hand, likely refers to the immediately previous exhortations within v. 16, especially ἐπίμενε, the call to perseverance. The sum of what has been exhorted is now described with the present active participle ποιῶν simply as "doing" (2 Tim. 4:5 is an especially relevant parallel).

The promised result, σώσεις . . . , is twofold, "both yourself and your hearers." The operative verb is σῴζω, which has as a general meaning, "save, keep from harm, preserve, rescue" (BAGD). Although there are those who argue that the salvation is from theological error, i.e., salvation in the sense of preservation (Bengel, Gromacki, Vine, Wuest), most commentators take σώσεις soteriologically and eschatologically (Alford, Bernard, Brox, Bürki, Calvin, Earle, Ellicott, Fairbairn, Gealy, Guthrie, Hendriksen, Hiebert, Huther, Kelly, Kent, Lenski, Moellering, Robertson, Scott, Simpson, van Oosterzee, and White; also J. Schneider, *NIDNTT* III, 215; W. Foerster, *TDNT* VII, 995). The other occurrences of σῴζω in the PE (1 Tim. 1:15; 2:4, 15; Tit. 3:5; 2 Tim. 1:9; 4:18) are clearly soteriological in orientation. It is true that διδασκαλία does deliver from error and bring to truth, but that seems to be included in the ultimate goal expressed in σῴζω (cf. 2:4; so also van Oosterzee). The salvation of the hearers is elsewhere depicted by Paul as the central goal of the ministry (cf. especially 1 Cor. 15:1, 2; 9:22; 2 Tim. 2:10; 4:5), and it is that hope in the living God who is the Savior of all believers that Paul has presented as the centerpiece of encouragement for Timothy in this section.

That a human being, here Timothy, is the subject of σῴζω is a phenomenon found elsewhere in Paul (Rom. 11:14; 1 Cor. 9:22; 7:16a, b), in James (5:20), in Jude (23), and with Jesus in the Synoptic Gospels (Mk. 8:35b par. Lk. 9:24b). Thus we see that the NT speaks of human agents in addition to the ultimate and absolute source, God himself (cf. the very helpful comments of Calvin). Jesus speaks of a man saving his life (Mk. 8:35 par. Lk. 9:24: σώσει αὐτήν = τὴν ψυχὴν αὐτοῦ, equivalent to σεαυτόν here) by the decisive act of "losing his life" for Jesus and the gospel, i.e., the surrender of saving faith (here by the perseverance that marks true faith; cf. again Col. 1:23 especially, and also 1 Cor. 9:24-27).

τοὺς ἀκούοντάς σου, "your hearers," is the natural way to refer to those who are the recipients of the gospel, since it was communicated orally. To Timothy's hearers the promise is extended with the same requirement for them as for Timothy, perseverance (ἐπίμενε αὐτοῖς). Timothy's διδασκαλία, like Paul's, is to encourage such perseverance (Col. 1:23; 1 Cor. 15:1, 2) for those whose ears are open to hear and thus can be truly called hearers (cf. 2 Tim. 4:1-5). Lenski summarizes well when he says that God alone saves (v. 10), yet he saves by means, "and it is thus that one who uses and applies these means can very properly be said to save both himself and others."

DUTIES TOWARD OTHERS: 5:1–6:2

Paul turns to duties toward various groups within the Christian community. As a transition from the previous section, he first addresses Timothy the minister in vv. 1 and 2 with reference to his relationship to those who hear him (4:16). He next turns to a group that merits special attention and care, widows (5:3-16). He then turns to the duties toward those who are called on to lead the church, the elders (5:17-25). Finally, aware of the particularly difficult role of some members, he turns to slaves and instructs them about their duties to their masters (6:1, 2).

HOW THE MINISTER SHOULD EXHORT OTHERS: 5:1, 2

Several times in the preceding section Timothy has been urged to apply the apostolic teaching to "the brothers," i.e., the fellow members of the Christian family (cf., e.g., 4:6). He has been called on to "prescribe and teach those things" (v. 11), to "let no one look down on your youthfulness" (v. 12), and to "give attention . . . to exhortation and teaching" (v. 13). The danger that might arise from such a responsibility is that Timothy might misunderstand such admonitions to require harsh and overbearing action on his part to carry out this task. Thus Paul immediately warns him not to carry out the necessary "prescribing" of these things (4:11) in an abusive way.

5:1 So v. 1 admonishes, "do not sharply rebuke" (μὴ ἐπιπλήξῃς). ἐπιπλήσσω,** a NT hapax (variant reading in Mt. 12:15f.; Lk. 24:43), means "strike at" or "rebuke" in the sense of "rebuke sharply" with a note of severity (MM). Such sharpness and severity are prohibited to Timothy. The prohibition extends to Timothy's relations with all the groups named in view of the fact that exhortation is given as the proper alternative course of action (ἀλλὰ παρακάλει) and is the operative verb for all the groups.

Paul begins this list of groups with the "older man." The singular is generic, as is evidenced by the plurals used for the following three groups. πρεσβύτερος (Pl.* 5x, all in PE: 1 Tim. 5:1, 2, 17, 19; Tit. 1:5; a comparative of πρεσβύς functioning here as a substantive) designated both age and office in that day as the equivalent word "elder" does today (used of age in Lk.

15:25; Jn. 8:9; Acts 2:17; see BAGD). Although some have thought that πρεσβύτερος is used here for church officers (as in 5:17), most commentators have recognized that the corresponding categories of "younger men" (νεωτέρους) and "older women" (πρεσβυτέρας) point to this as a category of age and sex rather than of office. The papyri contain several examples of this use of πρεσβύτερος in settings similar to that found here with advice given as to how one should relate to various groups that are older, the same in age, or younger (see MM; Dibelius-Conzelmann; Wetstein, *NT Graecum,* ad loc.).

Although Paul does not want Timothy to "sharply rebuke" an older man or anyone else, he does very much want Timothy to minister to them (cf. the adversative ἀλλά indicating a contrast to what precedes). Present imperative παρακάλει indicates the ongoing action demanded. παρακαλέω (see the data at 1:3) carries a spectrum of meanings that can be partially spanned by the translation "appeal to" (see BAGD). This occurrence of the verb follows a use of the related noun παράκλησις that is correlated with teaching (4:13), so its usage here is probably influenced by that association. Furthermore, the meaning of the verb here is also likely to be that found in 1 Tim. 6:2 (ταῦτα δίδασκε καὶ παρακάλει) where παρακαλέω is also associated with teaching. In both contexts, that which is taught is also to be urged upon and applied to the hearers. Thus here also the note of "appeal" or "exhortation" is in view.

Such pastoral admonition must be done, and with the respect due to one who is older. Thus Timothy must treat older men as (ὡς) he would treat his own father (ὡς πατέρα). πατήρ is used here in the sense of one's natural father, and Paul probably has in mind the command to honor one's parents (Ex. 20:12; Dt. 5:16; cf. Lv. 19:32; La. 5:12b).

"Younger men" (νεωτέρους, comparative of νέος) are to be exhorted "as brothers" (ἀδελφούς). Regarding disciples as family members is established by Jesus in the Gospels (Mt. 12:49, 50 par. Mk. 3:34, 35; Lk. 8:21; cf. Mk. 10:30). Timothy is reminded that in coming with the authority of a minister of Christ he is to regard those "younger," not as younger or inferior, but as family peers, i.e., "brothers," and conduct himself toward them in that way (ὡς ἀδελφούς).

5:2 "Older women" (πρεσβυτέρας,** a NT hapax, the feminine plural counterpart of the masculine singular form found in v. 1) are to be exhorted "as mothers" (ὡς μητέρας). μήτηρ is used here in the sense of one's natural mother (cf. especially Rom. 16:13). "Younger women" (νεωτέρας, the feminine counterpart of the masculine form in v. 1, found only here; 5:11, 14 in the NT; cf. τὰς νέας in Tit. 2:4) are to be exhorted "as sisters" (ὡς ἀδελφάς).

Although it is possible that ἐν πάσῃ ἁγνείᾳ qualifies Timothy's relationship with all four groups, it is more likely that it qualifies the last named relationship. ἁγνεία** (4:12) has the general meaning "purity" but more specifically can have the meaning "chastity," i.e., purity in the sexual realm

(BAGD, LSJM), which would seem to be the nuance intended here. Paul, with perceptive realism, gives this special word of caution for the situation where a male minister is called on to deal personally and privately with younger women (cf. 1 Thes. 4:3ff.; Mt. 5:28ff.). To heighten this concern he adds the word "all" (πάσῃ, rendered with ἁγνείᾳ, "absolute purity," by *NIV*).

Extrabiblical documents that give advice on how to relate to various groups have been referred to above (cf. MM s.v. πρεσβύτερος; Dibelius-Conzelmann). Two important differences mark Paul's words here in comparison with such documents: First is Paul's command that Timothy "appeal to" or "exhort" the various groups, especially the older members. The other documents are concerned only with the honor to be given and the proper relationship of younger to older, and do not even consider the question of instruction by one who is younger. The keynote of this passage is the responsibility and authority of a minister of God to give such instruction, albeit to give it with respect, and this makes it different from those accounts in its most central aspect. Secondly, the other documents speak of three categories, those older, peers, and those younger, whereas this passage speaks of only two categories, those older and those younger. The other documents say that younger men are to be treated as sons; in our passage they are to be treated as brothers. Here the Christian teaching of the brotherhood of believers is evident. The differences are more significant than the similarities.

CARE OF WIDOWS: 5:3-16

The Obligations of Descendants: 5:3-8

Paul sets the tone and direction for vv. 3-16 with the thematic statement in v. 3. "Honor" indicates that widows must be cared for (see below). "Who are widows indeed" indicates that discernment must be used in determining who needs care, and, as we shall see, who should provide the care. In the first subsection (vv. 3-8) Paul indicates that children and descendants, rather than the church, should provide for widows in their own family (v. 4). Then he describes who is truly a widow (v. 5) and who is not (v. 6). At the conclusion of this subsection he returns to the responsibility of the family to care for widows (vv. 7, 8).

5:3 With the second person singular imperative "honor" (τίμα), it might appear that Paul is continuing to instruct only Timothy, as he has in vv. 1 and 2. A closer examination reveals that he is instructing the church through Timothy. This inclusive note is sounded with the plural verbs in vv. 4 and 7 ("let them learn," "they may be above reproach"), with the repeated indefinite ("any") of vv. 4, 8, and 16, and finally with the explicit reference to the church in the summarizing words of v. 16b. Furthermore, the key terms that begin and end the section are plural ("widows," vv. 3, 16), which implies that others are in view. Paul may have been influenced by the second person singular imperative in the fifth commandment (LXX τίμα in Ex. 20:12 and Dt. 5:16, as here) and may have assumed that its application to all God's people would be as obvious here as it is in the Ten Commandments.

Paul's charge to "honor widows" (χήρας τίμα) echoes the repeated concern for widows found in the OT (Ex. 22:22, 23; Dt. 10:18; 14:29; 24:17-21; 26:12, 13; 27:19; Jb. 24:3, 21; 31:16; Pss. 68:5; 94:6; 146:9; Pr. 15:25; Is. 1:17, 23; Je. 7:6; 22:3; Zc. 7:10; Mal. 3:5), which is reflected elsewhere in the NT (especially Acts 6:1-6; Jas. 1:27). χήρα has as its basic meaning a "woman left without a husband" (see the excellent article by G. Stählin, *TDNT* IX, 440-65). Paul specifies that he is using the term with the properly attendant and necessary connotations when he adds "who are widows indeed" (τὰς ὄντως χήρας; the phrase appears in the NT only in vv. 3, 5, and 16). He will indicate what he means by the phrase in v. 5.

Paul's use of τιμάω here is surely influenced by its use in the fifth commandment. Moreover, the only other Pauline occurrence of the verb is a direct quotation of this commandment (Eph. 6:2), and use of the verb in the Synoptics most often reflects this commandment (6 of 10x: Mt. 15:4, 6; 19:19; Mk. 7:10; 10:19; Lk. 18:20). τιμάω means here not only "respect or revere" but "includes material provisions as well" (J. Schneider, *TDNT* VIII, 179; cf. also Jeremias). This is evidenced by several considerations: The duty to which children are called with reference to widows involves material provision, so that the church will not have to provide such aid (implied in v. 4, stated in v. 16). V. 16 encourages a woman to help any widows in her family so that the church will not be financially burdened and may help those without such help. The passage immediately following v. 16 uses the cognate noun (τιμή) for compensation (vv. 17, 18). Furthermore, the church already understood its responsibilities to widows in this way (Acts 6:1-6). Moreover, Jesus indicated that the injunction to honor parents included material help (cf. Mt. 15:5, 6).

τὰς ὄντως χήρας has been translated in various ways. "Who really are all alone" *(TEV)* is too restrictive (so Fee), "widows indeed" (*NASB;* cf. *RSV:* "real widows") is an accurate translation, and the paraphrase "widows who are such in the full sense" *(NEB)* catches the point. ὄντως is not being used to deny that others are widows in the normal sense of the word, but rather to signify those who qualify for the church's care. Paul will remind family members that they should care for their widows (vv. 4, 8, 16) so that the church can have the ability to care for ταῖς ὄντως χήραις (v. 16). His description in v. 5 will explain the phrase.

5:4 δέ implies some contrast and is best rendered "but." The contrast implied (stated in v. 16) is that descendants should take care of their own widows rather than the church. So this verse serves as an initial sorting out of responsibilities.

Paul states the matter in a first-class conditional sentence (εἰ . . . ἔχει) with an indefinite pronoun (τις) in the protasis and an imperative (μανθανέτωσαν) in the apodosis, so that in skeletal form it is a hortatory general principle: "if any widow has . . . let them. . . ." The condition on which the imperative is based is that a widow "has" (ἔχει) living descendants. Those descendants are designated by two plural terms, τέκνα and ἔκγονα. τέκνον, "child," is used here in the plural of immediate descendants of a parent. ἔκγονα** (a NT hapax), placed alongside τέκνα with disjunctive ἤ, in a general sense means "descendants" and more specifically "grandchildren" (Hesychius: τέκνα τέκνων). According to BAGD "the ancient versions understand it in the latter sense" here, and so do a number of the modern English translations. Although other descendants should not be excluded from Paul's statement of principle, grandchildren are primarily intended.

μανθανέτωσαν followed by the infinitives εὐσεβεῖν and ἀποδιδόναι indicates what should be done. Plural μανθανέτωσαν suggests that the plural objects of the protasis (τέκνα and ἔκγονα) have become the subjects of the apodosis (rather than χήρα, the singular subject of the protasis). Since the apodosis indicates that "parents" (προγόνοις) are the ones to whom a "repayment" (ἀμοιβάς) is to be given, the understanding that the τέκνα and ἔκγονα, not a widow, are the subjects becomes even more compelling. μανθάνω means generally "learn" and here has the nuance " 'appropriate to oneself' less through instruction than through experience or practice" (BAGD, 490; cf., e.g., Heb. 5:8; Phil. 4:11; and "let our people also learn to engage in good deeds," Tit. 3:14). This exhortation is apparently given to overcome reluctance or indifference to the task and responsibility and to remind children that this duty is not to be turned over to the church or to someone or something else. The plural nouns (τέκνα and ἔκγονα) and the plural form of the verb (μανθανέτωσαν) encompass all the children (descendants) in this responsibility. The priority of this matter, "let them first learn to practice piety in regard to their own family," is made clear by the word "first" (πρῶτον).

That which they are to learn to do is εὐσεβεῖν** (Acts 17:23), i.e., to be "reverent" or "respectful" (BAGD), to "live or act piously" (LSJM). Since true piety encompasses all of life, it will also include that which God requires as duties in human relationships. Thus *RSV* rightly renders the term as "religious duty" (so also *TEV*), and *NEB* renders it, more paraphrastically, as "duty to show loyalty" to the family. The one to whom the piety, or religious duty, is to be shown is τὸν ἴδιον οἶκον, "their own family." This construction, article plus ἴδιος plus οἶκος, is found in the NT also in 3:4, 5, 12, and in every case the meaning of οἶκος is "family" or "household" rather than "dwelling." ἴδιον is singular to agree with the noun it modifies, but refers back to the plural subject and is properly translated "their."

The phrase "and to make some return to their parents" is a further specification of that which the descendants need to learn to do (μανθανέτωσαν) and also of the piety (εὐσεβεῖν) they are to show. ἀμοιβάς** (a NT hapax; the plural here may be intensive but is common and may stand for the singular; see Lock, Spicq) means "return" or "recompense" and is used here in the sense of "repayment." ἀποδιδόναι means generally "give back," "restore," "return," and when, as here, it is used with dative of the person and accusative of the thing, it especially means "render what is due" (LSJM; so in most Pauline occurrences; cf. BAGD). The present infinitive signifies that they are "to keep on giving back" (Robertson). The combination of ἀμοιβὰς ἀποδιδόναι communicates forcefully the continued obligation "to repay what they owe" *(NEB)*. Repayment given to parents and grandparents is in a sense a returning of the care the children received from them. Those to whom repayment is to be made are τοῖς προγόνοις** (also in 2 Tim. 1:3), "parents, forefathers, ancestors" (BAGD; although often used of the deceased, it is used in Plato, *Leges* 11.931, as here, of the living). Since προγόνοις relates to the preceding τέκνα and ἔκγονα, the rendering "parents and grandparents" (by *NEB* and *TEV*) accurately conveys the meaning of the word in this context, which refers here primarily to a widowed mother or grandmother. "Parents" is an acceptable rendering if it is understood to include more than one generation.

Paul concludes this exhortation with the encouraging consideration that this is pleasing to God. γάρ signals that what follows is a reason that the preceding should be done. The reason is that "this" (τοῦτο, referring back to the apodosis) ἐστιν ἀπόδεκτον ἐνώπιον τοῦ θεοῦ (for a nearly parallel statement see 2:3). ἀπόδεκτον** (2:3) means "acceptable" and "pleasing" (see BAGD for two ways of accenting the word with possibly different meanings). The sense of the word here is that God welcomes this activity. Thus, although "acceptable" *(RSV, NASB)* is a valid rendering, the positive sense indicating how it is acceptable has rightly inclined the most recent English translations toward the nuance "pleasing" (*NIV:* "pleases"; *TEV, NEB* paraphrase with "approves"). ἐνώπιον (see 2:3) generally means "before," and often in the sense of "in the sight of," but here with the further nuance of "in the opinion or judgment of" (BAGD). The most basic motivation is that compliance pleases God.

5:5 Paul returns to the qualifying phrase that he has introduced but has not yet explained, "a widow indeed" (ἡ ὄντως χήρα), and describes such a person in this verse. καὶ μεμονωμένη, standing between the subject χήρα and the main verb, is in effect appositional to ἡ ὄντως χήρα and is the first and most basic description of such a person. μεμονωμένη** (perfect passive participle of μονόω, a NT hapax but a common classical verb) means "left alone" and describes a woman's plight as not only bereft of her husband but also without children to care for her. Implied in the particle δέ is a contrast between ἡ ὄντως χήρα in this verse and the widow in v. 4 who has children to care for her. Thus ἡ ὄντως χήρα, for whom the church should care, is one without a family to care for her.

She "has fixed her hope on God" (ἤλπικαν ἐπὶ θεόν). ἐλπίζω means generally "hope" and "embraces at once the three elements of the expectation of the future, trust, and the patience of waiting" (R. Bultmann, *TDNT* II, 531). ἐπί indicates the one on whom the hope is placed, i.e., "God." Placing one's hope on God is a hallmark of the believer; that the one praying has done so is a repeated refrain in the Psalms (see Hatch-Redpath, *Concordance,* I, 453f.). The perfect tense here indicates a past action with a continuing significance, i.e., such a woman has patiently trusted God, and still does, for her present life and for the future. She is trusting God for the special care he has promised to the widow ("The Lord . . . supports the fatherless and the widow," Ps. 146:9; cf. Dt. 10:18; Ps. 68:5). 1 Tim. 6:17 states, using our phrase of fixing hope on God, that God "richly supplies us with all things to enjoy." God meets the widow's needs through the care his people provide for her.

Her hope is expressed in her continuing (προσμένει, present tense) in prayers to God both day and night. προσμένει (see 1:3) means here "to remain" in the sense of "stay with" and denotes the constancy of her prayers. Paul has used the same two terms to describe the prayer life of the church (2:1). προσευχαῖς is the more general word for prayer, and δεήσεσιν, "entreaties," denotes more specific supplication. "Night and day" describes when the widow is involved in prayers. Paul always writes "night and day" (νυκτὸς καὶ ἡμέρας, 1 Thes. 2:9; 3:10; 2 Thes. 3:8; 2 Tim. 1:3), never "day and night," possibly because he started work before dawn and therefore began his prayers before dawn (2 Tim. 1:3; 1 Thes. 3:10; so Ramsay, *Church,* 85). The word order may simply be, however, the favored idiom of the writer. (Cf. the description of the widow here with that of Anna in Lk. 2:36-38.)

5:6 In contrast (δέ) with the "widow indeed" (ὄντως χήρα), another widow is described. Two things are said about her: (a) what she lives for, and (b) what her spiritual condition is. σπαταλάω** (also in Jas. 5:5 [see Hort's special note ad loc. in his *James*]; in the LXX see Ezk. 16:49; Sir. 21:15) means "give oneself to pleasure, live for pleasure," "live luxuriously or voluptuously," "live in indulgence." The specifics of this hedonistic and sinful life-style are not named. Whether it involved sexual sin cannot be said for certain, though this would be a temptation for a widow and a way to provide for financial needs. The contrast with the godly widow is striking: The godly widow trusts in God and seeks first his kingdom; this widow lives only for herself. Although this widow would likely think that she is really "living it up" and that the godly widow's life is really "dead," Paul's verdict is just the opposite. While being physically alive (ζῶσα; cf. 2 Tim. 4:1), she is as a matter of fact already spiritually dead (τέθνηκεν, perfect tense: "have died, be dead"; cf. Mk. 4:19; Mt. 13:22). The implication is that the self-indulgent widow is not a "widow indeed" (ὄντως χήρα), one who should be honored and cared for by the church.

5:7 Vv. 7 and 8 conclude this subsection by returning to the children and grandchildren of v. 4. Timothy is charged to prescribe all that Paul has just written, but in particular the responsibility of children and grandchildren to care for their parents (cf. Parry, Ridderbos, and White). This view of v. 7 is not shared by all. Fee, for example, takes the verse as referring to the widows. Considerations that must be taken into account are that those in view are referred to in the plural (ἵνα ἀνεπίλημπτοι) and that, by implication, they are referred to as presently active and responsible agents. The only explicit plural subjects in the preceding verses are the "children or grandchildren" (τέκνα ἢ ἔκγονα) who are exhorted to learn (μανθανέτωσαν) to practice piety by caring for their parents. Widows have not been addressed but only described, and in both cases (vv. 5 and 6) in the singular (ἡ ὄντως χήρα, ἡ σπαταλῶσα). Further, what is said about the true widow is less likely to be so explicitly prescribed (παράγγελλε) as are the duties and obligations of children.

That v. 8 focuses on the "children or grandchildren" mentioned in v. 4, flows out of v. 7, and shows how terrible a failure it is to neglect caring for one's own is also indicated by the appearance in vv. 4 and 8 of similar terms (τὸν ἴδιον οἶκον; τῶν ἰδίων καὶ μάλιστα οἰκείων) and of the specific concern for caring for one's family. Finally, it would seem that Paul is for the moment concluding his discussion (vv. 4ff.) of the family's responsibility for widows with vv. 7 and 8 before returning to the responsibilities of the church as a whole, which he actually began in v. 3. Thus vv. 7 and 8 understood together as a reference to the "children or grandchildren" give the most likely, and the most satisfactory, conclusion to this subsection.

If this is correct, then ταῦτα in v. 7 refers to the prescriptions of v. 4. The words ταῦτα παράγγελλε, "prescribe these things," were used by Paul before (see 4:11) to enjoin Timothy to "command" compliance with what is taught there. Here he does the same thing, and reminds Timothy of this previous requirement by adding the word καί in the sense of "also" (cf. Kelly). The reason for such exhortation is "so that they may be above reproach" (ἀνεπίλημπτοι**; see 3:2). Children and grandchildren are blameworthy if they do not care for their parents.

5:8 Here Paul expresses the terrible implications of not caring for one's own: It amounts to a denial of Christianity and an action and attitude worse than that of an unbeliever. δέ joins this verse to the preceding either as "a simple connective . . . without contrast" so that "it cannot be translated at all" (BAGD; so *RSV* and *NIV*) or as a contrast rendered with the word "but" *(NASB, NEB, TEV)*. If the latter, then the contrast is between being irreproachable by caring for one's own, or being a faith-denier and worse than an unbeliever by not caring for one's own. The εἰ δέ τις construction states the matter as a general principle both by its conditionality (εἰ) and by its indefiniteness (τις, "anyone"; see vv. 4, 16). So from beginning (v. 4) to end (v. 16), as well as here in the middle (v. 8), Paul is setting forth principles for the care of widows.

The sin is that anyone does "not provide" (οὐ προνοεῖ) for one's relatives and one's family. τῶν ἰδίων καὶ μάλιστα οἰκείων is Paul's way of delineating those who should be cared for (τῶν ἰδίων, οἰκείων), together with a note of special responsibility (καὶ μάλιστα) for the latter. ἴδιος in the plural as an articular substantive (elsewhere in the NT at Jn. 1:11; 13:1; Acts 4:23; 14:23) denotes those who are "one's own" and here especially one's "relatives" (see BAGD s.v.). Contrasted with οἰκείων by means of the emphasis provided by καὶ μάλιστα, τῶν ἰδίων refers to the larger family relationship and corresponds to the reference to "grandchildren" (ἔκγονα) in v. 4. Similarly, plural οἰκείων** (Gal. 6:10; Eph. 2:19; 1 Tim. 5:8) has the meaning here "members of the household" in the sense of "his immediate family" (*NIV;* cf. "his own family" in *RSV,* "his own household" in *NEB*). The καὶ μάλιστα** combination (Acts 25:26; cf. μάλιστα δέ in Gal. 6:10; Phil. 4:22; 2 Pet. 2:10) has the meaning here "and especially," highlighting within the larger family relationship the special responsibility to one's immediate family (cf. v. 4).

The apodosis states a twofold consequence. The first is that such failure to care indicates that that one "has denied the faith" (τὴν πίστιν ἤρνηται; note the perfect tense with its implications). ἀρνέομαι (Pl.* 6x, all in the PE*; see Riesenfeld, "ἀρνεῖσθαι") means here "deny," i.e., "repudiate" or "disown," in the sense of apostasy from the Christian faith. Denial is demonstrated by culpable failure. That which is denied is "the faith" (τὴν πίστιν), here referring to Christianity as that which one professes to believe (on this objectivizing of πίστις see on 3:9 above).

Paul joins (καί) to this appraisal the evaluation that such a person "is worse than an unbeliever" (ἔστιν ἀπίστου χείρων). χείρων, "worse," is a comparative of κακός used with the genitive of comparison ἀπίστου. ἄπιστος means generally "unbelieving" (or "faithless"). Here, correlated with τὴν πίστιν, i.e., the Christian "faith," an ἄπιστος is a "non-Christian" (the significance in all the Pauline occurrences). Such a person is "worse than an unbeliever" because Paul regards unbelievers as having "the word of the law written on their hearts," and therefore even unbelievers are known to "do instinctively the things of the Law" (Rom. 2:14, 15; cf. also 1 Cor. 5:1). Thus for a professed believer who has God's law ("honor your father and your mother") to fail to do what even many unbelievers instinctively do warrants the verdict that he is "worse than an unbeliever."

With these verses of admonition (v. 7) and warning (v. 8), Paul closes off this subsection (vv. 4-8) stressing the responsibility of children to care for their parents. Now he can return to the more general admonition of v. 3 and indicate how the church may wisely apply it to older, godly widows who have no family to care for them (vv. 9-15).

Enrollment of Widows to Be Cared For by the Church; Younger Widows: 5:9-15

Paul next turns to the church and its responsibility to widows. Vv. 9 and 10 indicate how the church should care for older and godly widows, and vv. 11-15 indicate why younger widows should not be given this status and should rather be encouraged to consider remarrying.

The existence of a list of "enrolled" widows is implied by the passive imperative of καταλέγω (a NT hapax in v. 9), which has as one of its meanings "select, enlist, enroll" (see BAGD and LSJM; *RSV,* "be enrolled"; *NASB* and *NIV,* "put on the list"; *NEB,* "put on the roll"). That this is a list of elderly widows without other means of support is clear from the context: The significance of the criterion of age — at least sixty years old — is borne out by its appearing first (v. 9), by the emphatic way in which it is stated (μὴ ἔλαττον), and by its reiteration (v. 11). Younger widows are counseled to marry again and avoid the difficulties that can arise for themselves, their families, and the church once they are on the list (vv. 11-15). Those on the list must also have manifested their godliness in a life of Christian service (vv. 9, 10; cf. v. 6) and must be lacking support by their children (v. 4; cf. v. 10). Paul also commands any female believer, apparently meaning any woman who is not married or does not remarry after being widowed, to assist widows in her family (v. 16a) and says that the efforts of families to care for their own widows will make it possible for the church to care for those widows who have no one to care for them (v. 16b).

Enrollment on the list involves a "pledge" (πίστιν) with reference to Christ that would be "set aside" if a widow on the list were to remarry (vv. 11, 12). The pledge is, therefore, to remain a widow and serve Christ in that capacity. The requirement of sexual fidelity while married (v. 9; cf. 3:2, 12) and of practical Christian service (indicated by specific examples in v. 10 and emphasized by the stress at the beginning and end of the verse on reputation for and devotion to "good works") might imply that the enrolled widow is to have a part in the church's ministry, though what tasks she is to carry out are not specified. Since such requirements are juxtaposed with tasks to be performed in 3:1-13, it is likely that the enrolled widow is to do some of the specific tasks named in v. 10 (caring for children, showing hospitality, assisting those in distress), as well as the general "every good work" mentioned there.

So a church may have a list of elderly and godly widows who have no one else to care for them and who commit themselves to serving Christ.

The church commits itself to assist these widows and in turn may ask them to perform certain tasks as need arises. Noting all the dimensions of this arrangement keeps one from drawing the false conclusion that the church does not help other widows who are either younger or who do not fully meet the requirements. But the passage does imply that the church enters into this permanent arrangement only with certain qualified widows and with mutually accepted commitments and possible responsibilities. Noting all the dimensions of the arrangement also guards against the erroneous conclusion that Paul is mandating a widows' organization in the church. The teaching of the passage is, rather, that the church only provides for widows when families do not. Thus, where every widow is provided for by her family there is no need for such a list. If, however, there needs to be a list, these are the requirements.

5:9 To be enrolled on the list a woman must already be a "widow" (χήρα). In accordance with vv. 3 and 4, she must be a "widow indeed" in having no family to care for her (cf. v. 16). She must also be "not less than sixty years old" (μὴ ἔλαττον ἐτῶν ἑξήκοντα γεγονυῖα). "Sixty was the recognized age in antiquity when one became an 'old' man or woman" (Kelly; for documentation see Spicq; Str-B III, 653) and would be the age at which remarriage becomes less likely as a general rule (cf. vv. 11, 12). Indeed, Paul makes this stipulation because he does not want to exclude or discourage remarriage as the normal, natural course that a widow might follow (vv. 11, 12; cf. v. 14).

Since a woman is already a widow when she is put on the list, the qualification "the wife of one man" must refer to her past life and conduct rather than to her present situation. The phrase ἑνὸς ἀνδρὸς γυνή appears only here in the NT (see above on the counterpart μιᾶς γυναικὸς ἄνδρα, 3:2, 12; also in Tit. 1:6). This phrase cannot be proscribing polyandry since women did not have more than one husband in that society at that time. Some (Bernard, Ellicott, Kelly) have maintained that it means that a woman must have been married only once and have appealed to both Jewish (Judith 16:22) and non-Jewish writings, as well as to tombstone inscriptions praising this as a virtue (see Kelly and Spicq and the illustrations in Wetstein). "Yet," as Lock says, "the permission to remarry (v. 14) points the other way; the writer would scarcely exclude from the official list a widow who on his advice had remarried and again became a widow." Therefore, Theodore of Mopsuestia's comment says it well: "If she has lived in chastity with her husband, no matter whether she has had only one, or whether she was married a second time" (II, 161). Thus the phrase demands a life of sexual and marital fidelity. *NIV* captures the meaning of the phrase with the words "has been faithful to her husband."

5:10 Such a woman must also be "well attested in good deeds" (BAGD). Some of these good deeds are specified, and the list is concluded by a final general reference to a woman having "devoted herself to every good deed."

ἐν ἔργοις καλοῖς μαρτυρουμένη, "having a reputation for good works," is followed in the remainder of the verse by εἰ clauses (εἰ with aorist active indicative for "simple" conditions that are assumed to be the case; BDF §371; Robertson, *Grammar,* 1004-27). These are connected grammatically to the main verb καταλεγέσθω (v. 9) and function as indications of what "good works," among others, are required of a woman to be enrolled. The last item, "if she has devoted herself to every good work," also suggests that the list is cumulative.

The first of these specific qualifications is the condition that "she has brought up children" (τεκνοτροφέω, a NT hapax), i.e., "care[d] for them physically and spiritually" (BAGD). Whether they were her own or orphans is not said. The other conditions that follow are oriented primarily, if not exclusively, to those outside the woman's family (e.g., "shown hospitality to strangers"), and the children mentioned here may well also be other than family members. ἐξενοδόχησαν** (a NT hapax) means "she has shown or given hospitality," which most likely includes hospitality to traveling Christians, particularly to those who come teaching and preaching (cf. the concern for hospitality in Mt. 10:40; 25:35; Rom. 12:13; 16:23; Heb. 13:2; 1 Pet. 4:9; 3 Jn. 5-8).

The next condition is that "she has washed the saints' feet" (εἰ ἁγίων πόδας ἔνιψεν). This requirement reminds one of Jesus' washing his disciples' feet (Jn. 13:5, 12, 14), thus doing what a gracious host was to do or have done (Lk. 7:44), and it indicates a woman's willingness to serve in a humble capacity in other ways (cf. 1 Sam. 25:41). Apparently Paul is not referring to something that had become part of the liturgy of the Lord's Supper, because then it would not serve as a unique qualification at all. Rather, he is referring to concrete deeds of care for weary and dusty travelers who are fellow Christians (ἁγίων, "saints," used as a substantive for Christians because they are regarded as holy in Christ and consecrated to God; see, e.g., the salutations of Paul's letters: Rom. 1:7; 1 Cor. 1:2; 2 Cor. 1:1; Eph. 1:1; Phil. 1:1; Col. 1:2; Phm. 5).

The last specific condition is that "she has assisted those in distress" (εἰ θλιβομένοις ἐπήρκεσεν). ἐπαρκέω** means "help" or "aid." Its usage in v. 16 (twice, the only other NT occurrences) indicates that the "aid" to be given is providing for the needs of others and caring for them (cf. v. 4), as in the provision of food and care for widows in Acts 6:1, 2. θλιβομένοις (present passive participle of θλίβω, "put under pressure, bring about distress," passive "be under pressure, be in distress") is best rendered here "those in distress" *(NEB).* Although this "distress" or affliction may well include persecution (as it does in Paul, e.g., 1 Thes. 3:4; 2 Thes. 1:6, 7), it would seem to be used in a more comprehensive sense here, as elsewhere in Paul (2 Cor. 4:8; 7:5, 6).

The concluding condition, "if she has devoted herself to every good work," indicates in general terms what must characterize the widow to be placed on the list and in effect indicates that the preceding were examples of those good works. Plural ἔργοις καλοῖς at the beginning of the verse is now replaced by singular παντὶ ἔργῳ ἀγαθῷ. παντί means "every," thus making this reference as broad and inclusive as the earlier one but also giving it a more intense and specific focus, i.e., "every good work," without exception. BAGD's suggestion (s.v. πᾶς 1aβ) is particularly apt for this phrase occurring in the final and summary position: "including everything belonging, in kind, to the class designated by the noun *every kind of*. . . ." ἐπακολουθέω is used here in the figurative sense of "follow after," i.e., "devote oneself to" (BAGD). The *NIV* captures this with its rendering "devoting herself to all kinds of good deeds."

The qualifications taken together depict one who is clearly past the time one usually remarries and past an age where she is likely to be able to care for herself, who is known for marital and sexual fidelity and purity, for good works, and especially for caring for children, for those in need of hospitality, for those in special need, and finally who devotes herself to not only these but to every kind of good work that God requires of his people. In short, the widow to be put on the list is an elderly, faithful, and godly Christian for whom the church should regularly and faithfully care and to whom the church could entrust, if the need arises, tasks she has already performed.

5:11-15 With v. 11 Paul commences a section (vv. 11-15) that specifies that younger widows should not be put on the list and that gives the reasons for this exclusion. The first reason (vv. 11, 12) is that if after being put on the list women remarry, they will in that way violate their pledge to Christ to serve him as widows and thus abandon a commitment to Christ. Secondly (v. 13), being cared for by the church might tempt women to become idle gossips and busybodies, and some might even fall into sexual temptation (the possible understanding of vv. 14b, 15). Paul therefore recommends, v. 14a, as a general rule, that younger widows remarry.

5:11 The strong disjunction between this section (vv. 11ff.) and the previous (vv. 9, 10) is indicated not only by δέ, but also by the contrasting contents. In vv. 9 and 10 elderly widows are to be put on the list (καταλεγέσθω). In vv. 11ff. "younger widows" are to be "refused" (παραιτοῦ) enrollment. Although who would be a "younger" widow (νεωτέρας, the comparative form of νέος) is implied by the age requirement of at least sixty (v. 9), the primary focus appears in v. 14 with the counsel to remarry and and bear children.

The clause comprising the remainder of v. 11 and v. 12 gives the first reason for this prohibition: When those who have been enrolled want to marry they thereby fall under the judgment of having broken their pledge of serving Christ as widows. The ὅταν ("when") clause indicates a very likely possibility that provides the condition on which the following clause, "they want to marry," depends. These two clauses then become the condition on which the judgment of v. 12 is based.

καταστρηνιάζω** (a biblical hapax) is a compound verb composed of στρηνιάζω and κατά, in the sense of "against," which requires that the object be genitive. The meaning of the uncompounded form expresses the strong impulse of sexual desire, which naturally makes such young widows "want to marry." This desire to marry means that they will need to set aside or annul the commitment they have made to serve Christ as widows. Thus Paul gives the main objection to enrolling younger widows in the very compact statement καταστρηνιάσωσιν τοῦ Χριστοῦ: "they feel the impulse of sexual desire that alienates from Christ" (see Rienecker-Rogers, *Linguistic Key,* ad loc.). This compacted statement is then unpacked in what follows.

5:12 Remarriage of enrolled widows has as its consequence that they incur judgment for breaking their first pledge. ἔχουσαι is used here in the sense of "having or including in itself, or bringing about or causing" something (see BAGD s.v. I.4) or "involving" something (see Thayer, *Lexicon* s.v.), and thus is properly rendered "incur." That which is incurred is κρίμα, "judgment," in the sense of "censure" (not in the sense of condemnation; cf. κρίνω in 1 Cor. 11:29, 31, 32, 34).

Such κρίμα occurs "because" (ὅτι as a causal conjunction) τὴν πρώτην πίστιν ἠθέτησαν. The phrase τὴν πρώτην πίστιν ("their first pledge," *RSV, NIV;* "their previous pledge," *NASB*) occurs only here in the NT. πίστις is used here in the specialized sense of "solemn promise" or "oath" (see BAGD s.v. 1b). πίστις with this meaning is used with the verb ἀθετέω, as here, in Polybius 11.29.3 and Diodorus Siculus 21.20, where, as here, the verb means "set aside" or "break."

Three options have been proposed for the meaning of this clause: The first is that the widow is breaking her pledge to her first husband. In obvious opposition to this is Paul's encouragement in v. 14 that a young widow remarry. Secondly, Fee suggests that remarriage amounts to abandoning Christ because, it is assumed, it is marriage to a nonbeliever. So the pledge she breaks is her faith in Christ. Although this view has the advantage of taking πίστις in a sense used elsewhere in the PE, it has the disadvantages of introducing a reference to a nonbelieving husband into the text and of missing the inherent contrast in the text itself. Vv. 11 and 12 indicate that remarriage itself for any "enrolled" younger widows carries with it an inherent turning from Christ and an inherent "judgment." But v. 14 makes it clear that remarriage *before* being "enrolled" does not carry that inherent judgment. The difference is that younger widows, by being "enrolled," have taken a "pledge" that they would "break" by marrying, and thus would "incur judgment."

The danger of this broken "pledge" is Paul's first reason for insisting that the church "refuse" (παραιτοῦ) younger widows. Thus the third view says that the "pledge" must therefore be related to their being enrolled as widows to be supported by Christ's church and must be a "pledge" to serve Christ as an "enrolled widow."

5:13 Paul's second and concomitant reason for refusing enrollment to younger widows is introduced with "and at the same time also" (ἅμα δὲ καί; BAGD s.v. ἅμα 1a indicates that the word is used as an adverb "denoting the coincidence of two actions in time"; Phm. 22 is the only other Pauline occurrence of the three words together). This reason is that they may become "idle" (ἀργαί) and, even more than idlers, "gossips and busybodies" (φλύαροι καὶ περίεργοι), saying things they ought not say.

"They learn through experience" (μανθάνουσιν, see v. 4) to be (εἶναι understood, see BDF §146.2; BAGD s.v. μανθάνω 4) "idle" (ἀργαί; Kelly suggests that the inferred infinitive is not necessary and suggests the idiom "they qualify as such and such" with a "touch of sarcasm implied"; so also Lock and Simpson). For Paul, to be "idle" or "lazy" ("inactive" in this sense) is inherently contrary to the Christian calling to serve God and is thus wrong (cf. 2 Thes. 3:6-12, where he refers to those not working as "busybodies," as here).

Paul says that such women "learn to be idle" περιερχόμεναι τὰς οἰκίας, literally, "going around the houses." One understanding of this clause is that they would be "misusing their opportunities in visitation" (Guthrie, similarly White). Another is that they are, as the *RSV* puts it, "gadding about from house to house" in the sense of wasting their time and that of others and even perhaps intruding (cf. Fee). Since φλύαροι καὶ περίεργοι are connected syntactically with μανθάνουσιν and περιερχόμεναι τὰς οἰκίας as much as ἀργαί is, the former understanding is most likely correct in that it provides not only the occasion to "learn to be idle" but also, if not even more so, the occasion to learn to be "gossips and busybodies."

Paul continues with an "and not only . . . but also" (οὐ μόνον δὲ . . . ἀλλὰ καί) conjunctional combination, which adds to his concern that the women become idle a concern that they become φλύαροι καὶ περίεργοι. φλύαροι** (a biblical hapax; see Spicq, *Notes* II, 949) designates those who are "gossips," i.e., as Paul indicates further, those "saying things they ought not to" *(NIV)*. περίεργοι (see 2 Thes. 3:11: περιεργαζομένους, "busybodies") means here "busybodies," i.e., those who pay attention to things that do not concern them (see BAGD) and who busy themselves about the concerns of others. Possibly Paul is using a wordplay here between ἀργαί and περίεργοι, as possibly also in 2 Thes. 3:11 (μηδὲν ἐργαζομένους ἀλλὰ περιεργαζομένους). "λαλοῦσαι τὰ μὴ δέοντα expresses the positively mischievous activity of the φλύαροι, as περίεργοι" (White). τὰ δέοντα (the neuter plural participle of the impersonal verb δεῖ; according to Abbott-Smith, *Lexicon,* s.v. τὰ μὴ δέοντα

= ἃ οὐ δεῖ) indicates the things that ought to be. With the negative μή and the participle λαλοῦσαι, the phrase indicates things that ought not be said.

5:14 Paul encourages young widows to marry, enter fully into family life, and thus eliminate the aforementioned occasions for temptation and criticism (the inferential οὖν links this consequent command, or exhortation, to the preceding). He uses the verb βούλομαι ("I want" in *NASB,* "would have" in *RSV,* "my wish" in *NEB,* "I counsel" in *NIV*) to express his apostolic direction. The direct personal involvement signified in first person singular βούλομαι is not unusual for Paul (this form in Phil. 1:12; 1 Tim. 2:8; Tit. 3:8; imperfect in 2 Cor. 1:15; Phm. 13; nominative singular participle in 2 Cor. 1:17). Paul directs this counsel to the νεωτέρας, used here without χήρας, which appears in v. 11, but with it still understood: "the younger (widows)." The counsel is "to marry" (γαμεῖν, Pl.* 12x, 9x in 1 Corinthians 7, 3x in 1 Timothy: 4:3; 5:11, 14).

It might appear that Paul is contradicting 1 Corinthians, where singleness is commended (7:7, 8, 28, 32-35), specifically even for widows (vv. 39, 40). Although Paul thus desired that others serve the Lord with the undivided attention of single persons, he recognized that whether God has given one the gift of singleness or the gift of marriage is decisive (1 Cor. 7:7). At the conclusion of 1 Corinthians 7 he is still expressing his own "opinion" (v. 40), which he has earlier expressed as a "wish" (v. 7), which he knew would not be right for all men and women. In 1 Cor. 7:39, 40, Paul expresses the judgment that a widow is "free to be married," but then expresses again his wish (see vv. 7, 8) that some be able to live unmarried, as he does, and serve the Lord in the happiness of undivided attention.

Now in 1 Timothy 5 the principle of acting in accordance with God's gift to the individual (cf. 1 Cor. 7:7) comes to expression as a general rule, without Paul's feeling the necessity to express the exception that he made in 1 Corinthians 7. Thus both passages express the same principle. The application in 1 Timothy 5 of Paul's own principle is that he now recognizes more clearly that being married before (i.e., being a widow) is, as a general rule, an indicator of how God has gifted one with reference to marriage and thus a reason to counsel remarriage (cf. already 1 Cor. 7:9). Paul may also be opposing the encouragement given by the culture to remain unmarried by its praise for the *"univira"* (see Lock and Fee at 1 Tim. 5:10).

The younger widow is not only counseled to remarry but also to "bear children" (τεκνογονεῖν,** a biblical hapax not found in Greek before this occurrence) and to "keep house" *(NASB)* or "manage their homes" (*NIV,* οἰκοδεσποτεῖν,** another biblical hapax not found earlier). The benefit of such a course of action is that it would "give the enemy no occasion for reproach" (μηδεμίαν ἀφορμὴν διδόναι τῷ ἀντικειμένῳ λοιδορίας χάριν). The infinitive διδόναι, "to give," is used in a parallel construction with the preceding infinitives, but in meaning it is dependent on them in the sense that, if the first three things are done (marry, bear children, and manage one's home, especially the first), then "no occasion for reproach" is left to be given. μηδεμίαν is used here as an adjective meaning "no." ἀφορμή means literally "the starting-point or base of operations for an expedition" and in our literature "occasion, pretext, opportunity for something" (BAGD). Paul does not want the widows' situation to provide such to "the one opposing," "the opponent, enemy" (BAGD s.v. ἀντίκειμαι). The singular participle may be generic, or it may refer to the devil. Paul uses the word elsewhere of humans and of the Antichrist. Here the context is not conclusive. Whatever the reference, the λοιδόρια** ("verbal abuse, reproach, reviling," BAGD; also in 1 Pet. 3:9) here would seem to be communicated by humans (cf. 4:1). Paul wants to remove the occasion "for" (χάριν, a preposition almost always appearing after the noun it governs) such "reproach."

5:15 Paul demonstrates the urgency of his concern by stating that some have "already" (ἤδη) turned aside to follow Satan. The ἤδη γάρ combination forcefully joins the temporal and the logical together and therefore gives greater urgency to Paul's warning. "Some" (τινες, indefinite plural) refers back to νεωτέρας in the preceding verse, the "younger widows," and is used here "of an indefinite quantity that is nevertheless not without importance" (BAGD). ἐκτρέπω is used in the NT and early Christian literature only as a passive with a middle sense of "turn, turn away" (BAGD). ὀπίσω is used here as an improper preposition with genitive, meaning "after." τοῦ Σατανᾶ (capitalized in *UBSGNT*, lower-case in *NA*[26]; NT 36x, Pl. 10x) means "the adversary" and is almost always in the NT used with the article, referring, as here, to "the Adversary in a very special sense, the enemy of God and all of those who belong to God, simply Satan" (BAGD). What is involved in this following after Satan is not stated, but its sinfulness is evident from the characterization itself.

5:16 Paul returns to the believer's responsibility for the widow in his or her family. Faithfulness to this responsibility will free the church to care for widows who have no one to care for them. The shorter reading, feminine πιστή, is better attested than the longer reading, which has both masculine and feminine, πιστὸς ἢ πιστή (Textus Receptus), and is to be preferred (see *TCGNT*). The female "believer" Paul thus refers to may be a young widow (or a single woman) who does not remarry and who has the means to care for another widow in her family. In this case, Paul would be encouraging such a woman to serve Christ in this way (cf. Tabitha/Dorcas and her provision for widows, Acts 9:36-42, especially v. 39). But it is also possible that Paul singles out the female "believer" here because the woman in a household would bear the main burden of caring for a widow. If this is the case, such a woman is particularly appealed to so that her husband and household may be enabled to do what God has called them to do. And it is possible that Paul particularly appeals to the female "believer" because of all these possible circumstances.

Paul's statement of encouragement is quite general, being a conditional clause introduced by εἰ followed by a τις that qualifies πιστή. πιστή, as noted above, is the feminine form of the adjective πιστός, which as a substantive, as here, means "a (Christian) believer." ἔχει, "has," is used here to indicate family relationship (see BAGD s.v. 2b, and the examples given there; cf. 1 Cor 7:2). χήρας, plural, might indicate that the woman appealed to has her mother and her mother-in-law, both widows needing care, or, following the previous reference to "children or grandchildren" (v. 4), the plural may refer just to her widowed mother and grandmother (and those of her husband, if she is married). ἐπαρκέω (see 5:10) means "help," "aid," or "assist."

The significance of this "support" (*NEB*) is signified by καὶ μὴ βαρείσθω ἡ ἐκκλησία. The verb βαρέομαι means here "be burdened" financially or by additional work and service that the church (ἡ ἐκκλησία) could utilize for others if family members would care for their own (ἵνα ταῖς ὄντως χήραις ἐπαρκέσῃ). This implies that the local church would, if necessary, care for widows not cared for by their own families. But the church should not assume the family's responsibility and be burdened with it, so that (ἵνα) it may care for and support (ἐπαρκέσῃ, see above) "those who are widows indeed" (ταῖς ὄντως χήραις), i.e., widows who have no family or children to care for them (see the use of ὄντως χήρας in vv. 3, 5, 16). Caring for widows in one's family is a double ministry: it not only meets their needs but also frees the church to care for widows who have no one to care for them.

Vv. 3-16 thus present Paul's directions concerning widows. The key statement (v. 3) is that true widows must be cared for (by the church, as explicitly stated in v. 16). But children and grandchildren must provide for their widowed mothers and grandmothers as the most basic act of piety, to gladly repay for care they received and because this pleases God (v. 4). Failure to do so amounts to denying the faith and makes one worse than an unbeliever (v. 8). The true widow has no one to care for her and looks to God alone, in worship and trust, for her needs (v. 5). The ungodly widow must not be supported in her sin (by implication, v. 6).

Widows whom the church should permanently commit itself to care for and support are only those over sixty (v. 9), i.e., those who are past the age of remarriage and of being able to support themselves. Since as widows under the church's care they may be called on to minister for the church, they must reflect the necessary godly characteristics, especially a history of service by good deeds (vv. 9, 10). Younger widows must not be enrolled as widows serving Christ in an unmarried estate, but should rather be encouraged to remarry and delight in marital joys and privileges (vv. 9 and 14). They should be refused entrance onto the list of widows under the church's care — with its pledge of singleness — because that pledge will bind them to a vow which they will perforce break (with dire consequences) when later they naturally want to remarry. Further, the service of young widows among the congregation is beset with inherent temptations which all can best avoid (vv. 14, 15).

In v. 16 Paul summarizes his teaching: Believers (here identified as female) should care for widows in their own families so that the church can be free to care for those widows who have no one to care for them. Thus both family and church between them will care for widows, the family its own, and the church those with no family.

COMPENSATION, DISCIPLINE, AND ORDINATION OF ELDERS: 5:17-25

Paul takes up another special group, elders. The connecting link is that elders too must be honored, and that honor, like that shown to widows, is shown by providing for them (vv. 17, 18). Other facets of their life must also be dealt with in an honorable way. Capricious and unfounded accusations must not be accepted as valid; rather there must be adequate witnesses for an accusation to be received (v. 19). However, when there is sin it must be publicly rebuked (v. 20). All these matters must be handled without prejudice or partiality before the presence of God, Christ, and the elect angels (v. 21). Paul further warns against haste in laying hands on individuals to put them into the office of elders (or to restore them after discipline and repentance). Such restraint will keep one from sharing in their sins as one responsible for their being in that position (v. 22). Paul interjects personal counsel for Timothy (v. 23) and then urges adequate time for a true evaluation of men before one lays hands on them (vv. 24-25).

5:17 Those to be honored are "elders" (πρεσβύτεροι, Pl. 5x, all in the PE: 5:1, 2, 17, 18; Tit. 1:5; in Acts of church officers: Acts 11:30; 14:23 [by Paul]; 15:2, 4, 6, 22, 23; 16:14; 20:17 [by Paul]; 21:18). Jeremias understands Paul to be referring to older men, as in 5:1, but it is more likely that he is referring to church officers because he refers to those who "rule well" and those who "labor in word and teaching." Moreover, Paul uses the same word to designate officers in Tit. 1:5, where the context has themes like those found here (appointing, Tit. 1:5; laying hands on, 1 Tim. 5:22; ability to exhort in sound doctrine, Tit. 1:9; laboring in word and teaching, 1 Tim. 5:17). In Acts Paul also refers to officers as πρεσβύτεροι (14:23; 20:17), and elsewhere in his letters, as here, he refers to church leaders as those who "rule," "lead," or "care for" (προΐστημι: 1 Thes. 5:12; Rom. 12:8). As in the preceding section Paul distinguishes "widows indeed" (ὄντως χήρας) from others who are widows in a broader sense of the word, so here with πρεσβύτεροι he speaks of a special class of "elders," church officers, as he does in Titus and Acts.

He speaks of the elders as καλῶς προεστῶτες. προΐστημι occurs only in Paul, and six out of his eight uses of the verb refer to officers and their activity in the church (Rom. 12:8; 1 Thes. 5:12; 1 Tim. 3:5; 5:17) or in their family (1 Tim. 3:4, 12), the latter serving as proof of their ability to lead the church (1 Tim. 3:4, 5). The participial form προεστῶτες is used here of one who has been placed before, or at the head of the church, and who has responsibility in that position both to "rule, lead, or direct" and to "be concerned for and care for" the church (for this dual understanding see the note above at 1 Tim. 3:4 and B. Reicke, *TDNT* VI, 701f.; contra MM; Greeven, "Propheten, Lehrer, Vorsteher," 32, n. 74). The perfect tense of the participle indicates that these men have been, and are now, so serving. Paul speaks specifically of those who do so "well" (καλῶς is used in the PE* exclusively as the measure of ministry, both in the family [3:4, 12] and in the church [3:13; 5:17]). As in the other occurrences, καλῶς connotes no pejorative comparison of others, but is simply the evaluation of one person's performance by itself.

As in Lk. 7:7 and Heb. 3:3, the meaning of ἀξιόω is "consider worthy, deserving," with the verb followed here and in Heb. 3:3 by the genitive specifying that which one is worthy of. Paul's choice of this verb may have been influenced by the saying of Jesus, ἄξιος ὁ ἐργάτης (Mt. 10:10; Lk. 10:7), which Paul quotes in v. 18. τιμή is used here in the same double sense as the related verb was in v. 3, i.e., "honor, reverence," but more particularly in the sense of "honorarium" or "compensation," as v. 18 makes evident with its reference to wages. διπλοῦς refers to this double sense of τιμή and has the meaning "double," i.e., "twofold," both "honor" and "honorarium."

The phrase beginning with μάλιστα gives a further delineation of these elders. The phrase may indicate a special subgroup of elders that is especially in view (μάλιστα taken as "especially"). But if Skeat is correct ("Especially the Parchments"), as I think he is, that μάλιστα can at times have the meaning "that is," then Paul is giving here a further description of those he has already mentioned. In this case οἱ καλῶς προεστῶτες πρεσβύτεροι are οἱ κοπιῶντες ἐν λόγῳ καὶ διδασκαλίᾳ.

κοπιάω, "work hard," "toil," is used by Paul more than by any other NT author (14x of 22x). He uses it of physical work (1 Cor. 4:12; Eph. 4:28; 2 Tim. 2:6 of the toil of the farmer), most often of his own mental and spiritual labors in the apostolic ministry (1 Cor. 15:10; Gal. 4:11; Phil. 2:16; Col. 1:29; 1 Tim. 4:10), and also of the work of others as spiritual leaders (1 Cor. 15:10; 16:10; 1 Thes. 5:12; 1 Tim. 4:10; here). With this verb he is self-consciously designating the work of these elders as a vigorous and laborious work.

They labor ἐν λόγῳ καὶ διδασκαλίᾳ. λόγος means generally "word," often in the sense of "speaking" (BAGD s.v. 1aα; cf. the nearest usage of the word and phrase, ἐν λόγῳ, 4:12). The anarthrous singular form with no modifier or contrasting term occurs only 6x in NT (PE 4x), with 2 Thes. 2:5 closest to the use here. The exact translation of λόγος depends on each context (cf. BAGD s.v. 1aβ). Here it is coupled with, but distinguished from, διδασκαλία, and most modern English translations have correctly rendered it here as "preaching" in the sense of exhortation and application. That which the preaching applies and which the hearers are exhorted to heed is "teaching" (διδασκαλία), i.e., that which is taught (cf. 4:6), although the activity of teaching could also be in view (4:13, 16).

οἱ κοπιῶντες ἐν λόγῳ καὶ διδασκαλίᾳ are most likely those Paul calls διδάσκαλοι elsewhere (1 Cor. 12:28, 29), a term that he also links with "pastors" as terms for distinguishable members of the same group (Eph. 4:11). It is likely, therefore, that here, too, he is speaking of a subgroup of the "overseers" that consists of those who are *especially* gifted by God to teach, as opposed to other overseers, who must all "be *able* to teach" (1 Tim. 3:2).

5:18 Paul appeals to a scriptural principle to undergird the imperative in v. 17. "For" (γάρ) links the imperative and the principle. The principle is true because God's authoritative writing speaks on the subject (λέγει γὰρ ἡ γραφή). γραφή (Pl. 14x, PE* 2x, also in 2 Tim. 3:16) means in general "writing" but is used "in the NT exclusively with a sacred meaning, of Holy Scriptures" (BAGD s.v. 2; see also G. Schrenk, *TDNT* I, 749-61). The clause λέγει (ἡ) γραφή or (ἡ) γραφὴ λέγει occurs almost exclusively in Paul (NT 8x; Pl.* 6x: Rom. 4:3; 9:17; 10:11; 11:2; Gal. 4:30; here). Since Paul regards ἡ γραφή as holy scripture, i.e., as God directly speaking, he uses the present tense, λέγει, to indicate the present and immediate relevance of the scriptural principle (see Warfield, *Inspiration and Authority,* 299-348).

Paul immediately quotes the principle. The first statement, Βοῦν ἀλοῶντα οὐ φιμώσεις, is found in Dt. 25:4 (LXX οὐ φιμώσεις βοῦν ἀλοῶντα) and is also quoted in 1 Cor. 9:9. "You shall not muzzle the ox while he is threshing" has a self-evident implication, i.e., the "ox" may acquire sustenance from its labors (ἀλοάω,** also in 1 Cor. 9:9, 10, "to thresh," i.e., by trampling over). "You shall not muzzle" (οὐ φιμώσεις) is a future indicative used imperatively as a prohibition. In 1 Cor. 9:10-11 Paul writes of this principle that "it was written" "for our sake" and applies it to humans (the plowman and the thresher) and then to the ministry: "If we sowed spiritual things in you, is it too much if we should reap material things from you?" What he says explicitly in this parallel passage we should understand as implied here.

The second statement, ἄξιος ὁ ἐργάτης τοῦ μισθοῦ αὐτοῦ, is identical (except for the omission of the connective γάρ) to Jesus' words in Lk. 10:7 (the parallel Mt. 10:10 reads τῆς τροφῆς for τοῦ μισθοῦ). Paul connects this statement to what precedes by a simple καί, which raises the question whether these words are, with those preceding, referred to by λέγει γὰρ ἡ γραφή and are thus regarded as a second citation of scripture (Fee says otherwise). NT writers do connect quotations of different portions of scripture with καί under similar introductory formulas (ὁ γὰρ θεὸς εἶπεν, Mt. 15:4; Μωϋσῆς γὰρ εἶπεν, Mk. 7:10; γέγραπται γὰρ ἐν βίβλῳ ψαλμῶν, Acts 1:20; πρὸς δὲ τὸν υἱόν [λέγει understood from v. 7], Heb. 1:8; διότι περιέχει ἐν γραφῇ, 1 Pet. 2:6). 2 Pet. 2:22 connects two proverbs with καί under a single introductory formula, "according to the true proverb," with the first from scripture and the second not. So the pattern would permit, even favor (and certainly not exclude), such a possibility here.

But the second quotation is not from the OT but is found in the Gospels as a saying of Jesus. Would Paul refer to this statement of Jesus as scripture? In his discussion of the same topic in 1 Cor. 9:6ff. Paul regards the teaching he sets forth to be that of Jesus (cf. v. 14; thus also Lock, Ridderbos). This would seem to exclude the idea (held by Calvin, Ellicott, and Huther) that Paul regarded ἄξιος κτλ. here as a quotation from a maxim used by Jesus rather than as Jesus' own formulation, and thus not as scripture. In 1 Cor. 9:14 Paul places this teaching on the same level of authority as the "ox" statement cited from "the law of Moses" (v. 9) and as the OT teaching about the rights of those who "perform sacred services" (v. 13). He emphasizes that authority by the introductory words and the content of the statement itself: "*So also* (οὕτως καί) the Lord directed those who proclaim the gospel to get their living from the gospel." Elsewhere in 1 Corinthians Jesus' teaching on marriage and divorce (7:10) and Jesus' institution of the Lord's Supper (10:23-25) are as authoritative for Paul as any word of OT scripture. Thus it would not be surprising that Paul refers here to Jesus' words under the rubric λέγει ἡ γραφή (see Ellis, *Paul's Use of the OT,* 36f.).

Furthermore, since ἄξιος κτλ. is evidently a quotation and is identical with Jesus' words in Lk. 10:7, the source of these words would seem to be Luke's Gospel. This raises questions about the dating of both the Gospel and this letter, i.e., whether Luke was written before 1 Timothy. Other solutions would be that Paul learned about this saying from Luke before the Gospel took final form, or that Paul knew of this saying through other means (so Barrett, Hanson; cf. Lk. 1:1-4 for both possibilities), and regarded the saying itself as scripture (so Guthrie, Lock, and Ridderbos). Since, however, γραφή usually refers to what is written and recognized as scripture and since the words quoted are found verbatim in Luke's Gospel, Paul's dependence on that Gospel is the only alternative that fits all the data (so Bouma, Hendriksen, Simpson, Spicq, who also refers to 2 Pet. 3:16). Uncertainties about dating should not automatically rule this conclusion out (so Bernard), since the necessary dates are both possible and plausible, even with 1 Timothy dated in the early 60s. But however Paul received the saying and however he regarded it, it is indeed the saying of Jesus reported in Lk. 10:7 (and Mt. 10:10).

ἄξιος is used in the saying in the sense of "worthy," i.e., "entitled" to wages. ἐργάτης means here "workman" or "laborer" (BAGD). Jesus uses the term consistently for agricultural workers, always with an application to the spiritual realm (e.g., Mt. 9:37, 38; 20:1, 2, 8; Lk. 10:2; in addition to Lk. 10:7 par. Mt. 10:10): He regards the worker in the kingdom as a real laborer who is thus worthy of his wages (τοῦ μισθοῦ αὐτοῦ). μισθός, "pay," "wages," is used in this saying by Jesus and Paul of payment for work done (cf. Mt. 20:8; Jas. 5:4). Jesus' saying states the justness of such wages, and has the effect of an ethical imperative (cf. 1 Cor. 9:11, which gives as a reason that beneficiaries of the labors should provide wages to ministers — a principle of fair reciprocity).

5:19 Paul turns to the subject of the fair handling of an accusation against an elder and of the elder who has sinned (vv. 19-21).

Because those in positions of leadership are subject to scrutiny, criticism, and rumors, Paul cautions Timothy not to "accept" or "acknowledge" as correct (BAGD s.v. παραδέχομαι) an "accusation/charge (κατηγορία) against (κατά) an elder unless" there are the requisite witnesses. ἐκτὸς εἰ μή** (a combination of ἐκτός and εἰ μή; 1 Cor. 14:5; 15:2) is a double (pleonastic) form of negation in postclassical Greek (BAGD s.v. ἐκτός) and means "unless" or "except."

That ἐπί means "on the basis of," i.e., "on the evidence of," rather than "before" in the sense of "in the presence of" seems most likely since this passage, like Mt. 18:16; 2 Cor. 13:1, which have the same use of ἐπί, reflects the OT teaching on the testimony given by witnesses (Dt. 19:15; cf. also Jn. 8:17; Dt. 17:6; Heb. 10:28). This understanding is shown to be correct for Mt. 18:16 and 2 Cor. 13:1 by the use of στόματος (in accordance with the Masoretic text and the LXX) after ἐπί. Even though στόματος is not used in 1 Tim. 5:19, the sense is the same as in Heb. 10:28, where ἐπί is also used without στόματος and where it is clear that it is the testimony of witnesses that is spoken of. δύο ἢ τριῶν μαρτύρων (δύο and/or τρεῖς with μάρτυς in the NT also in Mt. 18:16; 2 Cor. 13:1; Heb. 10:28) means, in essence, at least two witnesses. μάρτυς, "witness," is used here, therefore (as in the other texts based on Dt. 19:15), in the sense of one who bears testimony.

Paul is, therefore, reminding Timothy to follow the principle of Dt. 19:15 in church discipline. Jesus also applied this principle to church discipline in Mt. 18:16, where witnesses are said to be necessary "so that . . . every fact [literally "word"] may be confirmed," the witnesses being invited to sit with two people who are seeking to settle a personal or private sin (cf. Mt. 18:15 [variant reading]; Lk. 17:3, 4) that the witnesses did not themselves see. They become witnesses through this procedure. In effect, Paul is urging Timothy to follow this procedure found in Matthew 18 and the OT before the church accepts or acknowledges as correct an accusation against an elder. The process may consist of two or three witnesses bringing an accusation, but normally it would consist of two or three witnesses verifying an accusation that may come from only one individual before it is considered further.

5:20 Paul then indicates what should be done if an accusation is found to be true and the elder is, in fact, guilty of sin. Some (e.g., Hasler) have thought that vv. 20ff. leave the subject of elders and take up sin in general and the laying on of hands to restore penitent sinners. There is no indication, however, of such a radical break in thought, and the passage makes good, indeed better, sense when understood as still dealing with elders. Furthermore, nowhere else in the NT is laying on of hands clearly used in restoration of penitent sinners, though it is undoubtedly used with regard to appointment of elders (4:14; 2 Tim. 1:6).

Although the admonition concerning sin and public rebuke is not restricted to elders, since it is stated as a general principle, the context focuses on elders. The present active participle τοὺς ἁμαρτάνοντας is understood by some to denote continued or persistent sinning (cf. *NASB:* "those who continue in sin"; *RSV,* "those who persist in sin"). One implication would be that a person who is found to have sinned but is not at the moment engaged in the sin should not be dealt with as this verse indicates. Although the note of persistence may be intended by Paul, the more probable understanding is that the accusation is found to be true and the present tense is used to designate present *guilt* (*TEV* and *NEB:* "those who commit sins"). It is the committing of sin that is at issue.

Since the rebuke is to be public and is to be made on the basis of two or three witnesses, the implication is that either the sin is of a general or public nature, or, if personal and private, no repentance has been accomplished by the approach of two or three witnesses (cf. Mt. 18:15, 16). The implication of Mt. 18:15ff. is that a sinner is publicly rebuked ("tell it to the church," v. 17) only when the other steps have failed. Presumably, the same principles apply in this setting and are assumed rather than stated. What Paul is concerned for is that sin among the leadership not be shielded or hidden but be publicly rebuked. ἐλέγχω means here "rebuke," "reprove," or "correct" (BAGD) in the sense of "show someone his sin and summon him to repentance" (F. Büchsel, *TDNT* II, 474; cf. especially Mt. 18:15).

The reproof is to be made "before" (ἐνώπιον), in the sense of "in the presence of," "all." The question is: "all" of whom? Some commentators think that since the frame of reference is elders, "all" means "all the elders" (Bernard, Hendriksen, Lock, Ridderbos). This is certainly possible. But since the level at which the sin of the elder is being dealt with is that of two or three witnesses, the analogy with Mt. 18:15-18, particularly v. 17, "tell it to the church," would point to "all the church" as more likely (thus *TEV* and *NIV* render ἐνώπιον πάντων by "publicly"; cf. Bratcher, Calvin, Fee, Guthrie, Kelly).

The purpose of such public rebuke is ἵνα καὶ οἱ λοιποὶ φόβον ἔχωσιν. καί, "also," indicates that the disciplinary action was not only for the individual but "also" that it might have its result in οἱ λοιποί, "the others," or "the rest." It may well be that with the latter Paul has in mind just the other elders (so Bernard, Dibelius-Conzelmann, Hanson, Huther, Kelly, Lock, Ridderbos, and Robertson) rather than the whole congregation (so Brox and Wilson); but if a public rebuke would have that effect on the elders it would have the same effect on other believers, since the discipline would be no different for them than for the elders.

Paul wants that public rebuke to have the result that Christians φόβον ἔχωσιν, "may fear." ἔχω is used here in the sense of "have as one's own," i.e., so that they have φόβος as an appropriate inner characteristic in the face of sin and discipline (BAGD s.v. 2, especially 2eβ). φόβος is used here in the sense of "fear, alarm, fright" (BAGD s.v. 2aα) and is generally rendered with the word "fear" *(RSV, NEB),* though some versions paraphrase with "fearful" *(NASB),* "afraid" *(TEV),* or "warning" *(NIV).* But what are the believers to have fear about? Some answer that it is a fear "of sinning" (added by *NASB*). Certainly this is right as far as it goes, but the larger picture needs to be considered. The public rebuke brings about this fear. Thus the fear of receiving such a public rebuke is as much in view as the fear of sinning (cf. Calvin). Others are to be reminded by the public rebuke of the seriousness, shamefulness, and disciplinary consequences of sin. Since Paul is influenced by Deuteronomy's demand for two or three witnesses, it is likely that in this remark he is also influenced by Dt. 13:11, which indicates the result of an act of discipline: All (LXX πᾶς) Israel will be afraid (LXX φοβηθήσεται, the cognate to φόβος here) of the discipline and thus will withdraw from the sin. So likewise this passage.

5:21 The imperatives just given are solemnly enjoined on Timothy by this charge, which indicates how serious these matters are and how important it is that Timothy comply with them and do so with great justice. The "things" in view (ταῦτα), being plural, refer back to vv. 19 and 20 (see Bernard, Ellicott, who relates that the Greek expositors took it in this way, Fee, and Hendriksen), and not just to v. 20. Because of the seriousness of the charge, with its own implication of judgment, and because of the two key nouns (προκρίματος, πρόσκλισιν), which perhaps correspond to vv. 19 and 20 respectively, ταῦτα probably does not refer back to vv. 17 and 18, although this cannot be absolutely ruled out.

The charge is given by Paul (διαμαρτύρομαι, "I charge") before God, Christ, and "the elect angels" to Timothy (second person singular φυλάξῃς). διαμαρτύρομαι (used with ἐνώπιον τοῦ θεοῦ here; 2 Tim. 2:14; 4:1) has the sense here of "solemnly charge" *(NEB, NASB),* with the one giving the charge doing so as an apostle (cf. again 1:1 on Paul's sense of writing as an apostle; note the rather abrupt use of the first person singular verb).

Paul calls on the Father and the Son and on those who observe with them, the angels. ἐνώπιον τοῦ θεοῦ is used by Paul in this special sense in Gal. 1:20; 1 Tim. 5:21; 6:13; 2 Tim. 2:14; 4:1: "Before God" is a reminder that one is living and acting in the very presence of the God who gives life to all and before whom one is responsible (cf. 1 Tim. 6:13; 2 Tim. 2:14) and of the awesome reality that it is God who will be the Judge of one's actions (cf. 2 Tim. 4:1: "who is to judge . . ."). Paul correlates ἐνώπιον τοῦ θεοῦ κτλ. here with ἐνώπιον πάντων in the preceding verse: Not only must "all" the people of God see and be aware, God, Christ, and the angels see and are aware.

In 1 Tim. 6:13 and 2 Tim. 4:1, as here, "Christ Jesus" is joined to "God" in the ἐνώπιον construction: In 1 Tim. 6:13 we are reminded that Christ "testified the good confession before Pontius Pilate," and in 2 Tim. 4:1 that he "is to judge the living and the dead by his appearing and his kingdom." Thus Christ is appealed to both as one who did difficult things with great faithfulness and as the one who, on behalf of the Father, as part of his messianic rule at his appearing, will judge all humans and their deeds (cf. 2 Cor. 5:10; Jn. 5:22, 27; Acts 17:31). Since the appeal to Christ in 1 Tim. 5:21 is without such specification but uses the same phrase as these two passages, one, or both, of these perspectives may be the unstated assumption behind the usage here.

The combination of God, Christ, and the angels does not occur often in the NT (cf., e.g., Mt. 16:27; Mk. 8:38; Lk. 9:26; 2 Thes. 1:6, 7; Heb. 12:22-24) but adds to the solemnity of the charge. Angels (ἄγγελοι, PE* 2x: also in 3:16) designates here those good created spiritual beings who are God's messengers and who are associated in the scriptures with Christ's return and the work of judging (cf., e.g., Dn. 7:10; Mt. 13:39, 41, 42; 16:27; 24:31; 25:31; Mk. 8:38; Lk. 9:26; 2 Thes. 1:7; Heb. 12:22-24; Rev. 14:10, 14-20). "Elect" (ἐκλεκτῶν) is not used elsewhere in the Bible of angels (but cf. *Odes of Solomon* 4:8: "the elect archangels"), but here they are so designated to contrast them with the fallen angels (Jude 6; 2 Pet. 2:4) and to designate them as the chosen ministers of God who carry out his will (cf. Heb. 1:14) and who are "chosen to share in the judgment" (so Lock; cf. the verses listed above).

ἵνα is used in a subfinal sense (Robertson) to give the content of the charge and to serve as a substitute for an accusative with infinitive (cf. *NASB:* "I charge you to maintain"; *RSV, NIV:* "to keep"). Timothy is charged "to observe" or "to keep," or "to maintain" (possible meanings of φυλάσσω here; cf. Mt. 19:20; Lk. 18:21) ταῦτα, "these things," i.e., the requirements of vv. 19 and 20. He is to do so not only because he is observed and will be judged, but also because he is the representative of God and Christ as he does these things.

"These things" are to be done χωρὶς προκρίματος. χωρίς is used here with the meaning "without making use of something," "without expressing or practicing something" (BAGD s.v. 2bβ). προκρίματος** (a biblical hapax, but already known as a legal technical term in the second century BC; see

BAGD and MM) means "prejudgment" or "discrimination," i.e., preconceived judgment or prejudice. The phrase χωρὶς προκρίματος thus means without predetermination of either guilt or innocence, perhaps with reference to v. 19, or at least as a specific example where this principle must be applied. ποιῶν with μηδέν constitutes a universal negative, "doing nothing," indicating that no action should be done κατὰ πρόσκλισιν. κατά means here "because of," "as a result of," "on the basis of" (BAGD s.v. 5aδ). πρόσκλισις** (a biblical hapax) is used in the literature of the day in the unfavorable sense of "partiality." Paul indicates that leaning toward or favoring someone in discipline is always wrong.

In summary, the handling of accusations must be guided by the objective criteria of two or three witnesses, those who commit sin must receive a public rebuke, and all must be done without prejudgment or partiality.

5:22 Paul specifies measures to be taken to seek to prevent such a difficult disciplinary situation. An appropriate time span should be allowed (not "hastily") before laying hands on individuals to set them apart as elders, since this will go a long way toward eliminating the problem. Furthermore, such a precaution will also keep those who lay on hands from sharing responsibility for the sins of one they might otherwise have prematurely set apart.

The key word is ταχέως, which is used in its unfavorable sense, i.e., "too quickly," "too easily," or "hastily." That which should not be done "hastily" is χεῖρας ἐπιτίθει. ἐπιτίθεναι χεῖρας (or χεῖρα; the combination in the NT 19x; cf. ἐπίθεσις τῶν χειρῶν) is "to lay on hands" and is used with reference to several things in the NT. Since this section has been dealing with elders, it is natural to understand Paul to be using the concept here, as he has elsewhere, with reference to elders, i.e., for the public means by which they are set apart for the office of elder (so elsewhere in the PE: 4:14, which see; 2 Tim. 1:6). On "no one" (μηδενί) should hands be laid "hastily" to set him apart as an elder. Timothy, who with the other elders lays on hands (again 4:14), is commanded as the apostolic representative to see that the process of selecting an elder (cf. Acts 6:1-6) does not place himself (and the other elders) in a predicament.

Paul focuses on that consequence in the second part of the verse. μηδέ, "nor" or "and not," continues the preceding negation (μηδενί). κοινωνέω means generally "share," and here "participate," i.e., in sins (ἁμαρτίαις) in the sense of being responsible for them (see especially 2 Jn. 11; cf. Ezk. 3:18; 33:6, 8). By placing a person in an office that has as one of its qualifications that the person be "above reproach" (3:2), the one laying on hands will seem to be condoning the sins that that person commits (ἁμαρτίαις referring back to the ἁμαρτάνοντας of v. 20). The sins are those of others (ἀλλοτρίαις), but Timothy and the other elders will become responsible for those sins when they lay hands on too hastily.

The importance of this avoidance is emphasized in the concluding words: σεαυτὸν ἁγνὸν τήρει, "keep yourself pure," i.e., free from sin. The first accusative indicates who is to be kept (σεαυτόν), and the second the condition to be kept (ἁγνόν). ἁγνός means "pure" here in the moral sense, with the obvious implication of "free from sin" (cf. 2 Cor. 7:11; 1 Jn. 3:3; F. Hauck, *TDNT* I, 122).

5:23 This verse is a personal word to Timothy about his stomach and his frequent ailments that follows after the previous direct word to him (v. 22). It may have been prompted by Paul's knowledge that Timothy was drinking only water (the implication of the first part of v. 23), so that he might not become addicted to wine (3:3), as part of his attempt to keep himself pure (cf. Lk. 1:15; he might also have been influenced by the Nazirite vow of Nu. 6:1-4). Paul does not criticize his practice per se, but does encourage Timothy not to forego a little wine for medicinal purposes. Since Paul knows that his young colleague is certainly feeling the pressure and demands of the preceding verses, he pauses to express his concern for Timothy as a person and for his health.

μηκέτι means "no longer" or "not from now on" (BAGD). ὑδροποτέω** (a NT hapax) means "drink *only* water" (see LXX Dn. 1:12) and is thus to be distinguished from ὕδωρ πίνειν: Paul is not telling Timothy to stop drinking water altogether but rather to stop drinking water exclusively. In contrast (ἀλλά) to drinking only water, Timothy is urged οἴνῳ ὀλίγῳ χρῶ, with the reason given in the διά phrase. χράομαι means here "use" with the dative of that which is used. οἶνος (Pl.* 5x: Rom. 14:21; Eph. 5:18; 1 Tim. 3:8; here; Tit. 2:3), "wine," is "normally the fermented juice of the grape" (BAGD). ὀλίγος means "little" in terms of quantity. Paul carefully qualifies his recommendation of wine here by this word so that neither Timothy, nor any one, may misunderstand or misuse this statement (see Calvin); three of the other four Pauline occurrences of οἶνος (see above) have the same spirit of caution, and the fourth, Rom. 14:21, says that not drinking wine is better than causing one's fellow Christian to stumble.

Paul recommends that Timothy drink some wine "for the sake of" or perhaps "because of" (διά) his stomach (στόμαχος** is a biblical hapax [but see BAGD] that originally meant "throat," but soon extended its meaning to include "stomach" [see also LSJM, MM]) and his ἀσθενείας, "weaknesses," i.e., "illnesses" *(NIV)* or "ailments" *(RSV, NEB, NASB).* "Frequent (πυκνός) ailments" is very general, and Paul identifies neither Timothy's ailments nor what problem he had with his stomach (for discussion see Spicq, "1 Timothée 5:23").

5:24 Here and in the next verse Paul supplies the grounds for v. 22. Here he stipulates that although the sins of some people are so evident that one can make any early judgment about them and realize that they should not be ordained, with others sins only become evident after some time. Hence not laying hands on hastily will provide time for such sins to surface and eliminate the need for an accusation, two or three witnesses, and the public rebuke of an officer (and for sharing in the blame for putting such a one in office, v. 22).

τινῶν ἀνθρώπων, "of some men," placed first for emphasis, indicates an indefinite quantity. Although αἱ ἁμαρτίαι refers to any departure from God's standard of righteousness (see BAGD; G. Stählin, *TDNT* I, 295), it is undoubtedly used here with special reference to possible elders on whom Timothy might lay hands too hastily (ἁμαρτία occurs in 1 Timothy only in 5:22, 24 and ἁμαρτάνω only in 5:20, all of which are related). Some men's sins are "evident," i.e., "open" and "obvious" (πρόδηλοι; "the preposition [προ] does not appear to have so much a mere *temporal* as an *intensive* reference," Ellicott; similarly Parry). προάγω means here "go before" in the sense of "precede." The idea that some men's sins are so evident that they precede or go before them to "judgment" (κρίσις, Pl.* 2x: also in 2 Thes. 1:5) must refer to judgment by humans in order for it to be meaningful in this context (cf. Bengel, Huther; see Marshall, *Thessalonians,* 173).

Paul's real concern is with those whose sins are not so obvious, the existence of which warrants not being hasty in laying on hands (cf. 3:6, 7). These he speaks of as a contrary phenomenon with δὲ καί, "but also." Dative τισίν could be rendered "some," but the idiom for this second indefinite reference is "others"; the form of τινές is again placed at the beginning for emphasis. The plural verb ἐπακολουθοῦσιν, "they follow after," has as its understood subject αἱ ἁμαρτίαι. The import of this statement is that one must know some men for some time before their sins become evident, and since one wants to avoid unnecessary public rebuke and avoid participation in another's sins, it would be best not to be hasty with any man.

5:25 What is true of sins is "likewise also" (ὡσαύτως καί; for the evidence for the inclusion or omission of δέ between these words see *NA*[26]) true of "good deeds," τὰ ἔργα τὰ καλά, deeds in accordance with God's moral standard, the result of God's saving work in Jesus Christ (cf. Eph. 2:10). The parallelism with v. 24 implies that τινῶν ἀνθρώπων is to be understood after "good deeds." As with sins, so also with "good deeds," for some these "are" (the verb to be supplied) "evident" (πρόδηλα, see v. 24).

The last clause of v. 25 is open to two possible understandings based on how one understands ἄλλως** (a NT hapax), which means "otherwise" or "in another way." "Otherwise" might be related to the goodness of the deeds mentioned in the preceding clause, so that the things that "are" (the significance of ἔχοντα here, see BAGD s.v. II.2 and cf. Acts 7:1) "otherwise" are bad deeds or sins. Thus Paul would be reiterating and reinforcing what he said in the last part of v. 24. But it seems more likely that the contrast is to πρόδηλα, the "evident" quality of the good deeds. This would seem to be borne out by the words that follow, κρυβῆναι οὐ δύνανται, "they cannot be concealed," i.e., good deeds that are not immediately evident will become so, even though they are now otherwise (τὰ ἄλλως ἔχοντα). The parallelism with v. 24, suggested by ὡσαύτως, also speaks in favor of this understanding. If this understanding is correct, then vv. 24 and 25 are symmetrical and state the same truths, first about sin and then about good deeds. Thus delay in laying on hands can also, positively, make possible discovery of men whose worthiness is not readily apparent.

INSTRUCTIONS FOR SLAVES: 6:1-2

Paul now turns to slaves as another group, as he regularly does when he deals with different groups of Christians (Eph. 6:5-9; Col. 3:22–4:1; Tit. 2:9, 10), and as Peter does, following a similar pattern (1 Pet. 2:18-20). Paul also has words about slavery in 1 Cor. 7:20-22 and Phm. 10-21, which are written from a different perspective than (here and in the passages just listed) when he addresses one by one different groups of Christians. When he follows that procedure he appeals to God's will for the existence and permanence of certain social relationships: For marriage he appeals to God's creation order (Eph. 5:31) and to the marital relationship that God has instituted (vv. 22, 23; cf. 1 Cor. 11:3, 8, 9); for parents and children he appeals to the fifth commandment (Eph. 6:1-3). But for slavery no appeal is made to God's will for its existence; in fact, Paul encourages slaves to leave that situation, when leaving is possible (1 Cor. 7:21, see K. H. Rengstorf, *TDNT* II, 272), and masters to free slaves (Phm. 10-21; on the different perspectives see Knight, *Role Relationship,* 9-15).

Paul, nevertheless, does give counsel to slaves because he is persuaded that one can live as a Christian and bring glory to God even in that difficult situation (1 Cor. 7:20-22). The counsel given in the PE is like that of the Prison letters, written earlier, in focusing on the attitude of a slave toward his master (Eph. 6:5, 7; Col. 3:22-23; 1 Tim. 6:1-2; Tit. 2:9-10; cf. 1 Pet. 2:18). But the PE do not repeat the Prison letters' emphasis on the intrinsic value of work and the counsel that work be done as if for God and Christ (Eph. 6:5-8; Col. 3:22-25; on work as ordained by God cf. 1 Thes. 4:22-23; 2 Thes. 3:6-13). The PE do emphasize the evangelistic and apologetic aspect of the Christian slave's conduct, i.e., that slaves must serve and work in such a way that "the name of God and our doctrine may not be spoken against" (1 Tim. 6:1) and so that "they may adorn the doctrine of God our Savior in every respect" (Tit. 2:10). Furthermore, 1 Tim. 6:2 introduces a new problem, that of slaves being tempted to be disrespectful to Christian masters, while the earlier letters focus on the intrinsic value of slaves' work with little, if any, regard to whether a slave's master is Christian or not. These differences are generally credited to the different situations of the letters and their stylistic differences. In the case of 1 Timothy, addressed to Ephesus, Paul may have thought it unnecessary to repeat his foundational remarks about the intrinsic value of work made in Ephesians.

At any rate, the decisive factor for both 1 Timothy and Titus is apparently that so many slaves who have become Christians have non-Christian masters. The ever-present concern to evangelize these masters and not to set their minds against Christianity must be taken into consideration by those Christians who are nearest to them and are the Christians seen by these non-Christians more than any other, i.e., the slaves themselves. This evangelistic concern had a counterpart in the growing awareness of some slaves that Christian masters are brothers — and a misuse of this awareness. Paul seeks to correct this misuse in the more settled Ephesian situation (1 Tim. 6:2), where this would have become a problem, but does not mention it in addressing recently evangelized Crete (Tit. 1:5; 2:9, 10). As so often, not every argument needs to be, or is, used in every situation, only that which best answers the particular needs (cf. 1 Pet. 2:18-20). The common element in all the exhortations to slaves in the NT (the Prison letters, the PE, and 1 Peter) is that they urge the same basic response of respectful and submissive service.

Another important difference between the Prison letters and the PE is that Christian masters are not addressed in the PE as they are in the Prison letters. This difference is not as striking as it might first appear: In the Prison letters far more instruction is given to slaves than to masters (a ratio of four verses to one in both Ephesians and Colossians). Paul may think that the Christian masters in Ephesus (i.e., in 1 Timothy) have heeded the instruction given in Ephesians and that it is not necessary to repeat it. If disrespect toward Christian masters has become a problem (1 Tim. 6:2), this implies that these masters are not threatening their slaves, which Eph. 6:9 warned against, but are acting like brothers, which is being taken advantage of.

6:1 Whether Paul is speaking in this verse about the slave-master relationship in general terms or exclusively or primarily in terms of non-Christian masters is not easily resolved. In favor of the more general understanding is the generally unspecific nature of the verse (ὅσοι) in describing the slave condition, the word ζυγός, which designates slavery in general, the request made of slaves (which would apply in any situation) that they regard their masters as worthy of all honor, and negatively the lack of a specific designation of the masters as unbelievers analogous to that found in v. 2, where Christian masters are spoken of. It could be added, in the light of these arguments, that the motivation given in the ἵνα clause could be regarded as indicating a general concern for non-Christians observing Christian slaves, whether their own or those of Christians, not just a concern for non-Christians observing their own Christian slaves.

But the ἵνα clause with its evangelistic and apologetic concern seems to be decisive, so that, as v. 2 addresses the situation of the slave of a Christian master, so v. 1 addresses exclusively or primarily the situation of the slave of a non-Christian master. ζυγός can, then, be seen as indicating an oppressive attitude that regards slaves as property, which might be the attitude of a non-Christian (but not Christian) master, ὅσοι can be regarded as used in that context for slaves in that situation, and a need would certainly exist to ask slaves in that kind of situation to still regard their masters as worthy of all honor. At any rate, the following discussion will be carried on in the light of this preliminary decision and the various exegetical details will be tested as to whether or not they fit with it.

The first major consideration is the phrase ὑπὸ ζυγόν, "under a (or "the," understood) yoke." ζυγός (Pl.* 2x: here and Gal. 5:1) is used in connection with slavery in extrabiblical literature (see BAGD for references) and in the LXX (e.g., Lv. 26:13; Is. 9:4; Ezk. 34:27; 1 Maccabees 8:18). It is also used in the political sphere for domestic tyranny (cf. 2 Ch. 10:4f.; Gn. 27:40) and for oppressive rule by alien nations (Dt. 28:48; Is. 9:4; 14:29; 47:6; 58:6; for further LXX references see G. Bertram, *TDNT* II, 897). The yoke is used in a sort of parallelism with tortures and torments for an evil servant in Sirach 30:35 (= 33:26/27). The correlation with slavery is stated explicitly elsewhere in a phrase such as "the yoke of slavery" (genitive δουλείας with ζυγός, e.g., Sophocles, *Ajax* 944). The term is also used to express severity and harshness, as certain LXX occurrences indicate.

Unfortunately, this usage does not automatically answer the question of the word's significance here. Some have suggested that it be rendered "yoke of slavery," but that is not the actual construction here, and even those who do make such a suggestion admit that such a rendering is a bit redundant.

The other possibility is that this phrase is added to specify which slaves are in view. Thus Paul speaks specifically of slaves who are "under a yoke," i.e., those regarded as little more than oxen. Although the evidence is not conclusive, the construction, and especially the context, incline one to this view. It is doubtful that a Christian master would regard his slave as "under a yoke," but a non-Christian might.

ὅσοι, a correlative pronoun meaning "as many as," indicates "those who belong to a particular class or group" (Rienecker-Rogers, *Linguistic Key,* 632), that group being δοῦλοι that are ὑπὸ ζυγόν. δοῦλος means "slave," i.e., one who is subject "to an alien will, to the will of his owner," and whose service "is not a matter of choice" but "which he has to perform whether he likes it or not" (K. H. Rengstorf, *TDNT* II, 261).

Such a situation might seem to justify for slaves the worst kind of attitude and the least amount of service. But Paul urges slaves "under a yoke" to "regard their own masters as worthy of all honor." δεσπότης, "master," "owner" (NT 10x, Pl.* 4x, all in PE), is used of masters of slaves in this verse and the next, in Tit. 2:9, and in 1 Pet. 2:18. It does not necessarily carry negative overtones, as can be seen by its application to God (all other NT occurrences, including 2 Tim. 2:21). But Paul may choose the stronger word here rather than κύριος because non-Christian masters are primarily in view, or he may use it simply because it is the technically appropriate term. And he may have used κύριος rather than δεσπότης in Ephesians and Colossians because there he wanted to remind both slaves and masters of their relation to and responsibility to "the Lord" (ὁ κύριος, cf. Eph. 6:7-9 and 5:20; Col. 3:22–4:1 and 3:17).

It is suggested by some (e.g., BAGD s.v. ἴδιος 2) that ἴδιος is used here without emphasis, "their" rather than "their own." But it may well be that Paul wants to emphasize that slaves are called to certain tasks and attitudes with respect to "their own" (ἰδίους), in distinction from other, masters (as wives are asked to submit to their *own* husbands in Eph. 5:22; Tit. 2:5; 1 Pet. 3:1 and as bishops and widows are asked to govern and care for one's *own* house in 1 Tim. 3:4, 5; 5:4).

Paul urges that slaves "regard" (ἡγέομαι, PE* 2x, see 1 Tim. 1:12) their masters "worthy" (ἀξίους) of "all honor." He is thus asking them to make a self-conscious evaluation analogous to that which he elsewhere asks Christians to make in regard to civil rulers: The ruler may not be personally "worthy" (nor the government be regarded as satisfactory), but he in his position is to be so regarded (Rom. 13:1-7; Tit. 3:1, 2; for 1 Pet. 2:13-17 note the connection in the context). Similarly, Paul is asking for an attitude, and attendant actions, that focus on the fact that masters are in authority in the sphere of work (even though one is in that sphere as a slave under a yoke), and thus it is appropriate to recognize that position as worthy of respect. Simultaneously, he may also be asking slaves to regard their masters as fellow human beings who as such are worthy of such service and respect (cf. the admonitions of Tit. 3:1, 2, especially "showing every consideration for all"). That which they are worthy of is τιμή, "honor" or "respect" expressed in appropriate action. The construction πάσης τιμῆς can indicate that the honor or respect shown should not be partial or grudging, and it can also indicate that the honor should extend to various duties and actions.

The motivation for showing this respect is presented in the ἵνα μή clause: "so that the name of God and our doctrine may not be spoken against." Paul appeals to slaves to conduct themselves appropriately under their difficult situation in order that God and his gospel may not be ill spoken of by non-Christian masters, who would do so if they thought that God and gospel made slaves less respectful and poorer workers. τὸ ὄνομα τοῦ θεοῦ, "the name of God," is that by which God makes himself known and by which people speak evil of him or blaspheme him (cf., e.g., Ex. 20:7). The phrase τὸ ὄνομα τοῦ θεοῦ is found 3x in the NT (Rom. 2:24; here; Rev. 16:9; cf. Rev. 3:12 with μου), all three with βλασφημέω (cf. also Rev. 13:6). τὸ ὄνομα τοῦ κυρίου is used elsewhere in the NT, and τὸ ὄνομα τοῦ θεοῦ may be used in these three places in part because in these three places it is non-Christians who blaspheme, and the general name (θεός), rather than the covenantal name (κύριος), is more likely to designate the one whom they blaspheme.

Joined here to τὸ ὄνομα τοῦ θεοῦ by καί as that which might be blasphemed is ἡ διδασκαλία (see 4:6; 6:3), used here in the sense of "that which is taught." Tit. 2:10, a parallel in situation and in content, uses διδασκαλία and describes the "teaching" as τὴν τοῦ σωτῆρος ἡμῶν θεοῦ, i.e., teaching about God as Savior, i.e., the gospel. Slaves must not let their attitude and actions be a cause for God and his gospel to be "spoken evil of" (the best understanding in this setting of the various nuances of βλασφημέω; cf. Tit. 2:5; 3:2).

6:2 This verse admonishes slaves with believing masters (οἱ πιστοὺς ἔχοντες δεσπότας) not to be disrespectful just because their masters are Christian brothers. It urges them rather to let that be an incentive for even better service. δέ need not be translated (so *RSV, NEB, NIV, TEV,* BAGD). οἱ ἔχοντες is used here to indicate a relationship, namely, "those who have" believers as masters, i.e., who are under a believing master's control (cf. Col. 4:1). πιστοί is used here in the sense of "believers," i.e., Christians, as elsewhere in the NT (2 Cor. 6:15; 1 Tim. 4:10; 5:16; Tit. 1:16) and is put first for emphasis. δεσπότης is used again, as in v. 1, as the technical term for the "master" of a slave. Slaves who have Christian masters are commanded μὴ καταφρονείτωσαν, "not to despise (them, understood)," "not to look down on (them)."

The clause ὅτι ἀδελφοί εἰσιν, "because they are brothers," "gives the reason the slaves might have for despising their masters; it is not the reason for the command not to despise" (Bratcher, *Translator's Guide,* ad loc.). *RSV* captures the sense well: "must not be disrespectful on the ground that they are brothers." ἀδελφοί, "brothers," is used to indicate the spiritual relationship Christians have to one another, through Jesus Christ, as members of the family of God (cf. Rom. 1:13; 8:29; 1 Thes. 1:4).

ἀλλά, "but," introduces a contrast to μὴ καταφρονείτωσαν, which *NIV* and *TEV* render "instead." μᾶλλον is used here in an intensive sense, "all the more" *(NASB),* "all the better" *(RSV, NEB),* "even better" *(NIV).* That which is intensified is the imperative δουλευέτωσαν, which means here "serve" or "obey," although possibly with its stronger and more literal sense, "perform the duties of a slave" (cf. Eph. 6:7).

A second ὅτι clause gives the grounds for this imperative, i.e., because they (the masters) are believers and beloved. "πιστοὶ καὶ ἀγαπητοί must be the predicate of the sentence, which determines that οἱ τῆς εὐεργεσίας ἀντιλαμβανόμενοι, the subject, must be a description of the *masters* who have already been called πιστούς at the beginning of the verse" (Bernard). Both halves of the verse follow the same pattern: imperative with slaves as subject, followed by ὅτι clause with masters as the subject.

In the first ὅτι clause the masters are called ἀδελφοί; here they are called πιστοί, which answers to ἀδελφοί (Bernard). ἀγαπητοί (Pl. 27x) means "beloved." Paul uses the word in Rom. 1:7 of those loved by God and because of that fact to be loved by other Christians (cf. 1 Thes. 2:8). The latter usage, though informed and influenced by the former, is the prevailing usage for Paul and is to be understood unless the text specifically indicates that it is speaking of one loved by God (see BAGD s.v. 2 for passages in which Paul calls Christians "beloved" or "dear friends"; see further 1 Cor. 10:14; 15:58; Phil. 2:12; 4:1). God's love for both slave and master has made them brothers and brought them to regard one another as "beloved." Thus just as Paul asks the master Philemon to regard the slave Onesimus as a "beloved (ἀγαπητός) brother" (Phm. 16), so here he reminds Christian slaves that their Christian masters are "beloved."

οἱ ἀντιλαμβανόμενοι is used here in the specialized sense, which best fits the context (especially τῆς εὐεργεσίας), of "those who take part in receiving" (Lock) or "those who benefit by" (BAGD s.v. 3; Field, *Notes,* 210) with εὐεργεσία as its object. The suggestion that the masters are said here to be "those who devote themselves to kindness" (BAGD s.v. 2), although more in line with the usual meaning of the verb, puts the phrase badly out of step with the direction of the passage and therefore should not be followed (contra Kidd, *Wealth and Beneficence,* 140-56). εὐεργεσία** (Acts 4:9) means here "good deed," "benefit," or "service," or "benefit of service" (BAGD). The first century associated this word with the actions of one in authority who was a benefactor toward one under him (see Spicq). By the use of this word Paul turns the service of a slave into an act of bestowing good on another, even his master. Paul has thereby made the difficult role of a slave the means by which the slave can benefit his master. The slave has been reminded thereby that in the spiritual realm he is an equal, one who can also give. The brotherhood among slave and master should not encourage slaves to disrespect but rather to generosity and graciousness.

Paul adds the admonition ταῦτα δίδασκε καὶ παρακάλει, "these things teach and exhort," which is similar to the admonition added at 4:11. These two admonitions indicate a pattern in the letter, coming between sections of instruction for the church (here 5:1 [or 5:3] through 6:2) and more direct instruction of Timothy (here 6:3ff.; note σύ in v. 11). Before he turns to this more personal and direct instruction, just as at 4:11, Paul urges Timothy to be sure to teach and exhort the previously given truths.

ταῦτα is thus used in a similar formula in 4:11, and it is also used similarly in Tit. 2:15 (cf. 3:8) and 2 Tim. 2:14. In all of these cases it appears to refer to what precedes and not to what follows, and the pattern holds here also, where it includes all the material from the last personal section ending at 4:16 or 5:2. For the significance of δίδασκε, "teach," see 4:11. παρακαλέω (see 1 Tim. 1:3; Tit. 2:6, 15) has a spectrum of meanings, which can be partially spanned by the general meaning "appeal to." Used here with δίδασκε, the sense is that of appealing to those who are also being taught to apply the teaching to their lives. Timothy is to "urge" *(RSV, NASB* mg., *NIV)* the teaching upon them and exhort them to respond (*NEB* and *NASB* text use "preach"). The meaning of the corresponding verb in 4:11, παράγγελλε, "direct, urge, insist on," helps to pinpoint which nuance of meaning the virtual synonym παρακαλέω has in the parallel here.

FINAL INDICTMENT OF FALSE TEACHERS AND WARNING AGAINST LOVE OF MONEY: 6:3-10

Paul returns to his concern about false teachers (1:3ff.) and gives a summary description of what constitutes false teaching (6:3) as well as an indictment of such teachers (vv. 4-5). Not only are their teachings erroneous (vv. 3-5a), they also think that "religion is a means of (financial) gain" (v. 5b). Over against this Paul asserts the gain of true religion accompanied by contentment (v. 6). One should be content with the essentials of food and covering (v. 8), when seen in the perspective of birth and death (v. 7). He also warns of the dire results of an insatiable desire for wealth (v. 9) and concludes that such a desire is the source of all sorts of evil and may cause one to wander from the faith (v. 10).

FINAL INDICTMENT OF FALSE TEACHERS: 6:3-5

The indictment is presented in the form of a conditional sentence in which the condition is regarded as true. The protasis (the condition) is v. 3. The apodosis begins in v. 4 and extends to the end of v. 5.

6:3 Paul returns to false teachers for the third time (1:3-11; 4:1-5). The statement made about them is presented as a general principle (εἴ τις). Thus the rendering "anyone" for τις is appropriate, but, as in l:3-11, specific false teachers are undoubtedly in mind with this generic singular (Paul moves to plural ἀνθρώπων in v. 5). With the conditional clause, "if anyone . . . ," Paul asserts what he regards to be true and thus means "*since* someone . . . (does not so assent)."

ἑτεροδιδασκαλέω** appears in the NT only here and in 1:3. Thus it signals that Paul is returning to consideration of the same group of false teachers. It indicates that they "teach a (completely) different doctrine," i.e., one different from the apostolic teaching and therefore to be regarded as false (as the context here and in 1:3ff. evidence).

Paul describes the error of the teaching in that its "otherness" inherently involves not agreeing with (καὶ μή . . .) "the sound words of the Lord Jesus Christ." προσέρχομαι (Pl.* 1x; for the variant reading προσέχεται see *NA*[26]; *TCGNT*) means generally "come or go to" and is used here in the special sense of "agree with, accede to" (with the more classical negative μή with εἰ and indicative, only here in NT, see BDF §428.1; Robertson, *Grammar,* 1011; for this meaning see 1 Clement 33:8; Simpson; cf. προσήλυτος, "proselyte," one who has come over).

That which the false teacher does not agree with is "sound words" (ὑγιαίνουσιν λόγοις; for ὑγιαίνω see 1:10; for its use with λόγοι see 2 Tim. 1:13 and cf. λόγος ὑγιής, Tit. 2:8), "sound" in the sense of "correct," i.e., true in contrast with that which is incorrect or false. The "words" are those of Jesus. Specific words of Jesus are known and transmitted by Paul (e.g., 1 Tim. 5:18; Acts 20:28; 1 Cor. 11:23ff.). Paul also uses this kind of language to refer more generally to the message from the Lord, i.e., the gospel (1 Thes. 1:8). In the other occurrence of ὑγιαίνοντες λόγοι (2 Tim. 1:13), Paul can speak of himself as the proximate source, namely, "which you have heard from me" (ὧν παρ' ἐμοῦ ἤκουσας). Therefore, here, where "sound words" are said to come from Jesus, they "emanate from the Lord, either directly, or through His apostles and teachers" (Ellicott; cf. Jn. 14:26; 16:12-15).

Paul refers to Jesus here with the rather full designation τοῦ κυρίου ἡμῶν Ἰησοῦ Χριστοῦ, i.e., as the Jesus whom Christians acknowledge as the Messiah and as their Lord. This full designation is used in 1 Timothy where the authority and power of Christ are particularly in view (1:1, 2, 12; 5:21; 6:3, 14). That note is being sounded here: False teachers are not assenting to the words that have come from the source of authority, "our Lord Jesus Christ."

Paul joins to the foregoing a further description of that to which the false teacher does not assent, namely, τῇ κατ' εὐσέβειαν διδασκαλίᾳ. This is not a description of something other than the preceding but is rather a description of it in terms of its content (for τῇ διδασκαλίᾳ see 1:10) and results (κατ' εὐσέβειαν). The words describe the truth of Christianity seen as a whole. It is a life-changing message and thus it "accords with godliness" (so *RSV,* κατ' εὐσέβειαν; see Tit. 1:1); it is that which "promot[es] ([is] designed for) godliness" (Robertson; see further *idem, Grammar,* 609; this view is more likely than BAGD s.v. κατά II.7, which takes the phrase as adjectival). εὐσέβεια (see 2:2; 3:16; 4:7, 8) means here "godliness" or "piety," i.e., the life of reverence before and obedience to God.

6:4-5 In the apodosis of this conditional sentence the main verb τετύφωται is qualified by two participles, ἐπιστάμενος and νοσῶν, with the second contrasted to the first. The content of the second ("having morbid interests or desires") is given in a prepositional phrase with περί and two nouns. A relative clause (ἐξ ὧν) lists five results of what is described in this second participial clause. The ultimate reason for all that precedes (from τετύφωται on) is given in two participles (διεφθαρμένων and ἀπεστερημένων, genitive to agree with ἀνθρώπων), each followed by a noun indicating where or in what way the participle applies. The sentence concludes with another participial clause (νομιζόντων . . .) that includes an infinitival phrase and conveys the false teachers' evaluation of εὐσέβεια.

The main verb gives Paul's main characterization of the false teacher, that such a person τετύφωται** (elsewhere only 3:6; 2 Tim 3:4 in the Bible, but also a contemporary term [see BAGD], used only figuratively and usually in the passive, especially the perfect passive indicating a permanent condition [so Spicq]). Since the meaning "is conceited" is contextually indicated in 3:6, since that meaning also fits well in 2 Tim. 3:4, since the ancient versions also understood it in that sense here (see BAGD), and since that meaning coincides with Paul's evaluation elsewhere (1 Cor. 8:1), it is likely that that meaning is intended here (rather than "is blinded" or "is foolish"). In 1 Cor. 8:1-2 the reason given for this evaluation is that the person spoken of thinks that by one's own intellect, one has the answer or knowledge. That perspective seems to be involved here, since the false teacher is said not to agree with Jesus' words (v. 3) and is said to "understand nothing" (μηδὲν ἐπιστάμενος, v. 4).

The false teacher is said to be νοσῶν** (the verb is a NT hapax) used here figuratively of having a "sick" or "unhealthy craving." This craving is "for" (περί) ζητήσεις καὶ λογομαχίας. ζήτησις** has among its meanings that of "investigation" (Acts 25:20) and "discussion, debate" (Jn. 3:25; Acts 15:27). It is doubtful that either of these positive meanings is intended here since the word is linked with the pejorative λογομαχίας and because ζήτησις elsewhere in the PE in similar settings is clearly demarcated as negative by the adjectives "foolish" (μωράς, Tit. 3:9; 2 Tim. 2:23) and "ignorant" (ἀπαιδεύτους, 2 Tim. 2:23). Thus the likely meaning here is "controversial questions" *(NASB)* or "controversies" (*RSV, NIV;* cf. ἐκζήτησις in 1:4). Their other sickly craving is λογομαχίας** (a NT hapax; cf. λογομαχέω, 2 Tim. 2:14), literally "word-battles," or "disputes about words," which *NEB* well renders as "verbal quibbles."

From what has been said in vv. 3-4 (ἐξ ὧν) five results "arise" (γίνεται). The first-named, φθόνος (generic singular) means "envy" or "jealousy," i.e., holding a grudge against another out of desire for something the other possesses (D. H. Field, *NIDNTT* I, 557; cf. L. T. Johnson, "James 3:13–4:10"). ἔρις (also generic singular) is "strife, discord, contention" (BAGD). In all but one of its NT occurrences ἔρις is joined with a word for envy (φθόνος or ζῆλος). βλασφημίαι (the first of three plurals) here means "abusive speech" (BAGD s.v. 1; H. W. Beyer, *TDNT* I, 621; *NASB; TEV* has "insults") or "slander" (BAGD; *RSV, NEB*). ὑπόνοιαι** (a NT hapax) are "suspicions" or "conjectures" and with πονηραί refers to "evil suspicions" (cf. Sir. 3:24). διαπαρατριβαί** (a "heightened form of παρατριβή 'irritation, friction'" [BAGD]; occurring only here in the NT and extrabiblical literature, while παρατριβή is found elsewhere) means "mutual or constant irritations or frictions" (there is debate as to whether δια- implies "mutual" or "thorough").

The first two of these terms (φθόνος and ἔρις) occur together 3x in Paul, twice in vice lists (Rom. 1:29; Gal. 5:20-21; not in a vice list: Phil. 1:15). The third, βλασφημίαι, occurs elsewhere in vice lists, indeed only in vice lists in Paul, but of the three occurrences (here and Eph. 4:31; Col. 3:8) only this list also contains the first two terms. The last two terms do not occur elsewhere in Paul (or the NT). If there is an intentional pattern to this list, it may be something close to an alteration between inward thoughts and attitudes (φθόνος, ὑπόνοιαι πονηραί) and outward expression in words and actions (ἔρις, βλασφημίαι, διαπαρατριβαί).

The reason that these people have such characteristics is identified in the first two of the three participial clauses modifying ἀνθρώπων. διεφθαρμένων is from διαφθείρω, which generally means "spoil" or "destroy," and here in the moral sense "ruin" or "corrupt." Its perfect tense emphasizes the settled condition of being "corrupt in mind." In 2 Cor. 4:4 Paul explicitly says that "the god of this world has blinded the minds of the unbelieving"; the passive here also has the devil in view. That which has been corrupted is ὁ νοῦς, "the mind," here used of one's " 'attitude, way of thinking' as the sum total of the whole mental and moral state of being" (BAGD s.v. 3a; J. Behm, *TDNT* IV, 948ff.: "inner orientation or moral attitude"; cf. Ridderbos, *Paul,* 117-19).

Paul joins (καί) to the preceding the participial clause ἀπεστερημένων τῆς ἀληθείας. ἀποστερέω means generally "steal" or "rob"; here the perfect passive means "deprived" or "robbed." ἀλήθεια (see 2:4; 3:15), "truth," is used here as elsewhere in the NT "esp. of the content of Christianity as the absolute truth" (BAGD s.v. 2b). As in the previous clause, the perfect tense emphasizes the settled condition and the passive voice indicates that another, "the god of this world," has brought about this condition.

In conclusion Paul returns to the attitude of the false teachers and what they seek to gain by their εὐσέβεια. Another genitive participial clause qualifies ἀνθρώπων and voices what these people "think." They think εὐσέβεια (see 2:2; 3:16; 4:7, 8; used here as in 2 Tim. 3:5a), "religion," is (a means of) "gain" (πορισμόν,** also in v. 6; cf. Wisdom 13:19; 14:2). Paul elsewhere warns against money being a controlling factor in a church leader's life (3:3, 8; Tit. 1:7) and denies that he ministers for such a reason (1 Thes. 2:5). When he speaks in Tit. 1:11 of false teachers teaching "for the sake of sordid gain" (cf. Jude 11), he provides his own commentary on this statement. ἀφίστασο ἀπὸ τῶν τοιούτων should not be considered part of the original text for the reasons given by B. M. Metzger, *Textual Commentary,* ad loc.

The indictment of the false teachers is thus multifaceted and comprehensive. It begins with their heterodoxy (v. 3), which is correlated with their conceit and lack of real understanding (v. 4a) and their sick interest in mere controversy (v. 4b), turns to the maliciousness of life that flows from these characteristics (v. 4c), roots all this in spiritual blindness (v. 5a), and ends with their materialistic motivation (v. 5b). It is given to warn the church against such people.

GODLINESS WITH CONTENTMENT IS GREAT GAIN: 6:6-8

Paul picks up on the word "gain" (πορισμός) in v. 5 and affirms that in the true sense εὐσέβεια is, in fact, πορισμὸς μέγας. This section relates the true perspective that εὐσέβεια gives to the material side of life. Birth and death provide the vantage points from which to appraise the material things of life (v. 7) and to determine what is really necessary (v. 8a). Paul concludes by calling for contentment with these necessary things (v. 8b).

6:6 ἡ εὐσέβεια (see v. 5), "religion," with its power (in the sense of 2 Tim. 3:5b), "is" indeed πορισμὸς μέγας in contrast to (δέ, "but") the misunderstanding of its "gain" on the part of the false teachers. Paul says this not of εὐσέβεια alone, but of εὐσέβεια μετὰ αὐταρκείας. αὐτάρκεια** (also in 2 Cor. 9:8) was the term for a favorite virtue of the Cynics and Stoics (BAGD) and meant for them "self-sufficiency." Fee says of the analogous context of Phil. 4:11, where the adjective αὐτάρκης is used: "There [Paul] 'turned the tables' on the Stoics by declaring that genuine *autarkeia* is not *self*-sufficiency but *Christ*-sufficiency." Christ develops in the Christian the contentment "which freely submits to and delights in God's wise and fatherly disposal in every condition" (Burroughs, *Rare Jewel,* 19). αὐτάρκεια is joined to εὐσέβεια by the preposition μετά, which is used here "to show a close connection betw[een] two nouns, upon the first of which the main emphasis lies" (BAGD s.v. A.II.6). Hence εὐσέβεια, true Christianity, provides the contentment that each individual must appropriate, as Paul says in Phil. 4:11, "I have learned to be content." When the source (εὐσέβεια) is combined with the inward result (αὐτάρκεια), then there is "great" (μέγας) gain. In 4:8 Paul identifies the "gain" or "profit" of εὐσέβεια as "all things," "life" now and future.

6:7 V. 7 indicates the basis (γάρ) for the wisdom of contentment by bringing forward our possessionless entrance into the world at birth, which in turn sets the stage for the affirmation that we do not take anything material out of this world either. εἰσφέρω is used here with its literal meaning, "bring in." That it is first person plural may reflect the proverbial character of the saying as a whole, which echoes the truth of Jb. 1:21 and Ec. 5:15 and which is also known and expressed as a commonplace in Jewish and Greco-Roman thought (see Kelly, Spicq). εἰς τὸν κόσμον, i.e., into the place of human existence, makes explicit what is implicit in the εἰς prefix of the verb.

Emphatic οὐδέν makes the point that "nothing" material is brought with any person. The implication is that all humans have satisfactorily begun life without bringing with them any material things.

Paul then goes on to the perspective that death and departure gives. The preferred reading ὅτι (for variants see *NA*[26]; see B. M. Metzger, *Textual Commentary,* ad loc. for the reasons for this preference) presents the reader with a difficulty in interpretation. Rendering it "because" would seem to imply that what happens at death gives the reason that our existence at birth is as it is, and this is not what Paul is saying. Others suggest that ὅτι introduces a quotation, but this, too, seems unlikely. Perhaps the struggle reflected in the textual variants and versions points to the correct solution after all. The variants are not correct, but they have correctly understood what Paul intended. "The most natural solution of the problem is, that there is an ellipsis of δῆλον, or that ὅτι is for δῆλον ὅτι," i.e., "it is clear that" (Field, *Notes,* ad loc., referring to 1 Jn. 3:20 as a possible example; Hendriksen refers to Jn. 6:46 as an elliptical use of ὅτι).

οὐδέ joins the clause of the second half of v. 7 to the similarly negative first half. The second clause could be rendered somewhat literally as follows: "it is clear that neither are we able to take anything out," with "the world" understood from the first clause. τι is used here as a substantive meaning "anything" and provides a corresponding absolute (negative when taken in conjunction with the οὐδέ) to οὐδέν: Nothing in, neither anything out. δυνάμεθα, meaning "can" or "am able," is used here with the infinitive ἐξενεγκεῖν, from ἐκφέρω, which is the antonym of εἰσφέρω in the preceding clause and means here "bring out" or "take out." Together they express what the negative οὐδέ and the τι indicate we are *unable* to do, i.e., take anything out (of this world). That this is expressed in first person plural, "we," indicates the universality of this truth and its proverbial nature, and at the same time specifically encompasses writer and readers. Like the first half of the verse, this clause seems to echo Jb. 1:21 and Ec. 5:15. The implied conclusion is that acquisition of things has no ultimate or final benefit, despite what the false teachers supposed (v. 5; cf. Lk. 12:20).

6:8 This verse is the counterbalance to v. 7 and thus begins with δέ ("but"). It indicates that we do need certain things while living in this world, but delineates them as essentials and necessities (cf. Mt. 6:32) and encourages contentment with them.

ἔχοντες, "having," indicates possession. The things needful for earthly life are διατροφὰς καὶ σκεπάσματα. Both plural and singular of διατροφή** (a NT hapax) are used in Greek writings in the sense here, i.e., "means of subsistence, food, or sustenance" (BAGD). σκεπάσματα** (also a NT hapax) means "'covering,' of anything that serves as a cover and hence as a protection. Chiefly 'clothing' . . . but also 'house'" (BAGD). Whether a particular nuance is intended here is difficult to say; the plural probably means that it is not restricted to one or the other. "Sustenance and coverings," taken together, designate the necessities of life (cf. Mt. 6:25ff. and a similar twofold designation in Gn. 28:20; Dt. 10:18).

τούτοις, "these things," refers back to the immediately preceding two nouns and is neuter to refer to them by sense. ἀρκέω means in the passive "be satisfied or content with something" (BAGD). The future tense might be rendered literally "we shall be content" but more likely is a Hebraism with the force of an imperative, i.e., "let us be content" or "we should be content" (so Kelly; Ridderbos; N. J. D. White; Robertson, *Grammar,* 889; Alford, who cites in illustration Mt. 5:48). At any rate Paul delineates here the basics needed for contentment and the level at which our expectations, and hence our contentment, should be pitched. Whatever exceeds these basics can be gratefully received and enjoyed (6:17; Phil. 4:12), but should never be conceived of as a necessity so that it can destroy true contentment when it is lacking. Paul's teaching here reflects that of Jesus (Mt. 6:24-34; Lk. 12:16-32; cf. also Heb. 13:5).

LOVE OF MONEY IS A ROOT OF ALL SORTS OF EVIL: 6:9-10

Paul continues his treatment of one's attitude toward material things, but, in contrast (δέ, "but") to vv. 6-8, he now speaks of "those who want to get rich" (οἱ δὲ βουλόμενοι πλουτεῖν) and indicates the perils that attend them. V. 9a describes these perils in a verb with a prepositional phrase with εἰς and three nouns: Such people "fall into temptation, a snare, and many [evil] desires." V. 9b in an indefinite relative clause (αἵτινες) indicates that these people "plunge into" ὄλεθρον καὶ ἀπώλειαν, "ruin and destruction" (cf. Mt. 16:26; Lk. 12:20-21). V. 10a gives the reason (γάρ) for the foregoing in the principle that love of money is a root of evil. V. 10b in a relative clause (ἧς) indicates that what Paul has described in v. 9 has actually happened to some (τινες), so that they have "wandered away from the faith" and brought pain upon themselves.

6:9 The substantival participle οἱ βουλόμενοι describes a category of people in terms of their desire, which is then made specific by the infinitive πλουτεῖν: "those who want to be rich." The verb ἐμπίπτουσιν is used metaphorically to indicate what happens to such people, i.e., they "fall (into)," with the present tense indicating that which usually or normally happens and the prepositional phrase with εἰς and three nouns indicating that into which they fall.

The first is πειρασμός, which means here "temptation" or "enticement to sin" and is used here in the passive sense of that which "can be an occasion of sin to a person" (BAGD). The second is παγίς, which means "snare" or "trap" and is used here figuratively. Since διαβόλος qualifies the other two occurrences of this word in the PE, one of which precedes this occurrence (3:7; also in 2 Tim. 2:26), and since this context refers to "temptation," evil "desires," "ruin," and "destruction," it is likely that "the snare *of the devil*" is intended here (so J. Schneider, *TDNT* V, 593-95) and that Paul felt it unnecessary to add τοῦ διαβόλου this time (3:6, 7 also uses ἐμπίπτω, the only other occurrence in the PE).

The third noun governed by εἰς is ἐπιθυμίας, "desire," "longing," or "craving," which is used in both neutral (or positive) and negative senses in the NT. The negative sense far predominates (over 30x of 38), and that sense is made plain here by the qualifiers ἀνοήτους καὶ βλαβεράς. The will to be rich causes one to enslaved by "many" (πολλάς) strong desires (Tit. 3:3; contrary to contentment with what one has). These desires are said here to be ἀνόητος, "foolish," the primary emphasis being moral rather than intellectual (cf. J. Behm, *TDNT* IV, 961f.), and βλαβεράς,** i.e., "harmful" or "injurious" (a NT hapax used in extrabiblical Greek as the opposite of "useful" or "profitable"; see LSJM).

There may be a progression in v. 9 from temptation to entrapment to desires (cf. Jas. 1:14-15): If this is so, the indefinite relative pronoun αἵτινες refers to "desires"; if not, it probably refers to all three preceding nouns, in which case it is feminine in agreement with the second and third. It may be used here qualitatively, "such as," or simply in place of the relative pronoun (BDF §293.4; Robertson, *Grammar,* 728).

Whatever the antecedents, they "sink" or "plunge" (βυθίζω,** NT 2x: literal in Lk. 5:7; figurative here) people into "ruin and destruction." The figure is that of causing someone to drown. Those being drowned are τοὺς ἀνθρώπους. The definite article refers back to the plural subject, οἱ βουλόμενοι πλουτεῖν, and perhaps even to ἀνθρώπων in v. 5.

ὄλεθρος** (NT 4x: here; 1 Cor. 5:5; 1 Thes. 5:3; 2 Thes. 1:9) means "destruction" or "ruin" (see J. Schneider, *TDNT* V, 167ff.; H. C. Hahn and C. Brown, *NIDNTT* I, 465ff.), as does ἀπώλεια (NT 18x, Pl.* 5x: here; Rom. 9:22; Phil. 1:28; 3:19; 2 Thes. 2:3; see A. Oepke, *TDNT* I, 394-97; H. C. Hahn, *NIDNTT* I, 462-65). It has been suggested that this combination of two nearly identical terms, which is not found elsewhere, may suggest an intensification: "*utter* destruction" (BAGD s.v. ἀπώλεια). A number of modern English versions render the two as "ruin and destruction" *(RSV, NASB, TEV, NIV).* But because ὄλεθρος is used in 1 Cor. 5:5 of "destruction of the flesh" here and now, with the hope "that his spirit may be saved in the day of the Lord Jesus," i.e., for eternity, it has been suggested that ὄλεθρος refers here also to bodily destruction and ἀπώλεια to spiritual destruction (van Oosterzee, Kelly [possible], Spicq, Dornier), or that ὄλεθρος refers here to present destruction and ἀπώλεια to destruction (perdition) in eternity (so Vine, *Expository Dictionary,* I, 304; *NEB:* "ruin and perdition"; Robertson: "destruction and perdition"). Either or both of these suggestions that see a contrast between the two terms point to the most likely solution (which is not to say that ὄλεθρος cannot refer to eternity: it clearly does in 2 Thes. 1:9; cf. 1 Thes. 5:3).

6:10 To substantiate (γάρ) the preceding Paul presents the proverbial statement ῥίζα πάντων τῶν κακῶν ἐστιν ἡ φιλαργυρία, in which φιλαργυρία represents the desire on the part of οἱ βουλόμενοι πλουτεῖν. Statements like this were well known in both Jewish and non-Jewish works (see BAGD s.v. φιλαργυρία; Fee; Spicq; Dibelius-Conzelmann). The closest is "The love of money is the mother-city of all evil" (widely attested in Greek antiquity). It may be that Paul is citing a common proverb because it expresses truth (cf. Acts 17:28-29), or that he or the Christian community has modified such a proverbial statement (cf. again Acts 17:28-29) with the key word "root" (ῥίζα), or that he or the Christian community has coined this proverb. The second of these alternatives seems most likely, since proverbial statements about love of money are known, but none with the word "root" (ῥίζα). This may explain why the NT hapax φιλαργυρία, "love of money," "avarice," is used here rather than the term Paul usually uses for such, which is πλεονεξία. An equally plausible solution would be that Paul, as one who knows and uses the verb φιλέω, who uses at least five words compounded with the root φιλάο-, and who also uses the word ἀργύριον, knows, or has formed, a word like φιλαργυρία.

φιλαργυρία, "love of money," is what characterizes one who places his or her heart on possessing money, so violating the first commandment of the Decalogue, the commandment to love God (cf. Mt. 6:24 par. Lk. 16:13). Because this is an expression of sinful self-love in opposition to love of God (cf. "lovers of self" and "lovers of money" in 2 Tim. 3:2-4, a list concluding with the contrast "lovers of pleasure rather than lovers of God"; cf. also Jas. 4:4; 1 Jn. 2:15), it also violates the inherently related second great commandment (Mt. 22:39) to love one's neighbor.

The proverb states the matter as a principle: "Love of money is ῥίζα πάντων τῶν κακῶν," with these latter words first in the sentence for emphasis. Does Paul mean by ῥίζα "*the* root" *(KJV, RSV, NEB)* or "*a* root" *(NASB, TEV, NIV)?* Field (*Notes,* ad loc.) argues that the nature of the saying demands "the," understood as a hyperbole, and gives examples of anarthrous forms for which the English idiom would require the article. This perspective may be correct, but it is still noteworthy that the article could have been included and is not and that our understanding of the verse does not necessitate that the article be understood. In the light of these considerations, it is best not to insist on "the root" (cf. Kelly). ῥίζα denotes that from which something grows (cf. BAGD s.v. 1b) and thus the term itself designates love of money as a radical source of evil. This note is further emphasized by ῥίζα being placed first in the sentence.

Should the phrase πάντων τῶν κακῶν be understood as "all evils" *(RSV)* or as "all sorts/kinds of evil" *(NASB, NIV, TEV)?* Paul presents this proverb as substantiation of what he has just written in v. 9, where he says that "the will to be rich" causes one to fall into "many desires" (ἐπιθυμίας πολλάς). He does not assert that "all" desires result from "the will to be rich" but that "many" do. It is likely that the same perspective is intended by πάντων τῶν κακῶν here, thus "all sorts of evil." This is borne out by Paul's previous use of πᾶς for all sorts of human beings rather than for each and every person (2:1b, 4, 6; 4:10). So the proverb says that all sorts of evil have as their root source the love of money. κακῶν is used here in the moral sense, "evils."

Paul indicates in a relative clause that "some" (τινες) have longed for money and have wandered away from the faith and seriously harmed themselves. τινες, used here of "certain" definite people, referred to indefinitely (BAGD s.v. 1aβ), may apply not only to various people Paul knows in the church at Ephesus but, in particular, to the false teachers, who are never far from his mind when he sets forth these principles. It is Paul's reference to them as those who suppose that godliness is gain (v. 5) that precipitates this section. Furthermore, he began the section on the false teachers by referring to every such false teacher with τις (v. 3). Therefore, τινες in v. 10 may well return the discussion to the beginning in v. 3.

ἧς refers grammatically to its antecedent φιλαργυρία but logically only to the second half of the compound word, i.e., to ἀργύριον (so BAGD s.v. ὀρέγω). The verb ὀρέγομαι is used figuratively in the NT and here has the meaning "strive for, desire" or "reach for"; the participle is causal, giving the ground or reason for the action of the main verb ἀπεπλανήθησαν, which in its passive form means "wander away from." The preposition ἀπό indicates that from which they have separated (BAGD s.v. I.1), namely, τῆς πίστεως (1:2, 19; 3:9; 4:1; 5:8). Here πίστις with the article probably indicates the Christian faith in an objective sense that does not negate the subjective element of trust (see above on 3:9): Christianity can be referred to as ἡ πίστις because faith (trust) is such an integral part of becoming and being a Christian. Those Paul is referring to have strayed from "the faith" by straying from faith or trust in God and Christ as the central desire and love of their life (cf. 2 Tim. 4:10).

They have also (καί) done great harm (περιέπειραν ὀδύναις πολλαῖς) to "themselves" (ἑαυτούς). περιπείρω** (a biblical hapax found in Greek literature from the first century BC) means "pierce through, impale," here used figuratively to convey a terrible reality: They have pierced themselves (ἑαυτοὺς περιέπειραν). Their reaching out after money has brought the previously mentioned foolish and injurious sinful desires into their life (v. 9b), and these desires are the means of these self-inflicted ὀδύναις πολλαῖς. In the physical realm ὀδύνη** is used of pains like those of a wound, fracture, stabbing, or cut. When used with reference to the soul, as here and in Rom. 9:2, it refers to "mental distress" or "grief." It may refer to "the severe and piercing . . . self-accusations and pangs of conscience which will smite those who have defected out of love of money" (F. Hauck, *TDNT* V, 115; cf. also BAGD), of which Judas would be an example (Mt. 27:3-5), but if so would be, as in Judas's case, "the sorrow of the world" that "produces death" (2 Cor. 7:10). More likely what is referred to here are the griefs that sins themselves bring on the sinner, whether or not the sinner has any pangs of conscience. Such a person may have sorrow over the effects of sin on his or her inner self and life situation, but no "sorrow toward God" and no repentance, since he or she has turned away from the faith (cf. again 2 Cor. 7:10). Paul says here that those griefs are "many" (πολλαῖς), as were the foolish and injurious sinful desires (v. 9, ἐπιθυμίας πολλάς).

Paul began this larger subsection in v. 3 describing the false teachers and indicating not only their opposition to Jesus' words and "the teaching according to godliness" but also their other negative characteristics, concluding with the observation that they "suppose godliness is a means of gain" (v. 5). This prompted him to set forth the real gain of godliness, the contentment with life's basic necessities that accompanies godliness (vv. 6-8). In stark contrast to this are "those who want to get rich" (v. 9) and who have a "love of money" (v. 10). Paul describes the perils of such a love and indicates that its end is "destruction and perdition" (v. 9). Those who are characterized by it have strayed from the faith and have "pierced themselves with many pains" (v. 10). With this conclusion Paul has probably returned to consideration of the false teachers, thus ending on the topic with which he began this subsection.

FINAL EXHORTATION TO TIMOTHY: 6:11-16

Paul turns his attention from those who have wandered from the faith to Timothy and directly addresses him with a series of imperatives: "flee from these things" (v. 11a), "pursue" Christian virtues (v. 11b), "fight the good fight of faith," "lay hold of eternal life" (v. 12), and "keep the commandment" (v. 14). These demands are to be kept until the coming of Christ (v. 14). Paul's statement that God will bring about Christ's coming leads into a doxological statement about God (vv. 15, 16).

6:11 By combining the contrasting particle δέ with the personal pronoun σύ (used for emphasis), "but you," Paul has decisively contrasted Timothy with those who wander from the faith. The interjection ὦ is infrequent in the NT (17x, Pl. 7x) and is used most often before the vocative for emphasis (Rom. 2:1, 3; 9:20; Gal. 3:1; 1 Tim. 6:11, 20). Modern English translations no longer render it with "O," which has become rare with vocatives and might therefore convey to the reader a stilted sense, which is not what Paul intended.

(ὁ) ἄνθρωπος (τοῦ) θεοῦ** (here vocative ἄνθρωπε θεοῦ) occurs only 2x in the NT (also in 2 Tim. 3:17), but is used with some frequency in the LXX (for *'îš 'ᵉlohîm;* see N. P. Bratsiotis, *TDOT* I, 233) of men such as Moses, Samuel, David, Elijah, Elisha, and lesser known leaders, including some who remain anonymous. In later writings it is generally used of "the elect of God" (e.g., David in 2 Ch. 8:14) and in Hellenistic Judaism (e.g., *Epistle of Aristeas* 140) of a worshipper of Israel's God (J. Jeremias, *TDNT* I, 364f.; cf. Dibelius-Conzelmann). It is difficult to know whether Timothy is here being designated in the specific or general way. Perhaps Paul uses the phrase in a transitional sense uniquely appropriate to the NT situation, as signified by what he says about the "man of God" here and in 2 Tim. 3:17, which amounts to a general principle for every Christian, albeit addressed to Timothy. If this is the case, then the phrase harks back to the imagery of one who was uniquely a "man of God" but is applied here to one who is both a spiritual leader and at the same time an example to all believers of what each one should be as a "man of God" (cf. especially 4:12).

The first command to Timothy is to "flee from these things" (ταῦτα φεῦγε). ταῦτα has been used previously in 1 Timothy of everything mentioned in a previous section, and there is no indication that it is used otherwise here (see above on 3:14; 4:6, 11; 6:2, especially the last two). Hence, Timothy is to flee from all the errors and sins mentioned in the previous section. φεῦγε (Pl.* 4x: 1 Cor. 6:18: immorality; 10:14: idolatry; 2 Tim. 2:22: youthful lusts) means literally "seek safety in flight" or "escape" and in a moral sense "flee from, avoid, shun"; since it is used here in contrast to δίωκε, "pursue" (as in 2 Tim. 2:22), "flee" or even "run away from" is the preferred understanding (see BAGD s.v. 3). Such an action would be an appropriate response, given Paul's presentation of the extreme peril (see vv. 9-10).

Paul joins (δέ) to that negative command its equally necessary positive corollary, δίωκε δὲ δικαιοσύνην κτλ. As usual (cf., e.g., his "put off" and "put on" exhortations in Ephesians and Colossians), Paul indicates the positive steps necessary and does not simply warn against sin. διώκω is used predominantly in the NT, and particularly by Paul, either in the sense of persecuting someone, or in the sense of "following zealously after" or "pursuing" Christian virtues, as here (see Rom. 12:13; 14:19; 1 Cor. 14:1; 1 Thes. 5:15; 2 Tim. 2:22; cf. BAGD; A. Oepke, *TDNT* II, 229f.).

Six virtues are listed with no connecting links (as in Gal. 5:22-23). If "patience" may be considered to stand in the place of "hope," then the list here includes the equivalent of the common trio of faith, hope, and love (e.g., Rom. 8:25; 1 Cor. 13:13; cf. especially 1 Thes. 1:3: τῆς ὑπομονῆς τῆς ἐλπίδος). No two virtue lists of Paul are identical. But this list shares a number of key words and concepts with five other Pauline lists (2 Cor. 6:6-7; Gal. 5:22-23; Col. 3:12-14; 2 Tim. 2:22-25; 3:10): "love" (ἀγάπη, all six lists), "faith" (πίστις, here and in three of the others), "patience" (ὑπομονή here and in 2 Tim. 3:10; μακροθυμία there and in three other lists), "gentleness" (πραϋπαθία here; πραΰτης in four other lists), and "righteousness" (δικαιοσύνη, here and in three other lists). Only εὐσέβεια ("godliness") is present here and not represented in some other Pauline list (but ὁσιότης in Eph. 4:24, which follows δικαιοσύνη as εὐσέβεια does here, may be a virtual synonym). Outside the Pauline lists 2 Pet. 1:5-7 shares the most words with 1 Tim. 6:11 (εὐσέβεια, πίστις, ἀγάπη, ὑπομονή).

δικαιοσύνη, as used of humans in the NT, refers almost always to conduct that is in accord with God's will and pleasing to him (G. Schrenk, *TDNT* II, 198). Like all Christian virtues, this "righteousness" is brought about by the transforming work of Christ (cf. Phil. 1:11) accomplished in Christians by the Holy Spirit (Rom. 14:17), so that "the law's requirement" is fulfilled in those who "walk according to the Spirit" (Rom. 8:3, 4). Elsewhere Paul regards "all scripture" as the standard for righteousness (2 Tim. 3:17). εὐσέβεια (see 2:2; 4:7; in NT virtue lists only here and in 2 Pet. 1:6-7) designates in the LXX and in the NT "the duty that man owes to God," and is best rendered here by "piety" or "godliness" (BAGD).

πίστις in a list of virtues means either "faithfulness," i.e. "reliability," or "faith," i.e. "trust" in God. Occasionally Paul uses πίστις in the sense of "faithfulness" (cf. Rom. 3:3; Tit. 2:10; and perhaps 2 Thes. 1:4), and this has been suggested as one possibility for its meaning in Gal. 5:22. But that would be the exception in Galatians, where most of the 22 occurrences of the word mean "trust." Also significant are Pauline usages elsewhere, especially where, as here, it is followed by "love" and "patience" (e.g., 1 Thes. 1:3; cf. Col. 1:4; 1 Cor. 13:13), where the meaning "trust" is clear. A striking instance of that combination is in Tit. 2:2, where the controlling expression "sound in" makes it clear that there πίστις means "trust." In the comparable Petrine list, 2 Pet. 1:5ff., πίστις (v. 5) recalls v. 1, where "trust" is clearly meant. For all these reasons πίστις most likely refers here to "trust" in God rather than to "faithfulness."

ἀγάπη (see 1:5; 4:12) means "love," but, as so often, the object of love is not specified. Jesus' love command involves both God and neighbor (Mt. 22:37-39), and it is possible that Paul is following that pattern and intends both. Where, however, Paul indicates or implies the object of love, it is most often human beings (e.g., Rom. 12:9; 13:10; 14:15; 2 Cor. 8:7; Gal. 5:13; Eph. 1:15; 4:2; Col. 1:4; 2:2; 1 Thes. 3:12; 5:13; 2 Thes. 1:3; Phm. 5, 7). Humans seem to be the object in 1 Corinthians 13, which is followed by words similar to those here, i.e., διώκετε τὴν ἀγάπην (1 Cor. 14:1). Thus if a specific object is intended here, and it need not be, it would probably be humans.

ὑπομονή has a wide range of nuances, which include "patience, endurance, fortitude, steadfastness, perseverance, and expectation" (BAGD), and it is difficult to say which, if any, is intended here. It is utilized of persevering in good works (Rom. 2:7; 2 Cor. 12:12), of enduring persecution (2 Thes. 1:4), and of waiting patiently for Christ's return (Rom. 8:25). Thus Christian ὑπομονή is equally concerned with the attitude with which one endures, the actual perseverance, and one's confidence in the final outcome, all with a dependence on God's grace and a determination to serve Christ by means of the ὑπομονή (cf. F. Hauck, *TDNT* IV, 586f.). The word is probably used here in this comprehensive sense. πραϋπαθία** (a biblical hapax) means "gentleness" (cf. Pauline occurrences of its synonym πραΰτης: 1 Cor. 4:21; 2 Cor. 10:1; Gal. 5:23; 6:1; Eph. 4:2; Col. 3:12; Tit. 3:2; 2 Tim. 2:25).

These six virtues seem to group themselves into pairs (so Bernard and others, contra Hendriksen): δικαιοσύνη and εὐσέβεια represent one's relationship with God, πίστις and ἀγάπη are the animating principles of the Christian life, and ὑπομονή and πραϋπαθία are terms for the right ways of acting in relation to a hostile world.

6:12 Paul continues his exhortation to Timothy with ἀγωνίζου τὸν καλὸν ἀγῶνα τῆς πίστεως, "fight the good fight of faith" (cf. the nearly identical statement in 2 Tim. 4:7). The verb ἀγωνίζομαι** (also in Lk. 13:24;

Jn. 18:36; 1 Cor. 9:25; Col. 1:29; 4:12; 1 Tim. 4:10; 2 Tim. 4:7) and the noun ἀγών** (also in Phil. 1:30; Col. 2:1; 1 Thes. 2:2; 2 Tim. 4:7; Heb. 12:1) are both used of a struggle or a contest. It is disputed whether the idea behind these words as they are used here is athletics (Pfitzner, *Agon Motif*) or fighting (MM; cf. 1 Tim. 1:18, where military terms are used in a similarly structured clause: στρατεύῃ . . . τὴν καλὴν στρατείαν). The NT uses them for both (fighting: e.g., Jn. 18:36; 1 Thes. 2:2; athletics: e.g., 1 Cor. 9:25; Heb. 12:1). Although Paul may, or may not, have one or the other in view here, the emphasis in his figurative language here is not on a particular image but on the basic idea of "struggle": Paul wants Timothy to be willing to suffer for the gospel (cf. Phil. 1:30), to struggle in its service (cf. Col. 1:29; 2:1; 4:12; 1 Cor. 9:25; 1 Tim. 4:10; 2 Tim. 4:7), and to do so when he is opposed (cf. 1 Thes. 2:2).

The present imperative form of the verb suggests that this a never-ending struggle. The struggle is regarded as "good" (καλόν), both because it is engaged in for God and the gospel and also because it is inherent to the gospel's making its way in an evil world. That "the faith" is genitive (τῆς πίστεως) makes it unlikely that Paul refers to the struggle *for* the faith, i.e., for the content of the faith. He speaks, rather, of the struggle in which the Christian engages *because of* his or her faith and *through* his or her faith (cf., e.g., Bernard, Hendriksen, Kelly, Parry, Ridderbos, G. B. Wilson).

The imperative of the next clause, ἐπιλαβοῦ, is from ἐπιλαμβάνομαι, which means "take hold of" and is used here (and in 6:19) in the figurative sense "make one's own" (BAGD). This "second imperative . . . extends the metaphor to focus on the prize" (Fee). As with "run in such a way that you may win" (1 Cor. 9:24) and "I press on in order that I may lay hold of (καταλάβω) that for which also I was laid hold of by Christ Jesus" (Phil. 3:12), the imperative here extends the preceding imperative so that together they indicate the final outcome (note the asyndeton, i.e., that there is no conjunction between the clauses). Though the event is future, as the parallel passages just mentioned indicate, because "taking hold of" is regarded as a single event it is presented in a punctiliar aorist. Thus Paul tells Timothy: "Continually struggle the struggle of the faith, i.e. persevere, (and at the end) then once-and-for-all lay hold of eternal life" (cf. Phil. 3:12-14). αἰώνιος ζωή, "eternal life," life without end, is regarded as future in the Pauline corpus (cf. the other Pauline occurrences of the phrase: Rom. 2:7; 6:22, 23; Gal. 6:8; 1 Tim. 1:16; Tit. 1:2; 3:7).

Timothy has been "called" to this "eternal life" (εἰς ἣν ἐκλήθης, "to which you were called"). καλέω is used here, as quite often by Paul, of God's inner and effective call (see BAGD s.v. 2; K. L. Schmidt, *TDNT* III, 488f.; e.g., Rom. 8:30). Sometimes Paul states that it is God (the Father) who has called (e.g., Gal. 1:15; 1 Thes. 2:12; 4:7), and elsewhere the context usually signifies the same thing (e.g., Rom. 8:30; 9:11; 1 Thes. 5:24; 2 Thes. 2:14).

Therefore, when the verb is passive and the one who calls is not named, as here, God is to be understood as the one calling (for aorist passives of καλέω, as here, cf. 1 Cor. 7:18, 20, 21, 22, in the light of v. 17; Gal. 5:13; Eph. 4:1, 4; Col. 3:15).

In Paul's understanding God brings those he has called into the spiritual reality to which he has called them (cf. especially Rom. 8:30; also 1 Thes. 5:24). Hence that Timothy has been called (ἐκλήθης) by God to eternal life is the basis for Paul's exhortation to Timothy to struggle and to take hold of eternal life (cf. 1 Thes. 5:23-24). The reality of the call is evidenced in the activity of struggling (cf. 2 Pet. 1:10-11; 1 Cor. 9:24-27; Phil. 3:8-14).

The καὶ introducing the next clause has "simple copulative power, and subjoins to the foregoing words another and co-ordinate ground of encouragement and exhortation" (Ellicott). "God's is the prior action, but there must also be the response" (Fee). ὁμολογέω (Pl.* 4x: also in Rom. 10:9, 10; Tit. 1:16) means here "declare, acknowledge, confess" (BAGD) and to do so in faith (O. Michel, *TDNT* V, 209-11; cf. Rom. 10:9, 10). ὁμολογία** is used here in the passive sense of the "acknowledgement" or "confession" that one makes (BAGD). καλὴ ὁμολογία** is "the confession that is ordained, accepted, and confirmed by God," and it is καλή "because God demands it and man fulfils this command of His" (Michel, op. cit., 211 and n. 35; this phrase only here and in the next verse in the NT). The "confession" required was a public acknowledgment of Jesus (Mt. 10:32; Lk. 12:8) as the resurrected Lord (Rom. 10:9-10); elsewhere Paul calls this the "confession of the gospel of Christ" (2 Cor. 9:13). Paul appeals to that confession because it acknowledges Jesus both as the one who gives salvation and promises eternal life and as the Lord of one's life, whom one must serve (cf. Rom. 10:9, 10). Paul reminds Timothy of that historical moment when he made this confession "in the sight of" or "in the presence of" (BAGD s.v. ἐνώπιον 2a) a great number of eyewitnesses (πολλῶν μαρτύρων,** "many witnesses," the phrase only here and in 2 Tim. 2:2 in the NT), who would have been able to testify to it and thus to Timothy's public commitment, to which Paul now calls him.

What occasion is Paul referring to? Basically two answers have been suggested: (1) Timothy's baptism, when he confessed his faith (e.g., Bouma, Kelly, Lock, Spicq, Wohlenberg) or (2) Timothy's ordination as a minister of the gospel (Barrett, Hanson, Jeremias, Simpson; O. Michel, *TDNT* V, 216; Käsemann, "Formular"). A decision is not easy to make. God's call, mentioned in this verse, is usually related to confession of faith, and confession is usually correlated with baptism. But the cumulative effect of various factors in this context and elsewhere seems to tip the scales in favor of identifying the occasion of the "good confession" with Timothy's ordination: 2 Tim. 2:2, with its reference to "many witnesses," may indicate that what is in view here is an ordination situation. Since elders lay hands on the ordinand (cf. 4:14), it may be the elders that are referred to as "many witnesses," which would be appropriate, particularly since Paul has twice already appealed to Timothy's ordination (1:18; 4:14). In the context of this appeal to Timothy's confession he is being addressed as a leader, and so an appeal to his ordination would be apt. Furthermore, Paul appeals to Jesus' confession in the next verse with the same phrase — "a good confession" — and Jesus made that confession as part of his work as the servant of the Lord. This at least indicates that the "good confession" need not be restricted to baptism. Finally, an appeal to one's call by God to eternal life may fit with an ordination situation as well as with the occasion of baptism. Elsewhere Paul refers to God's salvation and call where he refers to his own appointment as "a preacher, apostle, and teacher" and does so to encourage Timothy to be a faithful minister (2 Tim. 1:8-14).

6:13 παραγγέλλω (see 1:3) means here "I charge," i.e., "I command" or "I direct." It is in the first person to express Paul's authority as Christ's apostle (cf. 1 Thes. 4:11; 2 Thes. 3:4, 6, 10, 12, especially vv. 6 and 12). Addition of σοι can be explained more satisfactorily than omission of it, since one expects the person charged to be indicated in the text (this variant reading correctly spells out what is implied in the text, and thus most ancient versions and modern English translations render the text accordingly, i.e., "I charge you").

Paul uses ἐνώπιον, "in the presence of," most often with reference to the members of the Godhead (see 2:3), here "God" and "Christ Jesus." God is described as τοῦ ζῳογονοῦντος,** i.e., as "the one who gives life" (cf. 1 Sa. 2:6 LXX: "the Lord makes alive"), not as the one who preserves life, as in Lk. 17:33; Acts 7:19. He give life to "all things," τὰ πάντα, used here of "humankind and everything else that possesses life" (BAGD s.v. 2bβ; cf. Acts 17:25). Paul's charge is, therefore, made in the presence of God the life-giver, with all the implications that that carries.

Christ is described as the one "who testified the good confession before Pontius Pilate." ἐνώπιον governs this part of the sentence also, and so καί joins Christ to God as those in whose presence Paul's makes his charge. For Χριστοῦ Ἰησοῦ see 1:1, 2. μαρτυρέω means here "bear witness" or "testify," and the aorist participle refers to a particular occasion in the past.

That particular occasion is specified in the prepositional phrase ἐπὶ Ποντίου Πιλάτου. ἐπί more likely means "before" here rather than "in the time of" (see BAGD s.v. I.1aδ; Kelly argues for the latter) since the former fits that actual historical occasion with its direct and personal dimension. Also, "before" would agree with Timothy's situation, since he was obligated to carry out his charge "before" people. Πόντιος Πιλᾶτος was the Roman governor of Judea (AD 26-36) who ordered Jesus' execution. He is thus repeatedly mentioned (49x) in the Passion accounts (Mt. 27:2-65; Mk. 15:1-44; Lk. 23:1-52; Jn. 18:29–19:38). Only here and in Lk. 3:1 is he designated by the nomen Πόντιος,** the "middle, gentile, or tribal name" of Pilate (BAGD).

Christ's "good confession" was his affirmative answer to Pilate's question "Are you the king of the Jews?" (Mt. 27:11; Mk. 15:2; Lk. 23:3; Jn. 18:33-37). The significance of this confession was that it provided the basis for the coalition among Pilate, the religious leaders, and the crowd — and thus the grounds for Jesus' crucifixion (see Jn. 19:12-16, especially v. 12; cf. Mt. 27:37; Mk. 15:26; Lk. 23:38; Jn. 19:19). Jesus' royal claim had been rightly recognized by the religious leaders to be messianic (Lk. 23:2), but they rejected it. Paul charges Timothy before Jesus as the one who made this "good confession" and in so doing willingly gave up his life to death on the cross (cf. Heb. 12:2).

6:14 The actual charge to which παραγγέλλω (v. 13) points comes in this verse. σε is direct address to Timothy, as was σύ in v. 11. The charge is that Timothy "keep the commandment." τηρῆσαι is used here, as τὴν ἐντολήν indicates, in the sense of "keeping" or "observing" a commandment (see H. Riesenfeld, *TDNT* VIII, 143-46 and n. 37).

τὴν ἐντολήν has been understood as referring here to (1) "the commandment" given at Timothy's baptism (Bernard, Dornier, Parry, G. B. Wilson); (2) one given at his ordination (Barrett, Brox, Ridderbos); (3) the injunction given in vv. 11-12 (Bürki, Easton, Guthrie, van Oosterzee, Weiss); (4) the commandment to persevere in his faith and ministry, as in 4:16 (Fee); (5) the whole charge delivered in this letter (Gealy, H. von Soden); (6) all that Timothy has been enjoined to do with respect to the ministry of the gospel and the government of the church (Calvin, Hendriksen); (7) everything entrusted to Timothy, by analogy with the "deposit" in 6:20 (Dibelius-Conzelmann, Hanson); or (8) the gospel viewed as a rule of life (Alford, Ellicott, Freundorfer, Huther, Kelly, Liddon, Lock, Spicq, N. J. D. White, Wohlenberg; some commentators' views are broader than these simple categories might imply, and some of the categories bring together commentators whose views are not quite in agreement).

The solution might appear to be intertwined with the understanding of "the good confession in the presence of many witnesses" of v. 12, but this is not necessarily the case. If the confession refers to Timothy's baptism, then on the surface (1) appears more likely. If it refers to his ordination, then (2) might appear more likely. But the understanding one has of v. 12 does not automatically determine the conclusion here since all the options are theoretically possible on either view of the "confession."

Each option has a certain plausibility to it within this context alone. Hence consideration must be given to use of ἐντολή elsewhere in contexts analogous to this one and to use of analogous terms in 1 Timothy. Paul does not use singular articular ἡ ἐντολή frequently; when he does, he refers to one of the Ten Commandments (Rom. 7:8-13), which seems unlikely here. In the non-Pauline NT letters ἡ ἐντολή is used in 2 Pet. 2:21; 3:2 (and in 1 John and 2 John of the love command, but that meaning has not been suggested here and nothing in 1 Timothy 6 would seem to warrant it). In 2 Peter ἡ ἐντολή is used "as a description of Christianity considered as a body of ethical teaching" (Bauckham, *Jude, 2 Peter,* at 2:21; at 3:2 he indicates that the term is used "in the same way").

Such a meaning for ἡ ἐντολή in 1 Tim. 6:14 would seem to be supported by the significance of analogous terms in the PE: Paul has designated the Christian faith as "the command" (ἡ παραγγελία, 1 Tim. 1:5), and in the conclusion of the letter (6:20) he charges Timothy to "guard the deposit," i.e., the Christian faith (τὴν παραθήκην φύλαξον). In 2 Tim. 4:7 he uses the same verb as he does here in saying that he himself has "kept the faith" (τὴν πίστιν τετήρηκα). Paul speaks, therefore, about the Christian faith as a command and as that which must be guarded or kept. This formulation of the matter was already presented by Jesus in the Great Commission, which in its Greek form (Mt. 28:20) contains the same verb, τηρέω, as 1 Tim. 6:14 and the verb ἐντέλλω, which is the cognate of ἐντολή.

Bernard, however, quotes 2 Clement 8:6 in favor of identifying the ἐντολή with the baptismal charge: "τηρήσατε τὴν σάρκα ἁγνὴν καὶ τὴν σφραγῖδα ἄσπιλον, ἵνα τὴν αἰώνιον ζωὴν ἀπολάβωμεν." Bernard understands the σφραγῖδα to be the "seal" *of baptism* (so also Lake, *Apostolic Fathers* I, 141). But 2 Clement itself says that it is giving the meaning here of Lk. 16:10-12, which it has just quoted, not, though the words are similar, of 1 Tim. 6:14. A few lines earlier (8:4) it says: "If we do the will of the Father, if we keep the flesh pure, and if we observe the commandments of the Lord, we shall obtain eternal life" (Lake's translation).

Bernard sees the same understanding in Cyril of Jerusalem, who quotes 1 Tim. 6:13-14 with τὴν παραδεδομένην πίστιν in place of ἐντολήν (*Catechetical Lectures* 5.13). But a number of others (Kelly, Lock, Spicq, N. J. D. White) cite the same words from Cyril to indicate that "the commandment" is understood by him to mean the Christian faith (category 8 above). This seeming contradiction is resolved in large measure when one realizes that several of the proponents of the view that the "commandment" is the baptismal charge (1 above; e.g., Dornier, Parry, Wilson) regard the content of the commandment given at baptism identical with that which the proponents of view (8) would regard it to be, i.e., the totality of the gospel's ethical demands. Views (4), (6), and (7) also describe the content in terms that are so close to the content of view (8) as to be hardly different except for their specificity of occasion or perspective. Brox expresses his view, that the "commandment" is the ordination charge (view 2), in part like view (7); thus this understanding of this view would, like view (7), nearly coincide with view (8) with regard to the content of the commandment. The other two alternatives, (3) and (5), refer "the commandment" to vv. 11-12 or to the whole letter and would seem to require that the text read "this," rather than "the," commandment. They also seem not to give adequate attention to the definiteness and absoluteness of the phrase "*the* commandment."

Therefore, six of the eight views would virtually coincide in their understanding of the content of the "commandment." The evidence from the NT seems to point to view (8) with its emphasis on the content. The differences between baptism and ordination that make decision so difficult and that mark most of the other views in one way or another should not blur or obscure that important point. Even the fact that Timothy is charged here as a Christian leader should not take away from the fact that everything that he has been commanded to do in vv. 11ff. is to characterize the life of every Christian, not just that of a Christian leader, and there is no reason to think that perspective has changed in v. 14.

Timothy is charged "to keep the commandment" ἄσπιλον ἀνεπίλημπτον, "without stain or reproach." ἄσπιλον means here "without stain, spot, or blemish," or "unstained." ἀνεπίλημπτον** (3:2; 5:7) means "irreproachable," or "without blame." The two adjectives seem to refer to the clause τηρῆσαί σε τὴν ἐντολὴν considered as a whole, Timothy's keeping of the commandment, rather than any one word within it. ἄσπιλον may refer to transgressions of the commandment, and ἀνεπίλημπτον to failures in keeping its positive aspects.

Timothy is to understand by the phrase μέχρι τῆς ἐπιφανείας τοῦ κυρίου ἡμῶν Ἰησοῦ Χριστοῦ that the charge to "keep the commandment" is an obligation laid on him and all Christians until Christ's return, i.e., for the entire Christian era, and that at Christ's return Christians will have to give account to Christ, who is "our Lord" (τοῦ κυρίου ἡμῶν). μέχρι does not mean that Paul believes that Timothy will be alive when Christ returns. Rather, this is the typical NT language of expectancy in relation to the time that καιροῖς ἰδίοις in v. 15 implies is unknown to any person (cf. Acts 1:7). ἡ ἐπιφάνεια** means generally "appearing, appearance," and is used in a religious context of the appearance of gods to bring help (see especially B. Gärtner, *NIDNTT* III, 317-20; Pax, *ΕΠΙΦΑΝΕΙΑ*). It is used in the NT only by Paul (2 Thes. 2:8; Tit. 2:13; 2 Tim. 1:10; 4:1, 8) and only of Christ's appearance, mostly his future appearing, as here (and 2 Thes. 2:8; Tit. 2:13; 2 Tim. 4:1, 8), but also his first (only in 2 Tim. 1:10). On "our Lord Jesus Christ," see 1:2. The full title is often used in contexts marked by solemnity to spell out and emphasize that Jesus is both Lord and Christ (e.g., the salutations in Paul's letters). Whenever a personal pronoun of possession is used, it is always ἡμῶν, "our," to emphasize the common standing that all Christians have to this Jesus as Messiah and Lord of them all.

6:15 Paul adds as an encouragement "which he will bring about at the proper time." I.e., God controls and determines the moment when his

Son will return as the victor and when the struggle shall be brought to an end.

ἥν has τῆς ἐπιφανείας as its antecedent and is the object of δείξει. δείκνυμι means here "show" in the sense of "make known," "manifest," or "bring about" (H. Schlier, *TDNT* II, 26). For the action of the Father in the epiphany of the Son see Acts 3:20; 1 Thes. 4:14. καιροῖς ἰδίοις (plural καιροῖς ἰδίοις** in the NT 3x: 1 Tim. 2:6; here; Tit. 1:3; singular in Gal. 6:9) means here "at the proper time" or "in his own time" (BAGD s.v. 1b, 2; see 2:6). Whether the subject of δείξει is the "he" (God understood) of the verb ending, to which the following descriptions of God are then in apposition, or the descriptions themselves as a complex subject, makes little difference in meaning.

As Paul presents the epiphany of Christ and indicates that this event is to be brought about by God, he is apparently drawn to speak of God's greatness and majesty that that revelatory event will reveal. The two adjectives μακάριος καὶ μόνος qualify the noun δυνάστης, as the one article ὁ evidences. δυνάστης** (NT 3x; only of God in the NT, but used in Hellenistic Judaism; cf. Sirach 46:5; 2 Maccabees 12:15; 15:3; 3 Maccabees 2:3) means "ruler" or "sovereign." The adjectival qualifiers give further perspective to God as "sovereign": μακάριος, "blessed," as an attribute of God occurs in the NT only here and in 1:11 (which see). Lock says that it designates "God as containing all happiness in Himself and bestowing it on men" (at 1:17). μόνος (used of God in Paul at 1:17; 6:15, 16; Rom. 16:27) means here, as elsewhere in reference to God, "only." God will bring about the appearance of Christ, he is the only real and absolute sovereign, and he is the sovereign who has and bestows all happiness.

He is also (literally) "the King of those who reign as kings and Lord of those who rule as lords." The implication of the fact that God is the "only sovereign" is now made explicit: He is the sovereign over every other kind of rulership. βασιλεύς, "king," is used not only of an actual monarch but also figuratively, as here, of the possessor of the highest power (BAGD s.v. 2; cf. 1 Sa. 8:7; Jn. 18:36-37). "King of kings" is not used of God in the OT but is in 2 Maccabees 13:4. κύριος, "lord," can signify, as here, one who is "master" and who has full control (see BAGD s.v. 1aα, 2a). "Lord of lords" is used of God in the OT (Dt. 10:17; Ps. 136:3). The two phrases are joined together in Judaism in 1 Enoch 9:4. The complete statement, "King of kings and Lord of lords," is found in the NT only 3x: here; Rev. 17:14; 19:16 (with slight variations). The statement in its entirety says that God is the possessor of the highest power over all who possess power and has full control over all who exercise control (cf. Is. 40:12-31; Dn. 4:35).

6:16 God is also "he who alone possesses immortality, who dwells in unapproachable light." ἔχων (see 1:12) means here "possess" in the sense of "have as one's own." Here μόνος (see v. 15) can best be rendered into

English by "alone" *(RSV, NASB, NIV),* though "only" is acceptable *(KJV;* J. B. Phillips, *NT in Modern English*). In either case the clause states that "immortality" (ἀθανασία,** 1 Cor. 15:53, 54; here; cf. ἄφθαρτος, "immortal," in 1:17, both used with apparently the same significance in parallel clauses in 1 Cor. 15:53-54 [Guthrie]) is intrinsically unique to God (cf. Ps. 36:9; Dn. 4:34; Jn. 5:26).

The second participial clause, φῶς οἰκῶν ἀπρόσιτον, is also governed by the definite article ὁ at the beginning of the verse. Thus both participles are substantival and describe God, and their descriptions are thereby closely linked together. φῶς, "light," is used by nearly all the writers of the NT, often of God (whether directly or indirectly). From Eph. 5:8-9 we may deduce that "light" with reference to God in the Paulines means "goodness, righteousness, and truth" (cf. holiness and truth in 1 Jn. 1:5-7; cf. also 1 Pet. 2:9). Here it says that God "dwells" (οἰκῶν) in light: Light characterizes his very existence (cf. Ps. 104:2). That light is "unapproachable" (ἀπρόσιτον,** a biblical hapax used elsewhere; see BAGD).

It is said further that God is the one "whom no person has seen or can see," which reinforces and further delineates the preceding clause. The absolute negative "no person" (οὐδεὶς ἀνθρώπων) states this truth from the point of view of actuality, as does Jn. 1:18 (cf. 1 Jn. 4:12). Not even Moses, with whom God spoke, saw God's face (cf. Ex. 33:18-23). The relative pronoun ὅν, "whom," has as its antecedent the two preceding substantival participles (ὁ ἔχων . . . οἰκῶν), i.e., God, not neuter φῶς. The second clause states the truth of the first from the point of view of ability. The key word δύναται, "can" or "is able," is used here with the infinitive ἰδεῖν and with the conjunction οὐδέ to indicate what one is not able to do, i.e., to see God. Paul is reflecting the OT truth that God is so holy that sinful mankind cannot see God and live (cf. LXX Ex. 33:20: "You cannot see [οὐ δυνήσῃ ἰδεῖν] my face, for no one can see me and live").

Paul does not make explicit here what he and others make explicit elsewhere when these elements are used. But certain connections seem to be intended by Paul's choosing to emphasize just these aspects of God's attributes in relation to his being the one who brings about "the appearing of our Lord Jesus Christ." When this great and majestic God brings about the appearance of Christ, who has already brought life and immortality to light (2 Tim. 1:10), Christ will enable Timothy to lay hold of eternal life (v. 12) and put on its attendant immortality (1 Cor. 15:51-57). That appearing will display "the glory of our great God and Savior, Christ Jesus" (Tit. 2:13). Our transformation, in which we shall become "like him" (1 Jn. 3:2; Phil. 3:20, 21), shall come about "because we shall see him as he is" (1 Jn. 3:2). The wonder and the glory of that appearing is that in it the transcendent God manifests himself in Christ and by that act makes himself available to us and bestows on us what we could never have and be apart from Christ. Thus we are to put on immortality, a characteristic that is God's alone, and to see him in Christ and be transformed (rather than destroyed) by that sight.

It is no wonder that Paul ends this marvelous and awesome description of God with words of praise: "To him be honor and eternal dominion." The relative pronoun ᾧ has as its antecedent the person in view in all the nominatives in vv. 15-16, i.e., God (the Father). For a consideration of what form of the verb is to be understood here, see the discussion and literature cited at 1:17.

This concluding doxology uses terms that correlate in inverse order with what has just been said about God and thus praises him in accordance with his character: "Honor" corresponds to the description of God as "he who alone has immortality and dwells in light," and the "eternal power" is that of the only Sovereign King and Lord. By τιμή, "honor," Paul prayerfully desires the reverence and respect that is due God (see 1:17; this word is used in praise to God and Christ in the NT in 1 Tim. 1:17; Heb. 2:9; 1 Pet. 1:7; 2 Pet. 1:17; Rev. 4:9, 11; 5:12, 13; 7:12; 21:26). κράτος (always used of God in the NT; in doxologies in 1 Pet. 4:11; 5:11; Jude 25; Rev. 1:6; 5:13; with τιμή only here and in Rev. 5:13) means generally "power" or "might" and also has the nuance "rule, sovereignty, or dominion" when referring to the ruling might of a great king (BAGD s.v. 1, 4; see also W. Michaelis, *TDNT* III, 905ff.). This power is αἰώνιον, "eternal."

The doxology ends with ἀμήν, "Amen," as do most NT doxologies (see 1:17). It is the writer's confirmation ("so let it be") of that which he has just written about God. Paul may also be seeking to draw out this response from his readers.

INSTRUCTIONS FOR THE RICH: 6:17-19

Paul provides instruction for those who are already rich, a provision he did not make when he warned against the desire to be rich (vv. 9-10). He warns about the danger of conceit and of fixing one's hope on riches (v. 17a) and urges the rich to place their hope on God alone, who has given all things for our enjoyment (v. 17b). Having established the proper relationship to God and to riches, Paul instructs the rich on how to use their wealth and live their lives (v. 18). Finally, he encourages them in that use of their riches by showing the benefit to be derived (v. 19).

6:17 οἱ πλουσίοι (here dative of those Timothy is to instruct) are "the rich" or "the wealthy" in the material realm, particularly those who do not need to work for a living (BAGD; see also Furfey, "ΠΛΟΥΣΙΟΣ," especially 245, 260f.). ἐν τῷ νῦν αἰῶνι serves as a limiting concept that sets the stage for Paul to speak about riches εἰς τὸ μέλλον in v. 19. αἰών can be used, as here, of "this present age or world," especially when it is qualified by some present time indicator (the phrase ὁ νῦν αἰών** appears also in Tit. 2:12; 2 Tim. 4:10).

The instruction Timothy is to give the rich is expressed in two negative infinitival clauses with the second qualified by a prepositional phrase. ὑψηλοφρονεῖν** (a NT hapax) means "to be proud, haughty" (BAGD) and is equivalent to the variant reading ὑψηλὰ φρονεῖν ("cherish proud thoughts, feel proud," the preferred reading in Rom. 11:20, where ὑψηλοφρονεῖν is the variant; BDF §119.5). The rich are tempted to think that their greater monetary value indicates that they themselves are of greater worth or value. Paul forthrightly charges them through Timothy "not" (μή) to think this way (cf. Rom. 12:16; Jas. 1:10).

ἠλπικέναι means here "to set or put one's hope." The perfect tense is used "by virtue of the continuing character of the hope formed" (BDF §341; Robertson, *Grammar,* 908; cf. the other NT instances of the perfect: Jn. 5:45; 1 Cor. 15:19; 2 Cor. 1:10; 1 Tim. 4:10; 5:5). The object of ἐπί, that on which hope is not to be set, is ἀδηλότητι, which is qualified by πλούτου, "wealth, riches," used here in the literal sense of "possession of many earthly goods" (BAGD). The phrase reads literally, therefore, "on the uncertainty of riches." This construction is equivalent in meaning to ἐπ' ἀδήλῳ πλούτῳ, but lays stress on the "uncertainty," at the same time putting genitive πλούτου first for emphasis (BDF §165). Paul warns against (μηδέ) such sin, which is also folly because of this uncertainty (cf. Ps. 62:10; Pr. 23:5; Lk. 12:19-21).

The rich are, instead, to set their hope "on God, who richly supplies us all things to enjoy" (v. 17c). ἀλλ' ἐπὶ θεῷ, "but on God," immediately, simply, and forcefully states, in contrast to ἐπὶ πλούτου ἀδηλότητι, the one on whom the rich should set their hope. (For the variant reading that adds τῷ ζῶντι after θεῷ see *NA*[26], and see *TCGNT* for reasons in favor of the shorter reading.) God is "he who supplies" (τῷ παρέχοντι) "to us" (ἡμῖν) πάντα, riches included. This is meant to encourage the rich to put their hope in the Giver and not in the gifts. ἡμῖν encompasses the entire community, both rich and poor, as it does elsewhere in the PE (2 Tim. 1:7, 9, 14; cf. Acts 14:17) and thus indicates that God provides for all. πάντα, "all things," is used here in the sense of "everything" (see πᾶν κτίσμα θεοῦ in 4:4). πλουσίως** (Col. 3:16; Tit. 3:6), "richly, abundantly," qualifies παρέχοντι and indicates the greatness of God's generosity in supplying all things to us. With this word Paul begins an instructive play on words and concepts going back to the previous πλουσίοις and continuing with πλούτου. In the next verse he will encourage the rich to emulate this generosity of God and "be rich (πλουτεῖν) in good works." In v. 19 he will encourage them to "lay up treasure" (ἀποθησαυρίζοντας) for the future. Here the phrase with εἰς specifies that it is "enjoyment," ἀπόλαυσιν** (also in Heb. 11:25), that is God's purpose for richly supplying us with all things. This enjoyment is not the self-indulgent living criticized in 5:6, notes Fee, but is thankful acceptance of God's good gifts given for us to enjoy (cf. 4:3, 4; Ec. 5:19, 20; Phil. 4:12).

6:18 Paul turns to a practical outworking of his command to the rich and of their setting their hope on God. The exhortation of the παράγγελλε continues to be spelled out in the three infinitives of this verse, each of which is dependent on that verb. There are four requirements in two groups of two each, the second item in each group enlarging on the first. This is most obvious in the second grouping, with κοινωνικούς dependent on the previous εἶναι.

Paul begins with the general word ἀγαθοεργεῖν,** "to do good," which is used elsewhere in the NT only in Paul's address at Lystra, where he speaks of God doing good by showering his good gifts on the hearers (Acts 14:17). The second infinitive here, πλουτεῖν, "to be rich," picks up on the wealth of God's generosity toward us (τῷ παρέχοντι . . . πλουσίως) and on the wealth of those to whom Timothy is to address these instructions (τοῖς πλουσίοις, v. 17). That in which they are encouraged to be rich is "good works" (ἐν ἔργοις καλοῖς; on plural ἔργα καλά in the PE see 5:10, 25; cf. 2:10). They are to do good and are to do so in a wealth of good deeds. In the former they imitate God (cf. Eph. 5:1); the latter is the way to be really rich.

εὐμεταδότους** (a biblical hapax) means "generous" (cf. the cognate verb μεταδίδωμι in Rom. 12:8 and especially Eph. 4:28), κοινωνικούς** (a biblical hapax) means "sharing what is one's own" or "gladly giving others a share" (F. Hauck, *TDNT* III, 809; cf. the cognate verb in Gal. 6:6; Rom. 12:13). The idea is for the rich to actually share what they have, which entails their personal involvement and sharing of themselves. This thereby expands and applies the previous concept (for a similar combination of these two concepts see Heb. 13:16).

Some have suggested that all four ideas in this verse indicate how the rich should use their money in Christian service. This is possible, certainly the last two do, and the following verse encourages the deeds of this verse by continuing the play on wealth, now in an eschatological perspective. But what is more likely is that Paul is instructing the rich through Timothy how they are to utilize both their riches and their lives in a truly rich way, i.e., by sharing and being rich in good deeds, and thus investing their lives (and their wealth) in that which will lead to permanent treasure.

6:19 The metaphor of wealth, which began in v. 18, is now extended eschatologically (Fee). The *RSV* ("thus laying up for themselves") and the *NIV* and the *TEV* ("in this way they will lay up treasure") express well the connection that ἀποθησαυρίζοντας has to the actions commanded in the preceding verse. Those actions were commanded because they are intrinsically good (cf. especially ἀγαθοεργεῖν and ἔργοις καλοῖς) and benefit others (so especially the last two). But now Paul says that those who do these good works provide benefit "for themselves" (ἑαυτοῖς). While doing good for others, they are simultaneously "storing up" or "laying up" (ἀποθησαυρίζοντας,** a NT hapax, in LXX only in Sir. 3:4; here accusative in agreement with the understood accusative subject of the preceding infinitives, i.e., the rich) "for themselves" θεμέλιον καλόν, literally "a good foundation" (here BAGD says that θεμέλιον is "about equal to 'treasure, reserve' "), εἰς τὸ μέλλον,** "for the future," indicating for what time the foundation is being laid up. "The future" here is the age that follows this age (for this sense cf. 4:8; Eph. 1:21).

A ἵνα clause indicates the purpose for which this storing up takes place. ἐπιλαμβάνω (here ἐπιλάβωνται, "they may take hold of") is used here in the same sense as in v. 12. ζωή is used in the PE* (as elsewhere by Paul) of the spiritual life God brings to the believer through Christ (2 Tim. 1:1, 10), which has a future dimension as well as a present dimension (1 Tim. 4:8) and which often is clearly demarcated as future by the designation "*eternal* life" (ζωὴ αἰώνιος, 1:16; 6:12; Tit. 1:2; 3:7). ὄντως (for the textual variants see *UBSGNT;* for the reasons for favoring ὄντως alone see *TCGNT*) is used here attributively, as are the other PE* occurrences (5:3, 5, 16), and means "real" or "true." In light of the reference in the previous clause to "the future" (εἰς τὸ μέλλον) and the parallelism of this clause with the second clause of v. 12 (which has the singular imperative of the same verb and αἰωνίου in place of ὄντως), τῆς ὄντως ζωῆς, "real life," must refer here to "eternal life" (cf. BAGD s.v. ζωή 2bβ). The two can be virtually interchangeable since in the NT that which makes life "real" is that it is indestructible (see 2 Tim. 1:10; Jn. 5:24; cf. R. Bultmann, *TDNT* II, 863f.).

What Paul says to the rich through Timothy is what he says to Timothy himself (vv. 11ff.), what he has said of himself (Phil. 3:8ff.; 1 Cor. 9:24-27), and what he has said to others (Gal. 6:7, 8): Good works demonstrate the reality of faith and salvation and are needed to receive eternal life (cf. Mt. 7:21; 25:34-40, 46b). Jesus also taught about the godly and generous use of wealth, which stores up treasure in heaven (cf. Matthew 6; 19; and 20; Lk. 12:33; 16:9). Similarly he taught that good works show that a person has an indestructible foundation (Mt. 7:25, using the cognate verb θεμελιόω). What both Paul and Jesus are saying is that one who has accepted God's grace and salvation must evidence it in one's life. Thus they are quite willing to say, as both an encouragement and a warning, that this evidence of salvation is a necessity for the reception of eternal life.

FINAL CHARGE TO TIMOTHY: 6:20-21

Paul draws his letter to a close with a final charge to Timothy, which calls on him to "guard the deposit" and does so in the context of warning him again against false teaching (vv. 20-21a). In doing so Paul returns to the concern with which he opened the letter (1:3ff.) and which has been a concern throughout (e.g., 1:18-20; 4:1ff.; 6:3ff.). As in Paul's letters to churches where he has labored and is known, no individuals are singled out for greetings. Paul concludes with a blessing (v. 21b).

6:20 Ὦ, an emotional interjection, is used here to add solemnity and urgency to his personal address to Timothy. Τιμόθεε, a vocative, is used to directly address his associate by name (cf. 1:18). The only other occurrences of Timothy's name in the PE* are in the opening salutations (1:2; 2 Tim. 1:2).

Timothy is to "guard" τὴν παραθήκην** (also in 2 Tim. 1:12, 14), "that which has been entrusted," "the deposit." This "deposit" has been identified with Timothy's own spiritual life, with his calling to the ministry, and with the apostolic teaching. Something like the first of these three views is probably demanded by the context in 2 Tim. 1:12. But the last seems to be demanded by the context here and in 2 Tim. 1:14, where "the deposit" is apparently the same as "the standard of sound words that you heard from me" (v. 13) and as the words heard from Paul that Timothy is later asked to "entrust" (the cognate verb παρατίθημι) to others (2:2, which thus combines the concepts used separately in 1:13 and 1:14). Here "the deposit" that Timothy is to guard is set in opposition to false teaching and is most likely, therefore, the Christian faith itself.

This combination of verb and noun, τὴν παραθήκην φυλάσσω, "guard the deposit," was commonly known and is seen in all three occurrences of the noun in the NT (here and 2 Tim. 1:12, 14; cf. παράδοσις in 1 Cor. 11:2; 2 Thes. 2:15; 3:6). It was used in the ancient world of the high obligation of having in trust another person's treasured possession, of keeping it safe, and of returning it as it was (e.g., Lv. 6:2, 4: LXX παραθήκη; cf. also Tobit 10:13; 2 Maccabees 3:15; for the Greco-Roman world see Barclay, "Paul's Certainties VII"; Spicq, "Saint Paul et la loi des dépôts"). Paul places Timothy under such a trust with regard to the gospel and its teachings (cf. 2 Tim. 4:7: "I have kept the faith").

Paul joins to the preceding positive command the necessary negative correlative, here expressed in a participial clause used in an imperatival sense (cf. Rom. 12:9, 16; cf. Brooks-Winbery, *Syntax*, 137f.). ἐκτρέπομαι, "avoid," is used in the NT in the passive form with a middle sense. What is to be "avoided" is designated first as "chatter" or "empty talk" (plural κενοφωνίας,** also in 2 Tim. 2:16). This "empty talk" is βέβηλος (so also in 2 Tim. 2:16), "profane" or "worldly" in the sense of "godless." Here Paul is apparently returning to his evaluation in 1:6, now using κενοφωνίας as a synonym for ματαιολογία. If that is the case, then the description of the false teachers' ματαιολογία in 1:7 may indicate what Paul means by βέβηλος here.

What Timothy is to avoid is also called ἀντιθέσεις** (a biblical hapax), "opposing arguments or ideas," a term that crystallizes what Paul says elsewhere concerning the false teaching and those who are involved in it (cf. 6:3-5; Tit. 1:9-14, especially v. 9; 2 Tim. 2:25; 3:8; cf. Schlarb, "Miszelle zu 1 Tim 6 20"). It is possible, as Bernard observes, that βεβήλους is to be taken with ἀντιθέσεις as well as κενοφωνίας, since the article appears only before κενοφωνίας. Paul acknowledges that these opposing arguments or ideas are called "knowledge" (γνῶσις), but asserts that in fact they are "falsely called" such (ψευδώνυμος,** a biblical hapax; cf. 1:7; 6:4).

6:21 Paul adds a relative clause to show what happens to those who profess the position described in the previous verse and why his command to avoid it is so crucial. The antecedent of ἥν is "falsely called knowledge." "Some" (τινες) "have professed" (ἐπαγγελλόμενοι; see 2:10), i.e., "have laid claim to" (cf. *NEB*), this erroneous system. Doing so has caused them to "depart" or "go astray" (ἠστόχησαν,** see 1:6; 2 Tim. 2:18) "with regard to" (περί) "the faith." "The faith" (τὴν πίστιν) is used in the same setting and with the same sense here as it is 1:19 (see the comments there), i.e., to designate both the gospel one believes, the Christian faith, and the belief that one has regarding its truth and in the one presented therein.

As in all of Paul's letters and in Heb. 13:25; Rev. 22:21, the final blessing begins with "grace" (χάρις), i.e., God's unmerited favor strengthening and enabling his people (see 1:2 on this word and on the verb to be understood). This χάρις is explicitly said to be "of (our) Lord Jesus (Christ)" in all Paul's letters except the last ones, Ephesians, Colossians, and the PE, in which χάρις is unqualified and the blessing is written as here, with only slight variations. At this stage Paul apparently thought it would be evident whose grace he intended. What is more striking than this change is that at the conclusion of every letter Paul prays that grace will be with the readers. This pattern manifests a foundational truth for Paul: For the ongoing life of believers the grace of Jesus is absolutely essential.

Plural ὑμῶν indicates that Paul expected this letter to be read to the believers, and it further indicates that all along he has had them, not just Timothy, in view. (For the variant reading singular σοῦ in place of plural ὑμῶν and on the question of the presence or absence of ἀμήν see *UBSGNT* and the discussion in *TCGNT*.)

COMMENTARY ON TITUS

SALUTATION: 1:1-4

Like other letters in the NT bearing Paul's name, the letter to Titus begins by identifying the author (1:1ff.) and the recipient (1:4a) and then expresses special greetings to the recipient (1:4b). It thus follows the form found in Greek letters of the day. But Paul expands each of the three elements of this form in a distinctly Christian manner (see above on 1 Tim. 1:1-2).

As in all his letters Paul calls himself Παῦλος. Except in those letters in which authorship is shared with those who are not apostles (1 and 2 Thessalonians, Philippians, Philemon), Paul identifies himself as an ἀπόστολος of Jesus Christ. The greeting is always a blessing of "grace" and "peace" (1 and 2 Timothy add "mercy," as do some manuscripts of Titus) and is almost always specified as being "from God the Father and the Lord Jesus Christ" (Titus alone refers to Jesus as "Savior"; 1 Thessalonians lacks "God the Father and the Lord Jesus Christ," and Colossians lacks "and the Lord Jesus Christ," but in both cases such words are used in the immediate context). There are other minor differences in the wording of the salutations (see above on 1 Tim. 1:2 for some), but the shared characteristics are most noteworthy.

The salutations in the PE specify that Paul's apostleship (or apostolic activity) is according to God's will or commandment, as do those in 1 and 2 Corinthians, Ephesians, and Colossians explicitly, and Galatians by implication. 1 Timothy refers at this point to God as "Savior" and to Christ as "our hope"; 2 Timothy adds "according to the promise of life in Christ Jesus." Both of these additional notes are found in slightly different forms in Titus. In the PE each of the recipients is designated τέκνον with the qualification ἀγαπητόν (2 Timothy) or γνησίον with a prepositional phrase regarding πίστις (1 Timothy and Titus).

Titus differs from 1 and 2 Timothy by its expansion of the section on the author. One of the two elements involved in this expansion is a description of apostleship in terms of its results among those to whom the apostle is sent (1:1b). The other is a statement concerning eternal life, encompassing God's promise in eternity, his manifestation of his promise in history, and Paul's being entrusted with the proclamation of that promised and manifested life (1:2-3). Both of these elements are similar to what is seen in Romans (cf. 1:1b and Rom. 1:5-6; 1:2-3 and Rom. 1:1b-4), which alone exceeds Titus in the expansion of the identification of the author.

These elements in the identification of the author appear later in Titus as important theological truths: The faith of God's elect and the knowledge of the truth according to godliness (1:1b) are to be the motivating concern for the elders (1:9-13). The people of God are urged to live godly lives (2:11ff.; 3:4-7), and the theological basis given for doing so includes the hope of eternal life (2:13; 3:7; cf. 1:2-3).

1:1 This verse contains the name of the author (Παῦλος), two designations of his role (δοῦλος, ἀπόστολος) with their respective indicators of relationship (θεοῦ, Ἰησοῦ Χριστοῦ), the results for which he labors (πίστιν ... καὶ ἐπίγνωσιν ἀληθείας τῆς κατ' εὐσέβειαν) and those for whom he labors (ἐκλεκτῶν θεοῦ).

For Παῦλος see 1 Tim. 1:1.

δοῦλος (see 1 Tim. 6:1) means "slave" and is used literally by Paul on several occasions (e.g., 1 Cor. 7:21, 22; Eph. 6:5-8; Col. 3:11, 22; 4:1; 1 Tim. 6:1; Tit. 2:9; Phm. 16, 18). The word can be used to designate the exclusive nature of man's relationship to God and is used by the LXX in the Psalms and elsewhere to describe this relationship to God (cf., e.g., Pss. 19:11, 13; 67[66]:17; 86[85]:2, 4, 16; 119[118]:17, 23, 38, 49, 65, 76, 84, 122, 124f., 135, 140, 176; Tuente, *NIDNTT* III, 595). Just as it is used for the members of the covenant community, so also it is used to designate its leaders, e.g., Moses (Ps. 104[105]:26), Joshua (Jos. 24:30[29]; Jdg. 2:8), Abraham (Ps. 104[105]:42), David (Ps. 88:4[89:3]), Jacob (Is. 48:20) (cf. Rengstorf, *TDNT* II, 268; BAGD s.v. 4). Paul connects the secular usage of δοῦλος, "slave," to the religious usage by designating the "free" Christian as "Christ's slave" (see 1 Cor. 7:22) and hence uses the term for members of the Christian community (Rom. 6:16; 1 Cor. 7:22; Eph. 6:6) and its leaders including himself (cf., e.g., for others Col. 4:12; for others with himself Phil. 1:1; for himself Rom. 1:1; Gal. 1:10; used as a principle 2 Tim. 2:24; cf. also σύνδουλος, Col. 1:7; 4:7). When qualified by a genitive in Paul it is usually Χριστοῦ (Rom. 1:1; [1 Cor. 7:22]; Gal. 1:10; Eph. 6:6; Phil. 1:1; Col. 4:12) rather than θεοῦ as here (and in Jas. 1:1 [where it is also qualified by κυρίου Ἰησοῦ Χριστοῦ]; 1 Pet. 2:16; Acts 16:17; Rev. 7:3; 15:3; cf. 2 Tim. 2:24, δοῦλον κυρίου). "But here, as elsewhere, the distinctive thing about the concept of the *doulos* is the subordinate, obligatory and responsible nature of his service in his exclusive relation to his Lord" (Tuente, *NIDNTT* III, 596).

Paul joins to the above designation his more usual designation of himself as an ἀπόστολος Ἰησοῦ Χριστοῦ (see 1 Tim. 1:1; note that Ἰησοῦ Χριστοῦ here is the reverse of the order found in 1 Tim. 1:1 and 2 Tim. 1:1, although Χριστοῦ Ἰησοῦ is found in some MSS here, see *NA*[26]). For ἀπόστολος see 1 Tim. 1:1. Paul refers to himself as "an apostle of Jesus Christ" in this opening section (as he does in his other letters) to indicate the role and authority with which he writes to Titus (1:4) and through him to the members of the churches on Crete (cf. 2:2ff., 15; 3:1ff., 8, and especially 15c: "Grace be with you all" [μετὰ πάντων ὑμῶν]).

His apostleship is κατὰ πίστιν ἐκλεκτῶν θεοῦ καὶ ἐπίγνωσιν ἀληθείας τῆς κατ' εὐσέβειαν. Although κατά might mean "in accordance with" here, the sense of the passage seems to be best captured by the *RSV* rendering "to further the faith of God's elect . . ." (cf. also Bernard, Brox, Hendriksen; Kelly renders it "in the interest of" and refers appropriately to Jn. 2:6; cf. also Jos., *Ant.* 3, 268). Just as in Rom. 1:5 Paul's apostleship is to "bring about the obedience of faith among the Gentiles," so here similarly his apostleship is "in the interest of" the πίστιν and ἐπίγνωσιν ἀληθείας of the ἐκλεκτῶν θεοῦ. πίστις would appear to designate here the subjective element of trust or belief, since it is followed by the genitive ἐκλεκτῶν θεοῦ and paralleled by ἐπίγνωσις. ἐκλεκτός (NT 22x, Pl.* 6x, PE 3x, Rom. 8:33; 16:13; Col. 3:12; 1 Tim. 5:21; here; 2 Tim. 2:10) means generally those "chosen or selected" and is used here, as elsewhere in the NT, "especially of those whom God has chosen fr. the generality of mankind and drawn to himself" (BAGD). The phrase ἐκλεκτοὶ (τοῦ) θεοῦ is used in the NT to designate Christians and to emphasize who it is that has elected them (the phrase is used only by Paul in the NT, Rom. 8:33; Col. 3:12; Tit. 1:1; it is also used in the LXX to designate God's people, 1 Ch. 16:13; Ps. 88:4[89:3]; 104[105]:6, 43; Is. 65:9, 15, 23). The entire phrase πίστις ἐκλεκτῶν θεοῦ reminds one of the statement "as many as had been appointed to eternal life believed" (Acts 13:48).

καί joins ἐπίγνωσιν to πίστιν as a joint object of the preposition κατά. For ἐπίγνωσις see 1 Tim. 2:4. With the definite article τῆς following ἀληθείας and preceding κατ' εὐσέβειαν Paul insists that ἀληθεία is that "truth" which pertains to or produces εὐσέβεια (cf. 1 Tim. 6:3, the only other NT occurrence of κατ' εὐσέβειαν). εὐσέβεια (see 1 Tim. 2:2) means here, as often elsewhere in the NT, "godliness" in the sense of a godly life, the life of one who fears and serves God.

The correlation of these terms characterizes the purpose of Paul's apostleship and highlights the perspective of his message and ministry. He constantly calls on his readers to turn to God in faith and to live in faith and is equally emphatic that God has previously chosen or elected such people (e.g., Rom. 8:28-33; 9:11). Similarly he constantly calls on them to know and understand God's truth so that they can "walk in a manner worthy of the Lord, to please him in all respects" (e.g., Col. 1:9-10). Here he knits all these aspects together with carefully chosen words (cf. 2:10-11; 3:8).

1:2 The logical connection between ἐπ' ἐλπίδι ζωῆς αἰωνίου and the preceding verse is not precisely clear and various possibilities have been proposed (see Huther and Hendriksen for examples). The preposition ἐπί does not in itself provide an answer. Analogies are provided by the occurrences of ἐλπίς in 1 Tim. 1:1 and of ἐπαγγελίαν ζωῆς in 2 Tim. 1:1, both in the section of the salutations of those letters related to Paul's apostleship, though in both cases in a slightly different construction than here, and with 1 Tim. 1:1 adding the qualification "our" (ἡμῶν).

Perhaps then this prepositional phrase at the beginning of v. 2 qualifies ἀπόστολος (cf. 1 Tim. 4:10), as does the preceding phrase, κατὰ πίστιν. . . . It would thus give an additional reason for Paul's apostleship (cf. BAGD s.v. ἐπί II.1bγ). If this is so, then this phrase speaks of the hope that Paul shares with the ἐκλεκτοὶ θεοῦ as he carries out his apostolic ministry and message. In 3:7 — the only other NT occurrence of ἐλπὶς ζωῆς αἰωνίου — Paul relates that he does share in this hope. The phrase should probably be understood to function here as it does there.

ἐλπίς (PE* 4x: 1 Tim. 1:1; Tit. 1:2; 2:13; 3:7) is used here and in the NT in the sense of "confident expectation" (as opposed to sight or possession: Rom. 8:24-25) based on God's promise. Sometimes the same hope is expressed in other words (e.g., "the hope of glory," Rom. 5:2; Col. 1:27). The combination ζωὴ αἰωνίος, "eternal life" (see 1 Tim. 1:16), signifies in Paul that endless future life which the believer will have as a gift from God through Jesus Christ (Rom. 5:21; 6:23; 1 Tim. 1:16; 6:12) and will enjoy in fellowship with God and his people.

The God who promised this eternal life (cf. 2 Tim. 1:1; 1 Jn. 2:25) "before the beginning of time" *(NIV)* is he "who does not lie." ἐπηγγείλατο (see 1 Tim. 2:10) is used here with the meaning "promised." Paul speaks elsewhere of God promising life with the cognate noun ἐπαγγελία (1 Tim. 4:8 and 2 Tim. 1:1). God's faithfulness to this promise is expressed negatively here with the adjective ἀψευδής** (a NT hapax), "who cannot lie." This way of speaking about God has its roots in the OT (e.g., Nu. 23:19; 1 Sa. 15:29), and this OT background is reflected elsewhere in Paul (e.g., Rom. 3:3-4; 2 Tim. 2:13) and in the NT (Heb. 6:18).

The time that God made this promise was πρὸ χρόνων αἰωνίων. The preposition πρό, when used of time, means "before" (see BAGD s.v. 2). Some have interpreted χρόνοι αἰωνίοι** (also in Rom. 16:25; 2 Tim. 1:9) as referring to the long period of time reaching back to when God made this promise to the patriarchs (e.g. Calvin; cf. *RSV, NASB, NEB*). Others (cf. *NIV*) think that Paul is speaking here of God's commitment before time began. The most compelling consideration is the meaning of the phrase (again with πρό) in 2 Tim. 1:9, where it relates to the time of God's purpose (πρόθεσις) and is contrasted with the "now" (νῦν) of Christ's first appearance. There the phrase is usually understood to refer to eternity (so *NASB* and *NEB*). Here, too, there is the same movement from the time of promise to the time of manifestation (Tit. 1:2, 3). Therefore, it is best to understand χρόνοι αἰωνίοι as referring to eternity here also. This would also be in accord with

Paul's perspective elsewhere, where he looks back to God's decision before time and the world began (cf. 1 Cor. 2:7: πρὸ τῶν αἰώνων; Eph. 1:4: πρὸ καταβολῆς κόσμου).

1:3 Paul now moves from eternity past to the manifestation in time and history of God's promise. φανερόω (PE* 3x: also in 1 Tim. 3:16; 2 Tim. 1:10; here ἐφανέρωσεν) means "reveal, make known, show." Here what is revealed is τὸν λόγον αὐτοῦ, God's message. There is a slight but understandable shift from the "eternal life" promised by God, referred to in the preceding verse, to "his word" here. According to 2 Tim. 1:10 (eternal) life is brought to light through Christ's work. But since eternal life is unseen and still in the future for believers, God makes known the truth about eternal life in what is called here τὸν λόγον αὐτοῦ, which in the analogous passage 2 Tim. 1:10 is said to take place διὰ τοῦ εὐαγγελίου. It would appear, therefore, that "his word" here should be understood as the gospel message (cf. the same correlation in Eph. 1:13; Phil. 1:12, 14; Col. 1:5).

This manifestation was made καιροῖς ἰδίοις, which may be rendered "at the proper time" (see comments on 1 Tim. 2:6; 6:15). God has determined the time of the manifestation (cf. Gal. 4:4; Rom. 5:6; see Lock).

Paul adds to τὸν λόγον αὐτοῦ the words ἐν κηρύγματι, "in proclamation" or "in preaching," thus, as elsewhere, carefully linking the essence of the gospel message to the apostolic communication of that message (cf. the closely analogous passages 2 Tim. 1:10-11; Rom. 16:25ff.). He says thereby not only that God has manifested the content of the gospel message but also that he has done so in and through the apostolic proclamation (ἐν with the dative to express manner or means).

Paul was "entrusted" with this task of "proclamation" (cf. 2 Tim. 1:10-11). Here he adds ἐγώ, "I," for emphasis, since he always remains amazed that he, who had been the gospel's arch-opponent, should be entrusted by God's wondrous grace with the proclamation of the gospel (5 of 7x in the PE* ἐγώ is used of this event: here; 1 Tim. 1:11, 15; 2:7; 2 Tim. 1:11; the other 2 are related to Paul's activity as an apostle: Tit. 1:5; 2 Tim. 4:6). A passive form of πιστεύω with the meaning "be entrusted with something" occurs 6x in Paul and nearly always refers to his being entrusted with the gospel and its proclamation (1 Cor. 9:17; Gal. 2:7; 1 Thes. 2:4; 1 Tim. 1:11; here; the one exception is Rom. 3:2).

κατ' ἐπιταγήν (see 1 Tim. 1:1) is used here with the meaning "in accordance with the command," which BAGD suggest is equivalent to "by command." Paul wants to make plain that his being entrusted with the gospel, i.e., his apostleship (see 1 Tim. 1:1), did not originate from humans (see Gal. 1:1, 11, 12) but is an "order" or "injunction" from God himself. Thus Paul refers in several of his salutations to this action of God, using ἐπιταγή (here and 1 Timothy) or θέλημα (1 and 2 Corinthians, Ephesians, Colossians, and 2 Timothy) with θεοῦ, or by directly repudiating any human agency (Galatians).

Here and in 1 Tim. 1:1 (see the comments on that verse) Paul adds to θεοῦ the designation τοῦ σωτῆρος ἡμῶν, "our Savior." He may do so because the readers of these two letters needed to be reminded that the one who has entrusted Paul with the gospel is indeed *their* Savior, so that this awareness might shape their thinking and acting as it shapes his (note where Paul refers to God as "Savior" in these two letters: 2:10, 13; 3:4; 1 Tim. 2:3; 4:10; "God our Savior" occurs nowhere else in his letters).

By thus referring to the "proclamation" with which he was "entrusted," i.e., to his own ministry, Paul returns to the purpose of his apostleship and thus concludes this portion of the salutation by giving further emphasis to that purpose. This clear statement of Paul's authoritative apostleship and its purpose of furthering the spiritual health and well-being of God's people provides for Titus the basis for communicating and carrying out Paul's sometimes forceful demands in this letter. Titus knows all these things, but by writing them to him Paul is making them very clear to those on Crete to whom Paul is ministering by means of this letter.

1:4 Here Paul indicates to whom (dative) he is writing this letter. Paul's designation of Τίτος (see **Recipients: Titus** in the **Introduction**) as his "true child according to a common faith" is nearly the same as his designation of Timothy in 1 Tim. 1:2 (see the comments on that verse). Here, however, he uses κατά in place of ἐν and adds κοινήν. κατά is merely a stylistic variation. Paul may use κοινός, "common," to remind Titus, the churches on Crete, and the false teachers "of the circumcision" (1:10; cf. v. 14) that he regards the uncircumcised Titus and himself, a Jew, as sharing the same faith (see **Introduction**, p. 9; cf. Gal. 2:3-4; 3:7-9, 14, 28-29). Titus, no less than circumcised Timothy, is Paul's spiritual child in this shared faith.

The greeting "Grace and peace from God the Father and Christ Jesus our Lord/Savior" so well articulated for Paul the essence of what Christians need, from whom they receive it, and in what capacity the members of the Godhead, who is this source, stand to Christians that he places it, with only minor differences, in the salutation of every letter (see the comments on 1 Tim. 1:2). In 1 and 2 Timothy he adds ἔλεος, "mercy" (for the textual variants in Titus, including those that add ἔλεος, see *UBSGNT; TCGNT*). Here alone he calls Christ σωτήρ, "Savior," rather than κύριος, "Lord." It is as if he anticipates the two crucial theological arguments that undergird his ethical exhortations in chapters 2 and 3, in both of which Christ as Savior is at the center (2:13; 3:6) as the one through whom God's grace has come to save us and to instruct and enable us in living godly (2:11ff.) and peaceful (3:1ff.) lives.

QUALIFICATIONS FOR ELDERS: 1:5-9

Like 1 Timothy, Titus plunges immediately into the business of the letter, since it is a letter to a trusted colleague. It has, therefore, no thanksgiving section, as do most of Paul's letters to congregations (and as 2 Timothy does). Paul begins by setting forth his reason for leaving Titus on Crete, namely to do the unfinished work and in particular to see that elders are appointed (v. 5). He writes this not because Titus needs the urging but to provide for him apostolic authority and direction in writing.

Paul then states the qualifications for "elders." He begins with the general requirement that they be "above reproach" and then takes family life as a most crucial proving ground (v. 6). He repeats the need that elders be "above reproach," now using the term "overseer" (ἐπίσκοπος) for the function "the elder" is to fulfill and strengthens that repeated demand by pointing out that the elder/overseer serves as "God's steward" (v. 7a). What Paul means by this is stated in terms of five characteristics that must not mark the life of an "overseer" (v. 7b) and six that must be found in the life of a leader of God's people (v. 8). Paul concludes by insisting that the overseer be steadfast in holding to the apostolic teaching so that he may carry out his two duties, which are to exhort in sound doctrine and to refute those who contradict it (v. 9). Vv. 6 and 7 are closely parallel to 1 Tim. 3:2ff.

1:5 The prepositional phrase τούτου χάριν** (as a preposition χάριν almost always follows its noun) indicates the reason or goal for Paul's leaving Titus on Crete, which is developed in the following ἵνα clause. ἀπέλιπον means here "I left behind"; the nuance of "behind" is seen clearly in the other occurrences of ἀπολείπω in the PE* (2 Tim. 4:13, 20; for the textual variants here, neither of which alters the meaning, see *NA*[26]). Κρήτη** (also mentioned in Acts 27:7, 12f., 21), the island of Crete, lies south of the Aegean Sea in the Mediterranean. As early as Homer (*Iliad* 2.649) Crete was known for its many cities, which may account for κατὰ πόλιν later in this verse. That Paul left Titus behind implies that he was with Titus on Crete. The occasion for this that best fits into Paul's life would be during a journey after Paul's release from his first Roman imprisonment (see the **Introduction**). From what follows, one can surmise that the two were successful in evangelizing various cities on the island but did not have time to return and strengthen the believers by setting the churches in order and seeing that elders were elected (for Paul's pattern see Acts 14:21-23).

Therefore, Paul left Titus to "set in order what remains and appoint elders in every city, as I directed you" (v. 5b). Middle ἐπιδιορθώσῃ** is to be preferred over the active (see *NA*[26] for the evidence for each reading; ἐπιδιορθόω is a biblical hapax here). λείπω occurs 6x in the NT but nowhere else with the sense that the participle has here. Literally ἵνα τὰ λείποντα ἐπιδιορθώσῃ means "that you might set right the things lacking." *TEV* has perhaps best captured the phrase in an English idiom with "put in order the things that still needed doing." That this is the proper sense is verified by the next clause, which indicates one thing that needed to be done.

καταστήσῃς (aorist subjunctive of καθίστημι) means here "appoint" or even possibly "ordain" (BAGD), as its only other occurrence in this kind of setting seems to indicate: In Acts 6:3 the apostles speak of the action they are about to take, that of putting the Seven (chosen by the congregation) in charge of the diaconal task by laying hands on them (v. 6). Similarly, in Acts 14 Paul and Barnabas do what Paul is asking Titus to do here, and the verb used is χειροτονέω, which could be rendered either "lay hands on" or "ordain." It would appear that both Paul, addressing Titus, and Luke in Acts 14 are compressing what takes place by speaking only of the last act, i.e., appointment or laying on of hands, and do not feel it necessary to relate the steps that lead up to that act (which are related in Acts 6). Moreover, Paul has not written the list of qualifications that follows in vv. 6ff. for Titus's benefit but more probably as a guide for the Christians on Crete, just as a brief list of qualifications was given to the Christians in Jerusalem to follow in their selection of the Seven (Acts 6:3). This similarity would suggest that the Acts 6 (and 14) pattern was operative here, and that would be a further indication for understanding καταστήσῃς as referring to the final act in the process.

κατὰ πόλιν is used in the distributive sense: "city by city" or "in every city" (BAGD s.v. κατά II.1d; cf. Acts 15:21; 20:23; also κατ' ἐκκλησίαν, Acts 14:23). This means that plural πρεσβυτέρους relates to each city that has a church: Several elders/overseers are appointed in each church. This corresponds to what was done in the cities of Philippi (Phil. 1:1) and Ephesus (Acts 20:17, 28; cf. 14:23; 1 Thes. 5:12, 13; 1 Tim. 5:17). πρεσβύτεροι here designates the officials who lead the Christian congregation (see the comments on 1 Tim. 5:17 and the excursus on **Bishops/Presbyters and Deacons** following the comments on 1 Tim. 3:8-13). Jeremias's suggestion that the term be understood here and in 1 Tim. 5:17 as "older men" and the clause here rendered "install older men" is rightly regarded by Dibelius-Conzelmann (and others) as "not possible linguistically."

Titus is to do this in accord with Paul's command. The clause with ὡς indicates the manner in which the activity should proceed (BAGD s.v. I.1;

cf. Col. 4:4; Eph. 6:20) and refers to what Paul has already said to Titus (aorist tense). He repeats it here in part by indicating the qualifications necessary for an individual to become an elder. With emphatic ἐγώ (as in v. 3) and the verb διεταξάμην ("I ordered, commanded"; cf. 1 Cor. 7:17; 16:1) Paul is providing for Titus (σοι) full apostolic authority to carry out this action carefully in compliance with the standards he gives.

1:6 Paul begins (as in 1 Tim. 3:2) by stating the overall requirement that a potential elder be "above reproach" (here ἀνέγκλητος, also used of church leaders in 1 Tim. 3:10 [deacons; see the comments there]; the synonym ἀνεπίλημπτος is used of the overseer/elder in 1 Tim. 3:2). As such, a man would not be open to attack or criticism in terms of Christian life in general or in terms of the characteristics that Paul goes on to name. This does not mean that an elder must be perfect, but it may be fairly said that each named characteristic marks his life. εἴ τίς (see 1 Tim. 3:1) ἐστιν, "If anyone is," causes the reader to expect a conclusion such as "Elect such a person as an elder." The conclusion is not stated, probably because Paul wants to list other qualifications, and then having done so, he considers it unnecessary to make explicit the obvious conclusion. The clause implies, therefore, that these requirements are what is necessary and that "anyone" meeting them is eligible.

μιᾶς γυναικὸς ἀνήρ, "the husband of one wife," indicates that marital and sexual fidelity are required of the potential elder. This assumes that the church officer is married (the usual situation in life) and thus prescribes fidelity in these terms. By inference it demands the same sexual purity of an unmarried elder, who is no more ruled out by this requirement than is the man with less than two children by the next requirement (see comments on 1 Tim. 3:2).

With "having children who believe, not accused of dissipation or rebellion," it is not demanded that the elder have children but only that, if he has them, they should be πιστά τέκνα (on τέκνα see 1 Tim. 3:4, 12). ἔχων is used here "to denote the possession of persons to whom one has close relationships" (BAGD s.v. I.2bα). The implication is that Paul is talking only about children who are still rightfully under their father's authority in his home (cf. ἐν ὑποταγῇ and the repeated τοῦ ἰδίου οἴκου of 1 Tim. 3:4-5).

Should πιστά in this clause be understood as "faithful" or as "believing"? The range of usage shows that either meaning is a possibility: The word can clearly mean "faithful," as it does several times in the PE, including once with a noun, as here (2 Tim. 2:2: πιστοὶ ἀνθρώποι). It can also mean "believing" and does on several occasions in the PE, again including once with a noun (1 Tim. 6:2: πιστοὶ . . . δεσπόται). The context here and the parallel in 1 Tim. 3:4-5, however, provide some important indicators: The qualifying statement here, "not accused of dissipation or rebellion," emphasizes behavior and seems to explain what it means for τέκνα to be πιστά.

Likewise 1 Tim. 3:4 speaks of the overseer "keeping his children under control with all dignity." In both cases the overseer is evaluated on the basis of his control of his children and their conduct. It is likely, therefore, that τέκνα ἔχων πιστά here is virtually equivalent to τέκνα ἔχοντα ἐν ὑποταγῇ in 1 Tim. 3:4. If that is so, then πιστά here means "faithful" in the sense of "submissive" or "obedient," as a servant or steward is regarded as πιστός when he carries out the requests of his master (Mt. 24:45f.; 25:21, 23; Lk. 12:42f.; 1 Cor. 4:2; cf. Thayer, *Lexicon;* Cremer, *Lexicon;* LSJM s.v.; R. Bultmann, *TDNT* VI, 175, all but Thayer giving "obedient" as one of the meanings for the word and referring to Xenophon, *Hellenica* 2.4.30; MM mentions a deed of sale in which a slave is described as πιστοῦ καὶ ἀδράστου, "faithful and not given to running away"; Horsley, *New Documents* II [1982] 53 gives an epitaph for a slave that says "I remain faithful [πιστός] as before" [cf. ibid. 3 (1983) 39]; Bultmann cites Hesychius: πιστός = εὐπειθής, ready to obey, obedient). This proposed understanding of the passage goes contrary to a consistent pattern in recent English translations *(RSV, NEB, TEV:* "believers"; similarly *NASB, NIV),* but the considerations cited above seem compelling.

The concluding part of the verse, μὴ ἐν κατηγορίᾳ ἀσωτίας ἢ ἀνυπότακτα, literally "not in an accusation of dissipation or rebellious," negatively qualifies πιστά and thus indicates what may not characterize πιστά children. The negative particle μή is used here, rather than οὐκ, probably because the participle ὄντα is understood with this construction (H. C. G. Moule, 155). μὴ ἐν κατηγορίᾳ** (the noun occurs in Jn. 18:29; 1 Tim. 5:19) can best be expressed in English by "not accused of." ἀσωτία** (here genitive of the content of the accusation) means "debauchery" or "dissipation" and is used in the NT of drunkenness (Eph. 5:18) and of associated vices of the non-Christian world (1 Pet. 4:4; cf. ἀσώτως in Lk. 15:13). Therefore the potential elder's children must not be guilty of "sensuality, lusts, drunkenness, carousals, drinking parties" (1 Pet. 4:3).

ἀνυπότακτα stands in tandem with the preceding prepositional phrase and its genitive modifier. Here it means "undisciplined, disobedient, rebellious," as it does in 1 Tim. 1:9, where it is used of those who are unwilling to be under God's will and law, and in Tit. 1:10 of the false teachers who "turn away from the truth" (v. 14). What must not characterize the children of an elder is immorality and undisciplined rebelliousness, if the children are still at home and under his authority. Paul is not asking any more of the elder and his children than is expected of every Christian father and his children. However, only if a man exercises such proper control over his children may he be an elder.

1:7 As Paul repeats here the requirement of "blamelessness," he introduces the functional title ἐπίσκοπος, "overseer" ("bishop"), for the elder, as he did in Acts 20:28 (cf. v. 17). He does so before he describes negatively and positively the traits that must characterize one who exercises oversight of others. He is not introducing another church office into the discussion (that of the overseer/bishop, as distinct from that of the elder) but is using another name for the same office (see the comments on 1 Tim. 3:2 and the excursus on **Bishops/Presbyters and Deacons**). With singular τὸν ἐπίσκοπον Paul continues here the use of the generic singular that began in v. 6 ("if anyone," εἴ τις) after the instructions regarding "elders" that began with the plural (v. 5). Thus Paul continues to focus on the elder/overseer as an individual.

ὡς θεοῦ οἰκονόμος gives the reason that blamelessness is needed (δεῖ; cf. 1 Tim. 3:2), ὡς, "as," being equivalent to "since he is" (Huther) and thereby introducing a basic characteristic of the elder/overseer (BAGD s.v. ὡς III.1a). An οἰκονόμος, "steward," is one chosen by his employer to manage his business or his household (cf. Lk. 12:42). The elder/overseer is a person chosen by God to be a manager and entrusted with the church as God's household (cf. 1 Tim. 3:5-6, 15). Therefore, his life must show that he truly is God's steward by displaying God's transforming grace.

Paul now lists five vices that must not characterize the elder, all negated by μή and all accusative in agreement with ἐπίσκοπον, the subject of the infinitive εἶναι (Robertson, *Grammar,* 1172). This list has a number of similarities with the list of five items in 1 Tim. 3:3 (see the two descriptions of the elder/overseer in Titus 1 and 1 Timothy 3 set in parallel columns in the discussion above of 1 Tim. 3:2): Two items are exactly alike and use words, πάροινος and πλήκτης, that appear nowhere else in the NT. The last two items in 1 Tim. 3:3 are also negated (by ἀ-privative), and the last is a synonym of the last term here. With these significant similarities between the two lists we might also expect to find some relationship between the remaining two terms in each list, the third and fourth in 1 Tim. 3:3 and the first two here.

αὐθάδης** (also in 2 Pet. 2:10) means "self-willed" or "arrogant." Its negation implies the corresponding virtue and thus may find its positive counterpart in ἐπιεικής (gentle, kind, gracious) in 1 Tim. 3:3. Aristotle (*Magna Moralia* 1.29; *Rhetorica* 1.9.29) identifies σεμνότης (cf. 1 Tim. 3:4) as the mean in the range in which αὐθάδεια is one extreme.

One who is ὀργίλος** (a NT hapax) is "inclined to anger, quick-tempered" (BAGD). The possible positive counterpart in 1 Tim. 3:3 is ἄμαχος, which means "peaceable" in the sense of not being contentious.

πάροινος,** "addicted to wine," and πλήκτης,** "a pugnacious man or bully" (BAGD), appear in the NT only here and in the corresponding list in 1 Tim. 3:3 (see the comments there and, for πάροινος, on 1 Tim. 5:23).

αἰσχροκερδής** means "greedy for money" (BAGD; cf. Lysias 12, 19, where it is used of those who take from others even though they have an abundance of what they take). This vice is mentioned in all the lists for officers in the PE (the same word [the only other NT occurrence] in 1 Tim.

3:8 [deacons]; 1 Tim. 3:3 has the synonym ἀφιλάργυρος) and in the exhortation of elders in 1 Pet. 5:2 (the only NT occurrence of αἰσχροκερδῶς), probably because it is such a strong and dangerous temptation (cf. 1 Tim. 5:9-10): When a person serves it, he cannot serve God (Mt. 6:24).

In this list of five vices Paul has singled out ways in which one may be gripped and controlled by the different sins of self: pride, anger, and desire for drink, dominance, or wealth. Being controlled by any of these disqualifies a man from the position of "overseer," one who leads others by serving as God's steward.

1:8 In contrast (ἀλλά) to those five vices, Paul names here and in the next verse seven virtues that must characterize the elder's life. The counterpart to this list is in 1 Tim. 3:2 and contains only five items: δίκαιος and ὅσιος, the fourth and fifth items here, are not represented there, perhaps because they were self-evident enough not to need mention on every occasion. The first and third terms in the list here appear identically in 1 Tim. 3:2, the second and sixth may represent ideas presented in different terms there, and the last, which consists of all of v. 9, refers to the same concept as the last word in 1 Tim. 3:2 (see the parallel columns in the comments on that verse).

On the first virtue in this list, φιλόξενος, which is the opposite of the first vice in v. 7, αὐθάδης, see the comments on 1 Tim. 3:2.

φιλάγαθος** (a NT hapax) means "loving what is good" (MM cite a late second-century AD papyrus document and render the word "a lover of virtue"). One is reminded of the list of good things that are commended to Christians in Phil. 3:8. An overseer's love for people is always to be correlated with a love for what God wants people to be. It is conceivable that this word corresponds to κόσμιος in 1 Tim. 3:2, especially if the latter means "well-behaved" or "virtuous" there.

On σώφρων see the comments on 1 Tim. 3:2.

δίκαιος, "upright, just, righteous," is used here of one who lives in accordance with God's law (BAGD s.v. 1; G. Schrenk, *TDNT* II, 190f.). It is used with this significance, "law-abiding" (BAGD), in the only other PE occurrence in reference to persons, in 1 Tim. 1:9. Paul is writing here, not about the fact that a person is declared righteous through Christ, but about righteous living (cf. his use of the related δικαιοσύνη in Rom. 6:13, 16, 18, 19). A general definition of this significance of the word is given in 1 Jn. 3:7: "the one who practices righteousness is righteous."

ὅσιος, "holy," is used here of a one who is "devout, pious, pleasing to God" (cf. by contrast ἀνόσιος in 1 Tim. 1:9; 2 Tim. 3:2).

ἐγκρατής (a NT hapax; Paul uses ἐγκράτεια in Gal. 5:23 and ἐγκρατεύομαι in 1 Cor. 7:9; 9:25) indicates one who is "self-controlled, disciplined" (BAGD). Probably this word is virtually equivalent to νηφάλιος in 1 Tim. 3:2 (cf. 1 Tim. 3:11; Tit. 2:2). Paul says in 1 Cor. 9:25 that the athlete "exercises self-control in all things" and applies that lesson to Christians as spiritual athletes, most vigorously to himself (vv. 26-27). That perspective is undoubtedly intended here for those who are to be leaders of the Christian community. Thus in a sense Paul has come full circle with this term: Now he states positively and generally in one word what he has stated negatively and specifically in v. 6 with several words.

Paul has sketched out with these few well-chosen words the characteristics that must mark an "overseer": He must love people and equally love virtue. He must be wise and prudent, must live in accordance with God's law, must be devoted to God and seek to please him, and must manifest genuine self-control. With this blend of characteristics, the Christian leader is equipped by God's grace to exercise the kind of oversight that a steward in God's house, the church, should exercise.

1:9 The last characteristic in the list that began in v. 8 is crucial, for without it the overseer cannot carry out the duties prescribed in the remainder of this verse. Paul uses ἀντέχομαι (always in the middle and with the genitive in the NT) here with the meaning "cling to, hold fast to, be devoted to" and thereby calls for the overseer's firm acceptance of ὁ πιστὸς λόγος, i.e., the "preaching" or "proclamation" that the prospective overseer/elder has heard and that is "faithful or trustworthy." At this time prospective elders were dependent on oral proclamation of the message, so Paul uses λόγος in the sense it has in 1 Tim. 5:17, "preaching," and πιστός in the sense it has several times in the PE (e.g., 1 Tim. 1:12, 15; 3:1; 4:9).

The prepositional phrase κατὰ τὴν διδαχήν between the article τοῦ and the adjective πιστοῦ is the key qualifier: The λόγος is πιστός, i.e., the message is reliable, when it is "in accord with the teaching." διδαχή, "teaching," is used here in the passive sense (see Rom. 6:17; 16:17) of that which is taught by the apostles (and by Christ). Paul refers to this teaching elsewhere with the related words διδασκαλία and διδάσκω (1 Tim. 4:6; 2 Thes. 2:15). Since what "has been heard" from the apostle is to be entrusted to "faithful men," whose task is to teach it to others (2 Tim. 2:2), Paul here designates as "faithful" proclamation that which is in accord with apostolic teaching.

The ἵνα clause that occupies the rest of the verse describes the practical and necessary task to be accomplished by one who is equipped by adherence to the reliable word. Holding to that word provides the basis on which an overseer "may be" (ᾖ) "able" (δυνατός; cf. Acts 18:24) to accomplish that task. Similarly, 2 Tim. 3:15, 17 says that the scriptures "are able (τὰ δυνάμενα) to make you wise for salvation" and that by them "the man of God may be adequate (ἄρτιος ᾖ) for every good work." Similarly, "able" here means equipped, in terms of knowledge and commitment, to carry out one's responsibility as an elder/overseer.

The responsibilities are twofold, as indicated by the καί . . . καί, "both . . . and," construction. Each is indicated by a present infinitive, the first παρακαλεῖν (see the discussion at 1 Tim. 5:1; 6:2). Here the meaning would seem to be "exhort" in the sense of urging one's hearers to accept the sound doctrine and respond appropriately to it. The exhortation occurs in the sphere of (ἐν; so Bernard) "sound doctrine" (τῇ διδασκαλίᾳ τῇ ὑγιαινούσῃ); in the first occurrence in the PE of this phrase (1 Tim. 1:10; also in Tit. 2:1; 2 Tim. 4:3), "sound doctrine" is said to be "according to the gospel," so that we may say that it signifies the teaching of Christianity. ὑγιαινοῦσα (PE* 8x, see 1 Tim. 1:10) indicates that the διδασκαλίᾳ is "correct," thus distinguishing it from that which is erroneous and thereby clearly identifying it as the teaching of Christianity. The activity called for here is also called for in 2 Tim. 2:2.

The second task is ἐλέγχειν (see 1 Tim. 5:20). A number of nuances are given for ἐλέγχω by BAGD, and various ones have been suggested for this occurrence, such as "refute," "confute," "convince," and "convict." But since all of them are plausible with the object that appears here, the substantival participle τοὺς ἀντιλέγοντας, some other determining factor must be sought. Since ἐλέγχω is used in v. 13 in a virtual enlargement and application of this statement, it is likely that the nuance there will also be present here. Probably because of the presence of the adverb "sharply" (ἀποτόμως) there, a number of the modern English translations that disagree here find themselves agreeing in v. 13 on the nuance "rebuke" (*RSV, TEV, NIV; NASB:* "reprove"). "Rebuke" (or "reprove") would seem therefore to be the likely nuance here also. A positive outcome is always hoped for with regard to those being dealt with here (see v. 13; cf. 2 Tim. 2:25-26), who are called οἱ ἀντιλέγοντες, literally "those who speak against." These persons are undoubtedly speaking against the sound doctrine just mentioned (cf. for this attitude Tit. 1:14; possibly 3:10; 1 Tim. 6:3, 20; 2 Tim. 2:16-18, 25-26; 3:8; 4:15).

The instructions in v. 9 correspond to the "able to teach" (διδακτικός; cf. 2 Tim. 2:24-26) requirement in 1 Tim. 3:2. By their explicitness they indicate what is involved in carrying out this particular responsibility of the elder/overseer.

Vv. 6-9 have presented the qualifications for an elder/overseer, God's steward. Such a person must be above reproach in his Christian life in general and in these special qualifications. His family life must demonstrate his fidelity and leadership ability (v. 6). He must not be controlled by any of the besetting sins of self (v. 7). He must love both people and goodness and must be thoughtful and prudent, obedient to God's law, seeking to please God, and self-controlled because he himself is controlled by God (v. 8). He must know and be zealously committed to the apostolic teaching and willing to teach it and to rebuke those who oppose it (v. 9). This last responsibility, especially that of rebuking those who "speak against," leads immediately into the next section and indicates the practical and necessary value of such leaders to the health and welfare of the congregation.

TITUS'S AND THE ELDERS' DUTY IN REGARD TO THE FALSE TEACHERS: 1:10-16

With causal "for" (γάϱ) Paul links this section with the preceding section. Here he describes the situation that demands that the elders "rebuke those who speak against" (v. 9). He indicates that the opponents are numerous and that their attitudes and actions are morally out of line (v. 10), their impact on families devastating (v. 11b), their teaching erroneous (v. 11c), and their motivation mercenary (v. 11d). He says that such false teachers "must be silenced" (v. 11a). To emphasize the seriousness of the problem and the threat these teachers pose, he quotes from one of the Cretan "prophets" a description of the evil that characterizes the Cretan people (v. 12). Paul says that the description is accurate, with the implication that it manifests itself in this situation, and that therefore such a situation calls for a sharp rebuke to disentangle such people from the error of the opponents (v. 13) and to call them away from the particular teachings and practices of those who turn away from the truth (v. 14). In the concluding two verses of this section Paul presents an even more radical critique and evaluation of those who hold to such error. First he deals in principle with the question of purity, and having stated the positive truth, he then states the principle that "to those who are defiled and unbelieving, nothing is pure" (v. 15). Then on this background Paul says of these who "profess to know God" that "their deeds deny him" and that they are "detestable and disobedient, and worthless for any good deed" (16).

Paul says several things about these false teachers, but gives no systematic description of them. Nevertheless, his reference to them as "those of the circumcision" (v. 10) and as those who "pay attention to Jewish myths" (v. 14) stands out and helps to identify them. He also describes them as those "who turn away from the truth" (v. 14). These last two descriptions taken together imply that the false teachers are, or have been, Christians and that they may be described as Jewish Christians (or predominantly so).

Paul speaks of other characteristics that, upon analysis, show that these teachers are very much like those in Ephesus mentioned in 1 Timothy and 2 Timothy. Furthermore, the concerns expressed here are much like those expressed in 1 Tim. 1:3-11, as seen in the following words and phrases:

Titus 1	**1 Timothy 1**
ματαιολόγοι (v. 10)	ματαιολογίαν (v. 6)
μὴ προσέχοντες Ἰουδαϊκοῖς μύθοις (v. 14)	μηδὲ προσέχειν μύθοις (v. 4)
διδάσκοντες ἃ μὴ δεῖ (v. 14)	ἑτεροδιδασκαλεῖν (v. 4)
καθαρὰ τοῖς καθαροῖς (v. 15)	καθαράς καρδίας (v. 5)
συνείδησις (v. 15)	συνειδησέως (v. 5)

In addition to these parallels, especially the reference to "myths," the concern for "human commandments" and the concern for ritual purity (Tit. 1:14-15) recall 1 Tim. 4:1-7, and the motivation of gain (Tit. 1:11) reminds us of 1 Tim. 6:5. Paul will not speak of false teachers again until Tit. 3:9-11, where he mentions "foolish controversies, genealogies, strife, and disputes about the law" (v. 9). Here, too, we see parallels with 1 Timothy (controversies, 1 Tim. 1:4; 6:4; genealogies, 1:4; disputes about the law, 1:7ff.; and strife, 6:4).

This false teaching is, then, like that found in 1 Timothy, but with a Cretan flavor as well. In sum, it is concerned with Jewish myths and genealogies, which apparently set the tone for the way in which it handles the law. It is ascetic but also rebellious and disobedient, it opposes the apostolic teaching and turns away from it, and it is motivated by gain. A similar teaching occurs elsewhere in the NT with other errors, and Paul opposed something like this Jewish asceticism already at Colossae (cf. Col. 2:16-17, 20-23). For a fuller comparison of all three PE on the false teachers see the comments on 1 Tim. 1:3ff.

1:10 The necessity and urgency of the elders being prepared to rebuke the opponents (v. 9) is now brought home by Paul's further description of the latter as "rebellious people, empty talkers, and deceivers," and in particular by the fact that they are "many" (πολλοί). (καί may have been added after πολλοί "in accordance with the rhetorical usage known as hendiadys" or left out by copyists who failed to recognize an original hendiadys [*TCGNT*]. With *NA*[25] it should probably be omitted because of the stronger manuscript evidence in that direction.) These people are ἀνυπότακτοι, "rebellious," most likely in the sense that they are unwilling to be subject to God and his law (see 1 Tim. 1:9, which may also have the false teachers in mind). As ματαιολόγοι** (a biblical hapax; cf. ματαιολογία in 1 Tim. 1:6; μάταιος in 1 Cor. 3:20; 15:17; Tit. 3:9), they are those whose talk is empty and of no value (cf. 1 Tim. 1:7) and "will lead to further ungodliness" (2 Tim. 2:16, which uses the synonym κενοφωνίας). As φρεναπάται** (a biblical hapax; φρεναπατάω in Gal. 6:3), they are "deceivers," those who mislead (cf. 2 Tim. 3:13).

The next phrase begins with μάλιστα, which is usually taken (e.g., BAGD) as "especially," indicating that most — but not all — of those Paul is speaking of are "of the circumcision." But Skeat ("Especially the Parchments") has brought together considerable evidence to demonstrate that in ad hoc documents μάλιστα may also mean "that is," in which case it introduces a further definition of the preceding term. If this is true here, which the references to "Jewish myths" (v. 14) and "disputes about the Law" (3:9) might support, then Paul is saying that all the false teachers are "of the circumcision."

In either case, that all or part of the false teachers were ἐκ τῆς περιτομῆς was a dominant characteristic. περιτομή means "circumcision" of the foreskin, and οἱ ἐκ (τῆς) περιτομῆς** were those of Jewish origin. The phrase is used in the NT once of Jews (Rom. 4:12) and otherwise of Jewish Christians (Acts 10:45; 11:2; Gal. 2:12; Col. 4:11), which is probably how it is used here — with somewhat negative overtones (as one senses with a different Jewish Christian group in Gal. 2:12). Acts 2:11 and 1 Maccabees 15:23 indicate that there were Jews on Crete, and Philo (*Legatio ad Gaium* 282) states that a large number lived there (cf. Josephus, *Ant.* 17.327; *Vita* 427).

1:11 With "who must be silenced . . . ," or more literally, "whom it is necessary to silence . . . ," Paul presents the essential demand placed on Titus and the leaders. This course of action was necessitated, as the words that follow indicate, by the devastation of families that was resulting from the false teaching. ἐπιστομίζειν** (a biblical hapax), "to silence," means, then, to prevent the teachers from spreading their teaching. Paul does not say here how this was to be done, but he does give some indication elsewhere in the letter. V. 9 calls for rebuking those who oppose, or "speak against," the apostolic teaching, and v. 13 also calls for rebuking them with the hope "that they may be sound in the faith." In 3:9-11 Paul tells Titus to warn a contentious person "once or twice" and to reject such a person if the warnings are not heeded (cf. Mt. 18:15-18; 1 Cor. 5:1-13). Apparently this pattern given by Jesus and by Paul elsewhere was known well enough by Titus that Paul did not feel it necessary to restate it here.

They are to be silenced "because they are upsetting whole families." οἵτινες is used here "to emphasize a characteristic quality, by which a preceding statement is to be confirmed" (BAGD s.v. 2b). It is well expressed by Ellicott's "inasmuch as they." ἀνατρέπω is used here figuratively of "overturning, destroying, or ruining." They ruin "whole" or "entire" (ὅλους) "households" (οἴκους; see 1 Tim. 3:4-5).

They do this by "teaching things they should not." Paul does not say here what those "things" are. In v. 14 he does specify that the false teaching involved "Jewish myths" and "commandments of those who turn from the truth," and in v. 15 he turns to the question of purity. The only "commandments" taught by the false teachers about which we have any knowledge from the PE are the prohibitions of marriage and certain foods mentioned in 1 Tim. 4:1-3, which would certainly fall into the category of questions of purity. If these prohibitions represent all or part of the "things" that Paul refers to here, then we can understand how the teaching devastates families: Might the prohibition of marriage involve ending existing marriages? But Paul may have more in mind here, since anything that causes an entire family to be moved from the faith could be spoken of in the words that we find here.

With "for the sake of sordid gain" Paul names what he thinks is the real motive for the false teaching. The preposition χάριν (see 1 Tim. 5:14), "for the sake of," indicates the goal of the teaching. Paul usually uses αἰσχρός** (exclusively Pauline in the NT: 1 Cor. 11:6; 14:35; Eph. 5:12) of that which is "shameful" or "disgraceful." κέρδος** (Phil. 1:21; 3:7) is "gain." These two words occur together only here in the NT, but the compound αἰσχροκερδής occurs in v. 7 and in 1 Tim. 3:8. Paul designates the "gain" as "shameful" or "disgraceful," not because he thinks teachers should not be paid (cf. 1 Tim. 5:17-18), but because they get it by teaching error (ἃ μὴ δεῖ), and because "gain" as the basic motivation for teaching what purports to be the Christian faith, as it was for them (χάριν), is "shameful" (cf. v. 7 and 1 Pet. 5:2: μηδὲ αἰσχροκερδῶς).

1:12 Paul attributes the brief quotation in the second part of this verse to τὶς ἐξ αὐτῶν, "one of them," the subject of εἶπεν, with ἴδιος αὐτῶν προφήτης in apposition to that subject. Both occurrences of αὐτῶν refer to the Cretans. ἴδιος, "one's own," heightens the force of αὐτῶν so that the two words together, "their own," make the prophet's identification with the Cretans very specific.

Therefore, Paul quotes an evaluation of the Cretans by their own fellow countryman and their own prophet. This gives a perspective that nothing else could. Paul affirms the truthfulness of that evaluation in v. 13a with "this testimony is true," a judgment that NT writers do not find it necessary to make of statements by prophets of God. This, together with the fact that this is the only place in scripture that a pagan is called a "prophet," implies that the term "prophet" is used here only from the perspective of the Cretans and not from the perspective of Paul and the Christian community.

The quotation is from Epimenides of Crete (sixth-fifth centuries BC), who is mentioned by Aristotle, Plato, Cicero, and other ancient writers. The work from which Paul quotes is not extant, but the quotation was attributed to Epimenides by some early Christian writers (e.g., Clement of Alexandria, *Strom.* 1.59.2; the commentaries of Chrysostom and Jerome). Others (e.g., Theodore of Mopsuestia) attributed it to a later writer, Callimachus (ca. 305–ca. 240 BC), because the first part of the quotation ("Cretans are always liars") is in his *Hymn to Zeus* 8. But Callimachus was not from Crete but from Cyrene and does not have the entire statement quoted by Paul.

That the Cretans (Κρῆτες,** also in Acts 2:11) were "always liars" (ἀεὶ ψεῦσται) was borne out by the use of the verb κρητίζω, "play the Cretan," to mean "lie" (see LSJM). κακός, which generally means "bad" or "evil," may have the sense "vicious" when coupled with θηρία; θηρίον means "animal," often "wild animal" or "beast," and is used figuratively, as here, of persons with a "bestial" nature (BAGD s.v. 2). γαστέρες refers literally to the inner part of the body, but when used figuratively of the entire person, as here, it means "glutton." Thus γαστέρες ἀργαί designates the Cretans as "lazy gluttons."

1:13 Paul now agrees with the Cretans' own spokesman's judgment. By doing so he is able to highlight explicitly the special problems that Titus and the elders on Crete face and to elicit consent from the Cretan Christians. But ἡ μαρτυρία αὕτη ἐστὶν ἀληθής, "this testimony is true," indicates more than mere agreement: It is Paul's certification that the evaluation is really true and not an extreme statement. Similar statements were made about the Cretans by Polybius (6.46.3: "So much in fact do sordid love of gain and lust for wealth prevail among them that the Cretans are the only people in the world in whose eyes no gain is disgraceful" [αἰσχρὸν . . . κέρδος; cf. Tit. 1:11]) and Cicero (*De Republica* 3.9.15: "Moral principles are so divergent that the Cretans . . . consider highway robbery honorable"). Paul is not making an ethnic slur, but is merely accurately observing, as the Cretans themselves and others did, how the sin that affects the whole human race comes to particular expression in this group.

The information given in the previous verse is the reason (δι' ἣν αἰτίαν, a causal conjunction phrase meaning "for which reason," "therefore"; BAGD s.v. αἰτία 1; cf. 2 Tim. 1:6, 12; Heb. 2:11) that Titus is charged with the responsibility to "rebuke" (ἔλεγχε) the Cretans. Since Paul says this in a section tightly joined to the preceding one (notice γάρ in v. 10), which speaks of the duties of elders/overseers (including the need "to rebuke," ἐλέγχειν, v. 9), it is evident that Titus is to do this through and with the elders/overseers. Paul calls for the rebuke to be given "sharply" (ἀποτόμως,** also in 2 Cor. 13:10) because he knows that only such a rebuke will get through to those who are described in v. 12. He does this out of concern for them, as the words that follow show, and in accordance with his principle of taking into account the person being dealt with (see the comments on 1 Tim. 5:1ff.).

Those to be rebuked are called "them" (αὐτούς) with no further qualification. Are they the false teachers previously mentioned, or are they Cretan believers who are starting to follow the false teachers? It could be argued that "that they may be sound in the faith" would best fit with the latter, i.e., those who are in the faith and need to be kept true to it, and that Paul would not expect the false teachers to become, as the result of a sharp rebuke, "sound in the faith." Furthermore, it could be argued that the end of v. 14 describes the false teachers ("who fall away from the truth") in distinction from gullible believers and that here Paul warns these believers not to follow the false teachings described there.

But 2 Tim. 2:25-26 shows that Paul could, indeed, conceive of the false teachers repenting. Furthermore, it is argued, he has had false teachers in view, and there is no evidence in the text that this perspective has now changed. If this is the case, then it could be argued that Paul is also warning the false teachers in v. 14 to give up following their erroneous ways and not to be those who turn from the truth.

But the decisive argument is that those who are to be rebuked (v. 13) are, in fact, distinguished from those "who turn away from the truth" (v. 14). αὐτούς refers, then, to Cretan believers who are disposed to follow the false teachers because of their own Cretan traits. This entails that Paul's focus did, indeed, move from the false teachers to the Cretan believers when he began v. 12, where the double αὐτῶν refers, not to "them, the false teachers," but to "them, the Cretans," in support of Paul's indication of how Titus and the elders should deal with the believers who have this Cretan background.

Paul's concern is "that they may be sound in the faith." The ἵνα clause indicates that a salutary outcome is the desired result of a severe rebuke (as elsewhere, e.g., 1 Cor. 5:5; 2 Thes. 3:14-15). ὑγιαίνω means generally "be healthy," i.e., not sick, and is used here in the figurative sense of "be sound" or "be correct" (see the comments on 1 Tim. 1:10). ὑγιαίνωσιν ἐν τῇ πίστει (cf. ὑγιαίνοντας τῇ πίστει in 2:2) refers, then, to their holding to the correct teaching (cf. v. 9) concerning the Christian faith rather than to the false teaching (note v. 14: "not giving heed . . . ," "who turn away from the truth"; on τῇ πίστει, "the faith," see the comments on 1 Tim. 1:19).

1:14 A requisite for and negative counterpart to the last clause in v. 13 is given in the negative participial clause here (so Huther). Thus Paul is saying that to "be sound in the faith" demands that one not "give heed to" or "follow" (μὴ προσέχοντες; see 1 Tim. 1:4; 4:1) the errors of the false teachers. Those errors are summarized here under two categories: (1) Ἰουδαϊκοὶ μῦθοι and (2) ἐντολαὶ ἀνθρώπων.

Paul uses μῦθοι (see 1 Tim. 1:4) to refer to "legends" that are contrary to the truth (e.g., 2 Tim. 4:4), as does the only other user of the word in the NT (see 2 Pet. 1:16). This is the only time that Paul calls the myths "Jewish" (Ἰουδαϊκοί,** a NT hapax, though other forms of the root occur in the NT and in Paul), but he also uses μῦθοι in a context in which he says that the false teachers want to be teachers of the law, i.e., of the OT law (1 Tim. 1:4, 7-11; see the comments there). There the "myths" are mentioned in the same breath as "endless genealogies"; when Paul returns to the false teachers in Tit. 3:9 he mentions not "myths" but "genealogies." It is likely, therefore, that the "myths" here are concocted stories related to the "genealogies" spun out from those given in the OT. Christians must not "heed" these "myths" for the reasons given in 1 Tim. 1:4.

The error in practice is designated "commandments of humans," ἐντολαὶ ἀνθρώπων. This phrase occurs only here in the NT, but its equivalent, ἐντάλματα ἀνθρώπων, occurs in Mt. 15:9 and Mk. 7:7, which quote the LXX of Is. 29:13, and in Col. 2:22, which reflects Jesus' words or Isaiah's or both and deals with a case of asceticism, as is also likely the case here. All three of these passages understand "commandments of humans" as what is put in the place of obedience to God and what he requires. This is also the understanding here, as the closely linked participial phrase, "who turn away from the truth," makes plain. Only in 1 Tim. 4:1ff., which deals with an error of asceticism similar to that dealt with in Col. 2:20-23, do the PE refer to actual commandments of the false teachers, and terms and concepts identical or similar to those used here are used there:

1 Timothy 4	**Titus 1**
"fall away from the faith" (v. 1)	"turn away from the truth" (v. 14)
προσέχοντες (v. 1)	προσέχοντες (v. 14)
"deceitful spirits" (v. 1), "liars" (v. 2)	"deceivers" (v. 10)
prohibitions (v. 3)	concern for what is impure (v. 15)
"every creation of God is good" (v. 4)	"all things are pure" (v. 15)

It is very likely, then, that the "commandments of humans" in view here are the same as or similar to those described in 1 Tim. 4:1ff., i.e., forbidding marriage and advocating abstention from certain foods.

Those who command these ascetic practices are those "who turn away from the truth." ἀποστρέφομαι means here "turn away from" or possibly even "reject" or "repudiate." The phrase occurs only here in the NT, but a nearly equivalent form is found in 2 Tim. 4:4, which speaks of "will turn away their ears from the truth" (ἀπὸ μὲν τῆς ἀληθείας τὴν ἀκοὴν ἀποστρέψουσιν). ἡ ἀλήθεια (cf. 1:1 and see 1 Tim. 2:4) is used here of "the content of Christianity as the absolute truth" (BAGD s.v. 2b). In 2 Tim. 4:4 it refers back to τὸν λόγον, "the word" of the gospel, which Timothy is called upon to preach (v. 2) as he does "the work of an evangelist" and fulfills his ministry (v. 5).

1:15 Paul most likely addresses the question of "purity" because it is one of the problems that the false teachers have raised in their teaching and, very likely, in their human commandments. First he states as a basic Christian principle that all things are pure to those who are pure. Then as a second principle he says that to those who are defiled and unbelieving nothing is pure. He concludes by saying that the very minds and consciences of such people are defiled.

καθαρός, "pure," is used 3x in this verse, twice in the first clause, literally "all things are pure to the pure ones," and once in the second, "to those who are defiled and unbelieving, nothing is pure." With πάντα καθαρά, "all things are pure," and οὐδὲν καθαρόν, "nothing is pure," Paul refers to ceremonial purity (as do Rom. 14:20; Lk. 11:41, both with πάντα καθαρά). With τοῖς καθαροῖς he uses the word in its moral and religious sense of "cleansed of sin" and "made inwardly clean" (cf. the other PE* occurrences: 1 Tim. 1:5 [see the comments there]; 3:9; 2 Tim. 1:3; 2:22; cf. also Paul's use of καθαρίζω: 2 Cor. 7:1; Eph. 5:26; Tit. 2:14). This religious and moral cleansing is accomplished by Christ's death (Tit. 2:14), which he applies to a person's life through his word and Spirit (cf. Eph. 5:26) and by which one's heart is cleansed, as the Jerusalem Council put it, by faith (Acts 15:9). It is in this sense that Paul speaks of "the pure" (τοῖς καθαροῖς).

1 Tim. 4:3-4 says virtually the same thing as the first clause of this verse when it says that Christians "know" that "everything created by God is good" and also, therefore, that "nothing is to be rejected" or regarded as impure or unacceptable for its God-intended use. The presence of πάντα, "all," here makes the statement absolute and unqualified (cf. πᾶν κτίσμα θεοῦ in 1 Tim. 4:4) and thereby shows that any human commandment that declares anything impure is, by that very fact, erroneous (the unstated but obvious lesson intended by beginning with this positive and absolute principle in a passage that deals with the error that contradicts this principle). Paul is not dealing here with the OT ceremonial laws of impurity, which did not deal with moral impurity but with things that God declared ceremonially impure so that they might serve as object lessons for spiritual matters. Peter's experience (Acts 15:15) showed that God had reversed this impurity by his own declaration (Acts 15:15).

In the second clause Paul, in contrast (δέ), deals with those who are οἱ μεμιαμμένοι (the first of two occurrences of the verb μιαίνω, both in the perfect to emphasize the continuing state), "the defiled." That those referred to are "defiled" specifically in the moral and religious sense is indicated by the further designation of them as "unbelieving": The most basic aspect of their defilement is that they have not believed and therefore have not been cleansed by God from the defilement of sin (cf. the comments above on οἱ καθαροί and the parallelism of these two clauses). These people are also said in the following verse to "deny" God by their "deeds" and to be "disobedient," both of which would indicate the ongoing defilement of "sins and vices" (BAGD s.v. 2).

ἄπιστος (here and 1 Tim. 5:8 in the PE*) consistently designates in Paul one who is an "unbeliever," who does not believe in Christ. Paul attributes this to the defiled here, even though (as he says in the next verse) they profess to know God, apparently because their commandments regarding purity demonstrate that they have not trusted Christ alone as the one who can cleanse their lives and make them pure. They are trusting in their asceticism to make them pure, but this reliance on oneself, as Paul says in Col. 1:18-19, is "self-abasement" and entails that one is "not holding to the head" (Christ). Such persons are, therefore, ἀπίστοι.

For the defiled and unbelieving "nothing is pure." That is, there is nothing that does not become defiled by their own religious and moral defilement. Paul seems to be applying the argument of Hg. 2:13-14.

ἀλλά before the concluding clause indicates not another contrast with the immediately preceding clause but, as Ridderbos points out, a further enlargement of the contrast already begun with δέ, as the repetition of the main verb μιαίνω bears out. By saying that the defilement is in "their mind and conscience," Paul signifies that it is internal and thus intrinsically moral and religious. αὐτῶν, "their," is placed before the καί . . . καί construction that closely links "mind" and "conscience" and is thereby emphasized and connected to both nouns. ὁ νοῦς (see 1 Tim. 6:5), "the mind," refers here to one's "way of thinking" (BAGD s.v. 3). Paul consistently regards "the mind" of the non-Christian as controlled by sin and therefore erroneous in its outlook (e.g., Rom. 1:28; Eph. 4:17; especially 1 Tim. 6:5 and 2 Tim. 3:8) and needing to be transformed by renewal (Rom. 12:2; Eph. 4:23). ἡ συνείδησις (see 1 Tim. 1:5), "conscience," is "moral self-consciousness." In short, Paul says that in both their understanding and their moral evaluation these people are "defiled."

1:16 On the background of the principles spelled out in v. 15, Paul turns to a specific evaluation of the false teachers. First, he acknowledges their claim: "they profess to know God." ὁμολογοῦσιν is used in the sense that they "declare publicly" or "claim" (BAGD s.v. 4) to "know" God. εἰδέναι, "to know" (the infinitive of οἶδα), is used here in the sense of a personal and positive relationship with God (BAGD s.v. οἶδα 2).

In contrast (δέ) to this profession, τοῖς ἔργοις (see 1 Tim. 2:10), "the deeds," or "their deeds" (with the article implying possession), are the means by which such people actually "deny" (ἀρνοῦνται; see 1 Tim. 5:8; 2 Tim. 2:12) God (the previous θεόν is assumed), the very one they claim to know. Paul does not make explicit what these deeds are. The similarities with 1 Tim. 4:1ff. noted above make it likely that Paul has in mind at least the kind of ascetic actions described there (perhaps with other deeds), by which these people reject what God gives to be gratefully received, deny the Creator's goodness, and show that they do not really know him who made all things good.

The next clause appears to be a further indication of why their deeds deny God, rather than a further listing of independent traits. "Their actual behavior denies their profession, for they are . . ." (Phillips, *NT in Modern English*). βδελυκτός** (a NT hapax) means "abominable and detestable" in God's sight. Since Paul has just dealt with the question of purity and with the defilement of those he is speaking of, the LXX of Pr. 17:15 may have come to mind with its statement that one who "pronounces the unjust just and the just unjust" is unclean (ἀκάθαρτος) and abominable (βδελυκτός) to God. Furthermore, the false teachers may have made similar erroneous judgments about Christians, thus deserving this identification. ἀπειθής means "disobedient" and may in this setting refer to the disobedience in view in 1 Tim. 4:3-4, that of rejecting the good gifts God has created to be received with thanksgiving, i.e., marriage and certain foods.

ἀδόκιμος basically means "not standing the test" and then, "disqualified," as here (cf. especially 2 Cor. 13:5; 2 Tim. 3:8). If we have understood correctly Paul's use of βδελυκτός and ἀπειθής, then this last characteristic can be understood as the conclusion that inevitably follows. If one is "detestable" because he judges the work of Christ inadequate for attaining true purity, and "disobedient" because he rejects the good gifts of God's creation, then that person is also so "disqualified" in God's sight that this unfitness extends to (πρός) anything and everything (πᾶν) that he does (cf. again v. 15b), with the result that no deed (ἔργον) of his can be good (ἀγαθόν) and acceptable to God.

Some have thought that those referred to here and in v. 14b ("those who turn away from the truth") are outsiders, Pharisaic Jewish leaders influencing false teachers "of the circumcision" (v. 10) within the Christian community. Hendriksen and Parry, e.g., say that the claim "to know God" is a Jewish claim. The radical and decisive language that Paul uses to describe these individuals probably influenced this view: It is assumed that these words would only be applied to those outside the Christian community.

But the error spoken of here is not what was typical of Jews. These false teachers are not the same as those combated in Galatians. They do not insist on circumcision and OT ceremonial rites. They have a more esoteric ("myths and genealogies") and ascetic ("human commandments," not commandments of Moses) position, parts of which may be found among Jews, but which was not typical of the main Jewish position. Paul's evaluation of these false teachers corresponds with what he says elsewhere in the PE about the false teachers in the church (e.g., 1 Tim. 4:1-2; 6:3-5, 10; 2 Tim. 2:17-18, 25-26; 3:5; see also Col. 2:20ff.) and to his indictment of false teachers in the Galatian Christian community (e.g., Gal. 1:9). Being "of the circumcision" they do have some views that come from the Jewish community ("myths and endless genealogies"), but their views go beyond Judaism. It is unnecessary, therefore, to say Paul has shifted from the false teachers within the Christian community to those outside. In accordance with his normal practice, Paul deals with false teachers in the church; he rarely, if ever, deals with those outside the Christian community, and there is no reason to suggest that he does otherwise here.

INSTRUCTIONS FOR DIFFERENT GROUPS OF BELIEVERS BASED ON GOD'S ENABLING GRACE: 2:1-15

In this section Paul gives instructions for various categories of believers (vv. 1-10). The basis for such instructions and for the expected responses is the instructing and enabling grace of God (vv. 11-14). In conclusion, Paul charges Titus to communicate these truths and apply them with full authority (v. 15).

THE INSTRUCTIONS: 2:1-10

Paul urges Titus to teach conduct in accordance with sound doctrine (v. 1) for five different groups: older men (v. 2), older women (v. 3), younger women (vv. 4-5), young men (v. 6), with Titus as an example (vv. 7-8), and slaves (vv. 9-10).

2:1 Paul contrasts Titus with the false teachers in a very simple but emphatic way, Σὺ δέ (see 1 Tim. 6:11). Titus is urged to "speak" in the sense of "teach" (imperative λάλει, which in 2:15 as well serves as a virtual synonym for δίδασκε, which is used in 1 Tim. 6:2 in a construction similar to Tit. 2:15; cf. Eph. 6:20; Col. 4:4). He is to speak "the things" (ἅ) that are "in accord with" or "consonant with" (πρέπει) "sound doctrine," the true teaching of Christianity (τῇ ὑγιαινούσῃ διδασκαλίᾳ; see 1:9; 1 Tim. 1:10).

2:2 The first to be instructed are the "older men." πρεσβύται** (also in Lk. 1:18; Phm. 9) is consistently used of older men in the NT and in extrabiblical literature (see BAGD). εἶναι and the other infinitives in vv. 2-10 may well function as imperatives (cf. Robertson, *Grammar,* 944; MHT I, 179). The older men are called "to be" (εἶναι), i.e., to manifest four characteristics. νηφάλιος,** though it also means "temperate in the use of alcohol," here probably has its other meaning of "sober" in the sense of clear-headed, as in 1 Tim. 3:2 (see the comments there) and 3:11, the only other NT occurrences. For a man to be σεμνός (see 1 Tim. 3:8) means that his actions and demeanor make him "worthy of respect," or "serious and worthy"

(W. Foerster, *TDNT* VII, 195). σώφρων** (see 1 Tim. 3:2; note σωφρονίζω in Tit. 2:4 and σωφρόνως in 2:12) refers to the prudent, thoughtful aspect of self-control (BAGD).

The fourth characteristic required of older men is ὑγιαίνοντες (for this word used with τῇ πίστει see 1:13), which is used here figuratively in the sense of "sound." Three areas in which they are to possess this characteristic are indicated with three dative nouns. Since these nouns are parallel and apparently used in the same sense and since the second and third, τῇ ἀγάπῃ (see 1 Tim. 1:5) and τῇ ὑπομονῇ (see 1 Tim. 6:11), require a subjective understanding, the first, τῇ πίστει, should be understood in the same way. Thus the older men should manifest a healthy "trust" in God, "love" toward others, and a hopeful "perseverance and endurance." These three nouns repeat the common NT trio of faith, hope, and love, with patience appropriately taking the place of hope (cf. 1 Tim. 6:11; 1 Thes. 1:3; 1 Cor. 13:13).

The four characteristics in this list are similar to the qualifications for officers given in 1:5ff. and 1 Tim. 3:2ff., and faith, love, and endurance should obviously mark all Christians. The latter probably implies that Paul believed that the older men should manifest, because of their chronological maturity, this spiritual maturity as examples for others.

2:3 Paul begins his instructions for the next group, "older women" (πρεσβύτιδας,** a NT hapax), with the transitional term ὡσαύτως (see the comments on 1 Tim. 2:9), "similarly" or "likewise," implying the repetition of the infinitive εἶναι. Furthermore, the terms in the list are all accusative, as would be expected if the infinitive were present or implied.

The first characteristic required of the older women, ἱεροπρεπεῖς** (a NT hapax), designates that which is "befitting a holy person," or as Lock puts it, "they are to carry into daily life the demeanour of priestesses in a temple" (the word is used of the conduct of a priest in inscriptions: see BAGD). They are to act this way since they belong to God by faith in Jesus Christ (G. Schrenk, *TDNT* III, 254). ἐν καταστήματι** (a NT hapax) means "in behavior or demeanor" (BAGD); "the noun denotes comportment or bearing viewed as the expression of one's interior character or disposition" (Kelly). Thus ἐν καταστήματι ἱεροπρεπεῖς encapsulates what Paul says about women in 1 Tim. 2:10.

μὴ διαβόλους (διάβολος 8x in Paul; of human beings in 1 Tim. 3:11; here; 2 Tim. 3:3) means here "not slanderers," "not malicious gossips." Concern for people can degenerate into this vice. Those usually considered most in danger of falling into it, because of their positive inclination, are hereby warned.

The perfect passive participle δεδουλωμένας, "enslaved," expresses what "much wine" (dative οἴνῳ πολλῷ) can do (cf. 1:7; 1 Tim. 3:3, 8; 5:23). Women, who have constant access to the food and drink of the household, are warned not to be captured and controlled by wine. Such a rudimentary warning may seem inappropriate, but 1 Corinthians (especially 11:21) shows how appropriate it was.

καλοδιδασκάλους** is a hapax not found elsewhere, but is not surprising for one who likes compounds, who uses καλοποιέω and νομοδιδάσκαλος, and who occasionally coins compounds (cf. especially verbs with ὑπερ-). The older women should be those who are "teaching what is good" — not in the sense of 1 Tim. 2:12, which is forbidden to women, but as is indicated by what follows, teaching younger women about their duties.

2:4 Paul continues here the characteristics required of older women and, at the same time, begins those that should characterize younger women, linking the older to the younger as those who teach what they themselves are and seek to be. The ἵνα clause is connected with καλοδιδασκάλους (v. 3) and identifies the purpose of the older women in teaching what is good.

σωφρονίζωσιν (a NT hapax; the variant reading σωφρονίζουσιν makes little difference in meaning; see *NA*[26] and Bernard's arguments for the adopted reading) is used here in the active sense of "encourage, advise, urge" (BAGD). Paul uses the positive τὰς νέας, "young women," with the infinitive εἶναι as the object of σωφρονίζωσιν (the only PE occurrence of noncomparative νέος, "young") and the comparative in v. 6, as in 1 Tim. 5:2, of the same age group (the comparative often has little comparative force; cf. the alternation in Diodorus Siculus 18.46.3-4). "Young(er)" covered a longer span of time than it does today, and Paul distinguishes "older" and "younger" with a degree of fluidity (see the comments on 1 Tim. 4:12; J. Behm, *TDNT* IV, 897; BAGD s.v. πρεσβύτης).

φίλανδροι** (a NT hapax used elsewhere in Greek literature; see BAGD) means, as the component parts of the word indicate, "loving their husbands." This word and the next (φιλότεκνοι) were used together in, e.g., an epitaph from Pergamus of about the time of Hadrian (Deissmann, *Bible Studies,* 255f.: "to the most sweet woman who loved her husband and her children"). φιλότεκνοι** (a NT hapax) is used elsewhere, as here, especially of women, of "loving one's children" in a positive and not indulgent manner (see BAGD).

It is noteworthy that the list of characteristics for young women begins with love for husband and children. This section thereby fills out the instructions to wives in Ephesians, Colossians, and 1 Peter, where the emphasis falls on fulfilling the role of submission and where love on the part of wives is not mentioned. It may seem strange for older women to be called upon to teach younger women to love their husbands and children. But this is put into perspective when we realize that Christians are constantly being taught in the NT to love, whether it be God or fellow Christians and neighbors (here the closest neighbor).

2:5 Paul continues with other things that older women should teach younger women (and which the older women are also to be). σώφρων (see

2:2) is the "prudent, thoughtful" aspect of being "self-controlled" and is the one term that is emphasized for each of these age and sex groups (vv. 2, 5, 6). ἁγνός (see 1 Tim. 5:22) means here "pure" in the moral sense. In the literature of the day it was often used of women in the sense of "chaste," but it need not be restricted to that meaning here or elsewhere in the NT.

οἰκουργός** (a NT hapax; for the variant reading οἰκουρούς and the reasons for the *UBSGNT* reading see *TCGNT*), literally "working at home," has been more aptly rendered by *NEB* and *NIV* by "busy at home." That is, women should be diligent homemakers (cf. 1 Tim. 5:14 in contrast to 5:13; cf. also Pr. 31:10-31 with its wide range of activities done by the wife as homemaker). Some commentators and versions, ancient and modern, have joined the following ἀγαθάς to this word and understood the two together, one as a noun the other as an adjective, as "good housewives" (so *TEV;* cf. the arguments, e.g., of Dibelius-Conzelmann and Hanson). This is certainly a possibility, but since the virtues up to this point have consisted of single items, it is more likely that these two words are to be taken separately (cf. the arguments, e.g., of Alford, Dornier, Kelly, Ridderbos, and Spicq; translated as such by *RSV, NEB, NASB, NIV*). Paul uses ἀγαθός frequently as an adjective in the phrase "good works," and substantively in speaking about "the good." Here, however, it is used as a human characteristic and probably should be understood as "kind," as probably also in 1 Pet. 2:18 (perhaps also Rom. 5:7; cf. also the related sense in Mt. 20:15).

It has been suggested that the six characteristics presented for young women to this point are grouped in three pairs. The first two, "loving husbands" and "loving children," could well be a pair and were joined together in literature of the time. The third and fourth, "prudent" and "pure," would present an interesting combination of wisdom and holiness, and the fifth and sixth, "busy at home" and "kind," would present a balanced combination of hard-working but also good-natured and considerate. The evidence for this suggestion is not compelling but is suggestive and plausible. Its plausibility is increased by the clear pairing of the first two terms, which may set a pattern, and is strengthened somewhat by the tendency of Paul and others to use pairs and other groupings (cf. 1:6-9).

If this suggested pairing is correct, it provides some explanation for the order of the list and may in turn suggest that a larger perspective is involved in the order of the three pairs. The first pair would present the main concerns of the wife/mother in her relationships in the home. The second pair would focus on her own piety, and the third would speak of her domain of activity and her attitudes and actions toward those around her. Such an overarching order may also be suggested by the fact that the list begins and ends — with the seventh item, yet to be considered — with the younger woman's relationship to her husband.

The present middle participle ὑποτασσομένας means here "continually submitting themselves," in the sense of voluntary submission. This submission is to be "to their own husbands." τοῖς ἀνδράσιν, literally "to the men," is used here in the special sense of "husbands," as the qualifying ἰδίοις makes evident (cf. 1 Cor. 7:2; 14:35; Eph. 5:22ff.; Col. 3:18f.; 1 Tim. 3:2, 12; 5:9; Tit. 1:6; 2:5; 1 Pet. 3:1, 5), and is in keeping with "a divinely willed order" (G. Delling, *TDNT* VIII, 41ff., especially 43). Paul uses ὑποτάσσω to refer to being under authority (ibid., 43f.), specifically of the relationship of women to men in the congregation (1 Cor. 14:34; cf. 1 Tim. 2:11: ὑποταγή) and to their husbands (here; Eph. 5:21, 24; Col. 3:18; so also 1 Pet. 3:1, 5). Such submission is based on the position of the husband as the "head" or leader of the marriage (Eph. 5:22-24; cf. 1 Cor. 11:3).

Paul does not feel it necessary to say that all submission is submission under God, with all that is involved in that truth (cf. Acts 4:19; 5:29), nor does he find it necessary to repeat what he says elsewhere about the equality of a woman/wife to a man/her husband (Gal. 3:28; 1 Cor. 11:11-12; cf. also 1 Pet. 3:7). This is so because that equality under God is part of the basic premise of the Christian faith and because Paul does not regard submission as problematic and needing explanation or qualification (cf. especially in his delineation of the headship of man the statement that "God is the head of Christ," 1 Cor. 11:3).

The concluding words, "that God's word may not be dishonored," may be more closely connected with the immediately preceding clause but should be regarded as referring to all that precedes (for an analogy cf. v. 10; see Ellicott). ὁ λόγος τοῦ θεοῦ is used here as in 2 Tim. 2:9 and Phil. 1:14 of "the message of God" (cf. Tit. 1:3). βλασφημέω, "speak evil of, blaspheme," is used in a similar context in Rom. 2:24, where Paul, applying Is. 52:5 (cf. LXX), writes of the Jews that "God's name is blasphemed among the Gentiles because of you," and he applies the same idea to Christian slaves in nearly the same words in 1 Tim. 6:1. The idea is again applied here with God's "word" in the place of God's "name." Paul thus encourages godly conduct by saying that it keeps God's message from being spoken evil of. Therefore, for a wife to fail to be submissive to her husband or to be unloving or impure, etc., would allow non-Christians to say that Christianity makes people worse rather than better and therefore that its message is not only useless but bad.

Fee and others are mistaken in understanding this argument to be saying that the conduct prescribed is simply that which is culturally acceptable, implying that Paul did not regard it as what is intrinsically right in God's sight. But Fee would presumably not regard the traits in this list other than the last one as merely cultural. The issue is Paul's view of submission of wife to husband. Fee is correct in assuming that Paul sees a motivation for good behavior in the view of non-Christians in the particular culture. And Paul does list things here that represent the norms of the day. But it is an error is to assume that what is unacceptable to non-Christians is therefore merely cultural and does not reflect a transcultural moral standard. Paul appeals to Gentile non-Christian perspectives here and elsewhere (1 Tim. 5:8; 1 Cor. 5:1) because he regards non-Christians as having in these cases a proper ethical sense, since "the work of the law is written in their hearts" (Rom. 2:15) and since they know right from wrong in certain basics even if they themselves do not follow this knowledge (Rom. 1:32).

It is particularly significant that when Paul uses the same kind of motivation in regard to Titus's own behavior (Tit. 2:8) he has more than a relative or culturally accepted standard in view: "Beyond reproach" and "having nothing bad to say about us" refer back to Paul's reference — from a Christian perspective — to "good deeds," "purity in doctrine," and "sound speech" (vv. 7-8). In the same way, Paul says that older women must be "teachers of the good" (καλοδιδασκάλους) to young women, "the good" then being described in the virtues listed, including submission to husbands. And Paul consistently uses the concept "good" of that which is good from God's point of view, not of that which society happens to regard as good. Furthermore, since the sections here on older men and women and younger men reflect Christian norms rather than merely contemporary cultural norms and are presented side-by-side with this section on young women and in a similar format, there is no reason to think that this section approaches behavior on a basically different basis.

Thus Paul does indeed appeal to young women to be concerned about the non-Christian's evaluation of misconduct, but precisely because he regarded that evaluation as correct, and because misconduct on the part of Christians would undoubtedly cause non-Christians to speak ill of the gospel as that which they perceived as being responsible for such misconduct.

Four of the seven virtues listed here for young women relate to marriage and the home. This is so probably because marriage and the home were the sphere of activity of the vast majority of young women and because Paul desired to minister to them in the sphere that they found themselves. He may also put the emphasis there partly as a response to the error of the false teachers (cf. 1:11, 14; 1 Tim. 4:3).

2:6 Just as the other groups must be urged, and the young women are to be taught by the older women, so "likewise" (ὡσαύτως; see v. 3) Titus is to "appeal to" or "urge" (παρακάλει; see 1:9 and especially 1 Tim. 5:1; 6:2) "the younger men" (τοὺς νεωτέρους; see 1 Tim. 5:1) to be what they should be in their Christian lives. The one characteristic that is to be urged on them is expressed in the infinitive σωφρονεῖν and has been urged on each of the other groups (σώφρων in vv. 2, 5; see the remarks there), probably because "to be of sound mind," i.e., "reasonable, sensible, and serious," is an overarching trait that assumes others that have been stated. But in a real sense σωφρονεῖν does not stand alone as the only characteristic asked of the younger men since the ways in which Titus is urged to be an example to them are also traits that they are thereby urged to have.

2:7 Here it must immediately be asked whether περὶ πάντα, "in all respects" (for this understanding of περί see BAGD s.v. 2d; Dana-Mantey, *Grammar,* 109), goes with the preceding words or with those that follow (for English versions on either side see the *UBSGNT* punctuation apparatus). It is asserted that taking it with the preceding words lets σεαυτόν carry its own force without detraction, but since σεαυτόν and περὶ πάντα represent different entities they do not necessarily interact with or detract from one another. It is also argued, with plausibility, that the wide scope of this phrase would give perspective to the one characteristic given for younger men, but it would be equally forceful if περὶ πάντα were taken with the following words, thereby giving the range in which Titus was to be an example to the younger men. The arguments are rather evenly balanced, and with whichever direction the phrase is taken the significance of vv. 6-8 as a whole is about the same.

Vv. 6-8 take a somewhat different form because Paul is seeking to accomplish two or three things at once. He is urging younger men to live godly Christian lives, and he is addressing Titus about his particular responsibilities as a minister and as an example to these men. But the focus on these two responsibilities of Titus dominates this section. Therefore, the characteristics named are influenced by Titus's particular position as a minister.

With σεαυτὸν παρεχόμενος τύπον καλῶν ἔργων (for this verb with the reflexive pronoun elsewhere in Greek literature see BAGD s.v. παρέχω 2a), "show yourself to be an example of good deeds," Paul turns to Titus as an example for the younger men (perhaps for all four groups; cf. ἡμῶν in v. 8 and 1 Tim. 4:12; see 1 Tim. 4:12 also on τύπος and 4:7, 12 on σεαυτόν) just as the older women were to be for the young women. The exact words τύπος καλῶν ἔργων (for pl. καλοὶ ἔργοι see 1 Tim. 5:10) are found here only in the NT, but Paul uses τύπος elsewhere in the sense of "example" with other words (Phil. 3:17; 1 Thes. 1:7; 2 Thes. 3:9; cf. also 1 Pet. 5:3; for the significance of τύπος see L. Goppelt, *TDNT* VIII, 248-50; De Boer, *Imitation,* 21-23, 86-89).

Some areas in which Titus must be "an example of good deeds" are presented in the words that follow here and in the next verse. With one exception, these words are in the accusative case and dependent on the verb παρεχόμενος. That one exception is the prepositional phrase ἐν τῇ διδασκαλίᾳ, "in teaching," which is placed first, perhaps for emphasis, and which qualifies one or more of the words that follow it.

διδασκαλία (see 1 Tim. 1:10) refers either to the activity of "teaching" or to what is taught, i.e., the doctrine. It is hard to sharply differentiate between the two nuances here. ἀφθορία** (a NT hapax, which probably explains the origin of the textual variants; see *TCGNT*) requires that Titus show "soundness" in either the content or the activity of his διδασκαλία.

σεμνότης** (also in 1 Tim. 2:2; 3:4), "seriousness," "denotes a high moral tone and serious manner" (Kelly) and may be a further indication of what Titus's διδασκαλία is to be like ("sound and serious in teaching"), or it may stand alone and indicate what his life itself should be like ("sound in teaching, serious . . ."). In favor of the former is the obvious emphasis on διδασκαλία so soon after a reference to God's "message" (v. 5). In favor of the latter is the use of σεμνότης elsewhere in the PE of persons, not things, and Paul's tendency, when referring to ministers, to refer to their personal life as well as to their work (e.g., 1 Tim. 4:6-16, where διδασκαλία is used in vv. 6, 13 and where a phrase analogous to this verse is found in v. 16). The question is further complicated by the fact that the next three words, λόγον ὑγιῆ ἀκατάγνωστον, can also be understood either as qualifying ἐν τῇ διδασκαλίᾳ or as standing as further characteristics on their own. This question, along with the meaning of διδασκαλία, is taken up in the comments on v. 8a.

2:8a ὑγιής (NT 11x) indicates that which is "healthy" or "sound" and like the verb ὑγιαίνω refers to that which is "correct." ἀκατάγνωστος (a NT hapax) means "not condemned" or "beyond reproach." This does not mean that Titus's speech or preaching (λόγος) should never be reproached or condemned by anyone, but that there should be no proper basis for such a reproach since what Titus says should be ὑγιής, i.e., in accord with the apostolic norm of what he should say. Here again we face alternatives in meaning, with λόγος referring either to Titus's everyday speech or to his preaching, although some would suggest that both are in view. In 1 Tim. 4:12 λόγος is used of speech in general, and there τύπος is used as it is in Tit. 2:7. 1 Tim. 5:17 and Tit. 1:9 are examples of use of λόγος with reference to preaching. The nearest equivalent to λόγος ὑγιής in the PE (ὑγιής does not occur elsewhere in the PE and λόγος ὑγιής occurs nowhere else in the NT) is plural λόγοι with the verb ὑγιαίνω, used of communication of the message of Christianity (1 Tim. 6:3 with reference to Jesus; 2 Tim. 1:13 with reference to Paul).

The alternatives for the separate words and phrases can now be considered as parts of a coherent whole. Is the whole section completely about teaching (διδασκαλία) and preaching (λόγος)? If so, then σεμνότης probably does qualify "teaching." Does "teaching" refer to activity and "preaching" to content? If so, then both ἀφθορία and σεμνότης may well describe the qualities of the one who teaches. Or do both phrases, the one about "teaching" and the one about "preaching," refer to content, with the second phrase appositional to the first? Or does the second phrase provide a further qualification of the "teaching" along with the two preceding words?

As an altogether different solution, we may ask if Paul speaks here of three distinct concerns, i.e., sound "teaching," a "serious" life, and "speech" (λόγος) that is beyond reproach. The attractiveness of this alternative is that the items listed here would then speak more directly to Titus's position as an "example of good works" for the younger men. Unfortunately, Brox's comments about several of the alternatives correctly apply more widely in this section: One cannot make such distinctions with certainty because all the various alternatives are possible.

2:8b The ἵνα clause reminds Titus that his life must be lived purposefully, so that what he does is not only intrinsically good and in accord with the "sound teaching" (v. 1), but also so that it has effect for good, with reference to the gospel, on those who observe him, especially those seeking an occasion to fault Christianity. Titus's conduct should not give any grounds for Christians to be accused of evil.

ἐναντίος (NT 8x) means either "opposite" or "opposed" according to the context. Here ὁ ἐξ ἐναντίας (cf. Mk. 15:39) means "the opponent." The definite article is used here in a generic rather than a specific sense so that the phrase refers to "anyone who may oppose" (cf. the plurals in 1:10-16 and the generic singular in 1:6-7). This "opponent" is probably to be identified as any of the false teachers already mentioned (cf. 1:14 and τοὺς ἀντιλέγοντας in 1:9), although it is possible that Paul is thinking more broadly of anyone who opposes Christianity, not only the false teachers but any pagans or Jews who might do so (cf. Bernard, Fee, Hanson, Kelly, and Spicq).

Paul wants this "opponent" to "be put to shame" or to "be ashamed" (ἐντραπῇ, aorist passive of ἐντρέπω; 2 Thes. 3:14 has the only other aorist passive of this verb in the NT) so that the opponent and others will realize that there are no grounds for speaking evil of Christians (μηδὲν ἔχων λέγειν περὶ ἡμῶν φαῦλον). Paul does not mean that Titus's good life will keep opponents from ever saying anything negative about Christians, but that it will not give an opponent grounds to accuse Christians of anything morally "bad" or "evil." The standard of judgment here is not what was unacceptable to that society, as some have suggested, but rather what is intrinsically "bad," as every other occurrence of φαῦλος** in the NT demonstrates (Jn. 3:20; 5:29; Rom. 9:11; 2 Cor. 5:10; Jas. 3:16).

It is noteworthy that Paul does not say "about you" (which a few manuscripts have added) but "about us" (περὶ ἡμῶν). He apparently uses the first person plural pronoun, which designates the Christian community as a whole (as elsewhere in Titus: 1:3, 4; 2:10, 12, 13, 14; 3:3, 4, 5, 6, 15), to indicate that the misconduct of any Christian, and especially of a leader in the church, will have consequences for the entire Christian community.

2:9-10a Because slaves are a distinct element in the church, Paul has a word for them when he addresses groups in the church (cf. Eph. 6:5ff.; Col. 3:22ff.; 1 Tim. 6:1ff.; also 1 Cor. 7:21f.), which is why they are here in a list otherwise based on age and sex. This section (vv. 9-10) assumes an unstated finite verb and therefore harks back either to v. 1 or to παρακάλει in v. 6. For the significance of δοῦλοι, "slaves," and consideration of the rationale for addressing slaves in an apostolic letter see the comments on 1 Tim. 6:1ff.

The response asked of slaves is stated in the infinitive ὑποτάσσεσθαι, "to subject oneself" (also addressed to slaves in 1 Pet. 2:18; elsewhere Paul uses ὑπακούω, "listen to" or "obey," Eph. 6:4; Col. 3:22). The same verb is addressed to Christians in other situations as well (Eph. 5:21; 1 Cor. 16:16; Rom. 13:1; Tit. 3:1; 1 Pet. 2:13; Eph. 5:22; Col. 3:18; Tit. 2:5; 1 Pet. 3:1, 5). Therefore, what Paul asks for is not unique to the slave situation but is a response that those under authority can appropriately be asked to render as part of their duty and responsibility to the one in authority. Slaves are asked to subject themselves to "their own" (ἰδίοις, with a focusing and delimiting significance) "masters" (δεσπόταις; see 1 Tim. 6:1-2). The latter term may be chosen here (and in 1 Timothy) because it more precisely describes non-Christian masters, a phenomenon which looms large in both passages.

Does ἐν πᾶσιν go with this statement or with the following one (see the *UBSGNT* punctuation apparatus for translations that follow either course). Huther presents what appears at first to be a forceful argument, i.e., that it should go with what follows since it is a matter of course with the former "whereas the same could not be said of εὐαρέστοι εἶναι, since that goes beyond the duty of ὑποτάσσεσθαι." Several commentators (e.g., Lock) argue that it should go with what precedes and that this balances best with ἐν πᾶσιν at the end of the section (v. 10). Paul's statement on the same subject in Col. 3:22 clearly joins the comparable κατὰ πάντα with the synonymous ὑπακούετε, and this is the most convincing and compelling consideration in favor of the same construction here (as Hiebert rightly argues; cf. also White, who also points out that Paul joins ἐν παντί to ὑποτάσσω in Eph. 5:24 and that "ἐν πᾶσιν elsewhere in the Pastorals is at the end of a clause," i.e., in 1 Tim. 3:11; 2 Tim. 2:7; 4:5; Tit. 2:10). Thus slaves are to subject themselves "in all respects," i.e., in all aspects of their service that a Christian slave can render without sinning.

They should also seek to be εὐαρέστους, "pleasing" or "acceptable" to their masters, i.e., to give satisfaction to their masters (BAGD, Bernard). Thus Paul asks for positive and winsome action in addition to passive submission (cf. Col. 3:22f.; Eph. 6:5ff., especially v. 7: μετ' εὐνοίας δουλεύοντες, "with good will rendering service"). And slaves are not to be ἀντιλέγοντας (Pl.* 3x: Rom. 10:21; Tit. 1:9; here), used here in the sense of "answering back" *(NEB)* or "talking back" *(NIV, TEV)*.

Paul gives two further instructions to slaves, one negative and one positive. μὴ νοσφιζομένους** (in NT only middle: Acts 5:2, 3) means "not putting aside for themselves" that which belongs to their masters, i.e., "misappropriating" or "stealing." Stealing would be a temptation to slaves, who could have access to many things that might not be missed in small quantities and who might justify their actions by saying either that the item did not count and would not be missed or that what they stole was justly owed to them anyway. It is evident here, as elsewhere, that Paul addresses slaves in their particular situation with its particular problems, but it is equally obvious that the problems addressed are not unique to slaves but are rather common to the situation of workers in general.

Instead (ἀλλά) slaves are to be those πᾶσαν πίστιν ἐνδεικνυμένους ἀγαθήν, "showing all good faithfulness." ἐνδεικνυμένους (in NT only middle) is used here of "showing" in oneself the quality spoken of. πίστις is used here in the sense of "faithfulness, reliability" (BAGD s.v. 1a; cf. Mt. 23:23; 2 Thes. 1:4), with ἀγαθής strengthening it (cf. Mt. 25:21, 23: δοῦλε ἀγαθὲ καὶ πιστέ). On πᾶς with ἀγαθός and a noun other than ἔργον see especially Acts 23:1. πᾶσαν is probably added here after ἀλλά to emphasize that this "good faithfulness" must extend to all areas, as opposed to a tendency evidenced by violations of the preceding two admonitions. πᾶσα πίστις ἀγαθή is not found as a whole elsewhere in the NT, and ἀγαθήν is found only here with πίστιν in the NT, but *BGU* 314, 19 has μετὰ πίστεως ἀγαθῆς and *P. Oxy.* 494, 9 (AD 156) has πᾶσαν πίστιν μοι ἐνδεικνυμένῃ, "showing entire faithfulness toward me" (MM).

Paul's presentation of the duties of slaves began, then, with a general request that they subject themselves to their masters in all things (v. 9a). This he followed with four principles arranged chiastically (positive, negative, negative, positive): be pleasing, do not talk back, do not steal, show all good faithfulness (vv. 9b-10a), with the first two addressing attitude and the third and fourth addressing fidelity.

2:10b Here Paul encourages slaves to live this kind of godly life in their difficult circumstances in a ἵνα clause that presents the "purpose contemplated by such conduct" (Ellicott). That purpose is that slaves may "adorn" or "do credit to" (κοσμῶσιν; see 1 Tim. 2:9) the teaching about God as Savior, i.e., that their lives may be so evidently transformed that they commend the gospel that teaches that this God saves people and changes their lives. Paul would have them do this "in all respects" and "in every way" (ἐν πᾶσιν; see v. 9). He has spoken about various aspects of their lives because each aspect should bring credit (and not discredit) to the gospel.

διδασκαλία (see 1 Tim. 1:10), "teaching," is used here as often elsewhere in the PE in the passive sense of that which is taught. The teaching in view (τὴν διδασκαλίαν) is designated by repeating the article τήν before the following words, τοῦ σωτῆρος ἡμῶν θεοῦ (for this phrase and the words in it see 1 Tim. 1:1), an objective genitive construction describing the content of the teaching. θεοῦ would seem to refer to God the Father since it does in the same phrase in 1:3. This identification is strengthened by the fact that the Father appears to be in view in this phrase elsewhere whenever no further identification is given (see 1 Tim. 1:1; 2:3; Tit. 1:3; 3:4).

EXCURSUS: MOTIVATIONS FOR APPROPRIATE CONDUCT: 2:1-10

Paul gives two motivations for the behavior that he asks of different groups of Christians in Tit. 2:1-10. The first is evidenced at v. 1, where Paul tells Titus to teach godly behavior "in accordance with sound doctrine." What Paul then writes for Titus to teach is, by definition, in accordance with this announced principle and thus comes from and agrees with "sound doctrine." This is the most basic and overarching motivation for the instructions that Paul gives.

A subsidiary and related consideration is the impact that the behavior of Christians will have on those around them. Paul mentions this three times in this section in different ways, negatively with reference to younger women (v. 5) and Titus (v. 8) and positively with reference to slaves (v. 10). These three situations actually deal with the same concern. The first and last represent the negative and positive sides of concern for how the Christian's conduct affects the gospel message. The second is like the first, but one step removed. Paul does not want ungodly conduct to give occasion for the gospel message to be defamed (v. 5). Instead, he wants godly conduct to commend the message (v. 10). Nor does he want Titus, the example for Christians, to be found guilty of moral evil (φαῦλον), which would provide a basis for attack on Christians and thus on the gospel message (v. 8).

These two factors both bear upon the behavior mandated. All of the actions mentioned in this section are demanded by Paul because they are intrinsic to "sound doctrine," i.e., Christianity. Therefore, they must characterize the lives of the respective groups in their respective roles. At the same time, non-Christians share the perspective of Christians on these matters and will notice failures in any of them, so that the gospel message will be adversely affected by the failures.

Since Paul is concerned for the impact of the conduct of Christians on non-Christians, it might be assumed that he is only asking for these actions because they were what was accepted in that culture — not because they are intrinsically right and in accordance with Christianity. That they were, indeed, the accepted patterns of behavior is clearly documented by many statements in literature of the time that commend a comparable list (e.g., for wives cf. Fee). The conclusion has been drawn, then, that what the culture demanded was a controlling factor for Paul's list, with the implication that in another culture with different norms not all of the virtues that Paul lists would be demanded, because then no one would be offended by their omission from the lives of Christians and the gospel would not be harmed.

For instance, Padgett ("Rationale") concludes that "the rationales of the *hina* clauses of Tit. 2 demonstrate to me that Paul's concern was not to lay down a law for all time, but to give temporary marching orders for the church, so that the gospel could go forth to all peoples" (p. 52). This conclusion provides for Padgett a resolution of what he considers a dilemma, namely, how Paul could call on women to submit to their husbands. His answer, in line with his major conclusion, is that in a society that regarded such submission as a virtue "it was necessary therefore to yield the right of women Christians to equality with men, so that the gospel could go forth" (p. 50; incidentally, the demand that wives submit to their husbands need not carry with it the idea that they are not equal: Paul links Christ's submission to the headship of the Father with the headship of husbands over wives [1 Cor. 11:3]).

This approach is misdirected on two counts. First, it ignores the principle that Paul says governs this section, namely that Titus should "teach what is in accord with sound doctrine" (v. 1, *NIV*) over against the false teachers, who were teaching "commandments of humans" (1:14).

Second, nearly every item in the list, when analyzed independently, can be seen as intrinsically right and not just in accord with the culture of that day, and every item agrees with what is said elsewhere in the NT. Certainly the interpersonal qualities asked of slaves (vv. 9-10) are intrinsically right for any working situation and are asked of the slaves for that reason. At the same time, slavery itself is not being taught as a norm (see the comments above on 1 Tim. 6:1ff.; Knight, *Role Relationship,* 9-15). Certainly for a wife and mother to love her husband and children and be sensible, pure, and kind (vv. 4-5) are intrinsically right and not just norms of first-century culture. It appears quite arbitrary, then, to single out the requests that women be homemakers and be subject to their husbands (v. 5) as something purely cultural. They are treated on a par with the other items in this list, and elsewhere Paul defends the latter of these two as a creation ordinance in the face of a cultural situation that wanted to go in the opposite direction (1 Cor. 11:3ff.). Similar remarks could be made about the list of requirements for Titus, but this is unnecessary since Paul says that a violation of any of them would be a moral evil (φαῦλος, v. 8).

Another way in which the demands in this section have been dealt with is by a methodology that places these culturally accepted norms and the ethical perspective of Christianity in tension with each other, with the conclusion that they cannot coincide or, if they do, what we have here in Titus is a sign of "early catholicism" and of a "middle-class morality" and must therefore be non-Pauline (so Dibelius-Conzelmann, e.g., at vv. 9-10: "It is in the emphasis placed upon such purely social values that the originally secular character of the parenesis is shown"; Kidd, *Wealth and Beneficence,* deals with this question of "middle-class morality"). But even elsewhere Paul commends what might thus be labeled purely "middle-class" social values in regard to the state and citizenship (Rom. 13:1ff.) and in regard to the work ethic (1 Thes. 4:11-12; 2 Thes. 3:6-12).

But even more importantly, as has been seen in the comments on Tit. 2:5, Paul regards non-Christians as having a proper ethical perspective on some basic matters (1 Cor. 5:1; 1 Tim. 5:8) because they know in their conscience certain basics of right and wrong, even if they do otherwise and approve others that do (Rom. 1:32). Their consciences reflect the fact that "the work of the law is written in their hearts" (Rom. 2:15). Hence Paul's appeal to wives to submit to their husbands, for example, is no less intrinsically right or part of the basic Christian perspective just because it was also commended by the non-Christian culture and society of that day. Since Paul commends and teaches this so consistently (as does Peter), it is, therefore, likely that this represented for Paul an example of where culture and society reflect "the work of the law written in their hearts" rather than a case where, as Fee says, "as with the list of virtues, this, too, assumes the cultural norm of what a good wife was expected to be like" (at v. 5).

GOD'S GRACE: 2:11-15

The previous section concluded with a reference to "the doctrine of God our Savior." This section gives that doctrine as the basis for the exhortations to godly behavior and thus begins with γάϱ, "for" or "because." The connection between the two sections, imperative and doctrinal, is the same as in Paul's earlier letters, the difference being that here the exhortations come first followed by an appeal to the theological basis (this order is also found sometimes in the earlier letters, e.g., Phil. 2:12-13).

Paul refers to the great act of God's grace appearing (ἐπεφάνη) and to that act bringing salvation to all people (v. 11). Then he speaks of that saving grace teaching us to say no to sin and to live truly Christian lives here and now (v. 12), while at the same time we look expectantly for the hope and glory of the second coming of "our Savior Jesus Christ" (v. 13). The reference to Christ as Savior returns the argument to the major point of this section. So in v. 14 Paul speaks of what Christ did and what he was seeking to accomplish thereby: He gave himself for us to free us from the rebellion of sin and to cleanse us to be his people, who want above all else to do what he wants (v. 14). Paul concludes by demanding that Titus teach the foregoing and to seek authoritatively to bring about an obedient response (v. 15).

2:11 "The grace of God" (ἡ χάϱις τοῦ θεοῦ; this phrase 15x in Pl.*: here; Rom. 5:15; 1 Cor. 1:4; 3:10; 15:10; 2 Cor. 1:12; 6:1; 8:1; 9:14; Gal. 2:21; Eph. 3:2, 7; Col. 1:6; 2 Thes. 1:12) is God's gracious intention toward mankind whereby, as Paul goes on to say, he saves, instructs, and enables people. Paul says that this grace "has appeared" (ἐπεφάνη, aorist passive), by which he refers to its unique historical appearance in Christ, which is communicated to us in the gospel, as is implied in the words "bringing salvation" and is further borne out by the comparable account in 2 Tim. 1:9-10 and by the only other occurrence of ἐπεφάνη in Titus (3:4ff.).

σωτήριος** is a predicate adjective agreeing with χάρις and means here "bringing salvation" (cf. again 2 Tim. 1:9-10; for this adjective followed by the dative see Thucydides 7.64.2; substantive elsewhere in the NT: Lk. 2:30; 3:6; Acts 28:28; Eph. 6:17). That the adjective is anarthrous, i.e., that it is a predicate adjective, means that "God's favour has appeared with saving power," whereas with the definite article it would make the noun phrase refer merely to "God's saving favour" (C. F. D. Moule, *Idiom-Book,* 114; cf. Radermacher, *Grammatik,* 117; for the variant reading with the article see *NA*[26]). σωτήριος picks up on σωτῆρος, "Savior," in v. 10 and looks forward to σωτῆρος in v. 13. What this salvation entails will be further delineated in vv. 12 and 14, as has already been the case in vv. 1-10.

The grace that has appeared is bringing salvation "to all people" (dative πᾶσιν ἀνθρώποις, attached to σωτήριος), i.e., "to all classes of men, even slaves, enabling all to live true lives" (Lock). Since salvation has come to all, all may be exhorted to live in a godly manner, as in vv. 1-10. Thus Paul uses "all people" here in the same sense that he has used it throughout the PE (cf. 1 Tim. 2:1-6; 4:10 and the comments there). More specifically "all people" in this soteriological setting equals "us" (ἡμᾶς, vv. 12 and 14) in the following verses, i.e., Christians, who are "a people for his own possession" (v. 14), just as "all people" in 1 Tim. 4:10 is clarified by πιστῶν, "believers."

2:12 παιδεύουσα further qualifies χάρις and further indicates the purpose accomplished by the appearance of "grace." The verb παιδεύω means both "instruct" and "discipline." Although both are possible here, the broader concept of instruction is more likely because of the instructions that follow (cf. Acts 7:22; 22:3; cf. also παιδεία in 2 Tim. 3:16).

The ἵνα clause that follows gives the content and goal of grace's instruction. Paul, as he often does, first speaks of a set of negative decisions that grace teaches Christians to make. These are expressed here by the verb ἀρνησάμενοι (see 1 Tim. 5:8; Tit. 1:16), which basically means "say 'no' to" with the further nuance here of "deny," in the sense of "renounce" or "give up" (cf. Riesenfeld, "ἀρνεῖσθαι," especially 217). Since the controlling verb παιδεύουσα is present tense and the following aorist verb, ζήσωμεν, is used with an ongoing present significance, it is best to understand the aorist participle ἀρνησάμενοι in the same sense, without denying that a decisive past choice does undergird every new expression of this renunciation. ἀρνησάμενοι is subordinate to the main verb ζήσωμεν, which means that we must be denying (or have already denied) "godlessness and worldly desires" as a condition for the positive goal to which we are called, i.e., so that we may live the Christian life.

ἀσέβειας** (also in Rom. 1:18; 11:26; 2 Tim. 2:16; Jude 15, 18) means "godlessness, impiety" in both thought and action. τὰς κοσμικὰς ἐπιθυμίας** (this phrase occurs only here in the NT but cf. 1 Jn. 2:16-17) are "the desires that characterize the world," with "the world" considered as the realm of disobedience to God and of sin (cf. κόσμος in Gal. 6:14). Paul returns to this concern in v. 14 when he speaks of "every lawless deed" (πᾶσα ἀνομία), which provides further insight into what he means here. It is likely that this couplet with singular ἀσέβεια followed by the plural ἐπιθύμιαι expresses the fact that grace teaches us to deny both the root principle, "godlessness, impiety," and its many concrete manifestations, "worldly desires."

Whereas the negative was governed by a participle, the next part of the verse is governed by a main verb, which demonstrates that the main thing that χάρις teaches us is the positive lesson on how we should live. The verb ζήσωμεν is qualified by three adverbs, σωφρόνως, δικαίως, and εὐσεβῶς, and by the prepositional phrase ἐν τῷ νῦν αἰῶνι. σωφρόνως** (a NT hapax, which, however, picks up on σώφρων in vv. 2, 5 [and in 1:8] and σωφρονέω in v. 6) means "in a self-controlled and thoughtful manner." δικαίως** (also in Lk. 23:41; 1 Cor. 15:34; 1 Thes. 2:10; 1 Pet. 2:23; cf. δίκαιος in 1:8 and a trilogy like what we have here, including this term, in 1 Thes. 2:10) means here "righteously" or "in an upright manner." εὐσεβῶς** (also in 2 Tim. 3:12), "in a godly manner," is used in the literature of Paul's time of a person's relation to God (BAGD). Here it is probably to be connected with Paul's opening statement in 1:1: "the knowledge of the truth that is according to godliness (εὐσέβεια)." These three adverbs seem to refer respectively to one's self, to one's relationships with other people, and to one's relationship with God, i.e., to thoughtful self-control, to uprightness in dealings with others, and to genuine piety in relation to God.

God's grace instructs us how we should live "in the present age," ἐν τῷ νῦν αἰῶνι** (this phrase also at 1 Tim. 6:17; 2 Tim. 4:10; cf. the synonymous ὁ αἰὼν οὗτος in Rom. 12:2; 1 Cor. 1:20; 2:6, 8; 3:18; 2 Cor. 4:4; Eph. 1:21 and ὁ αἰὼν ὁ ἐνεστώς in Gal. 1:4). Two nuances are probably intended by this phrase, the first being that God's grace does not simply prepare us for the age to come (v. 13) but also saves us for the present and teaches us how to live now. This nuance gives the temporal aspect of νῦν its due. The other nuance is the characteristic of evil and sinfulness that marks "the present age" in Paul's understanding of it and in his usage of this and similar phrases (cf. 2 Tim. 4:10; Rom. 12:2; Gal. 1:4). In this nuance the difficult arena in which Christians must live is given its due. Thus the need for the negative is recognized and particularly the demand to deny "worldly" desires, i.e., desires characteristic of this evil world or age. In particular this nuance takes into account that some are living under a this-worldly social structure, slavery, and that all must be aware that this present evil age will seek to use any misdeed on the part of a Christian against the gospel and against Christians (cf. vv. 5, 8).

Dibelius-Conzelmann have argued against Pauline authorship that the terminology used in this chapter and in this section in particular is more markedly Hellenistic than in Paul's earlier writings. But for one who made it his point to become "all things to all people" (1 Cor. 9:22) and who often used the language of his opponents or of the situation in which the particular church found itself (in, e.g., a number of terms and concepts used in 1-2 Corinthians and Colossians) it is to be expected that he would use such terms in addressing his younger Greek colleague in the Cretan situation. Thus the language and terms are in that sense quite Pauline, even though they may differ from language used in earlier and different situations. It is evident that Paul is not adopting the piety or ethics of the Greeks but using their terms to express Christian piety and ethics (as is always the case to some degree in the NT letters, by necessity, since the NT authors wrote in Greek). The language is being utilized and molded, and this is quite Pauline.

2:13 The participial clause that occupies vv. 13 and 14 serves as a further qualification of the verb ζήσωμεν. We live from the vantage point of "expectantly awaiting" and "looking forward to" Christ's appearing (προσδεχόμενοι; cf. Paul's use of the related verb ἀπεκδέχομαι in Rom. 8:19, 23, 25; 1 Cor. 1:7; Phil. 3:20; cf. the note of expectant waiting in the use of προσδέχομαι in Lk. 2:25, 38). Paul joins to the instructions given by grace about living the Christian life (vv. 11-12) this note of looking forward to Christ's appearing, so that the two give perspective to each other.

προσδεχόμενοι has as its object two nouns, ἐλπίδα, "hope," and ἐπιφάνειαν, "appearing," joined by καί and governed by a single definite article. The first noun is qualified by the adjective μακαρίαν and the second by the genitive construction τῆς δόξης, which itself in turn is qualified by another genitive construction.

Paul often uses the concept of "hope" of the expectancy that Christians have for the unseen and sure, but not yet realized, spiritual blessings that they will possess in the future in Christ (cf. especially Rom. 8:23-25). That "hope" (which is "laid up in heaven" for Christians, Col. 1:5) is for righteousness (Gal. 5:5) and for the grand inheritance of eternal life (Tit. 1:2; 3:7). Perhaps as fully as anywhere Paul speaks of this hope in 1 Thes. 4:13-18 as embracing several elements that are all inherently tied together, namely, Christ's return, the resurrection (or transformation) of all believers, and their being "always with the Lord" (and presumably with one another).

Whereas 1 Thes. 4:13 uses ἐλπίς of the subjective attitude of "hope" focused on these future realities, here Paul uses it of the objective "that which is hoped for" (as in Rom. 8:24; Gal. 5:5; Col. 1:5). The return of the one who brings all that Christians hope for is itself called "the blessed hope" (cf. Col. 1:27). This "hope" is called "blessed" (μακάριος) just as God was called "blessed" (see 1 Tim. 1:11) because it, like him, embodies and brings the blessedness for which Christians hope.

The single article before ἐλπίδα and ἐπιφάνειαν probably indicates that

Paul regards these nouns as referring to the same thing: The "hope" and the "appearing" are one event (cf. Robertson, *Grammar,* 786). This is borne out by the natural sense of the sentence, by the fact that elsewhere in Paul that which one hopes for is tied to Jesus' appearing, and by the use of τῆς δόξης, which elsewhere in Paul is attached to "hope" (Rom. 5:2; Col. 1:27), with "appearing" here. ἐπιφάνεια**, "appearing, appearance," in all its NT occurrences (6x, all Pl.: here; 2 Thes. 2:8; 1 Tim. 6:14 [see the comments there]; 2 Tim. 1:10; 4:1, 8), except for one (2 Tim. 1:10, Jesus' first appearance), refers to Jesus' second appearance, as is evidenced here by the words that follow.

The ἐπιφάνεια is said more particularly to be τῆς δόξης κτλ. Some have suggested that this genitive construction is a Hebraism and that the phrase should be rendered "the glorious appearing." It is more plausible, however, that the passage speaks of the appearance of God's glory rather than of the glorious appearing of God (ἐπιφάνειαν τῆς δόξης τοῦ μεγάλου θεοῦ). This is supported by the use of δόξα elsewhere with reference to Jesus' second coming, where it is not used adjectivally but as a noun indicating the splendor that will accompany and be manifested in that appearing (cf. Mt. 16:27; 24:30; 25:31; Mk. 8:38; 13:26; Lk. 9:26; 21:27; 24:26). Furthermore, Paul often uses δόξα followed by a genitive construction referring to God, as here (cf. Rom. 1:23; 3:23; 15:7; 1 Cor. 10:31; 11:7; 2 Cor. 4:6, 15; Phil. 1:11; 2:11; 1 Tim. 1:11). Finally, "the appearing of the glory of the great God" (ἐπιφάνειαν τῆς δόξης τοῦ μεγάλου θεοῦ) maintains the verbal parallelism between this verse and v. 11, which speaks of the appearing of the grace of God (ἐπεφάνη . . . ἡ χάρις τοῦ θεοῦ).

If this understanding is correct, then the appearing manifests the glory of "our great God and Savior Jesus Christ" (the reasons for understanding this to refer to one person are given below). This glory has a double aspect: Christians look forward to the appearing of this glory because therein "the Lord of glory" (1 Cor. 2:8) himself is finally and openly glorified before mankind. They also await it because in the appearing of this glory the blessedness that Christians hope for appears. Thus Paul has spoken here of the blessed hope and of the appearing of the glory as two aspects of one and the same event. When this glory appears so also will our blessedness appear (cf. 1 Jn. 3:2; Phil. 3:20-21; see Murray, *Romans* I, 161f. on the similar phrase "we exult in hope of God's glory" in Rom. 5:2).

But does τοῦ μεγάλου θεοῦ καὶ σωτῆρος ἡμῶν 'Ιησοῦ Χριστοῦ refer to one or two persons, or is there some other way to understand the verse in its entirety? (For a full discussion of this question see Harris, "Titus 2:13.") Essentially three views have been proposed: (1) that one person is in view and that the statement should read "our great God and Savior, Jesus Christ," (2) that two persons are in view and that the statement should read "the great God and our Savior Jesus Christ," and (3) that two persons are in view and that the glory of the one (God and Savior) appears in the other (Jesus Christ) so that the statement should read "the appearing of [him who is] the Glory of our God and Savior [= the Father], [which Glory is/that is] Jesus Christ."

The first of these views is supported by a number of modern commentators (Barrett, Bernard "with hesitation," Dornier, Easton, Ellicott, Freundorfer, Gealy, Guthrie, Hanson, Hendriksen, Hiebert, Houlden, Leaney, Lenski, Lock, Moellering, Ridderbos, Simpson, Spicq, and Weiss). In its favor is, first, that the "appearance" in the NT always refers to one person, Christ, not two (see the occurrences of ἐπιφάνεια cited above). Second, the hope of the Christian elsewhere in Paul is centered in Christ and his return (see the discussion of "hope" above). Third, the joining of two nouns by καί with one article, as here, usually designates one thing or person (see BDF §276.3; Robertson, *Grammar,* 786; idem, "Greek Article"). Fourth, the words "God and Savior" (θεοῦ καὶ σωτῆρος) are found together as a title designating one person in the Greek usage of the period (see the literature cited in MHT I, 84; Robertson, *Grammar,* 786; BAGD s.v. σωτήρ). Fifth, the following verse, v. 14, carries on the thought of this verse by referring back to it with the words ὃς ἔδωκεν ἑαυτόν, as if only one person, Christ, were in view (so Lock).

Sixth, "the exceptional use of μέγας with θεός may be more easily explained if θεός refers to Christ than if it signifies the Father" (Harris, "Titus 2:13," 269; cf. Ellicott and especially W. Grundmann, *TDNT* IV, 538-40). Harris gives the explanation that "if there is a use of the θεὸς καὶ σωτήρ formula and therefore exclusive reference to Christ, it would occasion no surprise if μέγας (and ἡμῶν) were added in opposition to the pagan applications of the formula: '*our great* God and Saviour, Jesus Christ' " (cf. Acts 19:27, 28, 34). Harris says further that Christ has shown himself to be "the great God and Savior" "by his sacrificial self-surrender to achieve their redemption and sanctification (verse 14)" (p. 270).

Interpretation (2) is also held by a number of modern commentators (Alford, Dibelius-Conzelmann, Holtz, Huther, Jeremias, Kelly, Schlatter, and N. J. D. White). In favor of it is, first, that Paul rarely if ever refers to Jesus with the word θεός (so, e.g., Huther). Winer states it more strongly: "Doctrinal conviction, deduced from Paul's teaching, that this great apostle could not have called Christ *the great God,* induced me to show that there is . . . no grammatical obstacle to taking καὶ σωτῆρος . . . Χριστοῦ by itself as a second object" (*Grammar,* 130 n. 2). Second, θεὸς ὁ σωτὴρ ἡμῶν (PE 6x, twice elsewhere: Lk. 1:47; Jude 25) is used elsewhere of the Father, which "does not make it probable that the whole expression is applied to the Lord Jesus Christ" (Alford). Third, σωτήρ "was one of those words which gradually dropped the article. . . . This being so, it must hardly be judged as to the expression of the art[icle] by the same rules as other nouns" (Alford; cf. Bernard). Fourth, since God the Father is referred to as Savior in v. 10 and as he who brings salvation in v. 11, it is highly unlikely that this title would now refer to someone else, namely, the Son (Abbot, "Construction of Titus II.13," 448, referred to by Harris, "Titus 2:13," 265). Fifth, the expression "great God" is a late Jewish term for God and would be an exception if applied to Jesus (Jeremias, who refers to the LXX, Enoch, Philo, and Josephus), and it is most in line with "similar epithets to exalt God's glory" (cf. 1 Tim. 1:17; 4:10; 6:15, 16, especially 1:11; so Huther). Sixth, while Paul regularly speaks of God and Christ side by side, "they are invariably distinguished as two persons" (Kelly; so also Huther).

Interpretation (3) was proposed by Hort (*James,* 47, 103f.) and has since been followed by others (e.g., Fee, Parry). It combines some of the considerations of the preceding two interpretations. First, there is only one appearance. Second, this appearance is that of Christ. Third, the title "God and Savior" go together so that there cannot be two persons in view but one. Fourth, "God" must refer to the Father, especially when μεγάλου is considered. Fifth, δόξα θεοῦ may have been a primitive christological title (Hort refers to Jas. 2:1; Eph. 1:17; 2 Cor. 4:6; Heb. 1:3; possibly 1 Pet. 4:14; also Rev. 21:11, 23; Fee appeals to the similar grammatical construction of Col. 2:2). Sixth, since this interpretation "resolves the difficulties and carries none of its own" (Fee), "Jesus Christ" should therefore be understood as in apposition to "the glory of God," and thus God's glory is manifested in the appearing of Christ.

Alford's argument (the third under interpretation [2]) explaining why σωτῆρος is anarthrous does not accord with the evidence in the PE, where σωτήρ is articular seven times and anarthrous only twice (excluding Tit. 2:13). In one of these instances (1 Tim. 1:1) "σωτήρ is anarthrous as being in apposition to θεός which lacks the article in accordance with the canon of Apollonius" (that "nouns in regimen must have articles prefixed to both of them or neither"); in the other (1 Tim. 4:10) "σωτήρ is anarthrous because it is predicative and adjectival" (Harris, "Titus 2:13," 274 n. 39; see also 268f. for Harris's treatment of other ways of accounting for anarthrous σωτῆρος, which, he shows, fail to carry conviction). That "God our Savior" refers to God the Father in the PE (the second argument under [2]) does not determine the reference of "God *and* Savior" or rule out its application to Christ, since Christ is also referred to in the PE as σωτήρ (3x of 9x, leaving this verse aside; in Titus, leaving this verse aside, 2x of Christ [1:4; 3:6] and 3x of the Father [1:3; 2:10; 3:4]). This makes the fourth argument under (2) inconclusive and points, in fact, to interpretation (1). Paul most likely does refer to Christ as θεός in Rom. 9:5 (see, e.g., the discussion and literature in *TCGNT;* Cranfield, *Romans,* ad loc.), which shows that the first argument under (2) and this aspect of the fourth argument under (3) are not conclusive. It is doubtful if the fifth argument under (3), that δόξα θεοῦ was a primitive christological title, has adequate evidence to sustain the hypothesis.

All three interpretations agree that but one person "appears," namely, Christ. Interpretation (3) says that the appearing is that of the "glory" of our great God and Savior, i.e., the Father, and that "Jesus Christ" is in apposition to that "glory," so that it appears in him. This position is attractive, but it requires an appositional reference that is quite far removed, and it is a solution that is certainly less obvious than the alternatives, or at least than interpretation (1).

Interpretation (2) has in its favor that it sees Paul using μεγάλου with θεοῦ in the same way that the LXX and late Jewish writers do (argument five), but argument six under interpretation (1) gives an equally adequate, if not better, explanation of the usage in the setting in which Paul writes. Interpretation (2) has against it that it separates "God and Savior," which was a composite title referring to one person in the literature of Paul's time (the fourth argument under [1] and the third under [3]) and which is joined by καί and one article and would be considered by all as referring to one person in the natural reading of the passage — if the words "Jesus Christ" were not present (the third argument under [1]). Interpretation (2) also has against it that it requires that anarthrous σωτῆρος be dependent on ἐπιφάνειαν, so that the passage speaks of "the appearing of the glory of the great God and (the appearing) of our Savior Jesus Christ." This construction would be strange for a NT writer in that it joins the impersonal (δόξα) and the personal (σωτῆρος ἡμῶν Ἰησοῦ Χριστοῦ) on the same footing. But even more fundamentally, there is no compelling reason to take σωτῆρος as dependent on ἐπιφάνειαν or to take καί as epexegetical when the more normal relationships are so much more likely.

The arguments in favor of interpretations (2) and (3) that focus on the juxtaposition of "Jesus Christ" and "the great God" are not compelling reasons for setting aside view (1), which is the natural and normal interpretation. Furthermore, the considerations of interpretation (1) that address this particular question are quite adequate. Therefore, we conclude that this section of the verse speaks of the appearing and the glory of one person, "of our great God and Savior Jesus Christ" (so *RSV, NEB, NASB, TEV,* which all give interpretation [2] in the margin, and of *NIV*).

With regard to the phrase τοῦ μεγάλου θεοῦ, W. Grundmann (*TDNT* IV, 538-40) quotes a number of OT references to proclamation of God's greatness in which "the basic monotheistic thrust in conflict with other gods is clear and unmistakable" (538f.). He then provides a number of examples to show that "in Hellenism, with its fusion of the oriental and Greek worlds, the phrase μέγας θεός is found everywhere" (539), as in the acclamations in Acts 19:28, 34. He concludes (see the arguments for interpretation [1] above) that Titus 2:13 adopts both the language of the OT and, more so, that of Paul's day to speak of Christ over against pagan cultic claims.

Paul refers to Jesus as σωτήρ (the word in NT 24x, Pl. 12x, PE 10x) six times (here; Eph. 5:23; Phil. 3:20; 2 Tim. 1:10; Tit. 1:4; 3:6). In the letter to Titus first the Father and then Christ are called "Savior" in adjacent sections in each of the three chapters (1:3, 4; 2:10, 13; 3:4, 6). Here Christ is called the Savior as the one who will bring the hoped-for blessedness through what he has done, as the following verse (v. 14) indicates, in his saving deed (giving himself for us) and its saving accomplishments (redemption from sin, cleansing for himself a people who will zealously do good deeds). Thus σωτήρ is used here as it is in the two non-PE Pauline uses of the title for Christ: It is set in a context like that of Phil. 3:20-21, in which "we eagerly await (ἀπεκδεχόμεθα) a Savior, the Lord Jesus Christ" because of the blessedness that his coming will bring ("who will transform the body of our humble state into conformity with the body of his glory"). And it is set in a context analogous to that of Eph. 5:23ff., in which Christ is the Savior who "gave himself up" for the church "that he might sanctify it, having cleansed it, . . . that he might present [it] to himself" (vv. 23, 25-27). Whenever Paul uses σωτήρ of Jesus, except once (Tit. 1:4), the context indicates some aspect of Jesus' work as Savior. The pronoun ἡμῶν here signifies those who already know him as Savior.

This verse concludes with the name Ἰησοῦ Χριστοῦ in apposition to the preceding designation, "our great God and Savior," thereby indicating precisely who it is of whom Paul has been writing. This is one of the infrequent, but important, occasions where Jesus is specifically designated θεός, "God." The others are arguably Rom. 9:5; Jn. 1:1; 1:18 (according to some manuscripts); 20:28; Heb. 1:8ff.; 2 Pet. 1:1; and possibly 1 Jn. 5:20. The use of θεός makes explicit what is implicit elsewhere in the NT, where Jesus is said to have the attributes of God, to do the work of God, and to receive the worship and allegiance due only to God. These references are infrequent, probably because the NT usually designates the Father as "God" and Jesus as "Lord" (cf., e.g., the trinitarian blessing in 2 Cor. 13:14 and Paul's argument for monotheism in 1 Cor. 8:4-6, where he writes of "one God, the Father," and "one Lord, Jesus Christ" [v. 6]).

2:14 Since this entire section (vv. 11-14) is governed and controlled by the motif of the saving and enabling grace of God in Christ (v. 11, the main clause), so that our expectant waiting for the blessed hope is spoken of as the appearing of "our Savior" (v. 13), it is not surprising that this reference to the "Savior" is followed here by a statement that sets forth the work of Christ as Savior in terms of what he did (the ὅς clause) and in terms of its intended result (the ἵνα clause). Although v. 11 speaks already of salvation and v. 12 of the results of salvation in the Christian's life, they do so in more impersonal terms (ἡ χάρις), in more instructional terms (παιδεύουσα), and without explicit reference to the work of Christ. Now that the person of Christ the Savior has been introduced into the flow of the argument, Paul presents Christ's work as Savior, i.e., his giving himself for us, and thus gives the basis for the salvation previously spoken of. Paul also presents the results that this deed accomplishes in the lives of the Savior's people and thus gives the basis for the effective instruction previously spoken of.

The antecedent of the relative pronoun ὅς is Ἰησοῦ Χριστοῦ, the only person (so we have argued) mentioned in the preceding verse. His saving work is set forth with the simple but profound words ὃς ἔδωκεν ἑαυτὸν ὑπὲρ ἡμῶν, "who gave himself for us," which seem to echo what Jesus said concerning himself (Mt. 20:28 par. Mk. 10:45). If they do, they embody certain changes from the Gospel form (some of which are already evident in Paul's previous statement echoing these words, 1 Tim. 2:6): The present tense is replaced by a past tense (understandable after the crucifixion; cf. 1 Tim. 2:6), "his soul" is replaced by "himself" (ἑαυτόν, the reflexive pronoun to indicate identity with the person acting; cf. 1 Tim. 2:6 and see below for the uniqueness in the NT of these words with the verb δίδωμι), "ransom" is omitted (because understood), and ἀντὶ πολλῶν is replaced by ὑπὲρ ἡμῶν (the personal replacing the impersonal since Christians are addressed, an analogous preposition being used; for the latter cf. again 1 Tim. 2:6).

ἔδωκεν ἑαυτόν refers particularly to the past and once-for-all act of Jesus giving himself up to die on the cross (here; 1 Tim. 2:6; and Gal. 1:4 with ἑαυτόν; in Mt. 20:28; Mk. 10:45 with τὴν ψυχὴν αὐτοῦ, all of Jesus — the only NT occurrences of δίδωμι with either of these singular objects; cf. παραδίδωμι in Gal. 2:20; Eph. 5:2, 25; Romaniuk, "Origine"). This self-giving is said to be ὑπὲρ ἡμῶν, "for us," i.e., for those who accept Christ as Savior (cf. σωτῆρος ἡμῶν, v. 13). The preposition ὑπέρ can be rendered "for" here in the sense of "on behalf of" or "for the sake of," but it is also possible that here it is equivalent to ἀντί, "in place of"; this is even more likely if this passage is considered a parallel to Mt. 20:28; Mk. 10:45 (cf. Robertson, *Grammar,* 630-32; Zerwick, §91; and especially M. Harris, *NIDNTT* III, 1196f. and the literature referred to there).

The ἵνα clause indicates with two verbs and a concluding phrase the purpose or intended result of Jesus' giving of himself. The first intended result is "that he might redeem us from every lawless deed." λυτρόω** (middle here and in Lk. 24:21; passive in 1 Pet. 1:18) means here "set free, redeem, rescue." F. Büchsel (*TDNT* IV, 350f.) thinks that here the idea of ransom is present (as in 1 Pet. 1:18) because the previous words refer to the "ransom" saying of Jesus (Mt. 20:28 par. Mk. 10:45). ἡμᾶς, "us," refers as before (vv. 12, 13, 14a) to those who know Jesus as Savior. Jesus' self-giving for "us" is effective and thereby he redeems "us."

ἀπὸ πάσης ἀνομίας, "from every lawless deed," with λυτρόω may reflect LXX Ps. 129:8 (130:8 in English versions; αὐτὸς λυτρώσεται τὸν Ἰσραὴλ ἐκ πασῶν τῶν ἀνομιῶν αὐτοῦ), Ezk. 37:23 (ῥύσομαι αὐτοὺς ἀπὸ πασῶν τῶν ἀνομιῶν αὐτῶν), or more likely a combination of the two (see below). By rendering ἀπό and the verb "to set us free from," the *NEB* has caught the meaning well. Singular attributive πάσης with no article includes "everything belonging, in kind, to the class designated by the noun," and thus nothing is excluded. ἀνομία means in its ethical sense, as here, "against the law," so that Christ by his death sets us free from all deeds done against or in opposition to God's law (cf. 1 Jn. 3:4). Christ liberates us from control by every kind of sin.

The second intended result is that Christ might "purify for himself a people for his own possession, zealous for good works." These words also seem to reflect various OT passages. λαὸς περιούσιος, "a people for his own possession," is found in the LXX in Ex. 19:5; Dt. 7:6; 14:2; 26:18, with the Deuteronomy passages expressing the concern for holiness found here. The language of the LXX of Ezk. 37:23 is also close to that found here: It speaks of a people for God (ἔσονταί μοι εἰς λαόν) that God will cleanse (καθαριῶ), having delivered them from all their transgressions (ῥύσομαι αὐτοὺς ἀπὸ πασῶν τῶν ἀνομιῶν αὐτῶν: note the close similarity to the previous clause here). Probably Paul is influenced both here and in the previous clause by the concept and language of the promise of the messianic age in Ezk. 37:23, which he sees as carrying out the earlier covenantal promises of Deuteronomy. Therefore, he combines the passages in this allusion, with the Ezekiel promise informed and shaped by the Deuteronomy covenantal language of περιούσιον, and then concludes with the summary phrase "zealous for good works," ζηλωτὴν καλῶν ἔργων, which may reflect his own way of expressing the concern of Dt. 26:18 ("a peculiar people . . . to keep his commands").

καθαρίζω is used figuratively in all its Pauline occurrences (Pl.* 3x: here; 2 Cor. 7:1; Eph. 5:26; cf. also Heb. 9:14) of moral and religious cleansing and therefore means "cleanse or purify" from sin. Whereas λυτρώσηται speaks of removing Christians from the control of sin, καθαρίσῃ speaks of removing the defilement of sin from Christians. In this way it recalls 2 Cor. 7:1, where the context (6:16) reflects Ezekiel 37, as does the present passage (i.e., Ezk. 37:27, which contains virtually the same words as Ezk. 37:23, which is reflected here).

The purpose of this action in Titus is twofold: so that Christ can prepare "a people for himself" and so that they will be "zealous of good works." The former is the ultimate concern. The "special" and "chosen" quality of περιούσιον with λαόν is appropriately represented in "a people for his own possession" *(NASB),* and "a people that are his very own" (*NIV;* cf. BAGD s.v. περιούσιος and with a slightly different emphasis H. Preisker, *TDNT* VI, 57f.; Cremer, *Lexicon,* 242f.; BDF §113.1; cf. for the concept 1 Pet. 2:9). With ἑαυτῷ λαὸν περιούσιον Paul is utilizing the covenantal formula and applying it, in fulfillment, to the NT people of God. This phrase replaces, in this allusion to the OT passages, the equivalent statement in Ezk. 37:23, i.e., "they will be my people (ἔσονταί μοι εἰς λαόν), and I will be their God."

Christ also wants that people to be, literally, "a zealot for good deeds" (accusative singular ζηλωτήν agreeing with and modifying λαὸν περιούσιον). ζηλωτής (Pl.* 3x: here; 1 Cor. 14:12; Gal. 1:14) means here "one who is eager or enthusiastic." Genitive καλῶν ἔργων, "good works" (see 1 Tim. 5:10, 25; 6:18), indicates what that one is eager to perform (BAGD s.v. ζηλωτής 1aβ). Paul was always concerned for good works (cf. 1 Cor. 3:13-14; 2 Cor. 9:8; Eph. 2:10; Col. 1:10; 2 Thes. 2:17). The good works of the preceding section (2:1-10) are seen here as "the proper *response* to God's grace revealed and made effective in the saving death of Jesus Christ" (Fee). With this phrase Paul has come full circle.

2:15 Paul turns to Titus and charges him to communicate "these things" (ταῦτα) with full authority to the members of the Christian community. This is the first occurrence of ταῦτα in Titus, but this usage reflects a pattern in 1 Timothy (see the comments on 1 Tim. 4:11; 6:2). The natural understanding is that ταῦτα refers to that which precedes in vv. 2-14, and this fits the pattern in 1 Timothy. Here ταῦτα is the object of all three following verbs, just as it is the object of several verbs in 1 Tim. 4:11; 6:2.

The three present imperative verbs, λάλει καὶ παρακάλει καὶ ἔλεγχε, indicate that "these things" are to be communicated continually (cf. the similar verbs in 1 Tim. 4:11; 6:2). With λάλει, "speak," Paul returns to the verb that he used to begin this chapter (v. 1) and uses it here as there in the sense of "teach," now including the great redemptive basis with the practical instructions. παρακάλει (cf. 1:9; 2:6 and see especially the parallel usage in 1 Tim. 6:2) means here "appeal to" or "exhort" or "urge," so that those taught appropriate "these things" and live accordingly. With ἔλεγχε, "reprove" or "rebuke" (concerning "these things"), Paul again picks up a word previously used (1:9, 13) and adds it here as a necessary third ingredient in view of those who contradict or resist, who either may be influenced by others to do so, or who do so by their own inherent tendency because of the remnants of sin (cf. 1:9). This "solemn admonition" should be given "to those who neglect their duties" or "who are slack or fail to respond" (Huther and then Hiebert; cf. the PE* occurrences in 1 Tim. 5:20 and especially 2 Tim. 4:2).

μετὰ πάσης ἐπιταγῆς, "with all authority," although possibly modifying only the last verb, probably modifies all three. Since Titus is to communicate God's truth, he is to do it with God's authority (here Paul applies to Titus's task a term he usually uses with reference to God, i.e., in Rom. 16:26; especially 1 Cor. 7:25; and in the other PE* occurrences: 1 Tim. 1:1; Tit. 1:3). The authority is inherent in the message because it is from God, as Paul indicates in 1 Cor. 7:6 by distinguishing what he says "by concession" from what he can say "by command" (κατ' ἐπιταγήν). To make this point plain and forceful Paul adds here the adjectival πάσης, "all" or "full." Elsewhere he reminds the minister that he must communicate authoritatively and with personal humility, gentleness, and patience (2 Tim. 2:24; 4:2).

Because God's truth is at stake, Paul goes on to charge Titus with another imperative: μηδείς σου περιφρονείτω, "let no one disregard you." περιφρονείτω** (a NT hapax; here with the genitive object σου) has as a possible range of meanings here "disregard, look down on, despise" (BAGD). Titus must let no one (μηδείς) disregard the message by disregarding him. Since this follows the previous charge, it is a further encouragement to "reprove" or "rebuke" anyone that does so. This charge is addressed to Titus, but it may also be written to support him in this task in the churches as the letter was read to the churches in Crete (cf. Calvin).

INSTRUCTIONS FOR LIVING UNDER RULERS AND WITH NON-CHRISTIANS BASED ON GOD'S EXAMPLE AND ENABLEMENT: 3:1-8

Here Paul instructs believers about their conduct and attitude with regard to civil authorities (in all or most of v. 1) and to "all people" in general (v. 2). In the light of the description in v. 3 of the "people" thought of, most likely this latter instruction is particularly concerned with Christians' relationships with non-Christians. Paul states that Christians also were once just as sinful and difficult to get along with as those he speaks of are now. But when the Christians were such, God was kind and loving to humanity (v. 4). Thereby God saved the Christians, though they had done no deeds of righteousness, simply because of his mercy (vv. 4-5). He did this through Christ by washing away the bondage of their sins and regenerating and renewing them by the Holy Spirit (vv. 5-6). Having declared the Christians righteous in his sight by his grace, God made them heirs who have the hope of eternal life (v. 7). It is evident that Paul wants this saying about God's mercy, kindness, and love toward mankind to be a motivation for Christians to perform good deeds toward sinful people, though he does not make this explicit in so many words. The lesson is so self-evident that he does not need to state the connection but simply says that this great redemptive truth should be "stressed," "so that those who have believed [in such a] God may be careful to engage in good deeds" (v. 8).

INSTRUCTIONS FOR LIVING UNDER RULERS AND WITH NON-CHRISTIANS: 3:1-2

With very few but telling words Paul gives his instructions. They can be few because, as the main verb (ὑπομίμνῃσκε) indicates, he is reminding the believers of what he has already taught.

The line between the words that relate to government and those that relate to one's fellow citizens and fellow human beings is not altogether clear. It is possible to take v. 1 as referring to government and v. 2 as referring to one's fellow citizens. Even with this division some say that government is not wholly forgotten in v. 2. Another view speaks of one or more of the last words of v. 1 as being more general. Or, going the other way, it is possible to see one or more of the words in v. 2 as referring to one's attitude and action with regard to government. In any event, the significance of v. 3 for understanding these two verses, and especially v. 2, must not be overlooked.

3:1 Paul charges Titus to continually "remind" (present active imperative of ὑπομιμνήσκω with accusative of the person and infinitives following) "them" (αὐτούς) of what he has taught about their relation to the state (for such teaching cf. Rom. 12:14–13:10). Those to be reminded are the Christians on Crete, not non-Christians, because only Christians have been previously taught by Paul. Paul addresses the Cretan Christians as a whole, rather than in separate groups as in 2:1-10, because what he now says applies to them all.

If the *UBSGNT* is correct in having no καί between ἀρχαῖς and ἐξουσίαις, as is found in some manuscripts, most of the versions, and the Fathers (see *TCGNT* for the argument), then we have a double asyndeton of two pairs, these two dative nouns and the two infinitives that follow them (cf. BDF §460.1). It is most likely that the second infinitive, πειθαρχεῖν, is not to be taken by itself and therefore absolutely, but rather that it is to be taken with both of the nouns. This would mean that the two nouns are governed by both of the infinitives. Parry suggests that "in each case the second word has the effect of qualifying the first: = 'to ruling powers which have due authority render the submission of an active obedience.' " This seems likely even if one might express the qualification differently.

ἀρχαῖς is used here in its sense of earthly "rulers," as the plural is also used in Lk. 12:11 (BAGD s.v. 3). ἐξουσίαις has as one of its meanings "the power exercised by rulers or others in high position by virtue of their office" (BAGD s.v. 4). It is used here in a particular application of that meaning, i.e., of "human authorities" as "the bearers of the authority" (BAGD s.v. 4cα). The other occurrences of the word in this sense are in Lk. 12:11 (with the plural of ἀρχή as here) and Rom. 13:1, 2, 3 (the only other instance in Paul, with the same subject under discussion).

The first infinitive, ὑποτάσσεσθαι, means here "to subject oneself" or "to be subject" and is used elsewhere in the NT with reference to secular authorities in Rom. 13:1, 5 and 1 Pet. 2:13. The second, πειθαρχεῖν** (also in Acts 5:29, 32; 27:21), "obey," is probably used here not in a general sense, because it is not used in that way elsewhere in the NT, but rather in the sense of obeying the "rulers and authorities." LSJM give "obey one in authority" as its basic meaning. Paul makes no qualifications here, just as he does not in Rom. 13:1ff. and as Peter does not in 1 Pet. 2:13. But we know from Acts 5:29 that this obedience is under God, and that, as Peter says there, there are times when one "must obey God rather than humans."

The next infinitive clause, "to be ready for every good deed," could be a request for readiness to perform good deeds in society in general or could refer to a readiness to do so in relation to government in particular. The general form of the statement would incline one to regard it as relating to society in general, but its position immediately after the demand to obey authorities suggests that it goes with this demand and explains what such obedience entails. In Rom. 13:3 and 1 Pet. 2:13-15 as well, doing good is mentioned in relation to the state. But even in these other contexts doing good is not restricted to that which relates directly to the government, even though it includes such — in submission, paying of taxes, etc. (cf. Rom. 13:6-7), but seems to include doing good in the larger context. The same is likely the case here, i.e., that the immediate connection is with the government but the statement is not meant to be confined to that.

"Every good work" (πᾶν ἔργον ἀγαθόν)** is nearly exclusively a Pauline phenomenon in the NT: It occurs 8x in Paul (2 Cor. 9:8; Col. 1:10; 2 Thes. 2:17; 1 Tim. 5:10 [see the comments there]; Tit. 1:16; here; 2 Tim. 2:21; 3:17) and only once elsewhere (Heb. 13:21). By using πᾶν in the singular and thus specifying "every" individual good work, Paul is speaking as broadly as possible and encouraging Christians to be "prepared" (or "ready," ἑτοίμους) "for" (πρός), i.e., to be "ready" and willing to do, whatever good work might need doing (cf. for the same phrase 2 Tim. 3:17, and especially 2 Tim. 2:21, which uses it with the cognate verb).

3:2 Paul continues his list of reminders with four more items. The first is μηδένα βλασφημεῖν, "to speak ill of no one." Does he still have government officials in mind here or is he now speaking in more general terms? In favor of the latter is the indefiniteness and breadth of the word μηδένα, "no one." Paul seems to be including any and all people under that word and thereby self-consciously broadening the horizon. Similarly, the conclusion of this verse says that Christians should show consideration to "all people" (πάντας ἀνθρώπους), and this wider perspective is picked up in v. 3. This is not to say that government officials are excluded, but only that they are not exclusively in view.

βλασφημεῖν is used here in the sense of "to speak ill or evil of," as in Rom. 3:8; 14:16; 1 Cor. 10:30. Paul is not saying by this admonition that Christians must be naive and never correctly evaluate and speak about the evil that they see in anyone, since this is what he himself does in 1:10-16. Rather, he is urging Christians to restrain their natural inclination to say the worst about people. As he puts it in Romans 12, Christians should not "pay back evil for evil to anyone" and should bless rather than curse those who persecute them (vv. 17, 14).

The next two items, ἀμάχους εἶναι, ἐπιεικεῖς, "to be uncontentious, gentle," go together, as the one infinitive governing them indicates and as they do in the only other NT occurrence of the first, albeit in reverse order, 1 Tim. 3:3 (see the comments there). ἄμαχος is used metaphorically in the NT and means "peaceable" in the sense of "uncontentious" (cf. 2 Tim. 2:23-24). ἐπιεικής** (also in Phil. 4:5; 1 Tim. 3:5; Jas. 3:17; 1 Pet. 2:18) means "gentle," "kind," with a concomitant note of graciousness (see the related noun ἐπιείκεια** in Acts 24:4 and especially 2 Cor. 10:1, where Paul urges his readers "by the meekness and gentleness of Christ"). It is often contrasted with severity in Greek literature. See Spicq's discussion of both words in *Notes* I, 263-67, and H. Preisker, *TDNT* II, 588-90 for the second word.

In the last item the participle ἐνδεικνυμένους (see 1 Tim. 1:16; Tit. 2:10) means here "showing" or "demonstrating." The verb (ἐνδείκνυμι) is used here in a way similar to that of 2 Cor. 8:24, where Paul urges his readers "openly before the churches [to] show them the proof of your love." Paul concluded the previous section of Titus on ethical admonition with this same participle and also with the same universal πᾶς (2:10: πᾶσαν πίστιν ἐνδεικνυμένους ἀγαθήν).

πραΰτης means "gentleness, humility, courtesy, considerateness, meekness" (BAGD; see also Spicq, *Notes* III, 570-81; Leivestad, "Meekness"). It may be best understood by its contrast to its opposites, roughness, bad temper, sudden anger, and brusqueness (see F. Hauck and S. Schulz, *TDNT* VI, 646, who give "mild and gentle friendliness" as the general meaning). English translations vary trying to find the right words to render this term with the qualification πᾶσαν: "perfect courtesy" *(RSV),* "a consistently gentle disposition" *(NEB),* "every consideration" *(NASB),* "always . . . a gentle attitude" *(TEV),* "true humility" *(NIV).* Whatever the nuance for πραΰτητα may be, Paul urges that it be shown not partially but fully (πᾶσαν placed before the verb for emphasis; see BAGD s.v. πᾶς 1aβ). πᾶσαν πραΰτητα is to be shown πρὸς πάντας ἀνθρώπους, "toward all people," i.e., "to everyone" without exception (cf. the occurrences of πάντες ἄνθρωποι in the PE*: 1 Tim. 2:1, 4; 4:10; Tit. 2:11). The double use of πᾶς is quite emphatic: Paul is urging "all" gentleness to "all" people.

This section deals, therefore, with Christians' relationships to both the civil government and to humanity in general. That Paul speaks of "all people" with non-Christians particularly in mind is made evident by the following verse, where he indicates by the use of "also" that the past condition of the Christians, i.e., their pre-conversion and thus non-Christian state, is what these "all people" are now like. His awareness of the sinfulness of "all people" and the call, nevertheless, for Christians to live with them in gentle and considerate ways leads to the next section, which identifies the theological basis for such action in God's own action.

THE THEOLOGICAL BASIS FOR LIVING WITH NON-CHRISTIANS: 3:3-8

By beginning this section with a statement that Christians "were once also" like non-Christians now are (v. 3), Paul does several things at the same time. He acknowledges that non-Christians are difficult to live with (e.g., "hateful") and thus that it is not easy to be gentle, kind, and considerate to them. In fact, he may be dealing with this factor as an objection that Christians might raise to his admonitions. At the same time he makes this fact part of the basis for his appeal to them (note γάρ). The Christians must consider that God's kindness and love for humanity was shown to such people, i.e., to themselves (v. 4). So Paul is only asking them to show to others, in the ways he has spelled out in vv. 1 and 2, the attitude that God showed to them when they were as sinful and hateful as the non-Christians now are.

God's attitude of kindness and love went so far as to save "us" (ἡμᾶς) because of his own mercy, not on the basis of our righteous deeds, but by a mighty inner transformation of the Holy Spirit (v. 5) whom he bestowed on us through Christ, whose work as Savior had accomplished such a great salvation for such sinners (v. 6). The result for "us" is that God, having declared us righteous in his sight on the basis of his grace, has made us his own heirs who expectantly look forward to eternal life in his presence (v. 7), those same people who "also once were foolish . . . , disobedient . . . , enslaved . . . , [and] hateful . . ." (v. 3).

Paul affirms the faithfulness of this "saying" (the content and extent of which will be dealt with in the comments on v. 8), which has summarized God's gracious salvation of sinners, and urges that its truths be "stressed" "so that those who have believed in [such a] God may be careful to engage in good deeds" (v. 8a). So Paul ends by indicating that the result of such a transformation and the awareness of such an attitude on God's part should cause Christians to "devote themselves to doing what is good" *(NIV)*, i.e., to the very things Paul has asked of them in vv. 1-2, which he says "are good and profitable for people" (v. 8b).

3:3 γάρ introduces the reason for the foregoing admonition, especially but not exclusively its concluding words, just as it did in 2:11ff. ἦμεν, the imperfect first person plural of εἰμί, is used here with the enclitic particle ποτέ (which is temporal here), "once or formerly," to describe in general terms what Christians were before their conversion (for this use of ποτέ in Paul, cf. Rom. 11:30; Gal. 1:13; Eph. 2:2, 3, 11, 13; 5:8; Col. 1:21; 3:7). Paul emphasizes the personal, as well as the collective, note already inherent in the verb by adding for emphasis the personal pronoun ἡμεῖς, "we," i.e., Christians (cf. 3:5, the only other use of ἡμεῖς in Titus: There that the saying is affirmed by Christians about themselves makes it evident that ἡμεῖς and the two occurrences of ἡμᾶς in that verse and the next designate Christians).

καί, used here with its meaning "also" or "likewise" (BAGD s.v. II.1), by its inherently comparative note adds to this statement of what Christians once were the clear implication that those with whom they are being compared (because they are distinguished from them), i.e., non-Christians (the group primarily in view in the "all men" of v. 2), are still as the Christians are described as having been (cf. the almost identical καὶ ἡμεῖς πάντες . . . ποτέ of Eph. 2:3 and the quite similar καὶ ὑμεῖς . . . ποτε of Col. 3:7).

That which we Christians "also once were" is now set forth in seven characteristics. The first is ἀνόητοι** (Lk. 24:25; Rom. 1:14; Gal. 3:1, 3; 1 Tim. 6:9), "foolish" in the sense of "without spiritual understanding" (Guthrie; cf. Eph. 4:18). The second is ἀπειθεῖς** (also in Lk. 1:17; Acts 26:19; Rom. 1:30; Tit. 1:16; 2 Tim. 3:2), "disobedient." As the usage in Tit. 1:16 seems to indicate, this disobedience is to God (cf. Paul's words in Acts 26:19 and his phrase "disobedient to God" in Rom. 11:30). This disobedience to God may be shown, however, by one's attitude and actions to those in authority; thus Paul urges Christians to be obedient to rulers in v. 1, since "he who resists authority has opposed God's ordinance" (Rom. 13:2), and describes the ungodly as "disobedient to parents" (Rom. 1:30; 2 Tim. 3:2). The third characteristic is πλανώμενοι (Pl.* 6x), a passive participle that should probably be understood here in the sense of "being deceived" (or perhaps "led astray"), since that seems to be the sense in the other PE occurrence of the participle (2 Tim. 3:13, there with an active form: "deceiving and being deceived") and in the other Pauline occurrences of the verb πλανάω (1 Cor. 6:9; 15:33; Gal. 6:7), in each of which he urges his readers not to be deceived about sin.

The fourth characteristic is expressed in a participial phrase, δουλεύοντες ἐπιθυμίαις καὶ ἡδοναῖς ποικίλαις, "enslaved to various lusts and pleasures." δουλεύοντες is used here figuratively of "being a slave to" (BAGD s.v. 2c) desires and pleasures (cf. Rom. 6:6, 16; 2 Pet. 2:19).

That which the Christians were formerly enslaved to is first of all ἐπιθυμίαι (see 1 Tim. 6:9; Tit. 2:12), which means generally "desires, longings, or cravings" (cf. BAGD). Although the word can and does have a neutral sense in the NT, it is usually used of "evil desire" in accordance with Greek and Jewish usage (as F. Büchsel demonstrates in *TDNT* III, 170f.). Often some qualifying phrase will indicate this (as in Eph. 2:3), but ἐπιθυμία can be used for sinful desire without any such addition (as in Rom. 7:7, 8; 2 Tim. 3:6 [?]; Jas. 1:14, 15; 1 Pet. 4:2; cf. Büchsel, 171). Certainly the other PE occurrences (1 Tim. 6:9; Tit. 2:12; 2 Tim. 2:22; 4:3) are used of sinful desire, which would appear to be the case here, even if it refers only to human enslavement to pursuing the natural desires of life as the chief purpose of being human (cf. Mt. 6:19-25, 31-33).

They were enslaved also to ἡδοναί,** "pleasures," a common Greek word used infrequently in the NT (Lk. 8:14; Jas. 4:1, 3; 2 Pet. 2:13, all but the last plural). In the other NT occurrences the word is used of sinful pleasure, and apparently this is true here also (cf. the Pauline compound φιλήδονος, "loving pleasure," which is analogous to the phrase here, "enslaved to pleasures," and which is regarded as the opposite of "loving God" in 2 Tim. 3:4). F. Büchsel notes that ἡδονή and ἐπιθυμία are closely related and offers as an explanation for that here that "when ἐπιθυμία is satisfied we have ἡδονή, and when ἡδονή is sought we have ἐπιθυμία" (*TDNT* III, 171 n. 36).

ποικίλαις (Pl.* otherwise only in 2 Tim. 3:6, there with ἐπιθυμίαι only) carries here its general meaning of "various kinds" or "manifold" and refers to both nouns. It may be last for emphasis (*NEB* [and *TEV*] also places it last, albeit with a slightly different construction: "We were slaves to passions and pleasures of every [all] kind[s]").

The fifth characteristic is expressed in another participial phrase, ἐν κακίᾳ καὶ φθόνῳ διάγοντες, "spending our life in malice and envy." διάγοντες** is used here in the sense of "spend one's life, live" with the accusative βίον understood (in this sense, with or without βίον, common in Greek writers; for examples see BAGD s.v.; LSJM s.v. II.1-2; in 1 Tim. 2:2 with βίον). The first thing that Paul says the Christians lived "in" is κακία, which when it is used in a list with other vices (Rom. 1:29; Eph. 4:31; Col. 3:8; 1 Pet. 2:1), as here, means something like "malice or ill-will" (BAGD), "the evil habit of mind" (Trench, *Synonyms,* §xi). The second thing that Paul's readers lived "in" is φθόνος, "envy," which is also used in lists of vices in Rom. 1:29; Gal. 5:21; 1 Tim. 6:4; 1 Pet. 2:1 (the first and last with κακία). "It is the grudging spirit that cannot bear to contemplate someone else's prosperity" or their success (Bruce, *Galatians,* 249, at 5:21).

The sixth characteristic is στυγητοί** (a NT hapax), which can mean either "hated" or "hateful" (see BAGD for occurrences in Greek literature, which tend toward "hated"; in 1 Clement it has both meanings: "hated" in 35:6, "hateful" in 45:7). BAGD note that the compound θεοστυγής before the NT had only the passive sense "hated by a god" but in Rom. 1:30 probably has the active sense "hating God," noting two later documents in which the active meaning is obvious. If στυγητός underwent a similar development, then the slightly more contextually suitable meaning "hateful" is to be understood here (*NASB;* cf. *NEB:* "odious ourselves"). If not, then the meaning "being hated," i.e., hated by humans, is to be understood (cf. *RSV, TEV, NIV*).

The seventh characteristic is μισοῦντες ἀλλήλους. The verb μισέω (Pl.* 4x: here; Rom. 7:15; 9:13; Eph. 5:29; with ἀλλήλους here and in Mt. 24:10) means "hate" or "detest." The reciprocal pronoun ἀλλήλοι, "one another," indicates the mutuality of this terrible hatred that sinners have for one another (cf. 1 Jn. 2:9, 11; 3:15; 4:20).

3:4 This verse begins with postpositive δέ, which contrasts the characteristics of God named here with the characteristics of our past condition listed in v. 3 and also contrasts the ὅτε clause here and its resultant outcome for us ("he saved us," v. 5) with the unstated but acknowledged condition, i.e., needing to be saved, presumed in the ποτέ clause in v. 3. A time framework is indicated by "when" (ὅτε) and "appeared" (ἐπεφάνη). The two nouns ἡ χρηστότης καὶ ἡ φιλανθρωπία enable us to understand this time reference.

χρηστότης** (NT 10x, all in Paul) is used of both humans (Rom. 3:12; 2 Cor. 6:6; Gal. 5:22; Col. 3:12) and God (Rom. 2:4; 11:22 [3x]; Eph. 2:7; here). In both cases the general meaning is "goodness, kindness, generosity" (BAGD; cf. the related adj. χρηστός in 1 Pet. 2:3, echoing Ps. 34:8 [LXX 33:9], and in Lk. 6:35). Wherever it is used of God it is related in the context to human salvation, as here. Eph. 2:7 is the passage the most similar in this way to Tit. 3:4: God does his redeeming work for those who "formerly lived in the lusts of [their] flesh" (Eph. 2:3; cf. Tit. 3:3) and is described as "rich in mercy because of his great love with which he loved us" (Eph. 2:4; cf. φιλανθρωπία here in v. 4, τὸ αὐτοῦ ἔλεος in v. 5, and πλουσίως in v. 6).

φιλανθρωπία** is found only twice in the NT, in Acts 28:2 of humans and here. Outside the NT it is frequently used of the virtue of rulers and their gods in relation to their subjects (see the references in BAGD; Spicq, 657-76; U. Luck, *TDNT* IX, 107-12). Here it refers to God's "love for mankind" (cf. Jn. 3:16).

Since χρηστότης and φιλανθρωπία occur together frequently in extrabiblical Greek literature (see BAGD s.v. φιλανθρωπία and the extended list of citations in Field, *Notes,* 222f.) and since singular ἐπεφάνη appears to indicate that the two terms are considered as one (so, e.g., Hendriksen, Lenski, and Lock), we may properly understand that it is God's "kindness-and-love-toward-mankind" that "has appeared." This attitude of God is contrasted with Christians' past attitude (v. 3) so that no one less than God the merciful Savior can be the norm for exhorting Christians "to be gentle, showing all meekness toward all people" (v. 2), since God showed to the Christians his "kindness and love toward mankind" when they were as "all people" are now (cf., e.g., Fairbairn, Huther).

This "kindness-and-love-toward-mankind" is that of "God" acting in his capacity as "our Savior." It is this attitude of God that secures the salvation of such needy ones, as the main verb in this sentence and its object, ἔσωσεν ἡμᾶς (v. 5), signifies. The flow of the sentence indicates that it is God the Father that is in view. All three persons of the Trinity are mentioned: The Father "saved us" (v. 5) and "poured out" the Holy Spirit on us (v. 6) "through Jesus Christ."

The temporal framework of 3:3-6. How and when (ὅτε) did this kindness-and-love-toward-mankind "appear" (ἐπεφάνη, second aorist passive)? ἐπιφαίνω** (NT 4x) means in the NT in the active (Lk. 1:79; Acts

27:20) "appear, show itself" and in the passive (Tit. 2:11 and here) "show oneself, make an appearance" (BAGD). Except in Acts 27:20 it occurs in soteriological settings. All the NT occurrences of the cognate noun ἐπιφάνεια refer to Christ's appearing on earth (2 Thes. 2:8; 1 Tim. 6:14; 2 Tim. 1:10; 4:1, 8; Tit. 2:13). Therefore, it is likely that the appearance of Christ is the occasion referred to by the verb here and in Tit. 2:11, in both of which Paul seems to be referring to the same event but in different terms: Both passages speak of God's saving actions as the basis for what Christians are told to do, and both do so by saying that a characteristic of God has "appeared" (ἐπεφάνη both times), bringing salvation or causing people to be saved (cf. Moffatt, *Love,* 214). We have seen above that "grace" and "kindness" (and "love") are inseparably linked in Eph. 2:4-7. Therefore, to ask how and when God's "kindness and love toward mankind" appeared is also to ask how and when his "grace" appeared. In 2 Tim. 1:9-10 Paul indicates that God's "grace" appeared in the first appearance of Christ and was brought to us through the gospel. Therefore, we can conclude that God's "kindness and love toward mankind" appeared in that same first appearance of Christ and has also been brought to us through the gospel.

Therefore, Tit. 3:4ff. has in view the same two time perspectives as 2 Tim. 1:9-10. "When" (ὅτε) and "appeared" (ἐπεφάνη) refer to Christ's first appearance, in which he "gave himself for us to redeem us from every lawless deed" (Tit. 2:13-14). God's salvation of Christians is based on Christ being their Savior, since it is only through Christ that the Holy Spirit is "poured out" on them and that the washing and renewing by the Holy Spirit, by which God saves, take place (3:5-6). But it would be a mistake to assume that the time references in 3:4-7 refer only to Christ's first appearance and not also to Christ's accomplishment of that salvation for particular Christians. Although "he saved us" (v. 5) is encompassed by the time reference of "when" and "appeared" in v. 4, it is nonetheless true that "he saved us" is further delineated by the time reference involved in the specific act in which Christians were saved, i.e., "through the washing of regeneration and renewing of the Holy Spirit, which he poured out on us" (vv. 5-6).

Furthermore, the other time reference in this context must not be forgotten. It is, after all, quite personal: "*We* (ἡμεῖς) also *once* (ποτε) *were* (ἦμεν) foolish" (v. 3). God's love in Christ has burst forth on their horizon, and this great eschatological event has now made them personally those who are saved, washed, regenerated, and renewed and thus no longer what they once were. This contrast between "before and after" is a recurring theme in the NT (e.g., Rom. 6:17-23; 1 Cor. 6:9-11; Eph. 2:2ff.; Col. 3:7ff.). Here as elsewhere this theme is related both to what has happened in Christ and also to what has, therefore, happened in believers. Titus 3 is thus like 2 Tim. 1:9-10, which says that Christ manifests God's grace by his appearance and which also reminds us that Christ does this "through the gospel."

The temporal location of "saved" (Tit. 3:5) is, therefore, in terms of the history of salvation, when God's kindness and love appear eschatologically in Christ and also, in terms of the experience of those involved, when they receive the "washing of regeneration and renewal by the Holy Spirit." The term "saved" is thus qualified from two sides. Salvation is accomplished in the appearing of God's "kindness and love toward mankind" in Christ and applied when the Holy Spirit is actually "poured out" on those who are thereby renewed.

3:5 The main clause of this verse, ἔσωσεν ἡμᾶς, "he saved us," is preceded by two prepositional phrases that deal with the basis for God's saving us. The first is a strong negation of any contribution on our part and the second is an equally strong affirmation that salvation is solely based on God's mercy.

With the negation Paul clearly rejects works as a basis for God's salvation, as he does elsewhere (Rom. 3:27, 28; 4:2-6; 9:11; Gal. 2:16; Eph. 2:9; 2 Tim. 1:9; cf. Marshall, "Faith and Works"). Paul makes more explicit what he is rejecting by adding to οὐκ ἐξ ἔργων, "not on the basis of works," the prepositional phrase τῶν ἐν δικαιοσύνῃ and a relative pronoun clause with the verb ἐποιήσαμεν and the personal pronoun ἡμεῖς, which both fall under the negation of the initial οὐκ.

The operative centerpiece is ἐν δικαιοσύνῃ, which is closely linked to ἔργων by the article τῶν and thereby describes the "works" in view. ἐν δικαιοσύνῃ occurs 8x in the NT, 3x with reference to God (Acts 17:31; 2 Pet. 1:1; Rev. 19:11) and 5x with reference to humans (Lk. 1:75; Eph. 4:24; 5:9; here; 2 Tim. 3:16). In reference to humans the phrase refers to an ethical response taught by scripture (2 Tim. 3:16), to the "fruit of light" (Eph. 5:9), and to what is acceptable to God (Lk. 1:75). Here it refers either to one's status as a child of the light having this "fruit of light" (as in Eph. 5:9) or, as Jesus and Paul sometimes use δικαιοσύνη, to human self-righteousness and efforts in the moral realm (cf. Phil. 3:6), or, more likely, to both together (cf. G. Schrenk, *TDNT* II, 202: The phrase here "corresponds materially, though not in detailed wording . . . inasmuch as ἐν δικαιοσύνῃ denotes the human attainment envisaged in Phil. 3:6, 9"). If it does refer to both, then Paul is telling the Christians that neither their present good works (cf. v. 8; Eph. 2:10) nor any pre-Christian efforts at good works are the basis for God's kindness and love toward them and for God saving them. The implication is clear: They must not wait until "all people" of v. 2 have become Christians or even until such people do some good work or something decent before they show them gentleness and kindness (vv. 1-3).

In the light of this understanding the meaning of the relative clause is clear: The action verb ἐποιήσαμεν is used to highlight further that it is the works of our activity that are negated (cf. Paul's use of this verb to highlight human activity in works in Gal. 3:10, 12; 5:3). Emphatic ἡμεῖς lays further emphasis upon "us" individual Christians, the very ones (ἡμᾶς) that God saves "according to *his* mercy." "We" did not "do" anything that could claim God's kindness and love or that would provide a basis for his saving us.

A strong affirmation of the basis for our salvation is now given. The adversative particle ἀλλά introduces a contrast to the preceding negative: *not* our works "*but* because of his mercy" (*NIV;* cf. 2 Tim. 1:9). κατά is used here with the meaning "because of" (BAGD s.v. II.5aδ; cf. 2 Tim. 1:9; 1 Pet. 1:3). ἔλεος is used 21x in the NT of the "mercy" of God/Christ toward people, and 10 of these occurrences are in Paul (cf. Rom. 11:31 and especially Eph. 2:4ff.; for the OT background cf. Ex. 34:6-7; Pss. 78:38; 86:15). αὐτοῦ is emphatic not only because of its attributive position (BDF §284.3; MHT III, 190), but also because of the contrast between the negation of what "we" did and the affirmation of "his" (God's) mercy as the basis for God saving us. God has mercy and pities our miserable condition and delivers us from it. Eph. 2:4ff. sets this mercy in the context of love.

ἔσωσεν (see 1 Tim. 1:15) is used here in the general NT and Pauline sense of spiritual salvation. Since this is the main verb of the sentence that includes vv. 4-7 and the focal point of vv. 3-7, all that leads up to the verb and flows from it enters into the understanding of what is intended by it. Plural ἡμᾶς indicates that it is a number of individuals who are saved, individuals who have been identified as sinners (v. 3). The time indicators (ποτε and ὅτε, vv. 3 and 4), combined with the aorist tense of the verb, signify that this salvation has already taken place and that it has delivered the Christians from what they were. The terms used in v. 5 describing the way in which they were saved indicate that it was accomplished by an inner cleansing of a new beginning and by a renewal wrought within by the Holy Spirit. V. 6 further indicates that this salvation comes about because Christ is Savior and therefore pours the Holy Spirit into the lives of Christians. One reason that God saved Christians is so that he might declare them righteous and enable them to become heirs who expectantly look forward to eternal life (v. 7).

The concept of salvation presented here is, therefore, grand in its perspective and inclusive in its accomplishment. The perspective is that God enters into history with his gracious attitude to act for us, transforming us now and making us heirs for an eternity with him. The accomplishment is that we are delivered from past bondage to sin, made here and now a new and transformed people who are indwelt by God's Holy Spirit, thus already declared justified at the bar of God's judgment, and finally made heirs of future eternal life.

This verse states that God saved διὰ λουτροῦ παλιγγενεσίας καὶ ἀνακαινώσεως πνεύματος ἁγίου. διά with the genitive is used with σῴζω some 9x in the NT (Jn. 3:17; Acts 15:11; Rom. 5:9; 1 Cor. 1:21; 3:15; 15:2; Eph. 2:8; 1 Tim. 2:15; here). Sometimes its genitive object is Jesus, the one "through" whom salvation comes, and sometimes it is an instrument or means through which salvation takes place (e.g., Acts 15:11; 1 Cor. 1:21; 15:2; Eph. 2:8; 1 Tim. 2:15). Nowhere else, however, does it speak as fully and explicitly about the content and activity of the means of salvation as it does here. λουτρόν,** "washing," is used here as a metaphor for spiritual cleansing, i.e., the removal of one's sins, as in Eph. 5:26 (cf. the cognate verb λούω in Jn. 13:10; Heb. 10:22 and the compound form ἀπολούω in 1 Cor. 6:11; Acts 22:16; for the possible connection with baptism see the comments on v. 8a).

The interrelationships of the string of genitives that begins with λουτροῦ are not immediately apparent, but there is no doubt that παλιγγενεσίας is dependent on λουτροῦ. παλιγγενεσία** (also in Mt. 19:28) is compounded from the adverb πάλιν and γένεσις, the verbal noun of γίνομαι, and thus according to H. Büchsel means "new genesis" (*TDNT* I, 686; for other studies of the term see Dey, *ΠΑΛΙΓΓΕΝΕΣΙΑ*; Ysebaert, *Baptismal Terminology,* 87-154 [88 on the meaning]). Büchsel (687) concludes that the word "seems quite early to have come into use outside the Stoic schools and to have become part of the heritage of the educated world, thus acquiring a more general sense" (so also Dey, 133, and Ysebaert, 90; Dibelius-Conzelmann acknowledge [150] that there are two points of difference between the use here and that of the mysteries, which they regard as the background for this passage; this identification of the background is regarded by Büchsel, Dey, and Ysebaert as not borne out by the evidence). In English versions it is often translated "rebirth" or "regeneration" (e.g., BAGD, *RSV, NASB, NEB, NIV,* but Ysebaert, 88, has some doubts about this). λουτροῦ παλιγγενεσίας might better be translated "the washing of a new beginning" or "the washing of conversion" (cf. Ysebaert, 134, 137; cf. Ezk. 36:25-28).

We cannot say with certainty why παλιγγενεσία occurs only twice in the NT, but Ysebaert's suggestion may be part of the answer: "The reason for its adoption need be no other than that which led to its use in this sense elsewhere: the want of a solemn term" (134). Another part of the answer may be that this is one of the few times that this particular truth is expressed in a somewhat creedal saying, that therefore a noun, rather than the usual verb form, is preferred here, and that this is the noun form best suited. The noun ἀναγέννησις, which is related to the verb forms usually used to present this truth in the NT, γεννάω and its ἀναγεννάω, is not itself used in the NT. Similarly, the "secret discourse of Hermes Trismegistus to his son Tat, concerning rebirth" consistently uses the verbs (ἀνα)γεννάω and the noun παλιγγενεσία of rebirth (W. Scott, *Hermetica* I, 238-55 [libellus XIII]; cf. Knight, *Faithful Sayings,* 97-100).

Is ἀνακαινώσεως dependent on λουτροῦ (so Barrett, Bernard, Bouma, Bratcher, Brox, Dornier, Ellicott, Freundorfer, Gealy, Hanson, Hendriksen, Huther, Jeremias, Kelly, Lock, Moellering, Parry, Ridderbos, Schlatter,

Spicq, Ward, Weiss, and Wohlenberg) or, with λουτροῦ, on διά (so Alford, Bengel, Fairbairn, Fausset, Guthrie, Hiebert, Lenski, N. J. D. White, and Wuest)? It appears that most of the discussion is focused, initially at least, on the wrong questions. Most of those who hold that ἀνακαινώσεως is dependent on λουτροῦ also hold that the "washing" is baptism, that it is baptism that brings renewal, that salvation is brought about by one action, not two, and therefore that "renewal" must be dependent on "washing" and not on διά. A number of the others hold that ἀνακαίνωσις elsewhere in the NT refers to progressive sanctification and thus refer it to that here and assume, therefore, that it cannot be considered part of the initial act of washing and regeneration; rather, it must be distinguished from that initial act. Therefore, ἀνακαίνωσις must be dependent upon διά. Some commentators candidly acknowledge that the problem cannot be solved simply by an appeal to grammatical and syntactical considerations, since both solutions are theoretically possible (e.g., Barrett, Bernard, Bratcher, Hiebert, and Kelly).

A further look at the content of the passage is needed before we return to this question. The concepts referred to by the string of genitives here are "washing," "new beginning," "renewal," and "the Holy Spirit." A similar cluster is found in Jn. 3:5 ("born of water and the Spirit"), and is apparently credited to the OT (in that Jesus expects Nicodemus to be acquainted with "these "things," v. 10). Ezk. 36:25-27 speaks of God cleansing his people and giving them "a new heart and a new spirit," indeed his Spirit. The cluster of concepts in Tit. 3:5, along with "through Jesus Christ our Savior . . . justified" in vv. 6-7, is also echoed, and in a similar order, in 1 Cor. 6:11, which says that Christians were "washed," "sanctified," and "justified" in the name of Christ and in God's Spirit. In these three related passages, therefore, the two concepts of water/washing/cleansing and God's Spirit are closely linked but also distinguished and are related to the inner transformation of humans. Furthermore, inner cleansing and inner transformation, though related, are distinguished in Ezk. 36:25-26 (and note that 1 Cor. 6:11 lists as separate concepts "washed" and "sanctified").

In Tit. 3:5 two of the four genitives precede καί and two follow it. Since the second and third of these words, "new beginning" and "renewal," are similar in meaning, the two most distinguishable terms are "washing" and "the Holy Spirit," as in the three related passages examined above. Here "washing" and "the Holy Spirit" are both paired with a term for inner transformation, again as in the three related passages. And, as in 1 Cor. 6:11, two terms are used for inner transformation.

Therefore, in Tit. 3:5 Paul considers this inner transformation from two different perspectives in a manner analogous to Ezk. 36:25-27 and 1 Cor. 6:11. He arranges the four genitive nouns chiastically with the most distinguishable terms first and last and with the terms for the result, the transformation, in the center. The first pair of genitives focuses on the need for cleansing from past sin: "washing" and a word that speaks of that washing as an inner transformation, a "new beginning" (cf. Norbie, "Washing"). The second pair focuses on the new life received and to be lived: The "Holy Spirit," the giver and sustainer of the new life, must do his work *within* Christians and so is joined to a word that speaks of such a new life as an inner transformation, "renewal."

If our analysis is correct, then, ἀνακαινώσεως is dependent on διά, not on λουτροῦ (which corrects the view taken in Knight, *Faithful Sayings,* 96f., 100). In ἀνακαίνωσις** (also in Rom. 12:2; cf. the related verbs ἀνακαινόω** in 2 Cor. 4:16; Col. 3:10 and ἀνακαινίζω** in Heb. 6:6) the basic root καιν- signifies that which is "new in nature"; the adjective καινός is used in this sense in the NT of the Christian who is a "new creation" (2 Cor. 5:17) and who is to put on the "new person" created in God's likeness (Eph. 4:24). Here, where the operative verb "saved" applies to those who were once enslaved to sin, it would appear that the sense of the explanatory noun ἀνακαινώσεως is "renewal" or "making new," i.e., the act of causing the "new creation" to come into being, "the first and unique renewing, the creation of a life that was not there before" (*TDNT Abridged,* 388; see J. Behm, *TDNT* III, 447-54, especially 453). It is on the basis of this *initial* renewal that the Christian and his or her mind *is being* renewed to true knowledge according to God's image, and hence the term and its cognate verb are used in this related sense elsewhere in the NT (e.g., Rom. 12:2; Col. 3:10).

πνεύματος ἁγίου indicates the one who accomplishes that initial renewal (cf. 2 Thes. 2:13: "salvation through sanctification by the Spirit"): The "Holy Spirit" is the one who directly effects the renewal. This initial "renewal" and the "washing of regeneration" mentioned just before are the twin aspects of inner transformation that were seen in Ezk. 36:26-27; Jn. 3:5-8; 1 Cor. 6:11: water/washing/cleansing and rebirth by the Spirit/renewal by the Spirit/initial sanctification. Here πνεύματος ἁγίου does not have the syntactical relationship with παλιγγενεσίας that it has with ἀνακαινώσεως, though it may be said on other grounds that the Holy Spirit does also accomplish the παλιγγενεσία. The combination πνεῦμα ἅγιον occurs only here and in 2 Tim. 1:14 in the PE* (17x in Paul); πνεῦμα by itself is used 2x in the PE of the third person of the Trinity (1 Tim. 3:16; 4:1).

3:6 Paul unfolds the saying further with "whom he poured out upon us richly through Jesus Christ our Savior." The relative pronoun οὗ refers to the nearest antecedent πνεύματος ἁγίου (and is attracted to its case), not back to λουτροῦ, as the following considerations would seem to indicate: The verb "pour out" (ἐκχέω, here ἐξέχεεν) is used of liquids and could be used with reference to the washing, but it is used in the LXX of Joel 3:1ff. and thus in the early church (Acts 2:17, 18, 33) of the Spirit, providing a background on which the usage with the Spirit here seems natural. Furthermore, that the pouring is "through Jesus Christ our Savior" again points to the Holy Spirit since the early church understood that the Spirit was poured out by Christ (cf. Acts 2:33: "having received from the Father the promise of the Holy Spirit, [Christ] has poured forth [ἐξέχεεν] what you see and hear").

This portion of the saying is a further delineation of the work of God that accomplished salvation. The subject of ἐξέχεεν is the subject of ἔσωσεν, God. ἐκχέω (NT 28x according to BAGD and *VKGNT,* who combine the forms ἐκχέω and ἐκχύν[ν]ω), "poured out," is used figuratively in the NT 8x, always with reference to the (Holy) Spirit (Acts 2:17, 18, 33; 10:45; Rom. 5:5 [God's love poured out through the Spirit]).

The adverb "abundantly" (πλουσίως,** also in Col. 3:16; 1 Tim. 6:17; 2 Pet. 1:11) makes explicit what is implied in "poured out," i.e., that God gave the Holy Spirit in a lavish way to each believer, just as the OT prophecies had said he would do (cf. Joel 2:28 [LXX 3:1]ff.; Ezk. 36:26ff.; 39:29; Is. 44:3ff.; Zc. 12:10; cf. J. Behm, *TDNT* II, 468f.: "the idea of outpouring, of the streaming down from above of a power . . . , is also used to describe the impartation . . . in which God imparts himself"). Because God himself poured the Holy Spirit out on Christians, the Spirit, as God's agent, accomplished salvation by renewing their lives.

ἐφ' ἡμᾶς indicates those on whom the Spirit was poured out, and in the context of this saying it describes the personal and direct nature of that action. Just as "we" (ἡμεῖς, v. 3) at an earlier time were personally enslaved to sin and lived sinful lives (v. 2), now we have personally been saved (ἔσωσεν, note the same ἡμᾶς as the direct object of that verb) through "renewal" by having the Holy Spirit poured out "on us" (ἐφ' ἡμᾶς). This is the fifth of six occurrences of the first person plural pronoun, which occurs in every verse from v. 3 to v. 6. Even when one makes allowances for the two (more common) genitive possessive forms (ἡμῶν), the occurrence of four nominative or accusative forms in as many verses is quite significant.

In all the NT passages in which the Spirit is said to be poured out "on" humans the preposition ἐπί is used, as it is in the LXX of Joel 3:1-2 (Acts 2:17, 18; 10:45; and here). BAGD (s.v. III.1bγ) relates that various verbs are used of the Spirit in connection with ἐπί and that the preposition in this case is used figuratively of the power that comes on a person.

διά with gen. 'Ιησοῦ Χριστοῦ is used to denote the personal agent through whom God has acted (cf. A. Oepke, *TDNT* II, 66-69; Jonker, "De paulinische formule"; for an especially significant Pauline use of διά ['Ιησοῦ Χριστοῦ] see 1 Cor. 8:6): The pouring out of the Spirit has occurred "through Jesus Christ our Savior," i.e., through Christ in his capacity as Savior — as Savior of those (ἡμῶν, "our") on whom he pours out the Spirit (cf. Acts 2:33, where Christ's exaltation bespeaks the triumph of his saving work and leads to his pouring out the Spirit, and Jn. 15:26, which speaks of the Spirit as the one whom Jesus will "send" "from the Father").

3:7 The affirmation that began in v. 4 moves on to its conclusion with a ἵνα clause that expresses the purpose of the main verb ἔσωσεν (v. 5). This part of the statement focuses on the present position of Christians ("being justified by his grace") and on their present privileged status and future hope ("heirs according to the hope of eternal life" or "of eternal life according to hope") that is the purpose of God's salvation.

δικαιόω (Pl. 27x, PE 2x) became virtually a technical term in Paul's writings, especially in Romans (15x) and Galatians (8x). But the verb is found in only one other earlier Pauline letter (1 Cor. 4:4; 6:11), and there it has two nuances of meaning, as it does in the PE (1 Tim. 3:16; here). Here it has the usual Pauline sense that it has in Romans and Galatians and in 1 Cor. 6:11, which, we have seen, is parallel to this passage (see above on v. 5). The aorist passive participle δικαιωθέντες indicates here a past action that "we" have been recipients of, that of being "justified," i.e., declared righteous in God's sight and forgiven of sins. It thus refers to a judgment made by God in which already, here and now, God has acquitted sinners and pronounced them righteous.

This declaration is τῇ ἐκείνου χάριτι: Its basis is "his grace." ἐκείνου may be used here as a demonstrative denoting the more remote object ("that one"), i.e., specifically going past Jesus Christ (v. 6) to God (the Father), the subject of "[he] saved" in v. 5. Or it may be used for emphasis ("*that* one," i.e., "*his*"). In either case, God, the subject of the entire sentence from v. 4, is most likely meant, God whose grace is operative for us in Christ (cf. 2 Tim. 1:9; Rom. 3:24). χάρις (NT 155x, Pl. 100x) is used here of God's "grace" or "favor," the attitude and action of one who does what he is not bound to do (BAGD). Therefore, justification is a "gift" made available "through the redemption that is in Christ Jesus" (Rom. 3:24; cf. the reference to Christ as σωτήρ in Tit. 3:6 and 2 Tim. 1:9-10).

The work of the Spirit in transforming and of God's grace in justifying coalesce in causing those saved to become "heirs of eternal life." That is, the ἵνα clause of this verse indicates the purpose of the salvation accomplished by God (v. 5), and the participial phrase with δικαιωθέντες indicates another aspect of that salvation. The "heirs" are, therefore, those who are both transformed by God's Spirit (v. 5; cf. Rom. 8:15-17; Eph. 1:14) and declared righteous by God's grace (cf. Rom. 4:13).

With γενηθῶμεν Paul states that those who have been saved and are justified have now "become" κληρονόμοι. κληρονόμος** (NT 15x) is used once in each of the Synoptic Gospels (Mt. 21:38 par. Mk. 12:7/Lk. 20:14) and in Heb. 1:2 of God's Son as "heir" and in the remaining NT occurrences (Rom. 4:13, 14; 8:17 [2x]; Gal. 3:20; 4:1, 7; Heb. 6:17; 11:7; Jas. 2:5) of the redeemed as God's "heirs." In both cases it is used figuratively of one who as God's son will receive something as a possession from him and who now stands in that privileged and anticipatory position. The possession to be received here is "eternal life" (ζωῆς αἰωνίου), a future unending life with God. The phrase ζωῆς αἰωνίου is used 4x in the PE* (1 Tim. 1:16; 6:12; Tit. 1:2; here) as well as elsewhere in the NT (for discussion see the other occurrences in 1 Timothy and Tit. 1:2).

Between κληρονόμοι γενηθῶμεν and ζωῆς αἰωνίου are the words κατ' ἐλπίδα. This phrase might indicate that the inheritance of eternal life is characterized by "hope" (ἐλπίς) and thus function as an intervening qualification: "that we might become heirs, according to hope, of eternal life." Or it might be joined more closely and directly with "eternal life" so that the first half of the statement is qualified by all that follows it: "that we might become heirs, according to the hope of eternal life." On either view the heirs are to receive eternal life, and that outcome and the position of the heirs who expect it is always in the attitude of hope. ἐλπίς (see Tit. 1:2) is used in the NT generally of "hope" and "expectation" and especially of "hope" pertaining to supernatural things spoken of in God's promises (BAGD; R. Bultmann, *TDNT* II, s.v., especially 531f.). Hope is also connected with the position of heirs in Rom. 8:16-17, 24-25, where "hope" is related to what is not seen but looked for (v. 24) and is said to be marked by patient and expectant waiting on God and his promised inheritance (v. 25; cf. Gal. 3:29; Heb. 6:17; Jas. 2:5).

3:8a: The extent and nature of the "faithful saying." Vv. 4-7 have spelled out the marvel of what God has done and has yet in store for his redeemed people — all on the basis of God's attitude of kindness and love toward them, which he was willing, at great cost and in the face of great hostility and opposition, to express to them. The unstated, but clearly evident, implication is that he calls on them, his "heirs," to express the same attitude toward sinners that he, God, has expressed to them and thus be true heirs who reflect their Father's character. V. 8 goes on to make this implication explicit.

πιστὸς ὁ λόγος is another of the five identical citation-emphasis formulas (1 Tim. 1:15; 3:1; 4:9; 2 Tim. 2:11). For a discussion of the meaning of the formula see the comments on 1 Tim. 1:15 and Knight, *Faithful Sayings,* 4-22. In brief, λόγος indicates that some "saying" is being cited, and πιστός indicates that Paul is commending the saying as "trustworthy" (for what follows cf. *Faithful Sayings,* 81-86).

The negative evidence regarding the identification of the "saying" is that nothing that follows the formula appears to be appropriate as a saying. The positive evidence is that several statements in the preceding verses could well be referred to as a "faithful saying," and the virtually unanimous opinion of commentators is that the formula refers to what precedes it. But to how much of the preceding verses? Dibelius-Conzelmann stand virtually alone in positing that the saying consists of vv. 3-7 (in their comments on 1 Tim. 1:15). The vast majority of exegetes identify it as vv. 4-7 (Alford, Barrett, Bernard, Bouma, Brox, Ellicott, Fausset, Hendriksen, Huther, Jeremias, Kent, Robertson, Simpson, Vine, Wohlenberg, and Wuest). A few identify it as vv. 5-7 or some part thereof (Easton, Lock, and Spicq). Kelly narrows his choice to vv. 5b-6, but then adds wisely that identification of the saying is difficult precisely because "Paul has clearly interwoven thought of his own with whatever traditional or liturgical material he has borrowed" (Gealy, who is apparently undecided, concludes his discussion with a similar note of caution).

It is true, as Dibelius-Conzelmann argue, that the first person plural gives a certain unity and continuity to vv. 3-7. But the use in v. 3 may be influenced by the following verses and adapted to them. Gealy notes that "vs. 3 is less rhythmical in form and liturgical in phrasing than vss. 4-7. Its list of vices would then . . . serve as the dark shadow against which the light of the Christian gospel shines the more brilliantly." The obvious relationship of v. 3 to v. 2, signalled by the introductory words "for we were once also" and, in content, evidenced by its nouns, speaks against it being part of a saying continuing with vv. 4-7. Furthermore, it stands as a separate sentence not necessarily or inherently related to vv. 4ff., while all the other "faithful sayings" consist of a single sentence.

Kelly argues that v. 4 should "probably" be excluded from the saying "since both *was manifested* and *God our Saviour* are in the idiom of the Pastorals." Furthermore, "since both 5a and 7 have a strongly Pauline tang, the extract may well be limited to 5b-6, i.e. the specifically baptismal section." The appeal to the "idiom of the Pastorals" and "a strongly Pauline tang" is, in fact, one of the best gauges of what is and is not part of an citation, provided it clearly distinguishes one part from another. But this cannot be so definitely done here. Vv. 5b-6 also contain Pauline and PE language: ἔλεος is found nine other times in Paul, four of them in the PE (excluding this verse); σῴζω appears twenty-eight times elsewhere in Paul, of which six are in the PE (excluding this verse). The close combination of ἔλεος and σῴζω is, it is true, lacking elsewhere in Paul, including the PE, but this is also true of ἔργων τῶν ἐν δικαιοσύνῃ (v. 5a) and ἡ χρηστότης καὶ φιλανθρωπία (v. 4), both of which are excluded from the saying by Kelly. Admittedly παλιγγενεσία (v. 5b) does not occur anywhere else in Paul and only once otherwise in the NT (Mt. 19:28). But the same is also true of φιλανθρωπία in v. 4, which Kelly excludes, being found elsewhere only in Acts 28:2 and then with humans, not God, as the subject in view. Consideration of Kelly's view thus shows not only that his criteria cannot with certainty limit the saying to vv. 5b-6, but also that the criteria, as valid as they are, simply do not serve to identify the saying.

Furthermore, Kelly's elimination of v. 7 would have the formula "faithful is the saying" jump over that intervening verse to the saying rather than refer to what immediately precedes it. This is contrary both to the normal expectation and to Paul's actual practice with the other "faithful sayings," in which the formula refers to the immediately preceding or following words.

Kelly's (and, e.g., Easton's) exclusion of the first part of v. 5 (beginning the saying probably with διὰ λουτροῦ) is based on the assumption that the saying is connected with a baptismal setting and therefore should begin with or be restricted to what relates to baptism. Kelly admits that "he saved us" and even the rest of v. 5 and perhaps even v. 4 are needed to complete the words and thought pattern that, it is claimed, begins with διὰ λουτροῦ. Since, as it is admitted, some words preceded διὰ λουτροῦ in the saying, why may they not be what we have in v. 5a and perhaps also v. 4? Easton's assertion that the theological statement of v. 5a "would be out of place in the hymn that follows" is not convincing. Both Kelly and Easton seem to include ἔσωσεν with v. 5a, but then treat it as necessarily introducing and as virtually part of v. 5b, which shows the difficulty of dividing the verse. Admittedly, this may show Paul's skillful blending of his argument with the saying, as Kelly in principle allows for. But it may more convincingly show that the two parts of the verse constitute one coherent thought, with ἔσωσεν as the verbal focal point that binds them together and is necessary to both parts.

Swete is "disposed to think" that the saying begins with v. 5 and regards v. 4 as "the writer's note of transition from ἦμεν γάρ ποτε κτλ. to the quotation" ("Faithful Sayings," 5). This is plausible, but since vv. 4-7 constitute a unit in both form and content and may as a whole be aptly designated a saying, there must be conclusive reasons for excluding v. 4. As it is, v. 4 signals the contrast in the saying to v. 3 that provides the reason for the admonition in vv. 1-2 by showing what God has done to and for those who were once also sinful (v. 3) in his great salvation (vv. 4-7). The bridge for the saying is thus the δέ added in v. 4 to set forth immediately the contrast and carry the reader from v. 3 to the saying. But even while we identify vv. 4-7 as the saying on the basis of these considerations, we must do so with the awareness that there is no evidence that will allow us to identify the saying with absolute certainty. (An early understanding of the saying as embracing vv. 4-7 is seen in the uncial Codex Sinaiticus, which separates v. 4 from v. 3 and joins vv. 4-7 [as noted by Ellicott and Simpson].)

The vocabulary of the saying is almost entirely what may well be called Pauline (for specifics see Knight, *Faithful Sayings,* 108). Of course, many of the words are not exclusively Pauline. Furthermore, some of the words are used in un-Pauline ways: Paul does not characterize human "works" (v. 5) with the term "righteousness" (neither does any other NT writer). ἀνακαινώσις (v. 5) in its only other Pauline (and NT) occurrence has a somewhat different emphasis. And φιλανθρωπία and παλιγγενεσία (vv. 4, 5) do not occur elsewhere in Paul's letters. These non-Pauline qualities are in accord with Paul's formulaic identification of these verses as a saying. On the other hand, he uses the sixteen or so words of the saying found elsewhere in his letters more often than any other single NT writer, and the first word, χρηστότης, is found only in his letters (10x). These considerations are insufficient to point to influence by any NT writer, except to say that the saying might have arisen in an area influenced by Paul.

A considerable number of commentators have associated "washing" (v. 5) with baptism. This hypothesis is strengthened by the concomitant focus on the Holy Spirit. In Acts and elsewhere in the NT baptism and the gift of the Spirit are related. Furthermore, the saying lays particular stress on initial inner change ("the washing of regeneration and the renewal of the Holy Spirit"), which is appropriate in connection with the initial rite of Christianity, which signifies such an inner change. And the saying is a terse creedal-liturgical statement that would be appropriate at Christian baptism. This is exemplified in its trinitarian structure (God, the Holy Spirit, Jesus Christ), which would be fitting in connection with baptism (cf. Mt. 28:19). The corporate or public use of the saying is seen in its use of plural pronouns. Some have suggested that it is a "hymn" or expression of praise. Against this is the fact that God is referred to in the third person rather than the first person. Perhaps the saying was an affirmation spoken by those receiving baptism or by such people and the congregation together.

But v. 5 refers to "washing," λουτρόν, and not "baptism," βάπτισμα, a term that was, of course, well known among Christians. But the Christian community apparently chose to use a term that would point more directly to human inner spiritual need and the inner spiritual reality brought about by God. The accomplishment of that inner reality is spoken of in the past tense in the aorist verbs ἔσωσεν and ἐξέχεεν (vv. 5, 6). Christians confessed, therefore, that God had already saved them through the radical inner washing of regeneration, and they did so at the time that they received that which signified that washing, i.e., baptism. They did not speak of baptism as saving them or as being the means of salvation but rather of a past action wrought by regeneration, which baptism symbolized and represented. In this setting they thus utilized (as in Rom. 6:1ff.; Col. 2:11f.; 1 Pet. 3:18ff., especially vv. 20-21) the forceful and picturesque language which speaks of the reality of the Holy Spirit's work under a designation that might also have been used of baptism.

3:8b-c Paul adds (καί) to the formula πιστὸς ὁ λόγος his specific direction to Titus (σε) concerning the utilization and significance of what precedes. The demonstrative pronoun (here τούτων), as in 2:15 and elsewhere in the PE (e.g., 1 Tim. 4:11; 6:2), refers to the entire preceding section, i.e., 3:1-7, and not just to the "saying" (the λόγος) in vv. 4-7. This is borne out by the reference here to "good deeds," which is the point of vv. 1-2 and the reason for citing the saying in the first place. So Titus is to speak about "good deeds," such as vv. 1-2 have prescribed and which are to be done even for sinners (v. 3), and about God's own attitude and actions toward us — as such sinners — in saving us and enabling us to do such deeds (vv. 4-7).

With the verb βούλομαι (Pl. 9x), which he uses elsewhere in giving apostolic instructions (e.g., 1 Tim. 2:8; 5:14), Paul expresses his desire that Titus do what is expressed in the infinitive that follows: "speak confidently," even "insist" (διαβεβαιοῦσθαι,** 1 Tim. 1:7) on "these things." ἵνα introduces the following subfinal clause or clause of conceived or intended result (Robertson, *Grammar,* 991; Burton, *Syntax,* 83; Deer, however, suggests that this use of ἵνα is imperatival as in vv. 13-14 and thirty-five other places in the NT ["Still More"]). The result that Paul intends from Titus's insisting on "these things" is what he expects of "those who have believed (trusted in) God," i.e., those who have come to know God's love and kindness, his Spirit's renewing work, and his great salvation. Paul thus introduces his usual insistence on faith with the perfect participle πεπιστευκότες, with the definite article οἱ signifying its use here as a substantive. πιστεύω with dative (τῷ) θεῷ occurs 5x in the NT (Acts 16:34; 27:25; Rom. 4:3; Gal. 3:6; here). Paul uses it twice of Abraham's trust in God as the great example of the believer (Rom. 4:3; Gal. 3:6), and in Acts 16:34 it is used of a new convert, the latter most analogous to the usage here.

Paul intends that believers "be careful" (φροντίζω,** a NT hapax but 15x in the LXX; cf. the related φρόνιμος, 5x in Pl.), i.e., that they be intent καλῶν ἔργων προΐστασθαι. Two understandings have been proposed for this infinitive clause both here and in v. 14: "to engage in (apply/devote themselves to) good deeds" (e.g., *NASB, RSV, NIV, NEB* margin) and "to engage in (enter) honorable occupations" (*NEB, RSV* margin). προΐστασθαι (NT 8x, all in Pl.) "literally means 'to stand in front of' and was the word used for a shopkeeper standing in front of his shop crying his wares" (Barclay; for documentation see Field, *Notes;* Lock). But this is neither the only meaning of the word in Koine nor even one of the two meanings found elsewhere in Pauline usage.

Furthermore, Field questions whether any instance can be found of καλὰ ἔργα with the meaning "honorable occupations." In this letter the phrase is used consistently of "good deeds" (cf. 2:7, 14; 3:1). Here Paul is repeating and reinforcing the appeal in v. 1 (as well as that of 2:14). Therefore, the context is decisively in favor of "busy oneself with" or "engage in" "good deeds" (see BAGD s.v. προΐστημι 2; cf. MM s.v. προΐστημι, using the Goodspeed translation: "make it their business to do good"; cf. Lock). On καλῶν ἔργων see the comments on 2:14.

That to which ταῦτα in the next clause refers is disputed. Opinion is essentially divided between it picking up on τούτων and referring again to what Titus is to "insist on" (Alford, Bernard, Ellicott, Hendriksen, Spicq,

N. J. D. White, and Wohlenberg) and it referring to καλῶν ἔργων (e.g., Bratcher, Fee). Huther says that it refers back to διαβεβαιοῦσθαι, but this seems too limited. Some argue that for Paul to attach the adjective καλά to the καλῶν ἔργων would be a tautology (Alford, Ellicott, Huther, Wohlenberg). Many commentators say that what follows in v. 9 and is contrasted to this final clause in v. 8 by δέ determines what "things" Paul has in mind here (Ellicott, Fee, White, and Wohlenberg). But here, too, the divided opinion remains, since v. 9 refers both to teachings (e.g., "genealogies") and to deeds (e.g., "strife"), so that some think that the matters of v. 9 are naturally contrasted with the "teaching" (Ellicott, White, and Wohlenberg) and others that they are naturally contrasted with the "good deeds" (e.g., Fee). Ridderbos holds that ταῦτα refers to the entirety of what precedes, i.e., vv. 1-7, and thus both to teaching and to the "good deeds" with which the section begins and which the teaching seeks to engender. This more comprehensive view is warranted by the broadness of what is excluded in v. 9.

With such a comprehensive view, it may well be that the two predicate adjectives, "good and profitable," refer respectively to the two parts of the entire preceding section. Thus καλά is not tautologically attributed to the "good deeds" but is an affirmation of the "praiseworthy" (BAGD s.v. 2b) character of the teachings about God's salvation (vv. 4-7). ὠφέλιμα τοῖς ἀνθρώποις would then refer especially to the benefit that "good deeds" have for "people," i.e., non-Christians, ἀνθρώποις here picking up the previous use of the word in v. 2, where non-Christians are primarily in view and where Christians are being urged to practice the consummate good deed of "showing every consideration for all people" (πρὸς πάντας ἀνθρώπους). Obviously such teaching with such an outcome of good deeds is "profitable," i.e., "useful and beneficial" (ὠφέλιμα,** also in 1 Tim. 4:8 [see the comments there]; 2 Tim. 3:16) for "people."

FINAL INSTRUCTIONS ABOUT FALSE TEACHINGS AND FOR DEALING WITH A ʽΑΙΡΕΤΙΚΟΣ: 3:9-11

Paul brings the body of the letter, and particularly the preceding section, to a close by returning to the subject of false teaching (cf. 1:10-16). Thus he contrasts what should be avoided in teaching and action (v. 9a) with what should be taught and done (vv. 1-8), and gives the reasons that such teaching and action should be avoided (v. 9b). Having told Titus what he should do about false teaching, he then gives him instructions for dealing with a αἱρετικὸς ἄνθρωπος (vv. 10-11).

3:9 δέ, "but," contrasts this statement and its contents with what immediately precedes. The action enjoined is περιΐστασο** (present middle imperative of περιΐστημι), a verb that has within its basic meaning the concept of "around" and which in the middle means "go around so as to avoid," and more succinctly "avoid, shun" (also in 2 Tim. 2:16; in 2 Tim. 2:23 Paul uses a similar verb, παραιτέομαι, which occurs in Tit. 3:10, with the noun ζητήσεις, which occurs here). What Paul urges Titus to constantly do he also thereby urges on all the Christians on Crete. He delineates four errors that must be avoided.

The first is μωρὰς ζητήσεις. Plural ζητήσεις (see 1 Tim. 6:4) is used once each in the three PE of an aspect of the false teaching: "controversial questions" or "controversies" (ἐκζητήσεις is used similarly in 1 Tim. 1:4). In two of these three instances the ζητήσεις are designated as μωράς, "foolish" or "stupid" (here and in 2 Tim. 2:23; since ζητήσεις is thus qualified by μωράς elsewhere and γενεαλογίας is not in its other PE [and NT] occurrence, it is appropriate to attach μωράς to ζητήσεις and not to γενεαλογίας). Elsewhere Paul tells Timothy to correct those involved with such controversies so that "God may grant them repentance leading to knowledge of the truth" (2 Tim. 2:23-26); thus "occupation with such questions is taken to be sinful and culpable" (G. Bertram, *TDNT* IV, 845; cf. also what Paul says about μωρολογία in Eph. 5:4-7).

The second error is γενεαλογίας** (see 1 Tim. 1:4), "genealogies," i.e., speculation about the origins and descendants of persons, which are erroneously thought to have religious significance.

The third error is ἔρεις. (Singular ἔριν was preferred in *NA*[25]; see *NA*[26] and *TCGNT* for preference of the plural.) ἔρεις (see 1 Tim. 6:4) occurs regularly in the Pauline vice lists (and is in vice lists in most of its NT occurrences) and means "strife" and in the plural "quarrels" or "dissensions."

The fourth error is μάχας νομικάς, "battles about things pertaining to the law." μάχας** is always plural in the NT (2 Cor. 7:5; here; 2 Tim. 2:23; Jas. 4:1) and is used "only of battles fought without actual weapons" (BAGD). νομικάς (NT 10x, PE* 2x, here and v. 13) is used here in the sense of "pertaining to the law" (BAGD; cf. νομοδιδάσκαλος in 1 Tim. 1:7). The law in view here is undoubtedly the OT law, with which the false teachers were especially concerned (1 Tim. 1:7ff.).

Each of these four errors is also mentioned in 1 Timothy, and two are mentioned in 2 Timothy. As has been noted, it appears that the same problem, or at least a group of similar problems, is being confronted in all three letters (see the **Introduction** and the comments on 1 Tim. 1:3ff.). The substantive elements here are "genealogies" and a misuse of the law. The atmosphere is one of strife and contention.

Paul concludes this exhortation by giving the reasons that such errors should be avoided: They are ἀνωφελεῖς** (also in Heb. 7:18), "unprofitable" — the opposite of the description of the teaching and good deeds set forth in vv. 1-8 (ὠφέλιμα, v. 8) — and μάταιοι, "idle" or "empty" in the sense of "useless" or "fruitless" (see 1 Tim. 1:6: ματαιολογία; Tit. 1:10: ματαιολόγος; cf. O. Bauernfeind, *TDNT* IV, 519-24).

3:10 Paul gives instruction in this verse and the next on how to deal with a αἱρετικὸς ἄνθρωπος. The adjective αἱρετικός** (a NT hapax) is used here of one who has chosen to follow the false teachings and practices described in v. 9 over against the apostle, Titus, and others in the Christian community who embrace the true teaching and its good deeds. Thus it may properly be rendered "heretical," as long as we do not read later ideas back into the text (cf. BAGD, Lock, and the use of αἵρεσις in 2 Pet. 2:1). Since this choice with regard to teaching and practice sets the one so choosing against apostolic teaching, it also makes such a person "factious" and one who is "causing divisions," which are also meanings of αἱρετικός. Paul uses this adjective in a pleonastic construction, perhaps for emphasis, including the noun ἄνθρωπον, the word used generally in Greek and in the NT for "human being," rather than using a simple substantive adjective.

It is only "after" (μετά with the acc., BAGD s.v. B.II.3) two admonitions have been given to such a person that the action then commanded may take place. μίαν καὶ δευτέραν combines a cardinal (for an ordinal) and an ordinal number, as was done elsewhere in Greek writings (cf. BAGD s.v. εἷς 4). νουθεσία** (also in 1 Cor. 10:11; Eph. 6:4), "admonition," includes both "instruction" and "warning" but with emphasis on the latter. (The verb νουθετέω, like the noun, is used in the NT only in Paul's letters [and in the account of Paul's labors in Acts 20:31] — with διδάσκω in Col. 1:28; 3:16 in the sense "admonish," i.e., speak so as to affect the will and disposition; cf. J. Behm, *TDNT* IV, 1019-22.) The two admonitions are obviously intended to turn such a person from his or her error, as in 2 Thes. 3:15; 2 Tim. 2:25-26, and are "a pastoral attempt to reclaim" (Behm, 1022). This procedure reminds us of Mt. 18:15-20, where one who sins is first dealt with privately and then semi-privately before the final step is taken. παραιτέομαι (PE* 4x: 1 Tim. 4:7; 5:11; 2 Tim. 2:23; here imperative παραιτοῦ) is used here in the sense of "reject" or "dismiss," i.e., remove from the fellowship of the Christian community (cf. 1 Cor. 5:11-13; 2 Thes. 3:14; Mt. 18:17-18).

3:11 Paul refers to the kind of person whom Titus and the church must admonish and dismiss with the definite article ὁ with the correlative adjective τοιοῦτος used as a substantive: "such a person," "one like that," probably meaning anyone who bears the qualities indicated (so 2 Cor. 10:11a; Gal. 6:1), though other occurrences of the term refer to definite individuals (see BAGD s.v. 3aα). One can take the radical action of dismissing such a person from the Christian community because the refusal of a "heretical person" to respond to two admonitions gives the grounds for such action and indicates the necessity for it. As in Mt. 18:17, the basis for taking the last difficult step is such a person's self-indictment ("being self-condemned," αὐτοκατάκριτος).

The dismissal is grounded in knowledge (εἰδώς, causal participle from οἶδα) of the "heretical" person's views and actions that has been gathered from contacts that the two admonitions have afforded (cf. Mt. 18:16: "so that every fact may be confirmed"). What is known is "that" (ὅτι) the person ἐξέστραπται** (perfect middle or passive of ἐκστρέφω, a NT hapax), which means either that he "has turned himself aside/perverted himself" (middle) or that he "is turned aside/is perverted" (passive). In either case the person has moved away from the apostolic message by choice (cf. the LXX of Dt. 32:20 and the use of simple στρέφω to mean "turn to something evil, be perverted" in Didache 11:2). The perfect tense is most likely used to indicate a settled position.

Titus and others will also know that such a person "is sinning," ἁμαρτάνει, the present tense most likely indicating the person's persistence in false views and activities in the face of the pastoral admonitions (cf. Mt. 18:17: "if he refuses to listen to them"). This combination of a settled persistence in chosen erroneous views and continued refusal to repent of sin enables one to know that such a person is (ὤν, "being") "self-condemned" (αὐτοκατάκριτος,** a NT hapax): The "heretical" person has shown himself to be clearly guilty and therefore has himself provided the basis for his dismissal (παραιτοῦ, v. 10).

PERSONAL INSTRUCTIONS AND GREETINGS: 3:12-15

This letter concludes in ways typical of Paul's other letters. He gives final personal instructions (vv. 12-13; cf. Rom. 16:1-2; 1 Cor. 16:5-12; Col. 4:7-9) and repeats a major concern of the letter (v. 14; cf. 2 Cor. 13:11; Gal. 6:12-16). He then sends final greetings from those with him and from himself to the believers in the place he writes to (v. 15a; cf. 1 Cor. 16:19-21; 2 Cor. 13:12-13; Phil. 4:21-22; Col. 4:10-15, etc.) and closes with a benediction (v. 15b; so all of his letters).

3:12 In this verse Paul lays plans for Titus to leave Crete and join him at Nicopolis for the winter. Ὅταν with the aorist subjunctive (here πέμψω) is used "when the action of the subordinate clause precedes that of the main clause" (BAGD s.v. 1b). Thus "whenever" either Artemas or Tychicus arrives to take Titus's place, Titus should then leave to join Paul (με).

Apparently Paul had not decided which of the two men to send, nor exactly when he would send one of them. There is no other reference to Ἀρτεμᾶς** in the NT. Acts 20:4 indicates that Τύχικος** was from Asia, a coastal province of Asia Minor, and that he and Trophimus were the representatives from the church there who accompanied Paul with the gift for the poor Christians in Jerusalem. Paul relates in Eph. 6:21 and Col. 4:7 that Tychicus is a beloved brother and faithful minister who will tell those churches about how Paul is doing; apparently Tychicus was the one delivering those letters. Since from 2 Tim. 4:10, 12 we learn that Paul sent Tychicus to Ephesus and that Titus went to Dalmatia, which is just up the coast from Nicopolis (see below on the identification and location of Nicopolis), we may reasonably assume that the plan outlined here did materialize and that Artemas was apparently the one sent to Crete. The plan was for Titus, when replaced by one of the two men, to "make every effort" or to "make haste" to come (both meanings for the aorist imperative σπούδασον are possible and both appear elsewhere in the PE* [4x: 2 Tim. 2:15; 4:9, 21], although the former is more dominant in Paul as a whole [7x: also Gal. 2:10; Eph. 4:3; 1 Thes. 2:17]; see BAGD).

Paul wants Titus to join him at Νικόπολις** (a NT hapax; see J. M. Houston, *ZPEB* IV, 436; G. L. Borchert, *ISBE* III, 534f.). Although several places were known by that name (see Zahn, *Introduction* II, §35, n. 3), the capital of Epirus best fits the time framework of the letter and the reference in 2 Tim. 4:10 to Titus being in Dalmatia, which was just up the coast from Epirus. Nicopolis was on the west coast of Greece about two hundred miles northwest of Athens on the the gulf of Ambracia (now known as Arta) near the Adriatic Sea (cf. Strabo 7.7.5). It was founded and named by Augustus in 31 BC and established as a Roman colony (cf. Dio Cassius 51.1; Strabo loc. cit.).

Titus is to come "because" (γάρ) Paul "has decided" (κέκρικα, from κρίνω) "to winter there," the perfect tense expressing a settled decision. The infinitive παραχειμάσαι** with ἐκεῖ, "to spend the winter" "there," indicates the decision that Paul has reached. He is not yet at Nicopolis, since he refers to Nicopolis as "there" (ἐκεῖ, "in that place," BAGD; cf. Rom. 15:24), not "here." Thus the subscriptions (see NA^{26}) that say that the letter was written from Nicopolis are not accurate.

Travel on the sea was difficult or impossible during the winter (cf. 2 Tim. 4:21), and Paul's experiences (Acts 27:12; 28:11) made him keenly aware of the need to make plans for the season. Use of παραχειμάζω by Paul or in connection with Paul (the Acts passages just mentioned; 1 Cor. 16:6) shows that he sought to spend his winters with Christians in strategic locations for gospel ministry. His choice of Nicopolis put him and Titus one step further west of the area where most of his labors had been concentrated and was most likely taken with a view to fulfilling his desire to go where the gospel had not been preached and, ultimately, to Spain (cf. Rom. 15:20-24).

3:13 Paul knows that two men will be going through Crete and commends them and their needs to Titus and the Christians there. They are probably coming from Paul and carrying the letter with them.

Ζηνᾶς** is not mentioned elsewhere in the NT. Here he is designated by his profession as τὸν νομικόν, "the lawyer," just as Paul mentions the professions of others on occasion (Rom. 16:23; Col. 4:14). The term is most likely used here of an expert in Roman law rather than Jewish law (so Spicq and Ridderbos; Lock regards it as indicating here an expert in Jewish law as in Matthew and Luke; cf. BAGD s.v. 2; Mason, *Greek Terms,* s.v.; on the training and duties of νομικοί in the Greco-Roman world see Taubenschlag, "Legal Profession").

It is quite likely that Ἀπολλῶς** is the Apollos referred to elsewhere by Paul and in Acts (Acts 18:24; 19:1; 1 Cor. 1:12; 3:4, 5, 6, 22; 4:6; 16:12). Acts 18:24ff. identifies him as a Jewish Christian from Alexandria who "was mighty in the scriptures" and "fervent in spirit" and speaks of his desire to go to other places to minister (v. 27). Therefore, it is not surprising to find Apollos going through Crete to his next field of labor. Since Zenas and Apollos are mentioned in the same breath and are both to be helped on their way and since we know that Apollos was a Christian worker, it may be assumed that Zenas his associate was also.

Paul commands that these men be σπουδαίως πρόπεμψον. πρόπεμψον is aorist imperative of προπέμπω,** which is used twice in the NT in the sense of "accompany" or "escort" (Acts 20:38; 21:5). It is used here, however, as is borne out by the following ἵνα clause, with the meaning "help on one's journey" by various means, including money, as it is predominantly elsewhere (cf. Acts 15:3; Rom. 15:24; 1 Cor. 16:6, 11; 2 Cor. 1:16; 3 Jn. 6). The journey thus spoken of in the NT is always related to Christian ministry, and those to be aided are those involved in such ministry (cf. especially 3 Jn. 7-8; all the other passages relate to Paul and his fellow workers and have the same implicit perspective).

The adverb σπουδαίως,** as was the case for the related verb σπουδάζω in v. 12, can mean either "with haste," in the sense of special urgency (Phil. 2:28), or "diligently, earnestly," in the sense of "do your best" *(RSV)* or "do everything you can" *(NIV)*. As with the verb the slight preponderance of usage falls in the second category (Lk. 7:4; 2 Tim. 1:17), and that is the preferred meaning here (BAGD s.v. 2).

The ἵνα clause gives the purpose for such help being given to Zenas and Apollos. Paul wants these two men to "lack" or "fall short of" (λείπω,** Lk. 18:22; Tit. 1:5; Jas. 1:4, 5; 2:15; here in the intransitive sense; see BAGD s.v. 2) "nothing." The verb is used here with regard to the necessities of life, as in Jas. 2:15 (and as is indicated by εἰς τὰς ἀναγκαίας χρείας in Tit. 3:14); "nothing" (μηδέν) recalls the reference to appropriate Christian generosity in 3 Jn. 6, which speaks of sending such workers on their way "in a manner worthy of God" (!) since they have accepted "nothing" (μηδέν) from Gentiles.

3:14 Paul again, prompted by the particular need he has just spoken of, calls on Titus to remind the Christians on Crete of the necessity of doing good deeds. The definite article οἱ with the first person plural possessive pronoun ἡμέτεροι implies that the pronoun qualifies an understood noun, so that the reference is to "our people," i.e., those who "belong" to Paul and Titus as fellow Christians (BAGD; cf. Rom. 15:4), those of whom Paul has used the first person plural pronoun ἡμεῖς in this letter (1:3, 4; 2:8, 10, 13, 14; 3:3, 4, 5, 6) and elsewhere in the PE. Perhaps Paul uses this construction to distinguish those who follow him and Titus from the false teachers and their followers as well as from non-Christian neighbors.

Paul wants the Christians to keep on "learning" (μανθανέτωσαν, present active imperative; see 1 Tim. 5:14) through the activity of doing (cf. the similar sense in Heb. 5:8). The infinitive following indicates the activity (for other examples see BAGD s.v. 4). What they are to learn is "to engage in good deeds," καλῶν ἔργων προΐστασθαι, which is repeated from v. 8 (see the comments there). This is an obvious attempt to drive the general lesson home with this concrete case. Thus they are to learn "also" (καί) with reference to this pressing need as well as in the more normal routines of life.

They are to learn this εἰς τὰς ἀναγκαίας χρείας. εἰς here either means "because of" (Dana-Mantey, *Grammar,* 103f.) or more likely has a purposive sense (MHT III, 266; *NIV:* "in order that"; *RSV:* "so as to"). τὰς ἀναγκαίας χρείας are literally "necessary needs," i.e., what is "pressing, urgent, and real" (χρείας; see especially Acts 2:45; 4:35; Eph. 4:28; Phil. 4:16; 1 Jn. 3:17).

Such concrete and evident cases of need on the part of fellow believers and Christian workers are opportunities in which the Cretan Christians must not fail to be doing good deeds. If they fail in such clear situations, they will indeed be in danger of being "unfruitful" (ἄκαρποι; cf. the unfruitful branches of John 15, especially vv. 2 and 6). Even though this statement is cast in the negative, it is given not so much as a warning as an encouragement (like 2 Pet. 1:8).

3:15 ἀσπάζομαι is the verb used for greetings in the conclusions of Greek letters (BAGD s.v. 1a; Exler, *Form,* 69-77, 111-13), including most of Paul's letters (Romans, 1 and 2 Corinthians, Philippians, Colossians, 1 Thessalonians, 2 Timothy, and Philemon) and Hebrews, 1 Peter, and 2 and 3 John. Those whose greetings Paul conveys, οἱ μετ' ἐμοῦ πάντες, may be either his fellow workers or all the Christians where he is. The exact phrase is not used elsewhere by Paul or in the NT, but πάντες in similar phrases refers both to all Christians (Phil. 4:22; 2 Cor. 13:12) and to Paul's "brothers," i.e., his fellow workers (1 Cor. 16:20; cf. the distinction between ἀδελφοί and ἅγιοι in Phil. 4:21-22). The one other occurrence in such phrases of "with me" (with σύν; μετ' is used here) is used in regard to the "brothers" (Phil. 4:21), so here, too, Paul may be referring to his fellow workers (so also Gal. 1:2 [σύν]; 2 Tim. 4:11 [μετ']). Paul's closing greetings are directed to singular σε only, as we would expect, in letters directed to individuals (here; 2 Tim. 4:21; Phm. 23; 1 Timothy has no such greetings). The "you" is, of course, the addressee of the letter, Titus.

Titus is directed to "greet those who love us in the faith." The recipients of this greeting are those who remain in the bonds of brotherly love in that "faith" (cf. Tit. 1:4; 1 Tim. 1:2) and are distinguished by this designation from others who are disloyal to Paul and his gospel. Paul uses the same verb, φιλέω, "love,"** in an even more forthrightly negative statement in the conclusion of 1 Cor. 16:22: "If anyone does not love the Lord, let him be accursed." He implies here that Titus is to make an appraisal of others with regard to their relationship to Paul himself, since only Titus knows the situation where he is and how individuals there stand with regard to Paul. That the apostle himself often made such appraisals of Christians, loving them because they were brothers in the faith and because their reciprocal love showed this reality, is seen in his repeated use of ἀγαπητός, especially in the plural and in the phrase ἀδελφοὶ ἀγαπητοί (1 Cor. 10:14; 15:58; 2 Cor. 7:1; 12:19; Phil. 2:12; 4:1; 1 Thes. 2:8; cf. 1 Tim. 6:2; Jn. 13:34-35; 15:12, 17; Eph. 6:24).

Paul's concluding benediction is "Grace be with you all." The letter thus ends, as it began (1:4), with God's grace (χάρις), since Paul is persuaded that grace alone brings salvation (2:11) and produces godly lives (2:12). χάρις is, indeed, used in the first and last chapter of every letter of Paul's, as also in 1 and 2 Peter and Revelation and at the beginning of 2 John and the end of Hebrews. The word expresses God's unmerited favor in Christ in its soteriological significance for the believer, saving, sanctifying, and empowering him or her (cf. the full discussion at 1 Tim. 1:2 and the very informative usages in Tit. 2:11; 3:7, where the significance of χάρις in the believer's life is explicated). Here Paul asks that this "grace" continue its work in the life of all in the church on Crete (for a discussion of what verb should be understood and what significance should be given to the benediction see the full discussion at 1 Tim. 6:21).

Here at the conclusion of a letter addressed to an individual, Paul concludes with plural πάντων ὑμῶν, "all of you," addressing all the Christians on Crete, to whom he has been speaking throughout the letter in the instructions he has given them through Titus. Plural ὑμῶν is used in this way in the concluding benedictions of each of the PE and in Philemon (see the comments on 1 Tim. 6:21). But here only in the PE does Paul add πάντων, "all," for clarity and emphasis (cf. πάντων in 1 Cor. 16:24; 2 Cor. 13:13; Eph. 6:24; 2 Thes. 3:18; Heb. 13:25; Rev. 22:21). The concluding ἀμήν "is absent from a variety of early and diverse witnesses" (*TCGNT;* see *NA*[26]) and was probably added by a copyist early in the history of transmission.

COMMENTARY ON 2 TIMOTHY

SALUTATION: 1:1-2

This letter begins like other Greek letters and the other Pauline letters with the author in the nominative (v. 1), the addressee in the dative (v. 2a), and words of greeting (v. 2b). The unique feature in Paul's letters is the expansion of each element with Christian elements. This salutation is nearly identical with 1 Tim. 1:1-2; for a fuller handling of those elements see the comments there. There are two differences: Here Paul says that his apostleship is διὰ θελήματος θεοῦ κατ' ἐπαγγελίαν ζωῆς τῆς ἐν Χριστῷ Ἰησοῦ, while in 1 Timothy he says that it is κατ' ἐπιταγὴν θεοῦ σωτῆρος ἡμῶν καὶ Χριστοῦ Ἰησοῦ τῆς ἐλπίδος ἡμῶν. Here Paul speaks of Timothy as ἀγαπητῷ τέκνῳ, while in 1 Timothy he calls him γνησίῳ τέκνῳ ἐν πίστει.

1:1 "Apostle of Christ Jesus" indicates Paul's special authority as one sent by Christ to act and write on his behalf (see further the comments on ἀπόστολος at 1 Tim. 1:1; for Παῦλος see there and at Tit. 1:1). The one who has directly appointed him is "Christ Jesus," i.e., Jesus who is the Christ, the one anointed and sent by God (see 1 Tim. 1:1). Although some find it unlikely that Paul would identify himself as an "apostle of Christ Jesus" in a letter to a personal friend and colleague, this self-designation is in place when one realizes that Paul is not just writing as a friend but with the authority of an apostle to instruct and admonish Timothy about his ministry and his responsibilities (note the imperatives in 1:14; 2:1, 3, 7, 8, 14, 15, 16, 22, 23; 3:1, 14; 4:5, 9 and the charge in 4:1ff.) and also to communicate to the Christians under Timothy's care the basis of authority for what Paul is asking Timothy to do (note plural ὑμῶν in 4:22 and the allusions to others in, e.g., 2:14).

Paul specifies that he is an apostle "by God's will," διὰ θελήματος θεοῦ. This phrase is found in Pauline salutations also in 1 Cor. 1:1; 2 Cor. 1:1; Eph. 1:1; Col. 1:1 (cf. Gal. 1:4 for a similar phrase; the phrase is also found in Rom. 15:32; 2 Cor. 8:5). Where it is not used in a Pauline salutation, an equivalent is used (κατ' ἐπιταγὴν θεοῦ, 1 Tim. 1:1; Tit. 1:3) or some other indication of the Father's will is specified (the Father is the assumed subject in Rom. 1:2ff.; in Gal. 1:1 Paul is an apostle "through" [διά] Jesus Christ and God the Father). διά indicates here that God's will is "the efficient cause" (BAGD s.v. A.III.1d). Paul describes this "will of God" at work in his life and especially in regard to his apostleship in Gal. 1:15-16 (cf. Gal. 2:7-9).

The following prepositional phrase expresses the aim and purpose of Paul's apostleship. κατ' indicates "the object and intention of [Paul's] appointment" to apostleship (Ellicott; cf. Tit. 1:1, where κατά appears to be used in the same way; κατ' ἐπαγγελίαν also appears in Acts 13:23; Gal. 3:29). ἐπαγγελία (Pl. 26x, PE* 2x: 1 Tim. 4:8 and here) is used almost uniformly in the NT of God's "promise" (BAGD s.v. 2a; cf., e.g., Heb. 6:13; 10:23; 11:11). "The content of the promises," even though different terms are used, "is always Messianic salvation" (J. Schniewind and G. Friedrich, *TDNT* II, 583). Paul utilizes the "promise" concept most fully in Galatians 3, where he indicates that what was promised to Abraham and to his spiritual descendants is fulfilled in Christ (the noun 8x: vv. 14, 16, 17, 18 [2x], 21, 22, 29; the related verb in v. 19). In Tit. 1:2, Paul speaks of the "eternal life" that God "promised (ἐπηγγείλατο) long ago" and has now manifested in his word.

The closest parallel to the combination ἐπαγγελίαν ζωῆς, found here, is in 1 Tim. 4:8. Genitive ζωῆς denotes the thing promised, "life" itself (see the discussion at 1 Tim. 4:8; 1:16; cf. 1 Jn. 2:25). ζωῆς τῆς ἐν Χριστῷ Ἰησοῦ specifies that the "life" spoken of is "the" life that is "in Christ Jesus," in Jesus as the Christ, the anointed one of God (cf. 2:10; for Χριστὸς Ἰησοῦς see the comments on 1 Tim. 1:1). ζωή is used in the NT "of the supernatural life belonging to God and Christ, which the believers will receive in the future, but which they also enjoy here and now" (BAGD s.v. 2). What Paul says here in brief form he says more extensively in the argument of Romans 6, i.e., that by spiritual union with Christ (v. 5), we now are "alive to God in Christ Jesus" (v. 11) and so "walk in newness of life" (v. 4) and have as "the outcome eternal life" (v. 22) "in Christ Jesus our Lord" (v. 23; cf. also 1 Jn. 5:11-12a).

The "in Christ" formula is characteristically Pauline (72x; elsewhere in the NT 2x in 1 Peter). The formula is found 9x in the PE* and 7x in 2 Timothy (1 Tim. 1:14; 3:13; 2 Tim. 1:1, 9, 13; 2:1, 10; 3:12, 15). For the formula ἐν Χριστῷ Ἰησοῦ see A. Oepke, *TDNT* II, 541f.; W. Grundmann, *TDNT* IX, 550-52, 561f. and the literature referred to there and in BAGD s.v. ἐν I.5d. Allan ("'In Christ' Formula," 117) emphasizes the differences in usage of this formula in the PE in comparison to the other Pauline letters and discounts the similarities, e.g., those cases in which it is preceded by the definite article, a difference already found in the other Pauline letters.

1:2 With the name Timothy in the dative case Paul designates the addressee of the letter. When the addressee is an individual (as in Philemon, 1 and 2 Timothy, and Titus) Paul refers to the warm and close bond that exists between him and the one addressed. In addressing Timothy and Titus, his younger assistants, Paul uses the affectionate term τέκνον preceded by a word that heightens its significance and thereby the status of the one in that role. In 1 Timothy and Titus that additional word is γνησίῳ followed by ἐν πίστει to indicate the sphere in which the term τέκνῳ functions. Here the word is ἀγαπητῷ (Pl. 27x, PE* 2x: 1 Tim. 6:2).

τέκνον might designate one or more of three possible spiritual relationships existing between Timothy and Paul: (a) spiritual sonship, Timothy being Paul's convert; (b) spiritual adoption and training, i.e., Timothy being Paul's adopted spiritual son; (c) spiritual youth in relationship to Paul as the older person in the faith. It is likely that at least both (a) and (b) are true. For full discussion see the comments on 1 Tim. 1:2.

Paul uses ἀγαπητός in Romans first of those who are "beloved" of God and called by him (1:7) and then of those who are "beloved" by Paul "in the Lord" (16:8; cf. 16:5, 12). Those who are "beloved" of God are "beloved" by one another (cf. 1 Tim. 6:2). Thus Paul can call the Corinthians "my beloved children" (1 Cor. 4:14, with Eph. 5:1, the only NT occurrences of plural ἀγαπητὰ τέκνα) and in the same context call Timothy "my beloved and faithful child in the Lord" (1 Cor. 4:17, the only other NT occurrence of singular ἀγαπητὸν τέκνον). Here ἀγαπητῷ τέκνῳ is undoubtedly meant to designate that same spiritual relationship to Paul even though the ἐν πίστει in 1 Timothy and Titus and the ἐν κυρίῳ in 1 Cor. 4:17 are not used here, since ἀγαπητὸν τέκνον can be used to designate that spiritual relationship without any further qualification (as in 1 Cor. 4:14).

Timothy was one of Paul's apostolic assistants who served faithfully with him in many situations and for him on various assignments. He is mentioned in all the Pauline letters except Ephesians, Galatians, and Titus. Much of what we learn about Timothy we learn from this letter, and each will be considered in turn as it is related (e.g., 1:3-7). For a synopsis of our knowledge of Timothy see the **Introduction.**

1 Timothy was sent while Timothy was on assignment in Ephesus (1 Tim. 1:3). Indicators in 2 Timothy point to Ephesus as his location when it also was sent: Onesiphorus is associated with Ephesus (1:18), and greetings are to be conveyed to his household (4:19). Tychicus is being sent to Ephesus and is most likely the bearer of the letter and perhaps a replacement for Timothy (cf. the epistolary aorist in 4:12). Alexander the coppersmith (4:14-15) may be the Alexander, probably to be associated with Ephesus, mentioned in 1 Tim. 1:20.

"Grace, mercy, and peace from God the Father and Christ Jesus our Lord" is the greeting that, with only slight variations, is in all of Paul's letters. The form here is identical to the one found in 1 Timothy (for full treatment see the comments on 1 Tim. 1:2).

THANKSGIVING: 1:3-5

Paul begins the body of this letter, as he does nearly all his letters, with thanksgiving to God. The thanksgivings in his letters express gratitude for God's grace in the life of the recipients and are usually related to the particular concerns of the letter.

Here (v. 3a) Paul thanks God for Timothy (implied) and relates that he remembers him in his times of prayer (v. 3c) and also reflects on his own service to God (v. 3b). He longs to see Timothy (v. 4a) because this will fill Paul with joy (v. 4c). His longing is made more intense when he remembers Timothy's tears (v. 4b). Paul is mindful of Timothy's "sincere faith," which was also possessed by his grandmother and mother (v. 5; cf. 3:14ff.).

On the basis of this sincere faith Paul makes his appeals to Timothy both forthwith (vv. 6-8) and throughout the letter (cf. 1:13, 14; 2:1, 3, 15, 22; 3:14). And on it is on the basis of Paul's serving God with a "clear conscience" (v. 3b) that Paul appeals to Timothy not to be ashamed of him (v. 8), to suffer with him (2:3), and to continue to follow him (3:10, 14). Thus two key motifs in the letter are mentioned in the thanksgiving.

1:3 χάριν ἔχω,** "I thank" (also in Lk. 17:9; Acts 2:47; 2 Cor. 1:15; Heb. 12:28), is used here (and in 1 Tim. 1:12) in place of the more usual εὐχαριστέω (Rom. 1:8; 1 Cor. 1:4; Eph. 1:16; Phil. 1:3; Col. 1:3; 1 Thes. 1:2; 2 Thes. 1:3; Phm. 4) or the less usual εὐλογητός (2 Cor. 1:3; Eph. 1:3). The phrase is found in the literature of the day, including the papyri (see BAGD s.v. χάρις 5), and is comparable to the Latin expression *gratiam habere* (Simpson). Paul expresses his thanksgiving "to God" (τῷ θεῷ) here as he does in all his thanksgiving sections.

The relative clause attached to θεῷ gives further insight into Paul and his religious life by affirming that Paul continually "serves" God. Robertson renders the present tense verb, which he says emphasizes the continual unbroken habit of life, "I have been serving" (λατρεύω, Pl.* 4x: Rom. 1:9, 25; Phil. 3:3). The verb is not the usual one for service. It is used in the literature of the day to indicate the execution of religious duties (H. Strathmann, *TDNT* IV, 62: "The ministry denoted by λατρεύειν is always offered to God"; cf. especially Rom. 1:9).

The second of two prepositional phrases, ἐν καθαρᾷ συνειδήσει, specifies the manner in which Paul performs his service. συνειδήσει (see the comments on 1 Tim. 1:5) means "moral consciousness" or "conscience." The term signifies that one is conscious of the rightness or wrongness (before God) of one's actions. καθαρᾷ συνειδήσει (see the comments on the only other NT occurrence of the phrase, 1 Tim. 3:9) is used here in the sense of a "clean," or better, a "clear conscience." Thus Paul is saying that he is seeking to live according to God's demands.

The first prepositional phrase, "from my ancestors," sets forth a linkage in Paul's life similar to that in Timothy's life (cf. v. 5). προγόνων** means literally "those born before" and is used here, as in 1 Tim. 5:4 (see the comments there), of one's "parents," "grandparents," or "ancestors." ἀπὸ προγόνων is best understood as "as my ancestors did" (so BAGD s.v. πρόγονος, citing several examples from inscriptions; similarly rendered in most modern English translations: *RSV, NASB, NEB, TEV, NIV*). Paul affirms here a continuity with the true faith of his Jewish ancestors, i.e., that he has not left the OT and turned to worship and serve another God, but, in recognizing Jesus as the promised Messiah, has continued to serve the God of Abraham (cf. Acts 23:1; 24:14; 26:6). Paul does not look back on his early life as a time of a bad conscience but as one of the terrible ignorance of unbelief with regard to Jesus (cf. 1 Tim. 1:13).

The relative adverb ὡς introducing the next clause "is almost equivalent to 'when,' 'as often as,' but adds the thought of the correspondence of the thankfulness with the thought of Timothy, χάριν ἔχω ὡς ἔχω μνείαν: to think of thee is to thank God for thee" (Lock). The neuter adjective ἀδιάλειπτον** (also in Rom. 9:2) is used here as an adverb with the meaning "constantly," indicating that Paul prays for Timothy on every occasion in which he prays. ἔχω . . . μνείαν** (also in 1 Thes. 3:6) is used here of remembering and mentioning in prayer, as the words that follow indicate. περὶ σοῦ occurs between the definite article and μνείαν to indicate that μνείαν has particular reference to Timothy ("you") and that he is the one whom Paul remembers in prayer (see BAGD s.v. περί 1g).

δέησις (see 1 Tim. 2:1) when used alone means "prayer," and in the NT and the literature of the day referred to prayer addressed exclusively to God (BAGD). ἐν ταῖς δεήσεσίν μου designates the prayers in which Paul remembers or mentions Timothy to God with thankfulness (cf. Phil. 1:4). νυκτὸς καὶ ἡμέρας, "night and day," is an idiom that occurs in the singular without further qualification some 15x in the NT, 8x in this order, always so in Paul (5x), and 7x in the reverse order (see 1 Tim. 5:5, the only other PE* occurrence). The phrase signifies that in the regularly recurring cycles of Paul's prayer life that correspond to the two main divisions of his daily existence he remembers Timothy in his prayers (the phrase of prayer in 1 Thes. 3:10; 1 Tim. 5:5; here; the other 2x in Paul are with reference to work). Some have punctuated the sentence so that νυκτὸς καὶ ἡμέρας is taken with the verb following in v. 4: "night and day I long to see you" (see the *UBSGNT* apparatus). The punctuation in the *UBSGNT* text, in which the phrase qualifies Paul's prayers, fits Paul's usage of the phrase elsewhere (see above).

1:4 Although vv. 3-5 form one long sentence, v. 4 is somewhat of an aside triggered by Paul's reference to remembering Timothy. Now Paul remembers the sorrowful parting they had and wishes that they could be together again, a wish that will be returned to in 4:9ff. ἐπιποθέω (Pl.* 7x: Rom. 1:11; 2 Cor. 5:2; 9:14; Phil. 1:8; 2:26; 1 Thes. 3:6; here) means "desire" or "long for" something. Here the participle is followed by an infinitive phrase expressing what Paul longs for: ἰδεῖν σε, "to see" Timothy (three of the seven Pauline occurrences of the verb are of desire to see people; two of those and one other are also followed by ἰδεῖν).

This participial clause qualifies either χάριν ἔχω or ἔχω μνείαν in v. 3, most likely the latter because it is nearer and because this would produce the most natural construction both grammatically and in terms of the emotions involved. But the choice makes little difference in meaning because both have to do with the same activity and occasion. The clause is a further description of what Paul remembers about Timothy, in prayer before God, and the entirety of v. 4 may be one of the things he asks for Timothy and himself.

Paul's longing is heightened by his remembrance of the tears of his colleague. The perfect participle μεμνημένος (from μιμνῄσκομαι) is used here in the sense of "remembering," "recalling to mind," perhaps even in contrast to "forgetting" (BAGD s.v. 1aα). What Paul remembers are the "tears" (τῶν δακρύων, Pl.* 2x, 2 Cor. 2:4; genitive of the thing following the verb) of Timothy (σου). The most likely recent parting that we have an account of is in 1 Tim. 1:3.

ἵνα χαρᾶς πληρωθῶ, "so that I may be filled with joy," denotes the purpose in view in Paul's longing to see Timothy. The passive tense of the verb suggests that it is God who does the filling (cf. Rom. 15:13), though it may simply be the usual construction of the verb when describing someone being filled with something. χαρά, "joy," is a recurring note in the writings of Paul, who uses the word more often than any other NT author (Pl. 21x, NT 59x). But he does not use χαρά in all his letters and uses it only once in Galatians, Colossians, Philemon, and 2 Timothy (only here in the PE*). It refers here to the joy of renewed contact with a beloved colleague.

1:5 In one sense this verse, the conclusion of the long sentence in vv. 3-5, indicates what has particularly prompted Paul's thankfulness to God, i.e., Timothy's "sincere faith." ὑπόμνησιν λαβών is an idiom that can mean that Paul has received an external "reminder" (ὑπόμνησις** is used in such a way in 2 Pet. 1:13; 3:1; the phrase only here in the NT). Guthrie and a number of others (following Bengel) suggest that Paul has just received news of Timothy. This is not improbable, but is only a conjecture. Lock allows for the possibility that Paul refers here to a "reminder," but also refers to places where ὑπόμνησις is used in the sense of "remembrance."

Whether Paul was prompted from without or from within, it was Timothy's ἀνυποκρίτου πίστεως that he remembers. ἀνυπόκριτος,** "genuine, sincere" (literally "without hypocrisy") is used here and in 1 Tim. 1:5 (see the comments there) of faith. Some have proved to have a faith less than genuine (cf. Demas, 4:10). In the midst of persecution and suffering, where fidelity is so very important (cf. 1:8ff.), Paul is thankful to God that he can remember Timothy as one in whom (ἐν σοί) there was a faith that neither wavered nor was double-minded, a genuine trust in God (cf. by analogy Jas. 1:6-8).

As with Paul himself (v. 3), so also with Timothy, what Paul commends in Timothy he finds as part of Timothy's spiritual heritage. Such a faith (ἥτις) "dwelled" (ἐνῴκησεν) "first" (the neuter adjective πρῶτον used as an adverb) as a spiritual reality in his grandmother and his mother. μάμμη** (a NT hapax) is used in Greek literature to refer to one's "mother" or "grandmother" (so commonly in the papyri; see MM), but its use here with μητήρ makes it clear that "grandmother" is intended. This is the only NT reference to Timothy's grandmother Lois (Λωΐς**), probably his maternal grandmother, since she is mentioned here with his mother. Eunice (Εὐνίκη**), his mother, is not named elsewhere in the NT but is mentioned in Acts 16:1 as "a Jewish woman who was a believer" (πιστῆς), apparently meaning that she was a Christian (cf. πιστός in Acts 10:45).

Paul adds for emphasis and as an encouragement to Timothy πέπεισμαι δὲ ὅτι καὶ ἐν σοί. The perfect passive of πείθω is used here with a present meaning and with a ὅτι following (as in Rom. 8:38; 14:14; 15:14; 2 Tim. 1:5, 12, the other PE* occurrences): "I am convinced that" expresses Paul's certainty that a genuine faith is "also" (καί) a continuing spiritual reality in Timothy (with the verb ἐνοικέω being understood from the previous clause with the prepositional phrase ἐν σοί), as it was in his mother and grandmother.

APPEAL FOR A SPIRIT-GIVEN BOLDNESS THAT WILL ENDURE SUFFERING: 1:6-14

On the basis of Timothy's "sincere faith" (v. 5), Paul appeals to him (v. 6: δι' ἣν αἰτίαν) to exercise that faith and stir up anew "the gift of God" that is in him, i.e., God's own mighty Spirit (v. 7). Because Timothy knows God's power and the reality of Paul's faithfulness to God, Paul therefore urges Timothy not to be ashamed of "the testimony of the Lord" or of Paul's imprisonment, but, rather, by God's power, to join Paul in suffering for the gospel (v. 8). Paul then gives a brief summary of the gospel in vv. 9-10: God saved us according to his own eternal purpose through the appearing and work of Christ, a work that abolished death and brought life and immortality to light through that gospel. Paul was appointed to proclaim that gospel and suffers because of that service (vv. 11-12). But he is not ashamed of that suffering (and Timothy must not be either) because he knows God and is convinced that God will "guard what I have entrusted to him until that day" (v. 12). With the anticipation of "that day," Paul charges Timothy to hold on to the ὑποτύπωσιν of sound words he has heard from Paul in an attitude of faith and love that find their source and reality in Christ (v. 13) and to guard "the good παραθήκην" by the Holy Spirit who dwells in him (v. 14).

1:6 On the basis of (δι' ἣν αἰτίαν as a causal conjunction; BAGD s.v. αἰτία 1) the reality of Timothy's genuine faith (v. 5) Paul reminds Timothy to "rekindle" (ἀναζωπυρεῖν,** a NT hapax; present infinitive of continuous action [Robertson]) "the gift of God." This metaphor from the rekindling of a dying flame (so Fee) does not mean that Paul thought that Timothy's faith was dying out, but that he should "fan into flame" *(NIV)* that special gift of God that he had received, i.e., make full use of it (cf. 1 Thes. 5:19). τὸ χάρισμα is used here in the sense of a special spiritual gift bestowed by God (τοῦ θεοῦ), as in some other occurrences in the NT (cf. 1 Pet. 4:10; Rom. 12:6; 1 Cor. 12:4, 9, 28, 30, 31).

From its association with laying on of hands here and in 1 Tim. 4:14 (see the comments there), this gift of Timothy seems to have been related to the ministry into which that act admitted him, so that the act was the occasion and the means by which (διά) God bestowed the gift. Therefore the gift was probably "a special enduement or anointing of the Spirit which Timothy received . . . to equip him for the work to which he had been called" (Stott). Paul refers to the event in a personal way here, "my hands," because he is making a personal appeal to Timothy. Paul knows that Timothy has the gift within him (ἐν σοί) because he was one of the instruments through whom God bestowed it, and therefore he can rightly call on him to stir it up.

1:7 The appeal in v. 6 is further motivated (γάρ) by the statement here about the nature of the "spirit" that God has given to "us." Is Paul referring to the χάρισμα of v. 6 under another designation, "a spirit," or broadening the discussion and talking about the "Spirit" who imparts the χάρισμα, or referring to the "attitude" ("spirit") that God has placed in "us"? The negative first statement in this verse has understandably inclined most modern English translations to use "spirit" with a lowercase letter (e.g., *NIV*), but the positive affirmation that follows seems to have the Holy Spirit in mind (so *TEV:* "Spirit").

Other factors point to the latter choice: Paul connects χάρισμα and the Holy Spirit in 1 Cor. 12:5, 7. When he writes about the πνεῦμα "given" by God (Rom. 5:5; 1 Cor. 12:7; 2 Cor. 1:22; 5:5; 1 Thes. 4:8, all using the verb used here, δίδωμι) and "received" by humans (Rom. 8:15-in context; 1 Cor. 2:12), he almost always refers thereby to the Spirit of God (exceptions are the quotation in Rom. 11:8 and possibly Eph. 1:17).

But since the statement here begins with the negative, the generic lower-case "spirit" is probably the best decision after all, as long as one recognizes that the positive affirmation beginning with ἀλλά does, indeed, refer to the Spirit of God. If this understanding is correct, then ἡμῖν, "us," refers to Christians in general (as in v. 9) rather than just to Paul and Timothy as those who have received a special χάρισμα (so, e.g., Lock and Parry), and aorist ἔδωκεν refers to the past action of God at the beginning of every Christian's life in giving his "Spirit" (cf. 1 Cor. 12:13; Rom. 8:9, 11, 14-16).

The "spirit" that God did not give is one of δειλία** (a NT hapax), "timidity" or "cowardice." Paul probably reminds Timothy of this both because of his own temperament and also because of the difficult situation in which he and Paul found themselves.

"But" (ἀλλά) God did give a spirit of δυνάμεως καὶ ἀγάπης καὶ σωφρονισμοῦ. Similar uses of the genitive with πνεῦμα are found in Rom. 8:2, 15; 2 Cor. 4:13; Eph. 1:17 and elsewhere in the NT (BAGD s.v. 5e). δύναμις, "power," is a characteristic of the Holy Spirit in the NT (Lk. 4:14; Acts 1:8; Rom. 15:13, 19; Eph. 3:16). The "power" that characterizes the Spirit is that which he brings into the life of believers as he indwells them. Thus believers are "strengthened with power through his spirit in the inner person" (Eph. 3:16) and enabled to have a ministry of accomplishment "in the power of the Spirit" (Rom. 15:18-19).

The Spirit is also characterized by ἀγάπη (Rom. 15:10), and it is through the Spirit that God pours out his "love" into the hearts of believers (Rom. 5:5). Thus for the believer "love" is the first evidence of the fruit of the Spirit (Gal. 5:22), and the believer lives a life of "love in the Spirit" (Col. 1:8).

Paul also says that the Spirit is characterized by σωφρονισμός (a NT hapax but see the occurrences of the other σωφρ- words at 1 Tim. 2:9, 14; 3:2). Since Paul can speak of one aspect of the fruit of the Spirit as ἐγκράτεια (Gal. 5:23) one should not find this related term foreign to Paul's way of thinking, as Hanson does. It is difficult to know which of its nuances this word has here (see BAGD): "making to understand," "making wise," and "admonition to do better"; "more rarely it can mean 'discretion' in the sense of 'moderation,' 'discipline' " (U. Luck, *TDNT* VII, 1104). Paul uses a cognate term, σώφρων, "prudent, thoughtful, self-controlled," when describing the characteristics of a bishop (1 Tim. 3:2). When Paul desires that the believer ascertain properly what the Spirit has given him (Rom. 12:3) and live and act accordingly, he uses the cognate verb σωφρονεῖν, "to have sound judgment," which seems in that context to combine the characteristics of prudence and self-discipline. Somewhat similar characteristics mark the description of the ministry of the Spirit of truth in Jn. 16:13: The Spirit "will not speak on his own initiative, but whatever he hears, he will speak." It seems likely that Paul's use of the cognate verb in Rom. 12:13 and the cognate adjective in 1 Tim. 3:2 are our best guides to his use of the noun here.

1:8 Because the spirit God gave us is not one of cowardice but of power, etc., Paul can "therefore" (οὖν) admonish Timothy not to "be ashamed," i.e., embarrassed (ἐπαισχυνθῇς, aorist subjunctive with μή as a prohibition; deponent passive with transitive use: Robertson, *Grammar,* 817f.; cf. Kee, "Shame") of τὸ μαρτύριον τοῦ κυρίου ἡμῶν. "The testimony" (τὸ μαρτύριον) is Christian preaching and the gospel generally (as in 1 Cor. 1:6; [variant reading in 2:1]; 2 Thes. 1:10; cf. especially the other PE* occurrence, 1 Tim. 2:6; BAGD s.v. 1b; H. Strathmann, *TDNT* IV, 504).

This testimony is "about" "our Lord" (objective gen. τοῦ κυρίου [like τοῦ Χριστοῦ in 1 Cor. 1:6]; *NIV, RSV,* and *NEB* have "to our Lord"). From this point on 2 Timothy uses κύριος without further identification (1:16, 18 [2x]; 2:7 [variant reading in 14], 19 [2x], 22, 24; 3:11; 4:8, 14, 17, 18, 22). Because of the earlier use of κύριος clearly identified as "Christ Jesus" (1:2), because τὸ μαρτύριον is more directly related to Christ (cf. 1 Cor. 1:6), and because one might more likely be in danger of being ashamed of Christ, a religious leader put to death as a criminal by Roman authorities and repudiated by Jewish religious leaders, than of God, it is most likely that κύριος here is a designation for Christ. Thus while Paul warns Timothy not to be ashamed of Christ, he also reminds Timothy, with the designation τοῦ κυρίου ἡμῶν, that Christ is the sovereign master of Christians' lives.

μηδέ, "nor," is used to continue the preceding negation (μή) and the previous verb (ἐπαισχυνθῇς; BAGD s.v. μηδέ 1a). Thus Paul urges Timothy not to be ashamed of him (ἐμέ) as one who is a "prisoner" (δέσμιον) in Rome (cf. 1:17; 4:16-17). It is striking that Paul refers to himself not as Rome's prisoner but as "his" (αὐτοῦ), i.e., "the Lord's" prisoner, with αὐτοῦ referring back to τοῦ κυρίου. His imprisonment is for no other reason than that he serves the Lord. Paul always refers to himself as a δέσμιος in this way (δέσμιος Χριστοῦ Ἰησοῦ, Eph. 3:1; Phm. 1, 9; δέσμιος ἐν κυρίῳ, Eph. 4:1). That he does so here gives Timothy perspective on Paul's imprisonment and thereby gives him reason not to be ashamed of the apostle.

Paul joins an imperative to the prohibition μὴ ἐπαισχυνθῇς with ἀλλά so that the thrust of the sentence shifts to the positive exhortation: "Do not be ashamed . . . , *but* join with me. . . ." The verb συγκακοπαθέω** (also in 2:3; here imperative συγκακοπάθησον; cf. κακοπαθέω** in 2:9; 4:5) means "suffer together with someone." Since the someone is not explicitly indicated, and since Paul, who is obviously suffering, is the one encouraging Timothy to suffer together with someone, it is often assumed that the someone is Paul (e.g., *NASB, NIV*), although others have left that an open question with "take your share of suffering" (e.g., *RSV, NEB;* similarly *TEV*).

τῷ εὐαγγελίῳ (dative of advantage) specifies that for which Timothy is to suffer, "the gospel," God's good news to mankind (see vv. 9-10). This is the first of three occurrences of εὐαγγελίον in 2 Timothy (also in 1:10; 2:8; elsewhere in PE* in 1 Tim. 1:11, which see). As always Paul's exhortation is based on God's enabling grace, and thus he exhorts Timothy to join with him in suffering for the gospel κατὰ δύναμιν θεοῦ, with κατά used in the sense of "in" or "by." δύναμις θεοῦ (in Pl.* in Rom. 1:16; 1 Cor. 1:18, 24; 2:5; 2 Cor. 6:7; 13:4 [2x]) harks back to the πνεῦμα . . . δυνάμεως of v. 6. Timothy can rely upon "God's power" because God's powerful Spirit is in him to give him that power (cf. Eph. 3:16, 20).

1:9 As is often the case with Paul, the mention of the gospel and of God triggers a statement of praise and thanksgiving or a kind of doxology (cf. 1 Tim. 1:17; 6:15f.; Rom. 11:33-36). Here and in the following verse he gives a further statement about God and his gospel (cf. 1 Cor. 15:3-4 and especially Rom. 1:2-4).

τοῦ σώσαντος is the equivalent of an explanatory relative clause and is generally rendered as such: "who has saved" (Burton, *Syntax,* §426). Paul wants Timothy to remember that God, whose gospel he is asked to suffer for, has saved him (for σῴζει θεός see 1 Cor. 1:21; Tit. 3:5). σώσαντος specifies what God purposed "in Christ Jesus" and manifested in him as "our Savior" (v. 10). Christ's work as Savior "abolished death, and brought life and immortality to light," and thus σώσαντος means that God has saved us from death and brought us life and its attendant immortality. ἡμᾶς, "us," in this general statement of truth designates the Christian community as a whole (cf. 2:11-13), even though it may be particularly applied to Paul and Timothy, as the designation of those "called" by God indicates.

καλέσαντος, also governed by the article τοῦ, further describes God. καλέω is used in the NT and especially in Paul of a "call" that is effectual (K. L. Schmidt, *TDNT* III, 489), i.e., of the choice of a person for salvation (BAGD s.v. 2). Most often in Paul, as here, it is God who calls (e.g., Rom. 8:30; 9:12 [11 in English versions], 24; 1 Cor. 1:9; Gal. 1:6; 5:8; 1 Thes. 5:24).

It is difficult to ascertain the precise force of dative κλήσει ἁγίᾳ, "a holy calling." Some suggest that it is dative of means or of instrument, "*with* a holy calling" (*RSV, NASB;* Schmidt, *TDNT* III, 492; BAGD s.v. 1; Bouma) because the calling comes from a holy God. Others take it as dative of interest: called "*to* a holy life" (*NIV; NEB:* "called to be saints"; Barrett, Kelly, Lenski, Lock, Robertson, N. J. D. White). κλῆσις (Pl.* 9x: Rom. 11:29; 1 Cor. 1:26; 7:20; Eph. 1:18; 4:1, 4; Phil. 3:14; 2 Thes. 1:11) is used in both senses in the NT (see the occurrences and BAGD s.v. 1, 2). The syntactical construction of τῆς κλήσεως ἧς ἐκλήθητε in Eph. 4:1 points to the first understanding, "*with* a holy calling." At the same time, the functional significance of the phrase in Eph. 4:1 is to call Christians "to walk in a manner worthy" of that calling. It may well be that the phrase here functions in that kind of double capacity.

Paul goes on to deny that God's saving and calling is "on the basis of" (κατά, BAGD s.v. II.5d; seen especially Tit. 3:5) "our deeds," as he does elsewhere (Rom. 3:20; 9:11; Gal. 2:16; and especially Eph. 2:9; cf. Marshall, "Faith and Works"). ἡμῶν carries on the persistent reference to the first person plural that marks this section (vv. 7, 8, 10, 14; cf. v. 2).

The introduction of a positive statement by ἀλλά after a negative statement continues a pattern seen also in vv. 7 and 8. God has not saved and called us because of our works, but "on the basis of" (κατά, BAGD s.v. II.5d) his plan and grace. πρόθεσις (Pl.* 6x: Rom. 8:28; 9:11; Eph. 1:11; 3:11; 2 Tim. 1:9; 3:10) has as one basic set of meanings "plan, purpose, resolve, will." Here, as in most of the Pauline occurrences (except 2 Tim. 3:10), it is used of the divine purpose. ἰδίαν, "his own," emphasizes that it is God's own purpose and no one else's. Since χάριν, "grace," is connected to ἰδίαν πρόθεσιν by καί, it is also governed by ἰδίαν. Thus salvation is not only on the basis of God's purpose but also on the basis of "his own" χάρις, the gracious intention of God. Paul also links these two elements, God's purpose or will and his gracious intention, elsewhere as the basis for human salvation. In Rom. 8:28 God's "purpose" is set in the context of his love (vv. 35, 39), in Rom. 9:11 in the context of his mercy (vv. 15f., 18), in Eph. 1:11 and 3:11 in the context of his grace (1:6-7; 3:2). One term emphasizes God's plan, the other his attitude and intention. For κατὰ χάριν* elsewhere in Paul see Rom. 4:4, 16; 12:6; 1 Cor. 3:10; 2 Thes. 1:12.

In the participial construction that follows singular τὴν δοθεῖσαν refers either to πρόθεσιν and χάριν as one, or, more likely, just to χάριν as that which is "given" to us (for δίδωμι with χάρις in Paul cf. Rom. 12:3, 6; 15:15; 1 Cor. 1:4; 3:10; 15:57; 2 Cor. 8:16; Gal. 2:9; Eph. 3:8; 4:7; 2 Thes. 2:16). God saved us and called us by giving his grace to "us" (ἡμῖν designating all Christians).

That he gave it "in Christ Jesus" signifies that it is brought to us in Christ's person and work. Paul speaks elsewhere of "God's grace" having abounded to many in "the one man, Jesus Christ" (Rom. 5:15), so that they received "abundance of grace" through him (5:17) and that "grace might reign through righteousness to eternal life through Jesus Christ" (5:21). Paul also says that God freely bestowed his grace on us "in the beloved" (Eph. 1:6). In every Pauline salutation God's grace is said to be from both Christ and God the Father, and nearly every concluding benediction in the Pauline letters wishes that "the grace of our Lord Jesus (Christ) be with" the recipients (Rom. 16:20; 1 Cor. 16:23; 2 Cor. 13:13; Gal. 6:18; Phil. 4:23; 1 Thes. 5:28; 2 Thes. 3:18; Phm. 25).

Grace was given to us in Christ πρὸ χρόνων αἰωνίων. When used of time πρό consistently has the meaning "before" (see BAGD s.v. 2 for the occurrences). But what is the meaning of the combination πρὸ χρόνων αἰωνίων** (Rom. 16:25; Tit. 1:2)? Except for the rendering of the *RSV*, "ages ago," there is a consensus among commentators and translations that the phrase, literally "before times eternal," is best understood here as "from all eternity" *(NASB, NEB)* or "before the beginning of time" *(NIV, TEV)*. This is in accord with Paul's perspective, which speaks of God's decision before time and the world began (1 Cor. 2:7: πρὸ τῶν αἰωνίων; Eph. 1:4: πρὸ καταβολῆς κόσμου).

1:10 Paul moves from God's eternal plan and the grace resident in Christ to the manifestation of that grace in the appearing of Christ as the Savior who accomplishes salvation by abolishing death and providing life and immortality. The shift is indicated by the verb φανερόω and the temporal adverb νῦν, "now," "at the present time," which is set in contrast to πρὸ χρόνων αἰωνίων (v. 9).

The feminine singular participle φανερωθεῖσαν agrees with χάριν, as did the previous participle τὴν δοθεῖσαν, and parallels that previous participle. That earlier clause related that God's grace was given to us in Christ "before the beginning of time." This clause relates that "now" God's grace has been "made visible" or "revealed" (other Pauline uses of φανερόω most like this one are in Rom. 16:26; Col. 1:26; and the other PE* occurrences, 1 Tim. 3:16; Tit. 1:3). This manifestation of grace has taken place "through" (διά) Christ's "appearance." Paul is the only NT writer to use ἐπιφάνεια** (also in 2 Thes. 2:8; 1 Tim. 6:14; Tit. 2:13; 2 Tim. 4:1, 8), "appearing" or "appearance," and he uses it exclusively of the "appearing" of Jesus in his first (only here) or second coming (the other occurrences). Paul thus states that God's grace was made visible in the earthly ministry of Jesus, in which this Jesus appeared in his capacity as "Christ," the anointed one (Χριστοῦ, see 1 Tim. 1:1f.), and as "our Savior" (τοῦ σωτῆρος ἡμῶν). Paul refers to Jesus as σωτήρ 6x in his letters (Eph. 5:23; Phil. 3:20; Tit. 1:4; 2:13 [see the comments there]; 3:6) and once in Acts (13:23). As the "Savior" Christ accomplished what Paul goes on to describe, and it is through those acts that God made his grace known and saved us.

καταργήσαντος μὲν τὸν θάνατον describes the effectiveness of Christ's work as Savior from a negative perspective. The μέν . . . δέ particles indicate both "connection and contrast" (Fairbairn; cf. further Robertson, *Grammar,* 1150-53). Hence θάνατον, "death," is defined in part by contrast to "life and immortality" (cf. Jn. 5:24). The "life" that is brought is not physical but spiritual life, and "immortality" itself speaks of life beyond physical death. Therefore, "death" here must be the spiritual death associated with sin (cf. Rom. 6:6 [the same verb]; 7:24; 8:2). Christ has "abolished" (καταργήσαντος) this death, so that it no longer has a hold on his people. Thus Paul speaks of Christ bringing "life" to Christians (cf. Rom. 6:4, 11, 13). When those who belong to Christ are resurrected, the last aspect of "death," physical death itself, will also be abolished (cf. 1 Cor. 15:26, using the same verb as here), and this, too, will occur on the basis of Christ's decisive work, which, according to Heb. 2:14, took place in Jesus' own death.

Christ has "brought life to light" (φωτίσαντος, Pl.* 4x: also in 1 Cor. 4:5; Eph. 1:18; 3:9). He has thus "not only shown it, but effectively manifested it" (H. Conzelmann, *TDNT* IX, 349). "Life" (ζωήν) here is the supernatural and spiritual life that was promised to believers in Christ (cf. 1:1). Christ embodies life (he speaks of himself as the life in Jn. 11:25; cf. Col. 3:4) and brings it to give to others (Rom. 5:17; 6:4; 2 Cor. 4:10-11; 1 Jn. 5:11-12). Paul joins to ζωήν the word ἀφθαρσίαν** (also in Rom. 2:7; 1 Cor. 15:42, 50, 53, 54; Eph. 6:24), "incorruptibility," "immortality," to provide the appropriate eternal dimension, just as he sometimes adds the word "eternal."

Christ has brought these great realities "through the gospel" (διὰ τοῦ εὐαγγελίου, this phrase in Paul* at 1 Cor. 4:15; Eph. 3:6; 2 Thes. 2:14), i.e., through the "good news" about his death and resurrection and about the significance of such for those who embrace that good news (cf. especially 1 Cor. 15:1-4 and then Eph. 3:6; 2 Thes. 2:14; 1 Cor. 4:15). The combination of "brought to light" with the prepositional phrase "through the gospel" joins the once-for-all historical redemptive deed of Jesus (his life, death, and resurrection) with the message about it and one's response (implied) to it. The two horizons are fused in this statement. That Jesus brought life and immortality to light in his life and resurrection is the essence of the gospel, and he brought life and immortality to light to the believer "through the gospel" message.

NA[26] sets vv. 9-10 in verse form as if it were a quoted statement (not so *UBSGNT*), and some commentators take the statement as such (Easton, Gealy, and Hanson), pointing to certain factors that seem to give this position credence (cf. especially Gealy's arguments). But other considerations favor taking it as written by Paul in the course of his argument. Kelly points out that vv. 9-10 are "subordinated syntactically to the preceding clause" and that "the ideas and language are Pauline." Indeed, certain words and phrases are exclusively Pauline, e.g., ἀφθαρσία, χρόνοι αἰώνιοι, or are used only by Paul in the sense they have here, e.g., πρόθεσις (furthermore, καταργέω is used 25x by Paul and elsewhere only 1x each in Luke and Hebrews; cf. Prat, *Theology* I, 397).

1:11 Having mentioned the work of Christ, Paul is now constrained to mention his own part in the ministry for the gospel, as he does elsewhere (2 Cor. 5:18, 20; Eph. 3:7-8; Col. 1:25; 1 Tim. 1:11-12; 2:6-7). The statement here is almost identical to 1 Tim. 2:7 but does not include the words "I am telling the truth, I am not lying" or the phrase "of the Gentiles" after the word "teacher."

εἰς ὅ refers to that "for which" Paul was appointed, with the antecedent of ὅ being εὐαγγελίου. ἐτέθην (aorist passive of τίθημι), which generally means "put" or "place," carries here the meaning "appoint" and refers to a definite past action (cf. C. Maurer, *TDNT* VIII, 157). The passive voice assumes that the reader will intuitively grasp that "by God" or "by Christ" is to be understood (cf. Gal. 1:1). ἐγώ is used for emphasis (cf. the other occurrences of ἐγώ in the PE*: 1 Tim. 1:11, 15; 2:7; Tit. 1:3, 5; 2 Tim. 1:11; 4:6, in which all but the second and the last refer to Paul's appointment to ministry, and even those are in contexts that deal with that topic).

The three terms κῆρυξ, ἀπόστολος, and διδάσκαλος (nominative case with the passive verb) designate different aspects of Paul's one ministry. κῆρυξ** (see 1 Tim. 2:7; 2 Pet. 2:5; cf. Paul's use of κήρυγμα [6x] and κηρύσσω [19x]), a term found in the culture of the day in both secular and religious senses, is the "herald" or "proclaimer" (see BAGD, MM). ἀπόστολος (see 1 Tim. 1:1), "apostle," is used here in the special sense of one directly chosen by Christ and sent with Christ's authority to speak for him (cf. Acts 11:14, 15; 26:16-18; 1 Cor. 15:8-10; Galatians 1). διδάσκαλος (Pl.* 7x) is applied by Paul to himself only here and in 1 Tim. 2:7 (but see Acts 11:26). In other uses of the word he either includes διδάσκαλοι in a list in which they are distinguished from ἀπόστολοι (1 Cor. 12:28, 29; Eph. 4:11) or uses it in a derogatory sense (Rom. 2:20; 2 Tim. 4:3). Most of the textual witnesses add ἐθνῶν after διδάσκαλος (all except ℵ* A I 33 1175 syr[pal]). But the *UBSGNT* editors "regarded the word as a gloss introduced by copyists from the parallel in 1 Tm 2.7, there being no good reason to account for its omission if it were original here" *(TCGNT)*.

What distinguishes these three aspects of Paul's ministry? κῆρυξ and διδάσκαλος emphasize his roles as evangelist on the one hand and teacher on the other. He may have added these two terms, both of which he uses of himself only here and in 1 Tim. 2:7, to his usual self-designation of ἀπόστολος to emphasize these aspects of his ministry in his letters to Timothy so that he could be a model for Timothy (and others), who is to serve as an evangelist (κηρύσσειν, 2 Tim. 4:2) and teacher (διδάσκειν, 1 Tim. 4:11; 6:2; 2 Tim. 2:2) but is not an ἀπόστολος.

1:12 *RSV, UBSGNT,* and *NA*[26] place a comma at the end of v. 11 and a period or raised dot after πάσχω in v. 12. In this way the intervening words form the conclusion to this long sentence that began with v. 8 and are divided from the words that follow πάσχω. Other critical editions (and all other translations noted in the *UBSGNT* punctuation apparatus) put the break between sentences at the end of v. 11. But it seems harsh to sever the intervening words from the following ἀλλ', and the phrase δι' ἣν αἰτίαν is found at the beginning of a sentence in its other PE occurrences (2 Tim. 1:6; Tit. 1:13; so also Heb. 2:11; cf. BAGD s.v. αἰτία 1), not at the end. Therefore, it is best to think of a new sentence beginning with the first words of v. 12.

δι' ἣν αἰτίαν functions as a causal conjunction with the meaning "for which reason," "therefore." "Because of" Paul's service in the gospel ministry he suffers these things, because suffering is tied up with the gospel in this evil world (cf. v. 8; 3:12). It is difficult to determine whether the adverbial καί goes with ταῦτα, "even these things" (Ellicott, Bernard), or with πάσχω, "I also suffer," i.e., suffering also is included in my appointment (Alford and especially Ridderbos).

Present tense πάσχω is used here of that which Paul is "experiencing" in the sense of "enduring" or "undergoing" (BAGD s.v. 3b). ταῦτα, "these things," is a comprehensive term that includes all that is involved in Paul's imprisonment (τὸν δέσμιον, v. 8), the only previous item to which this term could refer (and ἐπαισχύνομαι suggests a reference to v. 8, which has the same verb). Although the reader gains further insight into what is included in this ταῦτα as the letter progresses (e.g., v. 16: "my chains"), Paul most likely assumed that Timothy knew what he meant by it (cf. ταῦτα in 2:2).

The next clause, with ἀλλ' followed by οὐκ, takes away any false impression that "for this reason I also suffer these things" might seem to convey (cf. BAGD s.v. ἀλλά 2). Paul is not "ashamed" (ἐπαισχύνομαι, see v. 8) of the "gospel" (vv. 10-11; cf. Rom. 1:16), "the testimony of our Lord" (v. 8), and his own imprisonment as the Lord's "prisoner" (v. 8). V. 12 provides a word of explanation for the preceding sentence (vv. 8-11) and takes us back to the exhortation that begins that sentence: "Do not be ashamed. . . ." Paul indicates that he is not ashamed, even in his circumstances, so that Timothy will also not be ashamed, even if he also suffers.

γάρ signifies that the following words express the reasons that Paul is not ashamed: He knows (οἶδα) the one he has trusted and is persuaded of that one's ability to guard his trust. Perfect tense πεπίστευκα indicates "I have put my trust, and still put it" (Ellicott). Dative ᾧ is the object of this verb, but the antecedent of this relative pronoun is not expressed. Since both God the Father and Christ are mentioned in the preceding verses, it is difficult to know which in particular Paul has in mind. He uses the verb πιστεύω with both in the the PE. Since emphasis has been laid on God and his power (cf. vv. 6, 7, 8), it is probable that the Father is in view here as well (cf. 1 Thes. 4:14, where God is named as the one who acts with reference to the Christian dead).

With καί Paul joins to his certain knowledge of the one he has trusted his certain assurance of that one's ability to guard his trust. πέπεισμαι (perfect passive of πείθω; see v. 5), "I am convinced" or "I am certain," asserts Paul's confidence, the substance of which is expressed in the ὅτι clause that follows. The first aspect of Paul's confidence is that God is "able" (δυνατός; cf. Rom. 4:21; 11:23), with the aorist infinitive that follows indicating the ability of God about which Paul is so confident: God is able "to guard his trust." The infinitive φυλάξαι means here "to guard" or "to protect" in the sense of keeping what has been entrusted (τὴν παραθήκην) so that it is not lost (cf. v. 14; 1 Tim. 6:20; 2 Thes. 3:3). τὴν παραθήκην** (1 Tim. 6:20; 2 Tim. 1:12, 14, always with φυλάσσω) means "deposit," "property entrusted to another" (BAGD; see also the excursus in Lock, 90-92) and is used figuratively in the PE.

Paul uses ἐκείνη ἡ ἡμέρα, "that day," in this letter to designate the all-embracing day of God's final judgment (cf. 1:18; 4:8), as he (2 Thes. 1:10) and Jesus (Mt. 7:22; Lk. 10:12; 21:34) do elsewhere. NT usage most likely echoes the OT (cf., e.g., Zp. 1:15; see BAGD s.v. ἡμέρα 3bβ; G. Delling, *TDNT* II, 951-53). εἰς either "marks the limit or accents the duration expressed by the accusative" (Robertson, *Grammar,* 594). Therefore, Paul affirms here that God will keep his deposit "until" (εἰς) the judgment day (cf. Phil. 1:10 for a similar use of εἰς).

What does Paul mean by "my deposit" (τὴν παραθήκην μου)? Essentially two answers are proposed: The first is that the deposit is what God has entrusted to Paul, usually understood as the gospel although sometimes of his ministry: "what has been entrusted to me" *(RSV;* cf. *TEV, NEB).* The second is that the deposit is what Paul has entrusted to God, usually regarded as his life or himself: "what I have entrusted to him" *(NASB, NIV,* and the marginal alternatives in *RSV, TEV, NEB).*

Those in favor of the first view (Bernard, Bürki, Easton, Gealy, Guthrie, Huther, Jeremias, Kelly, Lenski, Ridderbos, Stott, Weiss; Barrett and Spicq with hesitation) note that the entire phrase (with the verb φυλάσσω) occurs only twice elsewhere in the NT, both in the PE, and argue that in those places (1 Tim. 6:20; 2 Tim. 1:14 — only two verses away) it has this meaning and should, therefore, here as well. Furthermore, they argue that the context is concerned about the gospel message that must be transmitted, not about Paul's own life. This understanding, it is said, would make a natural transition to the following verses, especially v. 14.

Those in favor of the second view (Alford, Bouma, Calvin, Fee, Hendriksen, Kent, Lock, Moellering, Robertson, Schlatter, Simpson, van Oosterzee, Ward, N. J. D. White; Barclay, "Paul's Certainties VII") argue that in this context the deposit is more likely to be what Paul has committed to God, e.g., his own life, since the statement speaks of God as the one who "guards" and of the deposit as Paul's ("my"). These two factors taken together distinguish this passage from the other two occurrences of the word (1 Tim. 6:20; 2 Tim. 1:4). In them, Timothy, a human being, is the subject of φυλάσσω; it is he who is to guard the deposit, which is not personalized as "my" deposit, as it is here. "My" with the deposit here seems more naturally to refer to what Paul has committed to another than to what has been committed to Paul.

This second view also fits this part of the verse, which is oriented to God's care of Paul. ᾧ πεπίστευκα, "in whom I have put my trust," has prepared the way for Paul to speak about the ability of the one in whom he trusts to guard "my deposit," that which Paul has entrusted to God, which in effect he has already identified as himself in the statement "*I* have put my trust." Furthermore, this perspective fits the letter as a whole and particularly this section, where Paul is encouraging Timothy to suffer for the gospel. Paul is concerned not only for Timothy's fidelity but also that Timothy be assured that God will take care of his suffering servant. Paul gives him this assurance by pointing out this reality in his own life (cf. Paul's references to God's care for his life throughout the letter, e.g., 4:8, 17-18, and the maxim that those who endure will reign with Christ, 2:12). For the appropriateness of this view of the "deposit" to what follows see below.

1:13 In the preceding verses Paul's emphasis was on not being ashamed and on an appeal for Timothy to join with Paul in suffering for the gospel. The reasons given were that God had accomplished a great salvation, which of itself should elicit such service (vv. 8b-12a), and that God was able to guard his suffering servants as he guarded Paul (v. 12).

In this verse and the next Paul returns to his direct appeal to Timothy (cf. v. 8). He emphasizes Timothy's responsibility to retain (v. 13) and guard (v. 14) the truth content of the gospel message in the face of the threats from false teachers (a matter to which Paul will turn more directly in 2:14ff. and that he will continue to deal with to the end of the letter, e.g., 3:1ff.; 4:3ff., 15). This appeal appropriately follows on the preceding statement and uses the key concept "guard the deposit" reciprocally. With his usual skillful way with words, Paul is saying in effect that as God has guarded the deposit of his life (and will guard Timothy's) so also Timothy must guard the deposit of the faithful account of the gospel that God has entrusted to him.

Before dealing with Timothy's responsibility to "guard" the content of the gospel, Paul first reminds him with imperative ἔχε of his responsibility to "keep" or "preserve" (BAGD s.v. I.1cβ) that content himself. That which he is to "keep" is the ὑποτύπωσιν "of sound words that you have heard from me." ὑποτύπωσιν** (also in 1 Tim. 1:16), placed first in the sentence for emphasis, is used here of the "standard" (BAGD; cf. also Ridderbos and Stott) that one must "keep" or "preserve," indeed, as the following parallel imperative clause indicates, that one must "guard" as a good deposit.

The "standard" is defined by the appositional genitive construction, ὑγιαινόντων λόγων κτλ.: It consists of the "sound words" that (ὧν) Timothy has heard from Paul, i.e., the contents of the apostolic teaching. ὑγιαινόντων λόγων** (the phrase only here and in 1 Tim. 6:3 in the NT) are "sound words" in the sense of "correct," i.e., "true" (on ὑγιαίνω see the comments on 1 Tim. 1:10). Paul speaks of himself as the source of the sound words because he understands himself, as an apostle, to be an appointed communicator of God's message (see Gal. 1:11-12; cf. 2 Tim. 2:2 on the phrase παρ' ἐμοῦ ἤκουσας**). Paul uses related but different terms to speak of himself as the communicator of a standard to be followed in his earlier letters (e.g., "tradition," παράδοσις, 2 Thes. 2:15; 3:6; 1 Cor. 11:2).

Timothy is to keep the standard "with" or "in" (ἐν) "faith" and "love" that are found only in Christ. "ἐν πίστει κ.τ.λ. specifies the principles in which ὑποτύπ. is to be held . . . the *sphere* and *element*" (Ellicott; cf. Bernard: faith and love form "the atmosphere in which the 'sound words' are to be preserved"). This construction virtually repeats the phrase used in 1 Tim. 1:14 (see the comments there). Timothy is to keep the standard while trusting God (ἐν πίστει) with the trust that is found only in relationship to Christ since it is found in Christ (τῇ ἐν Χριστῷ Ἰησοῦ). Timothy is also to keep the standard while he lives a life of love (ἐν . . . ἀγάπῃ), especially love to others, a love that is found only in relationship to Christ because it is found in Christ (τῇ ἐν Χριστῷ Ἰησοῦ). Paul is saying very plainly that the attitudes and actions of "faith" and "love" found in Christ are essential to one who is to preserve the apostolic standard.

1:14 Paul adds a second imperative and thus takes the exhortation a step further. That which Timothy is to "keep" or "preserve" (v. 13) he is now urged to "guard" (φυλάσσω,** also in v. 12 and 1 Tim. 6:20, which see), i.e., guard against it being lost or damaged (BAGD s.v. 1c), especially against false teachers and false teaching (see the context of 1 Tim. 6:20 and 2 Tim. 2:14ff., 25; 3:13-14; 4:3ff., 15). Since Timothy is the one commanded to guard the παραθήκην, "the deposit," it is something entrusted to his care (cf. the parallel in 1 Tim. 6:20), i.e., "the standard of sound words that he heard" from Paul (cf. 2:2 with the cognate verb παράθου). The deposit is called "good" (καλήν) to give emphasis to its value and truthfulness (cf. 1 Tim. 1:8; 4:6; Rom. 7:16). τὴν καλὴν παραθήκην is placed first for emphasis.

This guarding is not to be done in Timothy's own strength but διὰ πνεύματος ἁγίου τοῦ ἐνοικοῦντος ἐν ἡμῖν. διά here is used to indicate means and more particularly the personal agent (which is πνεύματος ἁγίου). Paul reminds Timothy again (v. 7) that he has the Holy Spirit dwelling (ἐνοικοῦντος; cf. v. 5 and especially Rom. 8:11) in him to enable him to carry out the ministry committed to him. Plural ἐν ἡμῖν, "in you," emphasizes that the Holy Spirit is present in all Christians, and that, therefore, he, Paul, knows as a personal reality the truth about which he writes (cf. 1 Thes. 1:5). Paul can exhort Timothy to guard the good deposit because he knows that the Holy Spirit is indwelling Timothy and therefore will be the one through whom Timothy will be able to carry out the exhortation (cf. Phil. 2:12-13).

The appeal has come full circle. It began with God's Spirit and his power and it has ended with the Spirit's enabling power. The flow of the account is striking. After urging Timothy to "stir up" the gift of God (v. 6), the imperatives follow one after the other, made more urgent by the recounting of what God has done and of what Paul has gladly suffered: "Do not be ashamed," "suffer with me" (v. 8), "keep the standard" (v. 13), "guard the deposit" (v. 14). The touchstone of the whole appeal is that God, by his Spirit within, is able to make his servant able (vv. 6-7). Thus Paul can appeal to Timothy not to be ashamed and to be willing to suffer for the gospel by God's power (v. 8). For God has shown his power in the very work of the gospel itself and in Christ, the suffering servant (vv. 8-10). Thus Paul is not ashamed even though he suffers for the gospel's sake because he knows of God's keeping power (vv. 11-12). Therefore, Paul concludes his charge to Timothy by commanding him to keep the standard of sound words, with faith and love in Christ (v. 13), and to guard the deposit through the Holy Spirit in us (v. 14).

EXAMPLES OF THOSE ASHAMED AND OF ONE WHO WAS NOT ASHAMED: 1:15-18

This section's connection with the preceding is that it provides negative and positive examples that make Paul's admonition to Timothy all the more relevant. First are the negative examples of those who "turned away" from Paul (v. 15). Paul knows that certain persons associated with Timothy's very area have "turned away" from him, and that is why he has asked Timothy not to be ashamed of him as a prisoner (v. 8). Second, he presents a positive example, also from Timothy's area, of one who was not ashamed of him. He recounts and praises Onesiphorus's concern and care, and thereby, without saying so, commends him to Timothy as an example to be emulated (vv. 16-18).

1:15 Paul purposefully relates an occurrence that Timothy knows about (οἶδας τοῦτο), which he specifies in the ὅτι clause: "All who are in Asia turned away from me." By 'Ασία Paul means the Roman province embracing the western parts of Asia Minor (now western Turkey) and having as its capital Ephesus. Aorist passive ἀπεστράφησάν recalls some event in which "all" "turned away from" him (με; BAGD s.v. ἀποστρέφω 3a; for the accusative after this passive verb see Robertson, *Grammar,* 484f.). Since this matter is implicitly contrasted with the personal help and attention that Onesiphorus gave to Paul (vv. 16-18), the turning away is more likely to have been personal rather than a falling away from the faith.

Who are πάντες ("all") οἱ ἐν τῇ 'Ασίᾳ? Some (e.g., Schlatter) have taken it that Paul is referring to all the Christians in Asia. This seems unlikely since not everyone there has done so (e.g., Onesiphorus, Timothy, etc.) and because Paul himself in specifying two names in this verse seems to have a more restricted group in mind. Thus most have taken the phrase to be referring to some particular group, some leaders or colleagues. Spicq (followed by Ridderbos) suggests that the phrase is a Hebraism for "all those *from* Asia," i.e., those Christians in Rome from Asia who could have stood by Paul but did not (cf. 4:16). Other solutions take the phrase to refer to the leadership who are now in (ἐν) Asia and who failed Paul in some way (cf.

Lock), either when he was arrested in their midst (Jeremias, Kelly, Simpson), when they were requested to come to Rome (Bouma, Hendriksen), or when they were in Rome (Bernard). Timothy knows about the event, but unfortunately we do not.

Paul singles out two individuals of that group (ὧν ἐστιν), "Phygelus and Hermogenes" (Φύγελος** καὶ Ἑρμογένης**), who are not mentioned elsewhere in the NT. They are most likely singled out as the leaders and perhaps also because Paul is most disappointed about them.

1:16 Paul turns from this disappointment, and its implicit appeal to Timothy not to do as these men have done (cf. 4:9ff.), to one who has greatly encouraged Paul and who is evidently commended to Timothy, Ὀνησίφορος** (also mentioned in 4:19). All that we know about Onesiphorus in the NT is found in these few verses (16-18).

Paul begins by expressing a wish for the Lord's mercy on Onesiphorus's family and ends by expressing the same wish for Onesiphorus himself (v. 18). It would appear that the principle of Mt. 5:7 is a guiding motif here. οἶκος (PE* 8x, 1 Tim. 3:4, 5, 12, 15; 5:4; Tit. 1:11; 2 Tim. 1:16; 4:19) is used here metaphorically for the "household" or "family," as it is in virtually all the PE passages. Onesiphorus and his family are distinguished probably because they were separated from one another. The suggestion that he has died will be considered when v. 18 is before us.

Paul wishes (Robertson, *Grammar,* 939) that the Lord "may grant" (δῴη, aorist active optative of δίδωμι, here; v. 18; Rom. 15:5; 2 Thes. 3:16, in all four expressing a wish) "mercy" (δῴη ἔλεος only here in NT, but cf. v. 18) to Onesiphorus's family because (ὅτι) of what Onesiphorus has done. The family is in Ephesus (cf. 4:19), so Onesiphorus was away from them when he ministered to Paul in Rome (v. 17). Paul wants Onesiphorus's family, which probably enabled Onesiphorus to provide for Paul's needs, to receive the same in return, i.e., "mercy," in the sense of having their own needs met (cf. ἐλεέω in Phil. 2:27). κύριος refers in the two preceding occurrences (vv. 2, 8) to Christ, and there is no reason to think that it is any different here.

ἀνέψυξεν** (a NT hapax) is a verb used of "reviving" or "refreshing" someone. Onesiphorus's "refreshing" of Paul (με, before the verb for emphasis) may have been through food that he brought to Paul, but it also undoubtedly came through his presence with Paul in itself (cf. 1 Cor. 16:17-18). He "refreshed" Paul πολλάκις, "many times" or "often."

Not only so, but Onesiphorus was not ashamed of Paul's "chain." ἐπαισχύνθη provides the verbal link with Paul's charge to Timothy in the preceding section (cf. vv. 8, 12). The implication is clear: Onesiphorus was not ashamed, so Timothy should not be ashamed. Although it is possible that ἅλυσις, "chain" (Pl.* 2x), is used figuratively here and in Eph. 6:20 of Paul's "imprisonment" (BAGD s.v. 2), it is more likely that it refers to the actual "chain" with which he was bound. All other NT occurrences of the word are literal, and this is how Paul uses the term in his comment recorded in Acts 28:20. Furthermore, Paul uses other terms when speaking of his imprisonment (cf., e.g., v. 8). If the literal understanding of "chain" is correct, it makes the comment even more vivid and striking: Onesiphorus was not ashamed to come to me even when I was bound by a chain.

1:17 ἀλλά is used following a negative statement to introduce a contrasting positive (as in vv. 7, 8, 9). Onesiphorus was not only not ashamed of Paul's chain, "but" even eagerly searched for Paul. When and where he sought and found Paul is indicated by the participial phrase γενόμενος ἐν Ῥώμῃ, "when he was in Rome" (cf. Mt. 26:6; Mk. 9:33; Acts 13:5 for this use of γενόμενος with ἐν and a place name). Here only in 2 Timothy is the city of Paul's imprisonment named.

ἐζήτησεν is used here with the meaning of "looking for in order to find" (BAGD s.v. 1aβ; cf. Acts 10:19, 21), with με specifying Paul as the one whom Onesiphorus was seeking. He sought σπουδαίως (the weight of manuscript evidence supports this reading over either σπουδαιότερον or σπουδαιοτέρως), i.e., "eagerly" or "diligently" (cf. especially Tit. 3:13). The result of his searching is expressed with καί and one expressive word, εὗρεν, "and he found" ("me" understood from the preceding με).

The conditions of this imprisonment seem to be much more difficult than those of the situation described in Acts 28:23, 30-31, so that it was necessary for Onesiphorus to search and to do so diligently. Paul expresses the episode in very personal terms because of his deep personal gratitude, and therefore refers to himself with a first person pronoun three times (vv. 15, 16, 17). He emphasizes the faithfulness of Onesiphorus's ministry not only with the statements themselves but also in the adverbs πολλάκις and σπουδαίως. He is obviously moved as he recounts the incident and therefore breaks off the account and expresses his thanksgiving for Onesiphorus's ministry by wishing that he will find mercy from the Lord "in that day," just as he found Paul and showed mercy to him (v. 18a).

1:18 δῴη is used here, as in v. 16, to express a wish. αὐτῷ refers back naturally to the subject of the previous verbs, which have themselves referred back to the name of Onesiphorus in v. 16.

The double occurrence of κύριος, as the subject of δῴη and with παρά, is puzzling. The intention might be to indicate that "the Lord" is both he who enables a person to find mercy and also he who gives mercy (cf. for similar double reference 2 Thes. 3:5; Gn. 19:24 LXX) or to eliminate the confusion that a second use of the personal pronoun (αὐτοῦ) might have occasioned. If the two references do not refer to the same person of the Trinity, then they refer, respectively, to the Son and the Father (cf. Mt. 22:44 par. Mk. 12:36/Lk. 20:42). In that case, the first would continue the practice to this point of using κύριος to refer to Christ (vv. 2, 8, and especially the parallel in v. 16) and would be in accord with the Pauline perspective that Christ by his person and work enables one to find mercy from the Father (cf. v. 9: "grace" is given us "in Christ Jesus"; cf. also 1 Thes. 1:10). The second occurrence of κύριος would, then, follow the pattern of the LXX, where κύριος without the article is God's proper name (Spicq; G. Quell, *TDNT* III, 1058f.).

With εὑρεῖν, "find," Paul makes good use of his sense of wordplay: May he who "found" me "find" mercy "from the Lord" (παρά with the genitive indicating from whom the mercy proceeds; cf. BAGD s.v. I; for God as the bestower of "mercy" in Paul see the use of the cognate verb in Rom. 9:15, 16, 18). The ἔλεος, "mercy," in view here is that needed by a human being and shown by God ἐν ἐκείνῃ τῇ ἡμέρᾳ, "in that day," the day of God's judgment (see v. 12). Since Onesiphorus ministered to Paul in the most extreme of cases, Paul in turn wishes for Onesiphorus "mercy" in the most crucial time, "that day" (a time that is very much on Paul's mind: cf. v. 12; 4:8). It is not as though Onesiphorus's service has earned his standing with God, since Paul still wishes for him "mercy." But at the same time Paul seems to be influenced by Jesus' teaching that at the judgment such evidences of mercy on one's part demonstrate one's true relationship to Jesus (cf. Mt. 25:36 in context).

It has been suggested that this reference to "that day" and to Onesiphorus separately from his family (v. 16; 4:19) means that he was dead (e.g., Bernard, Fee). This is, of course, a possibility, but the separate references may only mean that Onesiphorus and his family were apart from one another when Paul wrote, or that Paul wanted to express his appreciation not only for Onesiphorus's ministry but also for the support and understanding of his family. Paul speaks in 1 Cor. 1:16 about a man's household while that person is still alive and in 2 Timothy about "that day" in reference to those who are still alive, including himself alone (1:12) and with all believers (4:8). Furthermore, he can wish eschatological blessings for those who are living (e.g., 1 Thes. 5:23b). Therefore, that Onesiphorus was alive and separated from his family is as possible as that he was dead.

Some exegetes (Freundorfer, Spicq, Barclay, Bernard, and Kelly) take the view that this passage indicates that Onesiphorus was dead a step further and regard Paul's words as an example of prayer for the dead. But even if it is assumed that he was dead, Paul's wish is not addressed directly to God, as prayer is, but is rather a statement of what Paul hopes will be the case for Onesiphorus.

Paul returns to his statement of praise and appreciation for Onesiphorus by adding (καί) to the service that Onesiphorus rendered to him in Rome (vv. 16-17) service he rendered in Ephesus. διακονέω is used here in the sense of "serve" generally, i.e., of service of various kinds, with the accusative of the thing indicating the service rendered (BAGD s.v. 2; cf. Hermas,

Similitudes 2.10: διακονῆσαί τι ἀγαθόν, "to do some good service"). The variety and number of services that Onesiphorus rendered is indicated by neuter plural ὅσα, which can be translated "everything that" or "whatever" (BAGD s.v. 2; cf. *RSV:* "all the service"; *NEB:* "the many services"; *NIV:* "in how many ways he helped"). Paul may still be relating things that Onesiphorus did specifically for him, but that is not stated and he may be enlarging his praise of Onesiphorus and his commendation of his service by now referring in general to his service at Ephesus.

Paul concludes this section by indicating that Timothy personally (σύ) "knows" (γινώσκεις) about these matters since they took place in Ephesus (ἐν Ἐφέσῳ), where Timothy has been living and ministering. Ἔφεσος,** a seaport of Asia Minor in the plain of the Cayster River, is referred to as a center of Paul's ministry and of Christian activity several times in Acts (18:19, 21, 24; 19:1, 17, 26; 20:16, 17), twice in 1 Corinthians (15:32; 16:8), possibly in the salutation of Ephesians (1:1), three times in the letters to Timothy (1 Tim. 1:3; 2 Tim. 1:18; 4:12), and in Revelation (1:11; 2:1). σύ, the first of six occurrences in this letter (2:1; 3:10, 14; 4:5, 15), is added for emphasis. The neuter comparative βέλτιον** (a NT hapax), functioning here as an adverb, "well" or "very well," emphasizes even more Timothy's knowledge of the faithful service that Onesiphorus rendered in Ephesus (Robertson, *Grammar,* 277; cf. also Turner, *Grammatical Insights,* 90).

Paul gives at length in vv. 16-18 this example of Onesiphorus (and in v. 15 the negative example of others in Asia) so that it can serve as a reinforcement of his plea to Timothy not to be ashamed but to suffer for the gospel (vv. 13-14). Then, with that example in hand, Paul's very next words again appeal directly to Timothy: Σὺ οὖν, τέκνον μου (2:1).

THE APPEAL RENEWED TO SUFFER AS A GOOD SOLDIER OF CHRIST: 2:1-13

This section begins with "therefore" (οὖν), gathers up the preceding concerns, commands, and examples, and turns to a renewed direct address to Timothy (v. 1). Paul again urges Timothy to find his strength in God (cf. 1:6-7), in the "grace" in Christ (v. 1). He urges him to entrust what he has heard from Paul (cf. 1:13-14) to faithful men who will be able to teach others also (v. 2). These two verses serve as a transition, gathering up these two important emphases before Paul goes on to his call to Timothy to suffer. Thus God's power (and one's need to appropriate it) and God's gospel (and the need to faithfully pass it on) are the objective realities on which Paul bases his continual appeal to Timothy to suffer for the gospel.

That appeal is presented in military terms: Timothy is to suffer hardship as a good soldier of Christ (v. 3). V. 4 draws out the implications for the gospel ministry of one's being a soldier. Paul adds to that the images of the athlete (v. 5) and of the farmer (v. 6) as examples of the service that Timothy should render. Paul asks that the Lord will give understanding as Timothy reflects on these three mental pictures (v. 7).

Above all Paul asks Timothy to "remember Jesus Christ," who, although he was the descendant of King David, suffered and arose victorious from the dead, which is the keynote of the gospel (v. 8). For that gospel Paul also suffers even imprisonment as a criminal (v. 9), but his enduring such things has been the means by which the gospel has come to God's elect and by which they have obtained salvation (v. 10). Hence it has been well worthwhile (v. 10). Furthermore, such suffering or endurance for Christ is the common lot of all Christians, as the faithful saying so clearly says (vv. 11-13, especially v. 12). Thus when Timothy reflects on Paul's call to him to "suffer hardship with me" (v. 3) he must remember Christ and the gospel, the suffering and endurance that Paul has endured for "the sake of those who are chosen," and that this is the calling to which all Christians are called (with its glorious outcome).

BE STRONG IN CHRIST'S GRACE AND ENTRUST THE APOSTOLIC MESSAGE TO FAITHFUL MEN: 2:1-2

2:1 σύ, "you," is an emphatic personal address to Timothy. With οὖν, it contrasts him with those in Asia who turned away from Paul (1:15) and compares him with Paul and Onesiphorus (1:16-18). οὖν, "therefore," an inferential particle introducing the following exhortation (cf. 1:8), denotes that the exhortation is required because of what can be inferred from what precedes it. Thus it harkens back to two elements: the imperatives of vv. 8, 13-14 to suffer for the gospel, to retain the standard of sound words, and to guard the deposit, which all necessitate the enabling power of Christ's grace, and the defection of some (1:15) and the difficulties faced by those who remain faithful (1:16-18). These difficulties also make that power necessary. τέκνον μου (see 1 Tim. 1:2), "my child," a warm personal appeal to Timothy's spiritual relationship to Paul, adds the ever-present personal dimension to the robust imperative that follows (and to the imperative in v. 3).

Paul exhorts Timothy with the present passive imperative of ἐνδυναμόω, a verb that means in the passive "be strengthened," and thus also "become strong," and that is consistently used in the NT of spiritual strength (7x in the NT, all but one in Paul). The present tense indicates Timothy's need for continual dependence on God, i.e., "keep on being strengthened."

ἐν with τῇ χάριτι is, as Kelly says, "probably instrumental: 'by means of,' or 'in the power of.' " The repeated τῇ before ἐν Χριστῷ Ἰησοῦ indicates that this phrase modifies χάριτι and signifies that the "grace" is that found in Christ and in union with him (for ἐν Χριστῷ Ἰησοῦ in this letter see 1:1, 13; 2:10; 3:12, 15 and especially 1:9, where the phrase is used with χάριν; for an overview on the use of ἐν Χριστῷ and literature see M. Harris, *NIDNTT* III, 1192). This is in accord with most of the other Pauline occurrences of ἐνδυναμόω, where the one doing the strengthening is the κύριος (Eph. 6:10; 2 Tim. 4:17) or Χριστὸς Ἰησοῦς (2 Tim. 2:1) or simply ὁ ἐνδυναμῶν με (Phil. 4:13: "he who strengthens me"). χάρις is that which strengthens one to live the Christian life and to accomplish what God asks, whether it be in doing some activity or in bearing suffering. χάρις is God's gracious enabling power (cf. 2 Cor. 9:8; Tit. 2:11-14).

2:2 Paul combines with the need for personal spiritual strength (v. 1) the need to handle rightly and communicate faithfully the apostolic message (cf. 1:6-8, 13-14; 1 Tim. 4:6-16, especially v. 16, where this combination is succinctly stated). Timothy is to "entrust" to "faithful men" what he has "heard" from Paul, ἃ ἤκουσας παρ' ἐμοῦ (cf. 1:13). Paul uses ἀκούω to refer to his apostolic message because that message was so often given in oral preaching and teaching (for ἀκούω in this sense see Rom. 10:14, 18; 2 Cor. 12:6; Eph. 1:13; 4:21; especially Phil. 4:9; Col. 1:6, 23; 1 Tim. 4:16; 2 Tim. 4:17).

Paul refers to this message with the indefinite plural relative pronoun ἅ, which is appropriately rendered by the broad and indefinite terms "what" *(RSV)* or "the things [which]" *(NIV, NASB)* and which includes all of his teaching (cf. 1:13-14). He has made explicit this sense of the authority and permanent significance of his words on several earlier occasions (cf. 1 Thes. 2:13). He speaks of his teaching as "tradition(s)" (παράδοσις) received from him and to be held and followed by Christians (2 Thes. 2:15; 3:6-7) and commends the Corinthians for holding firmly to the "traditions" just as he delivered them (1 Cor. 11:2). He says of the things that he writes that they "are the Lord's commandment" (1 Cor. 14:37) and requires that his letters be read and shared with other churches (1 Thes. 5:27; Col. 4:16). So it comes as no surprise that what he has done throughout his ministry he now requires Timothy to do, i.e., to see that that teaching be faithfully entrusted to "faithful men."

Paul qualifies his statement about "the things that you have heard from me" with διὰ πολλῶν μαρτύρων. It is not immediately clear what these words mean. Some have suggested that διά be understood as "through" and that Paul is saying that Timothy has received Paul's message "through" the teaching and ministry of others. But that seems unlikely since Timothy has so often been with Paul and because it does little justice to the meaning of μαρτύρων, "witnesses."

Chrysostom (and others since him) suggested that διά be understood, instead, in the sense of "in the presence of" and that the μαρτύρων bear witness to what was taught and who received the teaching (for this meaning of διά see Lock; BAGD s.v. A.III.2a; Chrysostom wrote: "You did not hear in secret or privately, but in the presence of many, with all openness of speech"). Within this view, it is suggested that "witnesses" refers to those present at Timothy's "ordination" (1 Tim. 4:14; 2 Tim. 1:6) and that they bear witness to the fact that then and there Paul instructed him and entrusted to him the "sound words." Appeal is made to the fact that the only other occurrence of the phrase "many witnesses" (πολλῶν μαρτύρων) is found in such a setting (1 Tim. 6:12). It is doubtful, however, that Paul has this exclusively in view because not all of what Timothy heard from Paul was communicated to Timothy on that occasion.

This consideration has brought many to the probably correct position that the phrase is used in a wider sense (but not one that excludes the occasion of ordination). In that wider sense the witnesses (likely fellow ministers of Paul and Timothy) testify to the "soundness" of those words and to the fact that those words are the truth of God that should be passed on. That the witnesses are "many" also testifies to the truth that Paul has proclaimed those words openly and publicly (cf. Acts 20:20, 27). It is a public teaching testified to and known not just by Timothy or by some few friends and colleagues but by "many witnesses" (πολλῶν μαρτύρων, πολλῶν in the sense of "numerous," BAGD s.v. πολύς I.1aα; cf. Gal. 2:6-9).

ταῦτα, "these things," in the next clause refers back to ἃ ἤκουσας κτλ., to that which Timothy has heard from Paul. Plural ταῦτα emphasizes that Paul wants all that he has taught to be passed on. παράθου is second aorist middle imperative of παρατίθημι, which is used in the NT in the middle with the meaning "entrust" (Lk. 12:28; 23:46; Acts 14:23; 20:32; 1 Tim. 1:18; 1 Pet. 4:19). Timothy is to "entrust" "these things" "for safekeeping" and for "transmission to others" (BAGD s.v. 2bα).

That safekeeping is, indeed, in mind is signaled by the designation of those to whom "these things" are to be entrusted as πιστοῖς, "faithful." πιστοῖς is not used in this setting to designate them as "believing" (which is assumed) but as "trustworthy" and "dependable," ones to whom one can "entrust" such important truths. This imagery is seen also in 1 Cor. 4:1-2, where Paul speaks of himself, Apollos, and Cephas as "stewards of God's mysteries" (and in Tit. 1:7 he calls the presbyters/overseers "stewards"). In 1 Cor. 4:1-2, 17 Paul's faithfulness consists in his rightly communicating the mysteries of God and Timothy's in his faithfully handing on the public teaching of the apostle (that which he teaches "everywhere in every church"). The context signifies that this significance is intended here also. This point is important because there are those who are in opposition to the truth (v. 25), who will turn away from the truth and not endure sound doctrine (4:3-4). Furthermore, there are leaders who will oppose the truth (3:8) and who go astray from the truth (2:18). In such a setting, it is imperative that those to whom the teachings of the apostle are entrusted (to pass them on to others) be "faithful." Faithfulness negatively consists in their not losing, neglecting, ignoring, or falsifying (like the false teachers mentioned in this letter) what Paul has said, and positively consists of their "handling accurately the word of truth" (2:15).

Since the task committed to these faithful ones is that of teaching others also, it is certain that they are the same group of whom Paul wrote in 1 Timothy, the presbyters who "work hard in word and teaching" (5:17), and also in Titus, the presbyters/overseers who are "holding fast the faithful word that is in accordance with the teaching" so that they are "able both to exhort in sound doctrine and refute those who contradict" (1:9).

These "faithful" ones were men. Their task was "to teach" an audience that included the entire church, a task forbidden to women because of the men in the audience (1 Tim. 2:12; cf. 1 Cor. 14:34ff.). These presbyters/overseers were required to be men in view of their duty to rule over their own households (1 Tim. 3:4-5; cf. Eph. 5:22ff.; 6:4; Col. 3:21). Therefore, ἄνθρωπος is used here, as on occasion elsewhere in the NT (Mt. 19:5; 1 Cor. 7:1; Eph. 5:31) and in the LXX (1 Esdras 9:40; Tobit 6:7) and other literature, of " 'man, adult male' . . . in contrast to a woman" (BAGD s.v. 2bα; cf. 2 Tim. 3:8) rather than in its more general sense. As elsewhere in the NT the plural is used of those who bear this teaching responsibility (cf. 1 Tim. 5:17; 1 Thes. 5:12, 13; Eph. 4:11; Phil. 1:1; Acts 14:23; 20:17, 28).

Timothy is to entrust what he has heard from Paul to others marked by their ability to teach others (cf. Ellicott; BAGD s.v. ὅστις 2). Their teaching activity is future (future ἔσονται) in that it takes place after they have been entrusted with Paul's teachings. ἱκανοί (cf. 1 Cor. 15:9; 2 Cor. 2:16; 3:5) is used here in the sense of "competent, qualified and able" (BAGD s.v. 2) with the infinitive διδάξαι, "to teach" (cf. 2 Thes. 2:15; 1 Tim. 2:12; 4:11; 6:2), denoting that which they are able to do (Burton, *Syntax,* §376; cf. διδακτικός** in 1 Tim. 3:2; 2 Tim. 2:24).

ἑτέρους, "others," is used here, as often in the NT, in much the same sense as ἄλλος. It represents an indefinite number distinct from those who teach and most likely implies that they, or more probably some portion of them, will in turn carry on this process of teaching the apostolic message (cf. H. W. Beyer, *TDNT* II, 702). καί, "also," puts emphasis on ἑτέρους. Plummer is correct in suggesting that this brief reference to men being taught so that they can teach others gives evidence of "the earliest traces of a theological school." But the focus of the passage is on the absolute value and crucial importance of what the apostle taught.

SUFFER HARDSHIP AS A GOOD SOLDIER OF CHRIST: 2:3-7

With imperative συγκακοπάθησον (v. 3) Paul returns to the main reason that Timothy needs to be "strengthened in the grace that is in Christ Jesus" (v. 1). This section (and the next) drives home the need for suffering hardship as a good soldier of Christ with the imagery of the soldier (v. 4) being supplemented with that of an athlete (v. 5) and a farmer (v. 6). Paul concludes with an appeal for reflection, understanding, and application (v. 7).

2:3 συγκακοπάθησον, "suffer hardship with" (see *TCGNT* for preferring this reading over σὺ οὖν κακοπάθησον), resumes the exhortation given at the beginning of the letter (see 1:8). This exhortation will be included in Paul's last charge to Timothy (4:1-5, κακοπάθησον). As in 1:8 no reference is given for συγ-, and here as there it most likely refers to Paul because Paul applies this concept to himself in v. 9 (κακοπαθῶ) and uses πάσχω of himself in 1:12 following the use of συγκακοπάθησον in 1:8.

ὡς, "as," introduces the comparison: Timothy must suffer as a soldier. Paul uses military imagery elsewhere (e.g., 2 Cor. 10:3-5; Eph. 6:10-17; Phm. 2; see Pfitzner, *Agon Motif,* 157-86), though not always with the same words (στρατιώτης, "soldier," here only in Pl.*, NT 27x; cf. στρατεύω in Pl.* 4x: 1 Cor. 9:7; 2 Cor. 10:3; 1 Tim. 1:18; here; see O. Bauernfeind, *TDNT* VII, 701-13), often in a context of struggling against opponents of the gospel, as in 1 Tim. 1:18. Paul uses καλός, "good," here in the sense of praiseworthy or outstanding (cf. τὴν καλὴν στρατείαν in 1 Tim. 1:18). Genitive Χριστοῦ

Ἰησοῦ indicates the one who has enlisted Timothy and whom he serves as a soldier and prepares the way for the analysis in v. 4.

2:4 The statement in this verse speaks of the discipline needed to be a soldier. The operative verbs are "entangle" and "please." The soldier does not become entangled in things that would be a hindrance to his single-minded dedication to follow gladly the commands of his leader. The implication is that Timothy should not let anything in this life distract him, Christ's soldier, from pleasing and following Christ, his commander, even though such a course involves suffering hardship. οὐδείς, "no one," makes the statement a general principle. The participle στρατευόμενος (in Pl.* at 1 Cor. 9:7; 2 Cor. 10:3; 1 Tim. 1:18) places emphasis on the actual involvement of the soldier in his task. *TEV* has wisely captured that by rendering the participle with "a soldier on active duty." ἐμπλέκεται** is either passive, "is entangled," or middle, "entangles himself," and is used only figuratively in the NT (also in 2 Pet. 2:20) of the experience of one caught up in something. πραγματείαις** (a NT hapax) is used here and in other early Christian literature only in the plural and has the meaning "undertakings" or "affairs." τοῦ βίου is used here of earthly or everyday "life" (BAGD s.v. 1; cf. Lk. 8:14).

This assertion is given to teach Timothy through analogy, not as direct instruction. The analogy teaches that ministers should not be distracted by the normal affairs of everyday life in such a way that they cannot and do not give themselves wholeheartedly to their commander and his orders (cf. the same concern for every professed believer in Lk. 8:14, which is obviously meant in terms of priorities and not as an absolute). Paul concretely applies this principle in 1 Corinthians 9, insisting that ministers be paid so that they can devote themselves to their ministry (1 Cor. 9:7-14; cf. Gal. 6:6; 1 Tim. 5:17-18; Tit. 3:13-14; 3 Jn. 5-8). But this application is not absolute: Paul presents this argument for paying ministers together with an argument for the propriety of his own tent-making work (1 Cor. 9:12, 15ff.), noting, however, that he does that work to further his service for Christ, not in such a way that it distracts him from that service (vv. 18ff.). Thus this passage does not teach that Timothy, or any other minister, should withdraw from everyday life, but that he should not let it and its affairs distract him from service to his commander.

A ἵνα clause sets forth the purpose for this demand. A soldier is to be unentangled so that he is free to "please" (ἀρέσῃ; perhaps to "please" by good service, as Lock suggests, referring to Milligan, *Thessalonians,* at 1 Thes. 2:4) "the one who enlisted him as a soldier" (τῷ στρατολογήσαντι,** a biblical hapax). Paul uses the participial form probably because it emphasizes that a man is a soldier because someone enlisted him and entails that, therefore, he should serve that one. Timothy is Christ's soldier because Christ enlisted him (v. 3), and therefore he ought to serve him with unentangled service. The implication, following v. 3, is that such service involves suffering and that Timothy should be willing to please his commander by bearing such suffering.

2:5 Paul adds (δέ) the analogy of a law-abiding athlete as a model for Timothy. Adverbial καί, "also," indicates that this image is making much the same point as the preceding one (cf. Ellicott and *NIV:* "likewise"). This statement regarding the athlete is a general principle, as is evidenced by the generalizing ἐὰν . . . τις (BAGD s.v. τίς 1aγ; 1 Tim. 1:8) and especially by the concluding ἐὰν μὴ νομίμως ἀθλήσῃ. The principle is stated under the figure of anyone who "competes in a contest" (ἀθλέω,** a biblical hapax used twice in this verse; cf. E. Stauffer, *TDNT* I, 167f.; συναθλέω** in Phil. 1:27; 4:3).

Only with the apodosis (οὐ στεφανοῦται) with its exception clause (ἐὰν μὴ νομίμως ἀθλήσῃ) is the principle fully stated: "He is not crowned unless he competes by the rules." The principle is that, just as with a soldier, so also with an athlete there are things that must be done. στεφανοῦται** (also in Heb. 2:7, 8), "is crowned," refers to the wreath (στέφανον) that the victor wins as the prize (τὸ βραβεῖον) in the games of the day (1 Cor. 9:24-25; cf. W. Grundmann, *TDNT* VII, 615-36). 1 Cor. 9:25 also refers to a perishable wreath, indicating that the analogy points to an imperishable one. In 2 Tim. 4:8 we learn that the analogy points to a "crown of righteousness."

ἐὰν μή introduces the exception clause that qualifies the apodosis: One is not crowned "unless." The crucial word is νομίμως** (also in 1 Tim. 1:8), which is emphasized by its position. It means here "in accordance with the rules or laws of the athletic event" (cf. BAGD). Whether Paul was reflecting the requirement of some games that the athlete declare that he has trained the required number of months before being permitted to compete (see Kelly, Lock) need not be answered to understand the point of the analogy. The point is that the athlete must compete by whatever rules there are to gain the desired goal. νομίμως generalizes and leaves that point undefined, but in so doing makes the principle all the more forceful. For the Christian minister the point is that one of the laws of the Christian life is that God requires him to be willing to suffer hardship (v. 3; cf. 1:8). Paul makes this point explicitly in 3:12 (cf. Mt. 5:10-12 par. Lk. 6:22-23). The image of being crowned with a wreath has introduced the idea of blessing and reward.

2:6 The image of the farmer who receives his share of the crops reiterates the idea of reward and continues the emphasis on the need for suffering by the use of the qualification "hard-working" (κοπιῶντα). In this context the verb κοπιάω means "work hard, toil" but also carries, in the transferable lesson of the analogy, the nuances "strive" and "struggle" (BAGD s.v. 2). This word is one of Paul's favorites. He knows quite well its literal and physical significance from his own experience (1 Cor. 4:12) and urges such diligence upon Christians in their daily work (Eph. 4:28).

Against this backdrop of his own experience, he most often uses the term to refer to the effort and struggle needed in spiritual ministry (cf. especially 1 Cor. 15:10; Phil. 2:16; Col. 1:29; and elsewhere in the PE* 1 Tim. 4:10; 5:17). The participle presents the condition (Bouma, Ridderbos) necessary for the farmer, just as there were conditions necessary for the athlete and the soldier. Paul does not hesitate to present such a condition in this image and elsewhere because his exhortations are premised on the enabling power of the grace in Christ (v. 1; cf. 1 Cor. 15:10; Col. 1:29).

The image highlights not only the necessity for "hard work" but also the reward that results from such labor and carries on the note of reward sounded in the preceding image (v. 5). δεῖ with accusative τὸν κοπιῶντα γεωργόν and the infinitive μεταλαμβάνειν can be rendered literally "it is necessary for the hard-working farmer to receive." In idiomatic English the phrase is turned around with the hard-working farmer placed near the beginning of the sentence and the words "ought" *(NASB, RSV)* or "should" *(TEV, NIV)* rendering δεῖ. In any event, δεῖ expresses "the compulsion of what is fitting" (BAGD s.v. 6; cf. v. 24). μεταλαμβάνειν (here only in Pl.* although twice Acts has Paul using the word: 27:33, 34; cf. μετάλημψις in 1 Tim. 4:3) is used in the sense of "receive one's share of" (cf. G. Delling, *TDNT* IV, 10f.). The farmer receives his share of "the crops" (τῶν καρπῶν, literally "fruits," but as LSJM point out, usually "the fruits of the earth").

πρῶτον, "first," has been a puzzle for commentators. A basic question is whether it represents only something in the image of the farmer or is intended to carry over to Timothy's situation. (1) Calvin and others have suggested that πρῶτον be taken adverbially with the participle κοπιῶντα: It is necessary that the farmer should first labor, and then enjoy the fruits. But it is doubtful that the Greek can be properly understood in this way, and thus most commentators have rejected this solution (e.g., Ellicott). (2) Others have suggested that the reference here is to the "first share of the crops" that the supported minister is to receive (e.g., Dibelius-Conzelmann, Hanson; cf. 1 Cor. 9:7, 10). Fee correctly repudiates this position by saying that it "is totally foreign to the context." (3) If Paul does intend πρῶτον to carry over to Timothy's situation and refer to something that the minister shares in here and now before his future reward, then it might refer to his seeing the spiritual results of his labors in the life of converts. Paul does talk about the "fruit" of his missionary endeavor among the Gentiles (Rom. 1:13) and refers to those who have become Christians under his ministry as his "crown" (Phil. 4:1; 1 Thes. 2:19). But even this solution, although more in keeping with the context and flow of the argument, seems less likely than (4) the recognition that πρῶτον is simply part of the imagery and is not to be pressed in regard to Timothy's situation. The farmer's arduous labors are so certainly rewarded that one can speak of the farmer as partaking of the fruits "first," before anyone else does.

2:7 Imperative νόει urges Timothy to "consider," i.e., to contemplatively "think over" this series of analogies (represented by the relative pronoun ὅ; see *NA*[26] on the variant reading ἅ) that Paul has just finished "saying" (λέγω, a graphic first person singular present tense verb). Paul urges such contemplation "because" (as the *TEV* appropriately renders γάρ) he is confident that "the Lord will give understanding" (cf. Mk. 4:11 par. Mt. 13:11/Lk. 8:10).

It is difficult to decide whether Christ or the Father is intended by ὁ κύριος. ("It is a mark of the exalted meaning of the term 'the Lord' as the early Christians used it that it is not always easy to see whether they meant Jesus or the Father" [Morris, *NT Theology,* 167].) The title was last used twice in 1:18 of both persons, but the last occurrence there referred to the Father. Since Paul speaks elsewhere of the Father giving understanding (Eph. 3:2-4), it is likely that he is referring to him here (cf. also Pr. 2:6 LXX: κύριος δίδωσιν σοφίαν, καὶ ἀπὸ προσώπου αὐτοῦ γνῶσις καὶ σύνεσις). Furthermore, there is no identification of ὁ κύριος here with the reference to Christ in the next verse.

The predictive future δώσει, "he will give," is a promise that Paul gives to Timothy (σοι) in order to encourage the response that he has just urged on Timothy. This combination of a promise of divine enablement with an exhortation to responsible human activity recalls vv. 1 and 3. Paul urges reflection "because," as he says, in that activity the Lord will give "insight" and "understanding" (σύνεσιν; cf. especially Col. 1:9; 2:2). He says that the Lord will do so ἐν πᾶσιν, "in everything," i.e., in all the intended implications of the analogies in vv. 4-6 (ἐν πᾶσιν elsewhere in the PE in 1 Tim. 3:11; Tit. 2:9, 10b; 2 Tim. 4:5).

Paul has called on Timothy to suffer hardship and has placed before him three models for him to consider in that service: The soldier who pleases his commander and is not distracted from his service to him, the law-abiding athlete who gains the crown, and the hard-working farmer who receives his share of the crops. Together they speak of a vigorous and undivided service that is rewarded (cf. 1 Cor. 15:58).

THREE BASES FOR THE APPEAL TO SUFFER AND ENDURE: 2:8-13

The appeal to suffer hardship (v. 3) is now undergirded by two examples, Jesus (v. 8) and Paul (vv. 9-10), and by the fact that all believers recognize that they must endure for Christ (vv. 11-13, especially v. 12). Each of these three provides a reason for suffering and enduring. In the case of Jesus the unstated but implicit reason is that only through his suffering was redemption accomplished and death vanquished. Even he had to suffer. Paul suffers (v. 9) and is willing to endure all things so that "the chosen" "may obtain the salvation in Christ Jesus with eternal glory." In the case of all Christians, enduring is part of their calling, and the result of their endurance is that they "reign with Christ."

2:8 Paul urges Timothy always to "keep in mind" and "think about" (μνημόνευε, present imperative) Jesus Christ, the one raised from the dead, the descendant of David, who is both according to the Pauline gospel. This is one of the few places in the PE (1 Tim. 6:3, 14; Tit. 1:1; 2:13; 3:6) and the only place in 2 Timothy where Ἰησοῦν Χριστόν occurs in this order. This may reflect Paul's adoption of a phrase including the name as it was spoken in the Christian community, or it may be a stylistic variation. It seems most likely, however, that Paul intended to emphasize Jesus' humanity by placing first the name given at his birth (see the comments on 1 Tim. 1:1), since it would be meaningful to Timothy in this context (so Lock).

Timothy is to remember Jesus — the one set apart as God's anointed (Χριστόν) — as raised from the dead. Jesus' suffering placed him among the dead but the resurrection brought him out from them (νεκρῶν here means "all the dead," BAGD s.v. 2a with a list of occurrences; ἐκ [τῶν] νεκρῶν occurs 20x in Paul, 17x anarthrous and 16x with the verb ἐγείρω). The perfect participle ἐγηγερμένον lays stress on the fact that he is still risen (like the perfect verbs in 1 Cor. 15:4, 12-20; cf. Robertson). It is used syntactically as an adverbial participle in indirect discourse after the verb μνημόνευε: "Remember that Jesus Christ has been raised from the dead" (cf. Robertson, *Grammar,* 1041). Where Paul uses "raised from the dead" (ἐγείρω with ἐκ νεκρῶν) and indicates the one who does the raising, it is God the Father (both when the verb is active, Rom. 4:24; 8:11; Eph. 1:20; Col. 2:12; 1 Thes. 1:10, and when it is passive, Rom. 6:4). This consistent practice implies that the one who raises is God the Father here also. Timothy is to remember that Jesus is raised from death itself, and that triumph is to encourage him when he contemplates suffering hardship for Christ.

ἐκ σπέρματος Δαυίδ, literally "out of the seed of David," occurs in the NT only here and in Rom. 1:3 and Jn. 7:42. In both Pauline occurrences it appears in connection with the resurrection of Christ and as an essential aspect of Paul's gospel. That the Messiah is a "descendant of David" (idiomatically rendered) is also conveyed in all four Gospels, Acts, and Revelation (Mt. 1:1; 2:5ff.; 22:41-45 par. Mk. 12:35-37/Lk. 20:41-44; Acts 2:25-36; 13:23; Rev. 22:16) and is based on the God's promise in the OT (e.g., 2 Sa. 7:12ff.; Ps. 89:3f.; Je. 23:5). "Descendant of David" indicates Jesus' physical lineage (Rom. 1:3) and connects him to the promise that David's descendant would reign forever (again 2 Sa. 7:12ff.). As the promised messianic king of David's line, he suffered and was raised from the dead (cf. Lk. 24:26, 46). In fact, he entered into his glory and reign through such suffering (cf. again Lk. 24:26 and 2 Tim. 2:12).

The Davidic Messiah who suffered and was raised from the dead is the very essence of Paul's gospel. Genitive μου in κατὰ τὸ εὐαγγέλιόν μου ("according to my gospel," elsewhere in Paul in Rom. 2:16; 16:25) indicates who it is that tells this good news (cf. 1:11). Thus the phrase speaks of the good news that Paul proclaims (cf. BAGD s.v. 2bβ; 2 Cor. 4:3; 1 Thes. 1:5; 2 Thes. 2:14). On εὐαγγέλιον see the comments on 1 Tim. 1:11 (the other PE* occurrences are in 2 Tim. 1:8, 10; on Paul's references to Jesus' earthly life in his preaching see Lategan, *Die Aardse Jesus*).

2:9 The significance of ἐν ᾧ in the first clause of this verse is difficult to determine. The antecedent of the relative pronoun ᾧ is most likely εὐαγγέλιον, not Ἰησοῦν Χριστόν. ἐν has been understood in various ways, e.g., "in whose service" *(NEB)*, or in a causal sense, "for which" *(RSV, NASB, NIV)*. The latter commends itself through comparison with 1:12, where a similar transition is presented in the flow of argument (Ridderbos).

κακοπαθῶ** (also in 4:5; Jas. 5:13) means generally "suffer evil." What evil Paul suffers is related in what follows. μέχρι, "until," is used here of degree or measure, "even to the point of" (BAGD s.v. 1c; cf. Phil. 2:8; Heb. 12:4). Paul is suffering even to the point of δεσμῶν (Pl.* 8x), literally "bonds, chains," but more likely simply "imprisonment," as the word was often used (cf. BAGD s.v. 1), including the other Pauline occurrences (Phil. 1:7, 13, 14, 17; Col. 4:18; Phm. 10, 13). Paul's suffering is imprisonment "like a criminal" (κακοῦργος**), like one who has committed "gross misdeeds and serious crimes" (BAGD; see Lk. 23:32-33, 39).

In contrast (ἀλλά) to his imprisonment, Paul vigorously asserts that "the word of God is not imprisoned." He wants to make clear that his suffering and imprisonment does not hinder the gospel's progress (cf. Phil. 1:12ff.). ὁ λόγος τοῦ θεοῦ (Pl.* 10x: Rom. 9:6; 1 Cor. 14:36; 2 Cor. 2:17; 4:2; Phil. 1:14 [variant reading]; Col. 1:25; 1 Thes. 2:13; 1 Tim. 4:5; Tit. 2:5), "the word of God," is used by Paul to designate the message and teachings from God, sometimes with more emphasis on the central gospel content as here (and, e.g., 2 Cor. 2:17; 4:2; Phil. 1:14) and sometimes to refer to any particular truth that has been communicated (as in 1 Cor. 14:36; 1 Tim. 4:5; G. Kittel, *TDNT* IV, 115f. seems to recognize only the former).

οὐ δέδεται is a play on words, with δέδεται used figuratively with the negative to contrast with δεσμῶν. The importance of the statement is heightened by the perfect tense, which says, in effect, that God's word has not been and is not now "bound" or "imprisoned" (Ellicott). Paul will go on to say (v. 10) how his imprisonment has been used by God to bring God's message to those he has chosen and thus how it is worthwhile (cf. Phil. 1:12ff.: Paul's imprisonment has turned out "for the greater progress of the gospel").

2:10 διὰ τοῦτο (see 1 Tim. 1:16), "for this reason" or "therefore," is tied syntactically to the following prepositional phrase with διά and to the ἵνα clause, which together supply the reason appealed to by this phrase. Therefore, it is for this reason (cf. BAGD s.v. διά B.II.1), i.e., the salvation of the elect, that Paul endures all things. With this statement Paul shifts from the (συγ)κακοπαθέω verb forms (1:8; 2:3, 9) to ὑπομένω, which is also used in v. 12 in the "faithful saying." ὑπομένω means generally "remain," with the predominant note being that one remains instead of fleeing so that one "endures" in trouble, affliction, and persecution (BAGD s.v. 2; Pl.* 4x). Once Paul specifies what it is that one must endure (Rom. 12:12), but otherwise he uses absolute πάντα, "all things," "everything" (here and in 1 Cor. 13:7), or gives no specification at all (as in v. 12).

Paul's endurance is purposeful. He endures "all things" διὰ τοὺς ἐκλεκτούς, "for the sake of the elect." ἐκλεκτός (NT 22x, Pl.* 6x, 5x of humans, once of angels [1 Tim. 5:21]) refers generally to one who is or those who are "chosen." When Paul uses the word of humans, he usually places it in the descriptive phrase ἐκλεκτοὶ θεοῦ (here; Rom. 8:33; Col. 3:12; Tit. 1:1; in Rom. 16:13 he adds ἐν κυρίῳ); θεοῦ indicates the one who chooses (cf. the consistent Pauline usage of θεός as the subject, stated or clearly implied, of the cognate verb ἐκλέγομαι, 1 Cor. 1:27, 28; Eph. 1:4). The word thus represents "those whom God has chosen fr[om] the generality of mankind and drawn to himself" (BAGD s.v. 1b).

The elect are chosen "to obtain the salvation that is in Christ Jesus" (cf. Acts 13:48; see Hendriksen on this election). Paul believes that God has chosen from the generality of mankind some whom he will draw to himself; therefore, he is willing to give himself to be the instrument through whom they hear the gospel, are so drawn to God, and obtain salvation (cf. Acts 18:9-10). He can bear up under whatever difficulties because those whom God has chosen will respond and obtain salvation.

The ἵνα clause gives the particular purpose in view for those who are chosen. αὐτοί, "they," is used for emphasis and refers back to τοὺς ἐκλεκτούς. Adverbial καί ("also") puts emphasis on the αὐτοί. The meaning of καὶ αὐτοί, "they also," is in effect, therefore, "they as well as I" (Robertson; καὶ αὐτοί appears 40x in the NT, 7x in Paul, of which Rom. 11:31 is the only other place where αὐτοί represents the third person plural). τύχωσιν (NT 12x, Pl. 4x) means here "attain" or "obtain" with the genitive of the thing obtained (with this construction and general nuance in Lk. 20:35; Acts 24:2; 26:22; 27:3; Heb. 8:26; 11:35).

Paul is willing to endure all things so that "they" may obtain σωτηρία (NT 45x, Pl. 18x, PE*2x, here and 3:15). σωτηρία with the meaning "salvation" is found in the NT only in connection with Christ as Savior (BAGD s.v. 2), as here, "the salvation that is in Christ Jesus" (cf. 3:15; Rom. 1:16; 10:10). The "elect" must obtain salvation, and that salvation is in Christ. Thus here as elsewhere in Paul we find election in Christ (e.g., 1:10; Eph. 1:4ff.) and salvation in Christ.

σωτηρία here seems to be the present spiritual deliverance that has come into the life of the one who has obtained it by hearing the gospel and coming to faith in Christ. That it exists in the present is evidenced by the fact that a person may obtain it here and now — through Paul's efforts, by the apparent distinction between salvation and later "eternal glory," and by the description of σωτηρία as a present possession by the phrase "through faith in Jesus Christ" in its only other occurrence in 2 Timothy (3:15; cf. Rom. 1:16). Of course for Paul the concept of σωτηρία as a whole includes both present and future aspects, so that in another setting he can speak of it from its future aspect by saying that "now salvation is nearer to us than when we first believed" (Rom. 13:11).

μετὰ δόξης αἰωνίου, "with eternal glory," refers to the glory and splendor of the next life. Since δόξα (see the comments on 1 Tim. 1:11; 3:16) is used normally in the NT of God's glory, majesty, and sublimity, it is natural that it also be used of the future eternal state (αἰωνίου) and realm of existence in which his splendor is everywhere and immediately present and, as here, of that in which the redeemed participate in a marvelous and endless way as they behold his splendor in a full and direct way (cf. 1 Jn. 3:2; Rom. 5:2; 1 Cor. 2:8; 2 Cor. 3:18; Eph. 1:17; Phil. 3:21; Col. 3:4; 2 Thes. 1:9; 2:14; Tit. 2:13). In 1 Pet. 5:10 (the only other NT occurrence of δόξης αἰωνίου; cf. 2 Cor. 4:17: αἰώνιον βάρος δόξης) the "eternal glory" is said to be God's ("his," αὐτοῦ).

2:11-13 Paul now turns to the last of the three bases for endurance, which is the promised privilege of reigning with Christ. He does so by drawing Timothy's attention to a well-known "faithful saying" about the Christian life that has as one of its basic affirmations the necessity of enduring ("*if* we endure," v. 12a). The other statements of the saying remind Timothy that by union with Christ in his death Christians now live with Christ (v. 11), warn that denial of Christ, the alternative to endurance, carries the consequence of denial by Christ (v. 12b), and encourage sometimes faithless Christians that Christ remains faithful to them (v. 13). The saying as a whole thus provides a compact reminder to Timothy of the status of the Christian's life in and with Christ and does so in words that were acknowledged as recognized truth by Christian believers.

2:11a On πιστὸς ὁ λόγος see 1 Tim. 1:15 (cf. 1 Tim. 3:1; 4:9; Tit. 3:8). This occurrence of these words is undoubtedly used as the others were, as a combination "quotation and affirmation" formula. ὁ λόγος signifies that the words are a "saying" and πιστός commends the saying.

But does this formula refer to what precedes or to what follows (see Knight, *Faithful Sayings,* 112-15)? Of those who think that it refers to something in the preceding verses (e.g., Ellicott, Fausset, Holtz, Ridderbos, Schlatter, H. von Soden, Weiss, and N. J. D. White), most also take the general viewpoint that πιστὸς ὁ λόγος does not refer to a saying as such (e.g.,

Ridderbos). Many of these say that vv. 11ff., even if they are not what the formula refers to, are, in fact, a "saying" (e.g., Fausset, Holtz, and von Soden; White disagrees). Schlatter maintains that the formula always refers to a statement about salvation and thus that here it points to the soteriological statement that precedes it. But the use of the formula in 1 Tim. 3:1 has eliminated this necessity. Among the verses chosen by those who think that the formula refers to that which precedes are vv. 8 (e.g., Weiss, who also includes v. 9), 10 (Fausset), and vv. 4-11 (White).

Perhaps the most forceful objection offered to finding the λόγος in what follows the formula is that γάρ in v. 11 is out of place if the formula refers to vv. 11ff. (e.g., Ellicott and Weiss). This γάρ is understood as connecting vv. 11ff. to the preceding and therefore as a further demonstration that what precedes, not what follows, is the λόγος.

Among those who identify vv. 11ff. as the λόγος, some (Huther, Lenski, van Oosterzee, and Wohlenberg) take γάρ as "namely" and thus as emphasizing what follows in the saying. Most (Bernard, Easton, Gealy, Guthrie, Hendriksen, and Kelly), however, take γάρ as referring to what preceded the saying in the original hymn, of which only part is cited here. Fee, on the other hand, suggests that "the *gar* is probably explanatory — and thus intentional — but does not refer to 'this is a true saying.' Rather it goes back to all of the appeal in verses 1-10." Understanding γάρ as "namely" is somewhat unnatural and not in accord with the usual usage of the word. The other two suggestions are more plausible and may not be mutually exclusive, if Spicq is correct in suggesting that Paul paraphrases the first part of the hymn in vv. 8-10, intermingling his own thoughts and words. The words about Christ in v. 8 might be part of the original hymn, and thus γάρ might have referred to them in the original hymn and might still refer to them in this paraphrased form now. The συν- verbs in vv. 11-12 imply some preceding antecedent in the original setting of the larger saying and an antecedent in the present context. That antecedent is undoubtedly Christ. Thus vv. 11b-13 fit well with what precedes in their present setting and may play a similar role to that which they played in their original setting. Therefore, γάρ does not present an obstacle to πιστὸς ὁ λόγος referring to vv. 11bff.

Against referring πιστὸς ὁ λόγος to what precedes is the personal note that characterizes vv. 8-10 (v. 8: "*my* gospel"; v. 9: "*I* suffer hardship"; v. 10: "*I* endure"), which reflects Paul's situation as one in bonds. It is unlikely that Paul would use πιστὸς ὁ λόγος of something so personal since the other sayings connected with the formula do not do so. A further objection to v. 8 is its position some verses removed from the formula. V. 10b, with its rich soteriological content, would be a candidate for the "saying" were it not that Paul expresses in it why he is willing to endure all things, a very personal framework.

With vv. 11b-13 we find a different situation. Instead of the first person singular we find first person plural verb forms, conveying a corporate rather than strictly personal sense, which lends itself to a "saying" (cf. Tit. 3:5ff.). Furthermore, the structure of vv. 11b-13 is so striking that almost all commentators identify it as a "hymn" or "saying." The overall symmetry is found in four lines consisting of four conditional clauses. The structure of each protasis is the same: εἰ plus a first person plural verb. In the first two lines the verbs in both the protases and the apodoses are first person plural active, three of the four verbs have the prefix συν, and the apodoses consist of καί with the verb. In the last two lines the apodoses begin with κἀκεῖνος and ἐκεῖνος and the verbs are third person singular.

The content is as striking as the form. The correlation throughout is between "we" and "he" (Christ). In the first two lines this is manifested by the use of συν- in three of the four verb forms, a usage that speaks of the relationship of Christians ("we") "with" (συν-) Christ. This correlation is carried on in the last two lines by the "we" of the protasis being correlated to or contrasted with the "he" (Christ) of the apodosis (using the emphatic word ἐκεῖνος). The first two protases speak in positive terms, commending a particular kind of relationship to Christ. The third and fourth speak in negative terms of another kind of relation to him. The verbs of the protases present a chronological movement from past to present to future and then back to a consciously chosen present. The first two lines speak of a favorable outcome based on the condition. The third speaks of an unfavorable outcome based on the condition, and the last, as I understand it, speaks of a response not based on the condition but in God himself, as the additional clause after the protasis and apodosis indicates.

Some regard all of vv. 11b-13 as composed by Paul for the occasion (e.g., Lenski, White), but usually all or most of the four lines as a "saying" originally composed in a different situation. Some regard v. 13b as an addition by the author of 2 Timothy (e.g., Hanson, Hendriksen, Lock, von Soden). Others regard only the first two lines as the cited "saying" (above all Easton). But a number of commentators regard all of vv. 11b-13 as the saying (e.g., Barrett, Bernard, and Guthrie). The statement now stands as a whole consisting of vv. 11b-13, and we will deal with it in its present form. The origin of the particular elements will be considered as the question of a possible origin for the saying as a whole arises.

The saying seems to be cited because its emphasis on "enduring" (v. 12: ὑπομένομεν) undergirds Paul's statement about "enduring" (v. 10: ὑπομένω) and shows that endurance is a characteristic that marks the Christian's life (see further Knight, *Faithful Sayings,* 115f.). This stress is, therefore, both the semantic and ideological link to its setting. Nonetheless, Paul cites the saying at a natural transition point, "if we died with him, we shall also live with him," which is itself crucial to a proper understanding of the concept of endurance.

2:11b συναπεθάνομεν in the saying's first line poses two interrelated questions, that of who is referred to with συν- (also of concern with the second and fourth verbs of the saying) and that of the significance of "dying with." W. Grundmann states that the sense of συν- in Paul "is always 'together with' " (*TDNT* VII, 782). It is agreed that this συν- has Christ in view. This is clearly implied by the relationship of the three συν- verbs, because only of Christ would Christians say that they have died, will live, and will reign "with" him. This understanding is strengthened by the identification of the one referred to in the συν- with the one in view in the emphatic ἐκεῖνος in the apodoses of the last two lines of the saying.

Given that consensus, we turn to the second question. Some understand συναπεθάνομεν to refer to dying with Christ in martyrdom and thus understand the saying as a song of martyrdom (e.g., Bernard, Bouma, perhaps Fee, Huther, and von Soden). Others understand it as referring to a spiritual union with Christ in his death. Considerations favor the latter. Contextual significance is the first and major consideration: This "death with" results in "life with" (συζήσομεν) Christ (the apodosis). Furthermore, the wording of Rom. 6:8 is nearly identical, but the ideas are developed further in that context. Death with Christ is death to sin (Rom. 6:11), even as Christ died to sin once (v. 10); it is the crucifixion of the old person, the destruction of the body of sin, and release from the bondage of sin in crucifixion with Christ (v. 6). It is in Christ's death (v. 5) that Christians have died with him. And because they have been united with Christ (v. 5) they have died with him in his death, which brought about the inner death of the old person, release from bondage to sin (v. 6), and justification from sin. With this death comes the concomitant life. Gal. 2:20 (vv. 19-20 in Greek editions) expresses the same thought.

Other considerations that favor this view of συναπεθάνομεν over that which takes it as referring to martyrdom include, first, that dying with Christ is a strange way of referring to martyrdom. There is no example in the NT of such usage. Rather, the NT uniformly speaks of dying with Christ in reference to the spiritual death of Christians who have been crucified with Christ (Gal. 2:20 [19]) and who have therefore died with Christ to sin (Rom. 6:3ff.; Col. 2:12). Also the past tense of the verb speaks against it referring to a martyrdom yet to take place. The chronological progression in the protases of the saying (past, present, future, present) would be shattered by a reference to a martyr's death in the first protasis, and "enduring" would be taken as the result of a martyr's death. But "enduring" appropriately comes as the result of *spiritual* death with Christ. Therefore, the "faithful saying" begins with the believer's foundational spiritual experience and by means of the aorist presents it as an accomplished fact.

The apodosis presents a result that comes about on the basis of the fulfillment of the condition in the protasis. The future tense of συζήσομεν,* "we shall live with him" (the verb also in Rom. 6:8; 2 Cor. 7:3), signifies that this result comes after "dying with Christ." But is this the immediate future from the perspective of a past spiritual death, i.e., this present life, or a more distant future, i.e., life with Christ after death, or both? Here again the context of Rom. 6:8 aids our understanding. There, on the basis of Christ's present life "to God" (vv. 9-10), Paul concludes from συζήσομεν αὐτῷ that Christians should "consider [themselves] dead to sin, but alive to God in Christ Jesus" (v. 11). Since this statement demands that Christians "consider" themselves "dead to sin" now, the parallelism within the statement means that they should also "consider" themselves "alive (ζῶντας) to God in Christ Jesus" in this present life. As Christ now lives to God, so they are "alive to God in Christ Jesus." The life they are to live is a present "walk[ing] in newness of life" because they have been united to Christ in his death (v. 4). Thus they may not "still live" (ἔτι ζήσομεν) in sin (v. 2), because those who have been "united with Christ in the likeness of his death" certainly shall be also "in the likeness of his resurrection" (v. 5). They are now "alive from the dead" (v. 13).

It has been objected that future tense συζήσομεν in 2 Tim. 2:11b must refer exclusively to the future life after death (e.g., Huther, Wohlenberg) or the resurrection life (e.g., Ellicott, Weiss). If this argument were acknowledged as valid, it would apply with equal force to Rom. 6:8. But this would be to miss the whole thrust of Romans 6, which is concerned with the *present* effect of union with Christ in a Christian's life. The introductory question of Rom. 6:2 makes that perspective plain: "How shall we who died to sin still live in it?" There also the future tense is used (ἔτι ζήσομεν), and it refers to life here and now, as ἔτι, "still," makes clear. Rom. 6:8, as we have seen, says the same thing as 2 Tim. 2:11b: The one who has died with Christ will live with him — in the present. (Of course life with Christ goes on into the distant future as well: See especially 1 Tim. 4:8; Rom. 6:22; cf. R. Bultmann, *TDNT* II, 869.) Adverbial καί throws emphasis on συζήσομεν and highlights the fact that we are "also" united to Christ in his life just because we were united to him in his death.

2:12a ὑπομένω means generally "remain" or "stay behind." Among its derived meanings, that of "endure" in trouble, affliction, or persecution is dominant in the NT and is seen here in the second line of the saying (cf. LSJM; BAGD; F. Hauck, *TDNT* IV, 581f.). The NT relates what is involved in enduring: Believers endure hatred by all for Christ's sake (Mt. 10:22 par. Mk. 13:13; cf. Mt. 24:13), they persevere in tribulation (Rom. 12:12), they endure great sufferings (Heb. 10:32) and temptation (Jas. 1:12), and they patiently endure suffering for doing good (1 Pet. 2:20). This endurance is to continue throughout their lives, as the use of the present tense (in the four last-named passages) shows. Here also the present tense refers to continual enduring (cf. Hauck, 586: "In most of the NT passages ὑπομένειν refers to the stedfast endurance of the Christians under the difficulties and tests of the present evil age"). Since it is understood here that endurance is for Jesus' sake (cf. Mt. 10:22 par. Mk. 13:13), it was not necessary for Paul to say so explicitly. This is particularly so because of the three συν- verbs in this context, especially the fourth: The one with whom Christians will reign is the one for whom they endure. The NT concept of endurance always has an expectant eschatological note (cf. Mt. 24:13; 10:22; Mk. 13:13; Heb. 12:2; Jas. 1:12), which is present here also in the outcome of endurance, reigning with Christ.

The future tense of συμβασιλεύσομεν refers to an end-time situation that comes after the responsibility of the present tense ὑπομένομεν has ceased, since this state of existence for Christians has ended. This understanding of συμβασιλεύσομεν** is illustrated by its only other NT occurrence, 1 Cor. 4:8, where Paul criticizes those who think and act as if they are already reigning with Christ. He wishes that it were so and then speaks of this present age as one in which "when we are persecuted, we endure" (4:12). The theme of reigning with Christ recurs elsewhere in Paul and the NT (e.g., Mt. 19:28; Lk. 22:29-30; 1 Cor. 6:2; Rev. 3:21; 20:4, 6; 22:5). Here it is presented as an encouragement for enduring, and, as in the first line of the saying adverbial καί, "also," it lays emphasis on the future "reigning with Christ," which, though it is so different from the present experience of enduring, is "also" a result of that enduring.

2:12b The saying turns in its third line from steadfast endurance to the contrary action of denial. And with that it turns from comfort and encouragement to stern warning. It also turns to a future tense presentation of an awesome future possibility, i.e., that the professing Christian will deny the one he claims to have died with and to now live with. The resultant reciprocal action in the apodosis, "he also will deny us," makes it clear that the one denied is Christ, since ἐκεῖνος (here and in v. 13) after the συν- verbs, and in the context of the NT, signifies Christ.

ἀρνέομαι (Pl.* 6x, all in PE: here; 1 Tim. 5:8; Tit. 1:16; 2:12; 2 Tim. 2:13; 3:5) means basically "say no, deny," and is used in the NT of denial of a person with whom there was some prior relationship (see H. Schlier, *TDNT* I, 409-71; Riesenfeld, "ἀρνεῖσθαι"). This is its significance in a saying of Jesus (Mt. 10:33; Lk. 12:9) that may be behind 2 Tim. 2:12b. The particularities involved in denial of Christ come to light in Peter's denial (Mt. 26:69ff. par. Mk. 14:66ff./Lk. 22:54ff./Jn. 18:15ff.; cf. also Mt. 26:34f. par. Mk. 14:30f./Lk. 22:34/Jn. 13:38). Peter not only rejects the truth of the statements of the maid and others (Mt. 26:70 par. Mk. 14:68/Lk. 22:60), in particular he denies any knowledge of Jesus (Mt. 26:72, 74 par. Mk. 14:71/Lk. 22:56; cf. 22:61-62) and his relationship with Jesus (Mk. 14:69-70 par. Lk. 22:58/Jn. 18:26-27). The personal element in denial is also found in 2 Pet. 2:1 ("even denying the Master who bought them"; cf. Jude 4).

Denial of Christ manifests itself in various ways in the NT. It can consist in denying his name (Rev. 3:8) or faith in him (Rev. 2:13). It can thus take the form of forsaking or repudiating the Christian faith and its truths, particularly the truth concerning Jesus. In doing so one personally denies Christ (and the Father, cf. 1 Jn. 2:22-23). The denial can also manifest itself in the moral realm. Some may "profess to know God, but by their deeds deny him" (Tit. 1:16; cf. 1 Tim. 5:8).

The dire consequence of this denial is identified here in the form of a resultant reciprocal action (indicated by the κἀ, "also," a contraction for καί when joined to ἐκεῖνος): "He also will deny us." ἐκεῖνος ("that one" or "he") implicitly refers to Christ (see above). The denial by Christ (ἀρνήσεται) is that future final evaluation which he will make to his Father (Mt. 10:33) in the presence of God's angels (Lk. 12:9) when he returns in glory (cf. Lk. 9:26; Mk. 8:38; cf. also Mt. 7:23). The finality of his denial of those who have denied him will be as permanent and decisive as theirs has been of him, and will thus not be as in Peter's case, where forgiveness was sought and received. For that situation something else must be said, and to that the saying turns with its fourth and last statement.

2:13a The saying returns to the present tense in the fourth line with ἀπιστοῦμεν in the protasis speaking of what Christians might do or be and with the apodosis indicating Christ's response. This response is not a resultant reciprocal action, as in the third line, but finds its explanation in the nature of the one responding (ἀρνήσασθαι γὰρ ἑαυτὸν δύναται).

Does ἀπιστοῦμεν** (NT 6x: Lk. 24:11, 41; Acts 28:24; Rom. 3:3; 1 Pet. 2:7; variant reading in Mk. 16:11, 16) refer here to "unbelief" (so Alford, Bernard, Chrysostom, Ellicott, and Fausset) or to "unfaithfulness" (so Bouma, Guthrie, Hendriksen, Huther, Kelly, Kent, Lenski, Ridderbos, Weiss, N. J. D. White, and Wohlenberg)? The verb normally implies unbelief in the NT, and Ellicott concludes that there is not sufficient reason for departing from this regular meaning here. But it is more appropriate to say that in a slight majority of NT occurrences (4 of 6), i.e., in the non-Pauline texts, the word refers to unbelief, but also that the two Pauline occurrences can be interpreted either way. Furthermore, extrabiblical usage knows the meaning "disobey," under which "unfaithfulness" is a subcategory, along with that of "unbelief" (see LSJM and BAGD for references). These considerations point to the necessity of finding the meaning in this context. The key is that ἀπιστοῦμεν is answered with πιστός in the apodosis just as ἀρνήσεται answers ἀρνησόμεθα in the preceding line. Obviously what is in view in πιστός is God's faithfulness. Thus what is in view in ἀπιστοῦμεν, to which God's faithfulness answers, is "unfaithfulness" (so also BAGD; R. Bultmann, *TDNT* VI, 205, 208). This does not mean that temporary unbelief or lack of trust is not also present in the moment of unfaithfulness, for indeed it is.

But our understanding of ἀπιστοῦμεν here must be bound up with our understanding of this last statement of the saying in its entirety. Might this protasis be giving another, and perhaps worse, expression of denial (v. 12b), or is it giving an expression of the frailty of the believer, which is less than a hardened and final denial? The key is one's understanding of the apodosis, and so to that we must turn: Is Christ faithful to punish and repudiate because he cannot deny the justice and holiness of his being, or is he faithful to hold on to Christians because of his character of fidelity and the permanence of his promise?

ἐκεῖνος is Christ here as in v. 12b. It is he who "remains faithful." Paul's references to the faithfulness of God and Christ are strikingly uniform. This faithfulness is God's fidelity to his promises, and those promises relate to the positive outcome of human salvation (cf. 1 Cor. 1:9). Paul does not mention God's faithfulness as a basis for the certainty that the faithless will be punished, but as the basis for the assurance of the gospel promises (2 Cor. 1:18-20), for safety in temptation (1 Cor. 10:13), for protection from the evil one (2 Thes. 3:3), and for the sanctification and preservation of God's people (1 Thes. 5:24; cf. also Heb. 10:23; 11:11; 1 Pet. 4:19; 1 Jn. 1:9 [note πιστός]; Rev. 1:5; 3:14; 19:11). This understanding is also suggested here by μένει, "he remains," which with πιστός implies that Christ continues as the faithful one in his relationship to Christians. Though they change and become unfaithful (to him, understood), he does not change but has remained faithful (to them, understood). The Pauline and NT usage also suggests that Christ's remaining faithful here also includes his continuing adherence to the divine promises to his people even in the midst of their unfaithfulness. This understanding of the apodosis entails that the protasis most likely refers to temporary unfaithfulness and not to unbelief.

This fourth line of the saying is demonstrated in Christ's faithfulness to Peter even though Peter was so unfaithful that he denied Jesus (Jn. 21:15ff.; Lk. 22:31-32). While the apodoses in the first three lines of the saying result from the corresponding protases, here the apodosis is not the result but the opposite of the protasis. In the fourth statement in the saying, εἰ means "although," not "if."

2:13b Since the protasis does not, therefore, give the basis for the apodosis, a clause is added to give the reason (γάρ) for Christ's fidelity. Here ἀρνήσασθαι means "to say no, to belie, or to be untrue" to his own being (cf. BAGD s.v. 4; Riesenfeld, "ἀρνεῖσθαι," 208, 216; H. Schlier, *TDNT* I, 469, 471). Christ is faithful because of his own nature: He cannot (οὐ δύναται) be untrue to himself (ἑαυτόν). This reason is so necessary to the sense of the fourth line of the saying and to the saying as a whole that it must have been part of the original saying.

2:11b-13 The saying in these verses gives a helpful overview of key aspects of the professing believer's life. The first two lines encouragingly state the glorious results that accrue from one's identification with Christ, first in dying to oneself in union with Christ's death and second in enduring and suffering for Christ throughout one's life. The last two lines state the sad possibilities that an imperfect disciple faces in this life, denial and unfaithfulness. The saying sharply warns against denial, which can only expect denial in turn by Christ. But as a counterbalance comfort is offered to the disciple who is unfaithful by assuring him that Christ will remain faithful to him.

We can only offer a probable answer to the question of the origin of the saying. Since 2 Timothy was written from Rome, then it is possible that the church in Rome developed the first line by reflection on Romans 6 and by utilizing Rom. 6:8 in a contracted form. This is probable not only because of this link but also because the idea of dying with Christ is more fully developed in Romans 6 than anywhere else in the NT. Since Romans 6 relates death with Christ to baptism, it would be appropriate to conjecture that the saying was used in connection with confession of faith at the time of baptism. The third line seems to reflect Jesus' words in Mt. 10:33 and Lk. 12:9, cast here into the mold of the other lines. No very close similarity exists between the second and fourth lines and other NT statements. Thus one can only say that two likely sources have had their impact on the saying, and that the other lines were added as necessary when converts were confessing their faith and receiving baptism.

Paul has quoted the saying as a whole so that its various truths might have their impact on Timothy as he has called on him to suffer and endure for Christ (v. 3). In the light of that call, the second line's promise that those who endure will reign with Christ not only stands out in its relevance to Timothy's situation but is also set in the context of these other truths.

TIMOTHY'S RESPONSIBILITIES IN REGARD TO FALSE TEACHINGS: 2:14-26

This half of the chapter continues Paul's exhortations to Timothy, but now in the context of false teachers and false teaching (vv. 14-18, 23-26) rather than in the context of the non-Christian world, as has been primarily the case up to this point. On the background of the "faithful saying" in vv. 11b-13, with its demands for endurance and its warnings against denial, Paul charges Timothy to remind Christians about the danger of false teaching (v. 14), to handle "the word of truth" accurately (v. 15), and to avoid the error of the false teaching himself (v. 16), knowing particular false teachers who have taught that the resurrection has already taken place (vv. 17-18). Timothy and the church are to be encouraged, in the midst of this apostasy, by the truth that "the Lord knows those who are his" and by the fact that those who are his will abstain from wickedness (v. 19). Paul supports this point by the analogy of the cleansed and useful household vessel (vv. 20-21). To be that kind of vessel Timothy must flee youthful lusts (v. 22a), pursue godliness (v. 22b), and refuse false teaching (v. 23). As the Lord's servant he must be not quarrelsome but kind to all, patient when wronged, and able to teach (v. 24), and must gently seek to correct those in error so that they may repent, come to know the truth (v. 25), and escape the devil's snare (v. 26).

WARNING AGAINST FALSE TEACHING: 2:14-19

Here Paul warns against the error of the false teaching, specifies various forms of that error, and warns against the results of such error (vv. 14, 16, 18). He names certain false teachers who say that the resurrection has taken place (v. 17) and concludes with a counterbalance to the dismay that such apostasy might bring by asserting that God's solid foundation stands firm (v. 19).

2:14 The beginning of a new section is signaled by ταῦτα with the imperative ὑπομίμνῃσκε, "remind." Paul is still addressing Timothy directly, but now initially in terms of others, the "them" understood. The "them" could be Christians in general, but that Timothy is to warn them about the impact of their words upon "those who hear" (τῶν ἀκουόντων) suggests that Paul has in mind the "faithful men" of v. 2. If this is the case, he has returned to what seemed to be an isolated instruction in v. 2, but which is now seen not to be such. V. 1 is developed primarily in vv. 3-13. Now v. 2 is touched on again, not only by this brief word of instruction, but also by the instructions about what a godly teacher should be (vv. 15-16, 21-26). At the same time the preceding words to Timothy, vv. 3-13, in addition to the ταῦτα of v. 2, are the very things that he is to remind them of (on ταῦτα see especially 1 Tim. 4:11; 6:2). ὑπομίμνησκε (Pl. also in Tit. 3:1) is used here in the sense of "call to mind," "bring up" (cf. 3 Jn. 10). Timothy is commanded to bring to the minds of these men the very things that Paul has just brought to his mind.

The present tense of the participle διαμαρτυρόμενος following the present imperative ὑπομίμνησκε implies that the action of the participle is concurrent with that of the imperative. Because of the participle's dependence on the imperative, the force of the imperative carries over so that the participle is in effect a second command. διαμαρτυρέω (Pl.* 4x: 1 Thes. 4:6; 1 Tim. 5:21; 2 Tim. 4:1; in PE with ἐνώπιον τοῦ θεοῦ) means here "charge" or "warn." ἐνώπιον τοῦ θεοῦ, "before God," means here "in God's sight or presence" and is an expression used in assertions that call on God (cf. Gal. 1:20; 1 Tim. 5:21; 6:13; 2 Tim. 4:1; there is no essential difference in meaning in the variant reading ἐνώπιον τοῦ κυρίου; see *TCGNT*). The phrase reminds those charged that they are being called to accountability before God himself.

That which they are charged not to do is signified by μή with the infinitive λογομαχεῖν,** "to dispute about words" (a NT hapax that Robertson suggests was "coined by Paul from *logomachia* [1 Tim. 6:4]"; see *NA*[26] for the variant reading λογομάχει). Paul is not referring to "hair splitting" (contra BAGD) but to the kind of serious dispute about the meaning and significance of words relating to the Christian faith that results, as this passage indicates, in straying from the truth and saying that the resurrection has taken place (vv. 16-18; cf. the consequences of λογομαχία in 1 Tim. 6:4f.). One may also appropriately assume that this passage was written with the previous one about "words" in mind (1:13) and conclude that Paul is contrasting this conduct with what he commended there. Since Timothy has been retaining Paul's words and passing them on (cf. 1:13; 2:2) and since the false teachers were disputing them (cf. vv. 17-18), Paul charges those who would be faithful not to dispute about these words. This correlation is borne out by Paul's admonition of Timothy (as an example to those he warns) to handle accurately "the word of truth" (v. 15), i.e., the apostolic message.

They are not to dispute about words because there is no good result, literally, "for nothing useful" (ἐπ' οὐδὲν χρήσιμον; χρήσιμον** is a NT hapax known since the sixth century BC; see MM) or, in more idiomatic English, "useful for nothing" or "it does no good" *(TEV, NEB)*. And it is detrimental to the hearers. The outcome is the "ruin" or "destruction" (καταστροφῇ,** also in a disputed reading in 2 Pet. 2:6, which see) "of the hearers." Paul uses ἀκούω in a substantive participle construction twice in his letters to Timothy. In the other occurrence (1 Tim. 4:16) "the hearers" (τοὺς ἀκούοντας) are distinguished from Timothy, and it seems that here also Paul distinguishes between those who are called on to minister (cf. v. 2) and those to whom they minister, "the hearers."

2:15 Paul urges Timothy to handle accurately "the word of truth" and thus be a positive example to those he is "charging" of a faithful person and good minister. Paul sets before him the goal of serving in such a way that God will approve of his labors. He urges him with the imperative σπούδασον (see Tit. 3:12), which has the nuances here of "being eager and zealous" and "making every effort." Guthrie says that the word contains the notion of "persistent 'zeal.' "

This imperative intensifies the command expressed by the infinitive clause that it governs, σεαυτὸν δόκιμον παραστῆσαι τῷ θεῷ, "to present yourself approved to God" *(NASB)* or "to present yourself to God as one approved" *(RSV, NIV)*. The general meaning of "present" for παραστῆσαι "becomes almost equivalent to 'make, render' " here (also in Eph. 5:27; Col. 1:22, 28; so BAGD s.v. 1c). The second person singular reflexive pronoun σεαυτόν, "yourself" (placed before the infinitive for emphasis), focuses this command directly on Timothy. He is to seek to present himself "to God" (τῷ θεῷ; cf. the preceding ἐνώπιον τοῦ θεοῦ) as one "approved" (δόκιμον) by the God who examines his life and conduct (for this concept cf. especially 2 Cor. 10:18; cf. also ἀδόκιμος in 2 Tim. 3:8; Tit. 1:16). Paul "lifts the whole question of attestation out of the hands of men and sets it in those of God. God alone decides this issue . . ." (W. Grundmann on 2 Cor. 10:18, *TDNT* II, 258).

Paul develops this concept in the striking phrase ἐργάτης ἀνεπαίσχυντον, literally, "a worker unashamed." Paul (as did Jesus) applies ἐργάτης (Pl.* 4x) to Christian leaders (in a negative setting in 2 Cor. 11:13 and Phil. 3:2; in a positive setting here; and by analogy in 1 Tim. 5:18; cf. συνεργός in Rom. 16:21; 1 Thes. 3:2) because he regards the activity of the ministry as one of labor (cf. κοπιάω in Rom. 16:12; 1 Cor. 15:10; 16:16 [also with συνεργέω]; Phil. 2:16; 1 Thes. 5:12; 1 Tim. 4:10; and especially 5:17) and thus those involved in it as "workers" or "laborers." ἀνεπαίσχυντον** (a NT hapax; cf. Paul's use of ἐπαισχύνομαι, αἰσχύνομαι, and αἰσχύνη) means "unashamed" in the sense that he does not need to be ashamed of his work. The participle ὀρθοτομοῦντα qualifies ἐργάτης and together with the words that follow specifically describes how Timothy may be unashamed: by being a worker who handles accurately the word of truth (ὀρθοτομοῦντα τὸν λόγον τῆς ἀληθείας).

ὀρθοτομέω (found elsewhere independent of NT influence only in Pr. 3:6; 11:5 LXX) means literally "cut straight" or "cut right." There is a growing consensus that the stress is on ὀρθο- ("right") and not on τομέω ("cut") on the analogy of the similarly formed word καινοτομέω ("make a new assertion, renew"; cf. Lock, MM, Dibelius-Conzelmann [examples in n. 5]; H. Köster, *TDNT* VIII, 112). The imagery of a worker working with his materials carries through what began with ἐργάτην.

The material that this worker is to handle correctly is "the word of truth" (τὸν λόγον τῆς ἀληθείας). Only when he handles it correctly will he be unashamed (ἀνεπαίσχυντον). The rendering given in several of the modern translations, using a combination of the verb "handle" and some adverb such as "accurately" *(NASB),* "rightly" *(RSV),* or "correctly" *(NIV),* for the compound verb ὀρθοτομοῦντα with the phrase "the word of truth" as the direct object captures this relationship quite well.

Although Paul has used λόγος before in this letter (see especially v. 9) and elsewhere in the PE and has used ἀλήθεια before in the PE* (1 Tim. 2:4, 7; 3:15; 4:3; 6:5; Tit. 1:1, 14), this is his first use of the two together in the PE and his first use of ἀλήθεια in 2 Timothy. In Col. 1:5 and Eph. 1:13 τὸ εὐαγγέλιον is used to identify "the word of truth" as "the gospel." This fits the context here, where Paul has used "gospel" (τὸ εὐαγγέλιον) as the central concept (1:8, 10; 2:8). He has used the phrase "the word of God" (v. 9) and now refers to God's word as "the word of truth." "Truth" he uses in an absolute sense to contrast it with the error of the false teachers, the false teaching that contradicts and stands over against the word of God, the gospel. This contrast with falsehood marks his use of ἀλήθεια later in 2 Timothy (2:18, 25; 3:7, 8; 4:4) and elsewhere in the PE (e.g., 1 Tim. 6:5; Tit. 1:14; cf., e.g., Gal. 2:5, 14; 2 Thes. 2:10-12). The sense of the phrase here is probably best conveyed in the rendering "the message of the truth." To handle this word correctly is to handle it in accord with its intention and to communicate properly its meaning (cf. 2 Cor. 2:17; 4:2).

2:16 In addition (δέ) Timothy is also warned (just as he was to warn others, v. 14) to "avoid worldly empty chatter." Paul gives two grounds for this warning, one introduced by γάρ in v. 16b, the other by καί in v. 17a: Those who fail to avoid such chatter become even more ungodly, and their erroneous message harms others like a bad disease (cf. Smith-Beekman, *Analysis*).

The warning itself is quite simple and to the point. περιΐστασο** (also in Jn. 11:41; Acts 25:7; Tit. 3:9) means in the middle, as here, "avoid" or "shun." The present tense of the imperative characterizes the action as that which Timothy must constantly do. He is to avoid κενοφωνίας** (see 1 Tim. 6:20), "empty talk," which Paul characterizes here as βεβήλους** (1 Tim. 1:9; 4:7; 6:20; Heb. 12:16), "profane" or "worldly" in the sense of "godless." That Paul uses the same terms in 1 Tim. 6:20 probably indicates that he is dealing with the same false teaching here as there, where κενοφωνίας is a synonym for ματαιολογία in 1 Tim. 1:6. Thus his description of ματαιολογία in 1 Tim. 1:7 may indicate, in part at least, what he means by βεβήλους here (cf. also ματαιολόγος in Tit. 1:9 and the description there of the false teachers and their teaching).

The first reason (γάρ) for avoiding such talk is its dire effect on those who engage in it. Such people are referred to here with the third person plural verb προκόψουσιν, which could, admittedly, refer back to the talk itself, which was plural, so that the talk itself would be said to lead to further ungodliness. But the subject of this verb is the antecedent of αὐτῶν and ὧν in v. 17, which are specified by the names of two persons. Such people will "progress" or "advance" (προκόπτω,** Lk. 2:52; Rom. 13:12; Gal. 1:14; 2 Tim. 3:9, 13; all 3x in the PE of advance in what is bad), with the genitive following the verb indicating that in which they will progress, ἀσεβείας** (Rom. 1:18; 11:26; Tit. 2:12; Jude 15, 18), "ungodliness" or "impiety" in thought and action.

This construction is further qualified by the prepositional phrase ἐπὶ πλεῖον, which is placed first for emphasis and is best rendered "even more," "even greater." " 'They will arrive at an ever greater measure of godlessness' = become more and more involved in godlessness" (BAGD s.v. πολύς II.2c). It may be that these people regarded themselves as "progressives" and that Paul picks up the verb from their usage, ironically indicating that their progress is in ungodliness.

2:17 The coordinating καί joins the first clause of this verse to the preceding clause as the second reason for avoiding "godless empty talk" (v. 16). This time Paul speaks of the effect on others of such talk, "implying," under the image of a spreading disease, "that their teaching will feed upon, or eat away at, the life of the church" (Fee). Paul repeats λόγος and thereby sets "their" (αὐτῶν) "word," what is said by those who engage in this empty talk, in contrast to the "word of truth" (v. 15). ἔχω (here future ἕξει) with νομήν, literally "have pasture," was used figuratively in medical language of the "spreading" of an ulcer (see BAGD s.v. νομή 2 for extrabiblical parallels). The ulcer to which Paul compares this "word" is indicated by the conjunction ὡς, "as," and is that of γάγγραινα** (a biblical hapax but a medical term since Hippocrates, fifth and fourth centuries BC), "gangrene," i.e., decay of tissue in a part of the body where the blood supply is obstructed by injury, disease, etc., which continually spreads.

Having alluded to a group of false teachers by the use of "their," Paul specifies two such teachers (whose teaching will be indicated in v. 18a): ὧν ἐστιν Ὑμέναιος καὶ Φίλητος. ὧν refers back to αὐτῶν and to the subject of προκόψουσιν. Ὑμέναιος,** Hymenaeus, is undoubtedly the man referred to in 1 Tim. 1:20 (see the comments there), whom Paul had already "delivered over to Satan." Hymenaeus is still setting forth his false teaching and here is joined by Φίλητος,** Philetus, about whom nothing more is said in the NT.

2:18 This verse continues the thought begun in the last part of v. 17. The two men named there have "gone astray from the truth." Their error consists of "saying that the resurrection has already taken place."

οἵτινες, "who," is used here of two specific individuals and therefore takes the place of the simple relative pronoun (BAGD s.v. 3). ἠστόχησαν (see

1 Tim. 1:6) is used here with the meaning "deviate," "depart from" and is followed by περὶ τὴν ἀλήθειαν, indicating that from which they have departed. περί with the accusative is used metaphorically here with the meaning "in respect to" (C. F. D. Moule, *Idiom-Book*, 62) or "concerning" (Robertson, *Grammar*, 620). The concept τὴν ἀλήθειαν was introduced in v. 15 with the phrase "the word of truth" and is utilized again to represent the absoluteness of the gospel (cf. Gal. 2:5), as it will be later in this letter (2:25; 3:7, 8; 4:4).

These two men have departed from the truth by "saying that the resurrection has already taken place." The textual evidence favors the inclusion of τήν with ἀνάστασιν (see *UBSGNT, TCGNT*). Paul* uses ἀνάστασις of Jesus' resurrection (Rom. 1:4; 6:5; Phil. 3:10) and otherwise, as here, of a future decisive occasion when humans are to be raised bodily from the dead (1 Cor. 15:12, 13, 21, 42). Hymenaeus and Philetus are "saying" (i.e., teaching; cf. λέγω in 1 Tim. 1:7) that this "resurrection" ἤδη γεγονέναι. γεγονέναι (second perfect active infinitive of γίνομαι), "to have taken place" (see BAGD s.v. I.3) is further emphasized by the addition of the adverb "already," ἤδη.

Their teaching apparently related the resurrection only to the inner spiritual life. It was probably associated with a false asceticism and a low view of the material world, especially of the human body (cf. 1 Tim. 4:1ff.), and might have resulted from an incorrect handling of Paul's words (cf. 2 Pet. 3:16) about Christians being presently raised with Christ (Rom. 6:1-11; Eph. 2:6; 5:14; Col. 2:12, 13; 3:1-4; cf. Irenaeus, *Haer.* 1.23.5; for other early church references see BAGD s.v. ἀνάστασις 2b). Already in 1 Corinthians 15 Paul wrote against a similar (but not identical) form of error about the resurrection of believers, saying that such teaching calls in question Christ's own resurrection and is thus completely unacceptable.

The effect of such teaching is that "they upset the faith of some." καί introduces this result (see BAGD s.v. καί I.1f; cf. 2 Cor. 11:9 for a similar usage of καί). ἀνατρέπουσιν** (literal in Jn. 2:15; figurative in Tit. 1:11) is used here figuratively of "overturning, upsetting, or destroying" the faith of some. Indefinite τινων, "of some," indicates that some but not all of the Christians were affected in this way. Since τὴν πίστιν is "the faith of some," it most likely refers to their personal belief rather than to the body of faith, although the latter was certainly affected if what "some" had believed about the resurrection had been overturned by this new and erroneous teaching.

This error can affect how one regards Jesus' resurrection and its significance for one's future standing and hope for eternity, and thus also how one thinks of the Christian's present relationship to Christ and one's perspective on the body and conduct in this life and attitude to material creation. Therefore, Paul regards it as striking at the heart of Christianity and thus as a departure from the truth.

2:19 Lest Timothy and the Christians in Ephesus be discouraged about the inroads of this false teaching and its effect on some and perhaps even begin to wonder if a massive falling away is to follow, Paul reminds them about the stability and permanence of God's work. He bases this encouragement on two things: God's electing knowledge of his own and the fact that such true believers will abstain from wickedness. In doing so he utilizes statements from Numbers 16 that he quotes and summarizes here as permanent principles on which the Christians can rely.

μέντοι functions here (as it usually does in the NT) as an adversative, "nevertheless," to place the encouraging word that follows over against the discouraging report that precedes. Paul asserts metaphorically that the foundation laid by God in Ephesus and elsewhere stands — even though there are false teachers and some who heed their teaching. Some have suggested that Paul is referring to the gospel message under this imagery, and others that he is referring to the church. The latter is more likely since Paul has done so elsewhere (cf. 1 Tim. 3:15; 1 Cor. 3:10-12; Eph. 2:20-22), and this perspective is strengthened by his use of the house imagery in vv. 20-21.

θεμέλιος, "foundation," is used of either the "foundation" of a building or the elementary beginnings of a thing (BAGD). The two thoughts are combined as the imagery is figuratively applied to the church as the building that God builds (so rather consistently in Paul:* Rom. 15:20; 1 Cor. 3:10-12; Eph. 2:20; the exception is 1 Tim. 6:19; cf. K. L. Schmidt, *TDNT* III, 63f.). The adj. στερεός** (also in Heb. 5:12, 14; 1 Pet. 5:9; cf. στερέωμα in Col. 2:5), "firm, solid," is added to impress on Timothy the strength and permanence of this foundation, a note that the verb ἕστηκεν also takes up (cf. Is. 28:16). This foundation is "God's" (τοῦ θεοῦ), indicating its builder and owner, just as the "house" was "God's" (θεοῦ) in 1 Tim. 3:15. This in itself assures its stability and permanence, as Paul implies later in this verse. Now he says that God's firm foundation "stands" (ἕστηκεν, perfect active indicative of ἵστημι, used here intransitively), i.e., "stands firm," so that it cannot be overturned or destroyed (cf. 1 Cor. 10:12, where this verb is used in contrast to "fall").

The participial construction that follows is used "with a very faint causal force, illustrating the former declaration" (Ellicott). σφραγίς (Pl.* 3x: Rom. 4:11; 1 Cor. 9:2; 13x in Revelation) is used here of the mark or impression made by a seal, i.e., the inscription, and here that latter sense appears by extension (cf. Ex. 28:36; see G. Fitzer, *TDNT* VII, 939-53, especially 948; R. Schippers, *NIDNTT* III, 497-501, especially 500). Seals were used to identify objects and particularly to indicate ownership. Here the seal is the guarantee for the preceding declaration. The particular inscription to which Paul is referring with ταύτης, "this," is set forth in the statements that follow.

The first part of the inscription (singular σφραγίς) is the LXX of Nu. 16:5 with κύριος in place of ὁ θεός. Paul may have used κύριος because it reflects the Hebrew original *(YHWH),* which should guide our understanding of which person of the Godhead he has in view here, especially since he has referred to ὁ θεός in the preceding clause. He turns to Numbers 16 to give encouragement to Timothy and the Christians at Ephesus as they face false teachers and false teaching arising from their midst. As sad as the episode of Korah's rebellion was, it did not devastate the congregation of Israel, and false teaching will not devastate the church at Ephesus. The statement quoted here affirms God's ability to differentiate between true and false believers and becomes here the reason for believing that God's foundation stands firm in the present situation.

The second part of the inscription is joined to the first by καί and is probably a generalized summary of the exhortation in Nu. 16:26 that uses language found elsewhere in the OT, which in this summary form serves as a broad principle. The Lord identified those who were his by calling them to separate from Korah and those who followed Korah. Abstaining from evil is thus an integral part of the inscription and the second half of one great truth. God knows and chooses his people, and they manifest that reality by abstaining from evil.

πᾶς ὁ ὀνομάζων τὸ ὄνομα κυρίου appears to be a slight modification of a phrase in the LXX of Joel 3:5 (πᾶς ὃς ἂν ἐπικαλέσηται τὸ ὄνομα κυρίου), which is quoted in Peter's sermon (Acts 2:21) and by Paul in Rom. 10:13. If this is so, the verb ἐπικαλέσηται has been changed to ὀνομάζων, either to reflect the change from what one should do (call upon) to what one has done (called upon by naming), or the verb may be an alternative Greek rendering of the underlying Hebrew verb *(qarā')*. Paul's use of this phrase from Joel in Romans aids one's understanding of the component parts of the phrase. In Romans 10 calling upon the Lord's name is the expression of faith in the Lord (cf. vv. 11, 13 and especially v. 14). Therefore, here also to name the Lord's name is an expression of faith in him. (The occurrence of κύριος here may have caused Paul [in anticipation] to use κύριος, reflective of the Hebrew in the first half of the inscription, in place of ὁ θεός found in the LXX so that the two halves would contain the same word.) πᾶς, "everyone," makes the command absolute by addressing it to every person who names the name of the Lord.

The response that validates the claim to know the Lord that is made by naming his name (and that confirms the reality of being known by the Lord) is given in the command ἀποστήτω ἀπὸ ἀδικίας. The verb (second aorist active imperative of ἀφίστημι; see 1 Tim. 4:1) is used here in the sense of "keep away from," "abstain," "turn away from." It is not the verb used in the LXX of Nu. 16:26, but it does appear in the response in Nu. 16:27. Paul's attempt to summarize the principle involved in the passage as a whole (Nu. 16:26: "Depart now from the tents of these wicked men") with "turn away from wickedness" may have influenced his choice of the verb.

ἀδικίας means for Paul, as indicated by his usage (cf. Rom. 1:18; 2:8; 2 Thes. 2:10, 12), that which is contrary to the truth, i.e., "unrighteousness" and "wickedness." Hence the inscription commands not only a departure from immorality but also from the error that contradicts the truth and leads to such immorality. Therefore, the concrete application for the Christians in Ephesus is that they turn away from the errors of thought and practice of those who have gone astray from the truth (cf. v. 18).

THE VESSEL FOR HONOR, USEFUL FOR THE MASTER: 2:20-21

The purpose of this analogy about different vessels in a house is to elaborate on the second part of the inscription in v. 19, i.e., on the necessity of turning away from wickedness. The components of the analogy are presented in v. 20, and the analogy is applied in v. 21.

2:20 This verse states that in a large house there are various vessels, some εἰς τιμήν and some εἰς ἀτιμίαν. That some have gone astray from the truth (v. 18) provides the setting for referring to vessels εἰς ἀτιμίαν. Therefore, the large house is to be understood as the Christian community in its broadest sense, within which are false teachers, just as in the Korah situation (see above on v. 19). The analogy could represent society in general (Chrysostom), but that the imagery of the house has been used of the Christian community in 1 Tim. 3:15 favors that understanding here (Alford, Calvin).

Paul says ἐν μεγάλῃ οἰκίᾳ, "in a large house," probably because only in a large house would one find the variety of vessels that he mentions here, especially those that are εἰς ἀτιμίαν. He may also refer to a large house because thereby he can point to the Christian community in the broadest sense and speak of some of its "members" (vessels) as εἰς ἀτιμίαν. Nowhere else does Paul speak of the church or its members in such terms: It is in this setting, not as a generalized definition of what the church is or ought to be, that Paul uses this imagery.

δέ, "now," is a transitional particle. ἐν μεγάλῃ οἰκίᾳ, "in a large house," is "a locational or situational orienter" that "marks the beginning of a figurative illustration" (Smith-Beekman, *Analysis*). The particles οὐκ . . . μόνον and ἀλλὰ καί distinguish two classes within the category of σκεύη that will be carried through with the μέν . . . δέ construction, which relates the distinguishing prepositional phrases εἰς τιμήν and εἰς ἀτιμίαν to the two classes respectively. σκεύη is used here in the sense of "vessel" (cf. C. Maurer, *TDNT* VII, 358-67, especially 364).

Paul has on an earlier occasion referred to three of the four materials that he mentions here — χρυσός, "gold," ἄργυρος (NT 3x), "silver," and ξύλον (NT 2x), "wood" — in this order (1 Cor. 3:12, with cognate form of the words and with other words). There as here the first two are distinguished from the third as representing different categories. The fourth term here, grouped with the third, is ὀστράκινος, "earthenware."

The καί that introduces the μέν . . . δέ functions explicatively, "that is," "namely," indicating that the phrase that follows is intended to explain what went before it. The repeated relative pronoun ἅ is used here as a demonstrative pronoun with the meaning "some . . . others." Some vessels are εἰς τιμήν, literally "for honor," i.e., honored by the use to which they are put or the purpose that they have (cf. BAGD s.v. τιμή 2b; s.v. εἰς 4d). Likewise εἰς ἀτιμίαν, literally "for dishonor," means that a given vessel is dishonored by the use to which it is put or the purpose that it has (cf. Rom. 9:21, where the same two prepositional phrases are used, again with σκεῦος).

Therefore, gold and silver vessels are esteemed as honorable because they are used for honorable functions. Similarly, wood and earthenware vessels are regarded as dishonorable because they are used for garbage or excrement and are sometimes thrown out with their contents. The implication is that there may indeed be vessels like the false teachers in the professing Christian community, but their activity indicates that they are dishonorable.

2:21 Inferential οὖν indicates that the statement it introduces is an inference drawn from the last phrase of v. 20: Since some vessels are for honor, one should "therefore" seek to be one of them. This inference is presented in a conditional sentence introduced by ἐάν, "if." The condition is stated in general terms with the indefinite pronoun τις, "anyone" (on ἐάν τις see the comments on 1 Tim. 1:8). The condition to be met is specified in the words ἐκκαθάρῃ ἑαυτὸν ἀπὸ τούτων. The antecedent of plural τούτων is most likely the nearby plural relative pronoun phrase in v. 20b, ἃ . . . εἰς ἀτιμίαν, "some unto dishonor," which, as has been seen, speaks by implication of the false teachers. (It is possible but not likely that the antecedent of τούτων is the more distant ἀδικίας. Against this is not only that another closer antecedent would be passed over but also that ἀδικίας is singular.) The condition is that one cleanse oneself from the defilement of fellowship with "these" and the effects of their teaching and actions (cf. 3 Jn. 10-11). ἐκκαθαίρω** is used similarly in 1 Cor. 5:7 (cf. the uncompounded verb with the reflexive pronoun in 2 Cor. 7:1 in the light of what precedes it). ἐκ in the compound verb adds a perfective idea, which in this combination means "cleanse *thoroughly*" (cf. Robertson, *Grammar*, 597). The reflexive pronoun ἑαυτόν, "himself," is used because the action called for affects the subject.

In the conclusion, "he will be a vessel for honor," Paul explicitly uses the language of the analogy in v. 20. This use of the neuter noun σκεῦος, "vessel," sets the pattern for the use of the neuter gender in the three phrases that follow. Cleansing "from these" assures that one "will be" (future ἔσται) "a vessel for honor." This conditional sentence underscores the second half of the inscription in v. 19 and applies it to Timothy's situation. To be an honorable vessel one must depart from wickedness by departing from those who practice such (cf. 1 Cor. 5:11, 13; 2 Cor. 6:14–7:1).

The significance of the fulfillment of this condition is spelled out in the three phrases that follow. ἡγιασμένον (perfect passive participle) is used here in the sense of "sanctified" or "made holy" by having been cleansed from the defilement of sin and thus becoming one set apart for God and his service (see especially Eph. 5:26 where a similar [but not identical] sense of cleansing is conveyed by καθαρίζω, the uncompounded form of the verb used in the protasis of this verse). It thus reiterates the aspect of cleansing but in more personal spiritual terms.

εὔχρηστον** (2 Tim. 2:21; 4:11; Phm. 11) τῷ δεσπότῃ, "useful for the master," specifies the significance of this cleansing in terms of the vessel's "personal" relationship to the master of the house. It continues the image of the house with τῷ δεσπότῃ being the master of the house (cf. in the PE* 1 Tim. 6:1, 2; Tit. 2:9) and by analogy representing God (cf. Lk. 2:29; Acts 4:24; 2 Pet. 2:1; Jude 4; Rev. 6:10).

The end result is that the vessel "is prepared," i.e., has been put in readiness (ἡτοιμασμένον, perfect passive participle). The task for which (εἰς) it has been put in readiness is πᾶν ἔργον ἀγαθόν, "every good work," an apt phrase that fits the imagery of the house and also the application intended, the life of the Christian, especially that of the Christian minister. "Prepared for every good work" thus specifies how useful the vessel is to the master in that it is fit for every type of service. The phrase πᾶν ἔργον ἀγαθόν is used elsewhere by Paul some 7x (see 1 Tim. 5:10) of the wide range of good deeds that one is called to do as a Christian (cf. Eph. 2:10). Paul returns to this phrase in 2 Tim. 3:17.

TIMOTHY'S RESPONSIBILITIES AS THE LORD'S SERVANT: 2:22-26

This is the concluding paragraph of vv. 14-26. In it Timothy is again made the focus of attention as the Lord's servant. First he is urged to flee those "lusts" that may be a particular problem for him and to pursue the characteristics that should mark all Christians (v. 22). Next he is urged to refuse "speculations" because they "produce quarrels" (v. 23). Last of all, and at some length, he is reminded of his need to be a kind, patient, and effective leader-teacher who can be used to bring people to repentance and to knowledge of the truth and to lead them away from the captivity of error and the devil (vv. 24-26).

2:22 δέ provides a simple connection to what precedes. It is difficult to ascertain whether any contrast is intended. *NASB* renders it with "now" as a transitional particle without any contrast intended (see BAGD s.v. 2). Similarly, a number of modern translations *(NEB, NIV, TEV)* do not translate δέ at all, which is idiomatically possible when a simple connection is desired (BAGD).

Paul commands Timothy to "flee from" (φεῦγε, Pl.* 4x), i.e., "avoid" or "shun." Paul consistently uses the word in its imperative form to urge the Christian to avoid some particular form of sin (1 Cor. 6:18; 10:14; see 1 Tim.

6:11) and in the PE sets it in contrast with the command to "pursue" (δίωκε) various virtues. Here Timothy is urged to flee νεωτερικὰς ἐπιθυμίας. ἐπιθυμίας (see 1 Tim. 6:9), "desires," is usually used in the NT of wrong desires, as is demanded here by the context. There has been much discussion of what Paul has in mind here with νεωτερικάς** (a NT hapax), "youthful." The alternatives have included that this is a reiterated warning against the error of the false teachers, that Paul is speaking of the sensual sins of youth, and that he has in mind youthful sins of judgment and temperament. Some would find the answer in the contrast with the positive list that follows, so that the "desires" would be the opposites of the virtues commended.

V. 22 does not simply reiterate what precedes it but gives, rather, a wider perspective on what true sanctification means. It is added to forestall the false impression that avoiding fellowship with false teachers, essential as that is, is all there is to sanctification. As we have noted, Paul always uses "flee" (φεῦγε) in relation to particular sins, not sins in general. The specific relevance of "youthful" desires is found in the fact that Timothy is young (cf. 1 Tim. 4:12) and in the fact that the "desires" Paul has in mind may be especially problematic in Timothy's situation. The positive list that follows appears to be too general to help in identifying these "desires."

But it is possible that in what follows in vv. 23ff. Paul is making more specific what he has stated more generally in directing Timothy's work as the Lord's servant. His repetition of the warning about "speculations" (v. 23) may point to one of the besetting desires of youthfulness with which he is concerned. His words about not being quarrelsome, about being patient when wronged (v. 24), and about gentleness when correcting those in opposition (v. 25) may give us some idea of the contrary tendencies of youthfulness about which he is warning. In the final analysis we can only say that this is a possibility: Paul does not say explicitly what he means by "youthful desires." Furthermore, the characteristics warned against in vv. 23ff. are not unique to youth, though they are perhaps more characteristic of youth. (W. Metzger, in *"neôterikai epithymíai,"* identifies the "youthful desires" with the tendency to turn from the traditional to the new and alluring.)

δέ joins to the need to flee youthful desires four positive virtues, indicating that the negative needs to be followed by the positive (cf. 1 Tim. 6:11). δίωκε is used in the NT either of persecution or, as here, in the sense of "pursue," "follow zealously after" Christian virtues (cf. Rom. 12:13; 14:19; 1 Cor. 14:1; 1 Thes. 5:15; 1 Tim. 6:11; A. Oepke, *TDNT* II, 229f.). There are six Pauline virtue lists with more than three items (2 Cor. 6:6-7; Gal. 5:22-23; Col. 3:12-15; 1 Tim. 6:11; 2 Tim. 2:22; 3:10). Of the four virtues in this list "righteousness" is found in three of these lists, "faith" in four, "love" in all six, and "peace" in three. The list here thus shares three items with 1 Tim. 6:11 and three with Gal. 5:22-23, but in terms of the order and number of the virtues, the closest parallel is 1 Tim. 6:11.

δικαιοσύνη means generally "righteousness, uprightness." This virtue, as all Christian virtues, is brought about by the transforming work of Christ (cf. Rom. 6:13-19; Eph. 4:24; Phil. 1:11), which is accomplished in Christians by the Holy Spirit (Rom. 14:17; cf. 8:3-4). Paul indicates later in this letter that all scripture is profitable "for training in righteousness" (2 Tim. 3:17) and thereby sets up scripture as the standard of righteousness. δικαιοσύνη as human ethical action "is almost always used in the NT for the right conduct of man which follows the will of God and is pleasing to Him . . ." (G. Schrenk, *TDNT* II, 198).

πίστις, when used in a list of virtues, means either "faithfulness," i.e., "reliability," or "faith," i.e., "trust" in God. Paul does occasionally use πίστις in the sense of "faithfulness" (Rom. 3:3; Tit. 2:10; perhaps 2 Thes. 1:4), and that has been suggested as the meaning in the list at Gal. 5:22, but these occurrences are infrequent among the total of twenty-two uses of the word. Elsewhere, especially where, as here, πίστις precedes "love" (1 Thes. 1:3; Tit. 2:2; Col. 1:4; 1 Cor. 13:13), the meaning "faith" is clear. In the list in 2 Pet. 1:5ff. πίστις picks up the preceding reference in v. 1, where "faith" is clearly meant. All this points to the meaning "faith" here.

ἀγάπη (see especially 1 Tim. 1:5; 4:12) means "love," but here, as so often, the object of the love is not specified. Since Jesus' love command involves both God and neighbor, it is possible that Paul intends both here. Where, however, he indicates or implies an object it is most often fellow human beings (cf. Rom. 12:9; 13:10; 14:15; 2 Cor. 8:7; Gal. 5:13; Eph. 1:15; 4:2; Col. 1:4; 2:2; 1 Thes. 3:12; 5:13; 2 Thes. 1:3; Phm. 5, 7), and this seems to be the main focus in 1 Corinthians 13, which is followed by words similar to those here, διώκετε τὴν ἀγάπην (1 Cor. 14:1). Thus if some specific object is intended here, and it need not be, it would probably be fellow humans.

εἰρήνη (see 1 Tim. 1:2) in the NT and Paul denotes tranquility, harmony, and stability. In particular, the peace brought by Christ enables Christians to live at peace and to continually pursue that which makes for peace with one another (Eph. 2:14-18; Rom. 14:19; 2 Cor. 13:11; Gal. 5:22; Eph. 4:3; Col. 3:15). This note dominates Paul's letters and is most likely in view here.

The question arises whether μετὰ τῶν ἐπικαλουμένων τὸν κύριον ἐκ καθαρᾶς καρδίας, "with those who call on the Lord from a pure heart," goes with the last item or with all four, and also whether "with" (μετά) is to be taken as "in association with" or as defining the extent to which the attitude is to be pursued. "In the context calling for withdrawal from evil, it seems likely that Paul would suggest that Timothy not attempt to maintain peaceful relationship with those who are impure" (Smith-Beekman, *Analysis*). Thus this phrase is most likely a qualification of the last item and an indication in particular of those with whom peace should be pursued (contra W. Foerster, *TDNT* II, 416f.).

τῶν ἐπικαλουμένων τὸν κύριον seems to be another echo of Joel 3:5 and an abbreviated form of what is found in v. 19 and in Acts 2:21; Rom.

10:13; and 1 Cor. 1:2 (cf. also Acts 9:14, 21; 22:16). Here, in contrast with v. 19, Paul returns to the verb found in the OT and usually in NT citations of the Joel text. Because κύριον is either explicitly (1 Cor. 1:2) or contextually (Rom. 10:13) related to Christ in the use of this phrase elsewhere in Paul, one should probably assume that it is so intended here, since clear indicators otherwise are not evident in this context. ἐκ καθαρᾶς καρδίας** (the phrase elsewhere only in 1 Tim. 1:5 and in a variant reading in 1 Pet. 1:22), "out of a pure heart," i.e., one cleansed from sin, seems to be added to designate those who call upon the Lord, i.e, confess the Lord, in reality and who have changed lives (v. 19), reiterating the idea of cleansing (v. 21).

2:23 In further contrast (δέ) to the call to Timothy to pursue virtues is this admonition to refuse speculations. Timothy is commanded παραιτοῦ (Pl.* and PE* 4x: 1 Tim. 4:7, which see; 5:11; Tit. 3:10; here; in the first and last passages with reference to things), "refuse, reject, avoid, have nothing to do with" speculations. ζήτησις** (cf. ἐκζήτησις** in 1 Tim. 1:4) has among its meanings "investigation" (Acts 25:20) and "discussion, debate" (Jn. 3:25; Acts 15:27). Neither of these positive meanings is intended here since the word is clearly marked as negative by the adjectives "foolish" and "ignorant." That the word is used in 1 Tim. 6:4 in an essentially negative sense probably has inclined some to render it "controversies" (BAGD s.v. 2; *RSV*) or "speculations" *(NASB, NEB),* while its otherwise positive use may have inclined others to render it "arguments" *(TEV, NIV),* which lets the context and the qualifications indicate that here the word is used in a negative sense. In two of its three PE occurrences the activity is labeled "foolish" (μωράς, NT 14x, PE* 2x: Tit. 3:9) not only in the sense of "stupid" but also in the sense of "sinful and culpable" (G. Bertram, *TDNT* IV, 845). These arguments are further designated as ἀπαιδεύτους** (a NT hapax), i.e., "ignorant" in the sense of not informed. Perhaps the best explication of what Paul means by these two adjectives here is 1 Tim. 1:7: "They understand neither what they are saying nor the matters about which they make confident assertions."

The ground for this admonition is identified in the concluding εἰδώς clause. The participle εἰδώς (in Paul cf. 1 Tim. 1:9; Tit. 3:11; 2 Tim. 2:23; 3:14; Phm. 21; plural εἰδότες in Rom. 5:3; 6:9; 1 Cor. 15:58; 2 Cor. 1:7; 4:14; 5:6, 11; Gal. 2:16; Eph. 6:8, 9; Phil. 1:16; Col. 3:24; 4:1; 1 Thes. 1:4) is used to indicate *that* one knows and often, as here, is followed by ὅτι (only 2 Tim. 3:14 and 1 Thes. 1:4 are possible exceptions) introducing the clause that identifies *what* one is supposed to know. γεννῶσιν, literally "they beget or bear," is used figuratively in the sense of "breed" or "produce" with ζητήσεις understood as the subject. The "arguments" produce μάχας** (also in 2 Cor. 7:5; Tit. 3:9; Jas. 4:1, always plural and always used of nonphysical conflict; cf. BAGD), "quarrels." Because these foolish arguments are unedifying and particularly because they beget quarrels Timothy is to avoid them.

2:24-26 Paul turns from admonitions relating more directly to Timothy the individual to ones relating more to him (and others) as the Lord's servant(s) ministering to and relating to others, especially those caught up in the error of the false teachers. He states how the Lord's servant should relate to others (v. 24), how he should seek to help them (v. 25a), what it is that God will accomplish in their lives through his ministry (v. 25b), and finally who and what they need to be delivered from (v. 26).

2:24 Paul has said (v. 23) that foolish and ignorant arguments produce quarrels (μάχας). He now immediately joins (δέ) to that the forthright comment that "the Lord's servant" himself must not be quarrelsome (μάχεσθαι). Paul then moves by contrast (ἀλλά) to three things that the Lord's servant should be: "kind to all," "able to teach," and "patient when wronged." Paul reverts to a more general and indirect way of speaking, referring to the "Lord's servant," which would include Timothy and others, rather than referring directly to Timothy as he has done in the previous two verses. He does this so that this instruction will benefit not only Timothy but also others who serve in that capacity (cf. 2:2, 14).

Here Paul applies the term δοῦλος, "slave," to Timothy and others for the first time in the PE. The word bears the spiritual sense that it has when he applies it to himself in Tit. 1:1 (see the comments there) and to himself and his coworkers outside the PE (e.g., Rom. 1:1; 2 Cor. 4:5; Gal. 1:10; Phil. 1:1, of Timothy and himself; Col. 4:12). He also uses the word literally on several occasions. The word can be used in a spiritual sense of the exclusive nature of a person's relationship to God (so in the LXX in the Psalms and elsewhere; see R. Tuente, *NIDNTT* III, 595). Paul connects the secular usage to the religious usage by designating the "free" Christian as "Christ's slave" (see 1 Cor. 7:22) and thus uses the word of the members and leaders of the Christian community. "The distinctive thing about the concept of the *doulos* is the subordinate, obligatory and responsible nature of his service in his exclusive relation to his Lord" (Tuente, 596).

Here Paul uses δοῦλος of a leader in the Christian community, as the further descriptions of the task of the δοῦλος make evident ("able to teach," "with gentleness correcting those who are in opposition"). Picking up on the last title of deity that he used, κυρίου from v. 22, he designates the leader as δοῦλος κυρίου. Since Paul nearly always uses δοῦλος with Χριστοῦ (Rom. 1:1; Gal. 1:10; Phil. 1:1; Col. 4:12; cf. Eph. 6:5; κυρίου in 1 Cor. 7:22; θεοῦ in Tit. 1:1) and since that last occurrence of κυρίου probably had Christ in mind (v. 22), it is most likely that the κύριος here is Christ. That which is distinctive of the Lord's slave is that the Lord determines his conduct and activity.

δεῖ, the impersonal verb denoting compulsion of any kind, when used with the negative (οὐ here) conveys the idea that something should not happen (BAGD s.v. 6). The Lord's servant must not μάχεσθαι** (Jn. 6:52;

Acts 7:26; Jas. 4:1; except in Acts 7:26 of nonphysical fighting), "be quarrelsome" (cf. ἄμαχος, especially in 1 Tim. 3:3; Tit. 3:2).

With ἀλλά, "but," Paul introduces his description of what the Lord's servant must be. ἤπιον** (variant reading in 1 Thes. 2:7) signifies one who is "gentle" and "kind." And that characteristic and attitude is to be extended πρὸς πάντας, "to all," with πρός here in the sense of "toward" or "with" (BAGD s.v. III.4b; cf. Tit. 3:2). Although the Lord's servant may not be able to be at peace with all (v. 22), he is still called on to be kind and gentle to all.

He must also be "able to teach" (διδακτικόν,** 1 Tim. 3:2), i.e., to communicate "the word of truth" (cf. v. 15) effectively even to those in opposition (with correction, repentance, and appropriation of the truth being the goal: see v. 25). Finally, he must be ἀνεξίκακον** (a NT hapax), a word that "denotes an attitude of patient forbearance towards those who are in opposition" (Guthrie; cf. 1 Pet. 2:23).

2:25 The first part of this verse indicates the task that this teacher is to be engaged in and the last part the outcome that is sought. In effect the first half parallels the positive virtues of the preceding verse and relates them to the action necessary. Thus the three characteristics just named, "gentle," "able to teach," and "forbearing," correspond respectively to the three elements in the task to be performed — "in meekness," "instructing," and "those in opposition" (so Smith-Beekman, *Analysis*).

ἐν πραΰτητι denotes the manner in which instruction is to be given (see BAGD s.v. ἐν III.2 for examples of this usage). πραΰτης means "gentleness, humility, courtesy, considerateness, meekness" (BAGD; see Tit. 3:2; cf. Gal. 6:1). Its meaning may be further appreciated by its use in contrast to such opposites as roughness, bad temper, sudden anger, and brusqueness (see F. Hauck and S. Schulz, *TDNT* VI, 646 for references).

The specific task to be performed is παιδεύοντα (the verb in Pl.* 5x: 1 Cor. 11:32; 2 Cor. 6:9; 1 Tim. 1:20; Tit. 2:12), which has essentially two meanings: "instructing" and "practicing (some form of) discipline." Here both nuances seem to be operative. The concern for "knowledge of the truth" (v. 25) and that "they may come to their senses" (v. 26) both imply instruction. That those being instructed are in opposition and that the foremost concern for them is repentance (v. 25) implies some form of correction. The best understanding of the term here would be, then, that of corrective instruction, or simply put, "correcting" *(RSV, TEV, NIV).* The combination of this participle and the preceding prepositional phrase is a concrete example of the general principle enunciated in Eph. 4:15 of "speaking the truth in love."

Those to be corrected are τοὺς ἀντιδιατιθεμένους** (a NT hapax; cf. τοὺς ἀντιλέγοντας in Tit. 1:9), "those who are in opposition," or "the opponents," those who have begun to stand in opposition to the servants of the Lord and what they teach, either as false teachers themselves or as those influenced by false teachers. Here, as in 1 Tim. 1:20, Paul does not give up on the false teachers or their followers, but always hopes for and works for their restoration, as the following words demonstrate (cf. Tit. 1:13).

The hoped for outcome is: μήποτε δώῃ αὐτοῖς ὁ θεὸς μετάνοιαν εἰς ἐπίγνωσιν ἀληθείας, "if perhaps God may grant them repentance leading to the knowledge of the truth." μήποτε is used as an interrogative particle (BAGD s.v. 3bβ; cf. Lk. 3:15) with the idea of contingency (Robertson, *Grammar,* 988), "if perhaps," "in the hope that." Two things are said simultaneously in δώῃ αὐτοῖς ὁ θεὸς μετάνοιαν. The first is that "God (ὁ θεός) gives (δώῃ) repentance" (cf. Acts 5:31; 11:18 for other instances of διδόναι μετάνοιαν; cf. also 2 Cor. 7:9-10). It is he who changes the heart and turns a person around (cf. Tit. 3:5). The second is that in the case of the "opponents" all that Paul can say is that God "may" (subjunctive δώῃ expressing possibility but not certainty) give them repentance.

This possible outcome is described to give urgency and expectancy to the ministry that Paul has called for. The emphasis in this description is on God and his sovereign will, so that the ministry of "the Lord's servant" and the outcome that is sought may be kept in that perspective (cf. 1 Cor. 3:6). μετάνοια (NT 22x, Pl.* 4x: Rom. 2:4; 2 Cor. 7:9, 10; here), "repentance," is regarded in the NT as true acknowledgment of sin, sorrow for it, and turning from it (cf. 2 Cor. 7:9-10), in response to which God forgives sin (cf. Acts 5:31; Mk. 1:4; Lk. 3:3). Thus the correction seeks to produce a "change of mind" with regard to the erroneous ideas and deeds of the "opponents."

Concomitant with that repentance is "knowledge of the truth" (εἰς ἐπίγνωσιν ἀληθείας), i.e., a turning from error "unto" (εἰς) knowledge of the truth. The phrase ἐπίγνωσιν ἀληθείας (see the comments on 1 Tim. 2:4) is found in the NT almost exclusively in the PE, though its component parts are found in Paul's earlier letters with the same sense. In this phrase ἀληθείας represents "the content of Christianity as the absolute truth" (BAGD s.v. 2b). Therefore, the phrase as a whole indicates a person's coming to know and acknowledge that truth.

2:26 Here Paul gives the ultimate explanation for the opposition of the "opponents" — they are held captive by the devil — and thus also what is needed from that perspective, which is release from the devil's snare. In this way he moves back behind the human level (i.e., opposition) to the evil one and his hold on the life of those in opposition.

The devil's grasp is broken when the opponents spiritually break out of the intoxicating effect of that snare and "come to their senses" (ἀνανήψωσιν,** a NT hapax, see the extrabiblical references in BAGD). παγίς,** "snare," "trap" (used figuratively in Rom. 11:9; in 1 Tim. 3:7 "of the devil," as here; 6:9; literal in Lk. 21:35), is used figuratively here of the intellectual allurement of error. The trap is one that the devil sets for others. In the NT singular ὁ διάβολος with the definite article (30 of 37x in the NT) is always used of one particular powerful and evil spiritual figure, as in the LXX (e.g.,

Jb. 2:1; Zc. 3:1f.; 1 Ch. 21:1; see further BAGD; 1 Tim. 3:6-7; elsewhere in this sense in Paul in Eph. 4:27; 6:11).

The participial clause that follows expands on this reason that the "opponents" are in the devil's snare (ἐζωγρημένοι ὑπ' αὐτοῦ) and on what that involves (εἰς τὸ ἐκείνου θέλημα). The perfect passive participle ἐζωγρημένοι (literally "being captured alive") conveys the sense of "having been taken and held captive" and expresses the decisive hold that the devil has. (The verb ζωγρέω is used elsewhere in the NT only in Lk. 5:10; both here and there it is used figuratively in a spiritual sense of catching humans, albeit from opposite perspectives; for alternative suggestions on this verb and especially for αὐτοῦ and ἐκείνου see below.) ὑπό with genitive αὐτοῦ and a passive verb denotes the agent who has taken and held the opponents captive. Since the verb carries forward, and explicates, the previous imagery about the "trap" of the devil, αὐτοῦ most naturally refers to the devil, the nearest antecedent.

εἰς in the phrase εἰς τὸ ἐκείνου θέλημα points to the idea of purpose: The opponents were taken captive *in order to do* "the will of that one" (literally). τὸ θέλημα is used here in the objective sense of "what is willed, what one wishes to happen" and especially of "what one wishes to bring about by the activity of others" (BAGD s.v. 1cβ). ἐκείνου interchanges with αὐτοῦ here and thus bears the meaning "his" (see BAGD s.v. 1b and the references there) and refers, as αὐτοῦ did, to τοῦ διαβόλου.

ἐκείνου has, however, prompted other interpretations. ἐκεῖνος is most often used with the meaning "that" or "that one" to refer to a remote object. Some believe, therefore, that it refers to something other than the antecedent of αὐτοῦ, which is τοῦ διαβόλου. One view identifies the antecedent of ἐκείνου as God and set off the phrase from what precedes with a comma: "by him, to do his (that is, God's) will" (*RSV* margin; so also in the margin of *RV, ASV,* and *NASB;* in the main text of Moffatt). Thus Bernard, Ellicott, Jeremias, and Weiss understand the phrase as giving the result for those who repent: They now do God's will.

This view should probably be rejected for two reasons. First, ἐκεῖνος does not always refer to a remoter object; it is used elsewhere interchangeably with αὐτοῦ (see BAGD, Hanson). Second, this makes for a syntactically difficult reading, since ὁ θεός is quite some distance from ἐκείνου.

The second alternative understands αὐτοῦ as referring to "the Lord's servant" (v. 24) and ἐκείνου as referring to God: "having been taken captive by the Lord's servant to do God's will" (so Bengel, Lock, and Falconer). Here again, ἐκεῖνος need not refer to a distant antecedent. And with this alternative the syntax is even more difficult in that it takes αὐτοῦ as referring to a very remote antecedent.

Hanson has added to these reasons for understanding both αὐτοῦ and ἐκείνου as referring to the devil with his documentation of use of ἐκεῖνος after αὐτός with virtually the same meaning. Furthermore, he suggests two reasons that Paul may have chosen to use ἐκείνου here (if it is not to be explained merely by a desire to avoid repeating αὐτοῦ in the same clause). One is the use of ἐκεῖνος for one that is well known (one of the uses mentioned in LSJM; Hanson suggests this may be the significance in Wisdom 1:16). The other, which is somewhat similar, is that ἐκείνου might be used to give a slight emphasis (which Hanson says "is probably the case in Thucydides 4.29.3"). Either of these factors would offer a further explanation for the admittedly different usage in this passage. At any rate, that ἐκεῖνος is found elsewhere referring to the nearest antecedent is adequate grounds for acknowledging that the understanding of its usage here that is more satisfactory syntactically may well be correct.

2:24-26 This remarkable and helpful section sets forth the duty of the Lord's servant and the attitude with which he should conduct himself. The central focus of this duty is teaching and correcting those in opposition so that they may repent and learn the truth (vv. 24-25). The Lord's servant must seek to communicate this truth in such a way that opponents embrace it and abandon their error with proper remorse. God's servant thus seeks to be the instrument through whose efforts God brings them to himself.

At the same time, this passage calls on the Lord's servant not to be quarrelsome but to be kind, forbearing, and gentle, even when he is correcting opponents (cf. Mt. 11:29). Correction must not degenerate into quarrelsomeness, even when he is wrongfully opposed. The balance called for may be summarized in the Latin proverb *suaviter in modo, fortiter in re,* gentle in manner, resolute in purpose.

Paul also combines here the responsibility of the Lord's servant with his dependence on and recognition of God's sovereignty. The focal point is what God's servant is called on to do. But in the midst of this statement is interjected the truth that God alone gives repentance and brings people to knowledge of the truth, and that he does not do so as an automatic response to human labors. Paul speaks, rather, of God's action with the cautious language of "if perhaps" (μήποτε). We are reminded of Paul's earlier statement: "I planted, Apollos watered, but God was causing the growth" (1 Cor. 3:6).

THE CHARACTER OF MANKIND IN THE LAST DAYS: 3:1-9

Here Paul broadens the perspective on what he has just written by placing it in its larger eschatological setting and, in the same way, sets the stage for his encouragement of Timothy to even greater fidelity to the apostolic teaching and to the ministry to which he is called (note transitional σὺ δέ in v. 10 and σὺ δέ again in v. 14 after v. 13 has restated what was said in vv. 2ff.). Although Paul speaks of these "last days" (v. 1) with future tense verbs (vv. 1, 9), this is a future in which Timothy is already involved, since the passage is applied to him in his present situation (note the second person singular present tense imperatives in vv. 1 and 5) and since the activity of the false teachers is depicted as already occurring (in the present tense verb forms in vv. 6-8).

The passage as a whole comprises two closely related sections. After v. 1 sets the theme of difficulty in the last times, vv. 2-5 list the evil characteristics of mankind that make these times so difficult. Vv. 6-9 apply that description to the particular case of false teachers in Timothy's situation. The passage concludes by saying that the error of these false teachers will become so evident that their progress will be checked (v. 9).

3:1 Paul indicates with δέ a contrast with what he has just written. There the emphasis was on possible recovery of those in opposition; here, in contrast, is a fuller statement of the difficulties of the age. In speaking of that hoped for recovery, Paul does not want Timothy to be naive about the difficulty that "the spirit of the age" presents to his ministry. Thus he commands Timothy to "know," i.e., "understand" (γίνωσκε, present active imperative) "this" (τοῦτο). What "this" represents, i.e., what Timothy is to know, is spelled out in the ὅτι clause (cf. Robertson, *Grammar,* 699).

ἐσχάταις ἡμέραις,** "last days," is used here as elsewhere in the NT (Acts 2:17; Jas. 5:3; 2 Pet. 3:3; cf. Heb. 1:2; cf. further ἐν ὑστέροις καιροῖς in 1 Tim. 4:1 and the discussion there) to refer to the time of the Messiah, that last period of days before the final messianic action takes place. The concept and language are taken over from the OT (cf. Acts 2:17, quoting Joel 3:1; cf. further Is. 2:2). Here, as in 1 Jn. 2:18, where ἐσχάτη ὥρα is used, the phrase does not designate some yet-to-come period of days. Rather, Paul is reminding Timothy that the Christian community is living in the "last days," and, because that is true, he must come to grips with what characterizes those "days."

When the "last days" are present, "difficult times" (καιροὶ χαλεποί) "will be present" (ἐνστήσονται, future middle indicative of ἐνίστημι,** Rom. 8:38; 1 Cor. 3:22; 7:26; Gal. 1:4; 2 Thes. 2:2; Heb. 9:9; cf. A. Oepke, *TDNT* II, 544). The future tense here expresses certainty. Pl. καιροί, "times," is used here of a period of time as in 1 Tim. 4:1. That period of time is χαλεποί** (Mt. 8:28), "hard," "difficult," says Paul, because of the evil characteristics of mankind in those "times."

3:2-4 γάρ indicates that the list that follows supplies the reason for the "last days" being regarded as "difficult times": The evil characteristics of people living in these days make them difficult. Again the verb is in the future, "will be" (ἔσονται), because Paul is describing what will be true from the apostolic age on, not just what is true for Timothy's time. Here again the future tense is as much that of certainty as of futurity (cf. the future in that sense in vv. 9 and 13). οἱ ἄνθρωποι is used in its general sense of "human beings," "people," as it was in 1 Timothy (e.g., 2:1, 4, 5; 4:10).

The list consists of eighteen items in vv. 2-4, with a nineteenth added in v. 5. Five of the eighteen terms occur in the NT only here (φίλαυτοι,** ἀκρατεῖς,** ἀνήμεροι,** ἀφιλάγαθοι,** which has not been found elsewhere in ancient literature, and φιλήδονοι**), two occur elsewhere in the NT only in the PE (ἀνόσιοι** in 1 Tim. 1:9, τετυφωμένοι** in 1 Tim. 3:6; 6:4), and three others are found in the NT only here and in Rom. 1:29-31 (ἀλαζόνες** in v. 30, ἄστοργοι** and ἄσπονδοι** in v. 31). Four are shared with Luke-Acts (φιλάργυροι** in Lk. 16:14; ἀχάριστοι** in Lk. 6:35; προδόται** in Lk. 6:16; Acts 7:52; cf. Mt. 24:10; προπετεῖς** in Acts 19:36) and four occur several other times in the NT, two of them in Rom. 1:29-31 (ὑπερήφανοι 4x, including Rom. 1:30; βλάσφημοι 4x; ἀπειθεῖς 5x, including Rom. 1:30; Tit. 1:16; 3:3; διάβολοι 37x).

This lengthy list of items is presented naturally and conveniently without any connecting terms (cf. BDF §460.2). Furthermore, this asyndeton most likely "suggests that the same persons are not characterized by all of the evils itemized" (Smith-Beekman, *Analysis*). Like the list in Romans 1:29-31, this list reflects the evils of a pagan society. "At the same time Paul is indicting the false teachers, both by characterizing their existence as in keeping with these evils and by implying that they themselves fit many of the items in the list . . ." (Fee).

The list has a somewhat chiastic arrangement: It begins and ends with terms expressing similar concepts and has within this framework other matched groupings of terms working from the beginning and end of the list:

φίλαυτοι
φιλάργυροι
ἀλαζόνες
ὑπερήφανοι
βλάσφημοι
γονεῦσιν ἀπειθεῖς
ἀχάριστοι
ἀνόσιοι
ἄστοργοι
ἄσπονδοι
διάβολοι
ἀκρατεῖς
ἀνήμεροι
ἀφιλάγαθοι
προδόται
προπετεῖς
τετυφωμένοι
φιλήδονοι
μᾶλλον ἢ φιλόθεοι

The list begins and ends with words expressing a misdirection of "love." This suggests that what is fundamentally wrong with these people is that their life is misdirected and that the other vices flow from this misdirection. φίλαυτοι** (a NT hapax in v. 2, but cf. μὴ αὐθάδη, "not self-willed," in Tit. 1:7), "lovers of self," is put first, for when self rather than God (and others) is made the central focus of one's life all else goes astray (cf. Rom. 1:25; Philo, *Legum Allegoriae* 1.49: φίλαυτος καὶ ἄθεος). To this self-centeredness is joined that these people are φιλάργυροι (in Lk. 16:14 a characteristic of the Pharisees), "lovers of money," one of the basic traits of the false teachers (cf. 1 Tim. 6:5-10: φιλαργυρία** in v. 10; Tit. 1:11; warnings against this evil in 1 Tim. 3:3, 8; Tit. 1:7).

At the end of the list this misdirection of love is described in the revealing comparison φιλήδονοι μᾶλλον ἢ φιλόθεοι (v. 4b). μᾶλλον in the comparative construction μᾶλλον ἤ ("rather than") is used here with the meaning "instead of" so that μᾶλλον ἤ "excludes from consideration" φιλόθεοι (BAGD s.v. μᾶλλον 3c; cf. 1 Tim. 1:4). The phrase thus reads "lovers of pleasure instead of lovers of God," or, "lovers of pleasure and not lovers of God." Thus φιλήδονοι** (a NT hapax but cf. ἡδονή** in Tit. 3:3; Lk. 8:14; Jas. 4:1, 3; 2 Pet. 2:13), "loving pleasure," is the preoccupation of such people (cf. Rom. 1:31) and is said to be more important to them than "loving God." φιλόθεοι** (another NT hapax), "lovers of God," summarizes in one word what Jesus (citing the OT) said to be mankind's highest duty (Mt.

22:37-38 par. Mk. 12:28-30/Lk. 10:27-28) and is the concept Paul uses elsewhere to describe those who know God (Rom. 8:28; 1 Cor. 2:9; 8:3; Eph. 6:24).

The next layer of terms, working from both the beginning and the end of the list, focuses on pride and hostility toward others. Associated, therefore, with self-love is an attitude of arrogant pride and disdain for others. In the first two words of this layer, joined here as in Rom. 1:30, Paul describes these people as "boasters" (ἀλαζόνες, notice Pr. 21:24 LXX and the associated concepts there) and as "arrogant" or "haughty" (ὑπερήφανοι,** Lk. 1:51; Rom. 1:30; Jas. 4:6; 1 Pet. 5:5), i.e., as those who express their pride in both talk and attitude. Here again Paul mentions characteristics of the false teachers (cf. 1 Tim. 1:7; 6:4; see Trench, *Synonyms,* 98-102 on both words; Barclay, *More NT Words,* 85-89 on the second). The third word of this group, βλάσφημοι** (Acts 6:11; 1 Tim. 1:13; here; 2 Pet. 2:11), "evil speakers," "slanderers," is most likely used here of "abusive" speech against other people, just as the related verb and abstract noun are used elsewhere in the PE of an evil that Christians must avoid in their dealings with non-Christians (βλασφημέω in Tit. 3:2) and that is associated with the false teachers (βλασφημία in 1 Tim. 6:4).

The corresponding group of three words near the end of the list presents a similar perspective but in a nearly reverse or chiastic order. First, Paul speaks of προδόται, "betrayers" or "traitors." The deeds of the "betrayer" destroy interpersonal relationships as readily as the words of the "slanderer." The preceding word in the list is ἀφιλάγαθοι, "those who do not love the good," and that one is a "betrayer" may well be considered a result of, or at least be associated with, that dislike for good. After "betrayers" is προπετεῖς, "reckless," those who stop at nothing to gain their ends (as Kelly puts it). The last of these three items dealing with human pride and attitude toward others is τετυφωμένοι, the only participle in the list, "being puffed up" and thus "conceited." It also is mentioned as a characteristic of the false teachers (1 Tim. 6:4), and overseers are warned against it (1 Tim. 3:6).

The innermost part of the list, vv. 2c-3, consists of eight ἀ-privative words (one in a two-word phrase) surrounding the word διάβολοι. In each case the ἀ- negates some good quality, so that this group of words describes these people as not manifesting even the basic characteristics of human life that God's common grace usually affords. γονεῦσιν ἀπειθεῖς, "disobedient to parents," describes a behavior pattern that, when persistent and aggravated, is regarded in the OT as a clear sign that the person is rebellious (Dt. 21:18ff.). It may well be placed first in this group as the first step, or the most basic violation, in these violations of the natural order. Next is ἀχάριστοι, "ungrateful," which after γονεῦσιν ἀπειθεῖς may have special reference to lack of appreciation for the care given by parents (cf. 1 Tim. 5:4). ἀνόσιοι is most likely used as in 1 Tim. 1:9 (see the comments there) of those who are "unholy" in the sense of "disrespectful," there toward God and here toward other people (F. Hauck, *TDNT* V, 492). ἄστοργοι means "unloving" in the sense of without natural affection (see LSJM). στοργή is used of "love, affection," "especially of parents and children" (LSJM). Thus ἄστοργοι probably also has special reference to parents and children. ἄσπονδοι indicates those who will not be reconciled, i.e., who are unforgiving (see Trench, *Synonyms,* 193f.; see the possible synonyms, both NT hapaxes, ἀσυνθέτους and ἀνελεήμονας on either side of ἄστοργοι in Rom. 1:31).

In the midst of these ἀ-privatives is διάβολοι, which in the pl. refers to humans who are "slanderers" (so in the PE 3x: 1 Tim. 3:11 [see the comments there]; Tit. 2:3). This use of the word after the reference in 2:26 to those who are trapped by ὁ διάβολος may imply that such captives become like their captor. διάβολοι may well mark a turning point from a group of words, the five preceding α-privatives, that speak of decay of family relationships, to three ἀ-privatives that, with διάβολοι, have a wider perspective. ἀκρατεῖς are those "without self-control" (cf. Tit. 1:8). ἀνήμεροι, literally "untamed," designates those who are "brutal" or "fierce" (MM call attention to Epictetus 1.3.7, where those who forget their divine origin are likened to lions). The last of these three words is ἀφιλάγαθοι, which literally means "those not loving the good" (cf. the opposite, φιλάγαθον, in Tit. 1:8).

As noted above, the list goes on from this point in v. 4 with three terms depicting human pride and harmful dealings with others and then summarizes by saying that they love pleasure instead of God.

3:5 Paul concludes the list with words that specify that these evil characteristics affect even those who claim to be religious and Christian, as it has so evidently the false teachers and their followers.

The present participle ἔχοντες, "having," "holding," indicates that such people possess this characteristic along with the characteristics he has just named. They possess the μόρφωσιν** (in Rom. 2:20 with a different sense), the "form" or "outward form," of εὐσέβεια. εὐσέβεια is usually used in the PE* of the true religion, i.e., Christianity (so 1 Tim. 2:2; 3:16; 4:7, 8; 6:3, 6, 11; Tit. 1:1; of what the false teachers regard as a means of gain in 1 Tim. 6:5). The second half of this statement, which says that these people have denied "its (αὐτῆς) power," shows that εὐσέβεια (the antecedent of αὐτῆς) is used here of Christianity. Thus Paul is saying that many, among whom are the false teachers, are professing to be Christians and engaging in a form of Christianity without knowing its reality.

With the disjunctive particle δέ, "but," Paul sets a clear contrast between possessing an outward "form" of Christianity and possessing its "power." He says, in fact, that they have *denied* its power. ἠρνημένοι (see 1 Tim. 5:8) is used in the sense of "denying, refusing, saying no to" the reality that they profess, τὴν . . . δύναμιν αὐτῆς (2 Pet. 2:1 uses the verb in a similar context). Paul has used δύναμις twice before in this letter with special force and significance, indeed as a central motif. In 1:7-8 he assures Timothy that all Christians have been given God's Spirit, who endues the believer with his power, and asks Timothy to suffer for the gospel enabled by that power. In 1:9ff. Paul reminds Timothy that it is God in his power who saves us and gives us life. Here δύναμις is used of the power of God that is offered in the gospel, which those he describes have refused (cf. 1 Tim. 3:16). That they love pleasure instead of God (v. 4) signifies what is involved here: They have not embraced God, the source of power, but have made their own pleasure that which they seek and trust in.

καί connects the imperative clause that follows it with all that preceded in vv. 1-5 and thus also with the imperative in v. 1. Thus Paul simultaneously instructs Timothy to be knowledgeable about the difficulty of the last times, which results from the evil characteristics of people living in it, "and" exhorts him continually to "avoid" or "turn (himself) away from" (ἀποτρέπου,** a NT hapax, present middle imperative; cf. 1 Cor. 5:9-13) those who hold to an outward form of Christianity (the antecedent of τούτους). Thus Paul repeats the command given in figurative language in 2:21, now explicitly and directly applying it to Timothy's relationships with specific individuals (cf. Rom. 16:17).

3:6 Paul now turns to a subgroup of those he has just mentioned (ἐκ τούτων). γάρ indicates that this statement provides further explanation why Timothy must "avoid" such people. Present tense εἰσιν and ἐνδύνοντες speak of what is happening as Paul writes (see Ellicott) and provide another indication that the preceding future tense verbs do not apply only to a distant future.

What these false teachers do is described in the present tense participial clause. ἐνδύνοντες** (a NT hapax) can mean simply "entering," but it is used here with a negative overtone so that "creeping in" *(NASB),* "worming in" (BAGD, *NIV*), or "making their way into" *(RSV)* expresses the nuance better (the same idea is found in Jude 4 [παρεισέδυσαν]; 2 Pet. 2:1; Gal. 2:4). They enter "houses" (for τὰς οἰκίας see 1 Tim. 5:13) "to capture weak women." With the participle αἰχμαλωτίζοντες** (literal in Lk. 21:24; figurative in Rom. 7:23; 2 Cor. 10:5), "capturing," Paul continues the military imagery that he used in 2:26.

Those whom the false teachers seek to capture are designated with γυναικάρια,** a diminutive of γυνή (and a NT hapax used with similar significance in extrabiblical literature [see BAGD]), literally "little women," which is used here with a negative connotation. It is the immaturity and thus the weakness of these "childish women" that make them susceptible to the false teachers. Paul does not use the term to derogate women but to describe a situation involving particular women. That he uses a diminutive form shows that he is not intending to describe women in general.

The reason that these women are characterized as childish and weak is given in two qualifying participial clauses. The passive participle σεσωρευμένα** (the verb also in Rom 12:20, basically "heap or pile up") means here "overwhelmed," and its perfect tense specifies that this is a condition that these women are continually in (see Field, *Notes*). They are overwhelmed by their "sins" (ἁμαρτίαις, dative of means; elsewhere in the PE* in 1 Tim. 5:22, 23).

Not only are they overwhelmed by past sins, they are being continually led in the present (ἀγόμενα, present passive; cf. 1 Cor. 12:2) by a multitude of desires (ἐπιθυμίαις ποικίλαις, dative of means; on ἐπιθυμία see 1 Tim. 6:9; on its use with ποικίλος see Tit. 3:3). ἐπιθυμίαις is used here specifically of evil desires (as it usually is in the NT). These women's desires are ποικίλαις, "manifold," or "of various kinds." That their consciences are burdened by past sins and their lives controlled by such desires puts them in a weakened condition and makes them vulnerable to false teachers who "capture" them as followers.

3:7 The condition these women enter when they are thus captured is described as that of perpetual learners who never learn the truth. The neuter accusative plural participle μανθάνοντα (as does δυνάμενα) continues to refer to neuter accusative plural γυναικάρια, as did the previous participles, σεσωρευμένα and ἀγόμενα. They are "learning" from the instruction (μανθάνοντα) of these false teachers and are doing so "constantly" or "always" (πάντοτε, adverb of time in a negative sense here as in 1 Thes. 2:16).

Concomitant (καί) with this constant learning is the sad fact that they "never," "never at all" (μηδέποτε,** a NT hapax and adverb of time, an intensifying negative compound [Robertson, *Grammar,* 1173], here as the opposite of πάντοτε) are able to come to the knowledge of the truth, which is the opposite of what would be expected of those who are "constantly learning." The very falseness of the teaching itself makes them not "able" (δυνάμενα; cf. Mt. 23:15 and for the contrast 2 Tim. 3:15) to learn the truth.

εἰς ἐπίγνωσιν ἀληθείας ἐλθεῖν, "to come to the knowledge of the truth," is associated with being saved in 1 Tim. 2:4; εἰς ἐπίγνωσιν ἀληθείας is associated with repentance in 2 Tim. 2:25; and ἐπίγνωσις ἀληθείας is associated in Tit. 1:1 with the faith of God's chosen and with godliness (these are the other three occurrences of ἐπίγνωσις ἀληθείας** in the PE [see the comments on each passage], which appears elsewhere in the NT only in Heb. 10:26). ἐπίγνωσις ἀληθείας presents "the content of Christianity as the absolute truth" (BAGD s.v. ἀλήθεια 2b). "To come into" that knowledge is to acknowledge and embrace the truth of the gospel and be converted by it so that the things associated with this phrase in the other PE occurrences (repentance, faith, being saved, living in godliness) become a reality in one's life. The terrible consequence of the false teaching is that these women, who are so burdened, never really learn the truth that can make them free.

3:8 Paul turns to the false teachers, as is evidenced by the subject matter itself, by the use of masculine οὗτοι, and by the use of ἄνθρωποι in its more restricted masculine sense (cf. 2:2). He likens them to "Jannes and Jambres" who opposed Moses and says that they also oppose the truth because of their depraved minds.

δέ ties this verse to v. 6 as further grounds for the command in v. 5b and prepares the way for the comparison applied to the false teachers by οὕτως καί. The adverbial accusative τρόπον is the antecedent of ὅν, with which it is incorporated in the relative clause (Robertson). The phrase indicates a comparison, "in the manner in which," i.e., "(just) as" (BAGD s.v. τρόπος 1; cf. BDF §475.3; ὃν τρόπον** elsewhere in the NT in Mt. 23:37; Lk. 13:34; Acts 1:11; 7:28; 15:11; 27:25).

The Egyptian sorcerers who opposed Moses before Pharaoh (Ex. 7:11ff., 22) were called Ἰάννης and Ἰαμβρῆς in Jewish writings (e.g., Targum Ps.-Jonathan 1.3; 7.2; at an earlier date in CD 5:17-19). The names were also widely known in pagan writings (e.g., Pliny, *Natural History* 30.1.11), so Paul's reference to them would have presented no problem for the church at Ephesus (especially not for the false teachers, with their interest in genealogies [1 Tim. 1:4]). Even though the names do not occur in the OT text, there is no reason to doubt the reliability of the Jewish tradition (so Ellicott; for further discussion of the names and references to primary and secondary literature see BAGD; H. Odeberg, *TDNT* III, 192f.; Str-B III, 660-64; McNamara, *NT and Palestinian Targum,* 82-96).

Paul appeals to the OT episode to illustrate the point he is making about the false teachers (cf. 1 Cor. 10:4). Both groups take the same sort of action. Just as the sorcerers "opposed" (ἀντέστησαν, aorist) Moses in the past, so also the false teachers now "oppose" (ἀνθίστανται, present) "the truth" (both verb forms from ἀνθίστημι, which basically means "set oneself against"). Moses (Μωϋσεῖ, the dative required by the verb) is referred to 10x by name in Paul's letters. In the Corinthian correspondence, as here, the references are with one exception to events in Moses' life (1 Cor. 10:2; 2 Cor. 3:7, 13, 15). Here, even though in the first instance a person is opposed and in the second the truth is opposed, the two episodes are analogous in that opposition to Moses was really opposition to the truth of Moses' message (cf. Ex. 7:2, 13 with Ex. 8:18-19).

With the adv. οὕτως, "so," corresponding to the correlative ὃν τρόπον and strengthened in its comparative force by adverbial καί, "also," what has been said about Jannes and Jambres is applied to the false teachers. The latter are referred to in the demonstrative pronoun οὗτοι, "these," the antecedent of which is οἱ ἐνδύνοντες . . . καὶ αἰχμαλωτίζοντες (v. 6). That which they oppose is ἀληθείᾳ, "truth," the truth of the gospel (cf. ἐπίγνωσιν ἀληθείας in v. 7). Paul has used ἀλήθεια five times already in this letter (2:15, 18, 25; 3:7, 8) and will use it for the last time in 4:4.

The explanation for their opposition is given in the first of two participial clauses: These "men" (ἄνθρωποι in its distinctly masculine sense following masculine οὗτοι; see 2:2) are κατεφθαρμένοι τὸν νοῦν. νοῦς, "mind," is used here as elsewhere in the PE* (1 Tim. 6:5 [see the comments there]; Tit. 1:15) "as the sum total of the whole mental and moral state of being" (BAGD s.v. 3; cf. J. Behm, *TDNT* IV, 948ff.). Here τὸν νοῦν is accusative of respect (BDF §159.3; Robertson, *Grammar,* 486) with the perfect passive participle κατεφθαρμένοι (from καταφθείρω,** 2 Pet. 2:12): With respect to their minds, these teachers have been "ruined" or "corrupted" (see 1 Tim. 6:5), with the passive perhaps an allusion to the devil's activity (cf. 2:26 and the related verb διαφθείρω of the evil one in 2 Cor. 11:3).

The second participial clause gives the result of all this: The false teachers are ἀδόκιμοι (see Tit. 1:16; the opposite of δόκιμον in 2 Tim. 2:15), i.e., those who have "not stood the test" and are therefore "rejected" "with respect to" (περί; cf. 2:18) "the faith" (τὴν πίστιν, used here as in 2:18 and 1 Tim. 1:19; see the comments especially on the latter), i.e., the faith relationship with God.

3:9 Here Paul encourages Timothy by reminding him of the outcome that will meet the false teachers as it met Moses' opponents. In contrast (ἀλλά, Ellicott suggests "notwithstanding") with what he has written about their inroads into households, he wants Timothy to know that their impact will not continue because the "folly" of what they teach will become "obvious to everyone." With οὐ προκόψουσιν ἐπὶ πλεῖον, "they will not advance farther," Paul uses the same idiom that he used without the negative in 2:16 (see the comments there).

γάρ indicates that the second clause of this verse states the grounds for the first clause. ἡ ἄνοια αὐτῶν, "their folly," refers to the teaching of the false teachers. The best understanding of this phrase is gained from Paul's earlier appraisal of one aspect of the teaching: "They do not understand either what they are saying or the matters about which they make confident assertions" (1 Tim. 1:7). The reason that they will not advance further is that their folly will be "quite evident," i.e., "plain" and "conspicuous" (ἔκδηλος, a NT hapax; cf. LSJM) to "all" (πᾶσιν) who are exposed to it (cf. πάντες in 1 Tim. 4:15; 2 Tim. 2:24).

Paul makes his point by comparing (ὡς) the false teachers to Moses' opponents and by reminding Timothy that this happened with them "also" (καί): ὡς καὶ ἡ ἐκείνων ἐγένετο, literally "as also that of those came to be." ἡ recalls ἡ ἄνοια (see BAGD s.v. 9). The demonstrative pronoun ἐκείνων, denoting a remoter object, refers back to Ἰάννης καὶ Ἰαμβρῆς, the subject in v. 8. ἐγένετο, "became," is used with the adjective ἔκδηλος understood from the preceding clause. Paul says, therefore, that the folly of those men (Jannes and Jambres) also became evident to all. He is apparently referring to the failure of these opponents of Moses to repeat all the miracles that he brought about, which they sought to do to discount his message (e.g., Ex. 8:18-19 and especially 9:11). Thus it eventually became evident that their message was not true and was not to be followed. Paul says that the same will happen with regard to the false teachers at Ephesus.

In vv. 1-9 Paul has placed the difficulties that Timothy faces into the context of what characterizes the last days (vv. 1-7) and has compared them with the difficulties that Moses faced (vv. 8-9). Timothy and those at Ephesus have been forewarned of the difficulty ("realize this," v. 1), warned to act decisively in response ("avoid these," v. 5), and encouraged by what they know will be the outcome (v. 9).

CONTINUE STEADFASTLY IN WHAT HAS BEEN LEARNED: 3:10-17

Here Paul addresses Timothy directly and contrasts him with the false teachers by means of a twice-repeated "but you" (σὺ δέ, vv. 10, 14). The focal point of his instruction is the imperative to "continue (μένε) in the things that you have learned and become convinced of" (v. 14). The repetition of σὺ δέ signals, however, that there are two lessons, even if there is only one imperative.

The first lesson reminds Timothy of his long personal association with Paul, including Paul's persecutions and deliverance (vv. 10-11), and of the inevitability of persecution for Christians (v. 12). By recounting Timothy's past association with him and by stating this general principle Paul renews his call to Timothy to be loyal and to endure persecution (cf. 1:8ff.; 2:3ff.).

The second lesson follows a comment that evil people will proceed from bad to worse (v. 13) and calls on Timothy, in contrast to the false teachers, to keep to the teaching that he has received (v. 14) over against all corruption of it (cf. 1:13-14; 2:15). Finally, Paul reminds Timothy that what he has been taught he has learned from "the sacred writings" and that they, since they are inspired by God, are given not only to point a person to the salvation in Christ but also to teach, reprove, correct, and instruct so that a person may be equipped for a life of obedient deeds (vv. 15-17).

3:10 σὺ δέ combines the personal pronoun σύ, used for emphasis in contrast to others, and the contrasting particle δέ, "but" (this combination in the PE* also in 1 Tim. 6:11; Tit. 2:1; 2 Tim. 3:14; 4:5; cf. σὺ οὖν in 2:1, 3; σὺ δέ elsewhere in Pl.* in Rom. 11:17, 20; 14:10). Whereas those Paul has been speaking of have "opposed" Paul and his teaching, Timothy has "followed" the teaching of Paul and the various aspects of Paul's life that went along with and corroborated that teaching.

Paul uses παρηκολούθησας** (Lk. 1:3; 1 Tim. 4:6), "followed," in a double sense here. With some of the datives of association (Robertson) that follow it has the sense of "accompanying" or "being present at" events, e.g., persecutions and sufferings. But primarily, and more profoundly, Paul uses it in the sense of the "following" that takes place "with the mind" and that "understands" and "makes one's own" that which one follows, as in 1 Tim.

4:6 (cf. BAGD s.v. παρακολουθέω 1, 2). In this sense he refers to Timothy having followed his teaching, etc.

Paul lists nine things that Timothy "followed," prefacing the list with μου both for emphasis and also to indicate that it governs all that follows. The first seven are singular and are principles or concepts. The last two (in v. 11) are plural and give concrete examples of the seventh principle.

Paul begins with "teaching" (διδασκαλίᾳ; cf. 1 Tim. 1:10 and 4:6), i.e., what he teaches, because it is this primarily that he wants to contrast with the teaching of the false teachers (vv. 5-9). But since teaching never exists apart from the reality of the teacher's life and from the change that it has brought about in the teacher's life, he adds the marks of godliness that flow from the teaching and accompany it in his own life (cf. 1 Tim. 4:12, 15-16; 6:3; 2 Tim. 2:22-25).

ἀγωγῇ** (a NT hapax, cf. LXX Est. 2:20; 2 Maccabees 11:24) is a comprehensive term indicating Paul's "way of life," his "conduct" (cf. 1 Tim. 4:12, with a different word, and the statement about Paul's way of life in 1 Cor. 4:17). προθέσει (here only in Paul's letters of a human, elsewhere of God) designates his "purpose" or the resolute plan for his ministry (cf. Acts 20:20-21, 24, 27; 1 Cor. 2:1-5).

Having mentioned these general characteristics, Paul next characterizes his life with the usual Christian trilogy "faith," "love," and "perseverance" (cf. Tit. 2:2), with "patience" sandwiched in as something much needed by one who teaches in difficult situations, as he has reminded Timothy (in 2:24, albeit with a different word) and will remind him again (in 4:2, with the same word as here). πίστει is used as elsewhere in the PE (cf. 1 Tim. 4:12; 6:11; 2 Tim. 2:22) of trust in or absolute dependence on God. μακροθυμίᾳ probably carries the sense of "forbearance, patience" toward others, which it also has in its other PE* occurrences (1 Tim. 1:16 [see the comments there]; 2 Tim. 4:2; here for the first time in the PE in a virtue list; cf. 2 Cor. 6:6; Gal. 5:22; Eph. 4:2; Col. 1:11; 3:12) rather than its meaning of endurance, which would only anticipate ὑπομονῇ (see Trench, *Synonyms,* §53). Paul uses ἀγάπῃ (see 1 Tim. 1:5; it occurs repeatedly in lists in the PE, e.g., 1 Tim. 4:12; 6:11; Tit. 2:2; 2 Tim. 2:22), "love," here, as he usually does, of love for humans (cf. especially 1 Cor. 13:1ff.). He exhibited before Timothy what he asked him to pursue (2:22) and what he said the Holy Spirit has provided (1:5). ὑπομονή expresses the "endurance, steadfastness, and perseverance" of one who lives in the midst of the difficulties of this life kept and strengthened by Christ while awaiting Christ's return (see the other PE* occurrences, especially 1 Tim. 6:11; Tit. 2:2). Paul sums up in these words his ministry (teaching, conduct, and purpose) and his life (faith, patience, love, and perseverance).

3:11 With two plural nouns διωγμοῖς and παθήμασιν, and with ὑπήνεγκα, "I endured," Paul makes concrete the reality of his ὑπομονή.

διωγμοί** is used in the NT of "persecutions" suffered for religious reasons (Mt. 13:21; Mk. 4:17; 10:30; Acts 8:1; 13:50; Rom. 8:35; 2 Cor. 12:10; 2 Thes. 1:4). παθήματα means generally "that which is suffered or endured." Used with τοῖς διωγμοῖς it refers to "sufferings" endured as a result of persecution (cf. 2 Cor. 1:6-7; W. Michaelis, *TDNT* V, 930ff.). The qualitative relative pronoun οἷα, "such as, what kinds of," points to definite difficulties that Paul (μοι) experienced (ἐγένετο). It is neuter in agreement with its antecedent, τοῖς παθήμασιν. A second qualitative relative pronoun, masculine οἵους, agrees with διωγμούς, which follows it.

By repeating διωγμοί Paul focuses on "persecutions" and by naming certain towns he calls to mind actual events that Timothy "followed." These events Paul "endured" or "bore up under" (ὑπήνεγκα, aorist of ὑποφέρω,** also in 1 Cor. 10:13; 1 Pet. 2:19) in Antioch, Iconium, and Lystra, as related in Acts (13:45, 50; 14:1-5, 19). These towns were in the area from which Timothy came, and Timothy was aware of these episodes when he agreed to join Paul in the ministry (Acts 16:1-6). Paul mentions these earliest persecutions rather than later ones, probably because he wants to remind Timothy of his commitment to the apostle and his ministry from the very beginning and that from the very beginning that ministry has involved persecutions.

Paul adds the note of triumph in the Lord that marks his accounts of suffering and persecution: καὶ ἐκ πάντων με ἐρρύσατο ὁ κύριος, "and out of them all the Lord delivered me" (words very close to Ps. 33:20 LXX; cf. Paul's litany of difficulties and deliverances in 2 Cor. 4:7-9). He uses ἐκ in the sense of being delivered "out of" these persecutions, not in the sense of being kept "from" them. He rejoices because he has been brought through persecution and finally out of it (cf. "persecuted [διωκόμενοι] but not forsaken," 2 Cor. 4:9).

ἐρρύσατο (aorist of ῥύομαι) means here "he delivered, rescued." The deliverer is ὁ κύριος, Christ, the master whom Paul serves and who can and does preserve his servant (cf. 2:24 on who is in view with κύριος). Paul speaks in absolute terms with ἐκ πάντων, "out of them all." In every instance the Lord delivered him. And even when the last episode comes and leads to death, the Lord will still deliver, for then, Paul says, the Lord "will deliver me from every evil deed and will bring me safely to his heavenly kingdom" (4:18, with v. 17 the other PE* uses of the verb). Paul thus ends this catalog of what Timothy has "followed" emphasizing persecutions and the mighty Lord who always delivers.

3:12 Paul now states a general principle regarding persecution and attaches it to what he has said about his own experiences of persecution with postpositive δέ and καί, which together have the force of "and also": Just as Paul has endured persecutions so "also" this will be the case for Christians in general. πάντες . . . οἱ θέλοντες εὐσεβῶς ζῆν ἐν Χριστῷ Ἰησοῦ, "all who desire to live godly in Christ Jesus," is not a designation of a subgroup of Christians who desire a more godly life but rather a description of real Christians in distinction from those who follow false teaching. εὐσεβῶς ζῆν, "to live godly," is a description of the condition that grace brings about in the life of the one saved by Christ (cf. Tit. 2:11-12 and see the comments there for a discussion of these two terms). οἱ θέλοντες, "those desiring, those wanting," is used with the verb to express the will, purpose, or resolve (cf. Heb. 13:18; BAGD s.v. 2; G. Schrenk, *TDNT* III, 49) of those who truly want to be godly, in contrast to those who have only the form of godliness (cf. v. 5).

The godly life desired is found ἐν Χριστῷ Ἰησοῦ, i.e., in a living relationship with Christ through faith in him (see especially 1 Tim. 1:14; Gal. 2:20). With "life in Christ Jesus" Paul recalls the introductory statement in this letter (the infinitive ζῆν here, the noun ζωή in 1:1; this combination elsewhere in Paul only in Rom. 6:11 [with the participle ζῶντας]). "All" (πάντες) so characterized means for Paul "all" Christians (for πάντες with a plural participle in Paul to designate all Christians cf. Rom. 1:7; 4:11; 1 Cor. 1:2; Eph. 6:24; 1 Thes. 1:7; 2 Thes. 1:10), as in 4:8.

Thus, as a general rule, all Christians "will be persecuted" as Paul was (διώκω, the only occurrence in the PE with the meaning "persecute"; elsewhere in Paul with this meaning in Rom. 12:14; 1 Cor. 4:12; 15:9; 2 Cor. 4:9; Gal. 1:13, 23; 4:29; 5:11; 6:12; Phil. 3:6). This principle was already stated by Jesus (cf. Mt. 10:22-23; Lk. 21:12; Jn. 15:20) and by Paul, both on his first missionary journey (Acts 14:22) and in his earliest correspondence (1 Thes. 3:4).

3:13 This statement gives balance and perspective to the last by adding (δέ) the downward progress of "evil people and imposters" (cf. similarly v. 9). With πονηροὶ ἄνθρωποι, "evil people," Paul is probably referring again to mankind in this age (οἱ ἄνθρωποι, v. 2), using here the comprehensive adjective πονηροί in the ethical sense of that which is "wicked or evil" (cf. Mt. 12:35; Lk. 6:45; and especially 2 Thes. 3:2).

In vv. 2ff. Paul referred to some of wicked mankind as those who have a form of religion (v. 5) and as those who are false religious teachers (v. 6). Here also he appears to refer to the same category of people with γόητες** (a NT hapax). In this understanding καί has somewhat of an explanatory force joining the more specific γόητες to the more general πονηροὶ ἄνθρωποι (Ellicott). γόης means generally "sorcerer" but is probably used here in the sense of "swindler, cheat" or "imposter" (see BAGD for extrabiblical references; Paul uses it perhaps because Moses' opponents [v. 8] are designated by similar terms in Ex. 7:11). Whatever word may be used to render this Greek term, the intended meaning is clarified by the fact that they are those who "deceive" (πλανῶντες). Thus G. Delling says that γόης is "one who entices to impious action by apparently pious words" (*TDNT* I, 737f. in a helpful article).

Paul says that such people will "proceed" or "progress" (προκόψουσιν, in the PE* see 2:16; 3:9) ἐπὶ τὸ χεῖρον, literally "to the worse" (χεῖρον is a comparative of κακός). Their tactics and procedures will get worse and worse, as the first qualifying participle, πλανῶντες (active), indicates. That participle describes them as "deceiving" or "misleading" others (cf. Delling's comment, quoted above; see again vv. 6-7 and the other uses of the verb in Pl.*: 1 Cor. 6:9; 15:22; Gal. 6:7; Tit. 3:3).

The second participle, πλανώμενοι, describes these people either as self-deceived (middle) or as deceived by someone else (passive). The latter is most likely since Paul has already spoken about how the devil captures people (2:26) and also because in the only PE use of the cognate adjective in a context describing false teaching Paul speaks of "deceitful spirits" (πνεύμασιν πλάνοις) working "by means of the hypocrisy of liars" (1 Tim. 4:1-2). These people are thus deceived by the evil one and his evil spirits so that they believe their own deceptive message (cf. Rom. 1:21-25).

The statements that the false teachers "will progress to worse" and that "they will not make further progress" (v. 9) show that Paul can look at their progress from two entirely different perspectives. This verse recognizes that evil becomes intensively worse as time goes on. The other recognizes that the teaching of evil does not necessarily capture a wider audience as it becomes more intense and therefore does not become more extensive as it becomes more intensive.

3:14 With contrasting δέ and especially with emphatic σύ and the verb μένε, "remain," set in opposition to προκόψουσιν, "they will progress," Paul places Timothy and what he should do in sharp contrast with the progressive error of the false teachers. Timothy is to "remain" in the sense of "continuing" (present imperative μένε; cf. in the PE 1 Tim. 2:15; 2 Tim. 2:13; F. Hauck, *TDNT* IV, 576) in the things that he has learned.

οἷς is dative by attraction to the case of its unexpressed antecedent in its position following the preposition ἐν. What Timothy is to remain in is not indicated, except that it is what he has learned and has become assured of. ἔμαθες (aorist of μανθάνω; see 1 Tim. 2:11) is used here of what Timothy has "learned" through being taught, as the following clause demonstrates (BAGD s.v. 1). ἐπιστώθης** (aorist of πιστόω, a NT hapax), "have become convinced of," indicates that what Timothy learned he embraced as true and reliable. With this verb we see that Paul appeals not to traditionalism or to the status quo but to adherence to what Timothy has become convinced is true.

The encouragement to remain in such teaching is based on Timothy's knowledge of whom he learned it from. (Later Paul will appeal to the source from which Timothy was taught, "the holy scriptures" [vv. 15-17].) The participle εἰδώς, "knowing," is used here, as often by Paul, to ask the recipient to recall what he knows quite well (in the PE: 1 Tim. 1:9; Tit. 3:11; 2 Tim.

2:23). παρά with the genitive is used after ἔμαθες (and other verbs of learning), as often in Greek literature (see BAGD s.v. παρά I.3c), to designate the person(s) from whom one has learned. Here those persons are represented by plural τίνων (for the textual evidence for the plural see *NA*[26]). The further statement in v. 15 implies that his childhood teachers, Lois and Eunice (1:5), are included in this plural, but since this is an additional comment and not an epexegetical statement, it does not exclude Paul. Furthermore, the statement here recalls the beginning of this section, where Paul says that Timothy has followed his teaching (v. 10). Paul surely intends here to appeal to Timothy to continue in Paul's teaching since, as vv. 10-11 make clear, Timothy has known well the reality in Paul's life of the truth he teaches. Others who are included in that plural are then added in v. 15.

3:15 This verse adds another object of the participle εἰδώς (v. 14), as the conjunctions καί and ὅτι indicate (cf. Ellicott). Timothy also knows that (καὶ ὅτι) he has known (οἶδας) from childhood not only his teachers but also the source of the teaching itself, the "holy scriptures." βρέφος** is used of both the "unborn child" (Lk. 1:41, 44) and the "infant" (Lk. 2:12, 16; 18:15; Acts 7:19; 1 Pet. 2:2). ἀπὸ βρέφους, used in Greek literature with the meaning "from childhood" (see BAGD s.v. 2; cf. Mk. 9:21), implies that Timothy has known the scriptures from then until now. The Mishnah tractate *Pirke Aboth* (5:21), from the end of the first century AD, gives five years of age as the time that a Jewish child is fit for scripture (for other sources see Str-B III, 664-66).

ἱερὰ γράμματα, "holy scriptures," is not used elsewhere in the NT and is probably used here because of Timothy's Jewish background, since the phrase was used among Greek-speaking Jews to designate the OT (see BAGD s.v. γράμμα 2c; G. Schrenk, *TDNT* I, 763f.; cf. especially Josephus, *Ant.* 10.210; *Ap.* 1.54; *Ap.* 1.39f. enumerates the books of the Hebrew canon as comprising the Jewish scriptures). ἱερά was used to indicate the association of the scriptures with God (Philo defines ἱερός in *Quis Rerum Divinarum Haeres Sit* 171; see also G. Schrenk, *TDNT* III, 226-29). It is difficult to decide whether τά before ἱερὰ γράμματα is part of the original text or not (for manuscript evidence see *NA*[26]), but that makes little difference since the phrase was used with the same meaning with and without the article (cf. BAGD s.v. γράμμα 2c; G. Schrenk, *TDNT* I, 765 n. 13). It is commonly agreed that because of the technical character of the expression no article is needed (e.g., BAGD s.v. γράμμα 2c; Schrenk, 765; Dibelius-Conzelmann).

In the participial clause attached to ἱερὰ γράμματα by the (possibly repeated) article τά, Paul gives the central purpose of the "holy scriptures." In doing so he echoes Jesus' statements to the same effect (cf., e.g., Lk. 24:25-27, 44-47; Jn. 5:39, 46) and verbalizes what was evident in his own use of scripture in preaching to Jews (cf. Acts 17:2-3). τὰ δυνάμενα, "which are able," affirms that the ἱερὰ γράμματα have a certain innate ability, which is specified in the following infinitive clause (for this construction in Paul see, e.g., Rom. 15:14; 16:25; Gal. 3:21; Eph. 3:20). That which the scriptures are able to do is "to make wise unto salvation," as they did for Timothy (σε). "To make wise," σοφίσαι, means here "to teach" or "instruct" one about something. That about which the scriptures teach is identified as "salvation" (σωτηρίαν; see 2:10, the other PE* occurrence). σωτηρία is used in the NT of the spiritual deliverance from bondage to sin that Christ brings (see BAGD s.v. 2). Scripture's instruction does not itself bring salvation but points "to" (εἰς) it or leads one toward it (εἰς σωτηρίαν also in Rom. 1:16; 10:1, 10; 2 Cor. 7:10; Phil. 1:19; Acts 13:47; Heb. 9:28; 11:7; 1 Pet. 1:5; 2:2).

This salvation is received, says Paul here as elsewhere, διὰ πίστεως τῆς ἐν Χριστῷ Ἰησοῦ (διὰ πίστεως 15x in Paul — in Rom. 3:22 and Gal. 2:16 followed by Ἰησοῦ Χριστοῦ [Χριστοῦ Ἰησοῦ as a variant reading], in Phil. 3:9 by Χριστοῦ, in Gal. 3:26 by ἐν Ἰησοῦ Χριστῷ, usually with reference to some aspect of salvation, as here, and in Eph. 2:8 with σῴζω). διά with the genitive denotes that πίστεως is the means or instrument of salvation. πίστεως is used here in the active sense of "believing" or "trusting" in Christ as one's Lord and thus as one's Savior (Rom. 10:9 expresses what is in view here, and, like this passage, says in v. 10 that the result is σωτηρία). τῆς before ἐν Χριστῷ Ἰησοῦ emphasizes that "the" faith is that which is in Christ Jesus. Paul uses πίστις with ἐν followed by one or more of the names and titles of Christ several times (Gal. 3:26; Eph. 1:15; Col. 1:4; 1 Tim. 3:13) and thus specifies the object of faith by indicating the one "in," or upon, whom it rests (cf. M. Harris, *NIDNTT* III, 1212). The object of this faith is Χριστῷ Ἰησοῦ (cf. 1:1, 10; 1 Tim. 1:1-2).

3:16 The reminder of Timothy's long acquaintance with the scriptures and their central function (v. 15) leads Paul to conclude this section with a fuller statement on the divine origin and specific usefulness of scripture (v. 16) and on the purpose that it serves in the life of the man of God (v. 17).

The exegesis of this verse requires the resolution of a number of questions: Does γραφή refer here to various passages of scripture or is it used as a collective, and if the latter, what collection does it refer to? Does πᾶσα mean "every" or "all"? Is θεόπνευστος active or passive in meaning? Does it function as an attributive adjective ("God-breathed scripture") or as a predicate adjective ("scripture is God-breathed")? In other words, where should the understood verb "is" be placed, after γραφή ("scripture is God-breathed") or after θεόπνευστος ("God-breathed scripture is . . .")? This in turn is tied to whether καί is a conjunction between θεόπνευστος and ὠφέλιμος ("God-breathed and profitable") or an adjunctive adverb "also" ("God-breathed scripture is also profitable"). We take up these questions in order (for a helpful discussion of most of these questions see, in addition to the works cited below, House, "Biblical Inspiration").

γραφή (NT 50x [30x singular], Pl. 14x [9x singular]) was used in the Greek of the day for any piece of writing, but in the NT it is used only of holy scripture (BAGD s.v. 2; cf. G. Schrenk, *TDNT* I, 751ff.). This is borne out by its use here in parallel with ἱερὰ γράμματα (v. 15). Singular γραφή is often used in the NT of a particular passage of scripture (BAGD s.v. 2a; Schrenk, 752f.), and some have claimed that this is its only use (e.g., Lightfoot, *Galatians,* 147). Nonetheless, it is also used in the NT for scripture as a whole (see BAGD s.v. 2bβ for examples; Schrenk, 753-55; Warfield, *Inspiration and Authority,* 236-39). This understanding would seem to be demanded by 2 Pet. 1:20 ("no prophecy of scripture") and often even when a particular passage from scripture is quoted. In 1 Pet. 2:6, for example, the particular passage is said to be "*contained* in Scripture" (περιέχει ἐν γραφῇ; cf. Acts 8:32). The same may be said where scripture is personified (e.g., "scripture says," Rom. 4:3; 9:17; 10:11; Gal. 4:30; 1 Tim. 5:18; so also Gal. 3:8, 22). In 2 Tim. 3:16 we may well have another example of γραφή referring to scripture as a whole, but the answer to that question is tied up with the understanding of the use of πᾶσα.

πᾶς, when joined to an anarthrous noun, is usually understood as "every" (BAGD s.v. 1aα who, however, go on to say "scarcely different in [meaning] from the pl[ural] 'all' "; BDF §275.3; MHT III, 199; C. F. D. Moule, *Idiom-Book,* 94f.; Robertson, *Grammar,* 771f.). But this rule is not absolute: With certain anarthrous nouns, e.g., collectives or proper nouns (cf. Thayer, *Lexicon,* s.v. I.1c), the meaning "all" is intended (e.g., Rom. 11:26; Mt. 28:18; Acts 2:36; possibly also Eph. 2:21; 3:15; for more examples and further discussion see the grammars cited, especially Robertson, 772). Singular γραφή is used at least twice elsewhere anarthrously "as definite without the article" (Robertson, *Grammar,* 772, referring to 1 Pet. 2:6; 2 Pet. 1:20). Furthermore, it is used in the NT of "the scripture," i.e., almost as a proper name and certainly at times as a collective, whether with or without the article (cf. van Oosterzee; House, "Biblical Inspiration," 55f.).

For those reasons, it does not need the article, and "so far as the grammatical usage goes, one can render here either 'all scripture' or 'every scripture' " (Robertson). In the final analysis there is no essential difference in meaning. "All scripture" perceives scripture as a whole, and "every scripture" perceives it in terms of all its component parts.

But it seems more likely that Paul is contemplating scripture as a whole here and that he would say that the whole of scripture is "profitable for teaching, reproof, correction, and instruction in righteousness," than that every scripture passage is profitable in these ways. It is also more likely that he would say that the whole of scripture equips the man of God (v. 17) than that every passage does so. This understanding would also be in accord with his usage of the term in its collective sense in the phrase "scripture says" and would be more likely here since no specific passage is cited.

θεόπνευστος** (a biblical hapax) is a compound of the word for God, θεός, and the verb "breathe," πνέω, using the first aorist stem πνευσ-, with the verbal adjective ending -τος. The word may be properly rendered "God-breathed," though under the influence of Vulgate *inspirata* the more common, but somewhat less accurate, English rendering has been "inspired by God" (cf. 2 Pet. 1:21). If this is a passive verbal form, it indicates that scripture's source is the breath of God, i.e., that scripture itself is a result of that action. If it is active, it indicates that scripture is filled with God's breath and that it breathes out the Spirit of God. The latter was argued by Cremer in a later edition of his *Lexicon* (cf. pp. 730-32 in contrast with the other position, p. 282).

But Warfield demonstrates that in patristic literature the word bears "a uniformly passive significance, rooted in the idea of the creative breath of God" (*Inspiration and Authority,* 275; see further 245-96). He further indicates that this conclusion is confirmed by "the consideration that compounds of verbals in -τος with θεός normally express an effect produced by God's activity" (281; see 281f. for a list of more than seventy-five such compounds; cf., e.g., θεοδίδακτος, "instructed by God," 1 Thes. 4:9). He notes that this is in accord with "the Hebraic conviction that God produces all that He would bring into being by a mere breath" (286). Warfield's study has proved to be so convincing that BAGD list only his work in its bibliographic note on θεόπνευστος.

Is θεόπνευστος an attributive adjective ("God-breathed scripture") or a predicate adjective ("scripture is God-breathed")? Considering γραφή and θεόπνευστος by themselves, either view is grammatically possible. Roberts seeks to answer this question by appealing to use elsewhere in the NT of πᾶς with a noun and adjective and with no other word intervening in the sequence. In all such cases the adjective is attributive ("Note on the Adjective," following Spence, "2 Timothy iii.15, 16"; cf. also Roberts's "Every Scripture"; all three articles list twenty-one such passages; these data go against Simpson's and Kelly's argument that the adjective, if attributive, would precede the noun, at least as a general rule). The problem with appealing to this usage is that in each of these other occurrences the construction of the sentence did not permit the predicate adjective understanding. But here that alternative is possible. Furthermore, several passages in the list do, in fact, have intervening words (e.g., 2 Thes. 2:17; Tit. 2:10).

The only NT passage with the same word order (allowing for an intervening word) that also parallels πᾶσα γραφὴ θεόπνευστος by having a following καί and another adjective is 1 Tim. 4:4. There the adjective is a predicate adjective. This tips the scales in favor of understanding θεόπνευστος as a predicate adjective, though both alternatives remain possible. Also to be considered are the location of the understood verb "is," the force and meaning of καί, and the intended meaning of the passage as a whole.

The natural understanding of two adjectives connected by καί is that they are used in the same way, whether attributively or predicately. This favors placing the verb "is" before θεόπνευστος so that the two adjectives remain together as predicate adjectives (cf. again 1 Tim. 4:4). Compelling considerations would be needed to place the verb between them. Bernard (with others, e.g., Ellicott) argues that attributive use would make γραφὴ θεόπνευστος parallel to ἱερὰ γράμματα and that for Paul to make such a direct affirmation about scripture, that it is "God-breathed," would be irrelevant. But these arguments do not seem compelling. The latter is a subjective evaluation that not all find convincing. In fact, in a letter that restates many basic truths to encourage Timothy, it is not at all strange to find this truth emphasized, especially when knowing it will help Timothy use scripture for the purposes described in vv. 16b-17, which, in effect, follow from this fundamental affirmation. Furthermore, taking θεόπνευστος as attributive would imply that Paul did not regard all γραφή as God-breathed — a position that would be incredible, since by γραφή he always means scripture. It would also require that καί be understood as having the ascensive force of "also," which does not seem correct since in this construction "also" (καί) could just as well be omitted (cf., e.g., *NEB*). This understanding of καί is much less natural.

On balance it appears that understanding θεόπνευστος as predicate has somewhat more in its favor, though attributive use cannot be ruled out. In line with this and our discussion of πᾶς, we translate "all scripture is God-breathed and profitable [useful]," and in doing so agree in essence with most modern English translations (e.g., *RSV, NASB, TEV, NIV*).

Paul appears to be saying, therefore, that all scripture has as its source God's breath and that this is its essential characteristic. This is another way of saying that scripture is God's word (cf. Jesus' use of "scripture" and "word of God" in apposition to each another in Jn. 10:35). The same thing is also said when the NT uses "God says" for what is found in scripture, whether the words were originally spoken by God or not (see Warfield, *Inspiration and Authority,* 299-348) and when Paul insists that the message he speaks consists of words taught by God's Spirit (1 Cor. 2:12-13; cf. Heb. 3:7; Acts 1:16; 2 Pet. 1:21).

Therefore, what Paul writes to Timothy here embodies a conviction found throughout the NT and held by Jesus, his apostles, and other NT writers. Its particular significance lies in its absoluteness, first that relating to the extent of scripture (πᾶσα γραφή) and second that relating to the character of scripture (θεόπνευστος). Because "all scripture is God-breathed" Paul can state categorically that it is "useful for teaching, . . ." and that as a result of its fourfold work in one's life that "the man of God" is adequate and equipped (v. 17).

We have seen that Paul uses γραφή like others in the NT to refer to that which they regard as the written word of God. But is the OT all that he intends in the phrase πᾶσα γραφή? It would, indeed, be in accord with the context to conclude that he uses the phrase as a virtual synonym of ἱερὰ γράμματα (v. 15) so that he can say more about the origin and character of the "sacred scriptures" and indicate that their usefulness extends beyond leading to salvation to include all the aspects of one's life before God.

But another possibility is that Paul is enlarging on the previous reference by using another term and especially by his use of πᾶσα. He probably uses γραφή in 1 Tim. 5:18 (see the comments there) to refer to words of Jesus (found in Lk. 10:7). Another NT writer includes Paul's letters in the category of γραφή (2 Pet. 3:15-16). Paul insisted that his letters be read (1 Thes. 5:27), exchanged (Col. 4:16), and obeyed (e.g., 1 Cor. 14:37; 2 Thes. 2:15) and identified the words he used to communicate the gospel message as "those taught by the Spirit" (1 Cor. 2:13). In this letter Paul has praised Timothy for following his teaching (v. 10), has urged Timothy to continue in what he has learned from Paul (v. 14), has commanded Timothy to retain "the standard of sound words" that he has heard from Paul (1:13), has commanded him to entrust what he has heard from Paul to faithful men so that they could teach others (2:2), and has insisted that Timothy handle accurately "the word of truth" (2:15). After his remarks on πᾶσα γραφή he will urge Timothy to "preach the word" (4:2), i.e., proclaim the apostolic message, about which Paul has said so much in this letter.

It seems possible, therefore, that Paul by his use of πᾶσα γραφή is expanding the earlier reference to the OT to include those accounts of the gospel that may have been extant and perhaps also his own and other apostolic writings that have been "taught by the Spirit" (1 Cor. 2:13; cf. for this view, e.g., Stott). This understanding also fits well in this context. It provides a reason for Paul's use of πᾶσα and for his change from ἱερὰ γράμματα, an OT designation, to πᾶσα γραφή, a possibly more inclusive term. It would gather together Paul's concern for the preservation and communication of the gospel and the apostolic understanding and application of that gospel and place it on a par with the OT, as 2 Pet. 3:16-17 clearly does. And it would provide a clearer background for and transition to his demand that Timothy "preach the word" (4:2). However, we can only say that this is a possibility that should be considered alongside the other.

Looking at the question from a later historical perspective, it can be said that the unqualified statement that "all scripture is God-breathed" would apply to all the writings that belong to the category of γραφή, including those that were not extant when Paul wrote. Paul's statement is not that "these" certain writings are God-breathed and no others, but that "all" γραφή are God-breathed. The way in which he makes this affirmation gives us warrant to relate that truth to "all" of the NT, since it is recognized to be γραφή (cf. 2 Pet. 3:16-17, where this has already taken place in the NT age).

Paul adds a rather full statement about scripture's usefulness. He says that scripture is ὠφέλιμος** (cf. 1 Tim. 4:8; Tit. 3:8; cf. also Paul's use of the cognate verb ὠφελέω and noun ὠφέλεια outside the PE), "useful," in the sense of yielding a practical benefit. The benefit that scripture yields is spelled out in the πρός ("for") phrases that follow (cf. BAGD s.v. πρός III.3c).

Scripture is useful, first, for διδασκαλία (see 1 Tim. 1:10) in the sense of "instruction," "teaching." That is to say, scripture instructs one by means of its content (cf. *NEB:* "teaching the truth"). Similarly, Rom. 15:4 says of the scriptures (pl. γραφαί) that "whatever was written in earlier times was written for our instruction." There Paul makes a hermeneutical generalization to indicate to his readers why he is quoting a particular passage of scripture and applying its general truth to them. This is a practice that he, along with other writers of the NT and Jesus and the apostles in their preaching and teaching, followed regularly, as is evidenced by the large number of OT quotations and allusions in the NT (see also 2 Tim. 2:19; 1 Tim. 5:18, the latter referring to both Dt. 25:4 and a saying of Jesus as γραφή; Michel, *Paulus und seine Bibel;* Ellis, *Paul's Use of the OT*). It is this sense of the purpose of scripture that Paul is expressing in the four phrases here (cf. further his practice in Acts 17:2).

Second is ἐλεγμόν** (a NT hapax that appears in the LXX), used here in the sense of "reproof" or "rebuke." If the four purposes of scripture listed here are reflected in the four duties in 4:2 ("preach the word . . . reprove, rebuke, exhort"), then this hapax is elucidated by ἐλέγχω there. *NEB* paraphrases with "refuting error" (*TEV:* "rebuking error"). Third is ἐπανόρθωσιν** (a NT hapax; cf. ἐπιδιορθόω in Tit. 1:5), which is used in the sense of "correcting" or "setting right" (LSJM; see also Spicq), most likely with reference to conduct, as it sometimes was in extrabiblical literature (see BAGD for references; for the papyri see MM; for a different perspective see H. Preisker, *TDNT* V, 450f.).

Fourth is παιδείαν τὴν ἐν δικαιοσύνῃ. παιδεία** (also in Eph. 6:4; Heb. 12:5, 7, 8, 11) is used in the sense of "training, instruction" (cf. G. Bertram, *TDNT* V, 596-625, especially 624f.). The training in view here is training "in righteousness," i.e., it "is designed to produce conduct whereby δικαιοσύνη is actualised" (Bertram, 624, quoting Wohlenberg). δικαιοσύνη (see 1 Tim. 6:11), "righteousness, uprightness," is used here in the sense of "right conduct" (G. Schrenk, *TDNT* II, 210; similarly in 1 Tim. 6:11; 2 Tim. 2:22; Rom. 6:13; 9:20a; 14:17; Eph. 5:9).

Stott suggests that these four πρός phrases are arranged in two pairs, each with a negative word and a positive word, the first pair dealing with belief and the second with action ("creed and conduct"; cf. also Fee and Ridderbos). Thus he commends the *NEB* for the clarity of its paraphrase of each pair ("for teaching the truth and refuting error," "for reformation of manner and discipline in right living"). If this attractive suggestion is correct, it provides a distinction between ἐλεγμόν and ἐπανόρθωσιν and presents a natural chiastic order, since the positive term precedes the negative in the first pair (instruction and reproof) and the negative precedes the positive in the second pair (correction and training in righteousness). Stott goes on to sum up the importance of these words admirably: "Do we hope, either in our own lives or in our teaching ministry, to overcome error and grow in truth, to overcome evil and grow in holiness? Then it is to Scripture that we must . . . turn, for Scripture is 'profitable' for these things."

3:17 ἵνα with subjunctive ᾖ indicates either the purpose for which God intended scripture to be profitable (Robertson, Huther) or the result of such usefulness in a person's life (Kelly). The former is more likely. The desired result is that the man of God be ἄρτιος** (a biblical hapax), "'capable, proficient' = able to meet all demands" (BAGD). Paul makes this statement about one whom he designates as ὁ τοῦ θεοῦ ἄνθρωπος,** a description that can apply to any Christian in general or to Timothy and any other Christian leader in particular. Here as in 1 Tim. 6:11 (the only other NT occurrence of the phrase; see the comments there for full discussion) this designation is probably used in the general sense, though it may have been chosen here, and there, because it could also have special application to Timothy as a leader. The sense of the passage is that scripture is given to enable any "person of God" to meet the demands that God places on that person and in particular to equip Timothy the Christian leader for the particular demands made on him (cf. 4:2).

The concluding participial phrase strengthens the ἵνα clause by affirming that "the person of God" has been "equipped" by scripture "for every kind of good work." ἐξηρτισμένος, the perfect passive participle of ἐξαρτίζω, is used here with the meaning "having been equipped," or "having been fully equipped" (with the perfective use of ἐκ- [Robertson]; from the same root as the adjective ἄρτιος). That for which (πρός) the person of God has been equipped is πᾶν ἔργον ἀγαθόν, i.e., every aspect and task of the Christian life, and in Timothy's case, of the Christian ministry. The phrase πᾶν ἔργον ἀγαθόν, "every good work," occurs several times in the PE (see 1 Tim. 5:10) and elsewhere in Paul's letters. It signifies that without exception (πᾶν, "every," in the sense of every kind) God has equipped "the person of God" to do what is "good," i.e., what he has indicated in his scripture should be done, since he himself is the norm of all good. Since God created Christians for good works and calls on them to do good works (Eph. 2:10; Tit. 3:1; 2 Tim. 2:21), he has given scripture to instruct them so that they may know in principle what God expects of them and thus be equipped to do that particular "good deed" called for in each situation.

FINAL CHARGE AND FINAL TESTIMONY: 4:1-8

This section presents Paul's charge to Timothy (vv. 1-5), which is summarized in its own concluding words, "fulfill your ministry" (v. 5), and which is undergirded with Paul's testimony about his own ministry (vv. 6-8).

FINAL CHARGE TO TIMOTHY: 4:1-5

Paul's charge to Timothy is given in the presence of God and Christ and with special reference to Christ's return, kingdom, and judgeship (v. 1). The particular activity with which Timothy is charged is set forth in v. 2: preaching, reproving, rebuking, and exhorting. Paul commands that these be done constantly and with wisdom. They are to be done not only because the message and human need call for such activity, but also because of the deteriorating situation in which hearers will seek out a message more in tune with their own likes (vv. 3-4). Paul also speaks to Timothy in more general but also more personal terms about what he must be, do, and endure to fulfill this ministry (v. 5). The urgency of the task is highlighted by Paul's imminent departure, as the first verse of the next subsection indicates (v. 6).

These verses have an urgent tone, even though they are merely summarizing what has come before. They are dominated by a hortatory tone (cf. Smith-Beekman, *Analysis*): There are nine imperatives, eight of them spelling out activities that Timothy must engage in as aspects of his ministry and attitudes that must characterize him in his work (vv. 2, 5) and the last, "fulfill your ministry" (v. 5), summarizing the specific commands in this subsection and the demands made on Timothy earlier in the letter.

4:1 Paul begins this subsection with a charge that is made even more solemn by the witnesses before whom it is made — God and Christ — and by the reminders of the comprehensive judgeship and return of Christ. The deponent verb διαμαρτύρομαι, "I charge," is used to give an admonition emphatically (H. Strathmann, *TDNT* IV, 511f.), as it is in the other PE* occurrences, 1 Tim. 5:21 (a similar verb form followed by the same ἐνώπιον τοῦ θεοῦ καὶ Χριστοῦ Ἰησοῦ; see the comments there) and 2 Tim. 2:14 (a participle followed by ἐνώπιον τοῦ θεοῦ). The first person singular form gives the charge a direct and forceful quality and conveys the fact that the charge is given by Paul in his apostolic authority (cf. 1:1).

ἐνώπιον, "before," in the sense of "in the sight of, in the presence of," reminds Timothy that this responsibility is laid upon him and is to be carried out before none other than "God and Christ Jesus." Paul uses ἐνώπιον τοῦ θεοῦ in Gal. 1:20; 2 Tim. 2:14 and with καὶ Χριστοῦ Ἰησοῦ in 1 Tim. 5:21; 6:13; and here. God and Christ observe all that Timothy does.

In particular the one who became flesh as Jesus (cf. Mt. 1:21) and lived before God on earth as the one anointed to serve God (cf. Acts 10:38) will be Timothy's judge since he will be the judge of all people and their deeds (cf. 2 Cor. 5:10; Jn. 5:22, 27; Acts 17:31). The articular participle τοῦ μέλλοντος with the infinitive κρίνειν serves as a periphrasis for the future tense (BAGD s.v. μέλλω 1cβ). κρίνειν, "to judge," refers to the divine tribunal, as the direct objects ζῶντας καὶ νεκρούς, "living and dead," demonstrate (on κρίνειν cf. Rom. 2:16; Acts 17:31; for the concept cf. 2 Cor. 5:10). The phrase ζῶντας καὶ νεκρούς,** "living and dead," refers (as it does in Acts 10:42 with the noun κριτής and in 1 Pet. 4:5 with the verb κρίνω; in Rom. 14:9 the terms are reversed and a different perspective is present) to the whole of the human race at the time of the judgment, based on the idea that Christ will judge those alive at the time of the judgment and also those whose death has preceded it (cf. 1 Thes. 4:13-17). Just as the thought of the judgment by Christ of all people motivated Paul (2 Cor. 5:9-11), so Paul wanted it to motivate Timothy.

It is difficult to ascertain the precise meaning of καὶ τὴν ἐπιφάνειαν αὐτοῦ καὶ τὴν βασιλείαν αὐτοῦ, literally "and his appearing and his kingdom." Part of the difficulty stems from the fact that Paul has changed to a different form of construction with these two accusative modifiers. Most, however, take the construction to be the accusative used with swearing or adjuring (cf. BDF §149; see, e.g., 1 Thes. 5:27) following διαμαρτύρομαι and render it as the *NEB* does: "I adjure you by his coming appearance and his reign" (cf. *TEV* and *NIV*). Thus Paul adds as a further motivation the perspective both (καί) of Christ's "appearance" and (καί) also of his "kingdom," i.e., that he will also personally appear and inaugurate his kingdom. Paul develops and applies these concepts in the following verses.

From Paul's use in v. 8 of "on that day" (ἐν ἐκείνῃ τῇ ἡμέρᾳ) and the terminology of "longing for" the appearing, we see that ἐπιφάνεια** refers here (and there) to the second "appearance," or coming, of Christ, as it does in every Pauline occurrence except one (2 Tim. 1:10 is the exception; the word also appears in 2 Thes. 2:8 and 1 Tim. 6:14 [see the comments there]). In v. 18 the qualification "heavenly" (τὴν ἐπουράνιον) added to the phrase "his kingdom" (τὴν βασιλείαν αὐτοῦ) and Paul's statement that he "will" be delivered from every evil deed "into" (εἰς) that kingdom clearly demarcates that βασιλεία as "heavenly" and future (βασιλεία with a future reference 9 of the 14x in Paul: 1 Cor. 6:9, 10; 15:30; Gal. 5:21; Eph. 5:3; 1 Thes. 2:12; 2 Thes. 1:5; and these two PE* occurrences). In v. 8 Paul rejoices that "the Lord, the righteous judge," will bestow on him "on that day" "the crown of righteousness" as one of those who have longed for "his appearing" (τὴν ἐπιφάνειαν αὐτοῦ). In v. 18 he rejoices that the Lord will deliver him from every evil deed and bring him safely to "his heavenly kingdom" (τὴν βασιλείαν αὐτοῦ τὴν ἐπουράνιον). It appears from this that Paul has used these two concepts to encourage Timothy in the service he is charged to perform just as he uses them later on to express how these truths encourage him and ought also to encourage Timothy. Thus Timothy is to be encouraged to perform his task by the fact that Christ will appear and that Timothy himself will receive the crown of righteousness at Christ's appearing and be safely brought into Christ's future heavenly kingdom.

4:2 The content of the charge is presented as a series of five imperatives with a qualifying prepositional phrase. The first imperative, "preach the word" (κήρυξον τὸν λόγον), plays a dominant role, not only by being first but also by being amplified by the second imperative "be ready in season and out of season," and by the prepositional phrase with διδαχῇ at the end of this verse.

κηρύσσω is the verbal cognate of κῆρυξ, the "herald" whose duty it was to make public proclamation. The verb thus means "proclaim aloud, publicly" and is used in the NT of public proclamation or "preaching" of the message that God has given (in the PE* also 1 Tim. 3:16, which speaks of the proclamation about Christ among the nations).

The background for Paul's charge that Timothy proclaim τὸν λόγον is found in 2:9, 15, which speak of "God's word" and "the word of truth," i.e., the message and teachings from God. With this background Paul can use ὁ λόγος here for this "word" without further specification. Thus Timothy is charged to proclaim publicly that message from God and its truthful teachings (cf. 1 Cor. 15:2; Rom. 10:8, 14-15). This understanding is borne out by the following statements, which speak of the hearers not enduring "sound doctrine" and turning away from "the truth" (vv. 3-4).

The second imperative, ἐπίστηθι, with its two adverbs (εὐκαίρως ἀκαίρως) specifies how the preceding command is to be carried out. ἐπίστηθι (second aorist active) is from ἐφίστημι (Pl.* 3x: v. 6; 1 Thes. 5:3), which in the present and aorist has among its meanings "stand by." In the imperative it means "be ready, be on hand" (BAGD) or "be at one's task." εὐκαίρως ἀκαίρως are a paired wordplay on the word καιρός. εὐκαίρως** (Mk. 14:11) designates a time or season (καιρός) that is "good" (εὐ-) or "convenient." ἀκαίρως** (a NT hapax) designates a time or season that is "not" (ἀ-) good or "*in*convenient." Is this timeliness from the perspective of Timothy or from that of his hearers? From the emphasis in the next verse on time (καιρός) from the point of view of the hearers it would appear that the latter is the best choice. But it is possible that Paul is taking into account not only the hearers but also Timothy and his own inclinations, including his timidity (cf. 1:6-8). The essence of this clause is that Timothy is to be at the task of preaching the word whether the time is perceived to be good or bad (cf. Malherbe, "In Season").

The third imperative is ἔλεγξον (first aorist active of ἐλέγχω), used here with the meaning "reprove, correct." It is used elsewhere in the PE* of reproving one who continues in sin (1 Tim. 5:20; cf. Mt. 18:15), of correcting an opponent (Tit. 1:9, 13), and as one of the duties that Titus must perform with all authority along with λάλει καὶ παρακάλει (Tit. 2:15). It is probably best to consider its use here as containing a similar range of duties and activities. The fourth imperative, ἐπιτίμησον (NT 29x, here only in Pl.*), is used here with the meaning "rebuke," i.e., censure or prevent an action or bring it to an end (BAGD s.v. 1). In the third imperative Timothy is charged to speak to those who are in error or doing wrong and to attempt to convince them of that; in the fourth he is charged to tell those doing wrong to stop (cf. Trench, *Synonyms,* §4).

The fifth imperative (the fourth distinct action commanded) is παρακάλεσον (see 1 Tim. 6:2). The rendering "appeal to" comes close to spanning the spectrum of nuances the word has. Here the imperative, used alongside κήρυξον and the other terms, would seem to have the particular nuance of "urging" truths upon hearers and "exhorting" them to respond.

Just as the first command was qualified by the second imperative and its two adverbs, so also these last three commands (and perhaps the first also) are qualified by the concluding prepositional phrase ἐν πάσῃ μακροθυμίᾳ καὶ διδαχῇ, which indicates the manner in which they are to be done. The "patience" (μακροθυμίᾳ; see 1 Tim. 1:16; 2 Tim. 3:10) in view is that which is required by the tasks commanded and by the need for persistence and forbearance when dealing with sinful people in general and particularly when dealing with the difficulties that the next verse speaks of. πάσῃ, "all," before μακροθυμίᾳ is a realistic reminder to Timothy that the task is difficult and will require the greatest amount of patience. Timothy's work must also be done with full "instruction" (καὶ διδαχῇ). It is by διδαχή, by what one has been taught, that elders are able to "exhort" (παρακαλεῖν) and "rebuke" (ἐλέγχειν; see Tit. 1:9, the only other PE* occurrence of διδαχή). Here διδαχή is used in a related sense of what one teaches.

4:3 Introductory γάρ shows that the words that follow provide the reasons for the preceding charge. The imperatives in the preceding verse are warranted not only by the demands of the ministry of the word but in particular by the tendency of some professing believers to fall away from the truth.

Having used ἀκαίρως previously, Paul now gives some specifics about such an inconvenient "time" with καιρός (cf. 1 Tim. 4:1; 2 Tim. 3:1). Timothy is to be forewarned that such a situation will arise, and so Paul uses future ἔσται. Just such a time "will be" or "will come." This is an example of a NT pattern of warning about the effects of sin on people with the future (cf. 3:1-5; Lk. 21:12, 17; Acts 20:29-30). The future tense does not imply that the situation Paul describes has never arisen, but to warn Timothy of what he should expect so that he is not caught off guard or disillusioned.

The temporal particle ὅτε, used as a substitute for a relative pronoun, introduces a clause that indicates why the charge, and especially its qualifying words, is necessary. First Paul relates the negative response of some professing believers (elucidated in v. 4: "turning from the truth") to the teaching that Timothy will be giving. ἀνέξονται is the future of ἀνέχω (only middle in the NT), which means generally "endure, put up with," usually in the NT in the sense of "bear" or "forbear." Here it is used in the special sense of "hear or listen to willingly," as in Heb. 13:22 (cf. its use as a legal technical term in Acts 18:14). Paul says that "they" will "not" (οὐκ) willingly listen to and put up with ὑγιαινούσης διδασκαλίας (genitive following ἀνέξονται). ὑγιαίνουσα διδασκαλία** (the phrase elsewhere in the NT only at 1 Tim. 1:10; Tit. 1:9; 2:1), "sound doctrine," is said to be "according to the gospel" in 1 Tim. 1:10-11. As a synonym here for what Timothy is charged to communicate, it may be identified as the correct teaching according to "the word" (v. 2) of God (cf. Tit. 1:9; 2:1, which have contexts similar to the one here).

The second half of the verse, in contrast to the first (the transition is signaled by ἀλλά), says what "they" will do and why: "Seeking to hear what agrees with their own desires, they will accumulate teachers for themselves." ἐπισωρεύσουσιν** (a NT hapax) means "heap up" and is used figuratively here with the meaning "accumulate." The combination of this verb with διδασκάλους and ἑαυτοῖς signifies that these "teachers" are those that these hearers have handpicked "for themselves" and connotes that their teaching differs from that of Timothy and others who teach sound doctrine. This connotation is substantiated by the previous statement that these hearers will not willingly listen to sound doctrine and by the accompanying statement that these teachers are accumulated in accordance with the "desires" of the hearers.

κατά introduces the norm that governs their action (BAGD s.v. II.5). That norm is "their own" (ἰδίας) "desires" (ἐπιθυμίας), what "they" want to do and be. In other words, they have made themselves the measure of who should teach them and what teaching is acceptable. Paul's use of ἐπιθυμία in the PE indicates that he has in mind desire for what should not be desired (see 1 Tim. 6:9; Tit. 2:12; 3:3).

The participle κνηθόμενοι agrees with the subject of the verb, the hearers. κνήθω (a NT hapax) means in the passive "feel an itching." The object of the participle τὴν ἀκοήν, "hearing," stands here for "the ear," the organ with which one hears (so also in v. 4; cf. Acts 17:20). The clause means "having itching ears," but is used here, as BAGD says (s.v. κνήθω), as a figure "of curiosity, that looks for interesting . . . bits of information." BAGD add that "this itching is relieved by the messages of the new teachers" (cf. for this perspective Clement of Alexandria, *Strom.* 1.3).

4:4 In a concluding summary statement the ultimate action of these hearers is presented from two perspectives, on the one hand (μέν) with reference to the truth Timothy is to teach and on the other hand (δέ) with reference to the myths that their teachers teach.

The imagery of the "ear" continues in the first half of this statement: The hearers will turn "the ear" (τὴν ἀκοήν) "away from" (ἀπό) the truth. ἀποστρέψουσιν strongly implies that they once professed to hold to the truth that they "will turn away from," just as its usage in 1:15 implied a prior relationship (see Tit. 1:14, the other PE* occurrence). They turn away from τῆς ἀληθείας, "the truth," the message and teaching of Christianity regarded as the absolute reality. This is the third term that Paul uses in this passage to designate that which Timothy is to communicate ("the word," v. 2; "sound teaching," v. 3). With ἀλήθεια Paul returns to a term that he has utilized repeatedly in the PE and especially in these two letters to Timothy (including 2 Tim. 2:15, 18, 25; 3:7, 8) for the message and teaching that comes from God and that he has also used frequently in his earlier letters (see 1 Tim. 2:4 for the data).

The second half of the statement indicates that the hearers turn from the truth to "myths." ἐκτραπήσονται, "turn away," is used here as it is in the other PE occurrences, particularly 1 Tim. 1:6 (see the comments there). That to which they turn is signified with ἐπί. "Myths," τοὺς μύθους,** is used here, as elsewhere in the NT, to signify what is not true, is not historical, and lacks reality (see for data 1 Tim. 1:4; see also 1 Tim. 4:7). Here, where τοὺς μύθους are contrasted with ἡ ἀληθεία, that meaning of μῦθος is underscored (the same contrast is made in Tit. 1:14; cf. 2 Pet. 1:16). The definite article may signify that Paul is specifying the particular myths that are associated with the false teaching. For a discussion of the possible content of these myths see the comments on 1 Tim. 1:4.

4:5 In this concluding verse of the subsection, Paul returns to his direct charge to Timothy (which marked the first two verses) with a series of four imperatives. He contrasts Timothy with those described in the preceding verse with σὺ δέ, "but you" (which appeared earlier in 3:10, 14; see 1 Tim. 6:11).

The first imperative, νῆφε** (1 Thes. 5:6, 8; 1 Pet. 1:13; 4:7; 5:8), "be sober," is used in the NT only figuratively in the sense of being free from every form of mental and spiritual "drunkenness," and thus it comes to mean "be well-balanced, self-controlled" (BAGD). The present tense is probably used for this one command in the midst of a series of aorist imperatives because the qualifying prepositional phrase ἐν πᾶσιν envisions various situations that would require the continued action that the present tense represents: "in all things," "on all occasions and under all circumstances" (Fausset; cf. other PE uses of the phrase, e.g., 1 Tim. 3:11; Tit. 2:9, 10; 2 Tim. 2:7). The second imperative, κακοπάθησον,** repeats Paul's appeal to Timothy to "bear hardship patiently" (with him, συγκακοπάθησον in 2:3; see the comments there), even as Paul himself has borne such (2:9; the other NT occurrence is Jas. 5:13).

The third command is ἔργον ποίησον εὐαγγελιστοῦ, "do the work of an evangelist" (for a similar use of ἔργον see 1 Tim. 3:1). εὐαγγελιστής occurs only 3x in the NT. In Eph. 4:11 "evangelists" are mentioned between apostles and prophets on the one hand and pastors and teachers on the other hand in a list of gifts that Christ gives to the church. In Acts 21:8 "evangelist" is the designation of Philip, whose work in this capacity is presented in Acts 8 with the cognate verb εὐαγγελίζομαι as that of "evangelizing" or "announcing the gospel" (vv. 4, 12, 35, 40) with the intent that the hearers believe in Jesus (vv. 5, 12, 35, 36). This description of Philip's work together with the inherent significance of the term εὐαγγελιστής shows what the evangelist's task was. Paul wants Timothy to continue to evangelize even though he is working in a more settled situation and is not in a new and unevangelized territory as Philip was. This use of εὐαγγελιστής may indicate that Timothy is the "evangelist" or "missionary" for Ephesus and that Paul is encouraging him to continue that work. Or it may indicate that in whatever capacity Timothy serves he must continue doing the work of an evangelist. Cf. Paul's comments about Timothy's work in the gospel in Phil. 2:22 and 1 Thes. 3:2.

The fourth command, τὴν διακονίαν σου πληροφόρησον, functions as a summary exhortation embracing the preceding imperatives and any other aspect of Timothy's ministry. πληροφορέω** (Lk. 1:1; Rom. 4:21; 14:5; Col. 4:12; 2 Tim. 4:5) is used here with the meaning "fulfill," i.e., fully and completely accomplish and carry out the duties of his ministry (cf. Col. 4:17, where Paul [with Timothy] uses the synonym πληρόω to give a similar exhortation to Archippus concerning τὴν διακονίαν). Paul uses διακονίαν, "ministry," here with reference to Timothy (σου) just as he used the term with reference to the special service into which Christ has placed him in 1 Tim. 1:12 (see the comments there).

γάρ in v. 6 links the words that immediately follow with this subsection. Those words give further urgency to the charge here by indicating that Paul will no longer be present and give further encouragement by his own example and by the reward the Lord will give to his own (vv. 6-8). From this point on no other overall charge relating to the ministry is given to Timothy. Instead, the requests are specific (cf. vv. 9, 13, 15, 21).

Thus with the words of the solemn charge in 4:1-5 Paul in effect brings to a conclusion his words of instruction regarding Timothy's duties as a minister of Christ. This charge gathers up the concerns expressed throughout the letter and crystallizes them in nine memorable imperatives that begin with "preach the word" and end with "fulfill your ministry." With these imperatives Paul calls on Timothy to proclaim and apply God's word with much patience and careful instruction, to be clearheaded in every situation, to bear whatever difficulties such a ministry may involve him in, to evangelize, and to do whatever is necessary to accomplish the ministry to which Christ has called him.

PAUL'S FINAL TESTIMONY: 4:6-8

ἐγὼ γάρ signifies that this subsection serves as a further reason and motivation for the charge just given. That the time of Paul's "departure" is at hand is all the more reason that Timothy must take over much of what Paul has been doing. As Paul speaks of the conclusion of his ministry (v. 6), he is naturally drawn to reflect on that ministry. But here also he still has an eye on Timothy. He utilizes some of the very concepts he has used to encourage Timothy (in 2:1-7) to describe his own ministry, and thereby demonstrates that what he has asked of Timothy can be accomplished by God's grace at work in a person's life (v. 7). He also says that there is laid up for him a crown of righteousness in that day (v. 8a). Here also, as in vv. 6-7, he writes to encourage. So he says that the crown is given to all who long for the Lord's appearance (v. 8b).

4:6 ἐγώ is used here both to emphasize that Paul is speaking about himself and as a contrast to the emphatic σύ of the preceding verse. The contrast provides further reason (γάρ) for what has been previously said — *You* Timothy must carry on the ministry because *I* Paul am about to depart. This is the last ἐγώ in the PE,* and each time the word has been used for special emphasis (cf. 1 Tim. 1:11, 15; 2:7; Tit. 1:3, 5; 2 Tim. 1:11).

σπένδομαι** is used of the "pouring out of a drink offering" and here refers figuratively to what is happening to Paul. Paul may well be thinking of OT drink offering language in his use of the verb (cf. Ex. 29:40-41; Lv. 23:13; Nu. 15:5-10; 28:7), since he uses OT ceremonial language elsewhere and in Phil. 2:17 uses this verb with a word for sacrifice (θυσία). Here he alludes to the pouring out of his blood in martyrdom. He uses the present tense in its progressive sense (Robertson) to indicate the certainty of the event, as if it were actually taking place. "What was once a possibility [Phil. 2:17] is now a certainty" (Parry). He does not mean that his death will take place immediately, since he can ask Timothy to come be with him (vv. 9, 21) and bring him some items (v. 13). But he does indicate its certainty and that it is near. He uses, therefore, the temporal adverb ἤδη, "already," with the present tense to describe a process that is already taking place and that insures that outcome (notice also the passive voice of the verb).

The second half of the verse moves from the figurative to the more literal and joins (καί) to the vivid description of the process the stark statement of the finality of the end result. ὁ καιρός, "the time," is used with the qualifying phrase τῆς ἀναλύσεώς μου to designate the time in view. ἀναλύσεως** (a NT hapax), literally "loosing," is used of "departure" and figuratively of departure from life, i.e., "death" (cf. Philo, *In Flaccum* 187), here Paul's own (μου) death (cf. ἀναλύω in Phil. 1:23). The time of his departure ἐφέστηκεν. ἐφίστημι (Pl.* 3x: 1 Thes. 5:3; 2 Tim. 4:2), which means generally "stand by," is used here in the perfect tense with the meaning "is imminent," i.e., "is near at hand." The imminence of Paul's death is a poignant reason for his charge to Timothy.

4:7 With three graphic clauses Paul tells of his service for Christ. These clauses are parallel in construction, and that parallelism makes a forceful impact. Each consists of an accusative articular noun placed first and a perfect tense verb.

The first clause uses two cognate terms, ἀγών and ἀγωνίζομαι, to describe Paul's life and ministry in terms of a contest or a struggle (see the comments on 1 Tim. 6:12, the only other NT occurrence of this clause, for data, discussion, and literature; for the concept cf. especially 1 Cor. 9:25). These words were used in both the athletic and the military realms, and one need not decide which Paul has in view, if indeed it is one and not the other, because he uses the terms for both elsewhere and because the emphasis in his figurative use is not on the particular image but on the basic idea of "struggle."

Paul adds καλόν (as in 1 Tim. 6:12 and 1 Tim. 1:18 [see comments there on καλόν]) to make clear the validity and appropriateness of this struggle: The struggle is "good" (καλόν) because he has engaged in it for God and the gospel. Indeed, one must struggle for the gospel so that it can make its way in this evil world. The perfect tense of the verb, ἠγώνισμαι, signifies that Paul can make this statement about his entire ministry and that at the near conclusion of his life this fact stands established (as can also be said of the perfect tense verbs in the two following clauses).

Paul makes this observation to serve as a model for Timothy and to encourage him to rely on Christ's enabling grace (cf. 2:1). At the beginning and the end of 1 Timothy (1:18; 6:12) he admonished him in the same or similar words. In the second letter he has urged him to be a good soldier for the Lord (2:3ff.). Now he writes about the same struggle in his own life as something that has been accomplished.

In the second clause Paul uses τὸν δρόμον,** "the race course," in the same way in which he used it (according to Luke) in speaking to the Ephesian elders (Acts 20:24), i.e., as a virtual synonym for "ministry" (διακονία; cf. δρόμον in Acts 13:25). This course, Paul says, he "has finished" (τετέλεκα; cf. the synonymous verb τελειόω in Acts 20:24, which, with this slight difference, is the only other NT occurrence of this clause). Paul is affirming here that by God's grace he has fulfilled his ministry (cf. 4:5 [διακονία]; for Paul's use of race imagery see also 1 Cor. 9:24).

In regard to the third clause we must ask whether Paul uses τὴν πίστιν in a subjective or objective sense, i.e., whether he is saying that he has kept on believing or that he has preserved "the faith" intact. Or perhaps the clause is a fixed formula, as it is in other ancient writings, that refers to keeping one's trust (cf. Dibelius-Conzelmann), here with a Christian perspective. These all seem to be valid possibilities, so the issue must be resolved on the basis of context.

The three clauses in this verse are parallel, and in the other two clauses the nouns are objectifications of experiential phenomena, i.e., figurative expressions for the struggle that the gospel entails and the ministry that Paul has received. Therefore, "the faith" would appear to be used here in that same manner for "that which is believed," as it is elsewhere in the PE and in Paul (see the comments on 1 Tim. 1:19). Furthermore, since the other two verbs emphasize perseverance it is likely that this nuance of τετήρηκα is intended here as well. Therefore, Paul is saying that he has "persevered in the faith." At the same time, in a letter warning Timothy about those who corrupt and turn aside from the truth (2:18, 25; 3:8), in which Paul specifically urges Timothy to retain the pattern of sound words (1:13), to guard the treasure (1:14), and to handle accurately the word of truth (2:15), and in which he has just warned about those who will not endure sound doctrine and will turn away from the truth (4:3-4), it is also likely that he would speak, as a model to Timothy, of having "kept" or "preserved" "the faith." This use of τηρέω is in accord with its usage elsewhere with an impersonal object, where it "denotes the actual maintaining of the essential functions or realities of Christian life" (H. Riesenfeld, *TDNT* VIII, 143, citing Eph. 4:3; Rev. 16:15). This sense of "keeping" in terms of faithfully proclaiming and preserving the faith does not rule out the subjective sense, that Paul has "kept on believing," and even necessarily includes it: Paul perseveres in that which he preserves (cf. 1 Cor. 15:1-2).

Some have questioned the propriety of Paul making such statements about himself. Four observations may help to put this question in perspective: First, Paul puts the nouns first in these three clauses because he wants to emphasize the inherent value of the activity he has engaged in. It is "the good contest" or "the course" or "the faith" itself that has merited a lifelong "struggle" or "finishing" or "keeping" on Paul's part, as it ought to merit such on Timothy's part. Second, Paul does not speak in grandiose terms of his triumph but only of his attempted perseverance. He says only that he has struggled and fought, not that he has won. Third, Paul does not feel the necessity to repeat here what he has said earlier, which Timothy knows so well, i.e., that any perseverance on his part is brought about by God's grace within him (cf. 1 Tim. 1:12, 14; 2 Tim. 2:1; 4:17; Col. 1:29). Fourth, Paul is not exalting himself, but, as the context makes clear, is encouraging Timothy through his own experience of God's enabling grace.

4:8 This subsection (vv. 6-8) began with a statement about Paul's present status (v. 6), which led to reflection on his past life of ministry (v. 7). In view of all this Paul now speaks of what is in store for him and for others who share his longing for the Lord's return.

λοιπόν is used adverbially and can be construed either inferentially, in the sense of "therefore," or simply as an indicator of time, in the sense of "now" or "henceforth" (see BAGD s.v. 3αα, β). Since inferential use is doubtful in the NT (perhaps in 1 Cor. 7:29) and since the reason that Paul receives the crown is given later in the verse, it is best not to insist on this doubtful understanding.

Paul resumes the language of the games by speaking of ὁ στέφανος (NT 18x), "the crown" or "the garland" (elsewhere in Pl.*: literal in 1 Cor. 9:25; figurative, as here, in Phil. 4:1; 1 Thes. 2:19; cf. the related verb in 2 Tim. 2:5), which is qualified by genitive τῆς δικαιοσύνης. In the other NT occurrences of ὁ στέφανος with genitive nouns (1 Thes. 2:19: "of exultation"; Jas. 1:12: "of life"; 1 Pet. 5:4: "of glory"; Rev. 2:10: "of life"; 12:1: "of twelve stars"[?]) the genitive is appositional and epexegetic. Furthermore, in 1 Cor. 9:25 the adjectival qualification "imperishable" is used in the same way: To receive an imperishable wreath is to receive imperishability. Therefore, it is most likely that here, too, the genitive is appositional, so that the phrase should be understood as "the crown, namely, righteousness." Rather than being "the crown which will bring final justification" (W. Grundmann, *TDNT* VII, 629) it is much more likely that it refers to the permanent and perfect "state of righteousness" (G. Schrenk, *TDNT* II, 210) into which the Christian is brought by God (cf. Phil. 3:12-14, where Paul uses βραβεῖον, the "prize" in a contest, which is used interchangeably with στέφανος in 1 Cor. 9:24-25; cf. eschatological use of δικαιοσύνη also in Gal. 5:5). This crown, says Paul, is already "laid up" or "stored up" (ἀπόκειται,** literal in Lk. 19:20; figurative, as here, in Col. 1:5, which has an analogous expression; Heb. 9:27) for "me" (μου).

ὁ κύριος, who will give the crown, is Christ, since Paul identifies "the Lord" with "the righteous judge" (cf. v. 1) and speaks of longing for "his appearing." ὁ κριτής is used here of the supreme "judge" (cf. its use of Jesus in Acts 10:42; of God in Heb. 12:23; Jas. 4:12; 5:9). δίκαιος indicates that this judge is inherently and absolutely "righteous" and "just," and thus is qualified to judge justly and give "the crown of righteousness" (cf. Jn. 17:25; 1 Pet. 2:23; Rev. 16:5, 7; 19:2; cf. further G. Schrenk, *TDNT* II, 188). Paul declares in Rom. 3:25-26 that God's characteristic of being δίκαιος was demonstrated in Jesus' death, on the basis of which God justly justifies sinners; like justification, "the crown of righteousness" is a gift from "the righteous judge" presented on the basis of Christ's death and righteous life (cf. 1:10; Phil. 3:8-14). The Lord "will give" (ἀποδώσει, used elsewhere by Paul of God and the judgment in Rom. 2:6, utilizing language found in Pr. 24:12; Ps. 62:12) the crown to Paul (μοι) "on that day." The demonstrative pronoun ἐκείνη is used with ἡμέρα to designate "that" well-known and future judgment "day" of God (see the comments on 1:12).

Since Paul has spoken of himself in vv. 6-8a, he forcefully asserts at this point that this crown is given not only to him (οὐ μόνον δὲ ἐμοί) but also to "all" (πᾶσι) God's people. The ascensive force of ἀλλὰ καί gathers up those specified after it and includes them with the one specified by οὐ μόνον. πᾶσι has such textual support that inclusion of it is more likely than omission of it (see *UBSGNT; TCGNT*). Those who will receive the crown are defined in terms of their "love" for Christ's return (τὴν ἐπιφάνειαν αὐτοῦ; see 1 Tim. 6:14). ἠγαπηκόσι, used with reference to a future event (τὴν ἐπιφάνειαν) may be rendered "have longed for" (so *NIV;* cf. BAGD s.v. 2) as well as "have loved." The perfect tense signifies that this "love" has constantly characterized their lives.

With this participial clause Paul mentions that which characterizes all true Christians and in doing so echoes a motif that goes back to Jesus and his appeal to be alert and expectant with regard to his return (e.g., Mt. 25:13). Just as alertness for Christ's return is to characterize Christ's people (in Paul's letters, e.g., 1 Thes. 1:10; 5:6; 1 Cor. 1:7; Phil. 3:20; 1 Tim. 1:1; Tit. 2:13 [cf. Acts 24:15]), so also "love" for this return is to mark them. Paul leaves this note that all Christians long for Christ's return and will therefore all receive a crown of righteousness, which is particularly joyous and encouraging in the face of his departure, for Timothy to embrace and pass on. He thus ends this larger section just as he began it (v. 1): by referring to Christ and his return. Paul wants both Timothy, who continues to live, and himself, who dies, to live and die in the light of Christ's return and kingdom.

PERSONAL INSTRUCTIONS AND REMARKS: 4:9-18

In this section Paul gives instructions to Timothy regarding Paul's personal needs and relates to him several things about his personal situation. The personal character of the section is also evident from the appearance in every verse of a first person singular pronoun. Paul communicates three interrelated matters: his urgent request that Timothy come to him soon (vv. 9-13), a warning about Alexander the coppersmith (vv. 14-15), and a statement about Paul's own situation (vv. 16-18), which may also serve as a further encouragement for Timothy to come to him (see especially v. 16).

REQUEST THAT TIMOTHY COME SOON: 4:9-13

Paul's request that Timothy come to him as soon as possible (v. 9) — with Mark (v. 11) — is underlined by the departure of all his coworkers except Luke (vv. 10-11). His reference to Tychicus being sent to Ephesus (v. 12) is probably an indirect way of saying that Tychicus can take the place of Timothy and Mark and that they will then be free to leave Ephesus and come to Paul. He asks Timothy to bring him some specific items when he comes (v. 13).

4:9 The reference in v. 6 to Paul's impending death is the setting for this request that Timothy come to him as soon as possible. Imperative σπούδασον can mean either "hasten," or "make every effort, do your best" (σπουδάζω, PE*: Tit. 3:12 [see comments there]; 2 Tim. 2:15; 4:21, all but 2:15 requests for Titus or Timothy to come to Paul). Since the adverb ταχέως is added to convey the need for hurrying, it is more likely that the imperative is used in the other sense. Either way it conveys a sense of urgency.

The urgent request is for Timothy "to come" (ἐλθεῖν, used similarly in 4:21; Tit. 3:12). The personal nature of the request comes through clearly in the simple prepositional phrase πρός με, "[come] to me." ταχέως, "soon," a relative term, is given perspective by being replaced by πρὸ χειμῶνος, "before winter," in v. 21 (for its relative character see in Paul* 1 Cor. 4:19; Gal. 1:6;

Phil. 2:19, 24; 2 Thes. 2:2; 1 Tim. 5:22). This request presumes the usual time factor in the Roman judicial system, and particularly as it relates to Paul's case, and also takes into account the time for the letter to be carried to Timothy and for him to travel to Rome. Furthermore, Paul's requests for certain items to be brought to him (v. 13) also presume some time remaining for him when Timothy arrives. But at the same time, and more importantly, Paul writes as a man who is certain that he will not be released and that before long he will depart this life (v. 6) to Christ's heavenly kingdom (v. 18). In that light he writes urging Timothy to come to him as soon as he possibly can.

4:10 The explanatory γάρ signifies that this verse provides a reason for Paul's request in the preceding verse. He relates that almost all his coworkers have gone elsewhere and says (in v. 11) that he is nearly alone. The implication is that he is lonely and needs help and companions.

Paul's difficult situation is highlighted by his beginning with Demas, who has deserted him because of his "love of the world." Δημᾶς** is listed as one of Paul's "fellow workers" in Phm. 24 and under that designation is one of those who send greetings in Col. 4:14. BAGD and BDF (§125.1) suggest Δημᾶς might be a shortened form of Δημήτριος. Chapman ("Historical Setting," 364ff.) identifies the Δημήτριος of 3 Jn. 12 with this Δημᾶς, but this proposal is not conclusive.

Paul says that Demas "deserted" (ἐγκατέλιπεν, NT 10x, Pl.* 4x: Rom. 9:29; 2 Cor. 4:9; 2 Tim. 4:16; for the variant -λειπεν, which does not affect the meaning, see *NA*[26]) him (με) "because he has loved the present age" (ἀγαπήσας τὸν νῦν αἰῶνα). In this aorist participle of antecedent action "it is the inception of the action only which precedes the action of the principal verb" (Burton, *Syntax,* §137), i.e., Demas has begun to love and still loves the present age. Elsewhere Paul refers to ὁ νῦν αἰών,** "the present age, the present world" (also in 1 Tim. 6:17; Tit. 2:12), with ὁ αἰὼν ὁ ἐνεστώς (Gal. 1:4) and ὁ αἰὼν οὗτος (Rom. 12:2; 1 Cor. 1:20; 2:6, 8; 3:18; 2 Cor. 4:4; Eph. 1:21). Since it is an "evil" age (Gal. 1:4), whose God is the evil one (2 Cor. 4:4), Christians are not to be conformed to it (Rom. 12:2). Paul seems to be contrasting Demas's love with that which marks true Christians (4:8, the only other use of ἀγαπάω in the PE*), who love and long for the future appearance of the Lord. Demas's love for this world implies that he is one whose love for something else has taken the place of love for God (cf. 3:2, 4, where a compound of φίλος is used; cf. 1 Jn. 2:15).

In deserting Paul, Demas has gone to Thessalonica, a city in Macedonia on the Thermaic Gulf (Θεσσαλονίκη,** elsewhere in the NT in Acts 17:1, 11, 13; Phil. 4:16). He may be returning to his hometown, since he is mentioned in Phm. 24 with Aristarchus the Thessalonian (Acts 20:4; 27:2) and since two of the politarchs of Thessalonica were named Demetrius (Lightfoot, *Biblical Essays,* 247 n. 2).

Paul utilizes the verb "has gone" not only for Demas but also for two other fellow workers, naming the place to which each "has gone" (ἐπορεύθη, aorist passive of πορεύομαι, with εἰς and the place also in Rom. 15:24, 25; 1 Tim. 1:3). But the construction of the phrase with these two others, consisting of the person's name with the prepositional phrase, implies only this latter verb, not the earlier statement about desertion. Furthermore, that Titus has gone to Dalmatia, just north of Nicopolis, fits with Paul's earlier request (and presumed evangelistic strategy) for Titus to join him in Nicopolis (Tit. 3:12). Κρήσκης,** a rare Greek form of the common Latin "Crescens," is not mentioned elsewhere in the NT. Crescens is said to have gone to Γαλατία** (1 Cor. 16:1; Gal. 1:2; 1 Pet. 1:1; for manuscript evidence for this reading and the variant "Gallia" see *UBSGNT* and *TCGNT*). Γαλατία is almost certainly an area in central Asia Minor (for alternatives see the literature on Γαλατία in BAGD). Τίτος is Paul's well-known fellow worker (see the statements about his life and ministry in the **Introduction**). He has gone to Δαλματία,** Dalmatia, which is located in southern Illyricum across the Adriatic Sea from southern Italy.

4:11 The result of these departures is that the company of fellow workers has been reduced to one: Λουκᾶς ἐστιν μόνος μετ' ἐμοῦ, "Luke only is with me" (for this use of μόνος cf. Rom. 11:3; 1 Cor. 9:6; 14:36; Phil. 4:15; 1 Thes. 3:1). Λουκᾶς** is listed as one of Paul's fellow workers in Phm. 24 and is described as "the beloved physician" (ὁ ἰατρὸς ὁ ἀγαπητός) in Col. 4:14.

The remainder of this verse assumes that Timothy will come to Paul and states that he should bring Mark with him (μετὰ σεαυτοῦ). BAGD (s.v. 4) proposes that ἀναλαβών is used here as in Acts 23:31 and in extrabiblical literature (references in BAGD) in the sense of "taking along" a person who travels with someone. It is possible, however, that it is used in the more general sense of "take to one's self" (BAGD s.v. 3; so Thayer, *Lexicon*). Imperative ἄγε, "bring [him] along," is the key verb in this statement.

Μᾶρκος** undoubtedly refers to the one associated with Paul elsewhere in the NT. Hence "Mark" is the surname of John, son of Mary of Jerusalem and cousin of Barnabas (Col. 4:10) who accompanied Paul and Barnabas on the so-called first missionary journey but left them early during that journey (Acts 12:25; 13:5, 13). Paul did not want to take Mark on his next journey because of this desertion (Acts 15:37-40), but Mark proved himself after that time and came to be regarded by Paul as a fellow worker (Phm. 24; cf. 1 Pet. 5:13).

The reason (γάρ) that Paul wants Timothy to bring Mark with him is that Mark is "useful" (εὔχρηστος,** also in 2:21; Phm. 11, where what is said about Onesimus could just as well be applied to Mark) to Paul "for service." Paul has used διακονία for the "ministry" in which he was placed by Christ (1 Tim. 1:12) and for the "ministry" that Timothy is to fulfill

(2 Tim. 4:5). Furthermore, Paul regards Mark as his "fellow worker" (συνεργός, Phm. 24). For those reasons and because Paul wants Mark to come to replace other coworkers who have left, it is most likely that he uses διακονία here for the ministry of the gospel (rather than personal service). Cf. *NIV:* "because he is helpful to me in my ministry" (also *TEV*).

4:12 Τύχικος** is apparently the one who carried the letters to the Ephesians and to the Colossians, in which Paul calls him "the beloved brother and faithful minister in the Lord" (Eph. 6:21; Col. 4:7) and a "fellow bondservant in the Lord" (Col. 4:7). He was from Asia (where Timothy now is) and was one of those who accompanied Paul on his journey to Jerusalem with the collection (Acts 20:4). The terse statement here, "But Tychicus I have sent to Ephesus," together with v. 8, is probably written here for the same reason that a similar statement appears in Tit. 3:12. There Titus is told to come to Paul "when" (ὅταν) either Artemas or Tychicus have come to Titus, presumably because either of the two would take Titus's place. Paul says that he "has sent" (ἀπέστειλα, epistolary aorist) Tychicus εἰς Ἔφεσον (for Ἔφεσος see the other PE* occurrences, 1 Tim. 1:3; 2 Tim. 1:18), "to Ephesus," where Timothy is located and laboring (cf. 1:18). That place name, rather than the more usual "to you" (Tit. 3:12; Eph. 4:7; Eph. 6:21), is probably used simply to continue the pattern in v. 10.

4:13 While Timothy is "coming" to Paul (ἐρχόμενος; cf. the infinitive ἐλθεῖν in vv. 9, 21), Paul asks him to "bring" or "carry" (φέρε; cf. Acts 4:34, 37; 5:2) with him τὸν φαιλόνην. φαιλόνης** (a NT hapax, spelled φελόνης in some manuscripts) is regarded by most as a loanword from Latin *paenula,* which appeared at a much earlier date than the Greek word. The original form was φαινόλας or φαινόλης, which by metathesis (transposition) became φαιλόνης (see BAGD; MHT II, 106). The φαιλόνης, "cloak," was "a large, sleeveless outer garment, made of a single piece of heavy material, with a hole in the middle through which the head was passed" (Kelly). Since it served as protection against cold and rain, Paul may have wanted it because winter was at hand (v. 21) and also perhaps because his prison was cold. Whatever the immediate reasons, Paul wanted to recover essential possessions that he had left behind (ὃν ἀπέλιπον; see evidence for a variant spelling, which makes no difference in meaning, in *NA*[26]).

Paul left the cloak in Τρῳάς** (Acts 16:8, 11; 20:5, 6; 2 Cor. 2:12), a city and region in the northwest corner of Asia Minor. Troas was a seaport (Acts 16:11) and could easily be on a route from Ephesus to Rome. Therefore, Paul can ask Timothy to pick up the cloak on his way. Paul left it with Κάρπος,** "Carpus," presumably a Christian in that area, who is mentioned only here in the NT. (H. C. G. Moule conjectures that it was in Carpus's house that the Lord's Supper gathering mentioned in Acts 21:6ff. took place.) The best hypothesis is that the cloak was left when Paul was most recently arrested.

Paul also wants Timothy to bring "the books." βιβλίον (NT 34x, Pl.* 2x: Gal. 3:10) "is the most common word for the 'roll of a book,' a 'book,' or a 'writing' in the *koine*" (G. Schrenk, *TDNT* I, 617). In both the LXX and the NT it is used of any writing in general (e.g., Dt. 24:1, 3; Mk. 10:4; Mt. 19:7) and to refer to individual OT writings (e.g., 1 Ch. 27:24; cf. the related word βίβλοι in Dan. 9:2), particularly as "a solemn expression for the Book of the Law" (U. Becker, *NIDNTT* I, 243, referring to Dt. 28:58; Jos. 1:8; so also in Josephus [Schrenk, 617, n. 9]). Thus in the NT it is used in the expressions "the book of the prophet Isaiah" (Lk. 4:17) and "the book of the law" (Gal. 3:10) and by itself to refer to the Law (Heb. 9:19; cf. 10:7). Therefore, it is possible that Paul refers to the OT writings with plural τὰ βιβλία.

To make his request more specific, Paul adds the words μάλιστα τὰς μεμβράνας. μεμβράνα** is a loanword from Latin for the "parchment" used for making books (BAGD). There are two possible significances for Paul's phrase. The first is that it indicates which books, among all those that Paul asks for, he particularly (μάλιστα taken as "most of all, above all, especially") wants. The second possibility is that proposed by Skeat ("Especially the Parchments"), which understands μάλιστα as an equating or defining term so that the phrase is giving a further definition of all the books that Paul wants. On this view μάλιστα would be rendered "that is," and τὰ βιβλία and τὰς μεμβράνας would refer to the same thing. Skeat's documentation of μάλιστα with this meaning (in addition to the more common meaning) elsewhere in Greek literature and in the PE is convincing, which makes it possible here as well (cf. 1 Tim. 4:10; 5:17; Tit. 1:10[?]).

WARNING AGAINST ALEXANDER THE COPPERSMITH: 4:14-15

4:14 On Alexander see the comments on 1 Tim. 1:20, which probably refers to the same man, who may also have been the Jewish spokesman in Ephesus after the riot there (Acts 19:33-34). χαλκεύς** meant in particular "coppersmith" but came to mean in general "metal-worker." Paul does not specify the "much harm" (πολλὰ κακά) that Alexander "did" to him (μοι). It may be that Paul mentions Alexander here because the "harm" he did was to have Paul arrested: ἐνδείκνυμι, used here of what Alexander did, was used as a legal term meaning "inform against" (see LSJM), and Paul notes that Alexander "vigorously opposed our message" (so Fee and Spicq).

Paul expresses his confidence in God's retributive justice with ἀποδώσει αὐτῷ ὁ κύριος κατὰ τὰ ἔργα αὐτοῦ (a recurring statement in the OT, e.g., 2 Sam. 3:39; Ps. 28:4; 62:12; Pr. 24:12; one or more of these OT statements is cited in Rom. 2:6, where Paul uses the same verb and prepositional phrase as here). ὁ κύριος is undoubtedly the same "Lord," "the righteous judge," as in v. 8, namely Christ, whose "appearing" Paul longs for. At the future judgment day he "will recompense" (ἀποδώσει, future of ἀποδίδωμι, the same verb as in v. 8) Alexander "according to his deeds" (κατὰ τὰ ἔργα αὐτοῦ). This statement reflects the same convictions as 2 Cor. 5:10.

4:15 The preceding statement that Alexander did Paul "much harm" serves as the grounds for the warning here that Timothy should "guard against" Alexander. The connection is provided by adverbial καί ("also") and the emphatic pronoun σύ ("you" or "you yourself") used in a correlative contrast with the preceding μοι: "*You also* guard against him." Middle imperative φυλάσσου has the middle significance here of "(be on your) guard against," "look out for" with the accusative of the person to be guarded against (BAGD s.v. 2a; cf. Lk. 12:15; Acts 21:25; 2 Pet. 3:17). The present tense of the imperative indicates that Timothy must *constantly* be on his guard.

γάρ introduces a statement about Alexander's opposition, which is what Timothy must beware of. Alexander opposed "our" (ἡμετέροις, i.e., that of Paul and his fellow workers) teaching and presumably will continue to do so. λίαν (cf. Mt. 2:16; 27:14; Mk. 6:51; Lk. 23:8), "very much" or "exceedingly," placed first for emphasis, expresses the degree of his opposition. With ἀντέστη (from ἀνθίστημι), "opposed," Paul repeats the verb used in 3:8 (see the comments there), where he spoke of the false teachers' opposition to the "truth." Plural λόγοις, "words," signifies that Alexander's opposition was to their actual statements, i.e., the content of their message (plural λόγοι in the PE* in 1 Tim. 4:6; 6:3; 2 Tim. 1:13), and harks back to 1:13 and 2:2.

PAUL'S DEFENSE AND THE LORD'S PRESENT AND FUTURE PROVISION: 4:16-18

Here Paul relates that at his first defense no one supported him (v. 16), but the Lord gave him strength (v. 17a). As a result two things were achieved: The message was fully proclaimed and all the Gentiles heard it, and Paul was delivered (v. 17b-c). Paul remains confident that the Lord will continue to deliver him from every evil and bring him safely to the heavenly kingdom (v. 18).

4:16 Two general views are advocated with regard to what event Paul speaks of in the phrase πρώτῃ μου ἀπολογίᾳ, "my first defense." One is that it refers to an earlier imprisonment of Paul, probably the ("first") imprisonment in Rome recorded at the end of Acts, since Paul is before that court for a *second* time (so Eusebius, *HE* 2.22; Bouma; Hendriksen; Lock; Wohlenberg; Zahn, *Introduction,* II, §33; the most thorough defense is presented by Bouma, Hendriksen, and Zahn; cf. further Meinertz, "πρώτη ἀπολογία"). But most modern commentators (e.g., Bernard, Brox, Dibelius-Conzelmann, Fee, Guthrie, Jeremias, Kelly, Ridderbos, Spicq; see especially Ridderbos and Kelly) take it as referring to the first stage of Paul's present trial. Both views are possible and the arguments for them (presented below) cannot be considered conclusive.

The advocates of the first view argue that since Luke is with Paul (v. 11), Paul's statement here that everyone "deserted" him cannot apply to the present trial. Furthermore, the outcome of his house arrest described at the end of Acts appears to have been what Paul describes in v. 17: He says that he was "delivered out of the lion's mouth," and was able to engage in further ministry among Gentiles. That he was released and carried on his ministry is borne out by the PE (see further on Paul's "Release and Second Imprisonment" in the **Introduction**). But now Paul expects to die soon (v. 6).

The advocates of the second view regard it as unlikely that Paul would mention an earlier trial, the outcome of which Timothy already knew. It appears, rather, that Paul is informing Timothy about recent events. The "first defense" is thus the *prima actio,* the preliminary investigation in Paul's present trial. Paul was "deserted" either because his fellow workers had not yet arrived or out of fear had left him, or because the Christians at Rome, who unlike his fellow workers were in a position to "stand by him," did not do so. He was "delivered" (v. 17) in that he was not condemned at that first hearing and thus had time to write and ask Timothy to come to him before the next stage of the trial (vv. 9, 21). This would fit with Paul's view that his "deliverance" could finally lead to the "heavenly kingdom" (v. 18). Because the trial was public and was in the capital of the Gentile world, it might be regarded as the culmination of his work of taking the gospel to the Gentiles (v. 17; cf. Acts 23:11 and Paul's presentation of the gospel while on trial in Acts 26).

ἀπολογία (NT 8x) is used of Paul's courtroom "defense" (cf. especially Acts 25:16; Phil. 1:7, 16). Paul says that "no one" (οὐδείς) "came to his aid" or "stood by him" (παρεγένετο, BAGD s.v. 3). The verb is used in a special sense, and Kelly has suggested that it is that of coming as a witness or serving as an advocate. Unfortunately, we are unable to say who failed to do so and why. The exclusive nature of οὐδείς makes it clear that not even a single person stood by Paul, and the absolutely inclusive nature of πάντες makes it clear that "all," without exception, deserted him (ἀλλὰ πάντες με ἐγκατέλιπον; see the comments on v. 10 for the verb; cf. also 1:15).

As culpable as such action was, Paul does not put it in the same category as that of Demas (who left Paul out of love for the present world, v. 10), nor does he wish God's just retribution on them as he did on Alexander (v. 14). Perhaps he knows that those he is thinking of did what they did out of fear (as did Jesus' disciples, Mk. 14:50). For that reason he compassionately writes μὴ αὐτοῖς λογισθείη, "may it not be counted against them" (μή with the optative expresses a negative wish). λογίζομαι is used here in the sense of "count against" (cf. 2 Cor. 5:19; aorist optative in wish statements [or wish prayers] also in Rom. 15:5, 13; 1 Thes. 3:11f.; 5:23; 2 Thes. 2:17; 3:5, 16; 2 Tim. 1:16, 18; here only with the negative; cf. Wiles, *Paul's Intercessory Prayers,* 32).

4:17 Paul affirms that in contrast (δέ, "but") to these people (v. 16), "the Lord stood by me." For the third time Paul refers to ὁ κύριος (cf. vv. 8, 14). Evidence in those verses demonstrated that ὁ κύριος was Christ, and when the NT speaks elsewhere of "the Lord" standing by Paul or strengthening him, as here, Christ is apparently referred to (cf. Acts 23:11; Phil. 4:13). παρέστη (from παρίστημι) is used in the intransitive sense with the special nuance of "come to the aid of, help, stand by" (the one so aided in the dative, μοι; BAGD s.v. παρίστημι 2aγ). The aid provided was that Christ "strengthened" (ἐνεδυνάμωσεν) Paul, an experience that Paul has spoken of before (Phil. 4:13; 1 Tim. 1:12; 2 Tim. 2:1). Robertson aptly renders the clause as "[the Lord] poured power into me."

This strengthening was for the particular purpose (ἵνα) of enabling Paul to accomplish his assigned ministry, as has always been the case (see the passages just listed). If the clauses in this verse are in chronological order, then Paul's proclaiming the gospel preceded his deliverance, which would favor the view that vv. 16-17 refer to the first investigation in his current trial and that the proclamation was made during Paul's defense in court. Paul uses τὸ κήρυγμα here to designate "the proclamation" about Christ (Rom. 16:25), with which Paul had been entrusted (Tit. 1:3) as a herald (κῆρυξ, 1 Tim. 2:7; 2 Tim. 1:11). Here, as usual (1 Cor. 1:21; 2:4; 15:14; Tit. 1:3), Paul uses τὸ κήρυγμα absolutely because the content is understood.

Paul was very conscious of being entrusted with the κήρυγμα to proclaim it to the Gentiles (cf. Rom. 1:5; 16:25-26; 1 Tim. 2:7). When he speaks here of the κήρυγμα being "fully accomplished" (πληροφορηθῇ) "through me" (δι' ἐμοῦ), he is referring to the fulfillment of his particular responsibility, just as he has exhorted Timothy with the same verb to "fulfill" his ministry (4:5). Paul's mandate was to bear Christ's name "before the Gentiles and kings and the sons of Israel" (Acts 9:15). If he speaks here of an earlier stage of a legal process he is still involved in, then he has carried out the first and last parts of this mandate as fully as possible and now is in the court of the highest "king," Caesar himself (cf. Acts 25:11, 12, 21, 25; 26:32). For this reason he regards his defense in that setting (as before King Agrippa in Acts 26) as the fulfillment of the κήρυγμα entrusted to him. If, on the other hand, Paul is speaking of an earlier trial and subsequent release, he regards the further ministry that followed as the fulfillment of his mandate. The same could be said about "all the Gentiles/nations" having heard Paul, since καί is epexegetical.

Paul, like the other NT writers, uses ἔθνη for "nations" or "peoples" in general (e.g., Mt. 28:19; 1 Tim. 3:16) or for "Gentiles" in distinction from Jews (e.g., Acts 9:15; 1 Tim. 2:7; see 1 Tim. 2:7; 3:16). The phrase πάντα τὰ ἔθνη** (Mt. 24:14; 25:32; 28:19; Mk. 11:17; 13:10; Lk. 21:24; 24:47; Acts 14:16; 15:17; Rom. 1:5; 16:26; Gal. 3:8; 2 Tim. 4:17; Rev. 12:5; 14:8; 15:4; 18:3, 23) is used in the NT of both all nations (e.g., Mt. 24:14; 25:32; 28:19; Rom. 16:26) and all nations distinguished from Israel (e.g., Lk. 21:24; Acts 15:17; Gal. 3:8). Either understanding is possible here, regardless of what events Paul is referring to. Since, however, Paul uses the phrase here in connection with κήρυγμα and in 1 Tim. 2:7 refers to himself as a κῆρυξ in a context where he uses ἔθνη to refer to Gentiles, it is at least likely that the phrase is used in that sense here.

Paul obviously does not mean by πάντα τὰ ἔθνη any single gathering of all Gentiles, who then and there heard him. What he means is either that all those in attendance at his "first defense" (v. 16) heard him or that that occasion brought to completion the full representative complement of Gentiles to whom he was to preach the gospel. If the "first defense" was held publicly and Paul thereby was able to address a representative number of Gentiles in the Empire's capital, then he may say that "all the Gentiles" heard. Elsewhere in the NT "all the Gentiles" is used representatively with "all" referring to representatives (e.g., Mt. 28:19; Mk. 13:11; Rom. 1:5, "among all the Gentiles"; Gal. 3:8). That sense seems to be present here.

καί links ἐρρύσθην κτλ. to the two indicative verbs in the first clause of the verse, especially the first one, making this a second statement of what the Lord accomplished by his presence: The Lord not only stood by Paul, he also "delivered" (ἐρρύσθην, aorist deponent passive indicative of ῥύομαι; cf. 3:11) Paul ἐκ στόματος λέοντος (the two nouns occur in the NT, but the phrase is a NT hapax). Several understandings have been suggested for the final phrase: a literal lion in an amphitheater in which Christians have been thrown (impossible because of Paul's Roman citizenship, according to Robertson), Satan (cf. 1 Pet. 5:8), the emperor or the power of the Empire (Josephus refers to the death of Emperor Tiberius with τέθνηκεν ὁ λέων, *Ant.* 18.28), or some great danger, even death (cf. Ps. 7:2; 22:21; 35:17). Whether or not Jesus' reflections on Psalm 22 have influenced Paul at this point, it appears that Paul has been influenced by the parallelism of Ps. 22:20-21 (LXX 21:21-22: ῥῦσαι, the verb Paul uses here, ἐκ στόματος λέοντος). If so, then deliverance "from the lion's mouth" is a figure for being saved from the sword (Ps. 22:20). In v. 18 Paul appears to have been influenced by a line in the Lord's Prayer (Mt. 6:13); perhaps this has influenced his use of ῥύομαι here.

4:18 Following up on the preceding comment about the Lord's deliverance in a particular past situation, Paul now confidently asserts that the Lord will deliver him "from every evil deed" (ἀπὸ παντὸς ἔργου πονηροῦ).

Future ῥύσεται looks forward from the event just mentioned (v. 17, aorist ἐρρύσθην) and confidently asserts that in the future also the Lord will "deliver" Paul (cf. for this combination of past and future 2 Cor. 1:10). It appears that Paul uses here the language of a petition in the Lord's Prayer (ῥῦσαι ἡμᾶς ἀπὸ τοῦ πονηροῦ, Mt. 6:13). If so, then, continuing with his use of the title "the Lord" (ὁ κύριος, see v. 17), Paul applies the petition to himself with the personal pronoun με (ῥύσεταί με ὁ κύριος) and spells out the promise implicit in the petition by adding "every deed" (παντὸς ἔργου) to πονηροῦ (cf. Paul's earlier use of ῥύομαι with πᾶς in 3:11).

Singular attributive παντός with no article means "every" or "each" without exception. παντός ἔργου πονηροῦ is "every evil (i.e., hostile) action" (cf. G. Harder, *TDNT* VI, 557). The eschatological direction that Paul goes later in this sentence makes it clear that he is not excluding any evil that might be done to him, but only the power of evil to destroy him finally (Fee). The distinctiveness of the combination πᾶν ἔργον πονηρόν, found nowhere else in the NT (plural ἔργα πονηρά** in Jn. 3:19; 7:7; Col. 1:21; 1 Jn. 3:12; 2 Jn. 11; this is the only NT occurrence of the singular and of the phrase with any form of πᾶς) is further evidence that it is a Pauline adaptation of the petition in the Lord's Prayer, utilizing singular πονηροῦ from the petition.

Since he has mentioned his deliverance "from the lion's mouth," Paul wants to state clearly to Timothy that he expects his future deliverance to be heavenward and that this, too, is true deliverance. He speaks, therefore, about the ultimate and final deliverance and, because it is such, uses σώσει (also in LXX Ps. 21:22) as the appropriate verb. The pregnant construction σώσει εἰς, "bring safely into" (see BAGD s.v. εἰς 7 and the literature cited there), with "the heavenly kingdom" as the object of the preposition, implies deliverance from this world with all its evils and from death in all its aspects (for this future perspective of σῴζω elsewhere in Paul see Rom. 5:9-10; 1 Cor. 3:15; 5:5).

At least half of the Pauline occurrences of βασιλεία, "kingdom, reign," represent that aspect of Christ's (and God's) spiritual reign that believers will enter in the future (e.g., 1 Cor. 6:9-10; 15:24, 50; Gal. 5:21; Eph. 5:5; 2 Thes. 1:5). In 1 Cor. 15:24ff., as here (αὐτοῦ referring back to ὁ κύριος), Paul specifically identifies that "reign" as Christ's.

Paul uses both ἐπουράνιος, "heavenly," and οὐρανός, "heaven," of the realm that is distinguishable from earth (cf. especially 1 Cor. 15:47-49 and also Eph. 1:10; 3:15; Col. 1:16, 20). Several times Paul speaks of Christ as Master "in heaven" (ἐν οὐρανῷ, Eph. 6:9; Col. 4:1). The ἐπ- in ἐπουράνιος denotes that the word means "*in* heaven" (H. Traub, *TDNT* V, 538). Considering these factors, it appears that Paul is speaking of Christ's kingdom "in heaven" and saying that when he dies he will be brought safely into that kingdom and remain in it from then on (cf. 1 Thes. 4:13-18). In this heavenly kingdom Paul will "be at home with the Lord" (the best understanding of

2 Cor. 5:8). Here he expresses the same confidence that he expressed earlier when death was a possibility (Phil. 1:23), but now it is a certainty.

This statement about the Lord and his faithfulness evokes a doxology of praise, as elsewhere in Paul's letters (Rom. 1:25; 9:5; 11:36; 16:25-27; Gal. 1:5; Eph. 3:20-21; Phil. 4:20; 1 Tim. 1:17; 6:15-16). This doxology, like the other Pauline doxologies, expresses the desire that praise should be expressed through eternity (using αἰών) and concludes with the ἀμήν of affirmation. Only Gal. 1:5 is exactly the same as the doxology here. But four of Paul's doxologies use the doubled αἰών, as is done here, three in the same way as here (εἰς τοὺς αἰῶνας τῶν αἰώνων, 1 Tim. 1:17; Gal. 1:5; Phil. 4:20; only slightly different in Eph. 3:21). Most speak of praise (in its entirety or as part of or as the conclusion of a longer statement) with the word δόξα (1 Tim. 1:17 with τιμή; δόξα alone in Rom. 11:36; 16:27; Gal. 1:5; Eph. 3:21; Phil. 4:20). Three times Paul uses ᾧ, as here (1 Tim. 6:16; Rom. 16:27; Gal. 1:5). These doxologies and others in the NT usually consist of three or four (as here) component parts: the person praised (usually in the dative, here ᾧ), the word(s) of praise (usually δόξα with other words, here ἡ δόξα alone), a conclusion indicating the eternal duration of the praise (usually εἰς with αἰών in a single or doubled form), and usually an ἀμήν of affirmation.

ᾧ refers back to ὁ κύριος, which is a title for Christ (cf. again vv. 8, 14, 17, and now 18 for the contextual evidence). This would make this doxology and Rom. 9:5 (according to the best understanding of that passage) the only Pauline doxologies offered to Christ. For the form of the verb to be understood, whether "be" (εἴη or ἔστω) or "is" (ἐστιν), see the comments on 1 Tim. 1:17. δόξα signifies the luminous manifestation of God's person, his glorious revelation of himself (S. Aalen, *NIDNTT* II, 45). Used in a doxology, it expresses either the desire for that radiance to continue to be seen in its splendor and glory, or, in an echoing or mirror effect, asks that appropriate praise be given in response to it (see 1 Tim. 1:17).

Paul expresses the desire that glory be to the Lord εἰς τοὺς αἰῶνας τῶν αἰώνων (see the comments on 1 Tim. 1:17). Both the plural form of αἰών and the repetition of the word emphasize the "concept of eternity." The plural form presupposes "a plurality of αἰῶνες . . . whose infinite series," here emphasized by the twofold use of the term, "constitutes eternity" (H. Sasse, *TDNT* I, 199).

ἀμήν concludes this doxology as it does most NT doxologies. It expresses the stated confirmation ("so let it be," "truly," or simply "amen"; cf. BAGD) of that which the writer has just expressed (cf. Rev. 5:14), and probably also seeks to invoke from his readers the same response (cf. 1 Cor. 14:16; 2 Cor. 1:20; see H. Schlier, *TDNT* I, 337; H. Bietenhard, *NIDNTT* I, 99).

This section presents an interesting picture of the great apostle. He appreciates the company and assistance of fellow workers and expresses the need for the tools of his ministry ("the books, especially the parchments"). He is aware of the danger of false teachers and opponents (e.g., Alexander) and warns his younger colleague to be on his guard. His sense of God's justice gives him confidence that such opposition will be judged. He also feels keenly his desertion by "all" at his first defense. But his compassion wishes that the Lord not count this against them. In the midst of such disappointment over humans, he still desires the aid and comfort of his colleagues Timothy and Mark. And he desires it not just for himself, but also for the sake of the ministry to which Christ has called him.

Going beyond what Paul says here about human companionship is his expression of absolute confidence in the unfailing presence and care of the Lord. The Lord watches over Paul and delivers him, even from the most difficult situations, and enables him to fulfill, even in that moment of trial, the ministry to which he has been called. So grateful is Paul for such a Lord in the midst of such difficult circumstances that he breaks out into a doxology of praise and asks that that Lord be glorified forever.

FINAL REMARKS AND GREETINGS: 4:19-22

As the conclusion of his letter Paul has, as usual, certain greetings and a final statement of blessing. The greetings are to Prisca and Aquila and to the household of Onesiphorus (v. 19). Paul passes on greetings from Eubulus and three others and from "the brothers" in general (v. 21). Paul also mentions the whereabouts of Erastus and that Trophimus was left sick at Miletus (v. 20). This mention of coworkers who are not with Paul is appropriately followed by another request to Timothy to come to him, this time asking him to come before winter (v. 21). Paul's final words, as in nearly all his letters, are words of blessing (v. 22). (For an analysis of the closing portions of Paul's letters see Doty, *Letters,* 39-42.)

4:19 Paul begins with greetings to Prisca and Aquila. He uses the verb ἀσπάζομαι, which he normally uses to send greetings (Pl. 40x, all in the concluding verses of his letters). The imperative form, here ἄσπασαι, may be translated "Greetings to. . . "

Πρίσκαν** καὶ Ἀκύλαν** were the wife and husband team that befriended Paul in Corinth, whom he stayed with, and who worked with him as tentmakers (Acts 18:2-3). Aquila was a Jew and a native of Pontus (18:2). They accompanied Paul to Ephesus and remained there when he went on to Caesarea (18:18-22). Their Christian commitment and understanding was evidenced as they shared "the way of God more accurately" with Apollos (18:26). In Acts the woman is called Πρίσκιλλα, in Paul's letters she is called Πρίσκα (Πρίσκιλλα is a variant reading in Rom. 16:3; 1 Cor. 16:19). Paul calls them "my fellow workers in Christ Jesus" (Rom. 16:3) and mentions the church "in their house" (1 Cor. 16:19).

Prisca is usually named before her husband, and various theories have been proposed to explain this unusual order. It is possible that she was the more active Christian. Ramsay pointed out another case in which a woman was named before her husband probably because she was of higher rank (cited in BAGD s.v. Πρίσκα). It is also possible that placing Prisca's name first is an expression of Christian courtesy extended to her because she is a woman. In Paul's case in particular (and perhaps his attitude is also reflected by his companion Luke in Acts), it may reflect his gratitude in that the couple's hospitality toward him involved her in considerably more work. He names Aquila first only in 1 Cor. 16:19, where his mentioning "the church in their house" may recall the leadership role of Aquila in the church. These various theories are nothing more than that, and no conclusions should be drawn from them, particularly none that would contradict Paul's direct statements regarding the role of women in the church (especially 1 Tim. 2:10-15; also 1 Cor. 14:34ff.).

Paul's other greeting is to τὸν Ὀνησιφόρου οἶκον. τὸν οἶκον (PE* 8x: 1 Tim. 3:4, 5, 12, 15; Tit. 1:11; 2 Tim. 1:16) is used here metaphorically, as in virtually all the PE passages, for the "household" or "family" of Ὀνησίφορος.** Onesiphorus is mentioned only here and in 1:16, and all that we know about him in the NT is found in 1:16-18. His "house" is mentioned either because he is dead or because he is away from it. It is probably singled out because Paul appreciates the services the "household" has rendered, both directly and through Onesiphorus (see the comments on 1:16-18, especially v. 18).

4:20 In v. 10 Paul mentioned who had left and gone elsewhere. Here he brings Timothy up to date on two men who, for different reasons, have remained elsewhere and are, therefore, not with Paul in Rome (immediately after this Paul again asks Timothy to come to him).

The Ἔραστος** mentioned in Acts 19:22, like the one mentioned here, is a coworker of Paul and is associated with Ephesus and with Timothy. Therefore, it is almost certain that they are the same person. It is also possible that the Erastus mentioned in Rom. 16:23, "the city treasurer of Corinth," is the same person, especially since Paul's comment here about this Erastus is that he "remained in Corinth." An inscription has been found in Corinth mentioning an Erastus, "commissioner of public works" (*ERASTVS PRO · AED · S · P · STRAVIT;* see Cadbury, "Erastus"). Κόρινθος** is a city in Greece located on the isthmus of Corinth that served from 27 BC as capital of the senatorial province of Achaia and seat of the proconsul. The statement that Erastus "remained" (ἔμεινεν) in Corinth may imply that Paul was there with him.

Τρόφιμος** is an Ephesian (Acts 21:29) and was one of two from Asia in the group that accompanied Paul on his last journey to Jerusalem (the other from Asia was Tychicus, mentioned already in v. 12; the group included Timothy [Acts 20:4]). Jews from Asia falsely charged Paul with having brought Trophimus, a Greek, into the Jerusalem temple and stirred up the people in the city. As a result of this commotion Paul was arrested by the Roman authorities (Acts 21:27-36). This arrest led eventually to Paul's first journey to Rome. Paul "left behind" (ἀπέλιπον, a similar nuance in the other PE* occurrences: v. 13; Tit. 1:5) Trophimus ἐν Μιλήτῳ** (Acts 20:15, 17). Miletus was a port on the coast of Asia Minor near the Meander River and about thirty-five miles south of Ephesus. Paul stopped there on his last journey to Jerusalem and met with the elders of Ephesus (cf. Acts 20:15-38).

Paul left Trophimus at Miletus because Trophimus was ἀσθενοῦντα. The verb ἀσθενέω was used generally of the state of being weak. All its NT occurrences refer to physical illness (e.g., Mt. 25:39; Jn. 4:46; Phil. 2:26f.; Jas. 5:14). Though Paul on other occasions was the instrument through which individuals were healed (Acts 14:9-10; 19:11-12; 20:10; 28:8-9; cf. 2 Cor. 12:12), he did not always heal: On this occasion he left a fellow worker "sick" (cf. 2 Cor. 12:7-10). The implication of the verb "I left behind" (ἀπέλιπον) is that Paul was with Trophimus in or near Miletus when Trophimus stopped traveling.

4:21 Paul repeats his request for Timothy to come to him using the same imperative and infinitive as in v. 9 (see the comments there). But now, instead of using the adverb ταχέως, he uses the phrase πρὸ χειμῶνος. πρό is used with the seasonal designation χειμῶνος to signify the time before which Timothy should come. χειμών was used of both the cold season, "winter" (e.g., Mt. 24:20 par. Mk. 13:18; Jn. 10:22), and wintery and stormy weather (e.g., Mt. 16:3; Acts 27:20). Here the two meanings virtually coalesce since the season is probably intended precisely because then Paul will need his cloak (v. 13) and the weather will make sea travel impossible (cf. Acts 27:20 and context). Paul knows that if Timothy does not come "before winter" (usually regarded as from about November to about March; see, e.g., J. Kelso, *ZPEB* V, 806) he will have to wait until travel commences again in spring. Perhaps the most compelling reason for Timothy to "come before winter" is Paul's expectation that his trial and probable execution will not be put off that long.

Paul conveys greetings to Timothy from four individuals and from οἱ ἀδελφοὶ πάντες. The four, three men, Eubulus, Pudens, and Linus, and one woman, Claudia, are otherwise unknown in the NT. According to Irenaeus, *Haer.* 3.3.3, Linus was the first bishop of Rome after Peter and Paul (cf. also Eusebius, *HE* 3.2; 3.4.9). Paul's earlier mention of the departure of all his fellow workers except for Luke (vv. 10-11) implies that these four are not fellow workers. They are probably members of the church at Rome, since their names are joined to οἱ ἀδελφοὶ πάντες, which is probably a general designation for members of that church (see below). These four are singled out perhaps because they have a close relationship with Timothy going back to when he was in Rome with Paul (cf. Timothy's inclusion with Paul as author in Phil. 1:1; Col. 1:1; Phm. 1).

ἀδελφοί is used figuratively in the NT to designate Christians because they are members of a spiritual family through their relationship to Christ as Lord and Savior and to God as Father. ἀδελφοί in 1 Tim. 4:6 (cf. 6:2, the other PE occurrence in this sense) indicates those whom Timothy is to instruct and is responsible for, i.e., the Christians in Ephesus. Here the ἀδελφοί are distinguished from Paul's fellow workers, who other than Luke have left (vv. 10-11) and must, therefore, be the members of the Christian church in Rome. The universal term πάντες, "all," shows that Paul is including all those who properly bear the name ἀδελφοί, i.e., all the members of Christian family there (cf. elsewhere in Pl.:* 1 Cor. 16:20; 1 Thes. 5:26, 27).

4:22 The benediction, which is found at or near the end of each of Paul's letters, is given here in two parts. The first, with second person singular σου, is directed to Timothy, and the second, with second person plural ὑμῶν, is directed to everyone in the church in Ephesus.

For the final time Paul refers to ὁ κύριος, "the Lord," i.e., Christ (see vv. 8, 14, 17, 18), an identification that some copyists sought to make explicit (see *NA*[26]; *TCGNT*). On other occasions where Paul refers to "the Lord" in closing benedictions he speaks of "the grace of the Lord" (ἡ χάρις τοῦ κυρίου: Rom. 16:20; 1 Cor. 16:23; 2 Cor. 13:13; Gal. 6:18; Phil. 4:23; 1 Thes. 5:28; Phm. 25). He does not use that formula here, probably to save "grace" for the second part of the benediction and perhaps also to make this benediction more personal: Paul wishes that "the Lord" will be with Timothy as he has so evidently been with Paul himself (cf. especially vv. 17-18). μετὰ τοῦ πνεύματος ὑμῶν, "with your spirit," in some of the closing benedictions (Gal. 6:18; Phil. 4:23; Phm. 25) means the same thing as "with you" in others (μεθ' ὑμῶν, sometimes with πάντων, in Rom. 16:20; 1 Cor. 16:23; 2 Cor. 13:13; Col. 4:18; 1 Thes. 5:28; 2 Thes. 3:18; 1 Tim. 6:21; Tit. 3:15). Here Paul addresses singular μετὰ τοῦ πνεύματός σου to Timothy alone. This phrase makes it clear that Paul is speaking of spiritual presence, wishing, i.e., that the Lord will be spiritually present with Timothy in his inner person (cf. Rom. 8:16: "The Spirit himself bears witness with our spirit (τῷ πνεύματι ἡμῶν) that we are children of God").

With plural ὑμῶν in the second part of the benediction Paul turns to all the church members in Ephesus (on the textual variants, including the concluding ἀμήν, see *TCGNT*). Paul uses (πάντων) ὑμῶν alone or in the phrase τοῦ πνεύματος ὑμῶν after μετά in the closing benedictions of all his letters except Ephesians (where πάντων alone is used). With ὑμῶν he designates all the believers in the place he is writing to. He also uses χάρις in each of the benedictions (so also Heb. 13:25; Rev. 22:21). He explicitly calls it the "grace of (our) Lord Jesus (Christ)" except in his last letters, Ephesians, Colossians, and the PE, where χάρις is unqualified, probably because at this stage Paul thought it would be evident whose "grace" he intended. Thus Paul reminds his readers at the conclusion of every letter that they are dependent on Christ's unmerited favor, forgiveness, and enabling power (cf. 2 Tim. 1:9-10; Tit. 2:11ff.; 2 Tim. 2:1; for χάρις see the comments on 1 Tim. 1:2).

On the subscriptions added to this letter in a number of manuscripts see *NA*[26] and *TCGNT.* All of the subscriptions mention that the letter is to Timothy, most that it is the second letter to Timothy. Several say that Paul wrote it at Rome, usually specifying that he wrote it when he was before the emperor Nero the second time (e.g., the Textus Receptus; see the **Introduction** on when and where Paul wrote the letter).

INDEX OF MODERN AUTHORS

INDEX OF GREEK WORDS AND PHRASES DISCUSSED

INDEX OF SCRIPTURE REFERENCES

John

1 Corinthians

2 Corinthians

Galatians

Philippians

References to the Pastoral Epistles that occur within the commentary on the same passage are not included in this index.